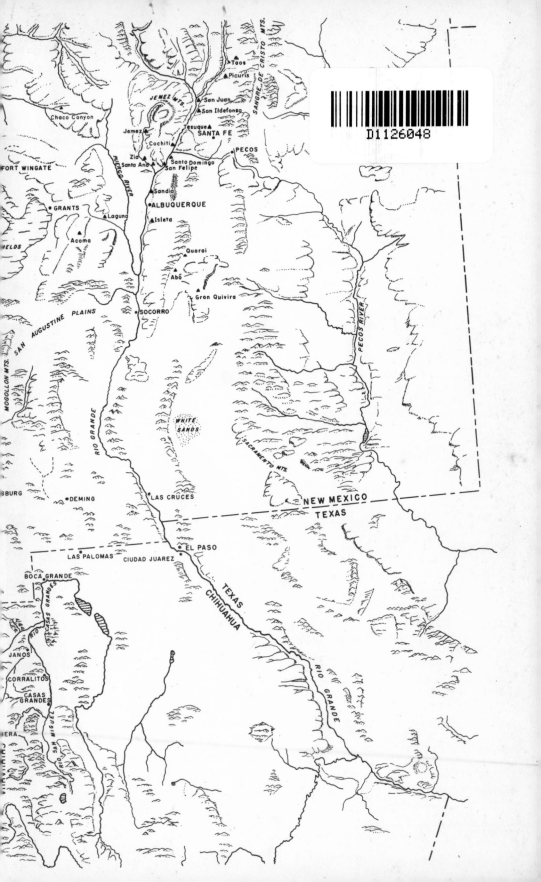

THE SOUTHWESTERN JOURNALS
OF ADOLPH F. BANDELIER

1883-1884

The Southwestern Journals
of Adolph F. Bandelier
1883-1884

EDITED AND ANNOTATED BY

CHARLES H. LANGE

AND

CARROLL L. RILEY

WITH THE ASSISTANCE OF

ELIZABETH M. LANGE

THE UNIVERSITY OF NEW MEXICO PRESS
ALBUQUERQUE

ACKNOWLEDGMENT IS MADE TO

Edgar L. Hewett
Founding Director of the School of American Research
and the Museum of New Mexico
who encouraged publication of the Bandelier Journals
and

Wayne L. Mauzy
Formerly Acting Director of the School of American Research
and Director of the Museum of New Mexico
who initiated editorial and financial arrangements
which brought publication to fruition

Manufactured in the United States of America
by the University of New Mexico Printing Plant
Library of Congress Catalog Card No. 65-17862
First edition

CONTENTS

ILLUSTRATIONS

The first four photographs in the illustrations are courtesy, Louis Latzer Memorial Library, Highland, Illinois; all others, courtesy, Museum of New Mexico.

DRAWINGS

From original sketches in Bandelier's journal

MAPS

PREFACE

THE PRESENT VOLUME is the second in our project to publish the South-western portions of the Adolph F. Bandelier journals. These journals were begun in the year 1880 and were continued on a more or less daily basis; they documented Bandelier's adventures in the Southwest, in Mexico, and in South America for almost a quarter century. After his death in 1914, the journals passed to his second wife and fellow scholar, Fanny R. Bandelier, who at one time intended to edit and publish them in three volumes (Hodge 1932: 370; see also Hobbs 1940: 122). In addition, there was once a plan by Fanny to publish the journals of the years 1886-89, the period in which her husband had served as "Historiographer with the Hemenway Southwestern Archaeological Expedition." There were to be notes by Fanny R. Bandelier and an introduction by Mary Austin. The volume was described as "An Intimate Glimpse into his daily life with its weal and woe." A prospectus of four pages was issued by The Press of the Pioneers, Inc., New York, carrying a date of 1934. The final page contained an "Appreciation" by Warren King Moorehead.

Adolf Bandelier's Journals should be of great interest to students of Southwest history and archaeology, as well as to the general public. Bandelier was our first Southwest historian and archaeologist, methodical, accurate and one who caught the spirit of the Pueblo-Cliff Dweller country.

Some of those who have since labored in the same field have not accorded Bandelier the praise he deserves. Both Cushing and Bandelier were true pioneers in effective research. Neither enjoyed the advantages which today accrue to explorers in the Painted Desert Land.

I have felt for many years both history and archaeology are deeply indebted to Bandelier. It is gratifying to know that his intimate record of travels and privations is now to be presented to the American public in an adequate way.

The present editors have benefitted from the typescript prepared by
Fanny R. Bandelier for that project although all entries have been and
will be checked against the original journal entries to assure complete-
ness and accuracy.

The journals were later willed to the Laboratory of Anthropology,
School of American Research, Santa Fe, New Mexico. At present, the
original journals—mainly handwritten—are among the collections in the
Library, Museum of New Mexico, Santa Fe.[1]

A major difficulty in bringing these journals to the public in published form has been the problem of basic editorial policy. Suggestions
have ranged from publishing verbatim to extracting only certain data
—ethnological, for example—and presenting them with extensive com-
mentary. In editing the Southwestern portions of these journals (1880-
92), we have attempted to steer a middle course between these extremes.

The journals contain day-by-day records of Bandelier's activities,
having served as both field notebooks and diaries. Their range is amazing; Bandelier was interested in almost everything about him and a
particular day's journal may contain information of interest to anthropologists, biographers, botanists, folklorists, geographers, geologists,
historians, and zoologists. Some entries have considerable literary quality, while others are written in such a cursory manner that phrases or
even single words comprise the entire record. Often, especially in the
early years, Bandelier's Continental European background comes to
light in the peculiar wording and frequently complicated structure of
his sentences. That he was, himself, aware of these shortcomings is
shown by the following excerpt from a letter to Lewis H. Morgan,
dated January 29-31, 1876 (White 1940: I, 260):

> There is in my way a great difficulty, which, however, I shall most
> assuredly overcome; the Spanish idiom is a foreign tongue, although it
> suits my taste & inclination better than any other,—and the English
> language, with all my efforts, still remains equally foreign to me. I have
> therefore, to translate from one foreign idiom into another.

It is perfectly obvious that Bandelier never intended his journals for
publication. Certain parts of them, much modified, later served as the
basis for published material (*Final Report, Islands of Lake Titicaca and
Koati, Documentary History of Zuñi*, etc.). The most striking feature
of the journals, however, is the candid, personal nature of many observations. Not only were field data given with on-the-spot comments,

but Bandelier had much to say about the people around him, whether Indian informants, colleagues, friends, or relatives. We see, through Bandelier's eyes, the daily activities, virtues, and faults of a great many people—some historically famous, others known primarily from the journals themselves. The journals, thus, provide vignettes that are especially valuable to anyone interested in the Southwest. Bandelier's often pungent opinions and criticisms must be taken for what they really were, one man's private comment on, and immediate reaction to, life about him.

In the edited journals, there is considerable annotation. This includes identification of historical figures and places, discussions of ethnographic data, etc. If no footnote is given for particular ethnographic information fully accepted by Bandelier, these data, in our opinion, were probably valid for Bandelier's time (in fact, descriptions of everyday life, religious ceremonies, political structure, and social relationships often apply almost equally today). On the other hand, Bandelier's interpretations and reactions often reveal a lack of sophistication, common to his day, in the social sciences.

As a matter of editorial policy, the following modifications in the original Bandelier journal entries have been made.

1. Certain types of entries—incidental information relating to the weather, occasional descriptions of background scenery, and unimportant calculations of elevations and distance—have been deleted entirely with no indication given. Bandelier regularly started each day's entry with weather data and occasionally interspersed additional comments later in the day.[2] When these serve no practical value, they have been deleted. Where weather conditions were pertinent to the day's activities, the comments have been retained. This policy applies to certain scenic descriptions as well. For example, the skyline of the Sandia Mountains has not changed in the past seventy years, and incidental, out-of-context references to it contribute little. The deletions are not indicated in the text, in part because such interruptions reduce readability. In addition, the rather haphazard way in which weather and other comments are introduced makes such deletion indicators as ellipses occasionally misleading. For example, Bandelier wrote on March 28, 1882, "Went to Governor Ritch at night. He was exceedingly kind with me. Made some confidential communications." This was followed immediately by a comment on the weather with no subsequent indication ever as to the nature of the confidences. Ellipses at such a point would very likely mislead the reader into thinking that the

editors had withheld sensitive material. We stress here that no such censorship has taken place at any point in the journals.

2. A number of sketches found in the original journals are not included in the published version. These are drawings of skylines, plots of fields, ground plans of pueblos, or maps of ruins, some of which were later published in the *Final Report* or elsewhere. We recognize, however, that certain sketches might have particularistic value to specialists, and so we have indicated with an asterisk (*) each point at which a sketch has been deleted. Such sketches, together with various measurements and azimuths, often give the illusion of considerable precision on Bandelier's part. In reality, these data were frequently so incomplete, or lacking in necessary base points, as to make them unusable. Similarly, notations of photographic plates have often been omitted. Bandelier's collection of plates has never come to light, and retention here of his numbering system and notes seems pointless. Should this collection ever be found, the original journals could be consulted.

3. Certain types of entries have been deleted in entirety from the present volume. These include copies of archival documents and lists of Indian vocabularies. Most of this material is to be included as special appendices in the final volume. As this special material normally does not relate to the everyday entries in the journals, no note has been made of its deletion. In the appendices in the final volume, however, each location in the original journals will be duly noted.

4. A special problem exists in the spelling of certain Indian names. Many spellings used by Bandelier have since been changed—for example, we now use Tewa for Tehua, Keres for Queres, Tiwa for Tihua, Zia for Cia. In these cases, we have shown the modern spelling at the first appearance of the term and from then on follow Bandelier's usage. In certain cases where Bandelier varied (Queres, QQueres, or Qqueres), we have retained only the most favored spelling and others will appear as variants in the appendices of the final volume.

5. Except for place names and various familiar terms, foreign words and phrases are accompanied by translations in the text, usually at their first appearance only. In addition, a glossary of foreign terms will be appended to each volume for the convenience of the reader. Entries in a foreign language of two lines or more are presented only in English, such translations being noted.

6. A few observations, recorded lineally by Bandelier, have been rearranged in chart form for greater convenience.

7. The variable dating systems used by Bandelier have been slightly

modified. Such usages as "24 Oct. '80," and other forms, have been standardized, e.g., "October 24."

8. The chaotic punctuation used by Bandelier has been somewhat modified to fit modern usage. Along these same lines, there have been occasional minor changes in sentence structure for purposes of clarity. Paragraph breaks are primarily those of the present editors. The use of italics (for unfamiliar Indian terms and some foreign phrases) is simply an editing policy. Bandelier, himself, was not consistent in handling these terms.

In preparing for the editing of the 1883-84 journals and for the diversified task of annotating the entries, the editors have added to their earlier experiences in the area of Bandelier's travels by travel and research in the Highland, Illinois, and St. Louis, Missouri, areas. In the Southwest, one or both editors worked in Santa Fe, Phoenix, Tucson, and traveled through much of the Rio Grande Valley of New Mexico, both sides of the New Mexico-Arizona line, southern Arizona, southwestern New Mexico, and northern Mexico.

These travels were of great benefit; in addition, newspaper files and similar materials have been most valuable in elaborating upon the cultural context of Bandelier's work in the last quarter of the nineteenth century. In this regard, we have been gratified to find the extent to which it is possible to recapture Bandelier's time and to supplement significantly his mere mentions of many individuals, frequently the "little people" so often bypassed by the mainstream of history.

Originally, it was the editors' aim to present each volume of *The Southwestern Journals of Adolph F. Bandelier* as a self-contained unit. The first volume (Lange and Riley 1966) included an extended introductory sketch of Bandelier's life; it was intended that subsequent volumes would have similar, but abbreviated, sketches—each to provide adequate context for the journal entries of the particular volume. However, since the completion of the first manuscript almost ten years ago, publication costs have risen to the point that such extensive duplication of data has become impractical.

Accordingly, our initial plan has been modified. In the interest of economy, this Introduction (the biographical sketch) has been reduced to a minimum. Occasionally, because of new data, we have revised statements made in the first volume. Normally, these revisions would be indicated in the Introduction or text to minimize possible confusion on the part of the reader. However, several changes are so basic that they are noted here in the *Preface* rather than being placed elsewhere.

These changes are primarily involved with identities and supplementary data regarding various members of the Bandelier family.

In the biographical sketch presented in our first volume (Lange and Riley 1966: 1-67), we placed considerable reliance on the study of Bandelier's life by Goad (1939). Subsequent research, however, has revealed the need to modify or correct a number of statements made in both of these accounts.

Our earlier statement, "In time, a second son, Emil Frederick, was born to the family." (Lange and Riley 1966: 7), was based on the account of Goad (1939: 15, 51, 52) in which the declared brother status of Adolph F. and Emil was reinforced by several references to the uncle-niece and uncle-nephew relationships between Adolph F. and Emil's children, Elizabeth, Gustave, and Emma (pp. 15, 53, 57, 58, 122). It now seems clear that Adolph F. and Emil were not brothers but, rather, were cousins through their fathers. (Probably, the two fathers were brothers; this has not actually been documented, but the relationship has been stated by Hobbs [1940a; 1940b] and others who had direct contact with members of the Bandelier family.)

For some time, in the course of preparing this second volume, we have been troubled by certain chronological discrepancies. Further research in church records at Breese (misprinted in the first volume as Breece) and in family papers still in possession of Elizabeth's daughter, Mrs. R. L. Ormsbee, Santa Fe, New Mexico, and of Gustave's son, Mr. George E. Bandelier, Stillwater, Oklahoma, has served to clarify the situation.

Emil's baptismal name was Paul Emile, in French, or Paul Emil, in German; he was born in the community of Sornetan, District of Moutier, Canton of Bern, on May 14, 1834, and was baptised June 6, 1834. Emil married Rosalie Lipps, March 17, 1858, in Sornetan; he died in Breese, Illinois, August 10, 1873. Emil's parents were Gustave A. Bandelier and Elizabeth neé Grüring. (Adolph F.'s parents were Adolphe Eugene Bandelier and Marie neé Senn.)

As of this time, the confusion in names, Emil Frederick as we published, following Goad, Emil as in the church records of his death, Emile as listed in a roster of Breese postmasters, and Paul Emile and Paul Emil as in the certificates of marriage, apparently is simply the result of multi-lingual communities and personal adaptations to changing circumstances. We have completely abandoned the possibility that Bandelier had a brother, Emil Frederick; aside from Goad's statements, there is no evidence whatsoever to support the existence of this or any other sibling.

Anticipating further new data as research progresses with the remaining journal entries, we will continue to make such corrections as the evidence dictates.

ACKNOWLEDGMENTS

PREPARATION OF A VOLUME such as this depends on advice, information, and guidance from a wide range of individuals and institutions in various places. We wish to express our appreciation to all listed below and hope there have been no omissions. If so, we apologize and assure any person inadvertently omitted that his contribution has been no less appreciated.

Of key importance in work on the first volume of this series were Mr. Bruce T. Ellis, Mr. Wayne L. Mauzy, Dr. Bertha P. Dutton, Mrs. Marjorie F. Lambert, Dr. A. J. O. Anderson, Miss Ruth E. Rambo, and Miss Gertrude Hill, all formerly or presently on the Museum of New Mexico Staff, Santa Fe. Some of these have also helped with this volume; in other instances, their successors have continued to assist us: Dr. Delmar M. Kolb, former Director of the Museum of New Mexico, and staff members Charles C. Proctor, Dr. John Polich, Mrs. J. K. Shishkin, Mrs. Jack Stacy, Susie Henderson, Terrie Young, and others. At the Research Laboratory of the Museum of New Mexico, we benefitted from the cooperation and assistance of Dr. George Ewing, Mr. Stewart L. Peckham, and Mrs. Kirk Bryan.

Many other individuals have also been generous with their help. We wish especially to thank Dr. Myra Ellen Jenkins, Senior Archivist, State Record Center and Archives, Santa Fe, who provided a number of new and valuable sources for the Bandelier period; Mr. Eugene Mc-Cluney, Acting Director, and Dr. Douglas W. Schwartz, Director, of the School of American Research, Santa Fe; and Mr. Charles Gallen-kamp, Albuquerque, who supplied details of Bandelier's early life. Dr. John M. Corbett, National Park Service, Washington, drew our attention to the Bandelier-Janvier correspondence, lending us his copy of this rare volume. Father Ernest J. Burrus, S. J., who recently published portions of the Bandelier-Collet letters, and Rev. Lowrie J. Daly, S. J., allowed us to examine photographic copies of the recently discovered *Histoire* manuscript; both have continued to assist in a variety of ways.

We also appreciate the great cordiality and cooperation received from present and former residents of the Highland and Edwardsville, Illinois, area. Professor Harvey Huegy, grandson of Bandelier's brother-in-law, Maurice, has provided valuable data on the Bandelier-Huegy families. Mrs. R. L. Ormsbee, Santa Fe, daughter of Elizabeth Bandelier Kaune, and George E. Bandelier, Stillwater, Oklahoma, son of Gustave A. Bandelier, were similarly helpful regarding Bandelier family materials. Miss E. Margaret Patton, Librarian, and Mrs. Corinne Wilson, Assistant, and Mr. David Schoen of the Louis Latzer Memorial Library, Highland, and Mr. Russ Hoffman of the *Highland News Leader* were most helpful. Mr. J. B. Menz, First National Bank, Highland, retired, was the only person interviewed who personally remembered both Adolph F. Bandelier and his father, Adolphe E.; we found his reminiscences most enlightening. Reverend Carl R. Schroedel, Pastor of the Congregational United Church of Christ, Highland, and Reverend Victor H. Schoen, Pastor, and Mrs. Myrtle Rutz, Secretary, of the Evangelical United Church of Christ, Highland, were all most courteous and helpful in work with their church records. Mr. Edward L. Bernays, President of the Edward L. Bernays Foundation, Cambridge, Massachusetts, helped with background of his family in Highland and St. Louis.

At Breese, Illinois, our research was furthered in the summer of 1969 by the assistance and interest of Mr. Charles H. Casey, widower of Mary Olivia Kaune; Reverend J. J. Kalkbrenner, St. John's Evangelical and Reformed Church; Mr. Erwin J. Mahlant, Publisher of *The Breese Journal*; and Mr. Urban Schwartz.

Assistance in various aspects of our fieldwork came from Alden C. Hayes, National Park Service, who provided data on the Gran Quivira-Jumano and other references, and from William Gibson, Don Morris, and Mrs. Garlyn M. Hoge of the Gila Cliff Dwellings National Monument; Mr. Bert M. Fireman, Curator, Arizona Collection, State University Library; Professor John A. Jones, Pennsylvania State University, and Father Kieran McCarty, O. F. M., San Xavier del Bac Mission. Personnel of the Silver City Historical Society Museum and of the Silver City Chamber of Commerce were most helpful during our visit there.

The Bandelier scrapbook cited repeatedly in the text of this volume was sent us by Dr. Fred Eggan, University of Chicago. Dr. Christa

Bausch, Ohio University, Athens, located and arranged for us to receive selections from files of *Das Ausland* in the Württembergische Landesbibliothek, Stuttgart, Germany. Nancy Kohlmeyer and Sarah Gehlert, students at Southern Illinois University, helped in preparation of the earlier stages of the manuscript. Mrs. D. Kathleen Abbass, research assistant at Southern Illinois University, has done most of the final typing as well as assisting with phases of the editorial work.

We greatly appreciate the fine support received from officials and colleagues at Southern Illinois University. Dean William E. Simeone, Graduate School, Dean Roger E. Beyler, College of Liberal Arts & Sciences, and Dr. Ronald G. Hansen, Coordinator of the Graduate Research Program, have been helpful in every way. Dr. Campbell W. Pennington and Dr. Robert H. Mohlenbrock aided with botanical identifications and Dr. J. Cary Davis, with glossary. Dr. Ralph E. McCoy, Dr. Ferris S. Randall, and Dr. John C. Abbott, Southern Illinois University Librarians, were most kind in offering their time and assistance.

As indicated on the title page, we have been most ably assisted in the preparation of this volume by Elizabeth M. Lange. From an initial involvement primarily with the indexing of the first volume, she has taken on additional tasks in assisting with various phases of the editing and research work. The significant increase in both the richness and number of informational footnotes has been one of the more tangible results of her greater involvement in the project.

Our special thanks go to the National Endowment for the Humanities whose grant, No. H 67-0-62, enabled us to complete this work.

C. H. L.
C. L. R.

Carbondale, Illinois

INTRODUCTION

THIS BIOGRAPHICAL SKETCH of Adolph F. Bandelier is intended primarily as background and context for his 1883 and 1884 journals. In the longer account of Bandelier's life presented in our first volume (Lange and Riley 1966: 1-67), we relied rather heavily upon Goad (1939). Reexamination of such works as White (1940), Hammond and Goad (1949), and White and Bernal (1960) and the utilization of additional sources including the Bandelier Scrapbook (n.d.), Radin (1942), Jacobs (1960), Burrus (1966; 1967a; 1967b), certain files of Das Ausland, to name but a few, have provided an appreciable increase in data per se and deeper insights into the life of Bandelier and his contemporaries.

While these additional sources would justify an expanded biographical sketch at this time, the decision has been made otherwise, as explained in the Preface. Some of this material, where especially relevant to the 1883 and 1884 journal entries, has been included here as footnotes. In a few instances, such information has been added to the following abbreviated sketch, either in the text or in the footnotes.

Adolph Francis Alphonse Bandelier was born in Bern, Switzerland, on August 6, 1840. His father, Adolphe Eugene, was a business or professional man with wide and educated interests, a fact that was to have considerable effect on Bandelier's young life. A few years after Adolph's birth, the elder Bandelier, as political winds shifted, decided to improve family fortunes by establishing a new life abroad. After a brief, disappointing visit to Brazil, he settled in the small Swiss community of Highland, Illinois, thirty miles east of St. Louis, Missouri, having been attracted there by the publicity engendered by the writings of the Köpflis (Kaspar Köpfli 1833; Salomon Köpfli 1842).

In 1848, Bandelier's father was joined by his wife, Marie Senn, his son, and the family maid, Annali Näfiger (Hobbs 1940a), and a home was established in Highland. The father, in 1854, joined with two other Swiss immigrants, Frederick C. Ryhiner, a physician, and Moritz Huegy, in the founding of a bank, the F. Ryhiner & Co. They had financial backing from the Gruner-Haller and Co. of Bern.

In 1855, Bandelier's mother died, and Annali stayed on to help with the family. Adolph was educated in the public school, supplemented by private tutoring in a variety of subjects. The family spoke German in the home, as did many in the community, and efforts were also made to ground young Adolph in correct French. Like his father, Adolph F. was active in numerous civic affairs such as the rifle club and the Turnverein, showing particular interest in the intellectual life of Highland.

In his scholarly interests, it is evident that Bandelier was influenced by the scientific work of Baron Alexander von Humboldt;[1] the two were said to have corresponded and may have met in the late 1850's. Earlier biographers, including the present editors (1966: 9), have stated that Bandelier studied geology in 1857 in Bern under Professor B. Studer and also that he studied law at Bern between 1865 and 1867. However, subsequent research (Charles Gallenkamp; personal correspondence) has indicated that the Studer episode was incorrect and that it was another Bandelier, probably a cousin, who studied law at Bern.

On January 5, 1862, Bandelier married Josephine ("Joe") Huegy, the daughter of one of his father's banking partners. During the 1860's, Bandelier published a number of articles of a climatological nature in the local newspapers and served as a recorder of these data for the Smithsonian Institution in Washington, D.C. He also lectured on a wide range of archaeological and historical subjects.

With the early 1870's, Bandelier's life changed significantly. He had been active, for a number of years, in assorted business affairs, a coal mine, a foundry, and other ventures, including some affiliation with the F. Ryhiner & Co. bank. Gradually, however, his interest in the business world declined, probably in part due to his father's domineering and often difficult personality. At this same time, Bandelier's scholarly activities and achievements increased. In 1873, he began to work on Spanish documentary sources for native Mesoamerica, teaching himself Spanish. That same year, he met Lewis Henry Morgan, a leading figure in American anthropology, who, in that period, was working out his famous theories on the evolution of human culture. A concomitant of Morgan's evolutionary reconstruction was the thesis that the American Indians had never progressed beyond the level of tribal social and political organization. Bandelier rapidly became a disciple of Morgan and an advocate of his ideas. In the years after first meeting Morgan, he spent much of his research energies trying to demonstrate that the Aztecs of Mexico had not attained a level of civilization but only a tribal-based barbarism. The intellectual development of Bandelier under Morgan and their interrelationships have been covered most competently by White (1940).

By the late 1870's, Bandelier was already a respected scholar, having published several monographs on ancient Mexican culture. In these writings and in his reviews of the works of others,[2] he displayed a thorough and rigid standard of research as well as a willingness to criticize those who failed to show similar discernment in their research. Bandelier was elected to membership in the American Association for the Advancement of Science in August 1876. Parenthetically, in November 1877, he became a naturalized citizen of the United States.

Although he maintained a sincere interest in Mexico, Bandelier's first fieldwork was not in Mexico, but in the American Southwest. In the latter half of 1880, thanks largely to Morgan's influence, Bandelier was sent to New Mexico by the newly formed Archaeological Institute of America, Boston; Charles Eliot Norton, the president, and Francis Parkman were prominent members of the Executive Committee. Leaving St. Louis by railroad, Bandelier arrived in Santa Fe on the evening of August 23, 1880.[3]

It is appropriate to comment here that Bandelier was embarking upon his fieldwork at an opportune moment in Southwestern history. Mining activities were attracting numbers of individuals into remote areas; military personnel, merchants, ranchers, and others, aided by the gradual expansion of railway and telegraph services, were increasingly active. Many of these people stood ready to facilitate his work, providing local information and then passing Bandelier on to friends or acquaintances elsewhere who could similarly assist him.

Bandelier quickly gained the friendship and interest of the Archbishop, John B. Lamy, and of the other churchmen, archivists and parish priests. He sought out the territorial officials, including Samuel Ellison, librarian, who had formerly been at Peña Blanca, some miles west of Santa Fe. Bandelier spent a few days investigating the archaeological remains at the rather recently abandoned Pueblo of Pecos, some twenty miles southeast of Santa Fe. Journal entries of that period clearly reflect his great enthusiasm and boundless energy as he entered this first period of active field investigations.

Perhaps through Ellison, Bandelier had formed the acquaintance of Father José Rómulo Ribera of Peña Blanca prior to his Pecos trip. Now, upon his return from Pecos, he accepted Ribera's invitation which, in effect, diverted him from earlier plans and suddenly launched his ethnographic field experience among the Pueblo Indians. He spent a fascinating, but very uneasy, few days at the ultraconservative Pueblo of Santo Domingo, on the Rio Grande a few miles from Peña Blanca.

Frustrated in his efforts there, Bandelier soon shifted a few miles northward to the Pueblo of Cochiti where his reception was much more hospitable, allowing him to begin an ethnographic study. During the autumn of 1880, the Cochiti guided him to nearby Frijoles Canyon and its prehistoric remains; Bandelier's enchantment with the area was immediate and the Rito de los Frijoles and environs continued to be a favorite spot throughout his life. (The area was designated Bandelier National Monument on February 11, 1916, by President Woodrow Wilson.) Bandelier returned to Highland and his family in time for Christmas, 1880; at the end of that year, his journal entries continue to express his great elation. On the last day of December, he wrote, "Thus the most important year of my entire life draws to a close. Thank God, thank God for every blessing, every sore, for weal and for woe, which He has been pleased to dispense. So far, so good, and there is hope for better. . . . Have no reflections to record. Future action is all that occupies my thoughts." (Lange and Riley 1966: 236-37)

In 1881, Bandelier finally gained his long-desired opportunity to work in Mexico. However, the Lorillard-de Charney Expedition, which he was to join, had disbanded in failure by the time he arrived in Mexico. Nevertheless, Bandelier spent several months doing independent work in Oaxaca and Puebla, aided and advised by his friend, Don Joaquín García Icazbalceta. Professional recognition came to Bandelier, in absentia, when he was elected to membership in the American Antiquarian Society in April 1881. Subsequently, on July 31, an important event for Bandelier occurred in Cholula, Puebla. On that date Bandelier became a Roman Catholic, García Icazbalceta standing as sponsor and the local priest, Dr. José Vicente Campos, officiating.

In March 1882, Bandelier returned to New Mexico under the auspices of the Archaeological Institute of America. During the remainder of that year and in early 1883, he engaged in extensive archaeological and ethnological studies, ranging in his travels from the Salinas region east of the Sandia-Manzano Mountains to Acoma and Zuñi.

While in the Acoma-Zuñi region, Bandelier formed the acquaintance of Frank Hamilton Cushing at Zuñi and came to be a great admirer of this unusual man. Leaving Zuñi, Bandelier worked his way west and then south to the deserts of southern Arizona. There he visited Casa Grande, Tucson and Fort Lowell, and Fort Huachuca. Bandelier then returned to Highland for the late summer and early fall; in late October 1883, he resumed fieldwork, first in the Rio Grande Valley and then, in the Silver City-Gila Cliff Dwellings area. In the spring of 1884, Bandelier continued the planned research of the Institute, surveying northern Sonora and Chihuahua, collecting data on the Opata Indians, the Apaches, and on many archaeological sites, including the extensive remains at Casas Grandes in Chihuahua. An interesting sidelight on this period was the news, widely reported, of his death at the hands of the Apaches. His refutation was dispatched to Highland, García Icazbalceta, and elsewhere, including Europe.

With the fieldwork for the Institute completed and the termination of his salary imminent (as of January 1885), Bandelier returned to Highland in the latter portion of 1884. In November, he departed for the East and for Europe, ostensibly to arrange for the colored printing of illustrations for research publications then being prepared, but also as an agent for his father to negotiate with the Swiss creditors of the F. Ryhiner & Co. bank, the condition of which was then deteriorating —as was that of numerous other financial institutions in the country at that time.

In most respects, Bandelier's trip was unsuccessful. The spring following his return from Europe brought financial disaster to Highland. Overextended in its investments and refused further aid by the Swiss financiers, the F. Ryhiner & Co. bank faltered and in late April 1885, a run occurred. The elder Bandelier, the only surviving member of the original partnership, fled, first to New Orleans and then to South America, leaving his son and the two junior partners to face the irate townspeople. Bandelier's brother-in-law, Maurice Huegy, committed suicide in late May; the other partner, F. C. Ryhiner, Jr., fled to Iowa (though later offering to return). Bandelier, himself, was the only principal still on the scene; the fact that he seems to have been no more than an agent for his father became an irrelevant detail in the minds of the townsmen. He was arrested and taken in custody to

Edwardsville, the county seat, where he spent the night in jail. Released the next day through the good offices of friends, Bandelier left for New Mexico, leaving Joe with her sister, Bertha (Mrs. Charles Lambelet), in Highland for the next several months. Bandelier never returned to Highland for any appreciable time after that.

Having lost their resources in an attempt to meet the bank's obligations, the Bandeliers found the next years difficult ones as they settled down to a new life in Santa Fe. A novel, actually begun in 1883 and written in German as *Die Köshare*, was finished in May 1886; published in 1890 in English as *The Delight Makers*, it was not an immediate success. Bandelier managed to sell several articles to a number of American and German publications; in 1886, he was commissioned by Archbishop J. B. Salpointe of Santa Fe to write an account of the missions of the Spanish Southwest[4] which was to be sent to Rome in 1888 for presentation at the Golden Jubilee of Pope Leo XIII.

Also in 1885, the Hemenway Southwestern Archaeological Expedition engaged Bandelier as historiographer, and for several years he worked on Spanish archival materials, both in this country and in Mexico. His bibliography and his scholarly recognition continued to grow in these years. (See bibliography included in this volume.) He made trips to both the living pueblos and the various archaeological sites, though there was some decrease in frequency and duration. A major event of 1888 was the return of Bandelier's father from Venezuela. Bandelier's closing journal entry for 1888 expressed the somewhat mixed emotions which this unexpected reunion prompted (Lange and Riley 1966: 54). "Another, so far, fortunate year. We have succeeded in bringing papa home, but with him we have secured a cloud on our otherwise happy sky. Well, God has so disposed, and we must take it as it comes."

By the early 1890's, however, Hemenway support was sporadic, and Bandelier decided that future work would be more rewarding if done outside the Southwest. In 1892, Adolph and Joe departed for the west coast, bidding the elder Bandelier farewell. On June 6, the Bandeliers sailed from San Francisco for South America, thus closing the Southwestern years.

In the autumn of 1892, Joe became ill in Lima, Peru, where she died December 11. A year later, Bandelier married Fanny Ritter, a young Swiss immigrant. Together, the two did far-reaching studies in Peru and Bolivia. Sent initially to South America on a collecting expedition by Henry Villard, New York financier and philanthropist, Bandelier later changed to the American Museum of Natural History, New York. A major publication from fieldwork of this period was Bandelier's *The Islands of Titicaca and Koati.*

Returning to the United States in 1903, Bandelier kept his affiliation with the American Museum until 1906, but then, after a publishing disagreement, he moved to the Hispanic Society of America. In his years in New York City, Bandelier also lectured at Columbia University, and between 1909 and 1911 served as a staff member of the Museum of New Mexico and the School of American Archaeology (now the School of American Research) in Santa Fe, although he never returned to the Southwest.

These were active years and yet a period of decline, as Bandelier's eyes failed and his general health worsened. Fanny read to him and helped in many ways. In late 1911, he recovered his sight sufficiently to accept a research appointment with the Carnegie Institution of Washington, going with Fanny to Mexico for several months in 1912-13. In the fall of 1913, the two embarked for yet another research trip, this time to Spain, for archival work in Madrid, Seville, and Simancas. It proved to be Bandelier's final trip; seriously ill almost from the time of their arrival in Seville, he died there March 18, 1914. Fanny continued their work for several months and extracted an important collection of primary documents on the American Southwest and northern Mexico, which was later published by the Carnegie Institution, Washington (Hackett 1923; 1926; 1937).

Throughout his life, Bandelier was first and foremost a research scientist. As his journals indicate, he spent long days on the trail, in good weather and bad, often afoot and sometimes without food and shelter. His amazing stores of energy made him ignore sickness, danger, and privations; his devotion to scholarly research is often awe-inspiring. Bandelier deserves to be better known.

THE JOURNALS OF ADOLPH F. BANDELIER

1883

JANUARY

At the end of the year 1882, Adolph Bandelier was working in the Salinas region east of central New Mexico. He spent the last week of 1882 surveying sites in the Gran Quivira and Quarai area on the eastern flank of the Manzano Mountains. This work continued into the new year, 1883.

January 1: May God be with us in the new year, with Joe, Papa, and *all*. He has been with us last year, and may He continue in this. We left at 11 A.M. with Don Ramón Cisneros. Snow very deep as soon as we rose a little higher. At the foot of the Loma Parda, about two miles northwest of the road, there are two pueblitos of small houses. I did not go to see them, and photographed the Mesa Jumana, time 18 seconds. Sky and light fair, but much reflection on the snow. The horses were not quiet, particularly mine. Up to Ciénega,[1] there was at least one and one half to two feet of snow.

At the Ciénega everybody was drunk. I reached Manzano at full gallop. The Padre [Louis Bourdier][2] was out, but he soon returned. At 4 P.M. we started at full gallop toward Punta de Agua, where there was a man sick with pleurisy. I made mustard plaster with great trouble and put it on. Returned at night.

January 2: I painted the whole day. A man shot himself at the máquina [saw mill?] of Eusebio García, so the Padre had to go there to administer. No danger. On the whole I am satisfied with the results. There are pueblitos on the lomas at the foot of the Sierra de Jumanas.

January 3: Painted. Manuel Luján came. After some fighting [arguing] with José [Olivas, Bandelier's guide], we arranged matters for tomorrow. Then a fierce snowstorm set in. But the snow is wet and melts almost as fast as it falls. The Padre is as kind as ever. Packed up my [photographic] plates.

JANUARY 4: The Padre is full of attentions and kindness. How can I ever repay him? I wrote cards to Padre Gromm [Grom],[3] to Brown,[4] to Joe, and to Professor Norton[5] also. The Padre stuffed us with all sorts of provisions and matters and things, so that our cart was loaded high. We had to eat first also.

At last, at 11 A.M., we started,—José on horseback, and we on the wagon. At Kuss',[6] I stepped off and borrowed his aneroid barometer. I then struck the Abó road and trudged along in the deep snow for nearly a mile, then turned off to the left through the field, fell into the arroyos, and finally returned, taking the wagon road to Punta de Agua. After having, in all, tramped about four-and-a-half miles in deep snow in about one hour, I overtook the wagon, and we went on to Punta de Agua. There we were informed that the road to Monte Solo was blocked by snow, and that we could not reach it today. So we decided to stay at the house of Jesús Salas overnight and to start in the morning. Altitude in front of the house of Jesús Salas, 7,035 feet.

Punta de Agua is about a quarter mile from Cuaray [Quarai], east-southeast. It is in a direct line, about five miles southeast of Manzano. I was told here that the people of Abó had been frightened on my [arrival], somebody at Manzano having told them that I came with the intention of taking away their lands and houses.

The Pueblo de Ojitos is about one mile from Manzano. Started there, thank God, at last. Don Manuel Luján gave me [various] names in the Navajo language. José Olivas gave me [several] in the Comanche idiom. Don Manuel Luján also told me a good story of the Zuñi Indians concerning the origin of the better (more moral) life among them. It resulted from incest.[7]

JANUARY 5: Had a very good night. It appears that there are small house ruins on the other side of the Arroyo de Quaua. Here, they find water in wells at twelve to fifteen feet depth. Left at 9 A.M. Snow deep to the foot of the Monte Alto, altitude there 6,600 [feet]. Then it [the snow] began to decrease. Altitude, Monte Alto, 6,760. Higher up, 6,950. The plain is very cold and bare, but as we rose it grew warm, and [there is] much sabino and piñón. Fine view to the north, the Sierra de San Pedro and the Pláceres very prominent. Camp in the

Monte at 1 P.M. Much chamizo, "yerba de la vívora,"[8] and zacate. Soil good. Limestone foundations of rock. While we were eating, the horses went off which caused much delay. We continued our trip, always up and down, crossing the Cañada del León, at an altitude of 6,700 [feet]. Then we entered into the Cañada del Aguaje, a rocky dry arroyo, running from the crest nearly east and northeast. . . .*

The camp appears good, but there are clouds rising northwest and west. From the ascent of the Aguaje the view embraces the whole Sierra del Manzano, Sierra de Sandía, Sierra de San Pedro, Sierra de Pláceres, and the Sierra de Santa Fé in an arc of a circle of about 60 degrees. Aguaje, altitude 6,995 feet; camp, 7,100 feet. The camp proved a very narrow one. We were already asleep when we heard shouting. To our reply, the answer came: "Buena Gente [Friends]." Four travelers on three horses and one burro came up, hungry and frozen. They were on the road three days from the Rio Bonito and were going to Sabinal[9] and [were] very glad to get to the fire. I hurriedly wrote a pencil line to Joe and gave it to them, requesting they mail it at Sabinal. It is our wedding-night, the twenty-second, and a memorable one. Oh, my God, it is only now that I begin to love her, as should have been the case years ago, and to find out how great a treasure she is to me. And so far, far away from her.[10]

JANUARY 6: Our guests left early, and after having hunted the horses, we finally left also at 9 A.M. Monte Solo is a round, flat hill, wooded, standing beneath the crest or brow of the mesa, where the latter bends nearest to the south and where it is also lowest. Thence the mesa trends to the southeast, treeless but very grassy. Land fertile, but no water at all. The rim is wooded all around, and along that rim the pueblos are situated, scattered above the cañadas. Many fine quartz pebbles are found on the surface, but no pottery. We traversed this cold, rolling basin, and on the last brow saw the Medano[11] with the church of Quivira[12] on it. The valley of the Medano is beautiful, fertile, grassy, with sabinos dotting it, but no water. On the northeast side there is a dry arroyo.*

The section presents itself as follows: the church and pueblo stand on the highest brow (not point) of a series of ridges running nearly east and west; the church overlooking the valley west and northwest. South of it there are a series of similar ridges also dotted with sabinos, with dry gulches between, about parallel, but lower than the one of Quivira. Beyond it, [are] wooded low mesas with steep banks. Surrounded by fertile fields or valleys, the Quivira has thus been a most favored spot up to [except for] the water, of which I cannot, as yet, find any trace. The pueblo is large, evidently at least three stories. Room or cells are sometimes very small, and the walls of well-broken limestone with soil or mud between. Many timbers protrude. Pottery [is] in abundance. Glossy prevails, but there is also black-and-white, smoky, black, and red. It is plain that any pottery except the glossy is exceptional and perhaps intrusive.[13] The church and convent is an enormous structure. The north wall of the church is forty-four inches wide; the east wall is wider yet. Took five photographs. We have a fine lodging.

Maize grows here perfectly without irrigation.[14] The nearest water east is the Ojo de la Gallina—twenty-five miles. North, the Mesteñito is twenty-seven miles. West, the Chupaderos, twenty miles. South, twenty-six miles, the Carizoso [Carrizo Mountain].

JANUARY 7: I took the compass and counted the rooms. The horses were gone again, so both men went after them. José returned, without the horses. They have fled south. He found a ditch, clearly an acequia, leading northeast. At ten meters above the base of House #1, and three-hundred-fifty meters northeast of it, there is a distinct old pond, about two meters deep, and forty meters in diameter. It had a rim of stone on the north side, and there also it was broken and a deep gulley trends down to the dry arroyo. Some distance to the southwest of it, there is another one thirty meters wide and two to three meters deep. At three hundred meters the acequia terminated in a third pond, flat, indistinct, and about thirty-five meters in diameter. Thus the water question is settled. Rain supplied the drinking water for the population, and the number of the latter could not have exceeded one thousand souls. There is much broken pottery around the ponds and along the acequia. [Bandelier here gives dimensions of various rooms.]* [There is an] old church opening east, . . . The total length of the edifice is 35.6 [meters], its width 7.4 [meters]. It is constantly smaller than both Abó and Cuaray. Manuel Luján is not home yet (at 3 P.M.).

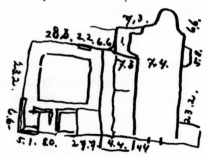

I am glad that the water question is solved. Thus another idol and myth is gone; it looks as if there had been two distinct pueblos at Quivira. Near the upper pond I found a handsome flint implement. There are places where pottery is found on the ridge. In the church, there are young sabinos. From the west side of the church, about one hundred fifty meters, is the foot of the ridge. Manuel Luján returned at 4 P.M.: no horses. There is a pueblo at the Lagunitas, four miles southwest. Pottery same as here.

JANUARY 8: Terrible night. Both men left early after the horses; they appear lost or stolen. It being exceedingly cold, I waited till about 8 A.M., and then started for the south-southwest. The hill of Quivira in that direction is not higher than 20 meters; then begins a grassy plain, three miles wide, rolling—dotted occasionally with sabinos. The grass in places [is] three feet high. This plain terminates at the foot of a bald ridge running about east and west. The foot of that ridge is 77.0 [meters?] below the hut at Quivira. A trench or road is visible, leading from it to the big church. The Loma Pelada itself is 35.0 [meters?] high and steeper than Quivira. On its very top are ruins.*

The structures are all so ruined that nothing can be discerned. Besides, there is a half inch of fine, slippery snow on the ground. Pottery [is] principally glossy, but also black and white, as at Quivira. On the top, there are foundations of single stones, three inches wide, well broken [well shaped? fragmentary?], set in the ground on edge.* For what purpose, I cannot imagine. Two estufas. Returned at 11 A.M.

Going about in the afternoon, I found a fourth pond, 35 meters west of House #9, and north of the church. It is the best made of all, at least 3.0 [meters?] drop [deep], and with a semi-circular rim, very plain from northeast by north to west. This rim appears to have been of stone, and it is covered with pottery. There are still two channels running down from it to the north and north-northeast. (José says they are "Desaguas [drainage ditches].") Thus the case is positive and plain. These ponds above the pueblo communicated with the large pond below the church by a channel running through the village. José found another small pueblo about west-southwest. Pottery glossy. Photographed the standing walls in the northwest corner of pueblo. At 4:30 P.M., I took the last view, the church and pueblo from the northwest. One [photographic plate] was lost through my fault. Don Manuel returned. No trace of the horses. They are evidently stolen. Tomorrow I have a hard day's journey before me.

JANUARY 9: Started at 3:30 A.M. and reached Punta de Agua at 3 P.M. on foot. Perfectly exhausted. Could not get any farther that day. Everybody is stunned by that unheard of feat. The snow is very deep from the Monte Solo on and walking barely possible. On an average, there are six inches of solid snow, but I broke through at every step, 35 miles 11 hours. Thank God for the strength He gave me. Salas will go for the cart tomorrow.

JANUARY 10: Reached Manzano at 10 A.M. The Padre came at 1 P.M., and a little earlier Juan José Pacheco of Sabinal [arrived], a very nice man. There is a great pueblo at Sabinal. It appears that, in 1879, the Rio Grande dried up below San Felipe for one or two months. On the contrary, it carried off the old town of Sabinal in 1856, cutting through a straight channel. I found here a number of letters from home, but none from the [Archaeological] Institute [of America]. Very tired. Painted.

JANUARY 11: Padre left for Chilili at 10 A.M. I painted. At noon, Manuel and José came with the horses and everything. But José is sick and even delirious. So I let him go with a horse, for he is useless further on. He shall sell the horse and turn over the proceeds to the Vicar General.[15] So I am left all alone. Called on Kuss. A letter from Joe. God bless her for everything. Wrote to her at night, but did not finish. Got shaved. Terrible operation.

JANUARY 12: Painted all day. Padre returned at 5 P.M.

JANUARY 13: Painted in the early morning. We left at 11 A.M. by buggy and road over to Punta de Agua. Juan de Dios Salas was sick. The smallpox is raging there too. Settled with him. Balance, $17.75 which the Padre will collect. Thence we drove to Cuaray, and Bernabé Salas led us to a hill northeast of the church, where natural rocks protrude, and where there is a slab, lying on the ground on which there is a carved inscription in Spanish. I could decipher the following: "lo puso."[16] At the foot there are some other words in the same kind of letters, which I could not make out, they being too badly blurred.

There are two or three other crosses painted on the rocks near by. I found no traces of pottery. Bernabé assured me that on the distant lomas around, particularly south, towards the mesa and in the monte, there is a great number of scattered small houses about. We examined the ruins again. I found less snow and more pottery. Measured three rooms and found them respectively: fronting south 5 x 9, 6 x 9, and 6 x 8 feet. Walls about 12 inches [thick?]. In the pueblo proper the pottery is glossy, but I found several pieces of finely corrugated and one or two pieces of black-and-white, also much delicate pottery, yellowish red, almost orange. I noticed traces of an almost obliterated estufa also. Finally Bernabé led us to a hill south of the east mound, about 50 meters in basal diameter, and 5.0 high, on the summit of which there are hollows indicating four or five cells which appear irregularly distributed. On the south side of the hill runs the arroyo; and there are "ojos [springs]," and there is a layer of sandstone flags, which appears [?] artificial, and runs northeast and southwest. The pottery on the entire mound is strictly small-house pottery, corrugated and indented, black-and-white, and smoky. There is much of it, and still I did not find a trace of glossy. The contrast between the pottery of this mound, and that of the other, which are about 20.0 [meters] distant [apart] only, is very marked and striking, and it looks as if there had been two distinct tribes settled at Cuaray.[17] Much flint and some obsidian are all over the ruins. We examined also the ruins of the convent. It was almost as large as that of Quivira. Several rooms, on the east side, are still entire, with white plaster on the wall, wooden lintels and ceilings. We returned by the Ojitos, and I examined the site of the old pueblitos about 1/5 of a mile from the road west-southwest. There are no traces of ruins and only a few pieces of black pottery. Painted all afternoon. There is a large pueblo at the "Tornillada" at the foot of the Mesa Jumana, eight miles from Abó. Shall visit it if I possibly can. From what I can gather the large pueblos are all below the crest of the mesa. The small houses are scattered through the monte and on that crest east and west, and the plateau of the mesa was absolutely unoccupied. Shall leave for Abó and the river [Rio Grande] Monday.

JANUARY 14: The Padre was called off to the Chiato hurriedly, to confess a woman who, while on the point of childbirth, has been suffering from a flow of blood which will probably kill her. He says that this happens frequently here. He knows no remedy. When he returned, Manuel Luján came. He tells me that, with the exception of the Parida, all the other ruins are at the foot of the mesa, whereas the small houses are above, on the rim or crest of the mesa. Went to Mass. Packed up my things,[18] settled with the Padre (very, very cheap in-

deed) and left on horseback for Abó at 1 P.M. The Padre came along
for about two miles. When I reached Ciénega, a furious snowstorm
broke out from the south. It lasted until I got about to the Loma
Parda. Was well received at Abó. There are two ruins at the Loma
Parda, one at the Ojitos de la Torneada, and one—it is said—above it,
on the mesa. There is one pueblo south of here, on the Cerro de la
Mina, one on the Cañada de Juan Luján, one on the Cerro Montoso,
the Pueblo de los Arroyos, etc. Shall go there tomorrow with Ramón.

They use, as remedies against small-pox, decoctions of "Rosa de
Castilla," "Manzanilla," etc.[19] Talked until 10 P.M.

JANUARY 15: We started at 10 A.M. for the east, and at the distance of
about a mile, across the cañada, reached the base of the Cerro Pelón.
Whereas the whole country around, except occasional bottoms and
valleys, is dotted with sabinos and cedros, this hill gradually rises about
150 feet in two platforms, grassy, but perfectly treeless. It is rather
broad, and contains ruins.*

There is very little pottery about, and what there is, is black-and-
white, small-house type, smoky, and plain. Nothing glossy, corrugated,
nor indented. Few flint flakes. There is no permanent water in the
vicinity. It is evidently a settlement of [two?] middle-sized houses,
neither of which was over one story high, and the whole recalls forcibly
the ruins on the plain of Cubero. Thence we proceeded to the northeast, following at first the Cañada de la Torneada, then turning into
the Cañada del Aguaje. The Mesa de la Torneada divides both [sep-
arates the two]. It is a bluff of red sandstone with outcroppings of
gypsum, abrupt and almost inaccessible at its southwestern point. It
is rounded; therefore, the name. At the crest it flattens into a lower
bench, wooded, which slopes down to the foot of the Mesa Jumana.
The mesa may be 200 feet high and the Mesa Jumana, with steep,
densely wooded slopes, rises about 500 feet. We ascended along the
bed of the deeply cut arroyo, a country of steep wooded and also denuded hills, often difficult to ride up or down, and entered the bench
about 1 mile west of the foot of the Mesa Jumana. Then turned to
the northwest and, 100 yards off, on a level open space, struck the
miserable temporary hut of Juan José Sanchez with the ruins of a
small pueblo. The nearest permanent water is that of the Ojo del
Aguaje. The foundations of the houses are plain yet.* The stone was
red sandstone, broken as best they could.

West of Building A there is a deep hole, an evident excavation, but

circular like an estufa. The pottery is glossy. An immense view to the
west and southwest opens here. The Sierra Fra Cristóbal, Sierra Magdalena, and the Sierra de los Ladrones open in full sight. The Sierra de
Socorro is still hidden by the range of cerros in front of Socorro. The
whole valley of Abó spreads out in full view. The wind (south) blew
intensely cold, and we left. Ramón told me that the 2 pueblitos at the
Loma Parda were similar to this one, only of red stone. But as he
spoke of another more interesting place south, about five miles off, I
concluded to drop the Loma Parda and to go to the latter point. We
rode quickly down to the Ojo del Aguaje and then struck across the
wooded and snow-covered hills, crossing dry cañadas, which all descend
from the mesa. At the head of some of them there are the cornfields of
the families of Abó, since the corn grows fine without irrigation, and
there are isolated stone ruins scattered through the woods. Two of
these cañadas form passes over the Mesa Jumana, with trails leading
directly across to Quivira. The southern and larger one, the Cañada
del Puerto Largo, is very fertile, and about five miles east of Abó, begins,
on the low banks of the vale, a series of ruins of evident "summer
ranchos" of Pueblo Indians. They are accompanied by glossy pottery
and are indicated by posts stuck in the ground. . . , and by forked
branches partly buried and partly scattered about.* Also loose stone
foundations. There are more of these ruins along the cañada upwards.
Some of the vigas [rafters] are six to eight inches in diameter, and the
edges evidently chopped off with a stone implement.* The horcones, or
forked branches [to support the vigas], are of various sizes, but the bark
is gone in every case. The appearance of the ruins indicates temporary
abodes only. Returned to Abó at 2 P.M. very highly pleased. Painted
till sunset. Unwell.

JANUARY 16: Am very tired and not well. The head is dizzy and heavy;
the back aches.[20] Shall probably not be able to go out today. Am [will
be] glad to get back to the river [Rio Grande], where if, as the case
might be, I fall sick, there is at least medical attendance near at hand.
I tried to brace up, but in vain, so I finally concluded to stay indoors. A
party from Ciénega told me that there were traces of ruins on the spot
where the chapel stands. Pottery is being found; also metates. The
storm of wind was very violent in the afternoon, and my own condition
very bad. Coupled with it were constant itchings as if I had body lice.
Maybe [so], the house and everything are filthy enough. The Padre
came at 5 P.M., blustering and bragging as usual about his own prowess.

The evening was quiet, but very cold. I felt somewhat relieved and shall start tomorrow. So the memorable trip to the Manzano and to Quivira has come to an end. Thank God! He has protected and assisted me in every way, and I can but attribute to him whatever results I may have gained.

January 17: We started at 8 A.M. ["We," here, included at least Bandelier and Father Bourdier of Manzano.] Last night Martín told me that he knew there was a still larger pueblo at the Torneada, on the other side of the Aguaje. It may be, but I do not implicitly trust [him]. The road descends into the Cañada Pintada and then turns to the right, always running in the very bottom of the dry arroyo. Sometimes the gorges are picturesque, the ridges are all wooded, and occasional rocks protrude. The strata appear undisturbed. On the crests of these ridges it is said that there are pueblos, mostly small houses. I do not doubt but there are a number of small houses scattered in the monte, but I still place no faith in the assertion, that there are a great many ruins of large pueblos.

As far as I can ascertain, there is a ruin at the Arroyos, one at the Estanque Colorado, at the Monte Solo, at the Mina of Ramón Cisneros, and a chain of ranchos on both edges of the Cañada de Juan Luján. At the Salada the first view is caught of the Bocas de Abó and the ranges which lie between us and the plain become all singularly bare and barren. There are hardly any trees on them at all. A circuit of nearly 12 miles must be made from the Salada to the Bocas, as the straight road is impassable. The Cerro Montoso (not Monte Solo, see above) stretches to the left.

At noon we entered the Bocas, a bleak denuded passage. No vegetation at all is visible; the rock appears to be plutonic. At least quartzitic. The west slope of the Manzano Mountains, while equally accidented [fragmented, hence broken?] as the eastern, and very similar to it, is totally barren and sterile. In the north there appears the Sierra de Sandía, beyond it the Sierra del Valle [Jemez Mountains]. The plain is totally level, grassy, treeless, and without water. The high ceja [rim] of the Rio Grande appears in the west; beyond it towers the Sierra de San Matéo.[21] In the southwest the lofty block of the Sierra de los Ladrones looms up handsomely, and nearly south the immense crest of the Magdalena Mountains. The Sierra de Socorro is barely visible in front of it. [In these observations, Bandelier seems to have been consistently misoriented about 45° south.] The plain was without snow, but the southerly wind very cold. I suffered a great deal from the cold.

We reached the Rio Grande at the Casa Colorada, 6 miles below Belen, and crossed cautiously as it carried ice and is at all times very treacherous. It is narrow and shallow, but full of changing sinkholes. Near the Casa Colorada is a pueblo, the Pueblo del Alto. Crossing the river, the western bottom is very fertile and densely peopled. First Jarrales [Jarales], then Pueblitos, then Manuelitas, finally Belen itself, a settlement scattered over four to five miles, of good solid people. There are no streets, the houses being too far apart. Father Gromm not being at home, we still remained [stayed anyway] and called on Mr. Becker,[22] to whom I gave a draft for $75. Exhausted and sick, I went to bed early, glad to be in bedsheets again. No sleep. Father Bourdier is full of body lice. Wrote to Pradt.[23]

JANUARY 18: Father Bourdier left early in the morning for Albuquerque. Got letters from Joe, the children, Rosalie,[24] and poor Evans.[25] [I am] slightly better, but exceedingly weak. Went to see a shoemaker. He is a German; in fact, nearly all foreigners [here] are Germans. Mr. Charles is from Bern; he is exceedingly pleasant and kind, and an excellent cook at that. I attempted to paint a little, but with bad success. Father Gromm returned at 9:30 P.M.; he is always the same good, kind man. I used *Agua sedative*[26] with fair effect.

JANUARY 19: Another letter from Joe. Such a good one! Am better, but still weak. Painted with better results. Very quiet. Talked with a prospective guide of the future.

JANUARY 20: Called on Mr. Goebel.[27] Very pleasant. Got my mail from Laguna. Painted.

JANUARY 21: Painted all day. Suspicious news from the Apaches. I shipped my photographs, box, etc. to Brown on the 20th. Am anxious to know how they turn out.

JANUARY 22: Painted pottery. At noon, Father Bourdier [returned from Albuquerque]. He reported intense cold at Santa Fe, and revolution in France.[28] I am well again and fit for work. There are pueblos at the Cerros and one at the Ciénega, on the road to the Rito Quemado. Bad Indian news confirmed.[29] Wrote to Mrs. Morgan.[30]

JANUARY 23: Father Bourdier left this A.M. No letters! Painted all day. Reports from the Rito Quemado[31] are very unfavorable. ——ito to Mrs. Gan. [?] Spent the evening pleasantly with Goebel. I am beginning to recover my lost sleep again.

JANUARY 24: Painted pottery all day. No letters yet, from no quarters. Began to write my report. The oldest book of the parish bears date 1793.

JANUARY 25: Photographs from Brown. Painted pottery all day and wrote my report at night.

JANUARY 26: Painted all day and finished my report. Tired. No letters.

JANUARY 27: Mailed my report. Got letter from Brown. 18 [photographic] plates OK. Painted all day. It appears that 50 to 60 years ago, this entire valley was timbered, sabinos, álamos, and mezquite growing in abundance. Since the settlements began, all this has completely disappeared. Wrote to Padre Campos[32] and to García [Icazbalceta][33] late. Wrote to F[rank] Bigler.[34]

JANUARY 28: Got photographs; OK. Painted all day. At sunset, visit from Becker. Wrote to Brown, returning photographs, and sent photographs to Bernays,[35] to Matthews,[36] to Frank Smith,[37] and to Rev. Adams.

JANUARY 29: My box came, totally broken. I had to send it to a carpenter at once. Painted all day, finishing at last the pottery from Quivira. At night had pleasant chat with Father Gromm. All ready to leave tomorrow. Wrote to Mr. Collett [Collet].[38]

JANUARY 30: Started on horseback at 1 P.M., following the road by the river, all through highly cultivated fields, with acequias in every [possible?] direction. I saw that, up to the Cerro de los Lunas, from the north, the right (west) side of the river is skirted by volcanic bluffs or hills. At Tomé a similar cerro juts out on the east side, near the shore. There is the Cerro de los Lunas, very high, craggy and picturesque, then a series of volcanic mesas, then the Cerro de la Isleta, and an unbroken line of steep mesas, merging finally into the malpaís of Albuquerque.

Reached Isleta at 4:30 P.M. and was very well received by Padre

Peyron.[39] The pueblo is large, and the houses have a Mexican appearance. Each house, often with a portal, is evidently for one whole family. I saw one estufa only, and they say that there is only one in all. There are two stores, José María Chavez and José Tondre.[40] The church is large, of adobe, as is in fact the whole pueblo.[41]

I had the advantage of seeing, the same evening, one of the well-informed men of the pueblo, José. He told me that tu-ay was the generic name for old houses or ruins. He denies having any knowledge of traditions among his people, but stated that the ruins south of Isleta are those of Piro villages.[42] "Los Lentes" are Piro. The pueblos south of the Manzano are Piro also. No name for the Quivira. The old Pueblo of Isleta was adjacent to the present one, . . . north of it, on the Mesa de Padillas. He says that they call the pueblos in general be-rein— Pueblos del Agua or Agua del Pueblos. There is a tradition here about the body of Fray Francisco Padilla, a monk buried in the church in a canoa [canoe or boat], that from time to time comes to the surface and is always in perfect condition. The last apparition took place in 1863 or 1864.[43]

JANUARY 31: Joseph Tondre came. The pueblo is divided into two sections [moieties]:[44] Ojos Colorados [Red Eyes] and Ojos Negros [Black Eyes]. Besides, it is divided into four quarters: white, blue, yellow and red maize.[45] I heard the distribution but could not note it. This is a secret. They have a cacique. Could not ascertain the aboriginal title, but they say distinctly that he is their priest![46] I started for the Mesa de las Padillas at 10 A.M. Through the cultivated, sandy, but fertile bottom for nearly three miles, then up the steep slope of black trap [lava] 23 heights = 36.8 meters = 119 feet.[47] The ruin is on the northern edge, . . .* The ruins show a one-story building [with two wings of 14 and 16 rooms respectively]. The pottery is mixed, glossy, and corrugated, also black-and-white. There is no obsidian, but much flint and trap or lava. The mesa is small and almost round. There is also black-and-white pottery at the foot of the mesa.

The Ojos Negros are called shi-pu-ne and the Ojos Colorados shure. The gobernador is called ta-bude, the cacique ay-cavede, and capitán de la guerra, cavede. An ancient Indian called on the Padre in the afternoon. From his statements, I gather that the old pueblo stood nearly on the present site, but there is a ruin on the other side of the river at the Ojo de la Cabra. [There is another] one at the foot of the Mesa de la Padillas, about three miles from this place. There is also a pueblito about [near] the cerro of Isleta. In fact, the entire volcanic range seems to be dotted at intervals with ruins. At night, the women here told me about many customs. When they bury, they purge like at Acoma, and they put food into the clothes in which the corpse is dressed. They also have the belief that the soul remains for four days upon earth. In the sepulchre they pour three to four tinajas [jugs] of water, but put no food. At the close of the 4th day, the whole relationship (todos los parientes) [all the relatives] bring food to the house of the deceased; the family washes itself, and then partakes of that food.[48] They have doctors, whom they call ya-añe.[49] They named to me four principal ones, but it is doubtful as to whether that number is accidental or permanent among them.

The tablas [headboards] in the dance are worn by the men. They dance the Baile del Pinito [Little Pine Dance] in September, when the men wear the tablas. [Also mentioned were] the Baile de la Tortuga [Turtle Dance] and Baile de los Ramos [Bough Dance, possibly Evergreen Dance]. They dance a good deal about the time of Christmas and New Year, and also in the week after Easter. These dances are public, but the rehearsals are secret! They also have public dances during which they compel the outsiders to remain out of sight! ([The reason for?] this is plain enough.) The Padre says that the doctors properly elect [more precisely, select] the governor and the war captain, and then present them to the people who nominally perform the election.[50]

FEBRUARY

FEBRUARY 1: The same woman also told me, and Padre Peyron confirmed the fact, from his experience among the Queres and Jemez, that four days after childbirth, the mother rises, as until that time the child is kept with her in bed, so as to preserve, as she says, "el calor de la madre [the mother's warmth]." Then, the child is named after the first object which [attracts the mother's] attention. If a star, the child is named star; if a flower, flower, etc. I inquired after the name asay or osay, but they could not give me any information. They also dance a Baile de la Flecha [Arrow Dance] and have a particular manta for it, highly embroidered. It is very old, and the only one in the pueblo. At the last dance, 12 women wore it in succession.[51]

Nicolás Lucero and his son-in-law, Ortiz, the former from Peña Blanca, the latter from Santa Fe, came by buggy to visit the cura [priest]. Bad news (ill conduct) from Padre Rómulo [Ribera, Peña Blanca];[52] also from Padre Brun![53] Left at 2 P.M. by [in] a violent sandstorm from the south. The road is dreary, but the country is mostly settled. I am told that the ruin in question is at the foot of Mesa de las Padillas. Sandhills and sandhills have to be traversed. The distance is 15 miles to the old town [Albuquerque].[54] The first person I met was Carlos Ruppe.[55] Went to Candelaria's.[56] Then to the new town and saw Will[iam M. Borchert].[57] He is sick. Has news from Annie [Borchert], who is with Joe. Saw Sanders.[58] Went home and wrote to Joe, dear good Joe! I am beginning to love her just now; as if we had been recently engaged.

FEBRUARY 2: Called on Dieckman, at the college,[59] but Fray Personé [Personnet][60] was not present. At Ruppe's. Then went to see the new town. Drew $100 for January and $100 for expenses. Called on Mr. Altheimer, etc. Sandstorm so violent that I cannot leave today, as I would have to face it, which is almost impossible. Shall see tomorrow. Returned to the hotel at 2 P.M., after mailing letter to Joe. Wrote to the *Ausland*.[61] Conflicting reports about the Apaches. Ordered a razor with guard, in place of the one I lost at Manzano and left $3.50 with E. J. Post[62] for it. It is one of the ugliest days I have seen on this trip; the driving sand is absolutely blinding, and the wind very violent although not cold at all. Wrote my letter. Mr. Huning[63] gave me valuable information.

FEBRUARY 3: They [Isleta] play a [form of the] game Patol; it is called *gui-ua-patol-ya-ua*. I saw it played.[64]

(*Na-be-se* [is their name] for the Baile del Pinito [Little Pine Dance].)

The foyer of the estufa is [formed by] a single transverse wall. The estufa is 11.5 [meters] in diameter, about 3.0 [meters] high of adobe,

and walls 14 inches thick. The Ojos Negros paint black and white; the Ojos Colorados, yellow! (Qu-share and Qui-ranna.)[65] Whenever a child is born in the pueblo, shots are fired. The pueblo of the "Lentes," a mile this side of Los Lunas, was Piro; so was the pueblito four miles south of Belen. I left at 10 A.M. and riding slowly, reached Isleta at 1 P.M. On the road, met Mr. Brock, an American, who entrusted me with a confidential mission for the Rito Quemado. We lost our way and wandered about till I got to Pajarito. Visited the estufa. It is well made. The women do not dance in the Baile del Pinito. Shall get additional vocabulary tomorrow. It appears that the [area] from Padilla to opposite Albuquerque is full of small pueblos.

FEBRUARY 4: Left Isleta at 10 P.M. Arrived at Belen early. Reception exceedingly friendly. Letter from F. Bigler and from Olivas. Nothing from the Institute [Archaeological Institute of America]. Painted still. My camera not yet done.

FEBRUARY 5: Painted all day. At night, wrote to Olivas and Bigler. The lack of news becomes very annoying.

FEBRUARY 6: Day very handsome again, but no news. Kept on painting. There are pueblos at the ciénega, or Ojo de la Jarra, and several in the Cañada de la Cruz. Two pueblos on the Rio Puerco close to its mouth. Night at Becker's very pleasant. Retired late.

FEBRUARY 7: Father Gromm left for Isleta. I painted all day, finishing up. Have 23 sheets now ready; on them 84 pieces of pottery and 11 ground plans of pueblos. Expected Frank [Bigler], but he did not come. Met Mr. Benecke!

FEBRUARY 8: Packed up my pottery in nine cigar boxes. Arranged with Frank Rivalé at $2 per day. Got my camera at last. It is well fixed. Took two photographs of Mr. Becker's baby. #3 and 4, time 11 and 12 seconds. At night, Frank [Bigler] returned with Father Gromm. No letters. Cannot explain this silence!

FEBRUARY 9: At Frank's [Bigler] request I changed the route, and in place of going to the Rito Quemado, shall go to the Laguna directly. Will start Sunday A.M. I mailed my paintings, and the letter to Dr. Longwill[66] about vaccination. Tomorrow, Frank will start for Albuquerque and return tomorrow night. My boots torn, gave them to mend. I hope I shall find letters at Laguna! If not, I do not know what to think of it. They have no cause for such a long silence. Shall write home tomorrow. A very positive letter. Whatever my faults may be, they have no reason to be so absolutely silent. Wrote to S. S. Robinson,[67] also to Mr. Gerdes[68] at Santa Fe. Sent receipt of postal order to Professor Norton. Wrote finally to Governor Ritch[69] too. Wrote to Gov. Terrazas at Chihuahua, enclosing letter of Governor Ritch and asking for circular to authorities. Frank changed his plans again and leaves tomorrow for Albuquerque and Laguna. Fixed my plates tonight.

FEBRUARY 10: Packed up. Wrote a short letter to Joe. Shipped valise to S. S. Robinson, Georgetown [New Mexico], and box with plates to Brown, also letter. Took leave of Mr. Goebel. Everything ready now for tomorrow. Shall go by the cerros and stay there overnight. Pancho is ready. Took the view from southeast of the church at 4 P.M. Dark, but lighted up in patches. #1, time 14 seconds. *Will require care in developing.* If good, the effects will be exceedingly fine. Took leave of Becker and he gave me $30. Spent the evening at the Belgians: Leyno and Danckenguy.[70] Pleasant.

FEBRUARY 11: Left with Francisco Rivalé at 10 A.M. We crossed the plain to the northwest and then ascended the ceja [ridge], which is not at all the vertical wall it appears, but a series of erosive hillocks and cuts, through which the road serpentines in rising up.* On the top is an extensive plain, through which the Rio Puerco runs from northwest to southeast in a broad depression. Along the west of it, about ten miles from the ceja, dark volcanic mesas run, the cañones emptying at about right angles to the Rio Puerco. In the southwest, the Sierra de Los Ladrones rises very abruptly in a pyramidal form. To the north of it extends the Sierra del Oso, plainly visible. Then lies the Ciénega with the large Pueblo of Ojo de la Jara. South of it the Santa Rita Valley with four ruins; beyond it the Cañada de la Cruz with *small houses*,* while other ruins are large and with estufas. In the northwest appears the Sierra de San Matéo heavily loaded with snow.

We crossed the Rio Puerco at 1 P.M. It is running with water now, although this is not often the case. The bottom is sandy with abrupt banks about eight to fifteen feet high. Its width varies between 30 to 100 feet. The plain adjoining is exceedingly fertile and yields maize well without irrigating. From time to time the river overflows its banks and does damage. The "Cerros," two volcanic isolated mountains, about 500 feet high, of lead or steel-gray trap, rise at the outskirts of the western mesa, where the Rio Puerco approaches it, mainly hugging the foot of the northern cerro. There the "Plazita" formerly stood, but the river swept over it three years in succession, and last year finally to such an extent that they moved over to this side so that the whole settlement is absolutely modern. Two miles from the Plazita, on the right bank, in the plain, stands the ruin on the other side. It was of adobe, and the walls are still visible in the same manner as at Puaray, but less distinct. I could not notice any estufa, but this may be on account of the fierce winds who [sic] blow across the plain. There is a remarkably brilliant display of pottery on the surface; glossy, and much more varied and handsome colors, for instance, a crimson chocolate-brown, a cream-yellow. The designs also are better executed, and the pottery is much better and thinner. All appears *new*. Fragments of metates, manos, and

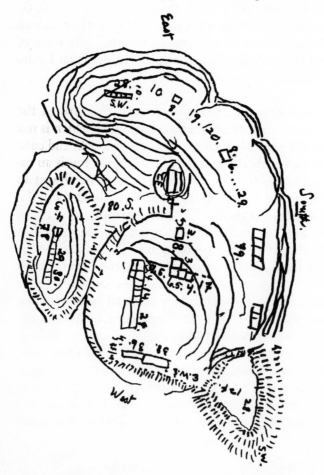

much obsidian in very large pieces. I never saw such a number of handsome fragments of pottery and of obsidian as here.[71]

We stopped at the house of Francisco Rel [Reál?]. He was not at home, but his family received us very well. Started on foot for the northern cerro, on the top of which is the ruin. The cerro is about two miles from the Plazita, and at least 400 feet high. Very steep and abrupt, difficult of describing. On the top there is a small house pueblo, scattered, built of plates [slabs] of trap, walls apparently piled up without adobe mortar. Pottery mostly red, painted black, but there are also fragments painted red outside, delicate [?], and white inside. Not a trace of corrugated and indented. Some flints, hardly any obsidian. Sky too gloomy for photography. To the north, the view extends beyond the cañón, the Chaca [Chacra Mesa], and the Cerro de la Alesna.

Night doubtful. There is much noise here about a Negro who has been concealed in a straw stack. We were careful about the horses. Above the cerro, there is no water. The woman of the house told me that, at one time, a party of Laguna Indians went to the river to sell pottery, but the Navajo murdered them all and left the pottery pieces strewn on the ground. This is well to know. The place is about 10 miles east of here in the plain. Five Lagunas were killed.

FEBRUARY 12: Started at 7:30 A.M. We rode very leisurely due north, up the Rio Puerco, then turned to the northwest, past the Mesa Redonda, and then into the plain to the Rito [on the Rio San José]. Sandstone formations all about. In the far north, the canyons east of the Sierra de San Matéo are visible; the Cañón de Juan Tafoya is very wild and inhabited by Navajos. The Rito is in a groove; the stream of the Rito at Laguna keeps [flows]; at the Rito, it sinks. Left Francisco at the Rito and started for Laguna. The road is very picturesque. Reached Laguna at 5 P.M. Mr. Bigler here. Stayed with Capt. Pratt [Pradt]. Got letters from home and from Mr. Parkman.[72] Thank God! Everything is all right.

It appears that each gens has its particular idols. He also tells me that 15 miles north of the "Cerros," in the Rio Puerco Valley, on the Mesa Colorada, there is a large ruin with pottery, identical with that of the "Cerros." There is a ruin three miles south of here; one, a half-mile; and another, one mile, west. South of Acoma, the ruins are mostly small houses. Witchcraft abundant here. They believe that putting a circle of twisted yucca above the head, and stepping into [under?] it, enables them to assume any form.[73] On the whole, everything is very favorable.

There will be a Chacuan [Chakwena][74] next Friday. There is evidently big immorality among the Pueblos. At Laguna, the organization of the Chacuan has successfully worked against it and abolished successfully the obscenities. But at Zuñi they are in full blast yet. We made 30 miles today. It appears that Mr. Cushing[75] expects us.

FEBRUARY 13: Got the names of all the clans: *Tzitz* [Water], *Qo-ha-yo* [Bear], *O-shatsh* [Sun], *Tzina* [Turkey], *Shruui* [Snake], *Ma-yo*, *Shia-huate*, *Shyu-amo* [Turquoise], (*Sushki* or) *Shutsuna* [Coyote], *Tyame* [Eagle], *Shash-ou*, *Yaqqa* [Corn], *Hapañi* [Oak]. They had *Mo-q'atsh* [Mountain Lion] also, but it is now at Zuñi. Several others have since died out. Besides these, we found out through Mrs. Pratt: *Qutz-Hanutsch* (antelope [clan]), *Tyope* (badger), and *Cica-Hanutsch* (a small bird, possibly a colibrí [Hummingbird Clan?]). In all 16 gentes. [Actually, these were clans; see fn 124.]

When a child is born, four days after its birth the mother gives it a name and hangs around its neck a large arrowhead of flint. Girls are often decorated with a bear's claw too.

I painted till about 2 P.M., making but little headway. At all events I must get over to Zuñi; if only to be alone again. [Too much Bigler?] At 3 P.M. went with Mr. Bigler to about a half-mile west of the pueblo. The village itself stands on a rocky bluff of sandstone, over the Rito which runs south of it. 150 meters northwest of the pueblo, after descending the steep declivity, and about 20.0 [meters] lower, is a long and flat ridge running south-southwest to north-northeast, which is covered with debris of rock, looking like a very old ruin. But it is evidently not a ruin. There is no pottery, only rarely fragments of flint. About 200.0 [meters] beyond is a similar ridge, parallel, on which are the remains of three small buildings of lava.*

On the southeast of the southern house, there is a circle which looks somewhat like a threshing ground. I found but one piece of pottery here, red-and-black. Considerable flint flakes, mostly red, and no obsidian. The houses look old and are built of lava blocks and plates [slabs]. Captain Pratt thinks that they are old. We returned through the pueblo. The houses are mostly two stories high, but there are also three-story buildings which now are abandoned. But the new houses are mostly one-story. They are built, like those of Acoma, of stones; sandstone, not lava, in adobe, and many or most, well plastered. The church is on the top of the hill, fronting east. It is not large, but neat. The plaza is not quite as large as that of Cochiti, much more enclosed, and is entered from the south side by a covered passage two-and-one-half steps wide. On that passage way is even a story built with a room, and the usual roof and ceiling.*

I am getting my journey [travel plans] into good shape, thanks to Messrs. Marmon[76] and Pratt, who are very kind. Merced de Pahuate, 1 Junio 1820, mentions a document stating that the "Rancho nombrado de Paguasti. . ." was purchased by the Indians of Laguna in 1769. The night was very interesting indeed. Messrs. Marmon and Pratt spoke in great detail of stories and of the country. There are several big lava flows. There is a crater at the Cerro Verde, south of the Rito, whence a lava stream runs north. Several flow from the Agual Azul [Agua Azul], from the Cebollita [Cebolleta Mountain].[77] It appears that south of the Cebollita, towards the Rito Quemado, there are a group of pueblos similar to [those of] the Cebollita, in shape as well as in stone work. There is one very large one down the valley on the high mesa, about 16-20 miles from the Cebollita, with an artificial water-tank. Near Agua Fria there is a very large crater, whence lavaflows run both east and west. Handsome ruins near-by. On the plains of San Agustín there are no ruins, so that there is a break south of the Rito Quemado, to Grant County.

Northwest of Zuñi, Mr. Cushing knows of 60 ruins which the Zuñi claim to have successively occupied. In regard to shi-pap, it is known here as a pueblo to the north, about the Rio Mancos and the Animas. The Zuñis believe that they came from beneath the earth, on the 4th floor.[78]

They have a story that at one time a young man lived solitary in a house, and that opposite there lived 2 young girls in another house. Both were alike; but one was good, and the other was a witch. The young man went over to see them, and falling in love with the good one, he staid there a few days. Afterwards they went to the village and became man and wife. He went to work in the field, and his wife brought his food. After she was gone, the witch came with food also and made him believe that she was his wife. Upon this the wife came also, and the two women got to fighting over it. In order to help his wife, the young man seized a stone, but mistook the witch, and killed his own spouse, while the witch flew off laughing in the shape of a crow. Inconsolable, he wept over his wife's grave every night, she appearing to him and consoling him. On the fifth night, she told him that she had to go now for the happy grounds in the west, whither he could not follow her. As he insisted, she said that the journey was long and tedious and that while she, being a spirit, would flit across the surface, he had to climb up and down the mountains and canyons, carrying his food along. He persisted, and so she finally told him to go to a room of her father's house and there get two feathers of the red eagle and bring them to her grave. He did so and stuck one of the feathers into her hair and the other he kept himself.

The next morning he prepared for the journey, and soon the whole pueblo saw a feather dancing along in the air. He followed her, and after a toilsome journey of many days, came to the entrance of the cave, where a broad staircase led down into the happy regions, and he could see the spirits in human forms enjoying themselves. Here his wife went down, while he could not enter. Disconsolate, he remained outside, sleeping at night in a small cave nearby. His food gave out, and he became weak and emaciated. Finally, a white owl visited him and asked his tale. She took him to another larger cave, and there promised to rescue his wife. The owl went to the cavern and flew over the heads of the spirits, fanning them to sleep. Then she persuaded the wife to come out, and at the staircase she resumed her body. The two travelled home together, but were strictly forbidden to hold carnal access. Near the pueblo, however, the pledge was broken. The wife vanished, and the young man returned alone, spending every night of his long life thereafter on his wife's grave.

Of the origin of the magicians, they say that they sprang from incestuous intercourse, while brother and sister were crossing a river. These are not the regular medicine men! In Arizona there is a story that a virgin went out and laid down beneath a piñón, and being naked, a drop of water fell on her navel, whence sprang the magicians. On the top of the inaccessible Superstition Mesa, a pueblo was converted into stones.

The Navajos worship the horned frog. They say that when the Giants were eating them [the Navajo] up, an old medicine man told them to take the hoods of these frogs, and to go through the country, showing the hoods, whenever the Giants would appear. This they did, and the Giants retreated before the sight to the verge of the Canyon de Chelly,[79] where, not looking back, they tumbled down and got killed.

They have a tale about a Giant pursuing a turkey, who flew to the top of a tree near a lake. The Giant, seeing the picture of the bird in the water, drank out the whole lake and died of it. The Laguna called Acoma also Shi-ui-ago; their belief is like that of Zuñi. They recollect the fruitless second attempt of Vargas to stamp out Acoma, and their flight to Zuñi and stay of 6 years there on the top of the mesa. They lived in caves also, and in the Sierra de San Matéo.

The Laguna call Sandia [Pueblo?] *Uashtatze*. The Tetilla [La Tetilla Peak]: *Qotit* [*Ko tyīt'*, Cochiti].[80] The little sticks, painted blue, are called prayersticks. The Navajo have the apachitas [apachetas] [like those] of Peru, stone heaps sometimes four feet high.[81]

Dr. Menaul sent me his first reader in Queres.[82] This pueblo is a mixup, with many Zuñi traditions, etc. The custom at Zuñi is, once a year, for all the marriageable girls to select a man to stay with them for three or four days and nights! At Taos, when the sun was eclipsed, they made a great noise and held many consultations. At last, the cacique made all the women of the pueblo over 12 years strip naked, and then race up and down the course until exhausted. The Zuñi do not permit snakes to be killed.[83]

FEBRUARY 14: Wrote to Joe last night. Received a letter from Mrs. Morgan, very kind and pleasant. Called on Dr. Menaul. Very pleasant. He has several splendid stone axes. Mailed cards to Joe, to Rev. L. Bourdier, Will B. [Borchert?], D. J. Miller,[84] and to John Becker. At 11 A.M., photographed the pueblo from the south side. Light brilliant. Plate #2, Time 7-8 seconds. View ought to be good. Dr. Menaul told me that about the Ojos Calientes near the Cañada Alamosa, there are numerous ruins. Appear to be small specimens of the quadrangular type with plazitas. Wrote to Mr. Cushing. Gave Mr. Brock's card to Major Marmon. Sent papers to Father Coudert,[85] Mr. Collet, and F. Smith.

In the dance of the Chacuan they wear masks and carry bows and arrows. Captain Pradt left for up the road at noon. The horse for Frank [Bigler?] only came at 3 P.M., and we immediately left for Acoma. About two miles southwest of Laguna we passed a low rocky mesita, of reddish sandstone, on the top of which is a pueblo ruin. I took the trail too far to the left, and that led us into the western cliffs, much eroded sandstone, where no descent was possible. So we returned to the north and finally struck the cañada to the east of the Cañada del Agua Escondida, at the outlet of which stands the station-house of Cubero. We reached that place at 7 P.M. and were splendidly received by old friend de Armond [de Armand] and his family.[86] Padre Schwarz was here, and so we spent a very pleasant evening. It appears that the books at Acoma are from the 17th century, at least he says so! My horse is doing admirably. I intend to have my horse shoed tomorrow if possible, as this is the only blacksmith on the road between here and Zuñi. We shall take 2 burros along with us, and start Sunday next, making 15 to 25 miles each day. The distance from Laguna to Acoma is about 18 miles.

FEBRUARY 15: In Acoma, there are clans: *Tzitz* [Water], *Tyame* [Eagle], *Shiahuate, Yaqqa-qotshini, Y. qu-qanyi, Y. qashia, Y. Pish-yuna, Qohayo* [Bear], *Oshatsh* [Sun], *Shru-ui* [Snake], *Ho-haqa, Tanyi* [Pumpkin], *Yssy* [Ivy], *Qutz* [Antelope], *Shyashqu.* Six estufas: *Tao-ta Qo-ritz, Tzi-ti-qa-a, Qosh-qash-tzitz, Shush-qatz, Hay-mat-atz, She-tshinitz.* Two more gentes [clans]: *Hapanyi* [Oak] and *Tzina* [Turkey]. 17 in all. Had my Chico shoed and then left at 11 P.M. [A.M.] for Acoma. It soon began a furious blow with sleet and snow, making progress almost impossible. We stopped a little while at Acomita, until the biggest snow had subsided and then started to cross the mesa. The storm lasted all the while, and the fog was so thick that the surroundings could not be seen. We got to the descent (on the path from the

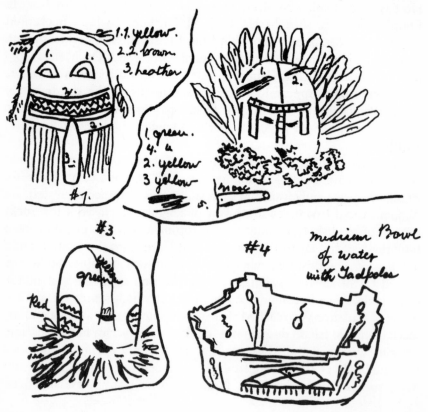

vadito [ford]) about 3 P.M., and the fog was such that we could hardly
see to the foot of the mesa of Acoma. Rapped Mr. Solomon Bibo[87] out
of his warm kitchen. He received us charmingly, and good care of the
horses was taken at once. Mr. Bibo lives in the convent. Faustino
showed us the place. There we met old Father Martín who received me
with open arms. In general, everybody is most affectionate with me. The
pueblo and the rock, in that snowstorm and the whirling fogs, looks
weird and magnificent. We changed our plans again in regard to Zuñi
and shall now go by railroad. It looks as if the passes would be blocked
by this time. Visited the most prominent places of interest. [Father]
Martín led us to one of the estufas. The moqatsh [firebox; literally,
mountain lion] is again different from anything I have seen yet. It is
smaller.[88]

Vaccination will be possible; they are prepared for it.

FEBRUARY 16: We left Acoma at 10 A.M. I vaccinated two small children. Rode down the cañada, and then crossed the foot of the mesa,
and took the direct trail toward Laguna. Reached Laguna about 2 P.M.
They were dancing the "Chacuan"—11 masks of the Chacuans, and
four dancers of another society. The dances are [obviously?] symbolical.
They had no drum, but pounded on a folded bag [leather, or rawhide?]
with a club, upon which was wound a red cloth. A stool and some food,
maize steamed in the leaf [husk], were placed in the middle of the
plaza. I could not study the figures [patterns] of the dance. Besides the
mask (#1), they wore skirts of dressed skins, the embroidered kilts and
scarfs, and in place of the skunk skins about the mocassins [sic], they
had embroidered in gaudily patched strips around the heels of their
mocassins. The rattles were painted green. Besides these 11 Chacuans,
there were four of another society with masks (#2 and #3). The
Chacuan carried bow and arrow; they were painted dark brown, with
[an hour-glass figure] painted white on each breast. The others were
painted red. No clowns. We went into the dressing rooms, were treated
very friendly, and served to eat. Saw the medicine bowl, with the
"Libella" [Libellula sp., the dragon fly] painted on the bottom. It is
cream-colored and dark-brown paint (#4). They had also the "Yapashi,"[89] [fetish, or symbols] that is, their substitutes. Wooden cylin-
ders, about six or eight inches high, painted green and white. #1 green;

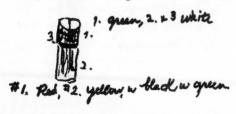

1. green, 2. & 3 white

3. 1.

2.

#1. Red, #2. yellow w black w green.

#2 and #3, white. Cornmeal and tortillas (sacred food)[90] were placed before them. There were several of them. They also had little boards of wood [early form of Kachina doll], which they do give to the children as dolls. #1 Red. #2 yellow, or black or green. The paint on the masks is all of Indian manufacture. Green paint is made of crushed copper ore. The feathers are also tinged yellow, ruddy, but there are some parrot plumes among them. The teeth of the masks are made of cornhusks, folded. The Chacuan claim the preeminence in the dance, and over all the other dances, and therefore, carry the bow and arrow. The dance lasted all day. Night fine, cold and clear. Painted awhile.

FEBRUARY 17: Went up to the pueblo. The dance continued. Visited a man who was weaving a plain manta.[91] The threads are stretched by pairs, two pairs facing each other.* He used a long shuttle, of dark brown wood, very highly polished.* He used a very dark-brown wool for weaving, but dark blue is also used. Got a letter from Joe, and one from J. Becker with $40.88. Handed the check to Captain Pratt, who is going to Albuquerque tonight yet. In Joe's letter there are complaints about Lizzie [Bandelier's ward]! She is young and regardless [heedless]. The best thing for her is to marry; then she will get those things out of her head and will soon sober up. But it is a great pity that poor Joe has no help now.[92]

At night, Captain Pratt's father-in-law [a Laguna Indian] came on purpose to talk. He is about 45 years old and has already ten grandchildren. Mrs. Pratt is about 22. She is a very pleasant woman. Conversation with Captain Pratt's father-in-law. The names of the estufas, as given by the Acomas, are correct. He says that formerly each clan had its particular estufa, but that now they are scattered [mixed memberships]. Each estufa belongs to a set of dancers, and the names are those of dances known to the Laguna.[93]

He says that from Acoma there came a man and a woman. The woman was Tyame [Eagle], the man Yaqqa-quishq [Blue Corn]. From Zuñi came a woman Shia-huate, a man Tzina [Turkey], from Cia [Zia] came Shutsuna [Coyote] and Yaqqa-Qotshiñe [? Corn]. The other clans came from the north, probably from the pueblo of Shi-pap. That pueblo they say is still standing, and nearby is a deep lagune [lake] with a whirlpool in it. Every clan has its Yapashi according to the name of the clan.[94] So Tzina has its turkey; Yaqqa has its corn; Qohayo, its bear, etc. As for deities, Sun is the first, then comes Moon, Stars, Sky (Hohaqa), Earth, Fire, and Air or Wind. Maseua [Masewa, the Elder

Twin War God] is a very powerful deity; he resides somewhere in the north, and his lieutenant [Oyoyewa, the Younger Twin War God] in the south. When they meet over the pueblo, then rain falls. They implore the assistance of Masewa in expeditions against the Navajo. Besides, they have, here, a goddess of the elements *Shihuane* [Shiwanna, the rain deity], *which they got from the Zuñi*. "Cuando hacen algun oficio" [When they have something official, *i.e.* some ritual or ceremony], they paint on one side of the wall a blue snake, on the other side a yellow snake, the tails towards the door, the heads meeting. Between the heads they paint the sun, the moon, masewa, a bear, and a puma. *Shyayaq* [Shayak] is known here as *She-eq*, and he says that the figures on the Potrero de las Vacas are *Qohayo* [Bear] and *Shyayaq* [Hunter—animal—lion]—*always placed side by side*.[95] The amulets are carried for protection, and when they kill game, they present it to the amulet as food and recompense. They claimed formerly that the *snakes* and other animals are people, men who have died and have taken animal shapes after death. Still, I could not find any trace of metempsychosis [transmigration of souls]; at least no positive proof of it. The Laguna first settled on the mesa southwest of the present pueblo, and also on the hill north of Dr. Menaul's. There a man called Shuti-Muti settled.

It appears that they have, also yellow, black, blue, red, and white corn. The loom for mantas. Name here *O-pash-tya-uasht*. On the floor, the loom is fastened into rings, made of wood and set in holes in the ground. The old man told me that it took him months to weave a manta.

At the close of the feast and dance, steamed corn was thrown about the plaza, to the great enjoyment of the boys and girls, and in general distributed among the people. Pratt got a whole basket full. The man

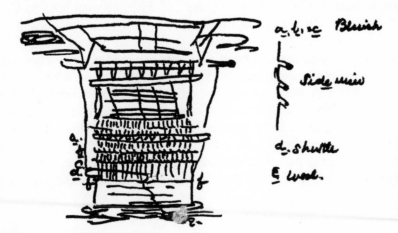

who came in last night was Hugh McBride from San Rafael, who now lives at the Cebollita. I arranged to stay with him for a few days. At midnight, Frank [Bigler?] left for Zuñi, and I got a letter from David Miller, and a charming one at that. Sent my boots to Albuquerque to be fixed.

FEBRUARY 18: Painted all day long, and made some headway. It makes a considerable difference if one is alone or not. I was alone nearly all day, except a few moments with Mr. Marmon and a few Indian calls. At night finished my journal. I had gone to bed at 2 A.M. and slept but little. Wrote to Joe a long letter, also a private and confidential one.[96] As soon as my boots come, I leave for Zuñi, at the risk of leaving unfinished work behind me.

FEBRUARY 19: Pratt did not come at noon. So I painted all day with tolerable success. Got a letter from Prof. Norton and began to write a report to him. Pratt returned at midnight with boots and cigars. As far as I can ascertain, there are no ruins about the Rito Quemado. In fact, the Sierra del Datil (Escudilla) and the Llanos de San Agustín have divided the migration, or rather the spread, of sedentary population into two branches, one west through Arizona to the Rio Gila, the other east to the Cañada Alamosa. On the eastern base of the Mogollones there are no ruins.[97]

FEBRUARY 20: Painted and fixed up matters for my departure. Went up to the school with Dr. Menaul. Very pleasant. He has a good idea about the numerous ruins. He says that many places containing pottery are the places where the Indians put food in vessels for their deceased. They do it still on heights. Passed the night [evening] in Dr. Menaul's office, writing. Wrote to Prof. Norton and Mr. Parkman, also to Collet.[98] Left at midnight for Manuelito [by rail].

FEBRUARY 21: Brilliant morning. The moonlight also was exceedingly bright. The country appeared to flatten out as we rose, and the mesa lowered. Did not sleep the whole night. About Fort Wingate,[99] the country became more picturesque, bare and bold rocks and crags lining the mesa. Sun rose when we reached Manuelito. Rocks grey. Extensive undulating mesas, covered with sabinos, spread out on all sides. Got to Bennett's! (or Houck's Tank! [present-day Houck, Arizona]) after 7 A.M. Very kindly received. But no horse nor Navajo. They had expected me yesterday and had an Indian ready, and as I did not come, he went away. So I left on foot about 9 A.M. for Zuñi. Distance 26 miles or rather 30 with the circuits.

I went first to the Agua del Coyote, seven miles. The mesas are undulating and thickly covered with low sabinos. Much cacti. Soil very sandy. Much mud. The agua, or lake, good water, lies in a handsome valley. It is southeast, about, of Bennett's. The trail then leads up the valley to the east-southeast toward an abrupt mesa, about 200 feet high. The soil is red. On top of that mesa an extensive view is gained over undulating mesas in all directions. No mountains in sight. Met some Navajo. Was entirely unarmed, but had no trouble. From the mesa I descended into a treeless gentle valley, always traveling to the east-southeast, then a long rise through timbered muddy slopes. Highly tiresome.

At last, from one of those ridges, probably the highest one, as snow lay in big patches, I saw to the east-southeast some isolated, very high mesas with abrupt walls and, to the south, a long ridge of distant mesas. This was Cibola, that is, the plain extending along the foot of the mesas; I kept trudging on along through the timber, very wearisome, as it is alternately muddy and sandy. At the northern verge of a depressed plain met F. A. Bigler riding back with a Navajo. He is perfectly delighted and full of "curiosities." It began to cloud in the west, and about 4 P.M., distant thunder was heard. Reached the northern limits of the plain of Cibola at 5 P.M.

It began to hail and to thunder. Lightning fell on the high mesa. I pressed on under the storm which was not very violent but still annoying. From the Agua del Coyote on, there was no more water, so I got very thirsty, as the snow did not allay, but rather increased, my thirst. The plain slopes gently to the southeast, but the path first goes around the northern mesas, gigantic masses of red sandstone with vertical fronts, timbered on top, then follows those fronts to the east and then descends into the plain going due south-southeast toward To-lo-yana, or Thunder Mountain. By that time it was night; the storm had ceased. My left heel was open and sore, but the sky was clearing.

I finally reached Zuñi (looking like a dark hill) at 7:30 P.M., and was received by Mr. Cushing and his family in the most charming manner. We had a long conversation. I must rely on his lecture before the Anthropological Society of Washington, D.C., for Indian mythology and creed. He is very remarkable and highly able. There are many things in it [Zuñi culture] which are identical with the Rio Grande Pueblos.

He is enthusiastic, and his enthusiasm might lead him too far, but there is not the slightest doubt but that he is honest, and that his mode of research is the true and correct one. He is in possession of a mass of *clearly coordinated facts* that are a perfect revelation and promise the greatest results.

Mr. Cushing [gave me a series of Zuñi terms]. The Zuñi River runs through the plain [of Zuñi]. It is called *Shi-uani Tshya-uana* and has its origin at the Ojo del Pescado and the Nutrias [Nutria]. In that plain are dispersed the eight or nine former pueblos of Cibola. To the southeast of Cibola rises the imposing Mesa of Toloyana [Thunder Mountain], 1026 feet high from its base. On it are the ruins of a pueblo and of a church.[100]

FEBRUARY 22: Somewhat rested, but still weary and fagged. Mr. Cushing has trouble in the pueblo. There is a man here, called Román Luna, half-Navajo, who is his bitter enemy. He tried to take his [Cushing's] life and has even stirred up an insurrection against him and the chiefs. The latter are on his side. As war chief of the tribe, [Cushing] is accused of not having done his duty. He offers to resign. This clearly indicates the democratic nature of their institutions.[101]

We first went to see the pueblo. It is built exceedingly compact, with narrow alleys, low passages, and thus recalls Cuzco.[102] The plaza is small but neat.[103] There are houses as high as seven stories![104] We entered many houses which are not very different from those of other pueblos. Only the rooms are larger and take the properties of spacious halls,[105] and the floors are not of earth, but of flags of stone set in common soil. They have small windows, low doors, also trap-doors, and their chimneys are large and square, more like those of the Acoma! There are 6 estufas, and Mr. Cushing believes that originally these estufas were really of the gentes, that they afterwards became phratral, whereas now they are held by the six principal bodies, or Orders, as he calls them. The latter are constituted, not any longer by gentes, but by individuals. There has been an evident development from the gens to a disintegration, a process which was probably stopped in the Rio Grande Pueblos.

The whole sociology shows the immense influence of religious creed

on institutions and is of the highest interest. The medicinemen elect
[nominate], but the council has the right to reject and thus bring on
new selections until they agree. There is consequently a right to *veto*.
A tribal council is composed of all the chiefs and those who were chiefs,
but the councils of the war captains are distinct from those of the civil
officers. There is one war chief for life. On the whole it is like the Rio
Grande Pueblos, though more primitive yet and less changed from
older times.[106]

The council met in the big plaza. It was a general meeting of the
pueblo and as such all the men "in good standing" with the tribe had
access to it. There were no ceremonies observed. The governor, Cushing, Mr. Wilson, and I, the chief priest and other old men and principals, sat on one side against the wall of a house, and other leading
chiefs and old men, so as to form an ellipse. The rest, many Navajo
among them, pressed about in a pack, standing and squatting. Those
of the inner circle, who appeared to be, and really were, the leading
principals,[107] smoked cigarettes, boys bringing in glowing coals and
embers. The governor directed the meeting so far as to keep order. Mr.
Cushing's opponent, a thick, heavy-set man, with a Navajo headdress
and a very wicked face showing clearly mixed breed, spoke long and
with great vehemence. He has been head-chief in former times, but
they had to remove him. His elocution was great, and his manner forc-
ible, passionate, pompous. He is a very impressive speaker. Cushing
also spoke, but only very calmly. We remained at the council until
sunset, and as the matter was then not yet decided, we returned home.

After nightfall, the head-chiefs all came, smiling and glad. They
brought news from the council. Cushing had previously resigned, and
they now came to beg of him to withdraw his resignation and accept
his situation as war chief again. In order to ascertain the true feelings of
the people, as no very positive expressions seemed to fall, they went
from one of the people present to the other taking his opinion on the
subject and the result was: One against Mr. Cushing, 2 neutral, and the
rest for him. (This mode of proceeding is certainly democratic enough.
In the discussion, however, strict deference is paid to age, and it appears that the fact that Mr. Cushing had all the old men on his side,
determined the result.) So this very important point is finally settled.
The influence of the priesthood is not so very great, else why the deference to popular voice and opinion?[108]

I could not write much, owing to constant talking and to that council matter. Mr. Cushing is speaking of going to Fort Wingate (40 miles), via the Nutrias, and to take me along.

FEBRUARY 23: I examined some of the houses from the outside. The pueblo is very compact, with passages and covered ways at right angles. It is built on a hill north of the river, and the northern houses are consequently built against and on the slope. In this manner they [?]. In consequence of this, the houses are 5 stories high on the south and 3 on the north; thus they are built against the slope. Mr. Cushing tells me that I need no plan, as I can have every detail at Washington. From the south side, the pueblo looks like a hill. Alona [Halona] is immediately opposite, on the other side of the river. Shall measure it if I can. The site of Zuñi was that of an old pueblo. In the afternoon went to see the church, which is not quite as large as that of Acoma, but after the same style, abandoned, plundered by the Washington party[109] in the most shameless manner, and falling to ruin in consequence. While there, I saw some marketing done just in the same manner as in Mexico, some products spread out on a blanket or a piece of skin or hide. There was corn; there was a piece of tanned leather, etc. Went to the store, but there is hardly anything in it. A Mexican told us that there were ruins near the Jarraloso. At [El] Morro,[110] there are several, one round one. There are said to be ruins near the Sierra del Dátil (cliff houses). Ruins near the Rito Quemado.

At night, they showed me a wand of parrot feathers. The top feathers are blue, and then there is a series of tiers of different colored feathers. Inside, there is an ear of corn with a heart of turquoise. (Mi-le) Corn Ear.[111]

FEBRUARY 24: Ruins of Pina-ua [Pinawa] situated southwest of Zuñi, about 2 miles, on a spur of a hill, south bank of Zuñi river. The river, after running from east to west bends to southwest, and the ruins stand about 200 yards east of the river. They are well built.

Sandstone is used, and the stones are well broken [shaped]. Walls 11 inches. No signs of estufas, and the whole looks suspicious. Still there is pottery, [including] corrugated and indented. It is also painted white-and-black, and black-and-red. Also modern pottery and obsidian. Nearby is a watchtower. It is probably two stories high, sunk beneath the ground. The upper story is, however, gone. There are steps of stone on the outside leading up to its floor.

I then proceeded to the east along the bluffs. On my way met, on the top of a hill, a stone monument in which a cornstalk was planted. That cornstalk had turkey and buzzard plumes tied to it, and several sticks, painted red, with feathers at one end, like long prayersticks. Mr. Cushing told me that these were the sacrifices made at the time of the presentation of the wand to the bearers of the wand by the Priests of the Bow. This sacrifice is made, figuratively, at the six points of the universe, north, south, west, east, above and below.[112]

The guardhouse is not a watchtower but a lookout to watch the crops. They are both ancient and modern. The one at Pina-ua has stone steps leading up to its top from outside, as in Peru. I then kept on to the east about two or three miles, examining the bluffs. They are of red sandstone, with occasional boulders of light colored rock. Traces of small houses are scattered throughout, with the very characteristic pottery. There are, in one of these houses, many prayersticks, black with plumes, smaller than the others.

I found, on the slope, another watchtower. This is two stories high, more perfect than the other, but more roughly made. Here, there are no outside stairs, but holes as in the pueblo houses to go up inside. Nor is the floor sunk beneath the surface of the ground, as [it was] in the first one. I then returned to Pina-ua and examined the grounds again. Found a ruined watchtower south of it. Only foundations left. On the heights east of Pina-ua, I found shells and old pottery, but no traces of houses. Ruins of Pina-ua are small. The Zuñi claim also to have made the white-and-black pottery, and as to the corrugated-and-indented, they still made it not long ago. Therefore, they also claim a part of the small houses—not all of them, however. The plain of Cibola is 30 miles long and 12 miles wide. I returned about 3:30 P.M.

At night, Mr. Cushing invited the old war priest to tell us a tale. It was the story of the poor boy of Pina-ua,[113] raised by very poor grandparents, who are badly treated by the rest of the people. Being fatherless, he gets it into his mind to search for his father and starts out for the west (Coç-luellan) where the gods of the Koko [Kachinas] dwell, the paradise! Reaches it on the fourth day. A lake[114] is in front of it, and a ladder descends through the water into a brilliant estufa where the deceased rejoin and dance. Does not find his father and goes back.

He then starts again to the south and gets to the house of the spiders which lead him to a great water, where he sees a snowy island. The spider builds a bowl for him and floats him on. On this snowy island, lives his father—a mighty handsome god, in perpetual bliss. He is recog-

nized and sent back on the rainbow. Chastises the rich people by killing eight of their daughters and brings them to the island, whence they are sent back to Pinaua as his wives.[115] The animals get jealous of his power and determine to kill him. The coyote undertakes the work and succeeds in changing him to a coyote while he himself plays his role. Becomes changed again, returns, but leaves the pueblo to wander with the youngest of his wives forever in the north. Thence sprang the Navajo.[116] Magic flute plays a great part; also, anointing the soles, the palms of the hands, the occiput.

FEBRUARY 25: *Shi-pap-u-li-me* is the name for the northern region. Rio Mancos, Rio de las Animas, etc. It is the *Shi-pap* of the Queres. There was to be a dance today, one of the kachinas. It is called the *Ko-Ko-ti-i-ua.* The so-called Mudheads (American expression) [Zuñian, Koyem-shi] opened the dance. There were ten of them. The heads are made of canvass [sic] covered with mud, and they present the appearance of imitations of fishheads, or of the head of a pig.[117] One drum accompanied them. The dance lasted about 15 minutes. It was often somewhat grotesque. The dancers were painted with mud and clothed in rather dilapidated black cloth. One drum.

Then came the *Qa-na-tshu,* 38 in number. They wore the headdresses, or masks, with sabinos and white flowers in them, which I have copied at Laguna. Their dance was all in a line → → → → →, then turning round one after another, ↓ ↓ ↓ ↓ ↓ ↓ ↓ ↓ ↓ and finally, ← ← ← ← ← ← ←. Their motions were quicker and better timed than those at Cochiti, and the costumes, though similar in every respect (masks excepted) to those at Cochiti, were bright and new. Mr. Cushing told me that this was because the river [Rio Grande] Pueblos commonly derived those articles from here, where they are kept very clean, and only sold after they grew old and torn.[118] At the head of these dancers was a Priest of the Bow in costume, with the wand, etc. The dance was very impressive, particularly with the many-storied background.

I then went to the ruins of *Qa-qima.** They are behind the southern spur of the great mesa (To-yo-a-la-na) on one of the debris heaps immediately jutting out from it, in a romantic and commanding position. The houses are of red sandstone, and tolerably well preserved. On a

sandstone shelf 15.0 [feet? meters?] above, there stand other buildings, and recent corrales nestle at the foot of the enormous rock of Toyoalana. The latter is a gigantic cliff, perfectly vertical. I found a little pottery; modern, black-and-white, red-and-black glossy, corrugated-and-indented.

The distance of Qa-qima from Zuñi is about five miles, but I went to the northern end of the mesa along its base (The whole mesa is six miles long and 1026 feet high.) and found the ruins of small houses scattered in rocky nooks and on shelves and hills of debris. Among them I found a guardhouse, facing the east.[119] It had on its northeast corner a small structure as follows, made of upright stones set in the ground.* It recalled to me similar objects found near the potreros of Cochiti, on the Potrero de las Vacas, and near Quivira. What it is I do not know. On the northeastern rim of the height of Qa-qima, there are upright slabs set on edge for defense.* Mr. Cushing says that the little square is a fox-trap, Hua-to-cia-A-K'e-lo-ye. Also a place of sacrifice.

After exploring the country around, I returned at 5:30 P.M. The dance was just ending with the usual distribution of food. At night, after having listened to Mr. Cushing's handsome poem (He is a poet of no mean qualities.),[120] and to a part of his paper, I had to tell the tale of Thor's voyage to Thrym[121] to the Indians. Mr. Cushing translated.

Then the old priest gave us a piece of Zuñi cosmology and astronomy. The Sun Father and Moon Mother created all things. The earth is a living being; it is flat, and both sides are inhabited. The sky surrounds it in the shape of an egg, and this shell revolves from east to west, the sun, moon, and stars being fixed. The lower side of this oval is dark, and when the dark side comes up, it is night. As light comes from the east, the east is the side of light and life; the west, the side of darkness and death. Therefore, they look and pray to the east, and therefore also they migrated from west to east, towards light and life. Mankind sprang from caves.

My things arrived safely. Near Qa-qima, on the rocks, there is a sun-house (?). I saw a beautiful vase* from one of the Moqui [Hopi] ruins, with a figure on it which they claim is the macaw. Possibly, but doubtful.[122] There were visitors again today, three Americans. They [the Zuñi] have an indiction of four years, four years together forming a day, and the next four years, a night.[123]

FEBRUARY 26: Shall go out to Matzaquia today. Above it, is a very sacred place, called Tonanchinahua. They have, every year about the

19th of December, the festival of the New Fire. They kindle it on Toyoalana, and there are four days of fasting, and ten days without sleeping. Three priests kindle it, starting in procession from the pueblo. Mr. Cushing thinks that the 13 sacred orders were originally phratral. The dignitaries are all hereditary in the gens of the Parrot![124] The 13 orders evidently indicate four original phratries. I am very well here, but must leave as soon as possible; else I lose too much time.[125] Everybody is exceedingly kind to me. The dance continues today, and day after tomorrow there is to be another, different one. Grand council tonight about religious matters.

Groundplan of the ruins of the pueblo of Matzaquia,* including the House of the Sun, which is new. The slab is about two feet high and made of grayish sandstone. The figure of the sun is a simple circle with eyes and mouth and no nose nor ears.

In front of the slab lay nine curiously shapen pebbles arranged in three rows of three each.

The threshold of this low and small structure was of stone, one smooth slab composing it. The opening faces east. The condition of the ruins of Matzaquia is worse than that of the other ruins. The pueblo stands about 200 yards southwest of the Rio Zuñi and is about two miles east of Zuñi. There is hardly any pottery about these ruins in general, and when I asked Mr. Cushing why such was the case, he told me that the Indians carefully picked up all the fragments, ground them, and mixing them with the clay, used them [as temper, or grog] for new pottery.[126]

(I write this on the 28th.) What I found here was mostly corrugated or recent fragments. Obsidian is met with everywhere. In the evening I painted, and Mr. Cushing read to me his last article. It is very interesting.

FEBRUARY 27: There are four Sayapa,* representing gigantic birds. The face is hidden by a painted tablet of wood.* The plumes are at least three feet high. The dance was opened by a round dance. A branch of piñón was planted in the square like a Christmas tree;[127] by its side was placed food. The dance is called Ya-e-o-ti-ua. Men and women and even children formed a circle around it moving* [counterclockwise] and singing. The drum was placed in the middle at the foot of the pine tree, and the drummer squatted to it. (This is a custom of the orders.) The dancers held each other by the hands. There appeared two horrible figures, painted white, naked,[128] a girdle of yucca fibres, with a branch of yucca across the small of the back and no other protection but a plume on the P.[enis?]. They wore a hood of buffalo hide. One [figure] was painted yellow; the other, red. A black mask with eyes and mouth, covered the face; around the neck were foxskins, and on the top of the head is a many-colored band with feathers sticking out horizontally. The only designs painted on the hood are those of the libella; on the back of it, a few black lines. These figures did not stay long, and then the dance proceeded along as before. In the act of the Sayapa, the priest (there were two of them) held a very curious wand. It was held in the middle by a handle, painted white, green, and yellow, with six feathers. It is called [Bandelier failed to complete this sentence.]

At night I painted while Mr. Cushing read to me some folklore. Highly interesting, particularly that of Atasaya, the man-eating giant, who was killed, according to one story, by a coyote; according to the other, by the twin brothers, Aha-yuta and Matzaluna. These tales greatly resemble those of the Popol Vuh, and are parallel to those of Hunahpu and Xbalanqué, in their conflicts with Cabrakan and Vukub Caquix.[129] I cannot help feeling, that while here, I live a part of the life of Mexico and Yucatan at its aboriginal period.[130] This is now the season of dancing and of games, and there will be another dance soon. Soon it ceases, and then begins a new life. Planting begins.

FEBRUARY 28: I went out to photograph. First took the pueblo from the northwest with Toyoalana in the distance. Plate #3, Time 8″. Then proceeded to the southeast and took the pueblo again, #4, Time 8″. Then took the church and the five-story houses, #5, Time 9″. Light fine. Time of day: between 10:30 and 12 A.M. In the afternoon, I painted a bowl or caxete [cajete]. Mr. Metcalf[131] is very kind with his assistance. His advice is highly valuable, for he is a true artist in every respect. Mr. Cushing and Mrs. Cushing, in fact the whole household,

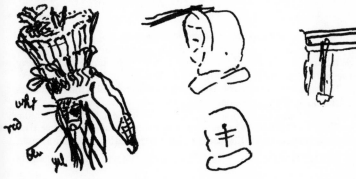

are very kind. So I lead a very pleasant life, but time flies and I must go southward. Mr. Cushing tells me that west and southwest of here, there are some ruins with magnificent pottery, well ornamented, and with brilliant colors. Particularly southwest of here, there is such a ruin. He owns two splendid vessels from a ruin near Moqui; one is #1, the other #2, with a very handsome pattern. It is red-and-black.[132] #1 has conventional figures of birds which Mr. Cushing says the Zuñi claim to be the macaw. This is doubtful, though it may be true. The Zuñi know the sun well, and have two suns, but these are different from the veritable Sun God. They also know the jaguar and paint it as a spotted panther. The skins of the bear and of the panther are only sacred on certain occasions, and used as medicine for certain diseases (the patient being wrapt up in them) but that otherwise they tread on them without respect. These skins which Mr. Cushing owns are frequently begged of him by the Indians for such medicinal purposes.[133] The story of the sun's name is interesting for its connection with Acoma, as well as for mentioning the buffalo as ranging about here. I saw today an Indian woman dressing stone with stone.[134]

MARCH

MARCH 1: Got a letter from Joe and one from Papa. Painted nearly all day at pottery. They danced again with the Mudheads as on the first day. Mr. Barthelmes [Barthelmess][135] came from Fort Wingate, also Dr. Cushing. [136] The latter brought the letters. They [the letters?] made a melancholy impression on me. It appears that the Zuñi use two kinds of red paint: red jasper and red ochre. They have six classes of pottery for household use. In general, the resemblances between Zuñi and the Mexicans are remarkable and strange.

It is evident that we are approaching discoveries of the greatest importance in ethnology, and eventually in the aboriginal history also.[137]

[The entry of March 1, 1883, actually began with the page (#30, front) reproduced here. It was one of the rare instances in the entire journals in which the writing or sketching was not done by Bandelier himself. The unsigned page may have been the work of Frank H. Cushing, W. L. Metcalf, or Miss Margaret W. Magill, each having some considerable talent along these lines. Other instances of a "guest" artist include the entries of March 18, 1883, with the work of Washington Matthews, and of March 19, 1883, with the work of Charles T. Gibson. Whether this cluster of sketches by others was a momentary fad, or whether Bandelier simply took advantage of the presence of several rather talented friends, there is little way of knowing.]

From what Mr. Cushing says the influence of the education of [by] priests is very great on the people. It is all oral. Songs are told to the people and learned by the young people by heart. Among these songs there is one, the principal and most sacred one, which he calls a national epic poem. It treats of the migrations of the Zuñi to their present place. Only the koko [Kachina(s)] can learn it, and it takes nearly 24 hours to recite it. The initiated is borne [escorted] into the pueblo by the mudheads.

The story of Montezuma,[138] as told by the Queres, is like that of Poyanque, whom the river pueblos call Pusha.[139] He came from *Shi-Pap-ulima* in the north with four feathers, introduced the sacred rites, and converted a dry season into a prosperous one, by the charm of his plumes. All the orders, except those of the Bow, venerate him, but the latter cling to Ahu-uta and Matzaluna. On the Twin Mountain, there is still said to exist the stone-pile erected by Fray Marcos Nizze [Niza], and portions of the wooden cross erected by him were still visible a few years ago. The Negro, Estévanico, is called by them the "Black Mexican," and they call English-speaking Negroes, "Black Americans."[140]

MARCH 2: Mr. Cushing promised to go to Toyoalana today with me. We started at 2 P.M. Dr. Cushing, Mr. Barthelmes, Abe [?], and I. I rode a mule. Proceeded to the northwest end of the mesa. There are pictographs: a six-footed mountain lion, two flute players, and a bust. Interesting.

Two ruins on top of Toyoalana.

The path winds around very steeply, along the edge of fearful [cliffs], through channels with still one and two feet of snow. At last we reached the top of the mesa at 3:30 P.M., at its eastern edge. The scenery is by far the grandest I saw in New Mexico, awful precipices, immense walls towering up on our right, and this was the easiest path of all, the others are terrific for dizzyness. Toyoalana is far more inaccessible than Acoma, and much larger. There are only 4 paths which lead up, and these can be easily defended.

Along the edge of the mesa there are still, as on the Potrero Viejo of Cochiti, piled up stones and rocks as barricades. The top is wooded, and the whole, on a larger scale, recalls the Potrero Viejo. We rode in search of [the shrine of] Matzaluna, and at last found it in a clear space. It looks very unimportant, but still is very interesting. (See picture). [No picture was found in the journal.] The statue is of wood, painted, but now out of shape, weatherworn, and very much defaced.

1ᵗ of March 1883.   # 3.0

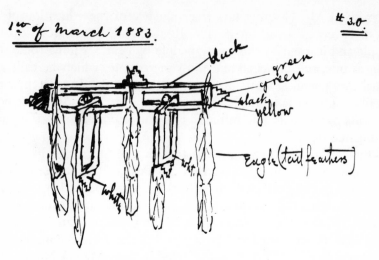

Eagle (tail feathers)

Body color. green
Outer edges black
Edges of terraces white bordered with black
Inner edges yellow.
Eagle feathers (ten in all) fastened on as indicated
save in pendant links which (in the sketch) are
provided only with one each, for sake of clearness.

Fluff of the ygii of the dance (suerō kéx)
Color of wood dark mahogany – hard wood of some
sort stained thus by long use. a,a,a, small
tufts of turkey feathers (dark) from the rump.
                              green with yellow end
                              black green inside (a)
          Teitwan or sacratied
          book and palets of the Shumakwe,
Eagle plumes as one above.

The ruins are scattered into 6 groups of which I measured only two. They are copies, so-to-say, of the pueblos of the plain. It appears that when they fled onto the mesa, each pueblo of below built its own for itself, close by the others, but still a separate and distinct group.[141] They are in rectangles, hollow, and the walls of sandstone, appear hasty work. Little pottery, since it is studiously collected by the Zuñi and ground into powder to be mixed with the clay for more pottery. What there is, has a hasty [crude] appearance. I saw some glossy pottery, but the majority is not glossy.

It is doubtful whether the Laguna and others who fled on top of the mesa occupied a separate building. When the Spanish army approached, it drew up at the northern base of the mesa, where now the

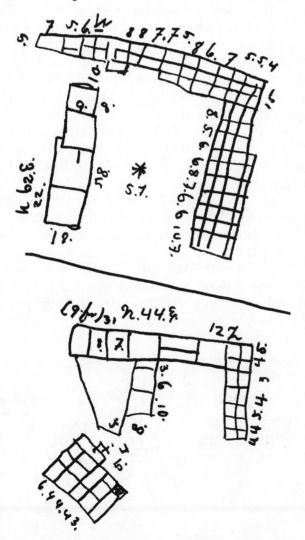

peach orchards of the Zuñi climb high up the slope. Trees dwarfish,
beginning to bud. To approach Matzaluna, I had to take off my boots,
so as not to [disturb?] the tracks in the light, reddish, sandy soil. There
is no water on the mesa, and as long as the Zuñi were up there, they
brought up the water from below, on one of those terrible pathways;
probably from Qa-qima. (The tradition is that at Qa-qima they killed
the Negro, Estévanico.) We descended after 4:30 P.M. and reached
the foot at dark. Then we rode leisurely home. There is no church
on the top of the mesa. On the whole, the mesa is the grandest thing
I have seen in New Mexico. All around precipitous walls are three to
five and 600 feet in height, and gigantic slopes of rubbish and cliffs
below, creeping up 700 feet in places.

The mesa is full of caves in which there are, of course, statues and
sacrifices. Mr. Barthelmes took his camera along, but like a true photographer, did not take any picture at all, because the weather did not suit
him. So I got no near [close-up] photograph of Toyoalana. At night I
drew the plat of the houses which I had measured, while Mr. Cushing
made for me a very handsome sketch of Matzaluna. The twin brothers
are nearly alike (Aha-yuta and Matzaluna), so that only a few feathers,
and perhaps one-sixteenth of an inch in height distinguishes them.[142]

I do not recollect whether I have already written down or not, that
there are, southwest of here, ruins with remarkably handsome pottery,
very bright colors. Mr. Cushing is of the opinion that this is only a local
exception, occasioned by the peculiarly favorable material within easy
reach. There are similar places west, near the Moqui pueblos. In either
case, the Zuñi do not claim the ruins as having been those of their own
settlements in former times.

"The Rattlesnake has come out," called the Governor to Mr. Cushing tonight, so there is to be no more folklore telling. Lest it might
bite you. This appears to be an allegory in allusion to the planting season approaching now, or even already begun. It is a pity, for these folklore tales are very handsome.[143]

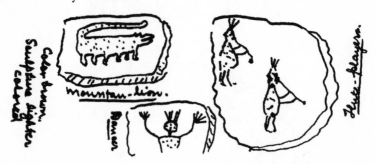

The pictures carved on the rocks [on Toyoalana] are as follows: color brown. Sculptures lighter colored. Flute Player. Dancer.

MARCH 3: I had decided to go to Hauico [Hawikuh], but there was no horse to be had, and besides, it was storming and blustering and snowing occasionally. So I stayed and painted all day. There is nothing very new otherwise. At night, the wife of Daniel Dubois came, a Mexican, on a visit. There are many ruins near the Venado (Ojo del Venado), about 25 miles west of here. The Aguas Calientes [present-day Ojo Caliente], where Hauico is, is midway about. The Ojo del Venado is on the banks of the Rio Zuñi in the same cañada, but lower down, since the Rio Zuñi flows to the west, into the Colorado Chiquito [Little Colorado]. Mr. Cushing painted [a picture of] his shield for me with the figure of the god *Achi-alatopa*, the goddess of the rainbow, and two pumas, on it. Day very ugly; still they will dance, tomorrow, the dance of the Mountain Sheep, which dance they have deferred now fully four years.[144]

MARCH 4: Dance of the *Haligo-oti-uae* [Mountain Sheep] today, although the weather was, if possible, uglier than yesterday. The dance was very peculiar. Na-yu-tshe officiated as high priest in the usual costume, but his head was bare. He held a wand of corn leaves [probably corn husks] and stood immovable (a handsome picture) before four men impersonating as many mountain sheep. They each bore a pair of pink horns with green zigzag lines*; the face was covered with feathers hanging down, and they were bent on two white staffs, imitating feet, so that they walked four-legged. Behind them another priest, with cap, but without his jacket, the body painted yellow, and the face covered with white [eagle] down, danced back and forth, holding in his hand a black bow whose string carried heavy black fringe of hair. With this bow he performed many symbolical motions (incantations) from and toward the animals. The latter wore a skirt similar, as to the borders, to that of the Malinche at Cochiti,[145] only its body was white. Around it [the priest] danced boys and girls in elaborate and brilliant costumes, very bright colors, and decidedly beautiful. Over the left [ear], each woman had a splendid imitation of the morning-glory (?), varied [probably as to color] in each case; on the right ear, [they wore a piece shaped] like the crescent moon. The boys wore a costume similar to that of Cochiti, but the paint was yellow. The mountain sheep knelt, danced, etc., in the center. The whole impressed me, as well as Mr.

Cushing (who had never seen it before), that it was an incantation to subdue the animal previous to starting on a great chase [hunt]. A body of singers, in common dress, and a drum made the music. The rhythm changed often; it was frequently rapid, and the motions, very quick. The roofs were densely packed with people, and the whole was a grand and imposing sight. The mountain sheep went out slowly, followed by the others, making long stations [pauses], performing rites.

Previously, Mr. Cushing had led me to a place where they made prayerplumes and sticks, tying them in little bundles covered with cornhusks. (The name of the god who apparently gave rise to the story of Montezuma is Po-shy-an-k'a, not Poyanque.) Mr. Barthelmes photographed the dance. I painted all afternoon. The dance was suddenly interrupted by one of the men falling dead. (Heart-disease and over-exertion.)[146]

At night, meeting of the Order of the Bow, and Mr. Cushing went.[147] He is Capitán de la Guerra, [War Captain], Ithcata Mosona. He carried a warclub with him. It is pitch-dark. In former times, when the Zuñi immigrated hither, as each band came, it had to build its own pueblo, and only gradually did they aggregate to larger clusters.

MARCH 5: Did not go to Ha-ui-qo, but staid at home and painted pottery. Mr. Metcalf then had the kindness to copy the beautiful jar from Arizona for me. Very good. We shall leave for Fort Wingate day after tomorrow. Inquiring of Mr. Cushing about the origin of the albinos,[148] he has told me that it was unknown, and that the tale of Gorman,[149] the American missionary, was not exact. The only American who ever lived at Zuñi previous to him [Cushing], was a party named Franklin,[150] who fell sick while passing through the pueblo and was nursed by the Zuñi who afterwards tried to keep him almost forcibly. It required the military to protect his exit.

So the end of my stay here approaches and with it the last pueblo where I intend to make studies.[151] There is a round tower near Nutria, and another one five miles from Fort Wingate. Mr. Cushing wears a badge of leather. (a.b.) Flints. The band is indicative of the number of scalps taken, by the rows of tresses, of which it is composed. There are

four rows when one scalp has been taken, and for every new trophy two rows more are added on each side. Two flint knives are added on each side. Every member of the Order of the Bow is compelled to secure a scalp before he is admitted, but he is strictly bound not to reveal the manner in which the scalp has been secured. The whole badge is worn as a talbart and is of deerskin grey because old.

The Indians here know of the northern light, though their notions are only very dim, as they see it only in the shape of a ruddy glow. As it looks, it is not unlikely that Mr. Cushing may join me at the Rito Quemado yet, thence to go southwest. Ha-ui-qo is said to be a large pueblo. Of Halona nothing is left to warrant the making of a ground-plan. Everything is built over by new houses and ranchos. The dropping dead of the man yesterday was, by some, attributed to the photographing, but the majority looked at it in a natural way.[152] If I must now sum up final results of my trip to Zuñi, they are, on the whole, very gratifying. Besides the very pleasant acquaintance of Mr. Cushing and his family, the information secured is extensive. But I see that these orders are not properly mystical; particularly the medicine orders show: that it is the knowledge of certain arts, which art is perpetuated through transmission by instruction, which constitutes the so-called tie of fraternity. Among the Indians, every special knowledge takes the shape of a magic art, of a medicine, and is the secret property of him who knows and therefore practices it. It is the beginning of castes and guilds. But only a beginning, and not the institution itself. Thus, while the warriors are all the able-bodied men of the tribe, the man-killers (Matalones [Matalotes] here) form a special body by themselves. So do the hunters, the fire-eaters, stick-eaters, etc.[153]

MARCH 6: I had further conversation with Mr. Cushing last night. It appears that the fact of taking scalps alone is not sufficient for membership in the Order of the Bow. It requires unanimity of vote. Neither does the taking of more scalps decide the rise in degree. Vote alone can secure it. This is very decisive. Men who have taken four and five scalps are not even members of the Order. These esoteric orders are very important for the *history of the growth of polytheism!!*

They danced the whole day, the dance of *Qoq-shi*, or Good Dance.[154] About 50 dancers, male and female, ten mudheads, and one priest of the bow. The men wore green masks with long black beards, and a multi-colored band at the bottom of the mask. The women wore plain white masks.[155] They danced in file, rapidly. There was a drum, and the dancers themselves sang, yelping, incidently, like coyotes. The priest of the bow carried a feather-wand and a medicine basket of clay [probably a pottery tray, or flat bowl] hung to his arm, as usual. It had a frog on it. The song was not as monotonous as the other songs which I heard with other dances. I find that the head offices are hereditary in the Parrot Gens. From the myths and folklore tales of the Zuñi a good map could be drawn illustrating their conceptions of the earth's geography. Co¢-luellan lies in the west, Shi-pap-ulima to the north (eight days journey). There would be in the far west great seas, and icy regions in the north and northwest. For the east their knowledge is limited, because it is the region whither they migrated. Zuñi would occupy the center of the world. Below, there would be a country, very hot, with naked people, fighting with sticks. North is yellow; west is blue; south, red; east, white. Upper region—many colored. Lower regions—black.[156] A-ue-clui-an is the horizon, also the upper border. The traditions of the Zuñi state that the first Spaniard ever seen by them was a man called "Nu-e" who came here very poor, with a long beard, and accompanied by two dogs who were then of a kind unknown to them. He made himself very disagreeable by reaching greedily and appropriating any kind of food. They held council and finally determined to send him off in the morning. But he disappeared in the night, and the priests told them that they had, with one bound [with one mind, i.e., decisively] sent him on to the south. This was evidently Alvar Nuñez Cabeza de Vaca! They also have a tradition that, about the time they killed the Negro [Estevan] at Q'aqima, many white Mexicans and Indians from Sonora came up and fought them. This was evidently Coronado![157] Wrote to Mr. Parkman tonight.

MARCH 7: At the request of Mrs. F. H. Cushing, I daubed the breastpin of Cochití into her album. Poorly done, but "causey du peu [What more can be said]." We left at 1 P.M. at last with two mules and a buckboard, with a full load of blankets and only a few provisions. The road leads up the Rio Zuñi, a turbulent muddy stream, through a handsome timbered valley, that is, the slopes of the mesas are timbered, while

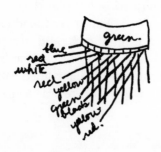

the valley itself is bare, but certainly fertile. We passed Heshota-¢lutzina* situated on the very brink of the river, north side. It appears to have been a small ruin. The river being almost not to be forded, I did not measure.

Our mules behaved very badly, would not go, so that Mr. Cushing had a very hard time driving. I never saw such animals before, for "cussedness," mulishness, and stubborness. We reached Heshota U¢la," 12 miles from Zuñi, in proper time. This ruin is polygonal, almost round, and also on the banks of the Zuñi River. It may have been two stories high; it is not very intricate, and of stone. The vertical side being outwards, the walls where decaying, fall outside. It had two estufas, one of which is round, and the other possibly quadrilateral. The pueblo, as Mr. Cushing soon discovered, had been originally devastated by Americans;[158] therefore the skulls and skeletons, and the great number of handsome pieces of pottery about. It is finely corrugated-and-indented, painted white-and-black, red-and-black, red-and-white, beautifully.

Ruins of He-Shota U¢la,* about 12 miles northeast of Zuñi. About five miles from it, west, Heshota-¢lutzina, a rectangular ruin, smaller. The Zuñi classify the beings into four classes: 1.) The unfinished one, animals and animal gods. 2.) The finished, man. 3.) [Bandelier omitted this one.] 4.) The Masters of the World. The pottery of Heshota U¢la is beautiful, and all kinds are represented: glossy, finely corrugated-and-indented, and very handsome dark-pink-and-white, red and white, brown and black. We found an entire skull of an adult, complete, the back part much flattened artificially, and Mr. Cushing found parts of five skeletons. Everything tends to indicate that the pueblo was stormed and hastily abandoned. We then turned to the north, into a rapidly rising well-wooded cañada and camped below the crest which overlooked the valley of Nutrias. The timber is high, beautiful pinabetes and piñones. Pools of water are found in many places, and the snow still lies in occasional patches. Then we made our camp in a lovely spot, certainly the most beautiful camp I have ever had.

MARCH 8: Very good night. But our abominable mules were gone. We hunted for them until 11 A.M., and then found them snugly concealed in the bush, not 50 yards off. Started at last at 12 A.M., mules worse than ever. It soon became apparent that one of them was probably sick. The sight of the valley is most beautiful, and it resembles the valley of the Ventana, only larger. Picturesque rocks line it on the north. They are of red and white sandstone, and cleft into pinacles by decay of tilted strata. Only one Zuñi rancheria [hamlet], the little Pueblo de Las Nutrias, stands at its northern edge. Sheep and horses pasture it.

About midway our mules gave out and in trying to assist Mr. Cushing to whip them up so as to reach Nutria, I fell overboard. After being pushed and dragged for about 15-20 feet, the wheel passed over my breast, bruising me considerably, but not injuring any limb or other part of the body. I picked up again, so far safe and sound. Thank God for it! I expected at least to lose my left leg, if not to be crushed.

We finally got to Nutria, which is a circular pueblo still inhabited as a summer village. I took a groundplan of it, hastily, and we agreed that I should stay here, as my bruises are slightly painful, while Mr. Cushing would go to Fort Wingate. The pueblo lies on a spur of a round rocky hump, to the west. There is much ancient and modern pottery on it, glossy, corrugated-and-indented, red-and-white, etc. Very handsome, and almost identical with that of Heshota U¢la. The lands of Nutria were donated to the Zuñi by the Spanish crown, but the Navajo also lay a claim to them, though ineffectually. Many Navajo are about, herding. Mr. Cushing today assured me that the Zuñi melted copper, silver, and gold, in small cups of burnt clay, that they had the blow-pipes and a kind of bellows, made of two bags with wood, and that this work in metal differed essentially from all Spanish or Mexican work.[159] Mr. Cushing left at 4 P.M. on the mule of a Zuñi who came to bring him the checks and Post Office order he had forgotten at home. The Indian remained with me at Nutria for the night.

MARCH 9: The situation of the pueblo [ruin at Nutria] is certainly a peculiar and handsome one. It is almost concealed from the outside and can only be seen at one to one-and-a-quarter miles distance, or else from the tops of the mountains surrounding it. It is tolerably large, and polygonal or "round" so-called. Has three estufas, made of red sandstone, and possibly three stories high. Cells [rooms] small, as usual. Pottery is not frequent, but what I found was corrugated-and-indented, white and black, and red and black. It appears to have been lately collected and carried away.

I returned to Nutria at 1 P.M., as my chest and hips are still very sore from the fall or accident of yesterday, and there is consequent lack of breath. Besides, am very hungry; had nothing to eat, and still have nothing but water and some strong tea. I write this at 4 P.M., and I have now been 30 hours without a morsel.

At 5:30 P.M., Mr. Metcalf and a big 4 mule train, laden with choice provisions, came. He brought me a letter from Mr. Cushing, one from Papa, and one from Lizzie with her photograph. Good, and good also so far. It appears that Pescado is also a round ruin, still inhabited at the present time. Passed a most cheerful evening. Mr. Cushing sent beer and segars, also whisky. I could not help but need stimulants this time, although my bruises are fast waning and disappearing. There are many Navajo about, and one came to see us. They remain and are, an ugly, thievish set.[160] I hardly know how I can return the kindness which Mr. Cushing has shown to me, and Mr. Metcalf also is of the kindest disposition and manner of action.

MARCH 10: On the whole, passed a bad night; though not on account of pain—only excitement, whiskey, and tea. We started at 10 A.M. with a splendid team. The road winds up to the top of the Sierra de Zuñi, which is not a flat mesa, but a series of parallel ridges, therefore hill and vale. There is much snow yet, but it melts and the mud is terrible. It would hardly have been possible for me to make the trip on foot at all. Beautiful pine trees compose the forest. It is not the low brush of the piñón and sabinos, but the dense stately timber, which I see now almost for the first time in New Mexico. It was very cold.

We reached the northern descent about 2 P.M. and then Mount Taylor appeared to the right. Before us the valley of Fort Wingate; a very handsome view, with its red walls of the mesa. To the west an immense mesa country extending to within 50 or 60 miles of Moqui. The Fort was reached safely, and then I went to the hospital where a very comfortable room was ready. At night, Dr. W. Mathews [Washington Matthews][161] called on me. Very kind. The Fort contains about 350 to 400 men. The buildings are good, neat, and clean. They are all of adobe, of which there is an excellent quality here.

MARCH 11: Sent a postal card home, and one to Mr. Menaul at Laguna. Dined at Dr. Mathews. Evening at Lieut. Huse.[162] Fine music by the band and very good meals.

MARCH 17: Having neglected to keep my journal, I must briefly resumé. The weather was very bad from the 12th to the 16th. Stormy, rainy, and snowing fast on the 15th. Today it is very handsome at last. I cannot work very well here owing to continuous interruptions. Still I painted two or three sheets. Mr. Metcalf left on the 15th A.M. and Mr. Cushing on the 16th A.M. Both were exceedingly kind to me, especially the latter. The surroundings are full of ruins, all small houses, and there are remains of acequias, also round towers. While here, I lost sheet #36 of my journal. [Sheet #36 never has been found.] Don't know how and when. It contains the groundplan of Toh-ya (Nutria) which is a round pueblo still inhabited. Am very sorry, but cannot help it at all. Dr. Mathews is an excellent man. He is a man of science and told me many interesting things. So he says the Navajo call all the ruined houses, without any exception, "Houses of those who were strangers to one another." He also says that the northern tribes have a winter house which is very similar to the small house, only it is of poles and bark, covered with mud. He sketches the plan as follows:* They also build chimneys or rather fireplaces, very similar to the chimneys of the pueblos. This is exceedingly important, as it shows the step from the temporary lodge to the pueblo house. The ornament painted by the Zuñi signifies the whirlwind. Also among the Navajo. Evening splendid. #1 and #4 photographs lost.

MARCH 18: Round tower five miles north of Fort Wingate, in what the Navajo call "Horse-Pen Valley."

Ruins of small houses in the same valley. The last one I could not measure. These ruins are very common in that section, and sometimes exceedingly small, evidently small watchtowers. Tall piñones grow in the ruins. Pottery corrugated-and-indented, white-and-black, and red-and-white. The round depressions appear to be the ruins of estufas. One had a distinct wall, well built, around it. The walls are commonly 11 inches thick, and are fairly well built. There are permanent water pools all about the bottom of the valley, and the soil is fertile. Timber all over it at present.

The day being very handsome, we left at 10 A.M. Dr. Mathews was kind enough to allow me to ride his wife's horse, a splendid animal. We rode to the west, through fine timber, P. contortus [P. contortus var. latifolia Engelmann, lodgepole pine] and P. edulis [P. edulis Engelmann, piñón] also a few occasional specimens of Abies douglassii.[163] The valley of Wet Springs is remarkably fertile, and the scenery very picturesque. The sandstone (carboniferous) is tilted on edge, so as to stand almost vertically, very much like the picturesque rocks at Nutria. On the whole the country is strikingly romantic and handsome.

The round tower is situated on a lovely spot. It is three stories high, 4.25 [meters] and about 0.60 [meter] of the upper story. Only the north side of the wall remains; the south side (whence the summer rain comes) has completely disappeared, and formed the rubbish over the hill and filled up the tower inside. The walls are in terraces. The lower

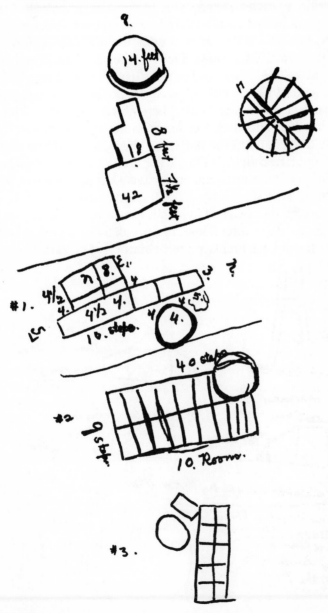

story is 1.06 [meters] thick, and the second story, 0.45 [meter]; and the third, as far as I could judge, about 0.30 [meter]. There are projecting stones set in on the outside, but not so as to form regular steps. The stonework is fair. The roof shows a large transverse beam, on which smaller ones rest. The ends of the beams, still partly visible, are imbedded in clay. Pottery black-and-white, and corrugated. Flint, but no obsidian. We then went to examine the small houses. I found a circular depression close to each and every one. In one case it was walled in and therefore a plain estufa. In the other two instances there was a basin, slightly wet, but no visible rim of foundations. The ground was also wet in the one which had a wall. The Navajo claim that these depressions were tanks, but I believe them to have been estufas. There is enough permanent water, without need of special tanks. Saw pottery; it is the usual characteristic kind. These three ruins are within 300 feet of each other, and there are many more, square ones, scattered through the timber and in the bottoms. There are said to be ruins opposite the Depot, near the Rio Puerco [of the West]. Saw some Navajo hogans or houses. They are rudimentary blockhouses. Their corrals are of brush, not of stakes.

The Navajo call themselves Tinne.[164] Dr. Gibson[165] tells me that the "Rees" [Arikara] have winter houses of a peculiar kind. They are oblong in some cases, and have fireplaces, not chimneys. Dr. Barthelmes took

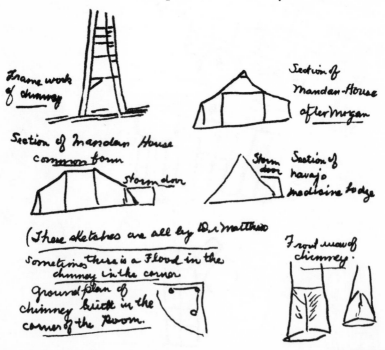

three negatives, but they were all broken on the trip. Finished my letter to Professor Norton tonight. The Mandan, Arickara, and Gros Ventre, are the tribes who built, within 100 years past, these chimneys. They are exact counterparts of the Queres *chimuni*, or *qoa-qa-shuma*. Four poles stuck against the wall, bound together by transverse sticks, and with grass wrapped around it, daubed over with clay.

On the whole, this chimney, which is evidently aboriginal, is the prototype of the pueblo chimney, and the winter lodge (which by the way is becoming permanent about Fort Berthold [North Dakota]) is the prototype of the small house of the pueblos.[166] In Navajo, Mount Taylor is called Tzotzil, or the High Peak. I talked to Juan about accompanying me, in case Román could not come. We had a concert tonight or rather in the afternoon. Among the Navajo the sun and the moon are twin brothers, therefore both male.

MARCH 19: Snow still lies in every valley. Wrote to Mrs. Morgan, and cards to Mr. Parkman and to Brown. The Navajo call the Moqui *Aya-quini*. The Tehua, *Na-sho-she*; Yutas [Utes], *No-ta*. They have a tradition that they formerly composed a part of the northern Tinne and were separated from them by a great fire. They once went to look for them and found them on the other side of a very deep cañón.

Am still waiting for Román. No sign of him yet.

MARCH 20: Dined at Mr. Mathews, in company with Mr. Riordan,[167]

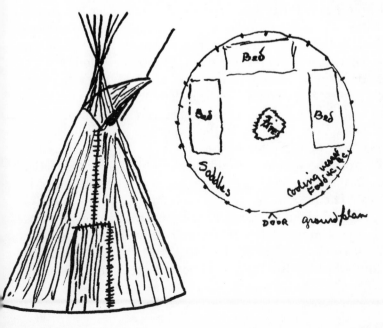

the Indian Agent at Fort Defiance.[168] Pleasant. At night began to write to Joe at last. The Navajo call the Apache *T¢i-i.*

Am absolutely on coals. No news from Zuñi; do not know whether Román is engaged or not. If he is not [available], then I shall talk with Juan, the Navajo, although I hate to do it, because I mistrust all the Navajo.

It appears that nearly all the Indians tribes have sodomy, and that these sodomites are dressed like women. They are tolerated only.

On the whole, I am not losing [wasting] my time here. There is a very large ruin 27 miles south of here, in what they call La Cebolla which ruin appears to be of the same kind as the ruin at the Cebollita, south of Acoma. Barthelmes has a photograph of it. Dr. Mathews told me that the Indians of Zuñi, when he asked them to show him the rooms of the oldest parts of the pueblo, replied that they could show him some, but not all. It appears to be their custom, when they abandon some of the lower rooms to move permanently into higher quarters and to fill up the former with rubbish and dirt. What connection may that have with Zayi [Sayil, or Zayil] in Yucatan? (La Casa Cerrada). Dr. Mathews thinks that the Navajo are largely a composite stock.[169] At present, they cultivate fields and irrigate, like the Pueblos themselves. Mailed letter to Professor Norton.

MARCH 21: Am very uneasy about Zuñi. Have no news at all. Begin to think of not going to the Rito Quemado, but to return hither [Fort Wingate?] from Laguna. Resolved to go to the ruins near the depot, and so started at 2:30 P.M., returning at 4:30 P.M. Secured groundplan and saw much pottery. It is plainly corrugated, indented with deep grooves, white-and-black, and red-and-black. Quality very good.*

The western basin or depression is a tank or pond; the other two are evidently estufas. I saw no trace of fields left, and the acequia itself is much obliterated. The Rio Puerco is eating on the north bank.

The road from Fort Wingate to the depot descends almost due north. Two ranges of rocky bluffs converge together, leaving a gap about a mile from the station. Beyond that gap lies the valley of the Rio Puerco. It is treeless, and the dark red soil is very fertile. There is also good grass. The river, a muddy swift-running creek, runs in banks vertical, jagged, and about 20 feet high. Beyond the bridge, 76 steps northeast, begins a range of low bluffs, and between them and the river runs the acequia. The Navajo claim that the latter was opened by them, at a time when the Rio Puerco did not run yet. This is doubtful.

The acequia is not wider than about two meters at most. On the bluffs, which are composed of grey limestone, at its western end and front, there are stumps of occasional piñones, showing that at one time low timber had grown on them. The ruins, which seem to be of regular type, are said to be scattered along the bluffs for over two miles, strung out on a line along the river, or ranged along or at the foot of the bluff. The whole length is 792.0 [meters or yards?] as far as I measured.[170] Then the bluff flattens out into the plain. The chief ruin is [on the bluff].* It is an apparent transition from the small to the large pueblo. The outer basin is evidently a tank, and it would not be too much to say that from it perhaps the fields below were irrigated. The smaller two are estufas. So is the [nearby] round depression. Every building, anyways considerable, has its estufa.

[MARCH 22: no entry made for this date.]

MARCH 23: Spent this day and the preceding in packing, finishing my paintings, and writing. Wrote to Joe, to Dr. Eggert,[171] to D. J. Miller, and to Mr. Griffin,[172] and mailed the letters. At last an Indian came from Zuñi with letters from Cushing. Román will not come; still the case is not hopeless as yet, but I must go to Zuñi myself after him. When I go there, there will be others ready. I talked to Juan, the Navajo, and visited him at his rancho or hogan. He was willing at first, but finally refused. It may be just as well as it is, though it makes the trip more embarrassing for me. At all events, I have to go back to Zuñi again, and not by the [Bandelier failed to complete this sentence].

Saw horned toads and lizards out. Of course, having packed up, I cannot write any more or paint, but went visiting. The kindness of Dr. Mathews is really extraordinary. So is General Bradley[173] and most of his officers. Sent $125 to Santa Fe today for account of Woodside.[174] Last night I wrote letters to Frank [probably, Frank Cushing] and to his wife. Reached Laguna at 1 A.M. [via railroad].

MARCH 24: Cold, but beautiful; found letters from Mr. Parkman, Bigler, Brown, and others. Also the photographs from Brown, that is, the old proof sheets, as he has not had time to make new ones. Wrote to Mr. Parkman and to Joe. Also to Brown and to Padre Brun. John Gunn[175] told me that there is a large ruin on top of a high mesa ten miles from here. Drill of Laguna Indians today. They look like monkeys in their jackets and helmets. What a pity, that the original costume has not been preserved. Last night, an Irish laborer, now busy at Agua Azul [present-day Bluewater] told me that there were ruins up the cañón. The day promises to be exceedingly ugly and disagreeable. Bad news from the Rito Quemado. Wrote card to Padre Gromm; also, to Bigler, and to Saunders[176] of Albuquerque, Reverend Ga[?], and to Father Mailluchet.[177] Captain Pradt came in, and after talking awhile, I started on horseback for Cubero. Had a lively ride, my horse being almost unmanageable.

MARCH 25: Left at 9 A.M. It was a splendid ride. Stopped an hour at Mrs. McCarthy's [McCarty's],[178] then followed the railroad track. Saw no signs of the houses covered by lava at all. About four miles from Grants, I found the Agua Azul in bad condition, the bottoms all over flowed. I finally crossed the river swimming, my good, excellent horse saving me. Chico is a splendid animal.

The overflow of the Agua Azul at this time is a phenomenon which occurs usually. But it is well to notice it. It explains why these fertile bottoms were not built upon by the aborigines. The latter had no means to check the inundation any. I recrossed the Agua Azul in front of Grants. I met there the cowboys of Mr. Latta[179] on a spree and went to pass the night at Don Provencher's.[180] Spent a pleasant evening with him.

MARCH 26: Frogs crying softly and almost timidly. Tried to get the boys out with me, but did not succeed. Waited at the spring till noon. The spring is splendid. A large pool of deep, crystalline water, extensive enough to allow skiffing, and many ducks in it. Rode over to Bluewater alone. About four miles from San Rafael there is a lagune [marsh] which has now overflowed and causes a great bend. To the northwest of it, a ridge. Beyond it the bluewater valley and ranch. This is a beautiful valley bordered by high volcanic mesas. Directly north and five miles off, stands an extinct crater.* The basin is only 30 feet deep about. The Agua Azul itself is a muddy torrent now. The soil is a very sticky red adobe underlaid by quicksand, and when soft, dangerous. Mr. Kuhns told me that he had bored for a well, 100 feet through the surface and drift. Then he struck volcanic sand; beneath it lava boulders, and finally solid lava, through which he passed 75 feet where the auger broke. He says that there is no water except springs, many of which are filled up by the Indians artificially, by sticks, wood, and dirt. Mr. Latta owns 216 square miles in a body, on which there are barely 300 acres of arable ground. The rest is pasture and low timber. Not a tie could be cut on the whole tract. But as a ranch it is a splendid property. They know of no ruins, but have found broken pottery. The boys came in late and rather down in the mouth, as Mr. Kuhns was angry. He is a big solid boy of 24 years and 6 feet 6 inches high. Received me kindly. Life rough. They have a bachelor home, and cannot allow women and liquor on the ranch. His half-brother, Samuel Kuhns, is a wise man. Spent evening quietly and pleasantly.

MARCH 27: Started at 7:30 A.M. Chico is lazy, and we had 45 miles before us. I followed the railroad, between it and the mesa, to the south. As I approached the [Continental] Divide, the higher timber descended the flanks of the mesa into the valley. The latter is waterless. On the north side of the valley begin the brilliant red bluffs of sandstone, so characteristic of this section. Their basis is often whitish-gray. The fronts are vertical walls frequently.

Three miles from Chavez,[181] where the Continental Divide begins, is the house of Juan Aragon. He keeps a little "wayside inn." While there, he told me that the spring in which he had watered my horse, had been filled up by the Indians. They had choked it with rubbish, with entire pottery (black-and-white), and the clay covering the whole was studded with flint implements of all kinds. There are several of those springs in this vicinity. In this spring, a wooden idol was found in the shape of a snake which a Navajo woman told him was "the charm of the spring." This piece of wood is now lost, and the pottery is broken, but I got three handsome flints: a large knife, broken or partly finished; [?] long, 0.065 wide, and 0.018 thick, and the other two knives, one of beautiful jasper, red and pink, and the other, whitish, finely dentated. All the ruins on the top of the mesa are small houses, so are those in the valley. But on the north side, nine miles away, there is a large pueblo with walls still standing. I examined one of the ruins.* The pottery is black-and-white and red-and-black. Near it is the usual depression which looks rather large for an estufa. We also found a number of very small stone-ruins like watchtowers.

The Continental Divide is barren, and the mesas on both sides of it form a level gap, through which the railroad passes. I went on through and over that gap, and reached Coolidge or Crane's (El Carrizo) at 4 P.M. The bottom west of it is very marshy, but I crossed it easily and then a wooded ridge, very handsome, into the plain north of Fort Wingate. Reached the Fort at 6:30 P.M. Chico has again been a brave little beast. He is very well, has not a wet hair, although we made 42 miles today. Found letters from Cushing, etc. All right at Zuñi, and they expect me there at once.

Everybody here is most friendly as usual. (N.B.) While at Laguna, the matter of Dr. Thomas[182] was discussed, and their expressions showed, that they were not in favor of his removal at all. There is evidently a community of interests. At San Rafael everything is upside down. The padre is at Albuquerque, because another attempt had been made at his arrest. He actually fled. But the cause of his arrest, aside from the case of Román Baca,[183] is that he refused to marry a 16 year old boy. Kuhns is bitterly opposed to both Mexicans and Indians. At Coolidge I met two Indians from Acoma.

MARCH 28: Am glad to be under shelter. I attended to Frank Cushing's matters early in the morning and had my horse shod. Then called on Dr. Mathews, taking lunch with him and Lieutenant Fornance.[184] Afterwards called on General Bradley. The old gentleman is again exceedingly kind and pleasant and gave me a wagon and everything I could hope for. I have made arrangements to leave my instruments here, to be shipped to Georgetown [New Mexico], while I proceed southward without them. It is better and safer. In this way I can go alone with Chico if necessary, having nothing but my saddlebags and two blankets to carry. I still hope to get Román when at Zuñi. Shall get my pants reinforced, new soles put to my boots, in fact, everything thoroughly overhauled. It is my last chance to have it done here. Barthelmes has two splendid negatives of the Dance of the Mountain Sheep.[185] They are really good. He is as kind as ever. Nothing from Laguna. General Bradley leaves for Santa Fe tonight. Colonel Crofton[186] and Captain Woodbury[187] called on me this afternoon. Very pleasant and kind. Lieutenant Huse is better, but a very tall and great "baby." This P.M., flags are at half-mast on account of the death of P.M. General Howe;[188] he was a personal friend of General Bradley.

Dr. Gibson came in and told me that he had heard the Sioux and other northern tribes formerly used flints for the heads of lances. He showed me an old Comanche lance made of an old, very elastic sword and fitted into the shaft (of willow-wood) by wet cowhide shrunk on. Dr. Mathews, with whom I passed the evening, showed me a process of twilling twine in three strings, used by the Navajo in making girths.

MARCH 29: Bought cartridges and towels. Got a letter from Padre

Grom. Had boots resoled and pants reinforced, putting on Troy's pants in the meantime. Wrote today to Padre Ribera, to Juan José,[189] to José Hilario,[190] to Don Nicolás Pino,[191] to Gregorio,[192] and to Don Joaquín [García Icazbalceta]. Wrote card to Dr. Brinton [193] and a few lines to Padre Grom. I then stepped over to Dr. Mathews again, and finally began to ship my various things by express, both to Joe and to Collett. To Joe I sent my paintings (21 plates), photographs, letters, journal for 1882, etc.[194] To Collett I sent the flints, requesting him to pay for them what he might deem necessary.

MARCH 30: I finished up my various duties and finally concluded not to ship my instruments, but to leave them at the Fort in Dr. Mathews' care. He will send them south to me, wherever I direct. Arranged for my departure. Lieutenant Fornance gives me an infantry soldier, a horse for the latter, and a pack-mule. Got everything together. Barthelmes will take my plates[195] at Laguna. Called on Colonel Beaumont,[196] Captain Waterbury,[197] Colonel Crofton, and finally Dr. Mathews, and Lieutenant Fornance. The latter gave me details about the so-called Spanish Fort, three miles from Pescado. It appears to be a parallel to the Cebollita near San Rafael. The stonework is as well done, and the ruin is large and round. My horse is in the finest possible condition. Everything is ready for departure at last.

MARCH 31: We started at 6:30 A.M. It was exceedingly cold and wet, and the wind blowing violently. We rode across the mountain through the storm, so as to reach Nutrias at 11 A.M. There, there was no snow at all, but the wind very violent and cold. The village is now inhabited, and we were kindly received. Ate our food in a house where they had five mantles of rabbitskins.[198] Clouds broke and we rode on. The road was perfectly dry and very good. Reached Zuñi after a very cold ride, at 6 P.M. Most kindly received. Think of it, Joe has written to Mrs. Cushing!

APRIL

APRIL 1: Román [i.e., the chance of Román's accompanying Bandelier] is far from being hopeless. The boy seems much attached to me, and the governor alone opposes. But I hope to break down the opposition yet. Mr. Cushing says that the Zuñi have a tradition, that three gentes, among them the Crane and the Rattlesnake, lived formerly in the small houses [as] there was no war in the country. When the war began, they aggregated in large pueblos.

I began to write at the *Ausland* paper again. At night, we spoke of the Abó paintings. It appears that the white-and-black-striped figure is one of the chief medicine men of the *ne-ue*, [Newekwe, probably] whereas the red-and-white, with vertical stripes, is a god: Poyatama. Thus it appears that the same customs and notions prevailed on the east side of the Rio Grande as on the west side.[199]

Mr. Cushing also told me about the origin of the Chacuani, or Chacuina [Chakwena]. It appears that, while they were traveling through Arizona on their migration hither, they were met at a certain place by a goddess who was invulnerable, and who headed all the bad spirits or demons against mankind. The two brothers (A. [Ahoyute] and M. [Matzewe]) then consulted about it and Matzewe mounted his magic net and had himself drawn up into the Sun. The Sun Father then told him that the said bad woman carried her heart in a rattle and that if he would strike that rattle with his thunderbolt, she would become harmless. So the eight storm gods transformed Ahoyute and Matzewe into two warriors, and they met the woman. Ahoyute sent his shaft and killed her, but she at once came to life again. Then Matzewe struck the rattle with his bolt, and it shattered. She at once became subdued, and passing into the earth, reappeared at the south with a band of warriors, but transformed into a beneficial protector of mankind. These [warriors] are the Chacuina.

APRIL 2: Last night, Mr. Cushing also told me the origin of the mula or macaw. It appears that one of their gods showed them two eggs of which he said they should select one. One of them would produce a handsome bird, beneficial to mankind, the other an ugly and noxious bird. The Zuñi selected the wrong egg, because it looked handsome and hatched it on the top of a mountain. Out of it came the crow, while the other egg, which was unsightly and dirty, was taken south by the god, where it produced the macaw.

Most of the day was spent in writing the *Ausland* paper and in negotiations about Román. The latter proved fruitless as far as the present is concerned, but two months hence he will go with me to Mexico surely. For the present, he will accompany me to San Juan [present-day St. Johns, Arizona]. Thus much is gained; the more I see of the boy the more I like him. Matters being thus far arranged, I spent the evening quietly in conversation. The ruined pueblo of *Tala-hogan* (Navajo) is the Ahuatu, Aguato, or Aguatobi [Hopi Awatobi, see Montgomery, Smith, and Brew, 1949] of the Spaniards. It contains the remains of a large church and has remarkably handsome pottery, even handsomer than that of Heshota U¢la. It was inhabited by the Moqui, and on account of constant friction about the hunting-grounds and rabbit-gardens (where they appear to have kept tame rabbits), the people of the other pueblos, six generations ago, fell upon and destroyed it. They murdered the men while in the fields and enslaved the women and the children. There are still descendants of them at Oraiby [Oraibi].[200]

The Zuñi also claim that the pueblo of Heshota U¢la was inhabited since the [Spanish] Conquest. There is any amount of charred corn in the ruins of Aguato. Mr. M[etcalf?] painted the jar from Moqui today for me; Mrs. Cushing, the watermelon bowl; and Miss Magill,[201] the Moqui basket. Thus I shall get two plates from Moqui and three personal souvenirs at the same time. It has been hard work to get Román, for the governor is bitterly opposed. The silversmiths here are Zuñi. The quality of the potters' clay here is splendid, and Mr. Cushing is right in attributing the advances in the art of pottery to local qualities of the clay.

APRIL 3: Mr. Cushing told me yesterday that near Aguato there were still drainage tubes of burnt clay, and that the fields are plainly visible. The governor told me that the ruins near Camp Apache are all of Zuñi origin, like those of San Juan.*

The names in Zuñi for a baby, a doll, and an idol are the same: *Ui-ha*. He-sho-ta-Tzi-nan, or Pescado (a round pueblo), was occupied permanently since the time of the Spaniards. ¢luellan is a larger place than a pueblo (he-sho-ta). The personal name is given and also publicly proclaimed at the time of initiating into a gens. The fields of the six *Chacui-mosona* are still cultivated apart, by all the people in common. It appears that they have, every year, eight rabbit hunts and eight deer hunts which are in charge of the Bow Order, whereas the antelope hunt is in charge of the Hunters [Society].

The beginning of the year is pictorially represented by the drilling of a firestick. The year begins about the winter solstice. The suntower is used as follows. In winter, they look through a notch in the western wall, over the pillar to the east. When the sun rises over a certain point, there in a line with the pillar, then it is midwinter or the beginning of the year. In summer they look from a pillar in the summer gardens to the sun tower. Sign of the year according to the Zuñi.

Six of their months are represented by the six colors; the others have different names. Nai-u-tshi keeps a calendar every year, but besides there exist, in scattered caves, many particular records of special events. Thus [there is evidence for] memberships [in their societies] for long periods. This explains why the pictographs are so much scattered, and often so far from the pueblos or ruins. Very interesting evening.

APRIL 4: I begin to be doubtful about Román, still I may do him injustice. He has not come as far [late] as 10 A.M. It appears now that the governor has again told him not to go! Went with Abraham to the spring beneath the hill on the north side of the pueblo. It is well walled in and covered.

The water is good and would be clear if the spring was cleaned out. Sandstorm most terrible all day. No possibility of leaving. Got my head washed by the governor's wife. At night the mail came in with letters from Papa, Joe, Mrs. Morgan, and Mr. Parkman. Professor Horsford sends me $100. Wrote to Joe, to Professor Horsford,[202] to Mr. Parkman, and also finished other letter to the *Ausland* dated "Acoma 20 May 1882."[203] Román has not come.

APRIL 5: Groundplan of the church of Ha-ui-cu.*[204] . . . The church is red adobe, whereas the pueblo is of red sandstone. This church stands at the foot of the hills, on the edge of the fields of Aguas Calientes [most likely, Bandelier meant present-day Ojo Caliente], a mile almost, northwest of the present summer pueblo. Plat of the ruins of the pueblo of Ha-ui-cu situated on a hill 14.4 [meters] high, or rather the southern spur of it, and about one-and-a-half miles from the spring of Aguas Calientes. There are no standing walls left, but foundations can still be easily traced, though much ruined. There is little pottery, and it resembles closely that of the plain of Zuñi and of Toyoalana in being glossy, and of a [?] pattern also. Much flint, and some obsidian. Further observations on following days. Left Zuñi at 7 A.M. and reached the Venado passing through a thunderstorm at 5 P.M.

APRIL 6:
El Pueblito.**

All these pueblos are on the ridge above the cañada north of it. The rock is sandstone, the soil sandy and light, and there are, of course, plenty of junipers and other small trees. This low monte extends all over the mesa. Several of these ruins are very far from the water, and it is therefore doubtful if the round basins are estufas, and not water tanks.

200 meters west of it, on same ridge.*

The condition of all these ruins is a very bad one. They are reduced to mere low mounds, some even have scarcely any stones left. The height of these mounds is from 0.30 to 1.00 [meter]. The basins by their side are almost obliterated; still they can be discerned. There are a great many of these ruins scattered all through the mesas on both

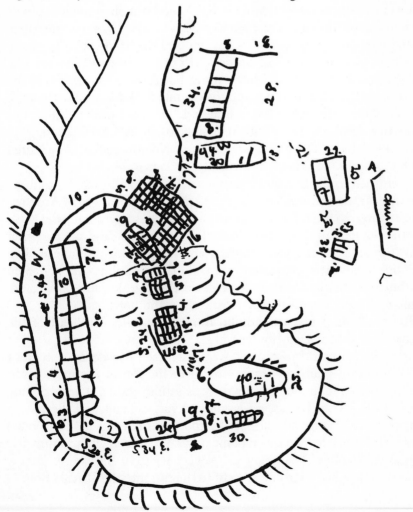

sides of the river. The pottery is black-and-white; red-and-black is also abundant, also corrugated-and-indented. Among the latter are some finely corrugated pieces, the corrugations being narrow and flat. . . .

I now resume yesterday's journal. The whole day was bitterly cold, and I soon got chilled through, while riding. I crossed Pina-ua [ruins] and went to the very end of the Zuñi plain. I then crossed over the spurs of the mountains south of Zuñi into a valley, and thence across hills of reddish sandstone into the very beautiful and fertile valley of Aguas Calientes. This valley is surrounded by hills of sandstone which terminate, on the east, south, and southwest in abrupt ledges. On these ledges the present summer pueblo is located. It absolutely recalls Acomita!

I went to the house of Antonico Barela and was charmingly received by him and by his old father, Juan Cristóbal Barela. I had seen the latter formerly at Zuñi. I, then, with a boy, crossed the fertile fields to Ha-ui-cu which place lies on a hill a mile north of the Aguas Calientes. The top of the hill is covered with the ruins, but there are ruins also at the bottom of the hill, between it and the church. Still it is smaller than the pueblo above. The whole is much ruined. There are pieces of flint, but I do not recollect any obsidian. The pottery is more like that of Toyoalana, but there is also some glossy. No corrugated or indented pottery was visible. Manos and metates of lava were visible.

I returned to the house of Antonico at 3 P.M., and there he told me the story of the abandonment of the pueblo, out of fear of the Apaches. They moved to the hill where some of the houses now stand, and there another church was built. But finally they moved to Zuñi, after a priest had been killed. Now, the pueblo is a summer pueblo, but there are two families living there permanently. I staid there until 4 P.M., and then Antonico accompanied me. We crossed the Rio de Zuñi on a handsome grassy plain, and then I followed on the north side.

Ruins of the pueblo at the Ojo Bonito, six miles southeast of the Venado, in the Cañada Bonita.* . . .

In order to reach this cañada, we crossed the Rio de Zuñi in front of [a Mexican] house and then crossed to the top of the mesa south and southeast. The foot of this mesa is sandstone; on it rests a wide layer of black lava. The ascent is bad and very difficult, but the view is magnificent. The cañada lies at the foot, and beyond it the wooded mesa is fully visible with the high mesa of Zuñi looming up prominently in the background. The mesa is not very wide, so that we crossed it soon, and then had a terrible descent to the east into the Cañada Bonita,

which is truly like her [its] name. It is a grassy narrow valley running
very nearly south to north. Not far from where it empties lies the Ojo,
with the ruins immediately above it. They are much destroyed, but the
pottery is very handsome, and somewhat similar to that of the ruins
of Heshota U¢la. It is glossy, black-and-white, finely striated, red-and-
black, corrugated, and indented. Among the glossy pottery, there is
some cream-colored; some painted green, red with white paint, etc.
Flint and obsidian are still visible. Manos, of the flat kind, of basalt,
lava, and quartzite, large and small. (It appears that the spring here is
not permanent. It dries up in the summer.) Groundplan of pueblo, a
mile south of the Ojo Bonito in the cañada.* Much ruined. Stone.
Pottery usual, but also red and white. No glossy fragments seen.

The Cañada del Venado, through which the Zuñi River flows south-
westward for about 20 miles, is narrow, and the mesas are high. Rocks
10 to 20 feet high line the bottom. The river itself runs in a deep bed of
red clay, like all along from Zuñi. There are but few passages [fords],
for the banks are precipitous. The place of the rancho itself is very
picturesque, a pleasant sunny spot, with a green lawn between it and
the river. I was very kindly received. (N.B. From the heights above
Aguas Calientes, I caught the first view of the Sierra Blanca in the
south, a long bold chain covered with snow, and today I saw it very
handsomely, also the Escudilla. They are visible from the top of the
mesas north of Zuñi, six miles off.) Talked a great deal about ruins,
which are very abundant on the mesas; small houses, much ruined,
mostly low and flat mounds. Much pottery is found. He showed me a
bowl in the shape of a small soup-, or sauce-, bowl, of reddish clay,
curiously wrought at the bowl, and the cover of a bowl. The bowl is now
broken, but the cover with the knob remains. Both appear as if turned
with a lathe (!?).[205] This cover is of brown jasper, covered with a thin
coating of clay!! Both objects were found buried in the ruins of the
Pueblito.

Otherwise, the pottery is of the usual kind, black-and-white, red-and-
black, corrugated and indented, and I found one kind, white, gray and
purple lines, which I had not seen before.[206] Quality good. Stone axes
are also found. In the river bottoms are said to be rock-carvings, and
in the rocks, clefts and caves containing pottery and traces of human
abodes. There is also a cliffhouse about. The mesas about were certainly
inhabited largely by small-house dwellers. Dubois (who is a Californian)
says that the Zuñi do not claim these ruins. The pueblos of the
Cañada Bonita are both very interesting, and there is a remarkable dif-

ference in that the large-house pueblo has handsome glossy pottery, whereas the other has it not. Found a mortar in the latter.

APRIL 7: I left at 8:30 A.M. and descended the cañada. On the south side, high black mesas of lava, almost hugging the river. On the north side, at some distance from the river, separated by a flat, grassy bottom, tumbled bluffs of red and yellowish-grey sandstone. In the walls of these is said to be a cliffhouse, or cave walled in, and many rock-paintings. I saw neither. About six miles from the Venado, and perhaps 500 [meters] from the river (north of it) lies the ruin in the accompanying groundplan.* The foundations alone are plainly visible. Pottery as usual, red-and-black, black-and-white, corrugated and indented, and red with white lines. About a mile farther on, on the south side lining the road and close to the northern bluffs, is a high ruin.* The pottery is the same. About seven miles from the Venado the mesas recede on both sides and appear to vanish; the grassy bottom spreads out.

Here there are the ruins of Tenney's old house, burnt down by unknown hands, four or five months ago. (Dubois is very bitter against the Zuñi although he says that they never molested him. He married a Navajo woman in first nuptials and has had three children from her.) Here, there is a windmill for a well. I met two of Tenney's boys. Crossed the river about 12 miles from the Venado (at a bad place) and began to traverse the plain to the south. The landscape is dismal. Flat, low mesas appear in the distance, sparsely covered with low, scrubby sabinos. The plain itself is grassy, but not a tree. It is the landscape of extreme barrenness.

As I ascended the plain, which there is fully six miles wide, to a barren, nude ridge, it became more and more desolate. I descended on the other side and saw before me a landscape, grassy plains and barren ridges, to the foot of the Sierra Blanca. The Escudilla becomes very plain, and in the east-northeast, a high pointed peak dimly appears. Grass is in occasional patches, and the Yucca bacata very prominent and large. Upon crossing the second ridge, I saw San Juan [present-day St. Johns, Arizona]. It lies in a desolate bottom, though of very fertile soil, but all around the hills, gravelly, are absolutely denuded of trees. The Rio Colorado Chiquito [Little Colorado River] is a roaring or rather rushing torrent of milky water; its banks are steep and vertical. The tower lies on the west side. Volcanic cones, clay-hills of dismal leaden and purple colors, spread into a mesa running southeast to northwest, east of the river, at a distance of two or three miles. The bottom between them and the river is moist and very fertile. But the landscape all around, for uncounted miles, is one of oppressive barrenness and death, endless views to the north, west, and east, over rolling plains with barren ridges and, in the far-off distance, thinly timbered plateaus. Between the Rio Zuñi, at Tenney's ranch, and the Rio Colorado here, there is not a drop of water, a distance of 20 miles, and no wood. The pyramidal peak to the east is the Sierra del Dátil. To the south of this, there is a high gravelly hill, along the slope of which runs an acequia. Mr. Barth[207] told me this acequia was formerly an old one and lined with mezcla. I want to see that white mezcla. Dubois has found actual drainage pipes made of it. The pottery is black and white, and grey, very old and washed. The ruins are almost entirely obliterated and have an appearance of very old, old age. It is possible that the rain, which has totally washed the hill may have advanced decay and obliteration. The hill which is about 20.0 [meters] high, runs from southwest to northeast. The mounds and depressions are barely visible.*

APRIL 8: Mr. Barth, 13 years old (born 13 May 1843), came from Posen [Germany] in 1856 to California; from California, he went to New Mexico in 1862. He has led an adventurous life. In 1865, he took the mail contract from Prescott (Arizona) to Albuquerque. In 1866 the same contract from Tubac (65 miles south of Tucson) to Prescott. Sold out the following year for $6000 and established a store at Cubero. Married in 1874 at San Rafael. From Cubero he moved here.[208] This place [San Juan] now contains about 200 Mormon families, and many Mexicans, mostly from Cubero. The Mormons are, as yet, a quiet, very industrious, agreeable set of people, and their influence is visible upon the Mexicans. The Mexican houses are nice, new and clean; the Mormon houses, on the west end, are shanties of wood as yet. But the Mormons will, very soon, have laid hands on the whole country, and as they are exceedingly coherent and clannish, nobody likes to see them. They are evidently pouring in in large numbers. Otherwise San Juan is a very pleasant place, were it not for the dismal nudity and barrenness of it. There is wood about 20 miles off, otherwise there is not a dwarfish sabino in sight. The ground is fertile, and the Rio Colorado Chiquito has a goodly body of water. It roars distinctly all day long.

I painted all day, and with good results. There is a show here of the most modest kind, and the whole family has gone to it, leaving me all alone in the house. I wrote postal cards home and to Mrs. Morgan. Prescott is 250 miles off. Holbrook, 65 miles. Concho, 15 miles. To the

Venado, it is 30 miles. On the whole it is mostly a grazing country, but the Mormons are fencing in on the east side of the river and farming. All the ridges appear very gravelly and barren. Excellent fresh butter, good milk, and coffee, etc. are here. But a glass of beer costs 25¢, so does a cigar. The bottle of beer, $1. Family very pleasant and kind. Chico appears tired. I begin to think of changing my plans, to leave Chico at Tucson, and to go to Chihuahua by rail. The more I think of it, the more it strikes me as best to get into Sonora, rather than to go to Chihuahua and to Coahuila.

APRIL 9: Daniel Dubois came last night. He speaks of ruins near the Concho, recently examined, which contain valuable things. Called on Don Pedro María Badilla,[209] Cura of San Juan, a lovely old gentleman, actually worshipped by everybody here. Wrote to Mr. Parkman, otherwise painted all day. Aristéo Varela told me of ruins 17 miles north of here with painted tiles, "cal y canto" [rough stone and mortar], etc. (Stuff [Nonsense!], for when I showed him my pottery, he said it was the same kind.)

APRIL 10: Started at 9 A.M., but soon got into low timber, and after wandering about for some time, lost my way. Tried several roads which all ended in the monte, and finally returned to San Juan. After taking dinner I started again, and taking the left-hand road, descended into the bottom of the Rio Colorado Chiquito. The borders are vertical bluffs in part. I followed the river upwards. The bottom is flat on the left bank; on the right bank it is always steep, with a series of high mesas behind. Gradually, high, abrupt bluffs began to appear on the left bank also, forming little valleys, in which are ranchos. The country is very picturesque, and the road as it winds around, is charming, though there are not many trees.

Finally, after passing the "Tule," I reached the beautiful valley of San José, or "Las Tusas," very fertile, and on a knoll, I found a small pueblo, which has been partly excavated, and the people are living in the old original rooms of the pueblo.[210] It is a denuded spot, with a very handsome view upon a grassy and well-watered valley. The place is full of stone hatchets.

I stay with José Jaramillo,[211] and write this in his dingy tienda. The people are the simplest in the world; more primitive than any I have met among the Mexicans as yet. Nearby there is Cushing's Cave, which contains many interesting things. The day has been tiresome, as I have travelled at least 25 miles, while the distance is not more than 14 miles.

APRIL 11: Took the groundplan of the pueblo. The walls are double in many instances, and well-made. An abundance of remains lies scattered about. Pottery, glossy, black-and-white, red-and-black, handsomely corrugated. Stone axes, mortars of lava, flat metates, manos. I found the walls to be 0.36 [meter] wide. Often they are double. Was shown an awl of flint. The acequia is at least five miles long, running from the Tule to two miles at least below here. The lands are very fertile. On the whole, it is a very favored spot. The mesas around have wood within two miles and the river an abundance of good water. The banks are steep; it runs in a cut of clay and loam; and the soil is very black and heavy.

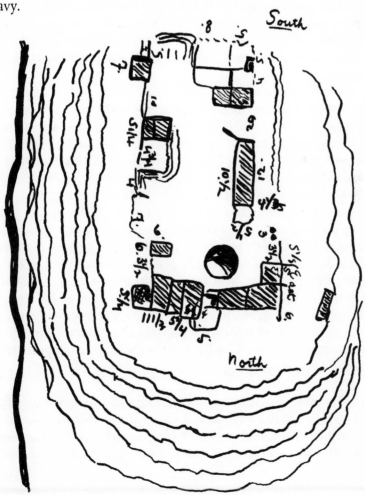

One mile southeast of San José de las Tusas, near the banks of the river, on the ranch of Eutymio Baca, lies a pueblo ruin.* It is much ruined. Pottery like the other, but there is also black with white lines and red with white. I found obsidian there. Much flint. Several old acequias run nearby, but to the northwest of it, as there is no space between the river and the brow of the hill (which there is about 8.0 [meters] above the river, and perhaps 100.0 [meters] to the southwest of it). We then crossed the north side of the river and visited the caves, which are numerous, and in many instances more fissures in the much tilted and disturbed [strata]. There are many prayersticks, much pottery, and I found remains of baskets like those of the Apaches, and finally a complete shoe [sandal]. It is of wickerwork.

The valley flattens out to the southeast. The rock is in general volcanic; the highest parts are black, the steep bluffs, standing up in the valley, are of red and yellow sandstone. The river is about 10.0 [meters] wide and runs swiftly. It rises and falls daily, reaching its highest point after sunrise. This is different from the Zuñi River, which is highest about 2 P.M.

Around the base of the rock of the caves, between it and the river, there are two small-house ruins.* The caves seem to pertain to them as the pottery is decidedly small-house pottery. The plume-sticks are of all kinds! red, blue, etc. On the plain, there are several estufa-like hollows, with pottery, which look exactly like the oldest remains at Pecos. I arranged with Manuel Chavez for tomorrow to the Concho. He told me that the Sierra Blanca was full of pueblos, and that there are many about the Escudilla and the Mogollones, although not in the mountains proper, but along their base. The Tusas appear as desolate, or rather, a denuded spot, but in reality, although somewhat exposed to winds, it is a very handsome fertile place, well chosen for an Indian settlement. There is a pueblo at the Tule and there, as well as on the eastern outlet of the acequia, are the remains of the white concrete which I shall see tomorrow. Rumors from the south are unfavorable; the troops have left Fort Apache,[212] Captain Dougherty[213] himself being in command of them. The Rio Salado [Salt River] appears to be full of ruins. Wrote to Cushing.

APRIL 12: Handsome day; warm, and very clear. Soon, however, a fearful wind arose from the west, and it blew all day with incessant violence. It was so strong that it almost blew me off the horse at times. We took a straight direction, across the mesas. The landscape is one of dreary and desolate barrenness. At the Tule, where there is a pueblo, which I did not see, there is the acequia. It is an exceedingly remarkable object. Laid on the ground, upon stones of which only fragments remain, it forms a concave trough, not deep. There are two of them, one of which is with vertical sides, ten inches deep, and two feet, six inches wide, and from three to five inches thick at the sides. The other is four feet, three inches wide and eight inches thick. The section is as follows.* The material resembles a ferruginous sandstone, or limestone, amygdaloid and somewhat crystalline. I took it for rock at first, and only after a little time, I came to the conclusion that it must be a concrete or mezcla of some kind. The whole is, as yet, an enigma to me. Thence on to the west, the country is horribly barren. The mesas are all black lava, appalling in their bleakness, and as far as the eye reaches, there is nothing to mitigate the effect except the Sierra Blanca and the Escudilla in the south. The valleys, equally treeless, have fertile soil, and one of them, where Tomás Avalos received us most kindly and gave us to eat, has fair water. There is some grass about.

Reached the Concho about 3 P.M. It is a handsome, well-sheltered vale, which is entered from the southeast by a rugged canyon of lava rocks, beneath which are two handsome ponds. At the foot of the rocks is the source of the Rio Concho, and on its banks, southwest, a recent Mormon settlement. The Mexican houses are on the east side, scattered. The valley is very fertile, but I paid 4¢ a pound for corn. No hay nor oats. But there is beer. I stopped at the house of Antonio José Ortega, although his wife alone was home. All the men, except one, are out; the women and children alone are here. This is the custom. I am suffering greatly from rheumatism in the small of the back, so much that I can hardly stand up. It is on the right side of the spine. The wind, which had slackened up a little at nightfall, soon rose again with great violence, and it blew a fearful gale all night. The roar was so great that all sleep was impossible. Sky all the while perfectly clear.

APRIL 13: Slept a little, after 4 A.M. Wind less violent, but very cutting. Although the cold constantly increased, we started at 10:30 A.M., ascending the mesa of lava. It was terribly cold. The wind furious, going through and through, so that we thought frequently of going back. No sign of life except prairie dogs. Yesterday we had seen antelopes, and the day before, two snakes. No trace of pueblos. All Lava.

Reached the rancho of Ortega at 5 P.M. almost frozen to death, stiff and sore from rheumatism. My companion, little Francisco Chavez, suffered almost more than I. We visited the source of the Rio Concho, but found no ruins. The rancho of Ortega is a lovely spot, but there is no permanent water, although he has some beautiful lagunes, which he constructed himself. This explains why there is not a trace of pueblos there. On the whole, I find that the villages are in groups, following the *permanent* water courses combined with wood. This is the country of the Venado.

Thence about 20 miles to San Juan, thence 13 miles to the Tule, 15 miles to the Concho, and 30 miles to Show-Low [present-day Showlow]. It indicated that the Indians settled on these favorable spots, changing around frequently about the main source of water. While the nomadic Indian roams over large surfaces, the sedentary Indian is tied to certain natural facilities. There he settles, and changes about around it, thus remaining nomadic on a limited scale.[214] Slept at the rancho. We are nine of us, including the Navajo woman who is the cook.

APRIL 14: I continued my way over a terrible road of lava. Treeless mountains, barren and exposed to the fierce wind. It was so cold, and the road so bad, that I walked most of the way. In the distant north a high double peak, heavily snowclad, appeared.*

The mesas around here are not as abrupt as are those of New Mexico. They are undulating wastes. At 11 A.M., I saw the skirts of heavy timber, pinabetes, in which is Show-Low. Reached there 11:30 A.M. It is a rocky vale through which the Rio de Show-Low, a small stream, trickles to the northwest. High pinabetes skirt it. It is a sunny spot, well-sheltered. On the southwest bank, lies a large handsome pueblo. Nothing but foundations remain, but they are very distinct. Pottery similar to that of the Tule and of the Cañada Bonita. Saw Mr. Cooley;[215] he promised me an Apache [guide]. Painted all afternoon. The mountains of the A.M. are the Sierra de San Francisco [north of Flagstaff, Arizona].

APRIL 15: It is Sunday, but we hardly notice it. At home they do!

[I made a] groundplan* of the pueblo[216] south of Mr. E. C. [C. E.] Cooley's house, and 180.0 [meters] west of the Show-Low River, on a hill with fertile bottom beneath it. Every room is distinct, but I found only one estufa. The walls are of sandstone, and were about 0.20 [meter] thick. The valley being very fertile, the inhabitants had their fields right beneath the house, as at Pecos; only on a smaller scale. . . . There is flint, and some obsidian, but very little only. The pottery is very remarkable. Corrugated-and-indented abounds; it is very fine, and painted. Some are plain red or pink; some have designs in bluish-black upon cream-yellow ground! The white painted pottery, with black glossy lines, is also very common. On the whole, the pottery is superior. Painted in the afternoon, and at night sent a postal card to Joe.

APRIL 16: I visited the ruins about a quarter mile south of here, a bare knoll surrounded by pines. There is a stone heap, indicating a ruined guardhouse near it. The ruins still show two small houses, much decayed, like those of the Venado. Pottery in all points similar to that of the large pueblo, but much older in appearance. Still this is no indication of greater age.[217] In the large ruin, excavations have been made, and thus fragments in a better state of preservation have been brought to the surface. In the small houses only the old surface pottery, worn by centuries, is lying about, also flint and obsidian. The walls here are partly lava, partly sandstone. After examining the ruins, I called on Mr. C. E. Cooley. The Apaches are organized in bands who live separate and have their own chiefs, and who only marry outside of their own band. When a man dies, his brother inherits his property, the wife or wives included. Thus there is clanship, with exogamic marriage, and descent in the female line. He knows of no traditions among them. They have medicine among them, but he knows of no secret societies.[218] He says that there are ruins about Springerville (Valle Redondo), and principally along the Rio Salado and the Rio Verde. Speaks of an acequia, 40 to 50 miles long. Spent the whole day with Cooley, Wolf, and Buell.[219] And how? [to what purpose?]. . . .*

Cooley says that a Zuñi chief told him they had the custom of building large corrales for the antelope hunts. They drove the animals into the corrals and slaughtered them there.[220] After the hunt they would go to the caves of the Tule and deposit plume-sticks, etc. in them. It is doubtful about my further movements. No Apaches are in sight, except a few renegades. Terribly homely chaps; they look much like the Navajos, but are smaller.

APRIL 17: Painted all day. There are no more ruins about here, but on the Rio de la Plata [Silver Creek] there are some. There are also many ruins in the Valle Redondo (Springerville). Mr. Huning [221] told me that there, the acequias of the ruins are higher up than those of the present farms. He also tells me that the corrals made of posts, with long lanes leading up into them and used by the Zuñi for large communal hunts, are exceedingly common about the Blue Water Region. The Zuñi claimed them as their own in former times.

The division of the Apaches into bands, located as groups or Rancherias, indicated localized gentes. These gentes or clans are often at bitter feuds with each other, but still they always are exogamic. Mr. Cooley denies the existence of traditions among the Apaches. This is doubtful.

APRIL 18: Painted all day. In the evening W. H. Wolf came in. There are ruins on Show-Low River, two miles below here, and also rock-paintings in the cliffs on both sides. Mr. Huning goes to Fort Apache tomorrow with me.

APRIL 19: I started in the buckboard with Mr. H. Celso sitting on behind and leading Chico who felt quite happy. We rose from the altitude of 6100 feet at Cooleys, through stately forests of pines, splendid straight trees, all *Pinus ponderosa*. The road goes through hill and vale, high mountainbacks, equally timbered, on all sides, and in the distance an occasional glimpse is caught of the snow-clad tops of the Sierra Blanca. The [Apache] Reservation begins about seven miles from Show-Low, near Clark[222] and Kinder's ranch, and the wild, heavily timbered mountain scenery, with an occasional fillet of water, closes in upon all sides. A new species of juniper[223] appears as we near the highest point of the Mogollones [Mogollon Rim], as this side branch or outlying skirt of the Sierra Blanca is called. The divide is 7400 feet high. Thence the descent is through steep and tortuous rocky roadbeds. All along the soil is very good, the wheel-tracks are deeply worn, and lay open a dark loamy sod. But the lava scattered all over makes it very rough. The highest point is about 17 miles from Show-Low. Then we descend towards White River. The grass turns fresh and green. Oaks appear, leafless yet, and the evergreen encino in large specimens. To the left of the road, bare patches, covered with excellent grass, skirt the canyon of the White River, which runs about east-northeast to west-southeast, a rocky cleft with vertical sides toward the road. There the rock is hard, black and grey lava.

On the other side, the slopes, often in vertical buttresses of red sandstone, rise at least 1000 feet. Dark pines sweep up past the perpendicular cliffs to the summit, which is accidented [broken], often bare, and then again covered with high pines. Eight miles from Fort Apache lies

the old former rancho of Mr. Cooley. The river at the foot of the cliffs
and at least 400 feet beneath the plateau of the road and of the timber,
forms occasional fertile bottoms at the foot of the canyon. In one of
these his house stood. The bottom is scarcely five feet above the river,
grassy, with fine soil, and acequias running through it. The house is
burnt down. The ruins stand close by. They were built of whitish hard
lava, and appear like a shapeless rubbish mass, about ten feet high.*
Pottery, finely corrugated and indented, painted in black and white,
grey and white, some unusually thick. In some the corrugations are very
delicate, in others coarse. It bears much resemblance to the pottery of
the pueblos of Show-Low. Still the corrugated ware, which largely pre-
dominates, is of finer, more intricate design. There is the usual design
of red-and-black, and black or red plain, but no glossy. The ruin is
evidently an old one, very old. It is sheltered at the bottom of the
vertical cliffs, and the sun gets into the valley only from the south, as
from east and west there are rocks obstructing the light of the sun.

Ascending, I counted the [my?] steps and found the altitude at least
400 feet. Above, at one-half mile distance to the northwest from the
brink of the canyon, lies the second ruin. It forms, with the first, the
following section.* Its appearance is about the same, also the pottery.
Trees have grown in it, [including] encinos, about 18 inches to two
feet around. Near by are two small-house mounds, about six steps by
four, and farther on there is the following ruin.*

Along the foot of the ruin at the bottom of the canyon runs an acequia built by Cooley. On the eastern rim of the northern wing, he
found two bodies extended, face to the east, feet outwards [?]. They
were evidently buried, as at Pecos, along the wall of the pueblo, facing
the rising sun. (Before we reached the ruins, and at about halfway, is
the so-called Post Office Hill. It is a ridge in the woods, and on it a pile
of stones, pebbles, rocks, twigs, of all description: of sabinos, cedars,
pines, live oak, etc. This pile corresponds to the apachitas of Peru,[224]
every Indian passing by deposits his offering in the shape of one of these
objects. Some of the boughs were very new and fresh indeed. The
people here believe that the Indians convey information to each other
by means of these deposits, and therefore have given it the name.) Soon
after leaving this spot, the valley opened and presented a most beautiful
appearance. The grass is green; *Verbena communis*, in bloom; sabinos
and live oak are in groves. The mountains around, rising to 1000 and
2000 feet, are clad in pine forest up to their rocky tops. The red sandstone shines through it in precipitous cliffs most magnificently. There

is verdure and life everywhere, handsomely contrasted by the bold crags and the deep cleft of the canyon of White River. The latter is a roaring mountain river; its waters are now milky, otherwise they are clear and limpid. Reached Fort Apache, a most beautiful spot, at the meeting of the north and east forks of the White Mountain River. We passed both forks, the water reaching almost into the buckboard. Splendid grass, tall yucca, sabinos, and oak. Kelly's Butte, a dome-shaped peak, is in full view. Stopped at Mr. Lacy's.[225] Reception exceedingly kind, by him as well as by Mr. Kirchner. Saw Dr. Henderson.[226] Captain Kendall[227] who commands the post now was of the utmost kindness. There are plenty of ruins nearby. About ten miles off there is a round watchtower. Many fires in the timber by the Apaches.

APRIL 20: Today was as disagreeable as yesterday was pleasant and delightful. With Sergeant Barnes[228] I walked up two-and-a-half miles along the east fork of the Rio de la Sierra Blanca to the first ruin. It is built of reddish-brown sandstone, in the usual way, but the pottery is painted and some designs are very intricate and entirely different from any which I had seen before. White-and-black-on-red ground.[229] Obsidian and flint. Manos, fragmentary metates, and entire doorsills of black lava abound. Bones had been dug out of them.[230] It is evident that this pueblo is more recent than those at Cooley's old ranch. It is 200.0 [meters?] south of the river, and the embankment denoting an old bed of it lies halfway. At the present day, the river overflows up to the latter mark.* Along that embankment willows grow, and on the foot of the Pueblo Hill a few large alamos, all of which are now leafing. (The alamos suffer greatly from mistletoe killing them as a parasite.) There are also wild walnut trees in the valley. Nearly opposite, on the north bank of the east fork, are ruins of small houses, but being on foot, we could not cross. An important ruin is six miles west-northwest of Fort Apache, in a canyon on the north side of the river.

The post is built very much like Wingate, but most of the houses are of logs, some of adobe and the guardhouse is of stone. But the spot is far more handsome. The deep precipitous canyon in which the two forks meet is about 150 to 200 feet deep, dark trap rock, often vertical. The scenery is picturesque and romantic in the extreme. But the day is horrible. Snow and sand or dust alternate. Mr. Barnes[231] told me that near the large ruin west-northwest he found a stone cist, two feet deep, and about two feet on each side, out of which he removed the fragments of a clay vessel, burnt, ashes, a metate, and a stone hammer. (Cremation.) In the afternoon Captain Kendall drove with me four miles west down the basalt, more picturesque, a deep black rugged canyon, charming vegetation. No rivers in that direction so far. Saw an old Mexican captive. The Apache name for Moqui is Ne-sel-she, for the Navajo Yu-ta-ha. The Apache women as a rule virtuous. These are the Coyoteros; those of San Carlos, the Pinal Apaches. But the women are badly treated and do all the work. The Apaches are very treacherous and well armed at present.[232] They begin to till the land now, but slowly.

APRIL 21: The whole day was colder and uglier than yesterday, and it snowed frequently. I improved my time in painting and writing up my diary, which I had somewhat neglected of late. Captain Kendall gave me much information. He has visited the Casa Grande and says it is a mud house, with walls seven to nine feet thick, built with cajones. He contends that it still contains six stories, but was originally eight stories high. It appears that the Rio Colorado is about the utmost western limit of the pueblos. In the Tonto Basin, there are many important ruins, and there, as well as on the Rio Verde, there are well built cliff-houses. Near one of the ruins in that region seven funerary urns were dug up, containing calcined remains, and at least 50 shoes [sandals], in rather perfect condition, of the same basketwork as the shoes of the Rio Che-yi [Canyon de Chelly?] and of the cave at the Tusas. It thus appears, if I combine with this the notice furnished by Barnes, that cremation as a mode of burial, after the Mexican fashion, has begun perhaps here already.

Mr. Lacy also tells me that the rooms at the Casa Grande are perhaps nine feet high, and the beams cut off with an implement of stone. An acequia (said to be 50 miles long) runs past the ruins, and the whole settlement appears to have covered about 600 acres (?).[233] On the whole, everything points to the Rio Gila as the line of future research. Here I am well treated in every respect. Mrs. Captain Dougherty[234] sent over a very polite note today, inviting me to dine with her. I went, and found Captain Kendall and his wife, Mrs. Lieutenant Gatewood,[235] and Mr. Lacy. The evening was pleasant, but rather insipid. Small talk and horse-talk. At night I fell dreadfully sick. I had eaten canned salmon, and this upset me completely. Vomiting, and finally strong diarrhea, ensued, and I spent a horrible night. Barnes called for awhile, but I was too ill.

APRIL 22: Spent a miserable night. Very weak and disjointed, but as the day is fine, we started at 9 A.M., Kirchner, Barnes, Soucy (Van Castle), Gomez, and I. Most magnificent scenery, the day splendid, and Chico rode like an angel. We crossed the rio about a half mile below the post, and then climbed a rugged declivity of lava on to a level cañada. It is the Cañada del Carrizo. It is grassy; [on the] left, mountains with mesa tops, but wooden slopes rise on both sides. The soil is fertile, but it has no water. Its direction is from north to south, and a dry arroyo, deeply worn in red sandstone traverses it, emptying into the river at the south. At the northwestern end of the cañada lies the pueblo, on both sides of the arroyo, which there is about 35 feet deep, with the naked and worn sandstone forming its sides. Tall pines grow in the arroyo and on the sides; the site of the pueblo itself has no trees. The village is scattered and appears like a combination of all three forms: outlying small houses, round enclosures, encompassing compact masses with a quadrangular court in their midst. The width of the walls I could not determine, but they appear to be of the usual size, and are of red and yellow sandstone, which crops out in the bed of the arroyo, forming its sides. The rooms are not always clearly marked, and even in the principal complexes they are hardly visible, the whole being one mass of rubbish. I could merely step it, as exact measurements would not be of great practical value. It was evidently a many-storied pueblo, mostly two stories, but in some cases also three stories. I could not discover any trace of tanks or cisterns, although they certainly must have had some permanent water nearby, as the river is about five miles off. The bed proper of the arroyo is rocky, worn in the sandstone, and thus not likely to have absorbed a former current, as at Quivira, etc. Still it is perfectly dry at present.

Nor is it likely that the two pueblos formed originally but one, the arroyo having cut through both, and thus compelled their abandonment.* The wearing out of 25 to 30 feet of red sandstone is an operation of far too long a period for that. As to the question whether both villages were simultaneously occupied or not, it is not possible for me to decide it. Nothing in the condition of the ruins indicates any difference of age; still, the similarity of the northern outhouses, in position and extent, might go to indicate that the village formerly stood on one side and that it was finally moved to the other and thence abandoned.

The two parts or pueblos also could have accommodated very nearly the same number of people. On the principle of two-three rooms to each family as a maximum, I find for the western pueblo 106 families, for the eastern, ninety-one, or between four and five hundred souls in each case. It looks as if the eastern pueblo had been abandoned first, since all the buildings there are on the brink of the arroyo.* The pottery is very handsome. It is all painted, red-and-black-and-white, red-and-white, black-and-white, red-and-black. Corrugated pottery is very scarce, only one piece being found, and that one painted dirty pink. Flint and obsidian was found also, but the latter is scarce. We spent a few hours there very well and I hope, profitably, although I was in a very bad condition. Sleep came on with such force, that on the way home I fell asleep while riding. We reached home at 4 P.M., very well contented. What Mr. Kirchner calls a Zuñi watchtower lies about ten miles from these ruins, in a mountain gap towards Cibiquiu [present-day Cibecue], on a round point. It thus has no connection with these ruins. At the post I was very sleepy, and thus went to bed early, and soon fell asleep. On the whole it was a great pity to have this beautiful day spoiled by yesterday's dinner.

APRIL 23: I painted all day. Many Apaches came in. I saw their cradle, which is much more elaborate than the pueblo cradle. In it they carry the infant on their backs. The hood or top is of wood and basket work, finely plaited, covered with red flannel and beads. A bow like that of the Pueblos forms the back, only it is flat. The baby is covered with

buckskin and fastened with buckskin straps. The men and women commonly wear many strings of glass beads, but they also wear little many-colored beans which they get from Sonora and prize very highly. I also saw a collar of an odoriferous root which they gather about here in the mountains. The earrings are pieces of iridescent shells from the Pacific coast. The men wear the bright headband of the Pueblos, only mostly with long pendants; often it is a piece of red flannel hanging down nearly to the waist. Their dress is in general more fancy, although cotton garments, trimmed red, prevail, also gaudy calico blouses. Their moccasins have a toe-protector in front. They are of buckskin with leggings attached, which often reach higher than the waist. The soles are of common thick hide. A strap of buckskin from above the heel, fastens around the ankle. (I bought one pair of moccasins with leggings for $2.)

Physically, they appear much more like the Pueblos than like the Navajos. They have the more delicate frame and smaller limbs of the former, and their eyes are an intermediate between both, though rather inclining toward the large, becoming Pueblo type. Although dirty, they are not unpleasant to look at. They wear their hair long. Several Navajos came to trade, and I could now easily distinguish both. The Apaches looked like familiar Pueblos types, by the side of the raw-boned, slit-eyed, wolfishly scanning Apaches [Navaho]. Both tribes conversed easily together. They are all painted, some red, some brownish across the cheek and nose, in patterns not unlike those of certain painted pottery, etc.* It looks hideous. I also saw some black paint. The women are small, thinner than the Navajos, and much more handsome. Their noses are aquiline. But they are filthy. The married women carry their hair loose and cut around; the girls wear it tied in a short chungo behind the head, to which is attached a convex tongue of red leather covered with brass buttons. It looks as follows from behind:* and hangs down to the back. Their dress is mostly cotton; they wear moccasins and the leggings like the men. It is very strange that the Apache women are generally virtuous! There are of course a few prostitutes, but very few only, and the great majority are absolutely inaccessible! What a great difference with the Navajos. Old Hannah, or Mrs. Transportation, as they call her here, is of course an exception. K.[irchner] sent her to me this p.m., and she is the most abject, filthy lewd looking and acting old "wh..." I ever saw. She stinks like a pest and knows nothing at all outside her "trade." Nearly all the other women are shy and decent, though friendly.

APRIL 24: Miserable day. Warm and clear, but an awful southerly wind. We had planned to go to the small-house ruins, but it was impossible. So I painted. K[irchner] sent me Old Francisca, a Mexican captive from Sonora, thoroughly "Apachized" and a very decent old woman and willing to talk.[236] She of course confirms the statements about the Rancherias marrying always exogamically, and says that marriage is mostly perfected by asking the girl. If the parents are willing, then the girl is purchased, the boy often sacrificing his entire chattels. If not, "muchos se casan por fuerza" [many are married by capture]. They believe in God, but call him "Dios" (!?) [Bandelier obtained other terms from this informant.]

Her statements in regard to ruins are indistinct. She once stated that the Apaches had built and afterwards abandoned them.[237] After stating that the Carrizo was formerly inhabited by the devil, she said that the devil is dead now, but that his brother lives. She also mentioned that the ruins are called "Qua" or "Ki," but about this I am in doubt. At sunset I am told that the Apaches are holding a great dance below, but that it will not be advisable to attend, as they are suspected of having made ti-suin [maize beer] and therefore going on a drunk, which would make it very dangerous. Suspicious rumors are afloat, of a collision at Cibiquiu, etc., but little reliance can be placed upon them. It is not impossible, however, that the corn, which the Apaches have been getting in from the post for the purpose of planting, may partly have become chewed up and fermented into ti-suin. If so, it would be a bad joke.

APRIL 25: Had a long visit from Francisca and two Apache chiefs this forenoon. They are remarkably like the Pueblo Indians. They again protested that they had no traditions, that they had always lived here, and feigned absolute ignorance in regard to the ruins and to the life after death. The soul goes into the air. This is, of course, "Shenanigan!" When I asked who made the stone axes and the pottery, the reply invariably was: "Quien sabe, quizás quando se puso el mundo." [Who knows; perhaps when the world began."] They do not claim to make any themselves or to have ever made any. Painted; wrote to Joe, also card to Prof. Norton. Mail came. News also that Wolfe is coming in.

APRIL 26: Mr. Lacy left for Prescott this A.M. Painted the stone hatchet of Barnes. It appears now that the cave 14 miles east of here contained empty jars with wicker inside,[238] and some sticks, also old basketwork.

Started up East Fork at 3 P.M. with Barnes. The bottom is narrow but very fertile. Gravelly hills, very steep and high, with live oaks, and tall pines, line the bottom. With the exception of one ruin, these are all on the hills overlooking the river. There are several small mounds indicating the watch towers, and two or three small-house ruins. The pottery is, for the nearest large-house ruin, *identical with that of the Carrizo and of the south side of East Fork.* These have the pottery of Old Ranch of Cooley's on North Fork, that is, corrugated and indented with exquisite corrugations, and also painted. Over all, there is much flint, and some obsidian. In the large-house ruin, I noticed two metates of black lava, elliptic, and one of these was deeply grooved only at one end. On the whole, the material excepted, they were similar to those of Las Vegas (N.M.). My compass is broken and demagnetized, so I could not take the bearings, except by approximation.

APRIL 27: Had a very long talk with Wolfe. He finally concluded to go. So I shall leave Monday and catch up with him at Black River. Painted all day and night, but am getting very weary of it. I am lame, and could not wear a boot now. My foot (left) is abraded from tying the moccasin too hard. Day painful. Wrote cards to Joe and to Cushing.

APRIL 28: My foot better, owing to vaseline. Mailed 14 drawings, and 55 sheets of my journal home today, in registered package. Also returned vaccinator to Dr. Longwill. To my terrible dismay, a dispatch was secured by Barnes stating my capture and murder by Geronimo,[239] of Ju's [Juh's] band, at San Cristóbal. I immediately telegraphed home, and wrote letters home, to Mrs. Morgan, Mr. Parkman, Will Borchert, to Mexico,[240] and to Cholula.[241]

APRIL 29: Dr. Henderson told me yesterday about the country west of Texas and east of Chihuahua. He says it is a dreary, parched, arid mountain wilderness, or else a thick chaparral, with no signs whatever of former pueblos, no ruins at all, except those of Spanish presidios. Barnes went to a cave, about eight miles east of here, and brought back from it a very large olla of basketwork, all Apache make, and subsequently claimed by them as such, and some rude black and corrugated pottery. The pottery looks very much like that of Sandia and Isleta. Near by there is a ruined pueblo, similar to that of the right bank, and it is said that these are the remains of an acequia or channel, cemented like that of the Tule. I wrote a long letter to Pretorius [Preetorius][242] on the Apache troubles. Captain Dougherty came. Very pleasant. He induced me to stay, and to go with him to the Carrizo, 30 miles north-west, where there are ruins.

APRIL 30: Painted all day. But my foot is very painful. Still I intend starting tomorrow with Captain Dougherty for the Carrizo, 30 miles northwest of here, where there is a ruin. The Carrizo runs into Salt River, and I shall thus secure the character of the ruins on another tributary of that stream. At the same time I am told that very important ruins exist on Eagle Creek, one of the tributaries of the higher Gila. These ruins are said to be southeast of here, and 25 miles east of Ash Creek. There are said to be standing walls left. (This would be in the San Francisco Mountains.) The cave found by Barnes yesterday is but a cache of the Apaches, but the pottery is ancient. They came and took the olla away from him, claiming it as their own. I am also told that the ruins on the Verde are mostly cliffhouses. Finally I am assured that there is a ruin on the very point of the high mesa opposite the post, but Barnes assures me that such is not the case. A man went after Wolfe today.

MAY

MAY 1: About noon, U-clemy, one of the leading medicine men came in. He was a handsome Indian and wore his medicine cap or helmet, of hide or leather. It is a cap, fitting rather closely, with two laps hanging down behind. There is a flint knife stuck into the rim of the cap. The whole is richly painted with intricate colors and designs.* It recalls much the Zuñi helmet.

It appears that these medicine men play a very conspicuous part in the wars and feuds of the Apaches! We left at 1 P.M. with Lawrence McCarthy (Private, First Infantry) and a pack mule. Followed the trail for three miles toward the large ruin visited Sunday before last, and then struck to the left, going in a northwesterly direction. We entered a deep valley, east of Kelly's Butte. High, wooded slopes, occasionally crowned with crags, shut it in on all sides. Vegetation strong, and the higher we rose, the taller grew the yuccas. Opuntia arborescens grows in large specimens, and the large-leafed, creeping Opuntia, in immense specimens. The valley, with its red soil, narrowed down to a mere rent, where the path winds between cedars, oaks, holly, etc., almost thickets, with tall pines scattered through them. Very wild and

very difficult in case of Indian warfare. We reached the crest, eight miles
from the post, and there a magnificent view opened to the west and
northwest. A vast undulating basin lay at our feet, bounded by a range
of high mesas. The valley is fertile, the grass is green, and groves of
timber are scattered through it. In the center rises a perfectly conical
peak, about 1000 feet above the plain.* It is of black lava, and its sharply
pointed top consists of naked crags. From the crest its foot is about
nine miles off. East of it, rises a huge, bald hump, about 2000 feet high,
of black lava also, an enormous mass. Otherwise, mesas with cliffs of
red standstone border the basin on the north, northeast, and east. The
tops are often craggy, but the seams appear horizontal. Almost in the
center of the valley lies Cedar Creek, a narrow trough, containing water
and groves of fine leafing cottonwoods. Carrizo Creek runs along the
western border of the basin in a deep canyon, whose fertile bottom
is sometimes a half mile wide, but at intervals almost disappears. Gorges
run into it at right angles, with small creeks in them. Otherwise, Cedar
Creek, which is 15 miles from the post, is the only water between it
and the Carrizo.

A rugged mountain country, well grassed and partly timbered, always
charming and romantic, and affording romantic outlooks on the high
ridges and crags bordering the basin, lies between the Cedar Creek and
the Carrizo. The descent into the Carrizo bottom is for about 100 feet
down an almost vertical cliff of lava, then a gentle slope of sandstone,
the whole about 500 feet deep. We slept under cottonwoods, near the
banks of a creek which comes down from the northeast. The trip has
so far been a happy one, very beautiful scenery and fine weather, but
my foot is very sore.

MAY 2: We rode up the valley three miles. It is a series of little fertile
bottoms, mostly on the west banks. Steep bluffs occasionally interrupt
them. The high mesa is visible at a distance of about eight miles; its
slopes are well wooded. With a light smoke hazing the bluffs, the
scenery is most charming, combining fertility with picturesqueness.
The creeks are all narrow, and rather sluggish, but the water is clear
and the bottom mostly rocky. The Apaches are planting in this valley.
The women are still wielding the hoe, and the men superintending the
work. It is the band of Sanchez,[243] leader in the Cibicu fight of 1881,
and a doubtful character, but very influential. They are a dirty crowd,
but very friendly. I saw several of their huts. They are like a half orange,
of boughs covered with pine branches, and finally with yucca leaves.

In front of them is commonly a square porch, like the "tapesto" of the Pueblos. Inside they look like temporary hog pens. It is a very primitive thing, but subject to be[ing] well-heated.

The ruins* stand on a natural platform, grassy, with a steep declivity to the south, and a high hill on which the houses were built, to the west of which the platform slopes again gently to the west and toward the creek. Here two creeks meet, one from the east issuing from a canyon into a small fertile triangular bottom, which lies at the southern foot of the ruin, and through which runs an old acequia with water, immediately at the foot of the pueblo; the fields were evidently here.

Apaches have spoiled the ruin greatly by building rude walls of stone, in the shape of horseshoes, over the hill.* It appears to have been open to the south and recalls the so-called "Sun-house" at Matzak's [Matzaquia] near Zuñi. The pottery is like that of the largest ruins near Fort Apache, painted pottery prevailing, while corrugated is scarce. Mortars of lava, and fragments of concave metates are seen. Very little obsidian and few flints. A well-polished slab of sandstone had Apache [?] carvings on it. Men on horseback. . . . We left about 11 A.M. and saw many young Apaches on horseback. One with a lance. At Cedar Creek, I saw an Apache violin and bow. a.a. is a slit. The cylinder is of wood, about 12 inches long and not quite 3 inches in diameter. It is, of course, fancifully painted. The bow is as follows. The sound of the chord is "thin" but can be varied, and while it is weak, it is not at all unpleasant. Reached the post at 6:30 P.M., highly pleased, but my foot so sore that I can hardly stand it. News of my death is in the papers, with obituary notice.

MAY 5: [No entries for May 3 and 4.] A succession of warm, fine, handsome days, but also of much suffering. My foot exceedingly painful. Wrote to Dr. Mathews, to Frank Cushing, and to Metcalf. Today the foot is a little better, and Dr. Henderson has given me a zinc salve which seems to work admirably. In general, I am treated with the utmost kindness. Today, Sanchez had an interview with Captain Dougherty and Gomez in my room. He wants rations, as they have nothing to eat. My obituaries are, so far, flattering, but this does not come into account with the fright and anguish of my poor people at home. I will not be able to leave the post for several days yet. When the Apaches go to war, they wear the feather cap, and strip down to the

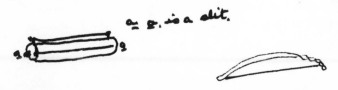

breech-clout, painting their bodies black. I painted some, but my foot has been so exceedingly painful that I did not do so much work as I ought to have done. I can't stand the trip to San Carlos yet and must wait until my sores heal up.

MAY 6 [and 7]: This day and the 7th were actually spent in loafing. Painted very little. Saw the Apache arrows for the chase of birds. They are round, of cane, with three feathers, and have a round, pointed wood as a point. One of them has a curious contrivance. On the wooden point, there was a quadrangle of four bits of wood around it, to prevent the arrow from going in farther. The arrows are tied with sinews. The local Apaches span the bows with three first fingers of the hand lying flat; the *Chiricahua*, with the tips of the fingers, almost the nails, pressed upon the cord. I wrote to Joe and to Bishop Salpointe,[244] also a letter of recommendation for Kirchner to Joe and Papa, and one for Capt. Dougherty to De Costa. Shall write to Brown tonight.

Provisions all in, and I shall have two men to go down with me tonight. My foot decidedly better. Everything is getting ready for tomorrow. My stay here has been about the laziest time of my whole trip, but the foot is certainly a good explanation, if not a sufficient excuse. The pain which I suffered was great. The Indians here and at San Carlos affect great hatred and dread of the Chiricahua. It is certain that the different bands often have bloody feuds and wage occasional warfare against each other. Thus I shall leave, going again into the

unknown. God alone knows my future, and I shall be contented, if He only allows me to see my wife and Papa again in the course of this year.

MAY 8: Capt. Dougherty was with me until 1 P.M. (These groundplans [ruins in the Gila bottom] belong properly to the 9th and 10th.*) After taking leave, and paying my numerous debts, I left that pleasant and hospitable place, particularly so through the kindness of Capt. Dougherty and Mr. Kirchner. My escort consisted of Sergeant Boggs and of Larry McCarthy. A pack mule, with ample provisions, had been added to our train.

The road leads up through the Seven Mile Canyon to the top of Seven Mile Hill. It is a rocky, picturesque, wooded gorge, and the circuit thus made is a long one to the southeast, south, and southwest. No change in appearance of vegetation. A little fillet of water trickles down. On the top of Seven Mile Hill, a broad flat, 12 miles wide, spreads before us to the south. On this flat are the graves of four men murdered by the Apaches last year. The flat is timberless, and the view extensive. In this flat we traversed Turkey Creek, which is always with running water. At the end of this flat, the mountains begin which encompass Black River. All the formation is volcanic lava, and the blocks protrude on the road.

The Canyon of the Rio Prieto (Black River) is very narrow and very picturesque. At a depth of about 500-700 feet foams the rapid river; there are fine trees all around, and vegetation clear to the river bank. A happy combination of grand rocks and beautiful verdure. The current is very strong, so strong that it would have swept the mule, and so we crossed on the ferry, which glides on a wire rope. The ascent is very steep. In high pine timber and very rocky soil, all volcanic, we crossed to 5717 feet at the "Tanks" ("Quartermaster's Tanks") in a rocky timber, near pools of permanent water. We had a hearty supper, and a good bed, but Larry's horse broke out and went off with Chico. Useless to look for them tonight.

MAY 9: Ice in the pools. Turkeys gobbling all around. Started at 7:30 A.M. and went up and down through timber and timber, lava and lava, a country absolutely [un?] inhabitable for sedentary Indians, to the summit (12 miles). There is water at least at two places, but always in dense high timber. From the summit an extensive view is commanded to the southeast, east, and south. A very steep, but not bare declivity, certainly 1000-1500 feet deep, leads into a canyon. Beyond it is a level and bare plain, and still beyond that appear lofty mountains. It is the Sierra Natanos, and far in the southeast, Mount Graham, 10,670 feet,[245] the Gila Range, and beyond it, Mount Turnbull.

At the bottom of Rocky Canyon, a change in vegetation began. The mescal agave appears occasionally, and *Opuntia arborescens*. Everything is greener. We crossed to Ash Creek, in the San Carlos Canyon, a low dry creek, with only occasional sheets of water, and a great many boulders, showing heavy [?] during the wet time. It is slightly timbered. Here an engagement took place with the Apaches in which Captain Hentig[246] was killed. Also several murders. From Ash Creek, the San Carlos Canyon diverges to the west and southwest; thence, the country rises in bald plains to the Gila Range, whose crest, Green's Hill is 697 [meters]. On the barren grass, very tall *Opuntia* dot the plain. From the brow of Green's Hill, a view expands over rugged lava peaks, very peculiar, beyond which appears Mount Turnbull.

The descent is often exceedingly steep and always very rocky owing to the lava. The yucca shoots up immense flower stalks, and the creeping *Opuntia* shows large leaves. The descent to the Gila is about 3000 feet in 13 miles. From the second highest ridge of the Gila, a remarkable change in vegetation appears. Cacti predominate. *Opuntia arborescens*, enormous, with blood red, not pink, flowers, creeping *Opuntia* in large leaves, flowering white and yellow, a pink flowering *Echinocactus*, mesquite, three kinds of yucca, and a horrible, green, thick, red and yellow flowering *Euphorbia*, with the gigantic pitahaya rising up on the slopes, form a remarkable assemblage of thorny plants. We reached the bottom of the Gila at 8:30 P.M. and camped under the cottonwoods, nearby the swiftly running river. Aside from Ash Creek, no trace of ruins. There, small old houses.

MAY 10: The bottom is very sandy and flat, with cottonwoods mostly killed by parasites. We left at 9 A.M. and proceeded through the sandy bottom, covered with sagebrush, mesquite, and an occasional cactus, to the crossing. No ruins there, except some remains of Apache "wickeeups." The bottom is not very wide, not over a mile, and it is hemmed in on the south by abrupt high slopes, too high for hills, and too low for mountains. These are capped by mesas, slightly wooded. The sides of these mountains are mostly bare, *red*, with aprons jutting out from beneath. The north side of the valley is broader, that is, the foothills run back more gradual and thus a longer distance. The mountains all around are barren, but their profiles are very picturesque.

On the whole, there is much resemblance with the Rio Grande. But still, there is more vegetation, and that vegetation, with its arborescent yucca and monstrous cacti is exceedingly striking. It is a foliage of mere thorns. On the road, I found the ruins of a small-house group. Pottery slightly different in color and design. Found one piece of corrugated only.

Arrived at San Carlos at 4 P.M. The buildings are on the site of an old pueblo and stand on a hill denuded and barren on the north side of the river. The post has good buildings, all of adobe. I could not, at present, determine as to whether or not these were large-house ruins. But from the compactness of the cluster, I should judge that it was a large-house pueblo (?). Everybody here states that the ruins in the Gila bottom are those of small houses, scattered, and in groups. Reception most friendly, and much information given. The ruins on Eagle Creek are large and compact. About Clifton, the cliffhouse abounds. There are cliffhouses about the Gila at old Fort Goodwin[247] and in the Gila Canyon. Lt. Davis,[248] who is very, very friendly, tells me that the Apaches, besides having the clan, also have "secret societies" like the Zuñi. On the whole, the Gila Valley is a "lower Rio Grande, running east and west." But it is well protected, and snow seldom falls in it. Ice forms occasionally to the depth of a half to one inch at most.

Nature here is different, and therefore must have modified the habits, manners, and customs of its aborigines. While the other rivers are more northern, one suddenly enters into a southern country on the banks of the Gila, running on the same latitude in a well-protected mountain groove. It is doubtful, however, whether there was a gradual change in the habits of life of the people, following the Gila. It looks rather as if at Casa Grande the lines of culture, coming down from the Verde, Salt River, and the Gila, had met and formed, so to say, a cluster with corresponding improvements in architecture.[249] There are many Apaches around here, and the information secured at Apache is confirmed. No obsidian at the ruins.

MAY 11: These ruins lie due south of the military headquarters (the old school buildings) at San Carlos. The foundations, of cobblestone, are plain. It is not unlikely that the walls themselves were of adobe.* No pottery as yet visible. To the south, there is a mound of rubbish, an elongated ellipse, about 0.80 [meter?] high, which I will have to measure yet. The whole of San Carlos appears to have been formerly a pueblo, and it looks as if it had been a large village of small houses.

Still it is not visibly clear. But the walls of the several clusters, as far as they can be traced, run at such diverging angles, that it can hardly have been a compact pueblo. The rooms, in general, appear much larger. San Carlos lies on the north bank of the Gila, on a bare eminence, rather broad. Very hot and very proper for an Indian settlement. There are fertile, though sandy, lands around it along the river. High and totally barren mountains encircle it. These ranges have picturesque outlines, but they are too angular, and there are no trees on the sharp crest. It appears to be all lava or at least volcanic rock, except opposite San Carlos where red sandstone and whitish limestone form the first tier of foot-rise [foothills]. I am told that there are ruins on the very top of Mount Graham. (10,600 feet high.) Broiling hot.

Left for Fort Thomas[250] at 1 P.M. The Gila bottom expands about nine miles west of Fort Thomas to a wide and greener basin, in which the yucca almost disappears, nothing but mesquite, cottonwood, and grass. This bottom presents a refreshing appearance. The mountains on the north advance closer down to the river and present a forbidding appearance of ruggedness and sterility. Reached Fort Thomas at 7 P.M., too late for the stage to Solomonville [present-day Solomon].[251]

MAY 12: Last night I was received and treated in the most charming manner by Mr. Wood,[252] by Colonel Evans,[253] and the officers. I went out, east of the little town of Marcey [?], and found these ruins on the very outskirts. They are plain, though reduced to mounds of light, sandy earth, perforated and undermined by tusas [prairie dogs?] and occasional stone foundations. The latter are similar to those at San Carlos. I become more and more impressed by the probability of the walls having been of adobe, as else there would be much more stone debris left.* There is no obsidian, hardly any flint, but bits of lava, large and small, which evidently belonged to metates and to manos. [One feature] looks like a tank, but was probably an elliptical building.

It looks as if there had been stone enclosures, or else large rooms, around the houses. The pottery is similar to that of the Gila bottom near San Carlos, only the characteristic black-and-white, and black-and-red reappears. But besides it, there is the same thick, reddish brown, unadorned pottery, and there is purple and cream. Saw no trace of glossy fragments, but as everything is much decayed, it might be that the gloss had been destroyed by decay. The ruins lie on the last terrace, gravelly hills, grassy, covered with low mesquite, and large mamillaria, often 15 inches in diameter. Went up town at 9 A.M. and met Lieutenant

Porter.[254] He introduced me to Mr. Collins and suggested a trip out to the ruins about eight miles east of Fort Thomas. So we started in an ambulance through the sandy bottom with sparse growth of mesquite, immense mamillaria, and an occasional arborescent yucca, following the road to Solomonville.*

About eight miles from Fort Thomas, we met the acequia in a bottom formed by sandstone bluffs receding from the river about three miles. It is higher than the surrounding ground by 0.15 to 0.20 [meter?], and does not show any trace of lining or concrete. It runs on an average south-southeast to north-northwest, with many bends, and has, on a length of about 350.0, four different ramifications [branches?]. Its width varies from 1.25 to 3.00 [meters?], the rims are slightly raised, and the center is consequently almost imperceptibly concave. The soil is very sandy, whitish, and movable, although evidently very fertile.

This acequia appears to run almost diagonally across a valley basin, formed by the bluffs of gravel and sandstone receding from the river in an irregular semicircle.* The acequia is of course not complete. From the foot of Mount Graham living streams run down to within five to six miles of the Gila, but they all sink at that distance from the river. We then proceeded and found, on a spur of the bluffs, a very handsome spring, around which there was some pottery, and faint remnants of stone foundations. The spring seems to completely pervade a hill, on the top of which is a deposit of black turf. Many willows. A Mexican told us that there was a ruined village about a mile southwest on the bluffs. We then crossed over to the Gila and about eight miles from Fort Thomas, at the house of Mr. J. H. Carlston (a Mormon), found the village. Surveyed on the other side. Much pottery. Also very large metates of black lava, shaped like a groove.* Mortars of lava, manos, two fine stone axes, flint arrowheads, and some obsidian. Also a con-voluted shell, perforated at the apex, and finally a block of stone, about 30 inches long, roughly worked, and indicating the beginning of a human statue. There are three more villages, similar in all points, on the other side of the Gila. Returned at 6:30 P.M. and met Mr. Solomon,[255] who tells me that the ruins at Pueblo Viejo are absolutely similar, namely, small houses. He also believes them to have been of adobe on foundations of rubble. He speaks of a large cave, about eight miles from Ash Creek, partly walled up, and with paintings inside. Was also told of large-house ruins near Fort Grant[256] (hollow rectangles).

MAY 13: From all I can learn, the valley of the Gila is exclusively occupied by small houses. The compact pueblos are on the tributaries, in the rugged mountains, both north and south. Left at 9 A.M. with a team of six mules, dragging 3200 lbs. At the crossing of the Fort Apache road, I found the ruins. They are foundations with very little pottery; in fact, I saw only one piece of corrugated ware. The foundations are of cobblestone, two rows being distinctly visible, set on edge.* Width 0.61 [meter]. They were evidently foundations on which was erected adobe. There are ruins at old Fort Goodwin, and ruins two miles east of the crossing, also ruins four miles from San Carlos on the road to Globe. All are said to bear the same character.

I reached San Carlos at 8 P.M. The Yumas and the Mojaves, when a man dies, burn the wickee-up and afterward cremate the body. A Mojave was accidentally killed yesterday, and today they burnt the hut and may cremate the body. The Apaches bury in the ground and cover the body with rocks. In the cave which Mr. Solomon mentioned, it appears there are paintings of various kinds. On Eagle Creek, there are also cliffhouses. On Salt River houses of adobe.* Large ruins at Mesa City [present-day Mesa], Tempe, and near Phoenixville [present-day Phoenix]. At Pueblo Viejo, the ruins are similar to those around here. My plan of the village eight miles east of [Fort] Thomas does not include all the buildings. The pottery proper has nothing very strange. There is black and white, white-and-black, white-and-yellow, glossy, etc. Also indented and corrugated.

MAY 14: Mr. Solomon described to me what appears to have been a mound of rubbish in the rear of his house at Solomonville. It was exclusively composed of fine white ashes. I painted nearly the whole day. Went to Dr. Pangburn,[257] and he impressed me favorably. He confirmed all that I learned concerning the Apaches in regard to their clans. He says that they have no tribal organization now, but formerly had war chiefs. They believe in spirits and in transmigration; the owl being particularly selected for that purpose. They destroy every article belonging to the deceased, so that he may have them after his death, as else he might return to get all his family. The Apaches also have a tale of the flood. The Yumas and Mojaves believe that, after death, the soul goes straightways to the west, where there is the last resting place, a place of eternal joy, dancing, and love making. At the entrance of this place, which they call Ē-nyarope, stands a guard, who comes in to see if he is properly tattoed on the chin and legs (as is the custom of the Yumas and Mojaves). If the tattoo marks are not there, the spirit is driven off. Whither such a rejected spirit goes, they do not know. They believe in witchcraft and punish witches (always women) by drawing them up by the hands until they confess. If they confess, they kill them. He related several circumstances of that kind. On the whole I felt deeply interested. Saw his gila monster. Wrote cards to Joe and to Prof. Norton.

MAY 15: We left at 10:30 A.M. and moved diagonally, through the channel in which the Rio de San Carlos runs. On the left a perpendicular wall of thinly laminated rock, picturesque. The river bottom is in all points similar to that of the Gila, lined with álamos [cottonwoods]. The soil is the same. The ruins are about five miles from San Carlos and extend to within 200 meters of the cottonwoods of the banks. They appear to have formed a village enclosed by an irregular stone wall, which connected single houses built along its line. In the center, about, is a basin or tank whose rim of stones is still visible. The Apaches have largely used the stone for their huts, which are now obliterated themselves, but the stones are scattered about and the excavations of the huts have greatly defaced the groundplan. The buildings are mostly on knolls, probably formed by decay of the adobe walls. In some places the walls appear to have been double also.* . . .

Pottery exactly similar to that of the Rio Gila. Some Apache houses are along the outskirts of the ruins.

These ruins are on a spur about three-fourths of a mile southeast of Gilson's ranch.[258] It forms a narrow ridge, steep and very gravelly. Hardly 15 [meters] wide. It may be that they are only former Apache dwellings. Still there is pottery exactly similar to that on the Rio Gila, and the walls where visible, are double.

These ruins* are a mile from Mr. Gilson's ranch, on a hill, . . . It is very gravelly, steep, and overgrown with mesquite and much yucca. The walls were evidently double, and about two feet thick. There is not enough stone in them to warrant the assumption that they were of stone; the foundations are of boulders and quartz, set upright, and they appear to have supported adobe walls. There is much pottery about in large fragments, and it clearly belongs to the Rio Gila type. There is no water near, but a dry sandy arroyo intersects the bottom south and east of Mr. Gilson's house, running east and west. Mr. Gilson's well is 90 feet deep.

The acequia, in the bottom, west and south of the ruins in the gravel bluffs, runs on an average from south to north, but issues from a depression between the hills and first runs southwest to northeast.* All the branches appear slightly raised above the ground.

The road (very dusty) winds past the "Triplets," and along the San Carlos River and in the groves of cottonwood covering its banks, until ten miles from the agency, where a high basaltic mesa narrows the river bottom for two miles. Cereus pitahaya grows on the steep and barren slopes of this mesa. Two miles farther on, the road leaves the river and turns into an open plain, with wooded border, and after passing through a rocky gap about 17 miles from San Carlos, .we look into the green basin where Mr. Gilson's ranch is. In the west rises the massive Sierra del Pinal, covered with timber to its very top, and in strange contrast therefore with the mountains around, which are otherwise bare, parched, rugged, and forbidding. Although higher, the Pinal, with green slopes ascending to its very foot, appears pleasant. The air is slightly cooler. Kindly reception by Mrs. Gilson, and was informed of the existence of ruins about one-half to one mile southeast, on the brow of a gravelly ridge running around the basin in which the house stands. I went and found them, also an acequia. All day I have travelled among the Apaches, and they were very friendly. They have their farms in the San Carlos bottom, and the best of them build new houses of upright posts and mud, with little windows like those of the Pueblos. Met one of them from the Carrizo. Very friendly.

May 16: I went out to the acequia. It seems doubtful now, still I can hardly refuse to believe that it is an acequia. The channels are mostly higher than the surrounding country and soil; they are of whitish sand, and there is some pottery strewn along it. Of course, there is great variation in the width, but nevertheless it looks as if there was a system of irrigation. Mr. Gilson informed me that there are ruins all along the bluffs. He also speaks of ruins near Riverside, toward the Rio Gila, but he cannot tell me what kind they were.

I left Gilson's about 10 A.M. and a severe rain storm set in from the east, which is the direction whence rain comes here. I went rather rapidly, and Chico is well disposed. As far as I could see, I ascended the same grassy flat, or rather low cañada, for about six miles. By the roadside lay a broken metate, and occasional cobblestones showed that there was population formerly. Also traces of acequias about three miles from Gilson's. At the end of the flat, I found and entered a gap through which the road winds upwards. Then a valley, finally a rugged, barren valley region, or rather deep gulches. Rained very hard, and I got to

Globe, a perfect mining town of 2000 souls, at 12 A.M.—distance 11½ miles. Reception kindest in the highest manner. Mr. McNally took me to his house. Dr. Hinnmann [?], Dr. Stallo,[259] Mr. Robb, Dr. Cook,[260] etc. Telegraphed to Mr. Parkman for money. There are many ruins, all small houses, south of here, but the principal ones are north and on the Salt River and Tonto Creek. At Wheatfield, the large houses begin. On Coon's Creek there is a natural cave with many paintings. In the center of it stands an immense stalactite which has a metallic ring. It shows the places where it was beaten for music; while all around, the floor is worn off by the feet of the dancers. Mr. Robb says the same thing from Cave Creek. Dr. Stallo has shoes, cloth, and cotton from the Tonto. They grew cotton there. Stone axes abundant. Pottery painted and corrugated.

MAY 17: The Pinal Range, which is right south of here, is covered with snow, an unheard of thing at this season. It rises to 9000 feet. Globe is 3600 feet. Had a long talk with Mr. Robb, and painted also. Called on Dr. Stallo. He gave me specimens of cloth, twine, pita [agave fiber], and cotton from the caves on Tonto Creek. The cloth is cotton; the twine is pita. Among his textile fabrics, there is a fringe or scarf, resembling somewhat the ornament of buckskin used by the matalotes. Around a nucleus of twisted rope is wound a tress of twine, from which fringes hang down. It is about 0.40 [meter] long. He has also some very fine axes. They are all of lava or basalt, long and slender, and the base is invariably straight. This form appears peculiar to Arizona axes south of the Tule. I have seen it now at Fort Apache, at San Carlos, at Fort Thomas, and find it again here and at the Tonto. Is it perhaps a genuine peculiarity?[261]

No reply to my telegram. The wires are all down. Mr. Holmes told me this evening that he excavated many ruins near Pueblo Viejo, and that the walls were invariably of "concrete," that is, of gravel and soil, and thus exactly similar to the walls of the Casa Grande and on Tonto Creek. The latter he describes as having been several stories high and 400 feet square, with a court, and a wall surrounding it, seven to eight feet high. The delay of the telegram is very annoying. Native copper occurs here, and Mr. Robb showed me a piece, evidently washed, which has accidentally the form of a broad spearhead. He thinks it is imperfect fusion! I am almost sure it is natural. Dr. Stallo has never seen any copper implements from ruins, but has heard of their existence. How immensely rich the country is in ores. Gold, beautiful native silver, horn

silver, silver glance carbonate of silver, all sorts of copper ores, iron, chromate of lead, molybdate of lead, etc. He says that an inferior turquoise is found south of Tucson, and has been pronounced such by Prof. Shepard of Amherst College. Wrote a long letter to Joe, I wrote until late again. My foot is well and I feel so far—good.

MAY 18: Got telegram, much to my relief. Left at 10 A.M. with Mr. Holmes, on Dr. Stallo's horse. The old gentleman is of the utmost kindness, and I do not know how to express to him my gratitude and feelings.* . . .

The country about Globe is perfect mining country. The valleys are deep gulches, bare and barren. The slopes are steep, rocky. Everywhere ore protrudes. It is copper, with silver, and iron. The great mineral belt extends from northeast to southwest, for a length of 35 miles and is about 15 miles wide. Some of the mines are evidently very rich. The rock is syenite and granite. The Sierra Pinal is a high timbered group with bare rocky tops, and absolutely deserted, with no traces of habitation from ancient times. Its northern slope is drained; the southern slope is parched, almost treeless and waterless. West of it are the Superstition Mountains, a series of abrupt high peaks with mesas, bordered by mostly inaccessible cliffs. On one of these is that plateau of which Capt. Pradt spoke to me. It is an old Apache camp in an inaccessible position. The Apaches through here were Tonto, who have become almost obliterated. The Aravaypas lived farther south. About two miles east of Globe is Bloody Tank, where Col. Woodson massacred 68 Apaches. It was a Cholula affair, the Americans preventing, by speedy action, being themselves slaughtered by the Apaches. It is justifiable, but no blame should be attached to Cholula, nor to Caxamarca neither.[262]

In the far-off west appears the Mezatzo [Mazatzal] Range. It is said to be similar to the Superstition [Range]. Vegetation similar to that coming down to the Gila. Ocoteas [Ocotillo, "Coachwhip"], mesquite, yucca, sahuaro, Opuntia. Mines and mines! Mr. Holmes told me that all the arroyos sink before they reach the main stream, then often reappear near the mouth of the rivers, but that the tendency is always to change the channel, and rather to recede than to advance in relation to the main water course toward which they are trenching or flowing. This is natural, their own drift filling up the beds in time.

On the tip of a hump, about 200 feet, vertical at the brim, very steep lower down, over a gulch in which there is cottonwood and a recent well where good water is from six to ten feet below the surface, stand the ruins. The walls are of stone, approximately broken [roughly shaped], well laid in mud, and not unlike those of Mitla and Tlacolula, but 0.86 [meter?] wide. The buildings are a kind of half-breed between Pueblo-type and detached houses, and were possibly but one story high. One room is excavated partly, showing the walls; the others are indicated by loose walls on the surface. Each of the two buildings has courts, whose corners are irregularly rounded. I found obsidian and much pottery. Among the latter the typical black-and-white, and the red-and-black is wanting; there is a black-and-white, red outside, and a [?]-white-and-black, identical with Fort Apache and the Gila. No finely corrugated pieces, but a coarse-corrugated cooking ware, painted red outside, and highly micaceous. Mr. Holmes pointed out to me a spot, five miles south, where the clay is found. It is filled with mica, washed down from the decomposed syenite and granite of the Pinal. He says there are ample evidences of the clay having been extensively dug out. For water, the aborigines in this pueblo went down to the gulch, and Mr. Holmes thinks that in former times the water rose to the surface. This is possible, for it is not very deep, and there are many cottonwoods. The top of the hill is absolutely denuded, but there are yucca, and also Ocoteas on the slope, so that heating material is readily obtained. A cedar post is still standing in the ruins, probably a fallen viga. There is no cedar nearer than the Pinal Mountains, but transportation for long and many miles was no object for the Indians.

In regard to fields, they may have cultivated in a limited measure at the bottoms, for the tops are too rocky. As they had only corn, irrigation was not necessary. The position was an excellent lookout and tolerably well-protected, being almost inaccessible on the southwest, north, and northwest, but easily ascended on the south and southeast. Mr. Holmes is not certain about the fact that the houses on the Gila had the walls also of vertical cedar posts filled in with concrete. But Dr. Stallo positively reiterated his statement. It is not impossible, however.

In the afternoon, we drove out a mile to a stalactite cave. It is very beautiful, though small. While riding out there, Mr. Salter told me that the ruins down Pinal Creek, eight or nine miles, begin to grow large-house type, and this was subsequently confirmed. Wages for miners here are $3.50 to $4 per day. There is no agriculture in the whole district worth speaking of. Garden patches in the valleys, and on Salt River, farms not exceeding 300 acres. Globe has a population of 1500 souls. But the ores are very rich. Wrote a long letter to Mr. Parkman. The band serenaded the railroad officials tonight.

MAY 19: Mailed two letters, and postal card to Mr. Cushing. Sent off show, silver ore, etc. to Joe. Painted and with fair results. But my pistol has not come yet. [Sketch of ruin visited May 18.]*

Pottery same as everywhere. The foundations appear to have been of large boulders mostly syenite and granite. There are a number of metates about which also were of syenite. This is quite a novel feature! The walls were evidently double and on the low hillocks formed in six places by the ruins there is a great deal of rock. It looks as if the walls had been of stone, heavy blocks, and in fact some excavations have laid bare such walls, which appear similar to those north of Globe, at the Aztec Mine. The ruin is extensive. It lies opposite the butchershop, a mile about from town on a promontory, about 25 feet high, formed of large drift and gravel, and terminating rather abruptly north and northeast. This is about as near a sketch as I can make it.*

Behind it rise higher slopes. The surface is nearly level, it is covered with gravel and has little grass, yucca and mesquite. The ruin appears to form several clusters of houses connected by courts. The courts are more obliterated than the rooms. Along the brink of the gulch, there is a line of very heavy boulders in great numbers and densely crowded, showing the existence formerly of a heavy wall of rude blocks. Mr. Eaton,[263] who went along, found a round perforated disk of micaceous clay.* Its thickness is about 0.002 [meter]. It is evidently artificial, and may have been a whirling disk, although it is rather thin and the hole in the center is only 0.003 [meter] in diameter, which makes it doubtful. [From Bandelier's sketch and the description, it is quite clear that this was a spindle whorl.] My compass is not quite in order yet. At Fort Thomas, among the stone implements shown to me by Mrs. Carlton,[264] there was a regular "Chunkey stone" of lava!

MAY 20: My pistol has not come yet. It appears the telegram was not delivered by Lieut. Davis. This is very singular. The feeling at San Carlos between the authorities and the mail contractors is exceedingly bitter. This is unfortunate. I met Mr. Connell[265] who took me home and showed me his fine Apache collection. If I had only had it before!

The most interesting articles of this handsome collection are two wands made of pine wood, from the Yuma. The wings are the sun's

rays. The four human figures are those of the four devils of the sun.
(Wrote to Prof. Norton and to Joe.)

On the other side are the four movements of the sun. I regret exceedingly that I did not have time to copy the whole. As it is, this
medicine wand is one of the most valuable things I have seen. I may
yet be able to copy it from memory. Besides, he has a Chiricahua head-

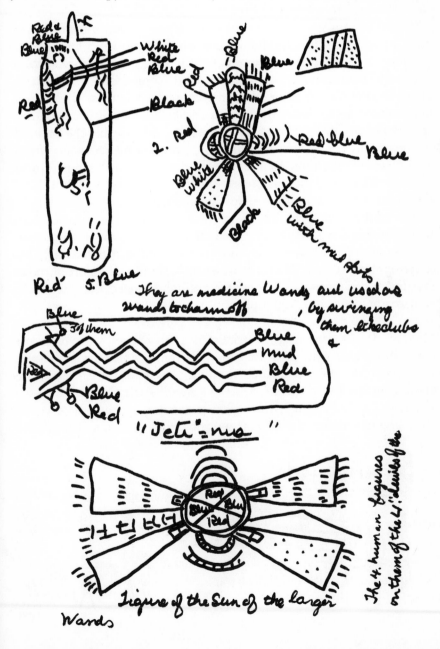

dress, used in the Dibbu dance.[266] It appears that only the Apaches use these headdresses in their dances; the Yumas and Mojaves have nothing similar to it at all. Mr. Connell, who has been post trader, says that there is not the least resemblance between the Yumas or Mojaves [and the Apaches], not even physically. Also that the Chinese learn the Yuma language very rapidly. This is at least very striking. The Yumas are properly a *coast* people![267]

He also has an Apache fetich [sic]. It is of wood and suspended by a string of buckskin. Besides, he has a stone axe from Fort Thomas, of that long slender form so common about here, and flat at the bottom, which approximates the axe. I have found [similar ones] at Calpan. There is evidently a number of strange things among these wild tribes, and if we connect them with the data gathered from Alaska, it cannot help furnishing material for many thoughts. Add to this the painted pottery of the Yumas, which bears strange resemblance to some of the old pottery of the ruins. I am constrained to look to the Yumas as a very interesting field of study, to say the least. Shall write to Prof. Norton about it, and tomorrow go to Mr. Connell again. At Mr. Hitchcock's[268] drug store, I found the following headgear of the Apaches, also belonging to Mr. Connell. One half of it is blue, the other yellow. It is bound together by sinews and by buckskin. It is exceedingly interesting. I must go to Yuma at all events. Somebody told me today that five miles south of here, on the road to Pioneer, there is a ruin with 42 rooms on the groundplan.

MAY 21: It appears that the Apaches in their dances, wear buckskin masks or caps over the face. Very thin, so that the features are visible through it. This corresponds to the painted masks of the Zuñi and the other Pueblos. The analogies seem to grow.[269] I left Globe at 10 A.M. and rode quickly through the valley, down Pinal Creek. The valley soon becomes deserted, but cottonwoods grow here and there. The

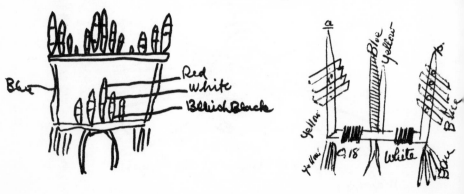

creek dries up fully. No change in vegetation.* The mountains on both sides are rugged and barren, the tops often craggy. About seven miles below is a rancho. A cowboy soon joined me and told me that opposite the rancho, about a half mile, on the side slope or lowest bluff, there are two large ruins close together, one of which contained 138 rooms. The walls are said to be still standing. Reached the "Wheatfields"[270] at noon.

The valley, which should be called a cañada, is very narrow. Here is a fine grove of high, stately cottonwoods, which covers the valley or pass, for it is only a quarter-of-a-mile wide. The quartz mill of the Mack Morris Co. is here, idle, for the ore has given out in the Richmond Basin, and they are clearly outside of the "Mineral Belt." I was admirably received by Mr. E. J. Flandin and his son, a charming boy. After lunch, we went to the ruins.*

There are two of them. The nearer one is due south, on the bluff above the dry creek. There are no trees, and the bluff is gravelly. The ruins are of stone, very heavy blocks or boulders. They form six small mounds, which are connected by foundations. It looks as if there had been at least six groups of houses, with courts or at least walls running from one to the other. South of it on the same plateau is the detached house.* Indistinct foundations alone remain. The pottery appears identical with that of Globe, but the red-and-black appears to change gradually into a thicker kind with some white lines also, and the black-and-white, while the designs are similar, decays differently. Perhaps owing to the clay only. Some flint chips, but I could not notice any obsidian. But I found an unexplainable fragment of dark blue soapstone, which looks as if a highly polished groove had been cut around it, so as to form a rim.

About a sixth-of-a-mile west of it is the larger ruin, which stands off of the edge of the bluff. It is slightly larger, and its principal feature consists of a long mound at the southern end of it. This mound appears to have been a two-story house for it was dug into the base and shows walls of heavy boulders laid in adobe. Some of the stones are broken; others appear to have been simply boulders, fitting the size. No clue could be obtained to the thickness of the walls. The mound is about 2.50 [meters] high, and may have contained three tiers of rooms. Beneath it, the rest of the ruin lies like a trapezoid. It is evident that a continuous wall surrounded it, on the inside of which were built houses from time to time, also perhaps courts. Here, too, are traces of isolated mounds, perhaps indicating single rooms or houses. But it is almost impossible to distinguish what was a house and what only a court.* The walls must have been thick and of heavy stone as the debris shows, and it is very hard to determine their direction. I did the best I could. At all events, it appears as if I had struck a still different kind of architecture. Houses of small sizes, connected by courts, so to say an intermediate type between the detached house village and the pueblo type. It is singular that there are most always two ruins close together, and that all are situated above the creek. The latter reappears as a running stream one mile farther west, so that the people of these pueblos had water within easy reach. In summer, after each rain, the creek is changed for a few hours into a roaring torrent, but it soon subsides. Pottery of both ruins similar. The corrugated ware almost disappears and when it is visible, it appears to be due more to careless smoothing. The cooking pottery is red and some very micaceous.

MAY 22: Painted all day. The name, "Wheatfields," comes from the fact that the Tonto Apaches cultivated wheat here in years past. Mr. Walbridge told me this evening that obsidian is found at Pinal, 30 miles west from here, in pebbles in a conglomerate (sedimentary formation) almost on the surface, beneath the soil. It is also found near Florence, 55 miles south of here, in a conglomerate also. Native copper is found at Mineral Creek, 25 miles southwest of Globe, in laminae, and in crystals. The strata are near the surface or at a depth of [?]. It is in a soft material, which could easily be removed. No serpentine. Beautiful chrysocolla is found near Lost Gulch. Clay beds proper do not exist, but [there are] many deposits that can be used for pottery, probably resulting from decomposition. At the Nugget Mill, about eight miles east, there is said to be a large ruin.

MAY 23: I left the good kind people at 9 A.M. Mr. Flandin gave me a "God bless You" on leave taking. It is the first time since I left Father Gromm and old Mr. DeArmond, that I received such a wish! I descended the valley which grew more narrow, for about two miles. It is overgrown with the same handsome large cottonwoods. There are a few houses of adobe, on the road. The canyon narrows as it goes down. The foothills even seem to disappear. Where the road turns sharply to the south to enter a gorge or rather, as Mr. Walbridge perfectly characterized it, a sandy wash, there are two foothills, high and steep, crowned by ruins.*
The one to the left appears to have had an inclosure of walls, [the

remnants of which are] still standing. I was very sorry that I could not visit it, but not knowing the distance, it was not safe for me to venture on a delay. So I entered the gorge. It rises continually for at least six miles, winding around in the strangest way. First southwest, then west, finally north, and then drifts to the northwest. Vegetation thorny. *Opuntia arborescens* reappears and a few scrubby cedars.* The Ocotillo is immense and flowers most beautifully. The mountains are terribly rugged, craggy, and bare. When I got to the crest, the view extended to Salt River, which could be seen distinctly lined by beautiful cotton-woods. The descent is very similar to that into the Gila Valley, only a clayey marl underlies the gravel. What there is of vegetation appears stronger, and there is more of it. I saw the yucca 8-12 feet high, sur-mounted by a flowering stalk of same height, all white with blossoms. *Opuntia arborescens* flowers red and yellow, and the pitahaya is in bloom, silky, pale, yellow. Reached the Salt River, a broad, blue, rush-ing and rolling stream, much wider than the Gila, with clearer water. But it is very alkaline. At Mr. Kenton's ranch, and partly where his house stands, there is a large ruin. Only foundations are left, and they are of very large boulders. Then there are heaps of drift gravel which indicate regular forms, and rows of boulders laid parallel, showing that the walls have been, like those on Pierce Creek, of heavy boulders laid in mud. Hardly any pottery is found, what I saw was pale red, and cor-rugated of a red color, like that at Show-Low, etc.

Mr. Kenton showed me a mano, lava, from the Rio Verde.* It is strongly similar to those from Mexico, and absolutely dissimilar to those of the Gila. The latter are all short, possibly owing to the form of the metate, as a narrow trough. I then kept on the Gila [Salt] bot-tom, crossing a low mesa or rather foothill near the river, on which there are large ruins, and pushed on into the beautiful green valley, planted with grain, emerald green, where the ranches of Mr. Danforth and of Mr. Robertson lie. I was most kindly received. There are two ruins to visit on this side of the river. I saw some beautiful pottery from the small ruin about 200 [meters] southwest of here, on the road. This is a distinct detached house with courts. There is hardly any pottery, and that is dark red and coarse, also white. Saw a small mano, of black lava, flat, irregularly prismatic. There is some little flint about. But no trace of obsidian. It [the ruin] is to the left side of the road, and very much deteriorated, like that at Mr. Kenton's. I secured considerable infor-mation.

Ruins* are very abundant about here. They appear to be of two kinds: large houses, and detached ones. There appears to be a fine cliffhouse or rather a cave house, five to six miles south of here. Mr. Vaughn, the teacher, assures me that "Cattle Creek," about 130-140 miles beyond the ruin west of Phoenix, is the western limit of the ruins in this latitude. A desert, [an] uninhabitable belt, 250 miles west, and 150 miles east of the river, flanks the Rio Colorado, and the ruins extend to that belt. Thus the limit at Prescott is 80 miles west of that city, but the main sections of ruins are south, on the Rio Verde, in the Sierra Ancha (which borders Salt River on the north) and farther south.

MAY 24: Left at 8 A.M., on horseback, for the cave dwellings. We rode down the river, past Archie McIntosh's[271] house, and about four miles in all, and then turned sharply to the south. The caves are visible at a great distance. We entered a deep canyon, where a spring rises.* The canyon is narrow; it has no bottom, only a dry arroyo, which is the outlet of the spring. This arroyo is shrouded in verdure, mesquite, thorns of all kinds, large cottonwoods, and walnuts. It is a perfect thicket, and difficult to get through. The slopes rising to the canyon are covered with boulders, and unfit for cultivation.

We first visited the lower cave*. The slope is exceedingly steep, difficult, on account of the cactus and of the crumbling, slippery, shale cropping out. The height is almost vertical at places. The entire height to the cave is 68 of my heights, or 109 meters, equal to 363 feet. The cave is large, and the eastern declivity (it faces to the east) is often vertical. The height of the cave is about 20 to 25 feet. Into it the house had been built. It is a perfect pueblo house, but small. The walls are of large stones, broken to suit, and laid in clay mixed with gravel, which gives it the appearance of concrete. The proportion of stone to concrete is about equal. I found many metates about, three of which were perfect. The manos are small, so as to work in the groove. Many of the roofs are perfect. They are of vigas, above them are either splinters or round sticks of ocotilla, above it reeds, and then two-and-a-half inches of mud. The floors, as far as visible, are black. There is some pottery about, handsomely painted, similar to that of the "Cerros" on the Rio Puerco, only much older.*

I found an old sandal, much fragmentary basketwork, rope, twine, and many corncobs. They are of the small variety, and I found one small piece of obsidian. No red-and-black pottery, but some faintly corrugated ware. The majority of the pottery, however, is dark red and very thick. The position of the pueblo is admirable for security and observation, but I cannot find any tillable lands short of two miles away. As to the timber, it is cedar as to the small cross pieces, heavy pine in regard to the central posts and the beams. There are several center posts, and one of them is hacked off even. Others are slightly bifurcated.

We then led the horses up to the spring, about a half-mile farther up the canyon, south, and to the foot of the second cave, which is about 400 feet high and steeper than the other. The slope is disintegrated shale, and hardly any cactus or shrubbery. Directly east of it is a very high mountain, with a big cave visible in it. The ruin is larger, but has not such an extensive view, owing to the mountains in front. Both ruins are burnt out. This was done by the Apaches who used to celebrate their dances in the ruins. So Mrs. McIntosh tells me. This ruin is mostly two stories high. The walls are of the same thickness, 0.30 [meter] on an average. The material is the same. In both cases, the stones are well-broken, but not hewn.

In the first ruin I found some arrow shafts made of canes, but not a single arrowhead. (It was very hot.) The lintels of the doors are of wood, several sticks laid across, some of the doors open to the front, but there are little square or quadrilateral holes. The roof is overhanging, or rather projecting, so that unless there is a driving wind from the east, which is said to occur very seldom, rain cannot affect the interior of the cave. Therefore, it is so well-protected and preserved.* It is evident, from the manner of construction, that the building was accommodated to the sinuosities of the ground. On the stories there were high parapets, and some of the rear rooms were open. There is also an inequality in the height of the various parts. I forgot to take the sections of the larger ruin, but it is so similar to the small one, that it will hardly make any difference at all. From the large ruin, rocks have wasted away, leaving the ascent possible from the north side only.* It was at all events a very strong place against Indians. The cavity is a stalactite cave, and there is possibly more in the interior. But the identity of these caves with those on the Rio Mancos in Colorado is very strange.

We left the cave about 3 P.M. and rode back. Met Mrs. McIntosh on horseback. She told me that the Apaches called themselves: "N'de."[272] Measured three ruins on the road to Mr. Robertson's, and saw a fourth one. They are similar to those on Pinal Creek, and of the small-house type. The valley is full of them, on both sides of the river. Pottery similar to the other, also black-and-white. There are springs in abundance; a beautiful one rushed out of the rock near McIntosh's. There is a smaller cave yet, which I did not, however, visit. The number of ruins, at least on this side of the river as far as I have seen them, is remarkable. They are scarcely more than a quarter-of-a-mile apart, and always on the gravel hills. There are none in the bottoms, which shows that there are or were periodical overflows. The appearance of the ruins is, otherwise, the same as that near Globe, and they are of the same type. The pottery is mostly coarse, common, cooking pottery. Still there are a few pieces of painted pottery, but all is much worn. On the whole, this Salt River is a much handsomer spot than the Gila. Vegetation is stronger, rank, but equally thorny. Snakes begin to appear. Lizards are quite frequent. Passed by another small ruin, but did not measure it. Saw no distinct traces of acequias, but there is a large one on the other side of the river. People are very kind to me. They are having a trial over some cattle stealing, which is imputed a hazard [of this area], of [from?] Fisk's[273] and Walbridge's ranch. It is done in rather a primitive style. The Apaches have not seriously troubled them of late, although they are always more or less afraid of them. My measurements of the caves are so far very exact*; the other ruins were only stepped.

I hear again the reports about the caves on Coon and Cave Creek. In the Sierra Ancha there are said to be but few ruins, as it is very rugged and barren on the southern slope.

MAY 26: Ruins* on the south side of road between Kenton's and Danforth's ranch, and on the bluffs at the mouth of Arroyo Pinto. The bluff [overlooking the Salt River] is vertical for about 25-30 feet; it is from gravelly drift.

The pottery is similar to the other, and at the same time like that of Fort Apache. There are many drift mounds also, which look very much like ruins, and some of them may be ruins indeed, since they are covered with pottery. Flint and obsidian are almost not present. The latter I did not find. On the south side of the road, about 300 meters, and not far from the banks of the Pinto lies the other ruin, which is by far the largest I have found in Salt River Valley.[274] It clearly shows the style of architecture. The mounds indicate houses, and these are connected by court walls,[275] so that the whole is an enclosure formed alternately by houses and court walls. There is but one entrance, and that can be easily defended. The houses were probably one story high, and the walls made of the usual heavy blocks of stone.* The disintegration of the walls leaves the huge blocks in heaps on the surface, whereas the crumbling binding material drifts away in the wind and rain. This explains the appearance of the ruins here as well as in Globe, as well as the gravelly clay of the cliffhouses explains the statement of Mr. Holmes that they were of concrete.

The day is hot, and I left at 5 P.M. Chico did not like to cross Salt River, which is very swift, and as broad as the Gila at San Carlos, but only "belly deep." The bottom on the other side is not as wide as that of the south bank, and it rises more rapidly. There is also a dense growth of mesquite, and the foothills, higher and more steep, are studded with *Cactus pitahaya* as with huge pillars.

I passed the ruin, leaving it to the left; it is three-fourths-of-a-mile above Armour Ranch and is well-surrounded with, and partly over-grown by, mesquite. Reached Armour's at sundown and was kindly received. They showed me a thin and very handsome slab of sandstone which had come from the top of the ruin, and a piece of copper, very much oxidized. It looked as if it had been beaten. They have found in these ruins corn and beans also, and some baskets. Also a little bell (?) of copper.[276] Stone axes were also mentioned. This ruin is mentioned as the largest one around here, but there are said to be many others, small ones, and similar to those on the south bank. The ruins extend into the Sierra Ancha and beyond it. In one of the houses they found a human skeleton.

MAY 27: This ruin* I visited late in the evening [May 26] before sun-down. It lies a half-mile east-northeast of Armour's, on the edge of the second tier of foothills. Nothing is left but foundations. This ruin shows the peculiarity again of the entrance to its gates, which I noticed in the ruins of this A.M. Pottery appears similar to that of the others, and the black-and-white predominated. On the first tier of hills, the boy showed me a place where they had opened a grave. The rocks are still visible, and they mark very distinctly an oblong hollow. They found, besides the bones, etc., a few arrowheads, and I noticed a number of very peculiar rocks on the spot. . . . It looks as if the roof had been about two feet (0.61 [meter]) thick.* Everything inside is charred and carbonized, as if the place had been burnt out (so were the corn and beans found in the rooms). The height of the excavation is 1.25 [meters]. Mesquite, which is of very slow growth, has grown large on top of the building. The height of this mound is 3.30 [meters]. . . .

It looks as if even the courts had been terraced! This would be very important! On the other houses or mounds, the partitions are plainly visible. As usual, there is no trace of the estufa. The pottery is, as usual, black-and-white, red-and-white, red with white-and-black, plain-thick-and-red, and chocolate-white-and-black. Very little corrugated, and none glossy. On the west side there is a gateway, reentering, and an oblong depression which might have been a tank! Saw a very handsome snake, but harmless.

From the conversation it appears that this ruin is regarded as one of the largest in Salt River, and that while there are some around the Sierra Ancha, the heart of the Sierra itself is too rugged and precipitous to leave room for human abodes.*

In this ruin the copper bell was found. It was not a bell, but a rattle; with a slit on the top. It was hammered, not cast.[277]

The Sierra Ancha itself forms the watershed. On its north side, the streams flow to the Colorado Chiquito and to the Rio Verde, and that side is well-watered. The south side, however, is barren, like the Pinal Range.

I hear a great deal about the Mazatzal [Range]. It is called the "Four Peaks," and there are said to be a great many ruins. But they are described to me as similar to those about here, large corrales with nothing but the foundations left, made of rocks. The ruins are said to be very thickly overgrown, and to be in inaccessible places, near the summit or crest.

MAY 28: Left early in the morning. I followed the first tier of height along the river for some time, and found this ruin,* as usual, on a promontory, to the left of the road. It shows but the usual form, and has little pottery, and only foundations extant. I thus rode on seven miles about due west, and out into a very barren country, away from the river, and directly toward Tonto Creek, whose green cottonwoods I saw. No ruins.

I then turned south and struck Tonto Creek opposite the ranch of Mr. Vineyard. Crossed it; it is a limpid stream, not deeper than two feet, and very firm bottom. Beyond, it is sand and gravel, overgrown with cottonwoods. Was directed to Mr. Flippen's ranch by Vineyard. It lies in the flat about one-third-of-a-mile southwest of Tonto, and at the foot of high, steep slopes, which descend abruptly from the Mazatzal Range. The ranch is but one grove of cottonwood and of gigantic mesquite. Well-received. But very hot. About 15 miles from the mouth of the Tonto, the Mazatzal Range approaches the creek and leaves thereafter no room for a bottom. The steep hills descend almost to the river bank; the Sierra Ancha remains about the same distance from the Tonto as it does from Salt River.

The foothills of the Mazatzal, even close to the crest, are dotted with ruins of the same character, namely: small houses with courts. On the east side, the ruins lie much lower, but they are never in the bottom, always on the first or second tier of hills or terraces, rarely beyond it inland. Mr. Vineyard came to visit Mr. Flippin. He speaks of many ruins. Tonto Creek inundates the bottom, and then always carries along much large gravel. Salt River is known to have risen to ten feet above its present level. I painted all afternoon. In regard to agriculture, the reports are less favorable even than farther off. Tonto Creek is a stock country, not a farming country at all. The aboriginal population must have subsisted upon corn and beans, which both grow well. But why these courts? They look so exactly like corrales! Mr. Vineyard spoke of graves, but they are evidently of the Apaches.

MAY 29: Left at 9 A.M. and rode over to Mr. Vineyard who climbed with me to the top of a high and abrupt hill west of his house, where I found this ruin.* The hill is very steep, and overgrown with all kinds of thorns. The ruin is made of the usual boulders, and it is clear that the people used these rocks as they came out of the drift, selecting them as to size and shape, and binding them with mud. Little pottery, mostly coarse, red, thick, cooking pottery. Some little obsidian, but it is very scarce. The painted pottery has nearly all disappeared. To what this singular fact may be due I cannot think. Has it been washed away, or have the inhabitants removed all their decorated ware? I crossed the Tonto again a half-mile above Vineyard's and followed the road in the sandy and gravelly bottom. No ruins there, but many on the terraces above, according to the statement. Bottom mostly covered with mesquite and "Cat's-claws" [Devil's Claws?, *Martynia*, sp.]. The cottonwoods range close along the creek bed. Distance to Cline's, nine miles. It is on the first terrace, and therefore barren; on the second terrace, above the house, lies this large ruin.* Several low mounds are quite prominent. Little pottery visible.

Among the pottery there are white-and-black, red-and-white, but hardly any corrugated ware. But I got some fair specimens of painted pottery, black-and-white, red-and-black, etc. No corrugated ware. Metates as usual of coarse granite. Since I left the Gila, the metates of lava have disappeared, and they are all of granite or syenite. They told me of a number of ruins across the creek, on the high points above its banks. and say that detached houses are at every quarter-of-a-mile. There are also remains of acequias on the other side of the river. Tonto Creek has a very mild climate. On the whole, it is a splendid valley for the meagre wants of an Indian population. The creek, as well as Salt River, is alive with trout. Gypsum (foliated) is found on Tonto Creek, and even abundant. But clay for pottery does not seem to be of good quality; it is largely mixed with pebbles and sand.

MAY 30: Started early for the ruins. They are a mile north of Cline's, on the left-handed side of the road,* on a perfect level, with the usual bushes of mesquite, "Tasajo[?]" and cacti. The columnar *Cerei* grow on the second tier above the river, and the ruins are on the first tier. The bottom of Tonto Creek is so gravelly and covered with drift that it cannot be cultivated at all, and in general, the hills along this and the Salado are the most gravelly regions which I have ever visited. The ruin is very characteristic. In the center of a large enclosure rises the mound. It form a "L," and its height is about 2.25 [meters]. The compartments are clearly marked, and from the amount of debris, it is either a two-story building, or else it has stood on a platform.

This latter question becomes more and more important. Otherwise, it appears that the walls were the same. The enclosure is in some places 2.50 [meters] wide, and it looks as if it had been a row of houses, only there are no traces of partitions, so that I must judge it has been a wide wall, perhaps filled up with earth between the outer and inner lines of stone, or these two parallel walls between which there was a passage to circulate. A road goes through, and the entrance was already there when the Clines opened the road in order to quarry the stones from the ruins. Their excavations are regular trenches, which, however, reveal nothing beyond the usual stone walls, in whose composition large drift enters, almost exclusively. The mound is surrounded by the usual rectangles and courts, though courts evidently. The idea strikes me more and more that, owing to the real scarcity of land suitable for culture, the small enclosures and courts might have been fields or rather garden plots? Pleasant chat with the Clines. They all state that there are more ruins yet farther north, in the Tonto Basin proper.

I started early, and the road led me almost exclusively along the first tier above the river. I found the faint traces of the two small houses there. They are at least three miles apart. Farther on, I came to the ruins on the other page.* They are extensive and have no central mound, but several small mounds. Their appearance is otherwise similar to that at Kenton's, and all the other large, "flat" ruins on Salt River and Tonto Creek. It may be that they are of older date than those of the central mound, and the latter has been levelled by time. But the pottery is the same, and there is a remarkable absence of corrugated ware. Saw no obsidian, and very little flint. Many metates, all of reddish and grayish granite. Mesquite bushes are growing freely among the ruins.

I then descended into the river bottom, which is narrow and very gravelly, totally unfit for cultivation, and has the usual growth of cottonwoods. On the south bank of a dry creek, running diagonally into the Tonto, I found a large ruin.* It has a mound in the shape of a horseshoe, which mound hugs closely the creek banks. Large mesquite trees have grown partly on it. Here the walls are of foliated gypsum, resting on foundations of very large rubble or boulders. The gypsum is translucent and transparent, and as it breaks off very regularly, the walls must have been very handsome.* As far as I could see the walls are at least 0.50 to 0.60 [meter] in thickness. Pottery is the same. No obsidian, but little flint, and metates of granite or syenite. The usual wall of circumvallation runs around the whole, it is about 1.0 [meter] thick, and the two rows of blocks on the outside of it are very prominent.*

Here, the southeast corner appears to be free of court and of compartments, and here also the wall is levelled to the surface of the soil. There are two distinct rubbish mounds.* One is on the outside, beyond the wall, about 50.0 [meters] off, and the other, at the southern line of wall, just beyond it, therefore outside the pueblo. On the whole, it is a very interesting structure. On the north bank of the arroyo, a ditch, possibly an old acequia, seems to run into it, or rather parallel to it. At that ruin, and opposite to it, bordering upon the creek, the second tier of hills assumes the form of a steep declivity of flesh-red, sandy rock. Large columnar *Cerei* grow on this almost vertical slope. Here again I descended into the bottom, rocky and gravelly as ever, and then crossed the Tonto to the ranch of Frank Cline. The bottom on that side is very similar to the one on the east, but the gravel deposits appear less wide.* "Tobe" Cline told me last night that within a few years, old springs have suddenly reappeared on Salt River. I followed the bottom for three miles to the ranch of Ward's. Then I turned into the mountains. It was ferociously hot. After reaching the plateau, I had the Reno Mountains right before me. They present a very forbidding appearance, rise very steeply, and have vegetation along the abrupt slopes, although the crests and tops appear exceedingly craggy. The mesa on

which I ascended merges into the foothills, or rather foot-slopes, of the
Sierra Mazatzal, as these mountains are properly called.*

The road winds up through gulches, and follows little valleys which,
while the slopes are barren with even little grass, are densely wooded
and have occasional springs. Not only cottonwood, but also walnut and
excellent mulberries, which are now ripe. I reached Fort Reno[278] about
two P.M., in terrible heat. The ranch of Dick Prather[279] is a very substantial structure; it lies in a basin, close by the ruins of the old fort,
which stand in an open space, from which an immense outlook is had.
To the south the valley of the Tonto expands; to the east, the whole
of the Sierra Ancha; to the north and northeast, Tonto Basin; in the
west side, the Mazatzal, only two miles off, rises in a long line of steep,
rugged high mountains. From Prather's house, the ground sinks to a
dry arroyo, and on this little slope, which is covered with groves of mulberry, walnut, willows, and cottonwoods, there are several springs. On
the other side of the creek rises a steep mesa, and at its brink lies a ruin.*
The slope is vertical in bands and places. Metates of granite in huge proportions, as thick as 0.30 and 0.40 [meter] lie about. The mesa runs
west and east and immediately from the foot of the Mazatzal Mountains. Like all the mesas here, it trends to the east, or Tonto Creek.
There is another, more extensive ruin on the road before reaching
Prather's. It is a flat one, but with a distinct, although low, small, central mound. The character of these ruins is identical with those lower
down. There are others near, and I was told that in Tonto Basin they
are absolutely alike, and not much larger, if any. This report is confirmed from every side. There are acequias there, and there is one in
the bottom of the creek below here. [Fort] Reno is a beautiful, almost
idyllic, spot, but Dick has it quite lonely up here, all alone. He cooks
well; we had excellent fish from the Tonto and potatoes. . . . Shall
stay here tomorrow, and visit an important ruin, the largest one known
to Prather, south of here.

MAY 31: Started with Dick Prather on foot about 8 A.M. The ruin*
lies about three-fourths-of-a-mile south-southeast of his ranch, in a
valley, and between two mesas. It is very handsome. No buildings are
visible, but the ground is exceedingly clean, and the foundations are remarkably distinct. It looks as if there had indeed been a raised platform
on which there stood buildings (small houses) and courts. . . . Hardly
any pottery is visible, but what there is, is not different, except in that
it contains some of the red corrugated ware. In the afternoon I painted.

The usual reports about ruins in the Tonto Basin came in. They confirm each other in that they speak of the ruins as similar to those of Tonto Creek and of Salt River. I passed two happy days at Reno, all in all; Dick is of the utmost kindness to me. Chico is lean; the grass does not agree with him.

JUNE

JUNE 1: I left Reno at 6 P.M. For nearly six miles, the road crawls up through the wild canyon, rising at least 2000 feet. There is not a foot of ground arable or even habitable; every eminence is shattered into crags. Lofty mountains rise on all sides, their tops are covered with crags, their slopes with vegetation. The road is horrible for wagons, almost impassable. From the summit, the eye plunges into the depth of Sunflower Valley.

Ruins at Sunflower,* above the house of Juan Soto, on hill of lava, densely overgrown. It is grassy, and almost lovely, but very narrow. Beyond are terribly rugged mountains, and in the blue haze of the far-off distance, ranges are seen which skirt the junction of Salt River with the Verde. It is a panorama of barriers, rendered lively and varied through the sharp profiles of the mountains alone. The rock around here is granite.

As I descended the naked slope, I met three Pima Indians; the first ones I ever saw. They were partly with pants, partly with naked legs, showing the breechclout. Good looking, their hair braided in tresses, artificially lengthened by other hair braided in. Sunflower Valley is very narrow, in fact it is only a gorge, with a little stream of water running through it, lined with cottonwoods. On a hill east of it, I found a ruin.* It is very old, much tumbled and overgrown, and its metates are again of lava! The appearance of the ruin is very old, and the pottery, mostly common, is very ordinary. It is very densely overgrown, which made it difficult to survey. I was told again, here, of the ruins on the tops of the mountains. There is mezcal agave here, and several Pima are baking the flower stalk in the ground, and thus sacharifying it. It is then peeled and dried, forming cakes, which taste exactly like pears preserved whole, and are excellent. They come to the mountains regularly for that purpose.

After dining at Juan Soto's, I rode on to Otero's ranch over a dreary series of very rugged ridges of granite, almost destitute of vegetation. It was fearfully hot. I reached the entrance of Barrell's Canyon and

Otero's ranch, a handsome green spot on the banks of a running creek, enclosed between high cliffs, about 4 P.M. Otero is not at home, but Ramón Miranda took good care of me and my beast. I am tired; the heat affects me considerably, and the eyes chiefly are weak. I see double frequently. At night I had the company of Mr. W. S. Logan of New York.

JUNE 2: My [carre(tero?) or com(pañero?)] Rafael Ochova, came at 8 A.M. and I overtook him about a mile beyond the ranch.

Ruin, a quarter-of-a-mile east of Jesús Otero's ranch, on high hill.* Little visible; pottery scarce and ordinary.

I soon got on the wagon, leaving Chico to follow as best he could, tied behind. It is a long tedious ascent, over rocky mountain ridges, sparsely covered with cacti, grand views to the south and east, but fiercely hot. Then a steep descent into a narrow cañón, at whose southern margin, almost closing it, rises "Sugarloaf" to a height of at least 1000 feet, nearly vertical. It is evidently trap or lava; the top is flat and it is said to contain ruins.*

On the west side is said to be the only mode of ascent, and the statement about ruins appears true. It is at all events a very safe place, and water is permanent in the creek at the foot of the mountain. We descend the canyon, and then again rose to a mesa, scrubby, terribly hot, whence we finally reached the banks of an arroyo which descends into the Rio Verde. On the right-hand side (going down) it is an absolute level, not very broad, with mesquite, tasajo, palo de fierro, some choyas [chollas], and *Peraskea gigantea*; on the other side, cliffs descend into it steeply. The mountains on the other side of the Verde are plainly visible. There is hardly an appreciable descent to the stream, which is encased by the usual gravelly bottom densely overgrown with cottonwoods. I could not discern any trace of ruins on the east side. Crossed the Verde, a beautifully clear stream with green water, about 3 P.M. Reached the Fort [McDowell][280] which is situated on the open plain beyond the cottonwoods, at 4 P.M. Reception kind. The country around is all level. Got letters and papers. Obtained nice quarters. News tolerable so far. Got to write. But I am almost used up, and my eyes hurt me badly. Must rest here for a number of days, and shall do so. Everything looks comfortable here and friendly.

JUNE 3: Painted the whole day. Lieut. Scott[281] and ten men left for

Phoenix this A.M., owing to silly trouble with the Maricopas. It is a foolish, ridiculous affair.

[June 4-June 6, no entries.]

JUNE 7: Wrote to Joe, to Bishop Salpointe, to McNally, to Lieut. Davis, and to Ochova. My eyes are very bad. I see mostly double. Am very lazy and have no energy at all. The nights are cool and pleasant, but my cold bothers me much. The "Phoenix War" passed off as expected, quietly and without bloodshed. Several Maricopa Indians called upon. They appear very similar to Pueblos, their braided hair excepted. Today one of them, an old man, wove a headband. They call their big water jars "Hä-ă." It is difficult, otherwise, to get anything out of them. They speak but little Spanish, and of course no English at all. They are quiet, unobtrusive Indians, who raise stock and good wheat crops.

Ruin on the parade ground of Fort McDowell.* The mound is very low, almost imperceptible. Very little pottery about. This is very natural, since the pottery has been pretty well obliterated through the use of the grounds. There are double foundations. . . .* This is a very doubtful ruin. Most people assert it to be that of the old guardhouse, which appears to have stood in the parade grounds. Still, I found some old pottery on the premises. Quién sabe? In the evening George Willcox [Wilcox] took me[282] to the ruin. It is [on] a handsome stream. Here, the banks are very steep, almost vertical, for about 20 feet, so that the section from the fort to the river is as follows,* the distance being about a quarter-of-a-mile. At (a) there is a plain ruin, which I shall measure tomorrow. Farther on, there is another small house indicated by a grave-like depression. (c) is the stump of a willow or mesquite growing in the ruin, and about 0.33 [meter] in diameter. Have a very bad cold.

JUNE 8: My cold is so severe that I could not speak until 8:30 A.M. Left on foot for the ruin. The central mound is about 1.75 [meters] high, and in some places flat stones are still visible, indicating the roof. It is much obliterated.* [To one side,] is a house of adobe, occupied by a soldier. There has evidently been much burrowing going on in the ruins [three rooms having been partially excavated]. There is a platform. The outside compartments are indistinct, and they have been despoiled greatly of the rocks once composing them. There are, so far, five or six rooms discernible. Pottery plain red and some black, not a single painted piece. No metates visible. I then went out from this slope, west, and reached the broken hills which compose the first tier. These hills, farther north, crowd to the very river bottom, and make it very difficult to expect ruins there. [Trough] metate of lava.* I wandered about five miles, until I reached the ranch of De Marbaix, a Belgian, who lives on a fertile bottom four miles north of the post. Such fertile valleys are frequent, and De Marbaix told me that they extend at least as far as 40 miles with interruptions of higher and lower hills hugging the river and almost encasing it in canyons.* . . .

Mr. De Marbaix told me that there were no pueblos up to 30 miles north of here. He described the ruins near Sears' ranch, as large-house type distinctly. He says that it is more in the shape of a rectangle, and that the other ruins north of it are similar. In the Sierra Ancha, north of the canyon of Salt River, there are still ruins of large houses several stories high. In regard to this ruin at Lederetta's, he says the houses contain 40 to 60 small cells, and that nearly each cell contained, buried under the floor, a skeleton; the skull being mostly well-preserved. The metate which his people use is a black, compact trap or lava, and comes from these ruins. In the ruins near this post, I found rough lava implements too. Not finding any ruin I returned by the road following the bottom. I noticed the ground to be very unfavorable for ruins and settlements. The Maricopas and the Pimas speak different languages.[283]

I painted all afternoon. Having some hopes of receiving my letters from Tucson tonight, I deferred, but nothing came except my eye protectors, which I sorely need for the outside glare.

JUNE 9: This ruin* is situated about a quarter-of-a-mile from the Verde, two miles south of the fort on a bluff to the left of the road leading to Phoenix.

Flint, some pieces of lava and lava chips. Did not notice any obsidian. Very little pottery, and what there is, is of the most common kind. I found a single piece, black-and-white decorated.

Although very hot, I left on foot about 8 A.M. and walked south. Soon found traces of mounds, but they are so mixed with rubbish from the fort that I could not unravel the two from each other. Beyond, and about three-quarters-of-a-mile from the fort, I found another ruin on the roadside. Low mounds, but extensive.* Around them, at a distance of from 75 to 60 steps, are the traces or rather vestiges of courts, showing it to have had the usual form. There is pottery about, all common, none painted. Going farther south, I struck the acequia. It must have been from one-and-a-half to three meters wide, and is now filled with fine white sand. There are many ramifications branching off to the right and left, irregularly, but I am not able to tell as to whether they are genuine or not; many of them are evidently washes. There are several dry arroyos coming down from the hills and terraces in the west, and the blending of these with the acequias makes it doubtful as to the real location of the latter. There are, along what appears to me to be the real acequia, vestiges of scattered habitations. The ruin [discussed above] is on the edge of the first foothills, on the very brink of the declivity, which, there, is very steep and covered with brush, while at the foot runs the acequia. The cottonwoods of the bottom grow at the foot, so that the acequia runs beneath their shadow.* There is an abandoned lime kiln, which was built there formerly by a Mexican. The ruins are in fair condition. Systematic excavations appear to have been made in front of the mound, and it may be that this mound either was large and has been reduced by digging, or else that there was a raised platform in front of it, to the south.* . . . Some of the debris indicates as if the walls had been originally composed of gypsum. But this is not sure yet, as the material is much disintegrated and very rotten. Fragmentary metates of lava. I returned at 11 A.M., well recompensed. I have now made up to date 1650 miles, of which Chico has travelled 1030.

JUNE 10: Started at 5 A.M. for Sugarloaf, reaching it about 8 A.M. Made the ascent and found: Nothing! It is an exceedingly tiresome climb of nearly two miles, on lava rock, and the top, while excessively rocky, does not contain a trace of ruins. This may have a bearing on the ruins supposed to be on the top of the Four Peaks! (Distance travelled 1670, of which 1030 with Chico; the poor little darling threatens to get sore withers.) Returned at 1 P.M. Thermometer 103.5°.

JUNE 11: Painted all day. Chico improving. Got my letters from Tucson. Thank God! Was so overjoyed that I nearly got tight in bar. Arranged for a trip to the canal tomorrow with Lieut. Scott, upon the Superintendent's [?] invitation. Had a long talk with John R. Freese. He appears to suit me.

JUNE 12: Started with Lieut. Scott at 10 A.M. on horseback for the canal. We crossed the Verde, about a mile below the post, and then con-

tinued on the first tier of terraces, across the rancho of Don Ben Velasco, into the triangle, where the Rio Verde runs along the eastern
slope of Mount McDowell, running into the Salado. To the east are
high and abrupt mesas. The junction of the two rivers takes place in a
sandy and gravelly bottom.*

Mount McDowell presents itself as a dark red, forbidding cliff, not
unlike to an immense castle, on which there are spots of very bright
verdure. It is on the north side of the Salado, southeast of Mount Mc-
Dowell, that the canal is being taken out by Mr. Trott. It passes through
a sandy but apparently fertile expanse, is 40 feet wide, and at least ten
feet deep. About a quarter-of-a-mile west of it runs what is termed the
traces of an ancient acequia. It is a tiny nook, runs along the edge of the
first tier of terraces, and is a streak of sand, encased by gravel, five feet
wide, and two feet deep.* It appears to have been filled up with sand.
If genuine, it compares with the modern enterprise as the work of
pygmies does with that of giants. There is west of it (between it and
Mount McDowell) among gigantic zahuarros and brush, a space with
much pottery, but no traces of buildings. After spending a very pleasant time there, we rode back along the Verde, crossing it again to the
east side, and at the distance of about five miles from McDowell, on a
level, close by the river bottom at the foot of the high mesas, found a
ruin. It is much shrouded by brush, and appears to have been built of
sandstone and concrete. Pottery black-and-white and red. Metates of
lava. Considerable flint, and many lava chips. Found a marine shell,
used in a necklace, etc. There may have been some gypsum along with
the concrete, but it is doubtful.

JUNE 12: The ruin has the usual form, but there is no central mound.
Still there are some compartments (always the smaller ones) more
elevated than the others. Dense brush, and some large mesquite, grows
over the ruins. We then rode up to the mesa. It is absolutely covered
with fine gravel and many pieces of pottery, and there are lines of
ridges visible, possibly indicating foundations. Still, they are so faint
that I would hesitate, and I could not well imagine of what kind of
material the walls were built, unless they be made of concrete which
has totally crumbled and disintegrated.

The view from the mesa over the valleys of the Verde is charming.
We then descended to the rancho of Velasco. On the little rises surrounding the foot of the mesa, there are other evidences of dwellings,
equally faint. But the pottery is different, and looks much more like

an older type of Maricopa pottery. It is pale flesh red and yellowish, with Indian-red decorations. There is also the common red kind, but there is no black-and-white, etc. Evidently the stone ruins and the obliterated vestiges have each a kind of crockery distinct from the other, and peculiar to each. The stone houses have not the red-and-yellow highly decorated ware of the other ruins.

After casting a glance at the ruins on Velasco's ranch, and agreeing upon visiting them tomorrow, I returned. It has been a delightful day, and on the whole very profitable.

JUNE 13: Started with the Doctor and George [Wilcox] at 8 A.M. Rode down to Velasco's ruin and found it similar to the one of yesterday. Only it looks as if a hard adobe, now out of its regular shape, had formed a large part of the material. Found a small piece of obsidian. Pottery common, except the black-and-white painted. The ruin is largely overgrown and seems to be elevated, on the average, considerably above the surrounding level. It may be debris only, but it may also be an originally artificial elevation.

Last night, Marion McCann confessed to me that the ruins on the Verde, 35 to 40 miles from here, were similar to those down here and on the Tonto. Reached the post about 11 A.M. Shall go to Tempe instead of Phoenix. Am going out to the ditch north of here this P.M. [Here, page 98 of Bandelier's journal is missing.]

JUNE 14: Left at 8 A.M. by stage. The country, after once passing Mount McDowell, becomes a desert. The choya, with its hideous thorns, is arborescent, and the zahuarro less frequent. The soil is sandy, but fertile as soon as irrigated. Reached the bottom of the Salado at 12:30 A.M. It is narrow, and has thick underbrush and cottonwoods, and the approaches to the river are heavily covered with drift gravel and boulders. Air more humid. Tempe lies on the river bank, rather high and thus beyond inundations. Immediately east of town, and descending abruptly into the river, rises Tempe Mountain, as usual rocky, barren, and rugged; an isolated peak. There are no trees on it, and near the top are said to exist rock paintings of some importance. East of Tempe, a broad mesa expands along the river. It is low and scarcely deserves the name. On it, stands the Mormon settlement of Mesa City, nine miles from Tempe.

Opposite, in the thick brush of the first tier of the river, on the north bank, is hidden a large ruin, reduced to a shapeless mound. Mr.

Hayden's[284] mill stands on the brink of the river. Stopped at Jesús García's. Kindly received. Painted all afternoon not withstanding the terrible heat. Formed the acquaintance of the Mormon Bishop Mc-Donald,[285] a friend of Moses Thatcher. There is a large ruin, a big mound, five miles east of here, on the mesa, and two acequias, one on each side of the river. The one on the north side runs nearly in a line with the great canal, that is, from 200 to 1000 feet from the river; the one on the south side is farther inland. Neither is lined. They are simply ditches, dug in the ground, from 20 to 25 feet wide (it is said?) and at most, six feet deep. Tempe is handsome with its row of trees, planted, but it is terribly hot and this heat very enervating.

This climate, with the warm winter, and the lack of precipitation (hardly two months of rain, July and August) had evidently exerted a vast and lasting influence on the aborigines. Two crops are frequently raised in one year. For wheat it is an excellent country. The Mormon settlement here is large, and there are also some Mexicans. Pima Indians come in frequently. Their jet-black hair is plaited, and a feather or some red cloth sometimes hangs down from it. The legs of the men are mostly naked except the breech-clout. The feet are naked. I saw them with turquoises in their ears, shells, etc. Many wear the striped (white-and-blue, black-, or brown-, and-white) undershirt. The women go with their feet naked; they wear a skirt of red calico and over it a loose blouse of white muslin, bleached, without long sleeves. Everything looks tropical. So does the type. Saw a Papago. He wore sandals like the Mexican "Cactli."[286] The men and women of the Pimas are very well-formed, but the women are said to be disgustingly loose, and to be purchased at any time for a dollar or two. Among the men there is drunkenness, for they make "Tisuin"! On the whole, the Pimas appear not unlike the Apaches.

JUNE 15: Went to the Mexican town of Tempe, with García. Where the house of Mr. Murphy[287] stands, almost due south of the mountain and on the edge of its slope, are several mounds, much ruined. The house stands on one of them. Although dilapidated, they show that they were artificial, and upon digging, they revealed adobe, stone axes, and pottery. I copied two of the axes at Mr. Murphy's, which took me nearly the whole afternoon. One of them is remarkably long, and this seems to be the characteristic of the Arizona axes, also that only one side of the edges is indented, that is, the groove for fastening does never run around the axe.[288]

JUNE 16: Left at 6 A.M. with García and a boy for the north bank of the Salado to visit a ruin.* . . .

We crossed Salt River, its thickly overgrown and gravelly bottom, the grand canal, and entered the perfectly level and open plain, which expands towards the barren and grotesque ridges and hills of granite ranging along the base of the mountains west of McDowell. On the left of the road is an almost impenetrable thicket six to seven feet high, which extends a little beyond the canal, but no trees. On the other, north, side, is the usual plain, over which zahuarros, low mesquite, palo verde, *Opuntia*, etc., are promiscuously scattered. The canal branches off from the river (deflects) and intersects, at a distance of about three miles from Tempe, the ancient acequia, which takes its head inside, and therefore west of the present channel.* It afterwards goes out of it. The ruin is about 75.0 [meters] north of this ancient acequia.

I must note here, that last night Sheet #98, which contained the record of the acequia seven miles north of McDowell, was carried off by the wind. I will briefly state, that the acequia is not over ten feet wide, and that we followed its winding course for over one-and-a-half-miles. Here is a copy of the drawing on #98. Also of the cross section, at a depth of two feet exposed.* It appears that they followed the level, using one of the sides of the slope as an embankment. Here in the plain, it is a common ditch, both banks being slightly raised. There is nothing wonderful in all these constructions, except their length, the one at McDowell being about 13 miles long, and with many curves about 25. The one here, which is much more straight, is perhaps about 20 miles.

Up to now, and in every case, the ruins stand outside of the acequia, and either near the head or the end! The ruin itself is an immense artificial mound supporting smaller mounds and foundations of stone.[289] The cross section from the southeast to the northwest corner, diagonally, is as follows, including the raised platform which surrounds it.*

The whole appears to have been built over without much regularity. The mounds show no traces of foundations and are much smaller in appearance than at McDowell and on Tonto Creek, but this may be due to contrast. Pottery in profusion, nearly all of the very common kind. Still there is some painted, red, on cream-colored background.* Flint, fragments of metates of lava, and some black pieces, apparently opaque obsidian. Around the whole structure there runs the elevated platform, on whose edge there was evidently a wall of stone, with much earth, clay, or adobe. There may have been an opening to that wall on the southeast side, but this is yet doubtful. The excavation on the east side is problematical. It has certainly not revealed any walls, and looks modern. More and more, against the assertions of all, I believe that there were two huge platforms, on the top of the highest of which there were the buildings. Around this mound lie profusely scattered, the foundations of small houses, some with mounds. . . .

There is a smaller one with a low mound about 200 steps north-northwest and a half-of-a-mile northeast. Between them are scattered foundations. The whole has been a village, but the question arises, why this bulky mound? This is highly important. Some of the remains of the foundations are as extensive as those with mounds. There is an enigma here, which I must carefully sift, and which I can only solve where there are free walls still standing. Have great hopes for Casa Blanca. Returned at 11 A.M. without my boy, whom I lost. He came afterwards, having fallen asleep and not hearing my calls. Painted all afternoon. Terribly hot. Wrote a postal card to Joe. Am considerably unnerved.

JUNE 17: Terribly hot. Gallardo[290] failed again. Painted. García brought me old Desiderio Palma, who speaks the Pima language perfectly. He says the Pimas and Papagos are one language and people, and that the Maricopa, Cócopa, and Yuma are one. That the Maricopa were warred upon by the Yuma, and Pima came to their assistance, rescuing them, whereupon the Maricopa settled near the Pima. But they do not understand each other, as the languages are totally different. The Pima still celebrate a victory over the Apaches.

When a man dies, the horse, the oxen, etc., which he personally owned, so also if anybody else dies, in fact in the case of the death of anyone, whatever belonged to him is killed or burnt or destroyed. The lands which were cultivated are immediately abandoned, and the huts burnt. Even the relatives, on both sides, burn their houses, in case of any death. (Montezuma's wife is called J'ooq. She was burnt.) Their medicine man, or Rechizero, is called maquay, also saysh-tshyuq. He can have several wives. The Pimas and Papagos call themselves O-tam, and the Pimas proper Giram-O-tam; the Papagos, To-jono-O-tam. What do these words mean? The Mexicans: Tshyutshqa. Blood revenge is very strictly observed. Each rancheria marries and intermarries, and while the personal names are all taken after plants and animals, there are no traces of the gens.

The Montezuma tale is, of course, repeated. He is represented as having been a great man, even the first man, and of having taught the Pima all they knew. I arranged with Desiderio for a Pima Indian to guide me to Zacaton [present-day Sacaton] tomorrow. It is Sunday, and there is movement in the place. Palma assured me that the Pima laid hardly any claim to these ruins; still they say that they were built by the people of Montezuma, and that when he returned, he found that these people had turned bad, whereupon he changed them into stones and destroyed the places. He also says that they keep the gavilán [sparrow hawk] and worship the eagle, of which they have a statue in a cavern in the Maricopa Range.[291]

JUNE 18: Splendid day. My Indian came, totally drunk; still we started. After passing through part of the handsome settlement of the Mormons, with neat houses, long rows of trees and gushing acequias, we turned south into the desert, bleak, sandy, and hot, little mesquite, an occasional zahuarro, etc. Terribly hot. On the northern border of the desert, saw some low mounds, inconsiderable, and isolated. No foundations. Reached Hayden's store at 1 P.M. Crossed the Gila, two thin films of water, not above the horse's fetlock, a sandy bottom, passed the Pima village and many acequias. The houses are round and square, of boughs, straw and dirt. The square houses are with bundles of straw. These are their storehouses. In summer they live in sheds only, and move out into the fields for that purpose. The south bank of the Gila is as dreary as the north side, isolated mountain clusters and peaks, bleak and barren, steep, rocky, and forbidding, rise up everywhere in the distance. There is no timber at all in sight, low underbrush, sparsely scattered, covers the white soil. Reached Sweetwater [Agua Dulce],[292] a desolate looking place, at 3 P.M. Reception very friendly. Chico again swollen.

JUNE 19: Started for Casa Blanca [293] at 7 A.M. on foot. About a mile from Agua Dulce [Sweetwater] a low mound (one height) to the left of the road. It is almost pure white sand.* Pottery of the usual kind. From a distance, the white mound of Casa Blanca looks gigantic, since it is on a high ridge, bleak and barren, treeless and shadeless. There is a Pima village around it, and a trading store belonging to Rittenhouse,[294] and kept by Joseph Fuchs (now Fox), an old German soldier. Examined the Pima houses. The winter house is round. A framework of four posts set in the ground, with forking ends upward, supports four poles laid across. Over these is laid a layer of sticks or canes, but principally sticks, and this is covered with a thick layer of mud and gravel, forming a gravel roof originally independent from the other parts of the building. They take green boughs or poles, bend them and tie them together and let them dry, forming a hoop; other poles they plant in the ground, bending them up until they touch the roof, and tie them to it by bark or fibre, and then slip down the hoops over them, fastening these to the poles by tying.

They leave a doorway of 1.60 x 0.67 [meters]. Then the whole is covered with wet mud and gravel, so as to form an impenetrable roof and wall. The mud, if the house is made in wet weather, is wetted. Against the foot of the wall they pole dirt around like a rim, and leave a depression around for the water to flow off into a ditch on the outside, or rather two semi-circular ditches. There appears to be the same size for all houses, about six to seven meters, in diameter, and the square houses measure the same size. These are after the same principle only square, the walls are made of upright bundles of long straw, and are not covered with earth, except at the base. The roofs are flat. The doorways are now closed with wood piled up before them.

. . . when the women have their courses, they are sent out the house and are compelled to sleep outside until menstruations are over and past.[295] I saw a number of their large grain baskets. They are made of straw, held together by yucca fibres. They are about four feet high and three feet in diameter. Besides these, they make the ornamented flat "xicara" [jícara], black and white, also painted. The black and white are both natural colors of the wood; the red and blue are painted. I also saw one of their apparatus for carrying, but could not sketch it. It appears a rather complicated machine.[296] The women do the work as among the Apaches; the men superintend only.[297] No weaving done by the Pimas.[298]

I then went out and measured the ruins. Cross section from west to east. The ruin is reduced to a white mound, on which foundations, about 0.50 [meter] wide, of white mud, are still plainly visible. These walls are not stone, nor adobe; they are white earth. There is

evidently a wall around it, of mud also, and that wall was around a raised platform. It had at least one mound. Pottery the same. Returned to Agua Dulce at noon.

Started for the Pima Agency[299] at 5 P.M. and reached the house of Reverend C. E. Cook [C. H. Cook][300] at 6 P.M. Reception kind. He completely discards the story of Montezuma, and says it is a Spanish and American importation. But the Pima have a story of a great re-former, whom they call Scepolo or Scepola,[301] who taught them arts and morals. His counselor was an eagle! (Cibola!?) They call the buffalo Cibolo. Tucson is *Styucson*, and signifies, a spring. *Ar-li-son* is Arizona! They have much to do with witchcraft, and kill witches or sorcerers. Believe in a future life, and strew meal to the souls of the dead, like the Pueblos.

JUNE 20: I painted nearly the whole day. On the north bank of the Gila, a mountain range extends from east to west, and approaches the river. It is barren and rocky and precipitous as usual, but on its foot-hills is a ruin which, from all the descriptions, is like those of the Rio Verde, Tonto, Upper Salt River, etc., namely: of stone, the foundations alone being visible. There is another ruin, on the north bank also, about eight miles northeast of the agency, which, however, being in a level plain, is a shapeless white mound. From that ruin a handsome painted jar was exhumed, which I copied. It was filled with human bones, well-broken, and although possibly not all the skeleton was there, at least every part of it was represented by fragments, even the skull. It had been sealed with mesquite gum and clay, but the cover was broken while exhuming it. This jar is of the same kind of pottery as at the Rio Verde, Lower Salado, Casa Blanca, etc., which dispels my doubts as to the fact of the latter being not ancient. I also painted a very pretty small stone axe. Dr. Ellis,[302] when he saw my wands, assured me that the Pima used similar objects in their cases of witchcraft. They bury them, and the party who accidentally finds them, is at once declared

to be the sorcerer or the witch. The Maricopa practice cremation, but I could not find out how. The water jar is called *ha-a*, the painted basket *Ual-ar*. Sent postal cards to Joe, to Mrs. Morgan, to Mr. Parkman, and to north Willcox.[303]

JUNE 21: Started at 8 A.M. The road follows the Gila bottom, which is less barren the farther east we get, the mesquite growing larger and more densely scattered. After passing between two mountain ranges, one on the north side of the Gila and close to the river, and the other to the south about four or five miles from it, we emerged into a broad plain on the south side. On the north side, there are low isolated mountains scattered between the river and the distant Superstition Mountains, giving it an appearance, not only of greater unequality, but even of being almost mountainous. The mesquite are growing larger and larger; passed Dempsey's handsome ranch, which lies on the outskirts of the Pima village of Black Water. Reached Walker's[304] (three-fourths-of-a-mile from Casa Grande) at 12 A.M. Most kindly received. Handsome spot. It shows that, wherever irrigated, this plain is exceed-

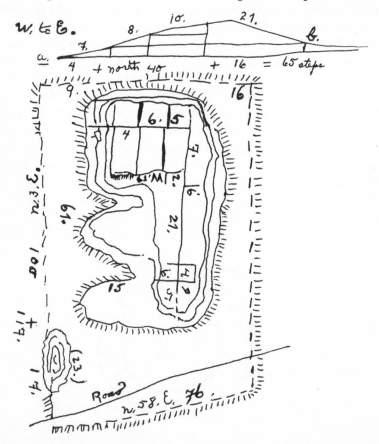

ingly fertile. After painting in the afternoon, I went out to the ruin. It stands a mile south of Mr. Walker's in the usual plain which is thickly covered with mesquite and some few zahuarros. In front of the house still standing are mounds on platforms with walls around them, or rather heavy parapets of earth. The central house is still three stories high, and there are walls around it which show two stories. No windows, but doorways, slightly narrower at the top than at bottom. Walls exceedingly thick.

From the decay it appears that the debris soon forms a solid mound, but still the debris here does not, through its mass, justify the assumption that the great mound at Tempe was anything else but a mound. Pottery red, also black, and some few pieces striped red, of the usual kind pertaining to Salt River and to the Verde. Saw a broken metate of lava. Between the main group, and the rancho, there are mounds on platforms. On the whole, the Casa Grande presents an appearance very similar to the groups of small houses on Salt River, Tonto Creek, and the Verde. It explains fully its principal features. I am now certain that two crops can be, and are, raised here in the same year. If desired, even two crops of corn could be grown, but this is never done. Planting in March, the corn would be gathered at the end of June, and planting again in July, it would yet fully ripen.

June 22: Splendid day. Hot, of course. Went out to the ruins with Rafael Lopez and measured the central group. The whole appears to have been surrounded by a wall of earth, which is now crumbled and partly obliterated by time and rains, but I am about sure that the houses did not stand on a platform. The decay of the heavy walls is very peculiar. They crumble away to firm mounds, like whitish marl, and to a comparatively small bulk. A house like the Casa Grande would thus dwindle down easily to a hill like the Casa Blanca! The vigas are still partly in the wall, partly burnt out. (This is recent destruction.) They were, according to Judge Walker, of different woods, pine, cedar, cottonwood, etc., thus showing that they gathered it wherever and as best they could, and not from one particular point only and of one particular kind. The cross-sticks or brush above the vigas were of arrowwood, Palo de fierra, etc. Above these, 0.30 [meter] of soil, and this layer is blackened, showing that blood was used to smoothen it. The whole ceiling is 0.61 [meter] thick. The walls are plastered, originally white, now oxydized, and very smooth. The doorways are tapering to above. There are airholes, but no windows; still on the north side there is a door on the second story looking out. What for? Unless there was a porch in front or a lower story. Of the latter there is no evidence nor trace. As to whether the house was three stories high on all sides, it is impossible to determine now. Judge Walker came; a charming man and thoroughly posted. He says that the material of which the walls are made is "natural cement."

This stratum crops out occasionally and underlies the soil in general. As it contains lime, it turns to a cement when piled up after being wetted and disintegrates again into marl. The floor is said to be a thick layer of the same material, but its depth I could not ascertain, neither that of the foundations. How the different stories communicated, it is impossible to conjecture; there is no evidence of stairs. Possibly ladders and trap doors. . . .

No obsidian found by myself, but obsidian chips and arrowheads have been found by other parties, also flint. Pottery in immense lots, all of good clay, but plain red and black, only a few pieces painted red. Metates of lava. Some stone axes were found there also, and a few trinkets. In the floor were found pockets, of the shape and size of an olla which we refilled with the small aboriginal beans. Also some bones were dug out; probably animal bones.

[Here Bandelier included a floor plan of the Casa Grande ruin, with various dimensions noted.]

Of the other buildings, only three walls (respectively three and two feet thick) are left. The partition walls run against the outer walls and not through, and the masses disintegrate first in large prismatic blocks, which tumble out and pulverize outside.

The Casa Grande is called by the Pimas "Vayq'y" also "Civanoqi" or the House of "Civano." Civano is said by them to have built it and inhabited it. His son settled on Salt River.* On the Rio Verde there lived a different tribe, and there was war between the two tribes. The Pimas claim to be the direct descendants of the builders of the Casa Grande and of the ruins about Tempe, etc., as high as the junction of the Verde and Salado. The Casa Grande is said to have been destroyed by people coming from the east in three large bodies. The Pimas claim to have been created here, and afterwards to have spread to the northward as far as the Rio Salado, then after their overthrow, to have passed to the south in part, where a part of the tribe still lives in Sonora. In Arizona there are still 4000 Pimas and 6000 Papagos. These are all Pueblo Indians to all intents and purposes.*[305]

They claim that one Creator made them, "T'yo-uot-Ămaque."

"*T'yo-uot*," Earth; "*Maque*," prophet. He came down to the earth and in his wanderings made man out of clay and breathed his spirit into him. They have a tale of the flood, out of which but one man saved himself, "*Ci-ŭe*," but he did it by taking refuge on the top of the Maricopa Mountains. This is the Montezuma, or rather he had been mistaken for Montezuma. The latter is [means] absolutely nothing. Still they have the tale of a migration to Mexico, via the Casas Grandes of Chihuahua, and two other stations. This may be Montezuma trash again.

The Pimas used to weave cotton, on the floor, or rather to net it. They formerly did not use the river for irrigation until about 50 years ago, when they began.[306] But they planted (at least the Papagos) their corn and cotton near the arroyos coming down from the mountains, and lined the beds of these with parapets which could be opened and the water conducted on the fields at every summer rain. This fully explains the acequias on the Rio Gila and at Gilson's. Mr. Walker says that the Pimas have a tradition that Civano had many women, all with handsome carrying-baskets. They have some turquoises, but use also green copper ore as ornaments. They make sacrifices in caves, and at times do not eat salt.[307] There are a few gentes, such as the Buzzard, "*Ni-ŭĕ*," "*Ni-ŭe-uöm-ŏ-qăr*." "*Uöm-ŏ-qăr*" dervied from "*ŭöm*," together, means a cousin, that is, offsprings of *two sisters!* Also the Coyote "*Pan*." This is the clan in full blast with descent in the female line.[308] About the secret clusters, '*Say-tyo-qap*" or medicine men are said to be fully organized. They hold secret meetings in the mountains at night. The "*Maqi*," or prophets, are the diviners, and are called upon to foretell issues of campaigns—they are like the "Ko-Ko" of Zuñi.[309]

The prophet, or a medicine man, as a substitute, always goes along. When at night the circle is formed with the fire in the center, the chief sits facing the fire and the direction whither they are going.* Then the master of ceremonies begins with the chant in a low measured tone, and after a while a warrior of promise places himself with his back to the chief and repeats the "*Savan-yo-qap*," an ancient song in archaic language. (Every male person is called upon as a warrior.) They had a central war chief, now dead. Also a civil chief "*Qo-e*" who settles all matters, civil and military, and the war chief was his assistant or minister. That civil chief also has military functions. The chieftaincy is so far hereditary, as his son, if capable and willing, succeeds mostly. But the old chief can select his successor, or rather deference is paid to his choice. At the war circle, after singing the songs, with responses, the chief speaks upon the campaign, etc., then calls upon the diviner to foretell. Everyone salutes him after [according to] the degree of relationship, and the prophet answers. Then he is saluted again. This is a common custom, to salute on and after the speech or transaction.

JUNE 23: Chiefs are elected by popular vote, but preference given to descendants of former chiefs.[310] Nearly every village has a council house, "tyĭ-in-qi." House of council. It is properly "House of Speech." A loud call or talk is called "Amoq," and as they have public criers they call him "Amoq-ö-tám." These criers publish [announce] everything in the morning, and everything is exactly as among the Pueblos. The Pimas claim none of the stone ruins proper. Fort McDowell, "O-ot-qom-vatqi" "Gravelly Ruin." There are men who are appointed to take care of the caves where they make sacrifices and preserve relics. This is among all the tribes. The acequia nearest the Casa Grande has been taken out about seven miles from Florence, east, or up the Gila. Know nothing about the upper Gila. The Pimas say that "Ci-ho," who survived the flood, was of small stature. There was an eagle who came into the pueblos and, assuming the form of an old woman, stole women and children. He stole a girl and made his wife of her. Ci-ho went to the bottom of the cliff where the eagle dwells, but it was inaccessible, until the girl cried down how to climb by means of a ladder made of sangrantado. The eagle was absent, and he [Ci-ho] changed himself into various forms until he finally got a shape which suited him. When the eagle came back, Ci-ho slew him with a sword, resurrected some of the bodies which were not putrified, and returned the girl home. At the time of Ci-ho, they already occupied the ruins, but they were built after the flood. Civano came long after. The Ancients are called by them "vi-pi-sets" great-grandparents (vi-cor, great grandmother!) also "ho-hoc-om," [Hohokam][311] the extinct ones ("ho-hoc," cosa acabada).

The Pima assert that the little plots of ground-like corrales which are so common in the ruins and always connected with the small houses after the [as at?] Tule and south of San Juan, were garden plots, fenced in or at least enclosed as if by curbstones, and that they were worked with shovels or spades made of Palo de fierro. Previously Mr. Walker had told me that the Pimas declared the isolated, scattered squares to be garden plots.

Went to the Casa Grande at 2 P.M. Measured the outskirts of the Casa Grande by stepping. They are shapeless mounds and breastwork-like dams or walls. Much pottery, painted also. Among it I found one piece—brown, painted black-and-white, as at Fort Apache and at Show-Low. The proper name for the Mazatzal Mountains is "Mas-a-sar." It is a Pima word. In the center of the tank there is a very large mesquite. The Apaches, they call "O-op." The Pimas are brave, and were inveterate enemies of the Apaches until six or seven years ago, when, the first Pimas went over there to trade with them. Horses for blankets, etc. The Apaches held a council as many were in favor of killing the Pimas. So they were finally escorted out of the reservation. Since that time occasional tradings take place.[312] The moths are exceedingly troublesome at night. Some musquitos [sic].

The Pimas have no knowledge of the Zuñi! There are ruins on the San Pedro. At the ruin between here and Zacaton a number of stone axes were dug out. Saw a piece of obsidian at the ruins today. It looks as if there had been a broken outer circumvallation around the main group of the Casa Grande proper. Last night I wrote to Joe, to Capt. Dougherty and to Dr. Mathews. The Pimas claim to have, with their settlements, reached as far as the Superstition Mountains. They call them "Qu-got," crooked. Mas-a-sar signifies the plain forks, from "Mas," plain, and "Sar," fork. Evidently an account [?] of the Four Peaks. The place where Ci-ho killed the eagle is not known. Neither is it known [where? or when?] the southern Pimas separated from the northern stock. But they positively assert that they were created here, and that the separation took place while their forefathers still inhabited these ruins.*

JUNE 24: Judge Walker asserts that there are no ruins beyond Gila Bend (west) and that the last ones there are fortifications only. Also speaks of walls closing the canyon at the Wheatfields, but hints that these might possibly be Apache. The Tontos may have made pottery.[313] The Pinal [Pinole] affair [was] an unjustifiable massacre by Woolsey.[314] Distance travelled till today: 1802 miles, of which Chico has made 1130. He is very well.

Spiders begin to appear at night, but up to this time I have not met a rattlesnake nor a mygah [gila monster?], centipedes nor scorpion. Have now, up to date, measured on this trip, 39 ruins in New Mexico, and 71 in Arizona, or 110 in all. In 1880, I measured 25; in 1882, 20, all in New Mexico, making a total of 84 in New Mexico and 71 in Arizona, or 155. To this should be added in Mexico, 11, or 166 ruins in three years. I believe that this is a fair work.[315] But do not let me become proud. I may fall at any moment. It is *His* work, and not mine. Thanks to Him for the power! Wrote cards to Barthelmess and to Kirchner. "*Styucson*" means Black Creek, or Spring. "*Oil-i-son*" (Arizona) means Little Creek, or Spring. Wrote a short letter to Mr. Parkman. Still we started for Florence about 10 A.M.

The distance is nine miles in the flat and sandy river bottom, or rather mostly over the edge of the first tier of foothills. They are, as usual, very gravelly. There is rather a conspicuous growth of mesquite and of the usual shrubs, etc. We crossed some old acequias, very deep in part, which have evidently been carried along the edge of the foothills. One of these acequias is said to pass north of Casa Grande, between it and the Rio Gila, thus leaving the ruin outside of the curve. These acequias show no lining at all.

Florence itself is near the Gila (south bank), almost in the bottom, on a sandy, hot, spot. Its population is about 800 to 1000. Houses mostly adobe, and the people did not strike me very favorably. Both the American and the Mexican parts of it do not look well. Still, I may have been predisposed against their looks, and therefore prejudiced.

Returning, we passed the ruins. Some walls have been excavated. They are of the same material as those of the Casa Grande, concrete, and 0.60 [meter?] thick. They show plainly that these kinds of mounds are but walls crumbled in, and if there is an artificial basis [prepared base], it is impossible to detect except through digging.* Pottery as usual. Stone axes were dug out of this ruin some time ago. About three miles southwest of it, a tank is found. It is well-preserved. West of it another group shows a distinct platform supporting a mound, part of which, at least, is formed by decayed walls, evidently. The whole ruin appears like a parallel to the "Casa Blanca" mounds. Still another group lies 268 steps north-northeast of these. All in a plain covered with mesquite, etc., no high trees, only brush and shrubs. It contains standing walls, very similar to those in the southwest corner of the court around the Casa Grande. Walls only 0.60 [meter?] thick. The tank lies 170 steps southeast from the last-mentioned group. These units form one group together. Pottery as usual.

We returned about 5 P.M., it being still exceedingly hot, though fine otherwise. Mr. Walker spoke to me extensively about the traditions of the Pimas concerning the Casa Blanca. They say that the Pueblos about Zacaton, after the Casa Grande had been captured and destroyed by irruptions from the east, made war upon the Casa Blanca, surrounding it with a hedge of brush, which afterwards, through the efforts of the medicine men, became transformed into live snakes. The tradition appears plainly as of an intertribal war. He also stated that the Pimas go out to the mountains for an occasional dance, that they have medicine baskets. The latter are adorned with feathers. They are baskets, not pottery.

JUNE 25: Left at 6 A.M. Rode 25 miles almost due south to the Picacho. About three miles north of the rancho of Manuel Ramirez there are some very old mounds, and an immense elliptical tank, partly broken down. This shows that these tanks, which are scattered over these arid plains, are not isolated, but always more or less in connection with ancient settlements. At the Picacho, the thermometer stood at 116° F in the shade. Mr. Walker had told me, previously, that the Papagos of today use such tanks in the Maricopa district. Chico is swollen, and so I took steps to ship him to Tucson. The country is horribly dry and shadeless, completely flat, with parched and rugged mountains along the horizon. The Picacho itself is a bold, steep promontory, and between it and a high chain to the north of it runs the railroad. I was told that there are other ruins, not far away, similar to those which I had seen. Slept at the rancho.

JUNE 26: Left by rail at 8 A.M. Chico was quite unruly at first, and very much afraid. Reached Tucson at 10 A.M. The country level, vegetation is the same [as that to the west]. Kind reception everywhere. Found a letter from Papa. Bishop Salpointe not here. Padre Antonio [Jouvenceau][316] told me that there are ruins on the Rio San Pedro, on the Arivaypa, and near Fort Lowell.[317] Sister [Maria] Euphrasia[318] directed me to Mrs. Black, 134 Stone Avenue, where I got a very good room.

JULY

JUNE 27 TO JULY 4: On the 1st of July I brought my horse over to Fort Lowell, turning it over to Dr. J. B. Girard.[319] It will thus not cost me anything at all. Tucson lies in an absolute plain, surrounded at some distance, by the usual barren and dreary ranges. Its present population does not reach 10,000 souls. There is a great deal of noise made, but on the whole, very little foundation for it. Left Tucson 4th of July and reached Deming at 6 P.M. It is, with the exception of the Rio San Pedro country, a desolate spot. (Scene of Apache massacres.) There is a good deal of mirage, vast expanses appeared as lakes, where there is no water at all around. Lordsburg is a wretched, miserable nest in a sandy, dreary, level, plain.

JULY 4 TO JULY 13: Reached Albuquerque at 4 A.M. on the 5th of July. Found Willie [Borchert] unwell, but Pauline and Annie [Borchert], etc., all right. Saw Eddy.[320] Always the same. Arrived at Santa Fe on the 6th of July. Reception overflowing in every respect. Frank Cushing here, and everybody else.[321] On the 7th Pauline came with Clara Huning[322] and Willie. I left Santa Fe on the 10th, A.M., with Messrs. Dr. Cushing and Gov. Sheldon.[323] Remained at Topeka on the 12th till 3 P.M. and arrived at home on the 13th at 9 A.M. Everybody well and happy, thank God. Joe looks happy and so does Papa, and I am so happy and joyful to see them again. Thank God a thousand times![324]

JULY 22: The 20th and 21st were devoted to the detestable affair with Gruaz.[325] I corresponded some, meanwhile. Got a letter from Mr. Parkman, from Dr. Eggert, Dr. Brühl,[326] and a card from George [Hoffmann].

At Santa Fe, Cushing told me that, on his trip south, to the Escudilla, he found ruins which, from the description, would be large-house pueblos, with the other type also represented, and that he met with what he calls a "cemetery." He also states that the traditions of the Zuñi reach [embrace the area] as far south as the foothills of the Escudilla, and that the Zuñi showed him an old historical painting on hide, which embodies their migrations. He made a facsimile of it.

I had a few callers, and made many calls myself. Today I am a little less lazy. Spent the evening on the farm.

JULY 23: Wrote at my report. It was awfully sultry in the afternoon, but towards evening it cooled off. Dr. Raab[327] spent the evening with me.

JULY 24: Got a card from Mrs. Morgan. Very reassuring and kind. Also translations from Dr. Eggert. Worked at my report, but am making very little headway as yet. It is dullness and laziness combined on my part, which prevents me from doing much.

JULY 25: Letters from Parkman and Mrs. E. L. Cushing.[328] Quiet morning. Wrote slowly, because I am extremely lazy and hardly fit to work. Shall try to evade going to Edwardsville if possible.

JULY 26 AND 27: I endeavored to escape going to the county seat, but it was of no avail. Had to go, for nothing! Called on Mr. E. M. West,[329] and dined with Mr. Bradshaw.[330] G[ruaz?] had for witnesses, George Roth,[331] and Kieburtz. He himself testified, the usual way. Must go back to Edwardsville on Monday.

[JULY 28-AUGUST 2: No journal entries found.]

AUGUST

AUGUST 3: Sunday stayed at home. On the 30th (Monday) went to Edwardsville. For nothing at all, because Metcalf[332] had gone. Had a long talk with B. E. Hoffmann,[333] and dined with Mr. West. Nothing new. At night [C. H.] Seybt[334] called for that note, and he settled matters very pleasantly so far. On the 31st and 1st of August I was busy writing to Boston about my publications. It [delays or problems in publication] is an outrage which must be stopped.[335] Got my Mexican drawings back on the 2d inst. This is very significant at all events. I received notification from Bohn[336] about a pretended overdraft. This is another outrage. I went down to Seybt and he proposed for us to meet here for the purpose. On the 2d wrote to Hospes,[337] to Bohn, to Parkman, to Greenleaf,[338] and to Mrs. Morgan. Received a letter from Hoffmann and one from Parkman on the 3d. Wrote and mailed letters on that day to Dr. J. B. Girard, Fort Lowell, to Bishop Salpointe, to Mrs. Black, Sister Euphrasia, and to Dr. B. M. Thomas.

AUGUST 4: Wrote to Padre Ribera and mailed letter. Returned contract or lease of Gruaz to A. T. Vallotton,[339] dated 28 April 1874, to F. A. Gleyre and Co., to Jacob Brunnschweiler.[340] He was at the machineshop of the foundry and busy. So I laid it on the lathe. Afterwards went to Blattner[341] and to Dr. Knoebel.[342] In the evening Seybt returned the note to me. I saw Vallotton, and he is willing to testify. At night Fritz[343] came and staid with us awhile.

AUGUST 5: Attempted to paint. Vallotton came, and he talked long about the foundry business. He is willing to testify that the business was in good condition when he left it, that it would have brought 5 to 6,000 dollars on forced sale, and that there were two lathes. While he was here two letters came, one from Dr. Mathews and another from Consul Gerlich. Very friendly both. The afternoon I spent on the farm, calling at E. Haller's with Joe for a short while. Wrote to Consul Gerlich at night and mailed letter. Mali's[344] birthday today. She is 33 years old.

AUGUST 6: Today I am 43! Wrote and mailed to [Don Joaquín García] Icazbalceta.[345] Got a letter, but nothing of importance. At night Joe had one of her attacks of faintness. Very violent, so that I got Dr. Mohr,[346] who pronounced it not dangerous. Thank God.

AUGUST 7: Joe well again though very feeble. Commenced work at the office this A.M. Fritz leaving for Dubuque today. Got letter from Dr. Gerlich and replied to him, arranging for Sunday next. Wrote to B. E. Hoffmann today.

AUGUST 8: Sent off a note to Icazbalceta and received a letter from Frank Cushing with $100 draft in it. Very, very kind expressions. Those good people out west compensate somewhat for the disagreeable things here, although I ought not to complain. God is always very good to me in every way. But I am lazy and hardly good for anything. Wrote but very little at my report.

AUGUST 9: Got a letter from Dr. Gerlich stating he could not come on Sunday next. I also got a very pleasant letter from Mrs. Morgan. Mr. Hadley called on me this morning. Wrote considerably.

AUGUST 10: Mr. Balsiger[347] called on me in the afternoon. Wrote much. At night we called on Mrs. Speckart[348] accidentally; it was beautiful moonlight. Small fire at the foundry in the afternoon.

AUGUST 11: Joe received a good letter from Celia Hoffmann;[348a] she is well again. At night I finished my report, 76 pages in all.[349]

AUGUST 12: All the women folks going to church. I wrote to John R. Freeze at [Fort] McDowell, stating hopelessness of the case. At 6 P.M. walked out on the farm and although it sprinkled, spent the evening very nicely, telling the folklore story of the "Poor Boy of Pina-ua." Returned at 9 P.M. Night very quiet, cloudy and pleasant. "Neutral tint" is an excellent paint. Wind northeast.

AUGUST 13: Wrote to Frank Cushing at last enclosing Joe's photograph. The whole day rather dull and cool. Spent the evening at Bernays'.[350]

AUGUST 14: Letter from Eddy, and one from Kirchner. Wrote and mailed letter to Judge Walker of Casa Grande, Arizona. At night, meeting at last about the coal mine. I cannot see how I should owe them anything, but to preserve peace, I agreed to give my note to Mr. Springer for $422.10 due 14th of May 1884, and with 7% interest. In case of a sale of the mine before that date, then this note becomes payable also out of the proceeds. Bohn surrendered his interest in the mine, and we promised to surrender his bond upon return of notes. Thank God for it; that much is over at last. The mine will be sold now.

AUGUST 15: Wrote to Atty. Springer, enclosing note for $422.10, and also to David Miller and to José Olivas at Santa Fe. In the afternoon I slept and when I awoke the sky was beautiful. No letters. At night wrote and went down to Bernays'.

AUGUST 16: At the office, J. Wildi[351] made a proposition for the wool-factory building.[352] I painted some, copied Dr. Joe Bernays'[353] "Das Römische Staatsrecht" which contains many very important points that connect with aborigines and began to write to Geo. Pradt. At night went to Uncle Kinne's.[354] Night hazy and sultry, afterwards cool.

AUGUST 17: Mails late. Wrote to Mr. Parkman enclosing sheets #1 to #5, inclusive, of my report and stating that I was copying the remainder for my use. Finished letter to Pradt and mailed it. There is much talk in town about the wool factory. Let them buy it, that's all! Got a short line from Springer. In the afternoon came the terrible news of the suicide of Louise Vulliet![355] It took place yesterday afternoon. Awful! At night Dr. Mohr and old Widmer[356] called.

AUGUST 18: Papa's birthday! Wrote to A. W. Metcalf and to E. C. Springer at Edwardsville. Got a letter from Springer with blanks. Am not worth anything for work. Funeral of Louise Vulliet at 4 P.M. Scandalous and insulting talk by the preachers Wallace[357] and Fiegenbaum,[358] and finally by Vulliet[359] himself. It is a shame, they are mere raving fanatics. Everybody was utterly disgusted. Spent the evening very pleasantly on the farm with Papa. I told the rest of the story of "The Poor Boy of Pina-ua."

AUGUST 19: Got a long letter from Mr. Parkman. Friendly but very serious. It is important in many respects, but he does not see the point. Sat down at once to write to him. Wrote nine pages and mailed the same day. Charles, Bertha, and Rosalie[360] spent the afternoon with us.

AUGUST 20: Received a letter from Sister Maria Euphrasia in Tucson. Painted with better success than before. Sent two more sheets to Dr. Eggert. Wrote for the "Ausland," at night, till 10 P.M.

AUGUST 21: Painted in the morning. Got a letter from Dr. Gerlich, and the terrible news about the deaths of Fernandez, of Manuel B. Otero, and of Whitney.[361] Fearful tragedy. Wrote to Dr. Eggert at once about the sad affair. Wrote to Collet, inviting him, Hilder, and Conant[362] for next Sunday. Evening fine so far, wrote at the letter to the "Ausland." Aunt B. A. Suppiger[363] died quietly today.

AUGUST 22: No letters. At noon news came of a supposed suicide of young woman Vogel, and finally about 3 P.M. the terrible news of the suicide of Robert Suppiger.[364] This is the most awful thing of all. Unfortunate Mary! No clue to the tragedy as yet. The suicide of young Mrs. Vogel is not confirmed. Informed George [Hoffmann][364a] of the terrible news, by letter.

AUGUST 23: Funeral of Aunt B. A. Suppiger. John Cavin committed suicide by hanging. Got a letter from Dr. Girard. Chico is well. Also got a letter from Collet. He will be here next Sunday. About poor Robert Suppiger, terrible developments loom up. It appears he is completely ruined, and may have taken along Mrs. H. and C. G. H. too! His father too is largely involved. How much is not known. Evening quiet. Wrote to Dr. Mathews and mailed letter tonight. Am sad and almost sick. Called on Mary, poor Mary; on old Bernard Suppiger; and on Uncle B. A. Suppiger.[365] What a difference!

AUGUST 24: Received a long letter from Padre Ribera; from Hilder,[366] a postal card. At 10 A.M. George [Hoffmann] came from St. Louis! Funeral very crowded. Over 175 people. Went with George and Emma. Short, by the [fraternal] lodges, but very decent. Afternoon on the farm with George, who left at 7 P.M. again. Began to write my novel (?).[367]

AUGUST 25: Got a letter from Metcalf. Mailed to Mr. Parkman sheets #6, 7, 8, 9, 10. Registered. Wrote nearly all day. It is delightful. At night Lizzie and Henry[368] came.

AUGUST 26: Collet and Hilder came. Letter from Frank Cushing. Wrote to Mr. Parkman, and to Frank Cushing, at night. The Missouri Historical Society proposes to publish my report, if the Institute permits it.

AUGUST 27: Got a terrible letter from Mr. Parkman. It completely upset me. I replied to him at once and remained more or less prostrate. It is incomprehensible.

AUGUST 28: Prostrate most of the time. Wrote two letters to E. H. Greenleaf. Received the manuscript of last year. Sent my drawings to Boston. Got Mrs. Cushing's photograph. Sunday quiet. Mr. Wilborn[369] called on me. But I am almost unfit for literary work. Worked hard at the office.

SEPTEMBER

SEPTEMBER 6: On the 3rd I went to St. Louis with Charles. His left eye was taken by Dr. Alt[370] at the "Pius Hospital." Operation very successful. At home, I found a comforting letter from Mr. Parkman. My back, however, became exceedingly sore, so much so that I could hardly walk and sit at all. Dr. Mohr treated me with morphine to little avail. St. Jacob's Oil proved after all the best. It began to improve only today. I received another very friendly letter from Greenleaf, and at the same time I forwarded to Mr. Parkman sheets #11, 12, 13, 14, and 15 of my report. John Neudecker, of Marion, committed suicide by shooting, today at 3 A.M. Horrible. Physical pain seems to have been the cause of it. On the 5th wrote cards to Dr. Eggert and to the Padrecito [probably Ribera]. On the 4th, a letter to Gov. Ritch. Today a letter to Greenleaf. Began a letter to Mrs. Morgan.

SEPTEMBER 7: I painted. At noon Papa did his best to start a fuss, but I avoided it as best I could. He insists upon that inventory being made at once, regardless of the fact that I cannot decently speak about it. Got a letter from Icazbalceta. Good. At night I had a long talk with Morris, and a very satisfactory one at that. Resolved to fix it tomorrow.

SEPTEMBER 8: Fixed up the inventory, and then agreed upon a plan of action principally in regard to real estate. Painted in the afternoon and slept a little while. It is of great relief to me to know how matters stand at the office, and as it is, I can do my duty towards the Institute and still be of service to the others. I trust that Papa will see it in the proper light now. A. Pagan[371] called.

SEPTEMBER 9: Dr. Knoebel called rather early in the morning, so that I could not do much work. In the afternoon I went out to the farm. At night wrote to Greenleaf again. Began letter to Dr. Bastian.[372]

SEPTEMBER 10: Wrote to Dr. Bastian. At night Henry came; the marriage is nearing. I painted with fair success.

SEPTEMBER 11: Botheration of the wedding begins. License, etc., etc. Mailed letter to Dr. Bastian. Wrote to Frank S. Bigler, but could not finish the letter. Ida Becker[373] came.

SEPTEMBER 12: Gustav[374] came. Much trouble and bustle in the house. Not less than six women in the kitchen. Mailed letter to Frank Bigler. Wrote to A. W. Metcalfe [Metcalf]. J. Donne came at night. Rehearsal! Tomorrow the "love-feast" begins. Seybt excused himself.

SEPTEMBER 13: Had to get up at 5:30 A.M. The trains (freight trains) going west, collided in the bottom of Silver Creek, thus delaying the passengers. The latter came up one hour behind time. August and Emily Becker,[374a] George and Cilla Hoffmann, Mr. and Mrs. Henry Hesse[374b] came. Very happy, but also exceedingly busy day. At night, all the St. Louis people left except Emily and Ida Becker, and Gustav.

SEPTEMBER 14: Everybody tired. Rest of the wedding. At 4 P.M. the old folks left all. Evening pleasant, but all very tired.

SEPTEMBER 15: Lizzie and Henry departed for their new home with Emily Becker. The house looks quite empty. Joe is tolerably well, but very, very tired. Am slowly returning to a normal state.

SEPTEMBER 16: Ed Leyh, and Dr. Kinner[375] came from St. Louis. Spent a pleasant Sunday all together. Dr. Mohr ate dinner with us, and Mr. V. Pfleger[376] took coffee. Dr. Kinner spoke beautifully about the geysers.

SEPTEMBER 17: Left for Greenville at 9 A.M. on horseback. . . . At Millersburg[377] met P. Streif's [Streiff's] son,[378] but he himself was not at home. At Greenville saw Judge Henry[379] and could easily arrange everything with him.

SEPTEMBER 18: Returned from Greenville again, via Millersburg, but Streif was not there. At home, I found a letter from Cushing. Everybody well at home so far.

OCTOBER

OCTOBER 9: I shall sum up as follows. On the 25th of September I went to Caseyville and spent the day with J. R. Miller,[380] examining the land and talking about it. In the evening I delivered a lecture before the Missouri Historical Society at the Polytechnic Hall [St. Louis].[381] [Here only notes on the weather and casual visits were made for several days.] Am unwell and rather desponding. No help from anywhere is to be expected at all. I must help myself, but only with God's help, otherwise not. Quite a correspondence went on in the meantime. Letters from Mr. Parkman, from Cushing, Mrs. Morgan, went back and forth. Kirchner sent me a set of photographic views, very handsome ones. Letters from Dr. Girard also. Wrote and mailed letters today to E. C. Springer, Edwardsville; Mr. Parkman; and to C. F. Kirchner, at Fort Apache.

OCTOBER 10: Painted all day. No letters, except for Papa, one from Mrs. Brossard. At night wrote to Capt. Dougherty, but did not finish my letter.

OCTOBER 11: Painted all day. Got a hopeful letter from E. C. Springer and a card from Greenleaf also. Replied to Springer. Were it not for the coal mine I might leave with a comparatively easy mind. Wrote and mailed to Capt Dougherty. Evening at Mary's.

OCTOBER 12: Letter from Henry. Preparing to leave. Wrote to the Ausland,[382] but did not finish the letter. The afternoon was spent pleasantly at Graffenried's and Wachsmuth's.[383] Only too pleasantly perhaps. I had altogether too much wine.

OCTOBER 13: Packed up. Spent afternoon at J. Schule's.[384] Night at Bertha's.

OCTOBER 14: Afternoon on the farm; evening at Seybt and Fritz. Everything ready so far.

OCTOBER 15: Made calls all forenoon. Left at 3:55 P.M. with Joe. Poor Papa. Arrived at the city, where George [Hoffmann] waited for us. All well at St. Louis.

OCTOBER 16: Went down town early and met Vallotton. He is ready. Then went to Ellison, and did not find him. Afterwards to Collett. Then back to meet Charley, with whom I went to Dr. Alt and again to Ellison without meeting him. So after leaving Charley, I wrote to Metcalfe requesting him to come over on Friday. Thence to George Engelmann,[385] recently ret'd [returned, or perhaps retired], and afterwards home. Letter from Bastian.

OCTOBER 17: Went down town again. Met Vallotton and looked for Ellison twice in vain, until at last, at 3 P.M. I met him at his shop. He leaves for southern Missouri but will come to Edwardsville next week if called upon. At Collet's, letter from Greenleaf with letters of recommendation to Generals MacKenzie[386] and Crook. At night went to Frank Horn's. Big supper. Cards from Greenleaf. Called at Consulate.

OCTOBER 18: Staid at home all day. Wrote to Parkman, to Greenleaf, to Mrs. Morgan, and to Mrs. Cushing. At night letter from Papa. All O.K. at home.

OCTOBER 19: Went down town. Saw Mathey about shell-beads. No letter. Yesterday, as no letter came, I concluded to write to Metcalf. Did it this A.M. and also wrote to General Crook and to Greenleaf. In the afternoon went to Bernays'[387] and got the $20, to Pretorious, to Mrs. Ryhiner,[388] to Hilder, and finally to Engelmann. Found telegram telling me that Metcalf and Blattner would be down tomorrow. This is unconceivable. Am very mad. Why could they not say so before? Wrote card to E. C. Springer.

OCTOBER 20: Met Metcalf at the Planter's House. Everything amply explained. Took no depositions, but arranged for Ellison and Vallotton to go to Edwardsville next Saturday 27th inst. All day with Henry. Dear good boy. Night at home. Saw old Dr. G. Engelmann. Got map from Boston.

OCTOBER 21: Joe sick in bed with headache. But thanks to Flower of Orange Water, it soon began to improve. Wrote cards to Ellison and Dr. Kinner, and sent my photograph to Ordwin [?]. Joe feeling slightly better, we went to August's at noon, George and I. Returned at 4 P.M. Joe was much better, but I concluded to leave tomorrow at 9:20 A.M. Spent a pleasant evening with the folks. August and Emily Becker, and Emilia Horn were here, also Streiff for awhile! After all had left, we drank to the health of Annie Borchert, it being her birthday.

OCTOBER 22: Left at 9:20 A.M. by Missouri Pacific. Joe is well again, and the taking-leave and separation, though painful, of course, is not as severe this time as formerly it used to be. In the car I met four Indian boys, just returning from school at "Hampton Roads." One of them, Pablo Rios, is a Papago from San Javier del Bac [present-day San Xavier del Bac]. His father is Ascensio Rios. Another, Frank Chisholm, is son of a Cherokee and of a Creek woman from near Shawneetown, Indian Territory. Another is also a Creek half-breed, and the fourth one, a Sac-and-Fox. Frank Chisholm is a lively boy and good looking. He goes after his mother, and regards himself to be a Creek Indian. He says the chiefs do not signify much. They have medicine men, also old women, but he does not attach to them any importance beyond their being "doctors." They believe in witchcraft. He says that, before he went to school, he seldom looked at an owl without thinking it was a witch. The same with the turkey buzzard. They have their dances, "stamping," with the drum; they paint themselves. (The Papagos also have their dances, but they do not paint nor dress, and they use the guitar and the big drum.) Frank tells me that they name the children, but without ceremony? Marriage commonly by robbery or by purchase. If the wife does not like him, she simply leaves him, and the "purchase money" is lost. They live mostly in log houses; some are of frame. Raise litle wheat, mostly corn, grass, and cattle. They make a beverage from crushed corn and water, called "Saf-gi" which is exceedingly refreshing. The boys left at Sedalia, except Pablo, who came with me to Topeka, where we arrived at 1 A.M. The Indian Territory is said to be a fine country, fertile, with springs and wells. Plenty of game, but no buffalo.

OCTOBER 23: Called at the A. T. and S. F. Office. Very kind, but I could not do anything in regard to the woolen mill. Wrote to Morris, to Joe (enclosing draft for $100), to Papa. At Popperdicks, there is a

magnificent marine oil painting by De Haas.[389] Got my pass extended to
30 November. The country to Jefferson City is exceedingly broken
and densely wooded. Beyond it is a fertile rolling prairie, with strips
and groves of timber. There is much more timber, however, than about
Highland. Wrote to Hospes also. On the train I met Col. Savage,[390]
manager of the coal mines of the A. T. and S. F. R. R., principally at
Raton. He told me that the coal is bituminous, not anthracitic. He
also assured me that there were no traces of pueblos around, nor even
spaces where pottery is found, but that in a crevice, about five miles
from Raton, they found an Indian pot or bowl, possibly recent, which
contained some water. It had been placed there, and then the crevice
was filled up with earth and rubbish.

On the train there were Lieut. Cruse[391] of Fort Lowell, and Lieut.
C. P. Elliott[392] of Fort Cummings.[393] The latter says that there are no
traces of ruins about that place.

OCTOBER 24: Fine view of Pike's Peak after we left Las Animas. It
came in sight again after we left La Junta. Heavily covered with snow.
Beyond La Junta sandy deserts appear, and as we proceed to the south,
small specimens of *Opuntia arborescens* turn up. Three ranges of mountains loom up in the west successively from north to south: The
"Cuerno Verde" southeast also covered with snow.* The "Trinchera"
very distant, and partly covered by a low range in front of it. There is
no snow on the lower and nearer range, and the main mountains are too
far away.* Finally the "Spanish Peaks" or "Huajatoyas." These are
exceedingly prominent and stately objects. There is snow on them
plainly visible. They are to be seen until we reach Trinidad, where they
disappear behind the cliffs of carboniferous sandstone. Trinidad lies in
a valley at the western foot of Fishers Peak. The Picket Wire River
runs by to the north, joining the Arkansas. Fishers Peak is the western
end of a long mesa running about east and west.* The *top* of the mesa
is *lava*, the bulk is carboniferous. Reached Raton at 8 P.M.

OCTOBER 25: Reached Santa Fe at 6 A.M. Went to breakfast with
Father Eguillon and then to the Exchange Hotel. Saw a great many
people; all very friendly. But the place is dead. Got from Jake Gold[394] a
little tambourine, recently made to order by the Indians of Tesuque
(called "*També*"). Began to paint it. Called at Brown's by invitation.
Also began to write to Joe, but was disturbed by Willison.[395] He told me
of another ruin; at the "Cañada del Pueblo," seven miles east of San

Marcos, and 16 miles from Santa Fe south. Large-building type, but now reduced to mere mounds, forming square with plaza. He also told me of three ruins about Silver City; one of which is in the town itself. Nothing definite about the shape and size.

OCTOBER 26: Painted at the tambourine. Jake Gold has two unpainted vessels from the caves of San Ildefonso, with plastic [appliqué] decorations representing snakes. They are simply black. The Indians of Santa Clara make today black vessels with indentations of a plastic nature, grooves and channels for decorative purposes. The wool factory business fairly started.

OCTOBER 27: Finished painting the tambourine in the afternoon, and returned it to Jake Gold at once. Saw Aaron Gold,[396] who requested me to look at his documents the next day. Took supper at Reed's.[397] After supper I went home to read, but was again delayed by calls. It is next to a bother, although well-meant and very friendly.

OCTOBER 28: Called on the Archbishop [J. B. Lamy],[398] on Mr. Farini,[399] on Major Blake.[400] The latter and his wife gave me many details about the pueblo of the "Nogal," on the northern spur of the Sierra Blanca. From their description it looks as if it was a compact house, communal type, pueblo. The cells are small, and the walls appear to have been of stone and mud, and thin. Pottery, black-on-white, or gray, and on red also. Few corrugated pieces. Asked about glossy pottery, but the reply was rather unsatisfactory. Mr. and Mrs. Blake both particularly insisted upon the existence of an old river bed, visible for 15 miles yet, very broad, on the east bank of which the pueblo of the Nogal was situated. He presumed that a large river, as wide as the Rio Grande, once ran past there, and that the upheaval of the malpaís south and southeast of the Chupadero had interrupted the course of that river, causing it to dry completely. They also say that the Mexicans have a tradition to that effect. All this is very doubtful though, but deserves to be noted carefully. There may be something in it withal. There is no permanent water except an occasional spring, but the arroyos run into the plains and flood them after every thunderstorm, just as they do in Arizona. Called round to say good-bye.

OCTOBER 29: Left Santa Fe at 3:40 A.M. Met Mariano Otero,[401] Jesús and Pedro Perea,[402] and Father Parisis[403] on the train. At Albuquerque saw the folks. Mailed letter to Joe, cards to Woodside and to Frank Cushing. Concluded not to go to Zuñi. Stevenson[404] here (Monday).

OCTOBER 30: (Tuesday) Wrote to Morris. Day was spent calling around. Concluded to go to Isleta with Pauline and Clara Huning. Not much lost and may be of some value. Eddy here all evening.

OCTOBER 31: Reached Isleta at 9:30 A.M. and went to Tondre's. Called at Jesús Chavez and at the Padre's [Peyron]. The latter not at home. Then visited the pueblo with the girls. The rooms are mostly larger than at the other pueblos, and much cleaner and nicer. They are preparing for the day of "Los Muertos," baking very good cakes, etc. These cakes are presented to the Church, and then the priest sells them back again to the people. Could not obtain any other information except that they came from the north along the Rio Grande, and that Chililí, Tajique, and Cuaray were Tigua Pueblos. About San Pedro they know nothing. There is a tale that, when the Piros left their villages below they came up to the Ojo del Coyote and upon leaving, they left an olla upon the fire with water in it and that this is the origin of the hot springs there. But whither they went is not known.

They say that all the Pueblos came from the north except the Zuñi, who came from the northwest to their place. The Apaches they call "B¢Lo-nin," and the Navajos "De-¢lonin." Had another confirmation of the matter of the "Ojos negros" [Black eyes] and the "Ojos colorados" [Red Eyes] and of their division into white, yellow, red, and blue maize, but could not determine how they were located. Spoke at length about the gentes of other tribes, but could not elicit anything. They denied positively having other clans than those of the corn. There are many Lagunas among them, and it is evident that these have kept their clans and their rites. Some of the Laguna dances are kept very secret.[405]

Of ruins, there are none on the west bank of the Rio Grande, but on the médanos [dunes] south of the Cerro de la Isleta there are at least two, one east and the other east-southeast of the pueblo. They think that these, together with the pueblo on the Mesa de las Padillas, were the original villages of the Isleteños, and that they were originally small, the people congregating into larger pueblos only of late.[406] The Mesa de las Padillas is called "Hyem-tu-ay." Their pottery are red bowls "Bu-ru" and black jars "Pa-bu-ru." "Ba" water; "fa" fire.

NOVEMBER

NOVEMBER 1: The proper name for Isleta is "*She-ui-gu-ba;*" for Sandia, "*Na-fi-a.*" The latter means: "dusty." They call the Mexicans "*¢la-fan.*" Left at 9:40 A.M. and met Román Baca and Don Felipe Chavez[407] on the train. They know nothing of the existence of a pueblo at San Antonio [New Mexico; on the Rio Grande some 75 miles south of Isleta]. Between Belen and La Joya, about the Sabinal, the country looks remarkably arid. Sand drifts are huge, and and the mesa behind Belen continues south interrupted only at the Sabinal by the mouth of the Rio Puerco, perfectly dry and with enormous heaps of drift and sand. This is near La Joya. At Alamillo, cottonwoods cover the river bottom, and thence on they continue to beyond San Marcial, with much more vegetation besides. Although the drift terraces become very heavy at San Antonio, the bottom is generally from a half to two miles wide on the west bank. The east bank is exceedingly bleak and denuded. About Polvadera the bottom disappears as the basal terraces of the Sierra Ladrona are shoved almost to the river front, but Limitar [present-day Lemitar] itself is very handsome.

North of Socorro, the Spaniards were compelled to march on the east bank, as there are two "Angosturas [narrow passes]," one at the "Barro" and the other above. Socorro is always handsome. About San Antonio, a hamlet situated on the drift terrace, with coke works and much coal, the "Sierra Oscura," and the "Soledad" appear. The Black Mesa at San Marcial is a unique object. We had a splendid view of the Magdalena [Mountains] and of the San Mateo [Peak], and then rounding the Black Mesa, entered the Paraje, at the foot of the Sierra Fra Cristóbal. It had rained and rained farther south in the southern half of the Jornada.[408] This latter is an undulating plain, covered with tufts of grama, with chaparro, palo verde as a little shrub, low mesquite and some yucca, only few of which are arborescent. It looks not at all barren. In the northern half, the soil is red and lava protrudes everywhere; the southern half is whitish, marly, and drifty.

The Sierra Fra Cristóbal is barren and frowning; the strata are uplifted remarkably to the northwest presenting this appearance.* The layers are very plainly seen. There are but few trees on the very crests. Slopes naked. The Sierra del Caballo connects with the former. It consists of a few gigantic lumps, one of which had a distinct saddle.* It is, if possible, more barren yet than the Sierra Fra Cristóbal. Between the latter and the Sierra de San Matéo,[409] extensive terraces, clad like the Jornada, slope down to the river, along whose banks álamos continue to be seen. Then broad terraces, farther down, extend into the interior where, through the rain clouds, I could catch a glimpse of the Sierra de los Mimbres. On the east, all was enveloped, else I would have seen the Sierra de San Andrés. Got to Las Cruces at 9 P.M.

NOVEMBER 2: Organos [Organ Mountains] in the east, 12 miles away, very handsome; northwest, the Cerros Narvaez with an old Spanish fort on top and an old Spanish village at the foot. North, the "Roblero."[410] Country level, but handsome. Las Cruces is a little Mexican town of 2,000 inhabitants. It is built Mexican fashion, one-story houses of adobe with a plazita. Church not large and without tower, only a belfry. The bottom is of course sandy, but still exceedingly fertile. Acequias cross it in every direction, and cottonwoods and willows grow in bunches, alleys, lanes , and groves. On the west, there are no mountains, the country slopes down in a broad terrace, at least 50 miles wide from east to west. On the north, besides the "Roblero," there is a distant mountain chain in the northwest, probably the spurs of the Mimbres. In the northeast, the Sierra de San Andrés; in the south, the Sierra del Paso.

I went to see Major Van Patten,[411] and met Capt. Pedregon[412] at the same time. Van Patten is very kind; he offers aid. There are some Piros here. He says that the tribes between here and Encinillas, south of El Paso, are the Piros, Piras, Mansos,[413] Senecús, Tiguas, Tchocoloches ("*Txocolouchque,*" giants, in Nahuatl, or "Tecolotes"??!)— finally the Tarahumares [Tarahumaras].[414] The latter are dark, tall, long black hair, straight, faces round, noses flat; they go almost naked, are gardening in the mountains, and they live south of El Paso towards Chihuahua. Of the Mansos, he speaks as of Pueblo Indians. It is singular that he distinguished between the Piros and Piras. Might not the latter have been the "Tompiras?" They still dance at Christmas, but all these customs are falling into disuse completely. They have no governor, but the "cacique" is often mentioned. They dance to the sound of the tombé! Made pottery. All this preliminary talk is doubtful, of course. But all, as far as I have seen them, assert, that there are no ruins along the river up to San Marcial, none in the Organos, and none west of the Mesilla. There are ruins at "Pa-chi-te-hú," 16 miles northwest from Fort Cummings, at the "Pueblo Encantado" of San Simón.

Still both Van Patten and Pedregon assert that, about 20 miles from this place, east, at the Cañada de las Tinajas ,there are rock-paintings! This would indicate a pueblo! It appears that water is scarce off from the river on both sides. I called on Father Laseigne [Lassaigne].[415] He told me that there was pottery in the Sacramento [Mountains] and on the Rio Hondo. Van Patten asserts that there are ruins towards Janos. The Mansos claim to have lived in the north too!?? Van Patten says that "Ju" is not Apache, and he has heard of the Tabosos and Pananas. There is a place called Toboso about Fort Quitman[416] in Texas. Met Mr. Daniel Fritz of Mesilla. He knows Guadalupe Miranda very well who now lives at Carrizal. The latter, from documents there at Santa Fe (up to 1836), says that Oñate moved up on the east side of the mountains. This is hardly posible, from the "Discurso." Still, it is well to note it. In that case the river would have changed its bed completely, from about 160 miles east of its present place to now. It has grown shallower in the past years; its channel 12 years ago was 18 feet deep; now it is only ten feet, and the old river bed is only a half-mile west of Las Cruces.

The climate has changed within 12 years. Earlier frosts have set in, and the freshets of the river have discontinued, showing a decrease in snows above. The rains have become more frequent in every season. The first crops are usually killed by frosts now. He also states that, since the past few years, a dew falls every night about 8 P.M. which withers everything. (I felt that dew tonight, returning with Major Van Patten.) There is much fever here, which has even been an epidemic among the Indians, but Capt. Pedregon states that this epidemic has been here in former times too occasionally.

I went to Van Patten at dusk and took supper. He says that, while there are pueblos on the southern slope of the Sierra del Sacramento, there are absolutely none in the Sierra de Guadalupe, but that there are in the Sierra Hueca in Texas, at Seven Rivers on the Rio Pecos (opposite the mouth of the Rio Peñasco), and towards the Rio Grande until Fort Quitman, but none east of it. West of the Rio Grande, there are several ruins beyond Chorreros or between the Rio Conchos and the Rio Grande. (This would about agree with the place where Espejo met the Jumanos villages in Chihuahua.) There are also ruins between El Paso and Janos and Presidio Viejo, but none in the timbered regions about Temoseche [Temósachi].

He then spoke of the Piros. They have their clans, and at Christmas night, they knock in crowds at each other's doors, calling the name of the clan, and begging for admission, singing in chorus a Spanish song in low voices. Admission is first refused on the ground that the clan is dead, but finally granted, as his relatives are still alive. They have their dances and many sorceries. He witnessed the feather dance, an act of witchcraft, for which purpose the sorcerers assemble in the estufa (!), a wreath of rushes (cañutilla [cañatilla?]) around their head. Six or seven feathers are made to dance alone, probably by friction. The estufa is a room entered into by a trap door from above. During that dance, they torture, pinch and punch with needles, etc., little dolls made of "corcho" (corkwood), representing the person whom they want to hurt. Compare Navajos! They worship the sun "*Olo*" and the moon "*Orno.*" They go to the housetops at sunrise, a "pregonero" first doing it. Then three men ascend to the belfry, their heads covered with the tilmas. When the sun rises, they uncover the heads and shade the eyes with the hands, the middle man using the right, the others the left hand. Thus they stand immovably gazing, until the shadow falls at their feet, when they turn back and descend. They strew sacred meal sometimes on the gates; they also strew salt (against witches). They keep idols, and *know nothing about Montezuma at all.*[417] It is the sun they are looking at, and not the return of Montezuma! At a certain moon, the girls reaching their maturity make a feast to it, but they are accompanied by four or five old women, and closely watched by the men at a distance, who let nobody approach. At Christmas Eve, they build huge fires in the mountains. On the night of St. John's Day (25 of June) the girls bathe in the acequia and then lie flat on the sand on their faces. An old woman then cuts off two inches from their hair with *an instrument which is not to be sharp.*

The cañutilla, or rush-circle, is a favorite material for witchcraft; they hang it above the main doors and on the corners of the buildings. Every dance begun at their homes at El Paso is also finished in Van Patten's house, since his wife was the daughter of one of their caciques!?? They hate the Apaches mortally and will not believe them under oath. Emilia showed me a beautiful manta (about 150 years old) worn by her mother. It is black, with a gold-trimming below and green embroidery. It is fastened over the left shoulder, and passes under the right arm. The women wear their hair loose; the men have "chungo" and "melotes."

They have plume-sticks, and when they want to know where a certain hidden object, or lost object, lies, they bandage the eyes of a man. He takes the plume-stick, places it on the end of an elastic chip or rod, the plumes upwards, vertically, and then bend the latter down, letting it suddenly go. This hurls the plume-stick upwards into the air, and when it falls, they look for the object in the ground. The same thing is done with a candle.

Mr. Wattlington told me that very large pottery [vessels] had been found at the foot of the Sierra San Andrés, near the Sandy Hill. The sand there is pulverized gypsum. The country east of the Organos is grassy "like the Jornada," but without water. Both Van Patten and Wattlington reject the idea of an ancient river there.

NOVEMBER 3: No letters! This is strange, if anything at all. I painted all day, finishing two sheets, one the Isleta pottery, and the other, the fetishes from Cochiti. Van Patten had promised to get me out in the morning, but he did not come, so I kept to myself all day at work. Frogs are crying like spring. Van Patten, to whom I showed my fetish drawings, recognized them at once and assured me that the Piros had similar ones, but of clay and of wood, and that they also carry them in a little bag of leather over the breast. Met Capt. Salazar today. Wrote and mailed postcards this evening to Joe, to Cushing, to the postmasters at Fort Wingate and at Tucson. Also wrote to García Icazbalceta, and to Fr. Campos. It appears that corn, here, would often give two crops; also apples. Grapes however would not do it. Finally, after mailing my cards, I wrote to the *Ausland* though not very long. The Indians here are completely Mexicanized, but they say that at El Paso they will not intermarry with Mexicans, although they do with other nations, except Negroes, whom they also shun and spurn. Is it the color only?

NOVEMBER 4: Stores closed, but bars open. No letters again. Mailed my two Mexican letters. Met Capt. Pedregon and spoke to him about the pottery. Wrote for the *Ausland*. Called on Father Laseigne and on Mr. Hildreth.[418] In the afternoon, I at last met Alberto Fountain.[419] He is a very good, attractive boy. There was a big funeral; I could not do anything at all, of course, so wrote to Padre Ribera and mailed him the little book. Called on Mr. Carbonnier. Left for El Paso at night. We crossed the pass about 11 P.M. by moonlight.

NOVEMBER 5: Headache. El Paso lies right at the foot of the eastern mountain forming the pass. El Paso del Norte at the foot of the western. In the distant east, the Cerro Hueco looms up. Did not find anybody at home for a long time. The town of El Paso del Norte is a big Indian village, below trees, except the two principal streets, where the houses are connected. The Indians mostly live in the "Barrial," [muddy place]. At 2 P.M. I could at last see the Cura Ramón Ortiz.[420] He told me that all the Indians (Mansos excepted) were transplanted hither in 1681, etc. The Mansos themselves are so mixed with the population that they have given up their nationality and language. Foundation of the church, 1656, Fray Martín de Hinajosa. Origin of the name of Gran Quivira being applied to the present pueblo. An ancestor of his, a Spanish officer, came hither at the beginning of this century, sent by the Spanish government after the Gran Quivira. He looked for it in the northwest and surveyed the Pueblo Bonito, etc.[421] But an old Jumano Indian, Tio [Uncle] Juan Largo, of Socorro, called attention to the present pueblo of Quivira, and thus the name remained. "Ju," "Nané," etc. are Apache "Janeros" and descend from the family of the "Baboso." They are the last of the tribe. Staid at Gallendo finally.

NOVEMBER 6: I walked over and found Nicomedes Lara or [y?] Leyva. He is alone in his house, his people left him; his wife is dead. Very soon became acquainted. He is a Manso! They have now forgotten their language completely and speak only Spanish. But he says that they know they came from the north and that they are Piros. He even says that some of his people (speaking of the Leyva) are at Zuñi! Of course, he began with the fib of Montezuma, but when I told him that I was adopted at Cochiti, he changed tune and interrogated me as to "que era la primera cosa en un Pueblo? [Who was of first importance in a Pueblo?]" When I replied to him it was the cacique, and told him the names in Queres and Zuñi, and told him of the governor and his lieutenant, of the war captain and his lieutenant, then he became satisfied I was "OK." He said that the old cacique, whose assistant he was [prior to the cacique's death], called him, the war captain, and his lieutenant, and told him they should, 11 days after his death, call together the people of the Pueblo, the principal men, and elect a new cacique of his own "blood" (!) He thus pointed to him, as he was "de la misma gente [of the same clan]." At the meeting of the principals, however, they looked to the fact of being of pure Indian blood from father and mother, and thus selected another one who, however, had not the knowledge required to fill the position. He particularly insisted upon the fact that the position of cacique was a very hard and responsible one, that he had to know a great deal in order to guide the Pueblo and to keep the peace among the people, and that his successor should be thoroughly informed in all the ways and means for that purpose.

I then asked him about the gentes, and he confessed that he was "blue corn," and that there was yellow, white, and red corn. He almost intimated that the office of cacique should be hereditary in the blue corn gens. He certainly knew all the other clans, but was not positive in regard to the fact that they still exist among the Piros, beyond the four colors of the maize! He evidently put me to quite a test of veracity and reliability.

On the 12th of December they celebrate their feast, first in the church; then the dance begins, men and women painted, both sexes with feathers on their heads but no headdresses, the hair of the women plaited. They play the "tumbé," of which he has one, made of a hollow tree, and covered with leather. They also had flutes formerly, but none any more. They sing old chants in their language, but do not understand them. The other Pueblos often deride them for their singing songs which they do not themselves understand. He has two large pieces of pottery which his mother made. One is red; the other is black. He finally complained that his people had no "médicos," and that consequently they were unprotected because the medicine men had to guide and to counsel and direct the tribe![422] This is of great interest and value in every way. It shows the true position of that class. On the whole, I am satisfied. These Indians make pottery and the recent pottery looks very much like that of the Pimas. It has the same paint and color. Only it is a little lighter in here, but the designs are remarkably similar. Painted in the afternoon, and then called on Mr. Boisselier, where I met Mr. Robert Fasnacht of New Orleans. Mr. Boisselier promised to give me a room tomorrow, and so I went over to El Paso to spend an hour with Mr. Fasnacht and then returned. The Rio Grande here is narrow but tolerably rapid.

NOVEMBER 7: Called on Nicomedes Lara and had a long conversation. It results from it that the pueblo of the Mansos was originally where the church is, because, there was the head of the acequia. At the "Reál," a pueblo of the Zumas existed, which is now abandoned, the Zumas having confounded themselves with the Spanish population. The Mansos originally lived in houses of branches and of straw or reeds, and only through the Spaniards were they brought to live in houses of adobe. In the sierra around here, the mountain sheep still exists. The Cura Ortiz told me that his great-grandfather, Don Bernardo de Mier y Pacheco,[423] Colonel of Engineers, about 150 years ago, surveyed the pueblos of the Navajo Country. Some of the plats were still at the City of Durango, in the hands of Señor Rascón. The story of the Gran Quivira of today originated thus about 100-120 years ago, for Tio Juan Largo, the "Jumano" Indian at Socorro, died 60 or 70 years ago, he being at the time over 100 years of age. Went with Mr. Boisselier and spent the night there.

NOVEMBER 8: Wrote and mailed letter to Joe and to W. Dessauer.[424] Got my room at last. It is exceedingly convenient for me. I called on Nicomedes and spent some time with him. The Mansos have seven war captains, the first, second, and five assistants. At the time of the Apaches the latter troubled them very much, and the people had to do all their planting together. They knew the red "Ara" here, but do not have it. The feathers which they use are eagle feathers and turkey feathers. From this talk I am led to infer that they look upon owl feathers as something very bad.[425] At night went to Padre Ortiz who gave me the first four books of the church extant, that is, the 2nd, 3rd, 4th and 5th, the first one being lost. The "Libro 2do de Bautismos, Año de 1682" begins 26 Sept. 1682 and terminates 1 Aug. 1696, and contains names of Mansos: Males, Females (Males as #1, Females as #2). [Bandelier here inserts a list of baptismal names.]

NOVEMBER 9: They killed a policeman on the streets of El Paso del Norte last night! Yesterday, Nicomedes told me that he had hunted all over the mountains, etc. of this neighborhood all his lifetime, but had never seen the slightest trace indicating ruins of ancient houses. This is conclusive.[426]

"Libo 2do de Defuntos, 1685" (from 1 Jan'y 1685 to 25 Febr, 1693). [Here again Bandelier inserts a lengthy list of names; this list is followed by others taken from "Libro Tersero de Defuntos, 1693," (from June 1693 to 1709), and from "Libro 2do de Casamientos, Año de 1707" (1707-1728).] My eyes were very much hurt by the study of these old books, so much so that I had to sleep in the afternoon. Here, the corn is planted in May; some of the wheat, in fall. The ground is irrigated before plowing for corn. They cover their vines in November. Called on Nicomedes Lara. He repeated to me the names of the gentes. There are six: "Rio azul," "Maíz negro, blanco, azul, amarillo, colorado." He again stated that they came from the north and lived in huts of straw and reeds until after the Spaniards came. . . . They had two tracts of communal lands, but the Cura Ortiz took hold of them under the promise of charging them half-rate for all funerals, etc. Now the lands are sold, and they pay full-rate! He got their papers. They have private real estate.

NOVEMBER 10: Lara told me last night that according to an old tradition of theirs, there should come at one time, from the north, people—Indians—but they would not be able to recognize them as such, although it would prove beneficial to them, and he is convinced that I am one of them. I let him believe it. Pious fraud!

About the Quivira, he says that they heard it had been a pueblo once, but now is a lagune, where they hear cocks crow and Indians sing yet today. He thinks the Quiviras dwelt there. Repeated again that they had no more medicine men.

I called on Padre Ortiz. He told me that the Zumas were wiped out by the smallpox epidemic in 1780, all dying but one, Camargo, who himself died 14 years ago, leaving only one son. The archives of El Paso were carried off and stolen by Mexicans, not by Americans. This was done for the purpose of stealing the lands of the Mesilla afterwards.

I left for Senecú at 3 P.M. The distance is six miles, all over and through a sandy flat nearly all cultivated and traversed by acequias with cottonwoods. A young Indian of Senecú joined me on the road. He is lieutenant of the war captain. There, as among the Mansos, one war captain, one lieutenant, and five "alguaziles [alguaciles]." He told me that, shortly [recently], upon the denunciation of a Mexican, they had been compelled to bury and conceal "hasta la madre" [probably a native fetish of some sort]. This he said with a wink!

I was most heartily received by the people. The cacique took me to his house at once, as a duty.[427] The governor, war captain, etc. called at night. The proper name of the Pueblo is "Tze-no-qué [Senecú?]." They claim to have come from Abó! Have no knowledge of Socorro or of any of the pueblos in the list of Oñate, their traditions are so far lost that even the cacique has forgotten the names of the gentes, although they exist. Tomorrow they will have the rabbit hunt, with sticks and bows and arrows. They have not exactly the same customs as at Cochiti, but they pay for each rabbit, one medio; for each hare, one Reál. The skins do not go to the cacique. They make the same pottery as the Mansos. Their merced [land grant] is in the hands of the heirs of Miguel Antonio Lobato at Bernalillo. They lived formerly about one legua [league] higher up, on the right bank of the Rio Grande, but the river changed its channel about 30 years ago, and the village was abandoned.

NOVEMBER 11: We started for Isleta [del Sur] "Tshia-iu-be-ga" on horseback about 11 A.M., the old good cacique going with me. Crossed the bottom, which is very fertile (consequently exceedingly muddy), overgrown with a thorny thicket, some cottonwood and small coralillos [?], then crossed the Rio Grande, which is neither deep nor wide and reached Isleta, a much scattered village near the banks. Saw Mr. Blanchard,[428] Father Personné, and Juan Severiano. The Tiguas are, like the Piros, reduced to about 40 families, but they have preserved more of their language. Still it is slowly dying out among the younger people. They claim to have come from the Manzano, that is, from that place and Cuaray, probably also from Chililí and Tajique. Know nothing of San Pedro, and of the Quivira but the name and a few tales. The ruins of Socorro are still above the "Presidio," but they have lost all knowledge of it and merely say that the people came from the same place as those of Senecú. Unable to ascertain more than that, we rode back. Their pottery is exactly the same as that of the Piros, and so are their drums. Their patron saint is San Antonio de Padua, and that of Socorro was San Miguel. I returned on foot, the mud terrible, and a cold easterly wind, blowing all night.

Called on Nicomedes who at last told me that he knows the language of the Mansos and gave me some names in it. He has trusted me fully as yet. They are exceedingly suspicious and wily, these people, and slow to trust. Nicomedes says that the office of cacique is hereditary in the blue corn [clan]; that of captain, in the yellow corn; and governor, in the white corn! He now says positively that he knows they came from the north, from New Mexico! About the Quivira, he thinks that the Queres inhabited it!?[429]

NOVEMBER 12: The Piros had confirmed the fact, that the Mansos originally lived in "jacales" only. So did the Zumas. Left early for El Paso del Norte. They were dancing the Matachinas. Met Tobler!? He is a worthless deadbeat and bilk. I left for a hiding place and for a place where there was a fire, as it was cold and windy from the east all day.

About noon the Indians came up from the southeast, a small band, six women, and girls, dressed in a manta of dark blue or black fastened over the left shoulder. It is embroidered beneath. Over it they wear a mantle of cotton goods, white or with print. They wear a white shirt under the manta. The manta has a waist. There is much embroidery, and necklaces about them. The top of the head has a knot of red and blue ribbons, which hang down the back; the hair is left long. Some of them had paint on their cheeks, brown "almagre [ochre]." They wear in each hand a handkerchief with something tied up in it. The men were dressed in citizens' clothes, with a rattle.

Nicomedes beat the drum, and around him, as usual, congregated the singers. It was, on a small and poor scale, a perfect Pueblo dance. They first danced in a line, facing the church, then made a few of the common figures, and finally we all went back to the house where, after taking an "aguardiente [a distilled beverage, perhaps mescal or sotol]" with the cacique, we squatted down to the dinner without forks, spoons, or anything. The "sopa" was of bread or rather a pudding (composition unknown); then came three courses of meat, but no vegetables at all. Water was the only beverage. It was, in every way, a Mexican-Indian, not a Pueblo, dinner. The "molle" [mole, chocolate-based sauce] was there too. After dinner I left and retired early, it being decidedly too cold. The Cura Ortiz assured me that there are ruined pueblos along the river.

NOVEMBER 13: Went to see Nicomedes but he was not ready yet. No letters! Cannot account for it. It is absolutely beyond comprehension! I returned to Nicomedes and went to the cacique. Manuel Guero with him. The cacique received us kindly, but Nicomedes insisted upon having him "give me what I deserved."[430] So we went to the kitchen hearth, and there went through the ceremonies. He first offered me pinole, which I strewed, first to the east, then to the south, to the west, and to the north. Then I had to smoke the cigarrito, to the east, south west, and north also, to above, and to below. They did the same.

Then a long conversation ensued, while I had to detail the custom of the nether Pueblos. We finally took dinner, and then the cacique took the pinole, strewed it outside on the path whence I came, and came back. Nicomedes then made four cigarrettes, and these were smoked in turn, each one taking four whiffs, to the east, south, west, and north. The stumps, when nearly finished, were deposited on the ground. Finally each one took pinole in his mouth and then threw some of it into the fire of the hearth. Afterwards we took our leave. Met Fasnacht. No letters! Don't know what to do!

It appears that the ruins are all those of Pueblos since the time of 1680. I forgot to state that, before we threw the meal into the hearth, we started out in procession, first the cacique, then Nicomedes, then I, then the cacica [cacique's wife, or female assistant (?)], to outside, smoked a cigarrette, and strewed maize, chewing some of it, and then returned inside. I think I played my part well!

Impatient, I went and took leave of everybody. The Cura [Ortiz] promised a copy of the "Auto de Posesión," of the church, which dates back to 1656. Went to El Paso, Texas, and slept with Fasnacht. On the whole I am well pleased with my trip, and the results are satisfactory. I do not think that a great deal more could have been accomplished. Met X. Nagely of Meyringon, who told me a great deal of Alex. Kayser, the man who married an Isleta girl by fraud and whiskey. He is still received as a member of the tribe with all the occult ceremonies. Of the Mansos, Piros, and Tiguas, there are of each, about 30 or 40 families.

NOVEMBER 14: Started at 8 A.M. The famous Pass is indeed, for an army, difficult. It is reduced to the river banks, and there are but few bottoms or level patches, otherwise, for certainly eight or ten miles. The stream is encased by steep lumps of gravel and drift, very tiresome to climb and descend, and often rocky crags. An army had certainly eight to ten miles of ugly toil. A perfectly level plain stretches out hereafter, with dense yucca, often arborescent, and much ocotilla and cactus. Gradually these thin out, the plain becomes lower and occasionally marshy, the banks for about a mile inland being dotted with cottonwoods. At Las Cruces the sky was clearing. But the country up to there is almost desolate, scarcely a house is visible up to Las Cruces. Was cordially received.

Got a letter from Papa. All well, thank God!!! A letter from Mr. Meysenburg,[431] one from Mrs. Morgan, and one from Kirchner. Wrote and mailed cards to Meysenburg, to Papa, and to Mr. Parkman. Wrote to German Consulate and to Mr. Whyte.[432] Had a long conversation with Dr. [George] Butjofsky [Butschofsky].[433] He is here since 1857, and has, in the U.S. Army, travelled down both banks of the Rio Grande to the Santa Rosa Cañón. He positively denies the existence of any ruins, older than 1680 on both banks!! Neither in the Sierra Hueca. But the tanks there have rock-carvings, and there is some pottery around them. (Water stations!)

Of "Ju" [Juh][434] he says that he is a half-breed, born and raised in the family of Manuel Barela at Corralitos, a very tall man, now old and covered with wounds, stern, much feared by his Indians, but brave and not as cruel an Nané,[435] who is full-blooded, no relative of Victorio[436]

and of rather pleasant aspect, but terribly cruel. Both are "Apaches
Janeros."

Met Major Llewellyn.[437] He speaks of ruins in the Sierra Blanca, and
especially along the Tularosa River, and says the Apaches, after the
Pueblos had surrendered to the Spaniards, turned upon the former
and destroyed them. Padre Laseigne told me the books at Isleta go back
to 1692. Most pleasant day with Dessauer.

NOVEMBER 15: Mailed letters to Mr. Whyte and to German Consulate. The name of Ju's old friend is Mariano Barela. Wrote and
mailed to Dr. J. B. Girard. Met Don Nestor Armijo. He estimates the
distance from the Laguna del Muerto to San Marcial at 40 miles; Dr.
Butjofsky, at 25 miles. No ruins in the Jornada, but it is not impossible
that there might be on the Rio Grande banks. Drew $40 on the Ger-
man Consulate at St. Louis and bought shoes and cravat, etc.

Called on V. P. [Van Patten, probably]. He is disorderly in his statements beyond all limits. Still he says (and I must pay some attention
to it) that the Mansos are idolaters today, that they have an underground place of three rooms, in the rock, lined with a white coating
(probably gypsum). He says that, in the war-room, scalps were hung
around, with figures underneath painted on the wall. That there are
different seats for the cacique, that the governor faces him, that there
is a life-size statue of a man on the right-hand side of the cacique's seat.
And a similar one, with a war club, on the left-hand side of the governor's. That in the centre of the room there is a stool with an idol on it.
He also speaks of many vessels, platters, bowls, etc., of singular shapes,
kept in the same place. But that everybody is led into it blindfolded!

There is something in all this, but it is told so confuse[d]ly that it is
very difficult to get at the real facts. I am very sorry to say that I could
not cross over to Mesilla and to see Albert[o] Fountain; it was not impossible, though difficult. At Padre Laseigne's I met Moises Vigil, who
talked a good deal about the murder of Charles Bent, and the "guerra
de los Chimayoses [war of the Chimayoses]."[438] The evening was delightful, but very chilly, on account of the brisk southwesterly wind.
Took leave of good old Dr. George Butschofsky, and promised to meet
him at Silver City soon.

NOVEMBER 16: Left at 10 A.M. as usual by train. Fare $17.60, I believe,
but was in such a big hurry that I forgot to count the change over and

above $2. The country north of Las Cruces, which I saw for the first time now in daylight, becomes almost a pass towards Doña Ana [present-day Dona Ana], and Fort Selden.[439] Similar, in rugged and rocky hills, to the pass above El Paso. The vegetation in general is similar to that of Arizona, only *Peraskia gigantia* is wanting almost completely. The Sierra de Doña Ana appears as an almost transverse chain, north of Las Cruces, approaching the river front and nearly hugging its banks on the east. I am undecided, however, as to whether Oñate went around it or not.

At Rincon I met Col. Forsyth[440] and approached him on the subject of "Ju." He looked at in in a very feasible light and arranged with me to go to General Stanley[441] tomorrow. Met Don Guadalupe Azcárate of Las Cruces, who also approved of my plan and gave me very valuable information. It appears that the heart of the Sierra Madre, that is, the six or seven valleys formed by the parallel ridges (running north and south) composing the chain (which is from 35 to 65 miles wide from east to west) is very grassy, warm in winter, and full of water in the shape of streams, etc. On the mountain slopes, there is an abundance of beautiful timber and all full of game. Into these valleys the Apaches retire and keep themselves in the winter. These valleys are shut in by terrible rocky and steep ridges, and access to these is exceedingly difficult from any side but Ju is least suspicious of an approach from the north. From Casas Grandes or from Babispe [Bavispe] he is ever on the lookout and even the route along the Sierra Madre either [both] east and west is very dangerous, on his account. Besides, I would, by taking eight miles north of Rincon on the east bank of the Rio Grande. This lies in the very heart of the Sierra. I can therefore hardly do anything approximately fair [reasonably significant] without the consent of Ju!

Azcárate also told me that there was an old pueblo at the "Perrillo," eight miles north of Rincon on the east bank of the Rio Grande. This would, then, be below the mouth of the "Jornada," and nearly at the junction of the Sierra del Cavallo and the river [Rio Grande]. There is nothing improbable in it, but still, I am going to see. He also thought it possible that there might be some ruins lower down, but I am very adverse to that belief for many reasons. We passed the Jornada and the high top of the Sierra Blanca, snow-clad today, loomed up above the Sierra Oscura and Sierra de San Andrés. It remained plainly visible until north of Valverde. Caught a terrible cold and am feeling very, very bad. Reached Santa Fe near midnight. Very unwell. Cough, fever, and headache. Went directly to Herlow's,[442] where I was exceedingly well received .

NOVEMBER 17, 18, AND 19: (WRITTEN 19TH) Sick and sick. Monday got a letter from Joe, thank God; she writes happily and contented and well. Dear, dear, little wife! I got fairly out of bed Sunday afternoon only, and spent a few agreeable hours with Mr. Koch.[443] But the least cold air makes me shiver. I am thoroughly spoiled. On Monday, I wrote to F. R. and Co. [F. Ryhiner & Co. bank, Highland, Illinois]. Have done what I could do. At night George Pradt and R. Marmon[444] called and staid in my room until 3 A.M. Am better. G. Pradt told me of the Thanksgiving Dance of the Lagunas which is now about to be celebrated soon. The Navajos perform remarkable sl[e]ight of hand tricks, like the revivification of a dry branch to a fruit-bearing tree, or shrub, in less than 15 minutes. (Perfectly Hindoo).

NOVEMBER 20: Meysenburg and I spent a charming day at the Rancho [present-day Bishop's Lodge] of Archbishop Lamy.[445] Most delightful scenery, etc. The Archbishop told me that there is a ciénega north of Pecos, near the Macho. It would be east of the high sierra. This might be the ciénega with the seven villages, mentioned by Oñate? Again unwell at night, feverish. Coughing a great deal. Pain on the right side.

NOVEMBER 21: Passed a most miserable night, coughing and feverish. Headache. Painted. In the afternoon, the headache became so bad that I could not stand it any longer. I did not know what I was doing at all. Dr. Eggert relieved me gradually, but still it was only after I had spent some time at Mr. Koch's that it almost passed away. Coughed and coughed.

NOVEMBER 22: Had an excellent night, coughing excepted. But the cough is loose at last. Went out and got a card from Dr. Girard. Met Sam Eldodt,[446] and with him called on the Archbishop. Met Amado Chavez[447] and arranged for a trip to San Mateo to see his pueblo.[448] I shall go with Eldodt to San Juan [Pueblo] for a few days. He tells me that Nambé has another name in Tehua! Also Santa Fe. But he could not recall the words. Shall try and find out. At night a telegram from General Crook. "In my judgment it would be impolitic for Prof. B[andelier] to go into the Sierra Madre. He could do no good and might make the Indians suspicious." Retired very late at night, having taken supper with Governor Ritch and had a long talk with Meysenburg.

NOVEMBER 23: Miserable night, coughing, coughing, and coughing. Rose completely exhausted. Had a long talk with General Stanley and resolved upon trying it—anything, anyhow, and anyway! I am better, but still coughing severely. Were it not for the cough, I would be all right, but that cough worries and troubles me. Went to bed early, and took a hot footbath. Saw Meysenburg!

NOVEMBER 24: Took a hot footbath, which relieved me greatly. Slept well. Left at 11 A.M. Reached Pojuaque [present-day Pojoaque Pueblo] at 2:30 P.M. 17 miles, passing Cuyamun-gue on the right of the road. The ruins of the old pueblo are still there, partly standing. It is near the confluence of the Tezuque [Tesuque] with the Nambé River, and three-and-a-half miles, by the road, from Pozuaque [Pojoaque]. A ridge, running down from the sierra, runs out near the confluence. Pozuaque, the pueblo with church, stands on that ridge, above the little plazita, where Mr. Leon Bouquet lives.

Nambé is higher up, and there is an old ruin four miles east, also. Northwest, opposite, is the terrible ridge, with fierce battlements and cliffs of sandstone, behind which is San Ildefonso. The country north of Pozuaque is very barren and arid. Constantly rising. Red cliffs to the right. We crossed the Arroyo Seco and then rose again to the north, barren hills of sandstone, eroded to fantastic forms. The view from the gate, or "Puertecita," is a very striking one. The valley of Santa Cruz de la Cañada lies at the very feet, with the village and church. The Chimayo Valley expands to the east of it. The Rio Grande bottom is plainly visible to the enormous cañones and potreros on the west side, above which the high Sierra del Valle [Jemez Mountains] rises. These cañones and potreros are very formidable. But the bottom valley itself is surprisingly fertile and beautiful. San Juan itself lies at the north end of the valley, almost opposite the confluence of the Rio Chama [and Rio Grande]. Reached [San Juan Pueblo] at 6 P.M.

NOVEMBER 25: Day very windy and cold. My cough is terrible indeed. The pueblo is clean and handsome. The men occasionally make bead-work, having learnt it from the Yutas [Ute Indians]. Their pottery is black and red. Both kinds are made alike, that is, painted with "almagre," but the red kind is taken out after being baked, whereas the other is, after baking, smoked thoroughly which, when polished, gives it the black lustrous color! The smoking is done with dung, but it may also be performed with straw. Painted all day at the "Qu'-huanĭfĭ," or macana [war club] from Santa Clara [Pueblo]. The evening I spent partly with Antonio, the sacristan.

NOVEMBER 26: Painted all day, finishing the war club. At night went to Antonio. The pueblo "de los Luceros," six miles north-northeast from here, an old ruin, is called "Pio-ge." Mr. Douglas[449] from Abiqiu [present-day Abiquiu] came. There is an ancient pueblo there, even two. The people of Abiqiu are merely "genízaros [mixed bloods]" from many different tribes; it is a modern settlement formed by the Spaniards, and the Pueblos. They have lost their languages, customs, dress, etc. completely, and are thoroughly hispanicised. The collection of Mr. Eldodt is a beautiful one. It contains splendid axes of stone, with handles, some very ancient pottery, a spearhead of lava or basalt, some very perfect arrowheads, a fetish of alabaster of very singular form, etc. In examining this valley, I can well conceive how the Spaniards, when they first came up here, settled in this region. It is exceedingly inviting, principally in fall. Fertile and handsome; the pueblos here were closer together.

NOVEMBER 27: The "Baile del Venado" [Deer Dance] is called "Pa-shyă-rĕ." The antlers are called "Pa-se." Antler "se" and head "Pa." Crown (yellow and green) "Ti-yu." Mr. Eldodt purchased a complete head dress of the Deer Dance. It is very original. Very unwell the whole day, almost unable to utter a loud word, and coughing. Mr. Douglas of Abiqiu asserted that, in opening a grave on the Rio Mancos, a corpse had been found, holding in its hand a war club like the one I have copied. I painted the medicine bowl from "Pio-ge," and in the afternoon took a short walk with Mr. Eldodt over to Yunque,[450] opposite. The actual plazita is built on the steep bluff above the railroad. It seems as if the old pueblo had stood on the river bank, or rather on the bluffs above. This valley is charming, and as far as fertility is concerned, the handsomest I have seen in New Mexico.

NOVEMBER 28: Almost speechless. Painted all day. Nothing new, as I cannot converse with anybody. But the kindness of Mr. Eldodt and of

Padre Seux[451] is beyond bonds and limits. At night retired very early.

NOVEMBER 29: Like yesterday, but a little better. Painted. At night had a long conversation with Don Juan García on Indian superstitions, etc. He told me of an occurrence at Santa Clara which clearly shows the power and office of cacique. On a first day of January (he being then County Judge) he was called to Santa Clara by an Indian to settle a dispute between the young and the old men of the Pueblo about the election of a new governor. The young men claimed to elect through a majority of votes; the old people claimed the usual form of nomination by the cacique! He decided in favor of the young men. He is very emphatic in his statement that at San Juan the same customs and dances were formerly practised in public as in other pueblos. The estufa here is rectangular.

NOVEMBER 30: Feel much better. Painted. Wrote to Joe, enclosing draft for $100. (Salary.) At night, went to see Atencio. There are seven clans here, but could only get the names of five: Deer, Eagle, Sun, White Corn, and Blue Corn. The former Pueblo of San Juan was at the "Pueblito" on the other side of the river and was called "Añĭmbŭ;" it was abandoned before the conquest of Oñate. Quitraco is on the "Rio del Oso" on the right bank; Camitria and Axol are also on the right bank, and so, probably is Xiomato, all opposite San Juan and not far from the river. It appears that, in 1598, all the pueblos of the Tehuas, San Juan excepted, were on the right bank. Tezuque, Nambé, and Pozuaque were formed after 1598, by people of San Ildefonso, Santa Clara, and San Juan settling there. This is very important.

At Santa Fe, the pueblo (à la Garita![?])[452] was occupied by "gente del chalchihuite [Turquoise Clan]." He positively affirms that the Tanos spoke the language of the Tehuas! The inhabitants of the pueblos across the river fled to the Moquis! So did the Tanos, but the latter also went to Santo Domingo [Pueblo]. The name for Ojo Caliente de José is "Po-ŏ-sĕ," and he intimates as much as that it was a Tehua Pueblo, as also Abiqiu! He says the name of the latter is Tehua. Of the Quivira he says that it was inhabited by "los Queres del Sur," meaning the Piros. The Manzano was a Tigua Pueblo![453]

DECEMBER

DECEMBER 1: Finished painting the headdress. At 3 P.M. we left for Santa Cruz, where Father Francolon[454] received me with the greatest possible kindness. He is beautifully fixed; his house is very elegant. The church books do not reach further [presumably, back] than 1726, but then, as Santa Cruz was the seat of the "Cofradía de Nuestra Señora del Carmen," it was [became] a kind of motherhouse, to which all the other parishes referred. So I found books of Jemez (San Diego de Xemes) here. Father Francolon told me that the people of Nambé were disappearing fast, and that it was attributed to a custom of either infanticide or of abortion prevailing among them. At all events there were some dark and singular agencies at work there, and he had noticed their introduction also among the people of Santa Clara. What it is, he is not capable of defining or finding out. The Governor of Nambé is a Navajo Indian.[455] Very ill. Cough exceedingly severe.

DECEMBER 2: Saw all the church antiquities, some of which are handsome. Left for Pojuaque at 2 P.M. Well received by Mr. Bouquet. It appears that the former church of Pojuaque was northwest of the actual pueblo, about three-fourths of a mile, and that it was abandoned about 80 years ago for the present site. But about 100 yards northwest of the pueblo of today there is a ruin, composed of ridges of stones (rubble) and dirt.* This was the old pueblo. There is a field in the depression of the old "plaza" and an estufa, but it is next to impossible to determine whether it was round or square. I found much jet-black obsidian and some painted pottery, among which a few pieces were originally glossy. There is no doubt of the fact that this ruin was occupied before the Reconquest,[456] but I doubt whether it was not built after 1600 A.D. [!!]

I asked positively about the matter of Nambé and was told that they were in the habit, until 15 years ago, of killing their most intelligent people under the pretext of witchcraft, and that this has greatly contributed towards depopulating the pueblo. Not longer than one year ago, a woman at Nambé was beaten to death by order of the authorities for having been the concubine of a married man. About witchcraft they know of the custom of pricking images, but have no knowledge of that of infanticides. (The engagement of 1837 took place at the "Arroyo Seco.")[457]

DECEMBER 3: Left at 10 A.M. in a two-wheeled cart. Cuyamunge is a very small ruin built of adobe. Walls about 0.48 [meter] thick. The plaza is easily recognizable. Reached Santa Fe at 3 P.M. and got a good letter from home. But I am exceedingly hoarse. Jake Gold told me that

Mr. Terry of the Metropolitan Museum wants to see me. He went to San Juan today.

DECEMBER 4: I painted the jar from San Ildefonso and in the afternoon I met Mr. Townsend. He stated to me that there were two ruins about seven miles north of Tezuque, also a ruin on the road, where the walls are exposed, showing cajón—work.[458] He confirms the stories about Nambé.

DECEMBER 5: Letter from Joe. Painted. Had a long call from Mr. G. Terry of the Central Park Museum. Also one from Padre Ribera!

DECEMBER 6: Col. Willison came in and gave me information about a pueblo 17 miles south of here. It is distinct from the one at the Cañada del Pueblo. Spent evening at Meysenburg's—foolishly—for my chest. Finished letter to Mr. Parkman, it covers 16 pages, and mailed it through the Hotel.

DECEMBER 7: Severe cough, etc. Painted. Had several calls. At night wrote and mailed to Joe, to Cushing, and to the German Consulate at St. Louis. My condition is alarming, and I concluded to go south at once.

DECEMBER 8: J. C. Pearce[459] was with me in the morning. Painted. At night had the visit of [Postmaster] Kuss of Manzano. Nothing new there. There is a report that a covered spring was found at the Quivira!? Went to Felsenthal[460] and glanced at his manuscript. It is dated 2 Nov. 1643 and bears title: "Carta de Justicia, Autos, y commissión, cometida al Sarg[ento] Mayor Francisco Gomez para la execución, etc." [Decree charging Sergeant-Major Francisco Gomez with the execution, etc.] It appears that seven Spaniards (officers in part) had been condemned to death, and had fled from justice. Their crime is mentioned as high treason and sedition, having informed the "Indios bárbaros" that the King of Spain was not their master, but that they should follow them and the priests! Against the latter the Proclamation of the Governor, Don Alonso Pacheco de Heredia, dated "En la Villa Real de Santa Fé," 26 July 1643, is exceedingly severe. It complains of the exorbitant "tequios" [taxes] demanded of the Indians by the priests, and declares that it is not the church, but the royal government on which the Indians depend. In fact it is as much against the church as against

Josephine Huegy Bandelier,
before 1880

Adolph F. Bandelier,
before 1880

Josephine Huegy Bandelier,
before 1880

Adolph F. Bandelier,
as a young man

Juan José Montoya and daughter, Cochiti

Jake Gold's Old Curiosity Shop,
possibly in 1886

"Tertio Millenial" Celebration, Santa Fe, 1883;
Apache Indian and Official in foreground

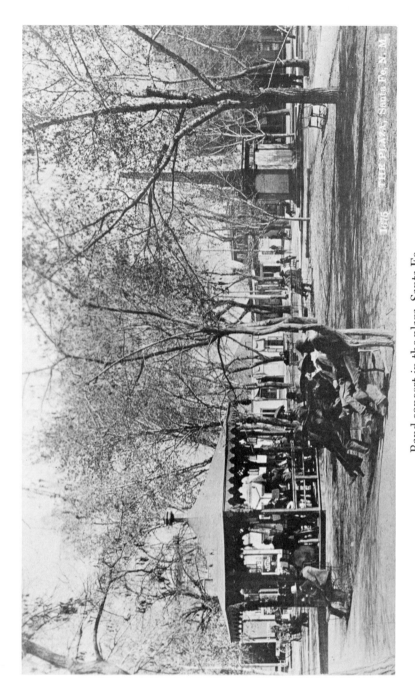

Band concert in the plaza, Santa Fe

Engraving of Exchange Hotel, Southeast Corner
of Santa Fe Plaza, after 1856

Plaza planted to alfalfa or other forage crop,
Santa Fe, c. 1880

Interior of Gold's Old Curiosity Shop,
c. 1880

Adolph F. Bandelier, aged 12,
from a daguerreotype

Josephine Huegy Bandelier, probably taken
during the Santa Fe years

Adolph F. Bandelier's father, A. E. Bandelier,
perhaps taken during the latter's stay
in Santa Fe

Adolph F. Bandelier,
in later years

Adolph F. Bandelier as a young man,
photograph taken at a
St. Louis studio

anybody else. It also mentions the Apaches as mortal enemies, and as if
they had always been so! A certain "estancia [hacienda]" is also mentioned on the banks of the Rio Grande, between the Pueblos of "San
Philipe" and "Sandía." Finally Santa Fé is mentioned as "Villa," and
it is ordained that [this document be] proclaimed "Por las calles" and
"al sonido de la caja" [through the streets to the sound of the drum].

There are also two letters, dated "Coarac" (Cuaray) Sept. 1643
(24th is the date of the first) and signed: Fray Juan de Salas "Capellán
[chaplain]." The whole document is exceedingly important in many
ways. It shows that there was open enmity between church and state,[461]
concerning Indian affairs in New Mexico. Wrote and mailed, through
Hotel, letters to Joe, Mr. Parkman, Amado Chavez, and cards to Pradt,
to Pauline, and to Dr. Girard. Large processions today and last night;
Cofradía de San Francisco parading the streets with music.

DECEMBER 9: Had an excellent night. Slept entirely without coughing
until 7 A.M. Finished my paintings early, packed them up, and mailed
them to Josephine.[462] Paid $1.14 for mailing!! Called on S. Ellison.[463]
He told me that he found, in documents of 169-? that Diego de Vargas
asked an Indian, who lived 20 days east of Santa Fe, about the Quivira.
That Indian replied that he knew of it, because they went there to steal
children. This shows again that the Gran Quivira of today was not
known under that name at that time.[464] Wrote cards to Pauline and to
Mrs. Morgan. Called on Gov. Ritch in the afternoon and had a long
talk with him. Dr. Eggert insists upon my staying here tomorrow.
Wrote for the "Ausland."

DECEMBER 10: Made final calls everywhere. Meysenburg went with me
to Father Defouri[465] and then to the train. José [Olivas?] was there too.
Went to Lamy[466] and then to bed.

DECEMBER 11: Left Lamy at 5 A.M. and went to Wallace [present-day
Domingo, or Domingo Station].[467] Walked over to Peña Blanca.
Rheumatism excruciating. Spent noon with Padre Ribera. Do not like
his appearance! Went back with him to Wallace. Met Father Parisis
there and Fred Tondre. Also Santiagito Tenorio from Santo Domingo.
Fred Tondre[468] told me that the old sacristan had found one of the old
pueblos I asked him about, but he did not recollect which. It is high up
in the sierra.

DECEMBER 12: Met Nathan Bibo[469] and Pedro Peria [Perea]. When we passed the Alameda, about nine miles below Bernalillo, they spoke of the old pueblo there. It is completely levelled, situated in the bottom lands, and filled up. It appears that, 75 or 80 years ago, the Rio Grande ran past there. It has since changed its channel. At Albuquerque we had rain. Pauline, Annie, and Will [Borchert] came to meet me, notwithstanding the rain. At Belen, very warm reception. Nothing new. The attachment of the Mexicans there is certainly serious. [?]

DECEMBER 13: All day at Belen. Pueblos at Casa Colorada, at the Jarales. Called on Leyno and Danckenguy. They say this weather is very extraordinary.

DECEMBER 14: Rode down to Socorro with Father Splinters![470] He says that on the Red River and Cimarron there are no ruins and no trace of pottery. Adolph Mennet[471] exceedingly kind. Longuemare[472] speaks of plastic [moulded?] pottery, two handles in the shape of snakes, black-and-white paints, [?], no symbolical figures, geometrical design only.* All found about western Tularosa.

DECEMBER 15: It is a great pity that Longuemare cannot be trusted! He says he discovered an old pueblo about 35 miles northwest of Socorro, near the Ladrones. He says also that, near that place, there are: "thousands of stumps of trees felled with stone axes," and that the ruins still contain the same "vigas." One thing appears certain, namely: that around Tularosa, and on the headwaters of the San Francisco, there are many and well-preserved ruins. Also, and this I had repeatedly asserted, that there are no ruins in the llanos [plains] of San Agustín! They are a barrier to the sedentary Indian. Left Socorro at 1 P.M. Traversing the Jornada, the Sierra Blanca appeared in full view. It is a majestic group or chain, deeply covered with snow. It remains visible from after passing beyond the Mesa of San Marcial to beyond Engle, or Ojo del Muerto. Stopped at Rincon, where I met Mr. Melchior [?], who introduced me to Huntington.

DECEMBER 16: Inquired [about the Sierra del] Perrillo, but nobody could tell me anything about ruins there. Antonio Sylva however told me, that nine miles south of Rincon, on the line of the railroad I would meet ruins. Rincon itself is a small place of huts and miserable adobes, 300 souls at most. Large railroad buildings. It was founded three years ago, and the majority of the people are still Mexicans of the lowest sort. Met accidentally a Spaniard, Enrique de Monte, who was going in the same direction. Rincon lies in a valley or sluice. The Rio Grande makes a bend of one mile to the north, then goes about west, and finally turns to the north.[473] North of Rincon is the Sierra del Perrillo, which is but a spur of the Sierra del Caballo. The Rio Grande bottom is covered with álamos! Going south along the railroad track, we traversed the cottonwood groves for about four miles. The bottom is fertile, somewhat marshy in places, and there are ranchos all along. They build them here of logs and dirt, but mostly of palisades [probably jacal structures]. The bluffs, which in the beginning remain at two miles from the river, are all remarkably jagged, crested, and divided into small eminences, which offer no room for contiguous villages. Vegetation on these bluffs is very scrubby. Mesquite, yucca, the latter occasionally in very large specimens, and an occasional palo verde. Coniferae I have not noticed.* But in the mountains back (north) of Rincon, there is said to be much mescal agave! I have not seen any.

After proceeding beyond four miles, the cottonwoods disappear, and an open bottom expands. This bottom is frequently intersected by channels indicating entries of the river, and the latter occasionally overflows. These encroachments are so common between here and El Paso, that there are at least 154 bridges or culverts on the whole stretch of 76.8 miles. The bluffs there approach the river in a curve as soon as they near the Cerro de San Diego, a high, dark red bluff, at least 1200 feet, almost verticle [sic], over the river bottom. Its profile is as follows from the north.*

An attempt to map it from the west would result as follows:* [view] taken on the west bank of the river, facing the cliff.*

Until there, the gravelly bluffs, small and with mostly sharp superficial crests, have been white, as if of marl, but it is doubtlessly a whitish conglomerate or breccia. At the Cerro de San Diego it turns into a red, lava-like cherty, quartzy rock, which is amygdaloid and drusic. There is a rounded mesa with mural front, similar in appearance to the top of Sugarloaf near Fort McDowell. Two Mexican boys told us that there was on top of it a stone enclosure, but I mistrusted and did not go. The little promontory cut through by the railroad is where the ruins stand. The river almost reaches the track. The ruins are reduced to mere foundations, standing on edge. They are made of stones and very much decayed. The rock is volcanic. Much pottery, striped, painted, and corrugated. The latter is painted, as at Fort Apache and Showlow. On the whole the pottery is extremely handsome. There is much red and brown flint, also white flint, but no obsidian there. Fragments of metates, of black, very amygdaloid, lava, also manos, are scattered about around.

The place is well selected for a village. The houses are small type, and only a few (three) are still visible. On the north side of the little mesa there is a flat traversed by an arroyo. In this flat they probably cultivated. The foundations look as follows:* The metate is simply concave without any rim to it or border.* Everything appears very old and decayed long ago. About a mile north of this place, there are gradual slopes again, with very fertile soil, and small ravines running through them to the railroad track. On these slopes there is much pottery and a fragment of metate. This latter has a rim as follows.* It is also of black lava. There are no traces of buildings left; still it appears that there has been a village or at least a few houses there. Otherwise there are no traces. As the bluffs recede from the river and become very rocky, the chances for settlements vanish. But beyond the Cerro de San Diego, south, there is a similar recess, terminating about Randall by another mountain range nearing the river. There may be a pueblo there. Made 21 miles today.

DECEMBER 17: Started for the "Perrillo" following the railroad north for one-and-one-half miles, then, striking east-southeast, descended into a bottom through which run several arroyos. On the banks of one of these arroyos, pottery was quite freely scattered, but not a trace of walls, foundations, or buildings. This bottom is fertile and may be irrigated from the arroyo, but the nearest permanent water, the river, is nearly one-and-one-half miles off. We then ascended the heights above the Arroyo del Perrillo. They are with sharp crests towards the river bottom, the whole region is much and variedly broken; there is hardly any room for houses. Vegetation scant, scrubby mesquite, palo verde, tasajo, yucca. (On Griffin's ranch there is a gigantic specimen of arborescent Yucca bacata, at least six feet high.) Very little grass. We explored the whole mouth of the arroyo, for a mile up and down, and found no trace of ruins or pottery, and then returned to Rincon, having made nine miles.

I painted in the afternoon, and wrote postal cards to Joe, to Mr. Parkman, to Dr. Eggert, and to Lieut. Elliott. Taking leave of de Monte, who has been my faithful and very useful guide, I reached Nutt at 8:45 P.M. Went to bed at once. Coughing.

There is no doubt but that the banks of the Rio Grande above

Rincon were settled. Priest told me that pottery was found in lots on the bluffs about Santa Barbara. Col. Rynerson[474] assured me that the arroyos of Palomas and of the Cuchillo Negro were probably occupied. Northwest of Fort Craig,[475] about 40 miles, there is a pueblo. As to south of Rincon, it is very doubtful. Neither at Randall nor at Fort Selden, nor at Doña Ana, has pottery ever been noticed. In the Sierra del Caballo, into which the Perrillo ascends, there is no water, except an occasional "tinaja [natural basin]." Such tinajas, together with holes for making mescal, are found three miles from Rincon. Not long ago [most of] these mountains were occupied by Apaches in large numbers, and the Perrillo, through which the road ascended towards the Jornada, was the scene of many a massacre. I presume Oñate ascended through that road or near it. For sedentary Indians, away from the river, there is no site nor place.

DECEMBER 18: Wind brisk northwest. Nutt is in a wide plain (15 miles from east to west and over 70 to 80 from north to south) perfectly level, grassy, and totally dry. At Nutt, which is on the eastern border, they have no water at all, but get it from Fort Cummings through Florida. Above the little place of Nutt itself rise high hills, capped with volcanic rims and boulders, sterile, absolutely treeless. They are the outcrops of the southern Sierra Magdalena, and remain as barren and desolate until they near the Rio Grande. These hills continue on the south side of the railroad for some time.

I walked over from Nutt to Fort Cummings,[476] 15 miles, which lies south of Cook's Peak (8790' about).[477] One grassy plain, with few *Opuntia*, yucca. Not a single tree in sight as far as the eye can reach, except some scrubby cedars, etc. on the slopes of Cook's Peak. The latter is a very bold, truncated pyramid, rising above dreary and steep slopes, intersected by rugged cañones. No vegetation. A beautiful flock of antelopes—25 or 30 heads—allowed me to approach within 20 yards at least and then sauntered off. To the north the plain is boundless, a few mountains only loom distantly; in the south it is bounded, at a long range, by the hills of the Goodsight chain. The whole is arid, and very unfit for population.

Fort Cummings itself lies at the foot of a low range, volcanic, and extending south of Cook's Peak like an apron, with two cones jutting out very prominently. The post (231 men and seven officers, mostly in tents around an adobe fort) is at the foot of these two cones. Reception most charming, Lt. Elliott of the greatest kindness, also Capt. Guthrie

and all the other officers, Lieuts. Mason,[478] Cecil,[479] Wheeler,[480] Peshine,[481] etc. There is a good spring near the fort, the only one near and
far. The mesa which is due south of the fort, extends in its lowest apron
to the railroad at Florida, opposite to which is the Sierra Florida, rugged
and cleft, like the Organos. The latter are plainly visible east. Las
Cruces is 50 miles off. Fort Selden, 53; Georgetown 42 miles. The hills
around Cummings are volcanic with much chalcedony and moss agate.

DECEMBER 19: Pleasant; painted. There are no ruins around here, but
the Apaches held the country for a long time and the cañón through
which the former mail route passed was the scene of innumerable
murders and massacres. Painted. Capt. Guthrie assured me that ruins
of mud buildings, with pottery, are found on the upper Missouri, in
Montana. He owned three complete vessels, painted. There is a cave
between Cook's Peak and Deming, which contained a few Indian
vestiges. Otherwise nothing. But everybody tells me of the Upper Gila
and of the San Francisco and of the Mimbres, for ruins.

DECEMBER 20: Painted. Am positive now that there was a pueblo at
Fort Selden also, on the very site of the Post. Pottery has been found
there and the report is common there that there was once a pueblo. It
is now totally obliterated. This is 19.1 miles south of Rincon. Its location was similar to that at [the Cerro de] San Diego, on a mesa projecting towards the river. Utmost kindness on the part of all officers. Met
Dr. Lacey, and John Burnside from Carlyle.

DECEMBER 21: Letter from Joe!! All well, thank God. But there is an
unexplainable mention about Mrs. Morgan! Yesterday and today I
painted with open doors! It snowed here last week, which is rare. Lost
Sheet #141 by the wind carrying it off. [This was recovered, or redone,
as the entry for December 16, which was on Sheet #141, demonstrates.]
It contained the notes about San Diego. I repeat here what is most
essential. Pottery painted, also corrugated and painted red, like that at
Showlow and at Fort Apache. Metates (only fragments) and manos, of
very drusic lava. Much red and brown Jasper about, in chips. Very
little flint and no obsidian right where the pueblo stands. But about a
mile north of it, on a more level space between the small hills about
the railroad track, I found much pottery, a broken metate, and a piece
of obsidian, a chip similar to those at Cholula![482]
Coniferae are scarcely seen in the region, only on the slopes, and

there they are dwarfish and scattered. The river encroaches much on the east bank, so that there are at least 150 bridges over such encroachments between Rincon and El Paso, a distance of 70 miles. The bottom is wooded up to four miles from Rincon, "alamos." Afterwards open and marshy. At the Cerro de San Diego, the bluffs reach nearly the river front, and the river itself makes a bend to the east. The west shore is mountainous, except the immediate bottom. The slopes appear arid and treeless, desolated. The cerro itself is an almost vertical wall towards the river, nearly a mile long, of red and brown volcanic breccia, with sharp mural crests and tops, apparently lava. The following would be a view from the north.* A Mexican boy told us that there was a stone enclosure on the top, and an American at Mr. Griffin's ranch told us that there were some rock-carvings in a ravine leading up to it. At the outlet, we found the obsidian, etc.

The ruins themselves are situated on a little promontory of breccia cut by the railroad track, and immediately joining Griffin's ranch, east of it. The foundations are plates of stone, planted in the ground vertically. Their thickness is about 0.12 [meter].* North of the promontory, and about 5.0 [meters?] below it, is a little plain traversed by an arroyo, which has every vestige of having been once cultivated. Probably the fields were irrigated through the arroyo. The remains of three houses are still seen, but there were probably as many more, at least. On all sides except northeast and southwest the mesita is bordered by abrupt ledges. The cerro is about 1,000 feet above the railroad.* This is the only site, in the whole nine miles, proper [for] a pueblo, and there may be another one at Randall's, nine miles farther south. Made 20 miles today. Returned at 4 P.M., walking leisurely.

DECEMBER 22: Mailed both letters A.M. I left at 11 A.M. in the ambulance. We struck the Nutt road and then turned due north, following a ravine. After about eight miles of travel, dwarfish holly appeared; the ravine grew deep and its sides rocky and precipitous. But the rain came at last from the west, and for about ten minutes it blew and rained so, that we were compelled to turn the ambulance and to lay by. We then entered Mule Cañón [Canyon], a very handsome narrow gorge, with beautiful rocky sides occasionally perpendicular, covered with lichens and green mosses. Along the arroyo running at the bottom, holly, oak, and small cedars grow in groves. It was very handsome. The sky cleared in the west, but a cold, cutting wind (northwest) blew. At Mule Spring, nine miles from Brockmann's, is the only permanent water of the cañón. The place is narrow and very rocky, still there is room for a small Indian settlement. Whatever soil is in the cañón is excellent, and there are small patches disseminated through it, so that there is a bare possibility of former Indian settlements in the cañón, though I could not observe any traces in various places.

Beyond Mule Spring the heights are reached and with them the country becomes again treeless. The Mimbres [Mountains] appear before us, and at their foot a cleft is indicated barely, in which the Rio Mimbres runs, but the bottom is not visible. In the west rises a remarkable mesa.* The hot springs are southwest and at a distance of 12 miles from the mill of Mr. Brockmann. It appears that the Rio Mimbres also loses itself in the sand beyond Hudson's Springs and at Deming. Deming is about 30 miles from here. Mr. Brockmann is nicely fixed. The valley is narrow, hardly a half-mile, and steep, absolutely denuded hills, treeless, descend into it. The river is bordered by cottonwoods; there are also willows, and very few cedars. Kind reception.

There are ruins here in the valley and on the hills, and many rock-carvings are scattered on loose large rocks on the hill slopes. Mr. Brockmann showed me some of them. They are very rude. He also carried me to the ruins a half-mile north of his house and mill. They are in the flat river bottom, about 100.0 [meters?] east of the river. Pottery very much alike to that of Rincon, though the corrugated kind, painted red, is lacking. No signs of metates visible, hardly any flint, but chips of basalt. The mounds are low, as most of the stones have been used for the construction of walls and enclosures. It shows that the walls of the buildings were of stone and mud. The whole has the appearance of the pueblos around Globe and at Wheatfields, but the mounds are lower, and show houses which did not contain over two rooms each. It looks as if they might have been on platforms, but the excavations made to a depth of one meter have revealed rubble, plates of stone of various sizes, uncut, and earth. It appears that a jar was taken out by Mr. Brockmann, with a very narrow mouth (olla) which contained a human skull far too large for the opening. [!!] On the site of Mr. Brockmann's house stood another pueblo, as evidenced by the platforms of rubble (about 0.10 or 0.08 [meter?] high) still visible in his plazita. Many skeletons have been found on the place. Two skulls, much decayed, were dug up while making the cellar, at a depth of 0.61 [meter?]. Also pottery, painted.

DECEMBER 23: Went out and measured the ruins. There is a broad, though not circular, depression near it, which shows traces of moisture, and is about 1.50 [meters?] deep, surrounded by a rim of earth, with small rubble and pottery. It is not an excavation for adobe, as a Mexican assured me positively. It must have been a tank! It is 36.5 [meters?] from the ruins. Some of the foundations stand on the edge, but the walls are so scattered, that it is very difficult to trace the true directions, and to measure their width is impossible. In one place, however, I could measure a double wall—0.61 [meter?] wide. There are several almost elliptical depressions, with high and broad rims, in front of the mounds.* They recall similar enclosures at San Lázaro, San Pedro, etc. [Galisteo Basin sites, south of Santa Fe]. There is a new stone building and adobe, very near the river or rather the acequia which runs the mill. The river is lined* with cottonwood.

Got through about 11 A.M. and went home to paint the groundplan, which is rather confused and not strictly correct in all the details. It is of course only stepped, and accurate measuring is impossible without digging. About 3:30 P.M., we went to copy the carvings. They are on the northern slope of a hill west of the house. They are evidently scratched out with a flint instrument or picked out. On the top of the hill is a circular depression, like an estufa 9.0 [meters?] in diameter, and 42.0 [meters?] east of it, a deeper one, 10.0 [meters?] across. Pottery, red and old, lying about, but I could not find any painted specimens. Little flint. No other traces of buildings or walls about.

There is a pueblo at the house of Juan Albino Baca, and miles below, at San Ysidro, three miles north of here, making five in all on a stretch of nine miles.

The climate here is not very cold; still there are damaging frosts in May. Pears generally freeze. Grapes and apples not. Ground very fertile. Potatoes excellent.

DECEMBER 24: Found a little bit of obsidian at the ruin. Otherwise no obsidian found so far. Mr. Brockmann suffered greatly from the Apaches. He tells me that, at Casas Grandes, metallic objects have been dug out, like frogs of copper, etc. The valley here, though narrow, is fertile and very valuable soil. There is also a pueblo seven miles north of here, at the rancho of Carlos Norero, an Italian, and on the road to Georgetown. There are also stories about pueblos in the mountains, but I could not ascertain anything positive.

Last night I was informed by Mr. Brockmann that he intended to go east next spring, so this A.M. I wrote a few lines of introduction to Joe

for him. It appears that in the "Valle de San Buenaventura" in Chihuahua, there are many ruins too, but Casas Grandes seems to be most
spoken of. The buildings are yet intact in part. There is little gold in the
Mimbres. The river overflows occasionally here, and then becomes a
very rapid and dangerous current. Still I do not believe that the old
ruins in the bottoms could ever be flooded by the river. About 9:21
A.M. Mr. Brockmann came back with Dick Hudson.[483] At the same
time Mr. Hermann Gruenewald came, and he told me of ruins one to
two miles south of this place. I thus determined to walk down with
him and examine the sites. I crossed the Mimbres (at one jump; it is
about 3 to 4.0 [meters?] wide and very clear water) and then followed
it south in the fertile bottoms whose rich black loam reaches to the very
foot of the barren hills. This bottom is wide, from a half to one mile,
and is all cultivated. The river hugs the bluffs on the other side very
closely, and it is lined with cottonwoods, willows, and ash. Some very
large trees. Above the bluffs, the abrupt top of Cook's Peak is plainly
visible.

Three-quarters-of-a-mile from the mill, on the rancho of Aniceto
Ribera, in the fields, there is the following ruin.* There are hardly any
foundations visible except on the south side. The rest of the ruins are
mounds which have no measurable walls and spaces covered with pottery and stones that evidently have been coarsely broken and used in
piling up walls. A little beyond there is another space where the rubbish, rubble, and pottery denote the existence of a building. It is about
quadrangular or slightly elliptical, pointing north with the major axis.
It is covered with pottery.*

In regard to pottery I would here state, once for all, that it is so far
the same as at the mill. It is identical with that of San Diego in the
black-and-white, and burnt-sienna-and-white, in the common red-and-
chocolate brown, but as far as the corrugated is concerned, I miss so far
the red paint. There is some little red flint, and a few pieces of white,
but everything is old and dilapidated and worn out. On the whole, as
far as I can ascertain, for six to eight miles south of Brockmann's mill,
there are pueblos and single houses at distances from one-quarter to one
mile from each other. The single houses are at the bottoms, whereas the
villages stand on low promontories at the foot of barren lomas. The
latter have no trees, as far as the eye can reach.

About a half-mile south of Gruenewald's, on the foothill, or rather
promontory, northwest of the ranch of Simon Erby, lies a pueblo.* The

ruins are reduced to mounds of broken stones where there were houses and to enclosures formed by scattered stones. There are, on the east and south side of the hills, on the slopes, stone enclosures, which lie lower than the hillocks indicating houses, and which look very much like garden plots. They are exposed to the sun. There is considerable pottery strewn about, and there are also some broken metates of porous and drusic lava.

Mr. Gruenewald told me that he carried off 100 waggon[sic]-loads of stone from these ruins. This is an exaggeration because he as well as other witnesses stated that the houses were not over one story high. The ruins are scattered in five groups, and the trend of the hill or tongue is from north to south. On the west side is an abrupt declivity, about 18.0 [meters?] high, and rocky; on the other sides the slope is gradual, but the rise, almost imperceptible, is to the north, or rather north of the highest group of ruins there is a gradual plain. At the foot of the hill is the fertile bottom, and the river is about 200.0 [meters?] to the east.*

On the whole there are few houses. Below there was an old acequia which ran from the river and parallel to it for about a mile. A modern acequia has been dug out along its course. Another place, 5.5 x 14 [meters?], in the bottom, showing signs of an old house. A mile south of it, a larger pueblo yet, and so they continue for six to seven miles down the river, until where it permanently sinks.

Spent it [the night] at Brockmann's pleasantly with the boys, Mr. and Mrs. Brockmann having left for Silver City, and so we were sole masters of the house.

The ruins here are evidently of the same kind as those at Globe and on Salt River, but the settlements were smaller, I have not, as yet, seen any one as large as those near Armour's and Kenton's ranches, and the big mounds also are lacking. The ruins on the hill between Kenton's and Robertson's, and on the hill above Cline's, pretty fairly represent the type. The pottery is, however, different, and the ruins are much more turned over and the walls are scattered and strewn around. They appear to be exceedingly old, and the flints and basalt chips are scarce. Saw no obsidian as yet. The metates and manos are of lava with large amygdaloids and druses. The positions are well chosen, and the soil is very fertile, so that it was easy for the people to live through [by means of] the crops they could raise. I particularly inquired for wood and posts. Enough timber grows along the river for "vigas" and for heating and cooking purposes, and the stream itself, clear and limpid, is not farther than a quarter-of-a-mile. Tried to write to Joe, but could not, on account of the boys' racket. So I joined them, and we went on till midnight—very jolly. It was a Christmas Eve, anyhow!

DECEMBER 25: Gruenewald came early, as we rose very late on account of last night's racket. This valley here is fairly settled, but has only been so for 14 years. Yesterday afternoon I met a relative of Nicomedes Lara of El Paso. The settlers are Mexicans from Mesilla and from El Paso del Norte. Formerly the Mimbres Apaches occupied the country, mostly the heights. Bloody fights have occurred in this neighborhood, the last one two years ago, when Lieut. Smith[484] and a man named Daly were killed, also two Negro soldiers, and several citizens. The affair took place in the Cañón del Gavilán. The mines appear to give out in the mountains, although loose gold is occasionally found. Copper ore is common; I saw handsome cuprite.

(Shall stop at Carlos Norero's tonight, eight to ten miles north of here. He is an Italian.)

Ruins on the rancho of Señor Carlos Norero, eight miles north of Brockmann, on the west bank of the Mimbres River, and about three-quarters-of-a-mile from it. They are mostly reduced to mere heaps, the stones having been used for building houses.*

I took leave of the good, kind boys at about 11:30 A.M., Fritz [Brockmann?] driving me up to Norero's where we arrived at 2 P.M. and were very hospitably received. The valley bears the same character everywhere, narrow; the river makes interminable and innumerable windings. The same osier (mimbral) [willow, or willow groves], cottonwood, and ash line its shores, and the fertile bottom is alternately on the east and on the west bank, with an occasional passage between steep, barren heights. The ground rises to the north, the heights also, and trees appear occasionally. Ruins are at San Ysidro, and occasional houses indicated by mere heaps of ruins or traces of foundations, are scattered. San Ysidro is a poor little hamlet, with a miserable chapel, three miles north of Brockmann's. At Norero's ranch, the valley is nearly a mile wide, the mountains are high on the west, steep and rocky; on the east their slopes line the river. Between the foot of the mountains and the river bottom, there are two terraces on the west side. . . . On the lower terrace, the ruins are situated, and nearly all the stones used in building the house of Norero and the three rent-houses south of it, are built of the walls of the ruins.

Sketch of Norero's place.*

The walls, where visible, have been of stone and mud; some of the foundations are double, but mostly only single rows of stones appear. Little pottery and of course like the other, little flint and no obsidian. Metates of lava. Norero says he found no wood and no axes nor arrowheads. But they dug out skeletons, the skulls being entire. They were dug out on the east side of the group of ruins and at a depth of scarcely over 0.40 [meter?]. Norero assures me that, while there are ruins on the terrace, very few and isolated buildings stand on the tops of the western hills. Away from the river there is hardly any water at all. Saw a metate, still in use at Norero's house, though broken in part.

Metate and mano.

Both are made of grey volcanic rock, and the mano is decidedly of porous lava. This valley is perhaps the handsomest one along the Mimbres. Tall trees of black oak, "Encino colorado," with edible fruit ("vellotas") [bellotas, acorns], are scattered along the heights. On the ranch north of Mr. Norero's, there are some traces of ruins, and on the second terrace, above the ruins through which cuts the wire-fence, there are several circular depressions, again without foundation, and almost without pottery.

DECEMBER 26: Left at 10 A.M. The valley remained the same, though gradually widening towards San Lorenzo, where it is about a mile-and-a-half wide. San Lorenzo lies on the west bank. Ruins south of Thompson's southwest of San Lorenzo, west bank of the Rio Mimbres.*

The river here is completely dry, as it sinks, even on this upper course, at intervals. The village, mostly Mexican, lies on a rather steep slope, as the river-ranges hardly afford room for any plaza. The ruins are very much destroyed, as usual. I saw some pieces of obsidian, however. Flint is very scarce. There is a huge circular depression on the north side. It is evidently a natural hollow between two ridges, but artificially closed on the north and south, so as to form a circular basin. My groundplan is not very exact; it is rather a sketch, but still of sufficient accuracy.

At San Lorenzo, Pomacena Archeta told me that there are large ruins at the headwaters of the Gila. I reached the Mimbres Mining and Reduction Works leisurely, the road being almost an even plain, whereas the banks continue abrupt on the east side. This plain is treeless, but every inequality of the ground, such as the river-hills, have isolated

junipers or groves of oak trees. The works are closed, and temporarily abandoned. Lack of ore! Mr. S. S. Robinson received me most kindly. A room was ready with every comfort and an old letter from Joe waiting. Mr. B. Rosenfeld[485] also was exceedingly kind.

DECEMBER 27: Finished my pottery from the Rio Grande, and painted one groundplan. There is a ruin right here. Traces of houses are on every promontory. The Reduction Works stand on the brow of the first terrace; here the plain of the valley disappears, and north of us the valley takes the shape of a cañón, narrowing down. Still there are level strips. Ruins are scattered all along. Mr. Robinson gave me a good idea of the metalliferous conditions of the country. The ore is in small quantities, in thin seamlets and grooves, in the Silurian limestone, and also along dykes of porphyry. . . . This abundance of ore scattered in small quantities seems to be the characteristic all over here and also in northern Mexico. I received some valuable information from him in regard to the drainage. The Rio Mimbres empties into Lake Guzmán, and that basin forms a separate region without outlet, into which the waters run from Corralitos, from Janos and even from Casas Grandes. This is an interesting fact, and the antiquities of that region must be carefully studied. Wrote a postal card home. The ore here is chloride and chlorobromide of silver. In the Burro Mountains native silver is found.

DECEMBER 28: Mr. Robinson left today, probably never to return any more. I painted. Met Mr. [J.?] B. Risque,[486] who gave me much information, confirmed by other parties. The ruins on the Upper Gila are cliffhouses, in sandstone, and built of sandstone plates. They are mostly small, the largest containing six to eight pieces [cells or rooms]. In some of them, the vigas are still seen. Shoes [sandals] of yucca, cloth, arrowheads and arrowshafts, pottery, and in one of them a copper pitcher (!!) clearly hammered, were found in them. That pitcher is now in possession of Mr. S. Brannan.[487] Native copper, in chunks and large sheets, is abundantly found at Santa Rita.[488] The Spaniards worked that mine in 1783, and many tools of copper, from the Spanish period, are met in the country.

At Gadden's [Gatton's] much pottery, intact, was met with in digging a well, and a large number of turquoise beads! This is on the Upper Mimbres. We called on Dr. Woods,[489] and he showed us an axe, which is of diorite. It has flanges. There is a large pueblo near his house, which

I shall measure tomorrow. Mr. Spiller showed me a skull dug out opposite the Reduction Works, directly above the river, in an old room.
The back part is artificially flattened.* There were two skeletons found
there, lying at right angles, the heads almost touching. There were ashes
and fragments of pottery, also very small pottery—entire, found with
them. On the highest mountain overlooking the Mimbres on the east
side, opposite Dr. Woods, there are two circular depressions, and there
many broken arrowheads were found. Metates are met with frequently.
The ruins extend to the high hills along the river too.

DECEMBER 29: Last night I wrote home a long letter. Painted. In the
afternoon I went to Dr. Woods, who gave me his stone axe. We then
measured his ruin.* It is fairly preserved. There are many very large
blocks of stone in it. The circular depression is interesting. On the
northwest side, there is a wall which runs partly into it.* On the south
side, there is like an entrance to it, formed by huge blocks of stone. The
ruin is of earth, but there are many stones scattered along it. The walls
of all the buildings were of rubble or cobble, and the foundations frequently set on edge. Returning, we called on Mrs. Winter.[490] She has a
number of turquoise beads. They are shaped and polished like those of
the Pueblos, also like the shellbeads.* Then she has a little ollita and a
little bowl, both plain, taken from the place where the skull was found,
and a stone mortar in the shape of a bear taken out of Gadden's well.
Finally, a magnificent olla, richly painted, from Casas Grandes. It is a
splendid piece. Painted until late.

DECEMBER 30: Painted all day. The Mimbres River loses its water 12
miles below Brockmann's, but in the rainy season it runs occasionally to
within 20 miles of the Mexican frontier. Its floods are often high
enough to submerge the bottoms, but they last only three days. They
occur in July or August. The advent of rain and its quantities are, however, very irregular. This, and the malarial fevers prevailing below here,
may have contributed to drive off the former aboriginal population. The
ruins are very old. I saw, near Dr. Woods'—a juniper tree 0.50 [meter?]
in diameter standing in the midst of a quadrangle of stone foundation.
The lowest point [temperature] reached here is +6°F. Snow falls occasionally, but never lasts. The soil is exceedingly fertile, every kind of
vegetable grows splendidly. Potatoes are fine and very good. But there is
a lack of water supply, and the river sinks at many places, even north of

here. Here it is a clear handsome brook, bordered by willows and osiers.

DECEMBER 31: I painted the jar of Mrs. Winter's. It is, I am satisfied now, from Casas Grandes, Chihuahua. Mr. Mager told me that about Central City and Fort Bayard[491] there are cliffhouses. The drainage of Silver City goes to the Mimbres yet. This is interesting, as it shows that cliffhouses exist equally on both sides of this "divide." I am now about through painting. I shall send home all the pottery, etc. I can get, and paint only such pieces as I cannot obtain myself. Mager, who has lived about the copper mines somewhat, says that he never knew anything about copper implements being found. No letters yet. I hope that nothing has happened. Still, there is no telling. Nobody seems to care about writing to me. This place is 5,940 feet; Georgetown, 6,750 feet, above sea level. Wrote short letters to Joe, to Dr. Eggert, Meysenburg, Eldodt, Padre Ribera, Padre Grom, Ad. Mennet, W. Dessauer, Lieut. Elliott, Dr. Girard, to Pauline, and to Frank Cushing. Retired after midnight. Happy New Year to dear Joe, Papa, and to all. May God have mercy upon me in 1884 also.

Goodbye 1883.
Thanks for everything received.

JANUARY

JANUARY 1: Happy New Year! At least to everybody, especially to the dear ones at home. Water frozen in my room. Returned the olla to Mr. Winter.[1]

Ruins* near the works, on the level plain north-northwest of my quarters. The foundations are of large blocks of stone. I did not do much today, but visited Mr. Winter and Dr. Woods. The latter was not at home. Received letters from Joe, etc. Thank God!! The letters are exceedingly friendly and kind. God bless dear Joe and Papa for it.

JANUARY 2: Left on foot at 11 A.M. The valley soon narrows, as the heights on both sides encroach upon the river, a clear, rippling stream, and not over five [meters?] wide. Fields extend along it for about one-and-a-half miles. There a string of ranchos nestles on bare spots or in nooks. There is the Widow Nicolai's on the left side, then Pratt's, and, five miles above the works, Hick's. Here the heights take the size and form of mesas on the right, and they shut down upon the river on the east. Ruins extend to here. Beyond Hick's there is continuous timber with few houses. Moulton's[2] abandoned sawmill, the government saw-mill, stand among tall, beautiful pinavetes. The heights seem to sink on both sides. At the government sawmill, I turn to the west-northwest leaving the Mimbres. There is a handsome ciénega at Stinson's ranch, without trees, and thence to the [Continental] Divide it is about two miles. The latter is wooded and cold. Beyond it the descent is rapid into a level, bare basin, in which Gatten's [Gatton's] ranch stands, at the out-skirts of the tall pines surrounding it on all sides. It can be seen at a glance that there was never any village in this bare spot. This is already on the Sapillo, and about one mile below, that almost dry creek is met with. Tall and beautiful pine timber, surrounding and partly over-growing rocky heights, covers the ground, and the road winds in and out between the high, picturesque rocks and cliffs. It is wild and cold scenery. At Moulton's mill, in a little vale with very picturesque, splendid pines, I met two boys of S .S. Brannan's with a waggon and drove with them home (four-and-three-quarters miles) a winding cañón with very picturesque, lofty timber. Crossed the Sapillo four times. The ranch of Brannan, where I was most kindly received, stands on the creek. The valley is narrow, but still leaves room for fields. On the heights above (northeast) a ruin. On the Sapillo very excellent water.

JANUARY 3: My foot is so sore that I cannot think of going to the Gila today. The copper pitcher is decidedly Spanish, not aboriginal. It is hammered, with handle to it and simply—*rivetted!* I asked particularly about copper finds, and Mr. Brannan assured me very positively that he never knew, saw, or heard of, any implements of copper or metal being found. He says that there are at Silver City copper vessels of very rude form, but even these he thinks are Spanish. Of idols, plume-sticks, etc., he never heard neither. At Mangas Springs, eighteen miles west of Silver City, a fetish of obsidian representing what he calls a dog (?) was found. This is not conclusive, however, The place was the residence of the famous Mangas Coloradas,[3] the Apache chief, and the fetish might have been brought there by the Apache from some ruined or some existing pueblo, or even by Pueblo Indians themselves, and lost!! Then he showed me a cup and saucer from Gadden's ranch (on the Sapillo!). These were exhumed he says from a "cache" at a depth of twelve feet. Mr. Ed. Moulton told me at eight feet. They are not taken out of the well, but near a spring; the upper layers were broken pottery, and then came whole pieces, many turquoise beads, white shell beads, and a cedar post. The latter was erect and thus might possibly indicate a buried dwelling. Mr. Gadden still has some of the pottery. Then again Mr. Brannan speaks of conical tubes of stone.* They are about 0.70 [meter?] long and tapering, and he says they are blowpipes used for smelting and reducing gold and silver. (Doubtful!!!)

The "cache" system seems to have been extensively practiced in this region. There are several caches, filled with ancient pottery, about Silver City. The system was to cover it up with several feet of tepalcates [potsherds] and then fill it with earth. Copied both saucer and cup. They do not match. Still they have the same thick and coarse pottery. The designs, though intricate, are coarse, and recall the coarsely "glazed" pottery of the Rio Grande in irregularity.

Went to the little hill northwest of Mr. Brannan's house and found the remains of foundations. Pottery, corrugated, brown, and black-and-white, exactly the same kind as on the *Rio Mimbres.** There are ruins all along the Sapillo, on the high hills, but they must be small. Lava metates, stone axes, arrowheads of obsidian and flint, awls of flint and of obsidian, are found. Heard many stories about the cliffhouses and caves on the Gila. The pitcher of copper was not found in a ruin, but along the trail nearby!!

Mr. S. S. Brannan told me of the custom of the Apache, whenever they pass one of the artificial stone heaps (as between Show Low and Fort Apache—last year), to deposit on it each one a stone and two twigs placed crosswise, the stone holding down the twigs.* Thus their number can be ascertained.

Got two visitors, Richard Dwella (D'Huellay) and Frank Hayes. The former spoke of old irrigation ditches in the Mogollones, and the latter of the same in the Clifton district, on the San Francisco River. Bad night, sleepless.

JANUARY 4: Left at 9 A.M. on horseback with Mr. R. D'Huellay. Followed the Sapillo for one-and-a-half miles and then took the trail into the mountains. Very rough and picturesque. No water. Splendid timber. Pinahuatl [Pinabetes?]. Reached Divide at 2 P.M. Magnificent view east to the Mimbres, north and west to the Mogollones, with the chasms of the Gila at one's very feet. Reached the Gila, a limpid mountain stream encased by lofty towering sandstone crags at 4 P.M. and then followed its course in the narrow cañones, with hardly any soil or bottom, to the Ojo Caliente, where I stopped with Mr. Nielsen who received me very kindly. Splendid rocks in front of us, about three to four hundred feet high, eroded into columns and spires in túnditas and other forms. Magnificent pine trees shoot up in the bottom, and every nook, every corner, of the rocks themselves, bears a pinavete, a piñón, or a sabino. The encinos are not common, but álamos line the course of the gushing stream. So I am on the Gila again! Am tired, 21 miles.

JANUARY 5: (The tops of the high mesas of the Divide are volcanic, making a horrible trail. The mouth of the Sapillo is about 20 miles west of here, and is a deep cañón; so is the whole course of the Gila for nearly 40 miles west and high up to the source which is 40 miles northeast from here. There is no snow visible on any mountain, and the tall grass has its stalks still green.) The *Rio Gilita* [Little Gila] empties into the Gila a mile south of the Ojo Caliente. All these tributaries flow in deep, stately cañones, very narrow and grand, but there is vegetation everywhere. On the whole it is a beautiful spot. The hot springs are right opposite, on the banks of the river, oozing out of the declivity.

Some of them steam very strongly. Approximate profile of one of the caves.*

Started for the caves about 8:30 A.M. The valley winds around, past the springs, to the west, and then forms a bottom scarcely a half-mile wide, heavily timbered with pines and cottonwood, also oak, which extends, accidentally wandering, and leaving very fertile bottoms, all timbered along the river, for nearly four miles.* These bottoms were originally timbered, and there are cleared spaces where Mr. Williams and Mr. Rogers have their ranches. The river, beyond the latter, runs near to the west side and the mountains there are picturesque vertical crags. The bottom expands to the east, and there are several treeless terraces which I examined and found old pottery with some traces of foundations, but so disturbed that it was totally useless to attempt any measurement. About five miles from the springs, after crossing the Gila six times, there is a very high rock of yellow volcanic breccia standing out boldly to the left.

At its foot a small creek meanders in a very deep cleft. It is not wider than the creek itself, or about one meter. On the south side, a high mesa with a timbered slope descends very abruptly. That slope, if it was only a little more inclined, would not be able to hold trees. The banks of the creek are so timbered and covered with brush as to make it almost impossible to penetrate. On the north side, trees grow up to about five to ten meters, then the slope gets rocky, finally vertical and overhanging in places, supporting a shelf above [on] which are the caves. The following would be the front of the north bluff, from its mouth to the caves.

The cross section at the caves would be as follows. Estimated height of the bluffs two hundred [meters?] at least.*

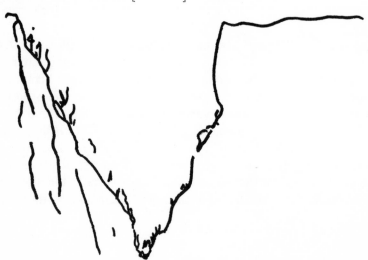

Above the caves, the bluff rises vertically, or rather overhanging. The caves which have been built are four in number, but the three easterly ones communicate naturally behind pillars. The middle cave of the three, which is the largest, is about ten meters high, and its roof bends over in front, so that protection against weather is absolutely perfect. As a place of concealment, it was beautifully selected, as well as of defence in case of direct assault, but for an enemy who would harass them, even with arrows, from the south side opposite, it was easy to keep them from water. From below, the buildings cannot be seen, and anyone might pass up the creek bed without noticing them at all.

[These caves constitute a major feature of present-day Gila Cliff Dwellings National Monument, New Mexico.]

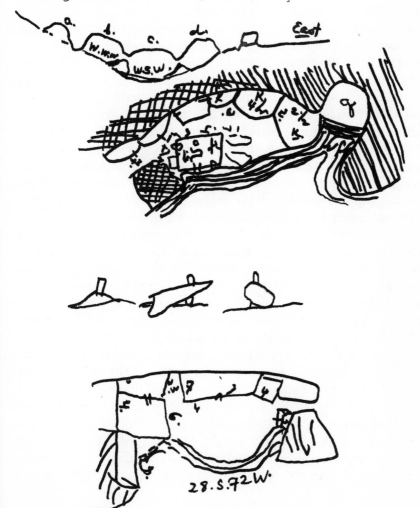

The ascent is not possible from the front, and very difficult from any side. East of the caves, there is another one, which is empty. (a.b.c.d.) are the buildings. They are narrower in front than in the rear.* No attempt has been made to level the floors by removing the rock, but there are black deposits of rubbish resembling manure!

K.K.K. are more like enclosures than like rooms. O. is the hearth. p.p. are the ends of a crossbeam, burnt down by the Apache. Immense masses of rock have fallen down from the roof; in some cases they have fitted the walls around them, showing that they were unable to move them. The hearth is in the center of the large room; it is of three flags, and the opening is mostly south. G. is an empty chamber walled up in front. But it is inaccessible without ladders and with my sore foot. Cave C. is the largest, that is almost two stories high.

For b. and a., see sheet #3.* Cave a. was walled up to the top in front, and the rear rooms had no roof as the absence of vigas and the finish on the top of the walls plainly shows. The beams are all pealed. The lintels are of two sticks of wood, sometimes half-round, and laid crosswise.* There are small air holes, one of them 0.20 [meter?] square, has two sticks of wood as lintel [presumably, sill] and on each side and a similar lintel on the top. A good deal of rubbish is all around. Very little pottery, visitors having picked it up. What I found was mostly corrugated, some of it painted red. Found one piece of painted pottery, black-and-white. Many corncobs, sticks, pita, and one fragment of a sandal. Of the latter, a great many have been carried off, also stone axes. The place as it is, is now rifled. I found a bundle of sticks, tied with pita. They had been dug up from the rubbish. There is hardly any flint and no obsidian at all. The walls are plastered inside and so daubed over outside, that they look almost like concrete. Practically, there are two retreating stories, the recesses in front having been converted into rooms by walling. The roofs, I am told, were like the pueblo, but the Apache burnt them down. The room of the caves slants inwards in c. and d.; the floor of all inclines outwards, mainly in a. and b. I descended, very painfully owing to my right foot, which is exceedingly sore, and crept out of the cleft. Almost impossible to walk. At the outlet of the cleft, there are some signs as of an old acequia, but it is doubtful. Flint chips abundant on the site near Rogers. Returned home at 3:30 A.M. [?] limping. It is our wedding night. I shall write to Joe.

There are other hot springs up the river yet. About eight to ten miles higher up, the valley widens, but it is an exceedingly cold country. Nearly two-thirds of the rooms in the caves were certainly without roofs. This is explained by the mild climate and the perfect shelter afforded by the caves. Saw a baldheaded eagle today. Game not very abundant. Skunks plentiful, also foxes, but no coyotes. Bear, mountain lions, and catamounts [lynx] occur occasionally, and, very rarely, elk. On the whole, this country affords safe retreats, but little room for pueblos. The aborigines were not very abundant, and their settlements necessarily small.

JANUARY 6: My foot still sore, so I remained at home and painted pottery. Am compelled to put all on one plate, cliffhouse and open air pottery. But as the same kinds are found in both places, it makes no difference. Previous to going to work, however, I limped to the top of the second terrace, or rather loma, southwest of the house, and found the remains above. The surface is treeless, and was so originally, and therefore selected for settlement by the aborigines.

It is important to note this fact, as it shows that they chose bare spots for settlement. This appears to be the rule, and the timber around gives little clue, therefore, to the age of the ruins. They consist of the usual foundations made of boulders, and flags set on edge. There is also the same sign of a small house (indicated by a low convexity, and a court or courts). Much pottery, corrugated like that of the cliffhouses or caves, red-and-white, black-and-white, and plain dark. Some white flint chips. No obsidian.

JANUARY 7: There are, on the hill, or loma, which I visited yesterday, two or three other places where the ground appears to have been originally "stirred up" and some faint traces of corners are visible. In all there may have been six small dwellings there, each one with a court.*

So cold that I could scarcely paint in the house. The water froze on the brush as late as 9 A.M. Painted all day. It grew handsomely temperate after 12 A.M., and lasted so until 4 P.M. Quiet. N. Nielsen was off all day again. My foot better, but still sore. Nielsen reported that on a high hill, opposite Rogers' ranch, west of the river, three miles above here, there is a large ruin, whose mounds can be seen from Rogers' house. Only foundations, he says. Shall go there tomorrow.

They have had scarcely any rain here this year, and the Gila has not been one foot higher than it is now; still it may occasionally overflow at long intervals. It thunders here at all times of the year, but real electric storms are rare. As usual, my foot is a little worse at night. The fountain [pen][4] suddenly began to work tonight, but we shall see tomorrow.

They are whimsical nuisances, that's all! But I shall try it in the field tomorrow. It is a lonely life here, and I am glad to leave day after tomorrow. I cannot do any painting at night, and the society of my good, kind Dane, Niels Nielsen, is not always the most spirited. Still we have enough to talk about. Were it not for the bitterly cold mornings, it would be splendid here. There is plenty of good, rough food. Since the day before yesterday we have venison! Mr. Williams was out hunting four days and shot four deer. Many conflicting land claims about here. Attempted to paint tonight, and succeeded to a very limited extent.

JANUARY 8: Sprained right foot slightly overnight, in bed. We had considerable amount of work to do and thus left only at about 10 A.M. My foot very painful again. I examined the stone heaps in the wooded bottom and found them to be only arroyo drift. At Mr. Williams, met him, Mr. Forbes, and D'Huellay. The ruins are directly opposite Mr. Jordan Rogers' new ranch, on a perfectly bare hill, about sixty-five meters high over the river. The main Gila there hugs the hills close. The ascent is rather steep, and there is a good deal of loose lava rock, but a good trail, though steep, leads up to it.* This trail is not old, it leads to the Gilita and to a cattle ranch situated on that stream.

On the very brow of the hill, facing south, south-southwest and southwest to west even, the ruins are situated, completely overlooking the whole valley, an admirable position for defence and observation, as behind it is a depressed plain, perfectly bare, so that for nearly a mile, on the elevation itself, not a mouse could move without being seen from the pueblo. The latter is small, and each group forms a distinct rubbish mound, and there are basin-like depressions separating each group and also among them. These depressions may be artificial in part, being the places where they dug out soil for the cement of the wall, but nothing else. The plain on the top is grassy.* The walls are of the usual volcanic rubble, laid in earth, but there is not a single wall standing, and it is difficult to trace the foundations owing to the rubbish. Much white flint in good, clear chips, some red and purple chips like porphyry or impure agate, are lying about. They are clearly artifacts.

I at last found a bit of obsidian! The pottery is the same in design, but there are many pieces which appear almost new and have a modern appearance. There is a thin, red pottery, and a red pottery, painted cream-and-white inside with black, very handsome, ornaments on it. Found one decayed piece with a hole, reamed on both sides.* Another piece, which I could not copy, has the following ornament, black upon white ground and evidently ancient.* Saw no metates, though I noticed a broken mano, of course of brownish black porous lava. [Sketch and height measurements.] On the whole the ruins are small, and they do not change my opinion that only small settlements, smaller than those on the Mimbres, but of the same style and design of architecture and much less of these, are found here. This is easily accounted for. There is no room and no agricultural resources here for a larger Indian population.

Mr. Williams showed me the sites of two more ruins, both within sight of the river, and both naturally denuded, high and treeless spots; one is about three quarters-of-a-mile east of the river bank and about one hundred to two hundred meters above it. Below Mr. Rogers', in a side cañón, are rock-paintings of snakes, lizards, etc., done in red ochre. Did not see them.

Very sore feet. Returned to Mr. Williams and then crept home where I finished my plate of pottery. Shall start for Brannan's tomorrow with Niels and D'Huellay. Am so far well pleased with the results of my journey to the Upper Gila.

Had to wait a long time until Dick D'Huellay came at last. Started on a burro. Went by Ailman's ranch.[5] Slept again very poorly, my feet improving. Niels Nielsen came along. The trail is indeed very picturesque, but the road is horrible in places, and no water except a few springs high up near the crest of the Divide, on the Sapillo side.

JANUARY 10: Left at 9 A.M. and as I started, it began to snow. Reached Moulton's before noon. Mr. C. G. Bell of Norfolk, Virginia, was there alone. Reception most kind. He showed me a fine collection of sandals, about seven pieces, which he had dug out of the cliffhouses on the Gila, also a ring for carrying water, and a piece of pita wound around with rabbit skin, evidently for a mantle similar to that made and worn by the Moqui! I began copying the sandal at once, but it is exceedingly difficult, being much dilapidated.

JANUARY 11 AND 12: Painted at the sandal. It is very difficult, and I doubt whether I can copy it fairly [accurately]. Mr. Bell assured me that he had himself assisted in digging out turquoise (!) two-and-a-half miles west of Santa Rita, at a small depth. It was in the Hanover Mine, was blue, turning greenish, and finally into white. John Fuller told me that on the Rio Grande there are ruins south of Fort Craig, on the west bank, and much pottery. He also spoke of an old acequia on the Rio

Bonito, and asserted that it was lined with cement! This lining was exceedingly hard, and only visible at the bottom. He says that the Prairie Indians tan their hides with brains! Pinos Altos, seven miles from Silver City, a rich gold camp, discovered in 1859.[6] Mr. Bell called my attention to the fact that no mocassins were ever found in cliffhouses. It appears that the latter were a recent invention!![7]

JANUARY 13: From Hick's place down, the ruins become nearly continuous. An isolated house measured 5 x 4 steps (3.7 x 3 [meters?]). Reached the works well but tired. Letters from home, from Father Grom, from Mathey, and from Lieutenant Elliott. All well, thank God.

JANUARY 14: Painted all day at the sandal. It is difficult beyond comprehension. I almost despair of making it. Sent a few lines to dear Joe. At night Mr. Rosenfeld gave me a short history of the copper mines of Santa Rita. It appears they were systematically worked by a certain Colonel Carrasco,[8] in 1801. (Others say 1810.) He had to work it according to Spanish mining laws, leaving pillars at stated intervals. It was afterwards, however, abandoned, and opened again and worked with very little caution. There is plenty of excellent ore, and the only thing that caused its abandonment now, was an ill-conceived scheme on the part of one of its owners to sell it for six million at London, in which scheme he failed utterly. So it remains idle! Tonight, I received plenty of letters. Papa's of the 15th December; Dr. Moore's of the 30th, Captain Dougherty's of the 18th October! They have travelled in every imaginable direction. Also a box which I do not know what it contains. Shall open it tomorrow.

JANUARY 15: Painted all day, and finished the sandal at last. It was a fearful job, and a very big undertaking at all events. Am very glad; both the news from home, and at the success with the sandal. Have not yet opened the box. Wrote four pages to Dr. E. M. Moore, Rochester.

JANUARY 16: I painted all day, finishing the ring for carrying water. Opened the box, and found it filled with sausage, which I distributed. I got another version of the Adam's Diggings[9] tale. It appears from the statements of a farmer that there are ruins in the Black Range (Mimbres), but mostly on both slopes, and not on the crests or tops. Risque left.

JANUARY 17: Wrote home, and Mr. [S. D.] Waters[10] took the letter along when he left for Deming this afternoon. Painted all day. The textile fabrics are all done at last, and I have begun at the corrugated-and-indented pottery. Slept at the superintendent's house tonight. Wrote to Governor Ritch and to Captain Dougherty.

JANUARY 18: I forgot to state that, last Tuesday, Risque and Carter brought me some handsome pottery and some arrowheads of grey trap, found opposite here, across the river, where there are considerable ruins also. Sent my letters to Georgetown. Painted pottery all day. At night wrote a long letter to Frank E. Robinson,[11] #15 Brainard Street, Detroit, Michigan, and a short one to Prof. Norton. My left breast aches.

JANUARY 19: Wrote to Greenleaf about brushes and paper. Painted pottery all day. Accident to Dr. Woods and to J. C. Winter yesterday, at Georgetown. The latter's foot is badly sprained. Painted at the caves till midnight. Mr. Winter told me of very remarkable remains found at Mangas Springs, in a big cave. Wands, idols, bows, mats, sandals, pottery, etc.

JANUARY 20: Painted the whole day. So did I Monday, Tuesday, and Wednesday. I got many handsome pieces of pottery, one entire bowl (yellow-and-white), a beautiful fragment painted white-and-black, two little pieces of indented pottery, very handsomely finished. Finally, Patrocinia brought me a most splendid axe, ten-and-a-half inches long, of dark green rock, possibly diorite and feldspar combined. It might also be a finely grained syenite. I painted so much, and so long at night, that I got very nervous, finally, sleepless, and unwell. So I abandoned painting on the afternoon of the 23rd and packed up. I have now, in all, 16 sheets complete (eight of groundplans, one of details from the caves, one of rock-carvings, five of pottery, and one of textile work), and three sheets begun. There are a number of ruins around the works, and they extend as far as three miles north-northwest along the Rio Mimbres. A considerable group, each cluster being small in itself, lies right opposite here, on the east bank, about forty [meters?].

JANUARY 20-23: [Sites?] above the river, on perfectly bare mesas. Besides, there are isolated square or rather quadrangular ruins promiscuously scattered. The following are three of those.* (All in steps!)

The latter contains a tall juniper tree in its center. Besides, there is one of the groups which I have selected as a fair specimen. This group lies on the west bank, about two miles above the works, on a bare slope to the left of the road going up. I was also shown a bone awl.* On the whole it appears that the river, wherever it is possible to settle it, was dotted by small villages with little provisions for defence. Mr. Rosenfeld tells me that they extend nearly to his ranch, and that there is a large one there with walls, crumbled, forming a mound. Much pottery was exhumed. He found a fireplace in one corner.*[12] This is the plan he drew for me of it. There are said to exist rock-paintings in that neighborhood. There would be much to do here, but I cannot stay any longer and must leave. Mounds are also said to exist near Mangas Springs.

Got a letter from Joe on the 22nd. All well.

JANUARY 24: Left with Otto Antonio. The road to Georgetown is a continuous ascent, very winding, through a narrow gorge or winding cañada, the slopes, very rocky, are covered with less timber. The road is very narrow sometimes. The country is so broken and rugged as to leave no favorable spots for Indian settlement. Georgetown is in a deep cleft, exceedingly similar to Globe in situation, only even more wild, and the steep rocky slopes timbered with oak and coniferae. Yucca appear more in profusion.

Met Mr. and Mrs. Smith.[13] He showed me exceedingly beautiful specimens of ore and two little pieces of whole pottery from Gatton's "cache." One is not deeply indented.* The other is a flat saucer after the manner of the one which I copied at Brannan's, but a little smaller. It is white, with black ornaments irregularly distributed. This is only an approximation. The former is not painted. Also cup and saucer, or bowl, plain, from the Mimbres.

After leaving Georgetown, we travelled, on a rather elevated plateau, cold, timbered, rocky, and waterless, from which a very beautiful view is enjoyed of the whole Mimbres chain. Yucca on this plateau becomes arboriferous, and the mezcal agave appears in small clusters. There is no water and too much timber for ruins to be expected. Beyond the Divide we fall again, and reach Santa Rita, in a valley at the foot of towering crags, very high. There is more open ground; still, as water is lacking, hardly any ruins can be thought of [expected]. This range of high, timbered mountains, with very picturesque rocky crags, perpendicular walls, extends from east to west, and south to Santa Rita to San

José. On their north side, the ground slopes gently upwards, with timber. Am told that there are no ruins.

At Whitewater, the country opens fully and becomes barren and bare as near Fort Cummings. In the southwest appears the Sierra del Burro, snow-clad, and there are patches even in this level waste. The Santa Rita heights form a long craggy mesa in the east. In the southeast Cook's Peak looms up. The vegetation shows nothing but arboriferous yucca. To the north-northwest is the Pinos Altos Range, whose lofty pines are plainly visible. Thus the country remains, barren and bare, undulations separated often, but not always, by arroyos otherwise dry. Not even the Whitewater is a permanent stream. Reached Silver City[14] at 4 P.M. It is in a very rocky basin, dreary, and with a cold draft of wind rushing through it.

JANUARY 25: Silver City has no running water. A dry arroyo traverses it, draining towards Deming into the Mimbres. Lower down a little water appears. The town is very dull now, but handsomely built. The side of the basin is exceedingly rocky, and appears to be of a very coarse breccia.

Last night wrote cards to Joe, to Dr. Eggert, to Lieutenant Elliott, and to Lieutenant Wheeler. Also a letter of introduction for Risque to Pauline.

Last night a polecat infested the year [surely, yard]. Cold and cloudy morning, exceedingly chilly. My lungs are very taken again. Coughing and very painful. Still, I went up to the northern outskirts of the city. There is a spring there, and indeed, on a knoll still inside the city limits, there are very faint limits and mounds which I surveyed and have mapped here.* Only few of the foundations are yet distinct. Of pottery, only very small fragments are left, but they appear very similar to those on the Mimbres and at Rincon even! Found a trace of flint and even of obsidian. The rubbish shows rubble walls in mud, but as a good many of the stones have been carried away, it is not possible to form a clear idea of the height of the buildings, but I do not think they were over one story.

On a hill about a mile from town, and whose base is about one-quarter-of-a-mile west of this knoll, is the ruin here platted.* It is much disturbed also, but as the slope is very steep on both east and west, and the ascent from the south over slopes and narrow crests with only a trail leading up to it, I do not believe that any rock was carried off, and, consequently, that the buildings were only one story high. The walls are of rubble and mud, as the excavation plainly shows, where a wall three-and-a-half feet high is still exposed. No thickness visible. Pottery the same as usual. Some of the largest enclosures are on the slopes, and were evidently enclosures and not houses. On the whole, the ruin is similar to that on the Gila opposite Rogers' ranch.

Returning, I copied the three stone axes of Mr. Howard. He showed me a rough plate of a ruin in the Black Range about five miles south of Fairview. It is enclosed by a *semi-circular stone-wall*. *a.* and *c.* are the ruins of *round towers*, whose original height he estimates at fifteen feet, and *b.* he mentions as a *tank*. The ruins are evidently small.* He showed me a flint awl also. The axes are of the usual well-known pattern.

I met many people, and left at 2 P.M. by train with J. B. Risque. The San Vicente flows permanently with water, somewhat below Silver City, the country still being rocky, but only for two to three miles. Afterwards it dries up, and the country opens and becomes a barren, naked plain all the way along, expanding treeless and waterless, uninhabited almost, north to the hills of Silver City; northwest to the Sierra del Burro; west as far as the eyes reach almost; south very far, the Hachas and the Tres Hermanas alone looming up in the distance; southeast to the Sierra Florida; east to Cook's Peak; and northeast to the Santa Rita chain, behind which the Mimbres loom up; and then around the northeast to north the Pinos Altos. In the far east, the Organos appear, and as we approach the high "Table Mountain" with the "City of Rocks" at its foot, [there is] Pachitihu and Hudson's Springs at the foot of bare and barren heights in the naked, open plain. [It is] a scene of aridity, monotony, and desolation, surrounded by high mountains, equal and more than that at Nutt and Fort Cummings. Deming, north of the Florida, is just alike—level, arid, and barren. Am told that the Sierra del Dragón is without water and ruins.

JANUARY 26: As we left, at 8 A.M., a permanent rainstorm seemed to be progressing. As far as the eye could see, only a barren, desolate plain was visible. The base of the Burros alone appeared, opposite to it some of the remarkably regular tops of Pyramid Range also. As a general thing, the country is absolutely treeless, the tallest plant being the yucca, but the mountains are covered with scattered and, as far as the distance permits to judge, evidently low, coniferae. As we approached the Divide, which is [before?] Steins Pass, it snowed fast. The Divide is at the foot of the Burros. At Steins Pass,[15] which is the southern spur of the Peloncillos, it was not as cloudy, but the country is terribly desolate and barren, also rugged. No water on the surface. Beyond it, is the grassy plain of San Simon, waterless on the surface except in some places of the Arroyo de San Simón. The latter rises on the eastern slope of the Chiricahua Range and runs in a slight curve towards the Gila, sinking before it reaches that river.

Below the surface, however, there is ample water obtained by sinking and boring. The San Simon Valley terminates a little south of the railroad and beyond it the Valle de las Playas begins extending into the very limits of Mexico. West of it the base of the Chiricahuas appears, skirting the plain and terminating at the north Mexican boundary. Railroad Pass is barren and arid; it divides the Chiricahuas from the Sierra Pinaleno in the north. Then follows Sulphur Spring Valley extending also southeasterly, bounded by the Sierra Dragón, where gold is mined now, and the Chiricahuas. The Dragones have no water at all on the surface. North of the road is the Sierra Salitre (Galino!). Then follows the narrow and broken valley of the Rio San Pedro, but Benson lies in a flat basin. Here vegetation becomes taller, and opuntia, palo verde, mezquite, are more plentiful. Shower of rain. (The Divide is almost a lake!)[16] Beyond it on the west are the Whetstone Range; north of the road, the Santa Catalina. We emerge upon still high open ground, the outskirts of the arid plains of Arizona. Tucson at 7 P.M. All well at Mrs. Black's, where I took the room with Mr. Neff.

JANUARY 27: Tucson is very lively on account of the Quijotoa Mine[17] which, at least on the surface, appears to be very rich. ¿Quien sabe? [Who knows?] Walked out to Fort Lowell and got letters from Mr. Parkman, Cushing, and Meysenburg. All right.

I was told that there are ruins at the Coyote. The plain between Tucson and the Fort is very arid, but the Riito [Rillito] runs past the Fort about one-fourth [mile?] from the north building, emptying, as a dry arroyo, into the Santa Cruz at Tucson. Below Tucson the Santa Cruz disappears, but is supposed to run to the Gila underground. North of the Riito the ground is in higher, rounded, and broken lomas, from which, at a distance of ten miles, the Santa Catalina rises abruptly. Returned from the Fort at night and on foot.

JANUARY 28: Painted all day. There are ruins in the southwest as far as a hundred miles from Tucson (cliffhouses) towards Sonoita, therefore probably about the Sierra del Ajo, or in longitude, west 113°. That country is called the Papaguería. Am preparing to go as soon as possible. Met Connell.

JANUARY 29: Painted. The force of climate is remarkable here. Green lettuce in fine heads is out in the gardens and in the open air. In the Father's garden, genuine maguey is thriving finely. Saw Dr. Thomas.

JANUARY 30: Painted. Was shown an arrow-sharpener of stone, handsomely carved, from southwestern Arizona. Handsome piece. Dr. Girard called, inviting me out to the Fort. Spent evening at Father Antonio's[18] and at Dr. Thomas'. [Ayenza?] offered me letters to General Topete.[19] Everybody advises me to avoid the Sierra Madre. Saw Connell's collection. It contains about seventy pieces, all new, among them some pieces from the Yumas. He says that the Yumas wear a kilt made of bark. This is interesting as compared with the skirt plaited of yucca, which Mrs. Winter mentioned as having been found at the caves on the Upper Gila! Am preparing to leave for the Fort.

JANUARY 31: Drove out to the Fort early, and took quarters at the hospital. Began at once to paint a canteen of corrugated pottery, painted red, which was found at the estanque, nine miles east-northeast of here. This is a permanent waterpool belonging to the Riito system. There are evidently ruins there. In the parade ground here, there are traces of low mounds, of undistinguishable disposition, and also much ancient pottery after the pattern of the lower Gila and Verde. There are ruins at Fort Grant, and Dr. Girard has a handsome stone axe from that place which is characteristic of Arizona, namely: crease only on two sides. Exceedingly like those of Silver City too. Painted.

FEBRUARY

FEBRUARY 1: Painted, but it finally grew too dark. At night, wrote home a long letter of four pages.

FEBRUARY 2: Wrote my journal, about which I had been very neglectful. There are thick, but low mezquites growing in the parade ground, among the low and nondescript mounds mentioned, and the pottery is scattered all over the ground. From Wheeler's Report, 1875,[20] and Dr. Rothrock's special Report (p. 122), I gather the following names of plants about Fort Apache: *Pinus ponderosa, Quercus undulata* (the common oak there) (p. 119.). In the Cubero plain, two kinds of grasses: *Brizopyrum spicatum* and *Sporobolus cryptandrus*. Between Ash Creek and the Gila (p. 122), the mezcal, *Agave paryyi* and *palmeri*, mezquite, *Algarrobia glandulosa*, the creosote plant, and *Larrea gigantea*. The *Dasylirion* is the saw-leafed yucca. The *ocotilla* is *Fouquiera splendens*. Estimates the height of the Santa Rita at 10,500 (p. 125). Rainfall at Camp Goodwin (Gila Valley) 32.78 [inches] of which 3.21, spring; 7.20, summer; 10.52 fall; and 11.85, winter. Old Camp Grant in the San Pedro Valley has fall, 6.43; winter 3.23. Tucson: summer, 4.30; Tubac: 10 inches. Fort Grant in the Aryvaipa [Valley]: 4,753′. Sierra Bonita (Mt. Graham): 10,516! The botanical name of the Palo Verde is: *Parkinsonia torreyiana*.

Rumex out in leaves!

Remains of ruins, northeast of the Fort [Lowell], half-encircled by the present acequia.* It appears to have been of marl, but it may have been an adobe house completely decayed and reduced to mud and dust. The walls, in their present state of decay, show a width of 0.75 [meter?] but as they are heaps rather than walls, it is impossible to find out how wide they originally were. The plan is doubtful, but at all events there is still no doubt that there has been a pueblo there, as there is too much pottery about. The latter resembles that of the Gila. There are also flint chips, though few, and some chips of basalt or trapp.

Farther to the southeast on the hills forming the second terrace of the Riito, there are other signs of former occupation, but nothing measurable. But along the road leading to the Ciénega, called the Mountain Spring road, there is an old channel, following that road at a distance of from one to twenty feet, exactly parallel almost [to the road] which has every appearance of having been an old acequia. This parallelism speaks against it, also the profile or cross cut in many places, which is that of a road track washed out by rain.* Also the width, which is that of the road itself. But in other places it deepens to a groove about 0.50 to 0.60 [meter?] deep, and of 0.40 width.* Then there is grass growing on both sides, giving them an appearance of perfect bordos [banks]. This again speaks for the acequia. The road, with the supposed acequia, skirts the gravelly hills . . . and on the other side a moist, fertile plain, converted now into a thicket of thorny shrubs, extends to the Riito. Two seeming desagües [drains] are visible near the point of the terrace, and near them the presumed ditch turns off to the east of the road and empties into a series of puddles or waterholes, in a thicket, which con-

nect with the present acequia. From these waterholes, the ground slants
more, and is traversed by numerous rills, all running towards the river
bed in various directions. It looks as if the ditch had been taken out from
the direction of the head of the Ciénega, which is 28 miles southeast,
and carried into the Riito.

Lieutenant Cruse spoke of ruins at Leopoldo Carrillo's rancho, seven
miles northeast, and Lieutenant Kingsbury[21] of stone foundations five
to six miles northeast. Caña agria.[22]

FEBRUARY 3: Letters from Joe and Frank Robinson. [Here, Bandelier
recorded a long series of botanical common names with genus and
species designations, probably taken from the sources cited on February
2.]

Met Lieutenant Reed [23] and Mr. Ouray [W. S. Oury].[24] There are,
according to the latter, many small ruins about the Estanqué Verde
[probably present-day Tanque Verde], but he knows of none at Huachuca[25] proper. Spent evening with Lieutenant Cruse.

FEBRUARY 4: The Riito is full of water, and the roar is loudly heard at
the hospital, a distance of a half-mile south.

[Here Bandelier quoted a paragraph from an article by Monsieur
Jamstel, entitled Le Progrès en Chine (Progress in China)].

Called on General Carr.[25a] Finished my report to Professor Norton,
but it was too late to mail it.[26] Examined the acequia again, and General
Carr assured me positively also that it was genuine. West of the Fort,
there are no ruins. The bottom of the Riito is very wide, and partly transformed into mud puddles today, but the main waters subsided already
in the forenoon and the rain is all gone. Wrote to Mr. Parkman.

FEBRUARY 5: Wrote home, upon receipt of a long letter from Papa and
one from John Fischer.[27] Went to Tucson in the afternoon with the
Dr. [Girard], Mrs. G[irard], and Lieutenant Kingsbury. Wrote card to
Dr. Mathews. Dined with General Carr. At night, I wrote letter to
Meysenburg.

FEBRUARY 6: Last night I wrote card to George Pradt. Got a letter from
Don Joaquín [García Icazbaleta], a note from Papa, and a letter from
the German Consul at St. Louis. Wrote to Cushing and to the Consulate. Lieutenant Reed affirmed today that, at Fort Sully in Dakota,
he found much pottery, painted and corrugated. He also described to

me a house at Fort Bechtold, in a village which is composed of the Mandans, Rees [Arikarees, or Arikaras] and Gros Ventres. This house had three rooms with skylights.* Only one door, and no window. In one corner of a room was a chimney made of sticks! (Compare Dr. Mathews last spring.) Lieutenant Reed has the first copy of Garrick Mallery's Dakota calendar, and he found it and communicated it to Colonel Mallery himself.[28]

FEBRUARY 7: Started at 10 A.M. Very despondent. The Institute cares not for publishing anything.[29] At home, there is not the condition which I should have there. Am about decided and determined to sever my connections with the Institute, and to return, perhaps even after this tour already. Still, there are other considerations yet in view. Time and God may bring relief.[30]

I followed the road. It avoids the Rillito, but what I suspect to be an acequia runs alongside of it for some three miles, and then turns left towards the Rillito. It leaves the question, as to whether it is an acequia or not, undecided. Vegetation, as the soil rises, changes into more arboriferous forms. Turning towards the southern point of the Santa Catalinas, the Sierra del Rincón appears behind them, its top still covered with snow. The rancho of Telly lies at the foot of this point on a sandy beach, where traces of pottery are still visible, and it looks as if there had been a ruin. Still, there is no permanent water on the surface. The sand drifts fearfully here; it blows in clouds even today. Thence I followed a dry cañada and then struck south-southeast across the high plain south of Sierra del Rincón rising to a barren pass, and then I turned due east into a deep rock gorge, sloping southwest towards Pantanos, but the road hugs the northern slope close and enters by a deep cleft into a pleasant vale, not a quarter-of-a-mile long, with a beautiful spring and Mr. Lick's house. It was 5 P.M. when I reached it, after having made twenty-two miles. The spot is very handsome.

This is "Mountain Spring," also called La Posta Quemada [Burnt Post]! The arroyo which descends, empties into the Rillito system. Here the Sierra del Rincón tapers out, and it is only five miles to the base of the Santa Rita's most northerly spur. The arroyo is dry except when it rains. Mr. Lick spoke to me of a cave about a mile from his house, where he found innumerable deer-prongs, skinning knives of wood, and broken pottery in ashbeds. There is also a ruin along the creek, four miles higher up. Rectangular foundations of stone. Lick tells me that there are water tanks in the highest crags and clefts of the

Dragones, and that there is no truth in the tale of a ruin on the top of Mount Graham. He is of the opinion that there are ruins around Fort Yuma.[31]

FEBRUARY 8: Started at 9 A.M. and went up along the arroyo. It descends along the southern base of the Rincón. The valley widens as it rises. Where the ruins are, there is much good grass. Otherwise, the vegetation is limited to yucca, dasylirium, and, on the mountain-slopes, zahuaros. The creek is running now. The country is not homely, but arid in its looks. Reached the Divide at noon, at the rancho of Miguel Torres, nine miles from Lick's house.

It is a long stretch, winding around the Rincón, bare and bleak, only yucca and dasylirium, and grass; very few zahuarros, except on the mountains, where they take the place of timber. At the ranch of Miguel Torres, on the denuded foot of the slope southeast of the Rincón, where there is no sign of water at all, I found, in a mezquite grove, the ruins above.* They are mere mounds, no foundations left at all, and as there is very little stone on the mounds, they must have been one story in height only. As to the material they were built of, it is not quite clear. They may have been of rubble, though there is hardly enough stone about to warrant the fact, and there is, on the other hand, very little soil. The great difficulty, however, is to conceive wherefrom they derived the water! Don Miguel Torres assured me that there is no permanent water on the whole Divide, and he knows of neither spring nor tank. That crops may be raised, is evident, by means of summer rains, but where the drinking water came from is the question. Flint chips, basalt chips, etc., are common, but no obsidian. Pottery is slaty grey, with red decorations, also yellow with red, plain brown, blackish grey, and red. Nothing [no pottery] corrugated at all.

Another ruin, now obliterated, stood where the house of Torres now stands. He excavated a metate there, but no stone axes. At Pantanos there was a ruin of a pueblo, which yielded a stone axe. Beyond this place, the ground still rises for two to three miles, bleak and barren, then the descent begins, over broken, bare hills, without any timber, into the San Pedro Valley. Distance six miles. In all, eighteen miles from Lick's! The valley is perfectly flat, and between vertical slopes ten to sixty feet high. It is marshy and about a mile wide. Got there at 4:30 P.M.

FEBRUARY 9: From the house of Mr. Thomas Dunbar,[32] where I stay and am well treated, the Whetstone, or Sierra Mesteña, is south-south-west. The Rincón is west-northwest; the Sierra Salitre east-northeast, and the Sierra Dragón southeast. Due south is the Sierra Huachuca and to the east of it are ranges far into Mexico, assuming the form of isolated groups. The Santa Ritas are almost west. Tres Alamos is on the right bank, about 25 feet above the river, which here hugs the east bank. It is not very wide, only about 20 feet, and is a red, very muddy stream. In general, the soil of the whole landscape has a very red hue, and the mountains in the distant north, near the Ojos Calientes of Dr. King,[33] show a red hue.

East of the house, a barren plain extends to the foothills of the Sierra Salitre, and north, the houses of Tres Alamos rest on the lowest spur of a gravel terrace, studded with mezquite, and superposed to that plain, domineering the river which hugs its foot. It is indented with lateral arroyos. There has been a pueblo at Tres Alamos, and a mile north of it, on the terrace, are other ruins.* They are composed of a stone polygon, evidently an enclosure connected with a mound (building) at its northwestern angle. North of it is an irregular quadrangle of mounds, covered with rubble and pottery, and still northwest, there are mounds, some of which bear the usual foundations. The buildings may have been of stone, although there is not much rubble about, but at all events they were only one story high.

Still north, beyond the arroyo, through which the road passes to the mouth of the San Pedro, there are other ruins, foundations of rubble, very distinct. These appear to have been outlying buildings. No obsidian. The flint and basalt or trap chips are abundant, so is pottery, which is identical with that of the Divide. Nothing corrugated or indented. Prismatic manos are found also. The ruins, as a group, are larger than those of the Mimbres, but the compartments are not larger than the largest ones there. What the polygonal enclosure was, I am unable to guess. There were no buildings inside, and there is even hardly any pottery. I could not learn of any other ruins in the immediate vicinity, but it appears that the San Pedro is dotted to its mouth with them, and that there are only caves without houses in them, but that they contain "relics."

I concluded to go south, to Huachuca, and thus descended to Benson, following the marshy valleys. It bears the same character, and the hills on the east side are steep, barren, and gravelly. On the west side, the ground is more gradually sloping, but three miles north of Benson, a cluster of gravelly hills and little mesas rises abruptly. On the whole, there is but one terrace above the bottom, then come the foothills, and the river approaches both banks alternately. Cross-section of valley,* rather ideal, of course.

Reached Benson [founded 1880] at 4 P.M. Benson is a miserable nest. Only one street. On the southwest, gravelly, barren hills; east a gravelly range of hills between it and the San Pedro. Everywhere timberless bottom, arid, treeless hills, and barren, dismal, bleak mountain chains in the distance. Desolation all around me, despondency within. God and Joe alone keep me up. Chico was livelier today.

FEBRUARY 10:[34] (Sent card to Dr. Girard last night.) After a conversation with Mr. Lagarde of San José (California), now mining at San Pedro in Sonora, I concluded to go ahead to Contention [Arizona]. Chico is livelier and much better off. Started at 10 A.M. The valley presents, throughout, the same appearance as far as Saint David, the Mormon settlement. The bottom is about one-and-a-half to two-and-a-half miles wide, the gravelly bluffs encroach upon it from time to time, or here and there an isolated hill, or group of hills, or little mesa, stands up.* For six miles, I followed the left bank and satisfied myself that there are no ruins, as the bluffs are too sharply crested. There may be some on the east side, where the flat appears more conspicuous and wide; still it is doubtful, as the people are uniform in stating that there are no ruins at all. There is much more mezquite scattered over the flats than farther south, and while it is all shrubby and scrubby, seldom five to six feet high, the trunks are thick on the face of the ground, but they divide into branches as soon as they rise above the surface. Yucca and zahuarro have almost completely disappeared.

About six miles south of Benson, the hills close in upon the river on the west side, and the east side alone extends as a bleak, but fertile, flat which, on an average, is about 20 to 40 feet above the San Pedro. The latter, a stream rendered muddy by the washings of the mills above, runs in a channel cut vertically about ten to fifteen feet deep and about 25 feet wide. Here, the Mormon settlement of Saint David lies, about a mile east of the San Pedro, and nine miles from Benson (eight by the railroad—about ten by the road). North of the town, I found traces of ruins. Pottery similar to that at Tres Alamos, but nothing defined. The flat here is about three miles wide to the east. On the west side, there are but few semi-circular basins left between the advancing gravel hills, and on the verge of some of them are springs, which leads to the supposition that there might be ruins there. On the east side, the springs are so far scarce. The hills then gradually sweep around towards the river, until they close in upon it, five miles south of Saint David. Hereafter, the slope disappears and nothing remains between the river and the hills, but a bottom which is scarcely a mile wide across from east to west. Before reaching this point, however, and about three-and-a-half miles north of Contention, on the flat, marly or clayey mounds appear, evidently ruins, covered with the same pottery as at Tres Alamos, scattered in a group of about ten, at various distances from each other. No obsidian, but flint and trap. At Saint David, fragment of a lava metate. Reached Contention (seventeen miles by the road) at 3 P.M.

Stopped at Mr. Larrieux's a half-mile south of a little dilapidated place, on the high bluff east of the river, are vestiges [of ruins]. . . . They have been uselessly dug into and senselessly disturbed by A. W. Chase, rifled of all their painted pottery, and are difficult to trace owing to about two dozen trenches. At the foot of the hill and west of the road, parallel to it, runs an acequia, one-and-a-half to two meters wide. Of the ruins, only a few rubble foundations remain. (There is very little rubble there, so that it is doubtful as to whether more than the foundations were of stone!)

FEBRUARY 11: Wrote home last night. Mailed it today. Bad night, severe headache. Chilly. Still, I crossed the river, visiting the rancho of Mr. Larrieux, about a mile north-northwest of Contention. A beautiful spring gushes out there, and on the top of the hill, southwest of the house, are traces as of an old house, but as there was no pottery, I was unable to ascertain anything. I then followed the bluffs down until nearly opposite the town, but while they are scrubby and thorny, there are no signs of ruins.

Met poor Mr. Alex W. Chase. What a wreck!! He showed me his drawings of antiquities found here and at the Grand Central Mine, two miles above. There is first a frog, out of what he calls "green jade." (Doubtful [probably diorite].) Its length, he gave at about 0.10 [meter?]. Then an axe of the same material, and identical in shape with those from Silver City, etc. Pottery painted, and, he assures me, corrugated! He is very positive about the latter being found on the San Pedro, and even in quantities. It is not impossible, since it is found at the Estanque Verde! At the Grand Central, he mentions two "forts," which were still filled with rubbish, so that the rooms could be excavated. This indicates here three pueblos. But the poor man speaks so indistinctly that I can barely understand one-fourth of what he says.

He showed me an axe or tomahawk of stone, slender, copied by him from the same locality. A stone axe, like those of Silver City, was found in an old mine in the Dragones, near Cochise's[35] stronghold. A cowboy, who had been a soldier, affirmed to me that in Cochise's fort there are signs of ruins like those at Grant's and near Phoenix, and much pottery. He states the same thing from the "Chiricahui's" [Chiricahua Mountains]. Still, I doubt it yet very much.

There are also rumors about a ruin near Tombstone. Everything is very doubtful. Mr. Chase, as well as Mr. Weiss, discredits the story about the Dragones. One thing seems certain, namely: that "Cochise's Stronghold," which is in about the northern half of the Dragones, is high up between crags and rocky clefts, perpendicular from the outside, properly a well-watered, fertile valley. Water is permanent there, and there is no impossibility of its having been inhabited. But the lower slopes of the chain are arid and absolutely barren. Mr. Larrieux seriously doubts the accuracy of the cowboy's statement about the Dragones.

FEBRUARY 12: Began to write to Mr. Rosenfeld. We started at 9 A.M. and drove across the plain, rising first to the terrace above the San Pedro, and then southwest. About nine miles away, we crossed the Arroyo de Barbacomari, which is permanent. It is a small fillet of water which runs in a cañada about a half-mile wide, low hills, covered with a scrubby vegetation, descending into it from both sides. The Huachucas are covered with snow, and the upper part of them is covered with pines. The cañones are studded with two kinds of oak. Reached the Fort [Huachuca] about 1 P.M., and found all my friends from [Fort] McDowell there. Captain Tisdall,[36] Lieutenant Scott, and all the other officers. Major Chaffee[37] is in command. Dined with him. He advises me strongly not to risk too much about Babispe [Sonora]. Around here, although the arroyo is permanent to the Fort, nothing has been found as yet.[38]

FEBRUARY 13: Took a stroll with Lieutenant West.[39] The view from the heights southeast (of here) is very extensive. Mount Graham is covered with deep snow, and to the north of it is visible another snowy crest, which must be beyond the Gila. In the east, and beyond the Dragones, the Chiricahui are plainly visible. Below the Tombstone Range is the Sierra de la Mula, southwest of it, in Mexico, the isolated crest of San José, and beyond the Mula, and south of the Chiricahui, rises the peak of Cocospera. In the Sierra Madre, the ruins were found southeast of Babispe, in a very wild, inaccessible country. Lieutenant West is not positive, but he thinks that there are ruins on the Babispe. Lieutenant Forsythe [Forsyth][40] is positive about it. At San Bernardino there is nothing; still Lieutenant West found a white flint spear head. Painted.

FEBRUARY 14: Painted all day. There is a handsome axe of greenish diorite from these surroundings; otherwise, I could not ascertain anything from around here. Saw two handsome metates. Don't know where from. Received an offer from Lieutenant Stoutzenberg[41] to accompany me into Mexico. The Fort is very handsomely situated, at the outlet of a deep, wooded cañón, and between high slopes, covered with grass and a few oaks. The bottom has many handsome oak trees. Finished letter to Rosenfeld.

FEBRUARY 15: Copied the little tablet of Lieutenant West, which comes from Tempe. It was found in connection with skeletons. The latter are reported as lying on their backs, therefore full length, and with extended arms, holding in one hand an olla with some beans. A recent paper also states that near Tempe, in an excavation, a shell was found incrustated with turquoise![42] This looks very much like the Sha-atze of Cochiti. Lieutenant West also tells me that the so-called mines at and about Prescott are only pits used by the Indians for getting out mineral paint, red oxyde of copper, green and blue carbonates. Lieutenant Forsythe speaks of ruins at Mud Springs, northwest of San Bernardino. I am at a loss what to do! Dined at Lieutenant Stoutzenberg's; he cannot come along. Mailed letters to Rosenfeld and to S. D. Waters. Wrote report on ruins of Santa Fe County [New Mexico],[43] and letter to Governor Ritch.

FEBRUARY 16: Mailed the letter, etc. to Governor Ritch. Lieutenant G. L. Scott left, with me "in charge," and a fine train, for Barbacomari Creek [present-day Babocomari River] at 10 A.M. Lieutenant Scott says the proper name is "Barbacombri." Whether "Barbacoma," "Barbacomiri," or "Barbacombri" is correct, I cannot tell. We reached the station and then turned upstream to the west. The creek is narrow, but permanent. The character of landscape is the same as lower down.

Rounded hills, sparsely covered with grass, mezquite, and some yucca, though not many. The bottom is fertile, but not wide, and indented as usual by the hills encroaching upon it. One mile, about, above the station, a high promontory juts out into the bottom, and near to the river. On it stands a new corral, and there are low mounds of pebbles, it is not possible to determine whether they are artificial or not. At all events, they cannot be measured.

On the east of this hill, a sloping platform descends like an apron. This apron was distinctly occupied by a village, but only the few ruins here sketched can be measured on the surface.* The foundations are, as usual, of rocks set on edge, and there are low irregular mounds of red earth. One of the enclosures embraces a low mound. A number of basalt chips, flint chips, but not a trace of obsidian, are loose about. The pottery shows no trace of corrugations or indentations, except in one piece, when it may be accidental. The prevailing pottery is plain, reddish, grey, and yellowish, often as thick as 0.008, and even 0.011 [meter?]. The painted pottery is different from that I saw on the San Pedro inasmuch as it does not show any of the red on yellowish ground. It is white with black ornaments, alike [similar] to that of the Casa Grande, red on white ground, and one piece I found had red and black ornaments on whitish ground. But the strangest thing of all was the find of the well-known red pottery with black geometrical lines. The last time I saw this type was on the Upper Salt River, if I correctly remember. Why this break, I cannot imagine. Still, I found three pieces of it. Not a single metate of lava was noticed, but quite a number of granite and of quartzite, and manos of greenstone. The metates are very primitive, mostly huge boulders, worn out into a disk-like basin with the rim only on three sides. There are also very thin metates, closely resembling a thick dish.

The pueblo must have been quite extensive, if the amount of pottery is a criterion, but the houses were not over one story high, judging from the rubbish. We then ascended to Fort Wallen,[44] which lies on a promontory on the north bank. Not a trace of pottery, although we searched very diligently, and as for flakes of trap, I did not see any. But there was a very large broken metate there, of red rock, with granite and quartzite. Still I could not find out where it came from. There are signs of foundations, but, since there is not a trace of any artifacts, I am at a loss to declare their origin. The creek there is quite deep, and we crossed again to the south side. On a high and bare loma stands the ruin here delineated.*

It is a large enclosure, indicated by stones set on edge, and it has on the southwest side a group of low mounds very much out of shape, red

clay, and it seems to indicate a configuration similar to that at Tres
Alamos. But it is so washed that any conclusion is dangerous, except
that inside the enclosure there was no building. Pottery, flakes, and
metates are plain and like the others. We followed up the river about
the ruin and crossed a marshy bottom to the house of "Judge" Laty,
who keeps a saloon also. There are foundations there, of the usual form
and size, and also on a knoll west of the place. The ruins show white
concrete, and the walls are nearly two feet thick. It may, however, not
be aboriginal. Pottery similar and rather scarce. The valley here is narrower as the Mesteñas are closing in upon the river from the north.
On the south side the usual broken mesas, rounded, extend to a great
distance.* Here we were already northwest of the Sierra Huachuca.

Turning back, we entered these mesas through a broad and arid
cañada, driving due south-southeast, and to the northwestern edge of
the Sierra, on which there appears a cluster of wooded slopes with dark
green cañones between them. There is much snow on them. Along the
northern base of the Huachucas, a picturesque park of oak trees, with
much yucca and grass, extends to the Fort [Huachuca]. We reached the
latter at sunset, having driven 23 miles today. Painted my groundplans
at night. On the whole, the day has been satisfactory. I have satisfied
myself that the creek has been inhabited. While I am not quite clear
as to any possible modifications in the architecture, it is very strange
that the old pottery should be so different from that on the San Pedro.
In fact, it approaches that of Globe and of San Carlos more than any
other. The metates resemble in shape those about Fort Thomas, also
those of Salt River, Globe, and Fort Reno, and their material is that
of the latter three places. The ruins, on the whole, are very much
destroyed and have the appearance of very great age. So has the pottery.
The latter is not as abundant as in other localities.

FEBRUARY 17: There is a cave in the Sierra, on its northern slope, but
I heard only of stalactites and nothing else. Lieutenant West called.
Day lazy, and did very little. Dined with [Messrs?] Vandevers, and then
wrote to Dr. Girard. Lieutenant West called again.

FEBRUARY 18: At 2 A.M. fire broke out in the kitchen of Mrs. Blum's,
and the building, that is its wooden parts, soon blazed. Got up and
moved under an oak tree. Sky clear, but a high wind. The soldiers came
rushing up and in an instant crowned the roof. The whole thing was

carried on very properly, in military style and without confusion, Major Chaffee giving his orders from below. By 4 A.M. the fire was quenched, but the building was well gutted. I then retired to bed again.

Breakfasted with Lieutenant West and then moved over to Messrs. Vandever Brothers, as Mrs. Blum intends to "quit." Met Captain Overton.[45] He told me that in a cave near Fort Grant, many sandals, plume-sticks, little bows, etc., had been found, and also fine stone axes. It rained sporadically all day, and I wrote to Mr. Parkman, to Joe, and to Don Joaquín [García Icazbalceta]. Dined at West's again, and then spent an hour with the boys of H Troop, 6th Cavalry. They had two splendid axes from the neighborhood of Fort Verde.[46] One of them was excessively large; the other, which I copied, was smaller, but had flanges and the groove or crease nearly all around.

FEBRUARY 19: We left at 11 A.M. José María Córdova and I. Travelled along the Sierra Huachuca. The mountains are traversed by wooded cañones, emptying into arroyos, which now are running, but which are mostly dry in summer until the rainy season. The oak trees follow the arroyos like little promontories into the barren slopes which descend towards the San Pedro. Beyond these slopes, and on the other side of the Rio, similar slopes, although more wooded or rather more scrubby, expand to the rugged hills of Tombstone, and the high Sierra de la Mula. Córdova told me that only the northern part of the Sierra del Dragón is thus called, and on account of a Mexican dragoon who died there, but that the southern part—Cochise's Stronghold—is called Sierra Peñascosa [rocky]. It well deserves its name.

The Sierra Bonita (Mount Graham) is very prominent in the north-east, deeply snowclad. We followed the Sierra Huachuca all day to past the large mill, which derives its ore from the Sierra de San José, also called de la Gallina. Here, on a high oak-covered ridge or spur of the mountain, the distant peaks of the Sierra Madre appeared beyond the peak of Cocospera. To the south-southeast, the San José, an isolated mountain-notch, looms up magnificently. Its top is covered with snow. Descending through the oak grove, the Cananéa appeared, also snow-covered. From the oaks (two kinds, the "encino," with oblong leaves, and the "vellota," with very glossy spinated leaves), we descended into the plain, reaching Ochoaville (Palominas) after sunset. The view is extensive, but arid and dreary; no trace is visible of the small Rio San Pedro, in the barren, grassy plain, which slopes up to the Sierra de San José. Turning back towards the north, the Sierra Mesteña presented a remarkable appearance. In the crests and tops, reverberation had cut up gaps of the most singular character. It appeared about as follows.*

The Tombstone Mountains are also completely changed. As the sun set, the original views returned. Very kind reception at Palominas. Don Fortino Paredes and Don Vicente Ciganán [Cigarrán?] offered and gave me letters [to] everywhere. Important ruins at Turmote, but none here. Sierra Bonita invisible.

FEBRUARY 20: Examined the gravel heap which constitutes the soil on which Palominas lies, but found no trace of pottery. Lagarde and Marmolejo came. Left with Lagarde about 11 A.M., following the river on the west. The scenery is always the same. San Pedro is on the west. side of the river. Met Don José María Elias, Señor Nájera, and the other officers. News from Puebla and Cholula. Ruins at Magdalena and at Santa Ana. Exceeding affability on the part of the people. In the course of conversation I found that the bulk of the ruins are near Tenarate [?] and Santa Cruz, on the south flank of the Sierra Huachuca.

FEBRUARY 21: Left about 8 A.M. following the San Pedro on the right (east) bank. Crossed the boggy and miry bottom, with difficulty, and then ascended the level, grassy plain; nothing else but grass, arid and terribly desolate, until to that pueblo.* The pottery is not painted. Metates and flat, prismatic manos. No water in sight. Stone foundations are visible, but there is not much rubbish about. Caught up with Lagarde, Vicente Ciganán, and Marmolejo. Descended into the Cananéa, a lively stream, and one of the sources of the San Pedro. The latter has three or four branches. Tenarate lies on one.

Reached the Cananéa, a well-fortified rancho with two round towers, and then entered the gorge to the Pinal. Very picturesque. Highly romantic. Crossed the little brook at least thirty times. Vegetation fair. Oak trees, much yucca and dasylirium, opuntia, agave, and the high, snow-clad summits have pines. General Pesqueira[47] and Don Epitacio Paredes received me hospitably. Around Tenarate there are eight to ten ruins, and there is a hill with fortifications in a spiral, and another one ten leagues northeast. Pottery painted. Stone axes, metates, etc., and carved rocks. (Today made 27 miles.) On the representations of General Pesqueira I concluded to change my plan, going to Arispe [Arizpe]. Bad sleeping in the wooden cabins, but not so very high and cold, although this is the highest point in Sonora.

FEBRUARY 22: The General left early with almost everybody. I followed on foot, and went with Julian Zubia to the mine, which is in a cañada, four-and-a-half miles southeast. The Sierra de Bavispe plainly visible, and even the Sierra Bonita still appears in the distant north. We descended into a deep, wooded cañada. The trees are oak, of the usual two kinds. The slopes of the hills are covered with gravel, making walking very difficult. Went to the mine and returned. Slept with Julian Zubia and his aged mother. It appears that, in Opota [Opata],[48] "Ba" signifies water and therefore all the names with "Ba" are Opota. Babacomari, Bacanuchi. (Don Epitacio Paredes tells me that Vacapa may mean Matapa or Matope of today; also that in his opinion, Nexpa is the Rio Fronteras. This I still doubt.)

On the whole, there are no ruins in the interior of the Sierra Cananéa, but on the east flank there are two, the one on the San Pedro road, the other, three miles east of Pinal (or the mill of General Pesqueira) at the Paredón Colorado. On the 18th of May 1883, six inches of snow fell at the Cananéa. The Apache still roam around here sometimes, but they are not very dangerous. Farther south they are worse. Am undecided as to whether I go west or not. Distance travelled today, on foot, 15 miles.

FEBRUARY 23: Left with Victor Espinosa at 9 A.M. On the southwest of Cananéa, in the open plain on the very brink of the cañada, are the following ruins.* Nothing but foundations and heaps of rocks remain in the fully barren grassy plain at the brink of the valley. Could not see any pottery. We then struck east across the plain for ten miles, when we descended into the exceedingly broken and difficult country of the Ojo de Agua. Here there is another adobe fortification like that of the Cananéa, only with square towers. Abandoned also. The valleys are narrow, very deep, covered with grass, and few oak trees. Ruins north of the rancho of Don Joaquín Bonorand. . . . He left home in 1871, and he has been here now 21 months. This ruin is disseminated [scattered].* Below, there is a very gravelly plateau. The pottery is mostly plain, but there are painted specimens. These are like those of the Babocomari, only the white-and-black and the red-and-black are not there. Little flint. The metates are of lava and of a coarsely grained hornblendic rock. The manos are prismatic and flat. No arrowheads, and no stone axes. [There] is an oblong enclosure, made of large blocks, partly broken; it has no pottery nor flint, and inside it is perfectly smooth and cleaned up. It may be Apache; still the communication with the old village is apparently plain! It is almost impossible to form a correct idea of the shape of the houses, beyond that they were separate, detached dwellings for one family only, and that stones, of various sizes, boulders and pebbles, from larger than a half-bushel down to my fist, entered into the composition of the walls. More than one story high, they were not. I am undecided yet as to whether the walls contained much soil or not. Detached small buildings—few in number, are scattered along the rim.

Now I return to the journey from Cananéa to Los Fresnos. The following is a plan made by Mr. Bonorand.* From beyond the Sierra de los Ajos, an arroyo with rainwater runs to the Ojo de Agua. Beyond the Ojo de Agua, the road follows exceedingly narrow gorges. The river must be crossed and recrossed at least 30 times. Rocky and picturesque. A very dense thicket of willows, with cottonwood, oak, and later on, occasional ash trees, covers the bottom, Few spots are open, for instance, the Cañada Ancha to the left of the road. At Los Fresnos the thicket opens and the heights expand in slopes, less trees and less rocks. It snows here in winter. Delightful reception and night. News so far good.

FEBRUARY 24: The ruins here are southeast of the rancho, on the east bank of the river, and overlooking its lower bottom. They are on an apron, which has but very few trees, and is very gravelly. The mounds are numerous, but not large, and they are very low, showing that they have been washed a great deal, and that they are old.* There is much broken pottery about, some pieces corrugated, others plain, and very few painted. The painted are like those of San Pedro and Tres Alamos. It is impossible to determine the character of the buildings. Gravel mounds are so mixed up with the rest, that, since everything is covered alike with bits of pottery, it is impossible to form an idea of what is natural or not, or at least it is exceedingly difficult. In many cases I am in doubt yet.

The color of soil, grey; slightly reddish hue. Mounds of same. Very slight depression, like a faint basin, probably from contrast with surrounding ridges and low mounds.

On the east-northeast of the apron, a high steep hill, grassy slopes, and occasional oak trees and tall yucca, dasylirium, rises abruptly. It overlooks the bottom and the country north, east and south.* On its top is an oval mound, or rather enclosure, and 34 steps beyond it, a heap of broken stones, like a recent boundary monument, without any twigs or leaves whatever. There is no pottery in connection with it, and it is in all points similar to the other ruin. The stone foundations of the rectangles are mostly of small stones set into the ground at a depth of only 0.08 to 0.12 [meter?], apart from each other from 0.03 to 0.15 [meter?] and very seldom touching. They cannot have been foundations of houses; rather lines of demarcation, enclosures of fields, than anything else. They mostly enclose depressions, and rarely, elevated areas, although the latter case also occurs. They are similar in form and size to those so common in New Mexico and in Arizona, but the rocks are smaller, and they are more closely alike those from the Babocomari. Obsidian I have not found yet. Of stone axes I have merely heard, but the reports around here are very contradictory. There seem to have been so many settlements made during the time of the Apaches and Spaniards, and abandoned out of fear of the latter, that it is impossible to determine without seeing what is ancient or not. The greatest difficulty is to find the rivers, although I am on the right track now. The country is not very safe; the Apache were here as late as last June, but it is not as terrible as it looks.

[W.] C. Streeter is at Nacosari [present-day Nacozari]. The yucca is tall, there are some opuntia, no zahuarro, few if any ocotillas [ocotillos], and no pines. Of game, deer and antelope, bear, [?]; I am now going to Bacuachi and finally to Nacosari. On the road to Nacosari there are two ruins, of graveyards, they say! Jesús Duarte assures me that there are ruins at San Agustín, east of the Organos. The country of the Cananéa was once inhabited by the Seris[49] who have now dwindled down to four-to-five hundred men. There is considerable traffic on this road, even by waggons, although it is not very good. Many mines.

It grew warm at noon, and I went to the lower apron attached to the hill on which the first ruin stands. Here there is a perfect village, and the foundations, although disturbed, are still plain. They were composed of large and smaller blocks, the latter being used to fill up the interstices between the former. In one place these foundations are very plain, and show a thickness of 0.50 [meter?]. It is clear that the thin foundations are not those of houses. Found a fragment of a flint knife. The usual metates and pottery are about. Six miles south of here, at Los Conejos, on the west bank, there is another ruin, and a stone axe has been found there. Shall see tomorrow.

In the afternoon I painted pottery. The metates of the ruins are not of lava only, but they are also of other rocks. They are mostly massive, but also thinner, only the surface is worked, and they have no feet. The pottery is very much broken, and everything in general is very old and looks exceedingly dilapidated. I omitted to state that near the Ojo de Agua, there are signs of ruins too. These consist of rocky fragments of a metate. The character of complete destruction of these ruins is very remarkable. It is exceedingly strange, compared with the good state of preservation of the ruins in northern New Mexico and in Arizona. Still, it is not altogether surprising. The climate becomes more moist the farther south we go; consequently, the greater is the disintegration.

FEBRUARY 25: I left with Ciganán and Tomás Jácome, late in the forenoon. The valley of the river is narrow, but always wooded; the heights are steep, rounded tops and rather barren. At the rancho of Hofstadt I got an axe, a handsome specimen. There are signs of a ruin there, also at Los Conejos, about a mile farther south, on a site on the left hand [side] of the ruin [valley?], and a mile farther south on the right hand [side]. They are, however, so undistinguishable, except for a few bits of pottery and a few gravel heaps, flint and basalt chips, that I could not make out anything at all beyond assuring myself of the fact that they existed. From that point we crossed over on the trail, somewhat rough, cutting off a mile and into the river valley again. The Cerro Colorado is also said to contain ruins of the same character. They call them sepulturas because the gravel heaps look somewhat like graves, although they are round and probably natural. At a distance of 20 miles from Genovérachi the view expands. The Sierra de Bacuachi, followed on the south by the Púrica, rises boldly in the east, a broad stately chain, somewhat wooded, and with a few specks of snow on the latter.

Below, other ranges loom up. The valley of Motuticachi soon opens; it is sandy, broad, covered with mezquite, a few cylindropuntia, Uña de Gata [cat's claw], and some stunted palo verde. Along the river, blooming willows and cottonwoods. The soil is red and gravelly, but fertile. The river commonly sinks there till [up to] Bacuachi, but now it has water, a clear running water. It almost completely sinks below Ures, but the Rio Yaqui and the Rio Mayo are both very deep to the sea. Bacuachi proper is a small village with a church, on a high bluff above the river, built of adobe, and much decayed. It contains six-to-seven hundred souls, and has been terribly bothered by the Apaches until about six years ago. These Indians reduced it almost to nothing. Now it picks up again. The valley is also called de las Higüeras [of the fig trees]. There are ruins at Motuticachi, at Cañada de la Cruz, and others scattered around. Pleasant reception at Domingo Durón's. Bad night because of a serenade with acordeon by José María Córdoba and Ciganán. Met Mr. Cumming. Concluded to go to Nacosari.

FEBRUARY 26: Chico refuses to eat. Got shaved, a fearful operation. There are stone axes here, I am told, and some have been found at Ures. I copied the one from Los Conejos. Other axes have been found near Banámichi [Banámiche] and even possibly around here. Copied pottery. Was very much discouraged for awhile, but Chico is picking up again.

In the afternoon I went to the Cañada de la Cruz, about two-and-a-half miles north-northwest of Bacuachi. In the angle formed by the road and the cañada, on the top of the bald, mezquite-covered bluff, are the remains of two groups forming one small village. They are very indistinct, however, and it is barely possible to discriminate between what is mound and what is gravel pile. Many very small bits of pottery, mostly painted red inside, are scattered about, much trap chips, some white flint, but no obsidian. Saw manos, but not one metate. Very few foundations are measurable. The houses are small, and probably of one room only. The material was evidently rubble and red mud, large rocks being used for the foundations. General plan.*

The whole is very unsatisfactory, still it is at least something. At night I got some further information. There are some ruins in a cañón west of Guassabas, 15 miles from the road between it and Oposura, but they are only rock foundations. Of caves or cliffhouses, I could not hear anything at all as yet. Specimens of mounds.*

FEBRUARY 27: Began to write home last night. Started with Don Miguel Valencia on horseback for Motuticachi at 10 A.M. We followed the road as far as the Cañada de la Cruz. There, on the little apron northeast of the ruins which I measured yesterday, I found ruins, . . . reduced to mere scattered blocks of stone, partly still planted into the sod. There is little pottery about, and it is reduced to little bits. It is plain and reddish, but I could not find any painted and decorated pieces. Of metates, there is no trace there.

From this spot we crossed over to the mesas leaving the road and the river to the right, and hugging the high ridges which are spurs of the Manzanal [Range] to the left. These heights are bare. On the spurs east of the conical peak in those ridges, there is said to be a ruin. We descended into the valley of the rancho[s?] of Durón and Valencia. Here the river, winding around the mesas to the west, loses its water and enters a narrow rocky cañón going south. The valley is very fertile and covered with álamos. I got here a very fine stone axe which was picked up in a side cañada, probably a float or drift, which has drifted down from the mesas north. We followed up the river to the east, about a mile and then ascended the mesa west of the river.

Here, we met the ruins on sheet #30.* They are far better preserved than any I have yet seen in Sonora. Much pottery is about, but all broken into small fragments. I found no decorated fragments, and one piece of indented pottery, painted Indian-red, many metates, mostly syenite and granite, and I cannot find any of lava. But the manos are sometimes of lava, sometimes of hornblende, and they are small, flat, thin, and prismatic. The metates are heavy blocks, ground, also dish-like plates [mortars?]. There are more spaces showing the marks of habitation than I could put in on my survey, but on the whole the settlement was not very large. The single houses approximate to the square shape, and besides there are some of them which are plainly connected with enclosures. Besides, there are isolated enclosures.

The latter show the distinctive features which I already observed at Los Fresnos, and there is considerable difference between them and the ruins of the houses. The latter commonly show low, very low, mounds of red earth and of gravel, with large blocks of broken stones scattered or still planted.* The depth to which these blocks of foundation are planted does not exceed 0.30 [meter?] and they seldom go to 0.15. On the promontory, there is an almost square ruin which appears to have been a lookout, as it stands on the very brink and overlooks the valley of the Sonora River. This valley may have been cultivated, because it is fertile; but on the other hand the river here is without water for half of the year. About a half-mile southeast of the ruin, on the other side of the river and against the hill slopes, there is a permanent pool of water—"ojo" which appears to have been used as a supply for the pueblo formerly.

We returned by way of the road by which we came yesterday. I am considerably in doubt as to my further movements. The country is decidedly insecure, but on the other hand it is the nearest way in every respect. But again there is hardly any considerable stream of water near Nacosari except the Rio Cumpas or rather the Rio Oposura, which, however, is not permanent. I finally concluded to go to Arispe and thence on to Cumpas.

Chico is not well. He goes and runs well, but does not eat any barley and very little, if any, hay. I don't know what to think.

FEBRUARY 28: Copied the stone axe and pottery all day. Carlos Loaysa went off to see the mine, but John Hohstadt [Hofstadt], the two Smiths, and Charley Cunningham stayed with me. It was not always very pleasant, but the last three speak no Spanish, so I had to keep them company to a certain extent. At night, Mr. Bonorand came with Jesús Duarte and I spent the evening with them. Duarte is full of mines, and knows of pueblos everywhere in the sierra, but as they are always connected with some old mine it is doubtful as to whether they are not old Spanish mining camps. The ruins, which I saw yesterday, may be termed: La Mesa del Agua Caliente and those of the Cañada de la Cruz, El Pueblito. Don Miguel Valencia, however, does not know as to whether there are any hot springs near or not, but there is a permanent tank west of the mesa. From here, the Picacho is very prominent, and it somewhat resembles the "Navajo Church" at Fort Wingate. It is due west.

FEBRUARY 29: Everybody left this morning. Wrote and mailed letters to Joe, to Dr. Girard. Lieutenant West,[50] and to Ad. Mennet. Am waiting for [Don Estanislao] Alvarez. Loaysa left me letters of recommendation to Chinapa, Arispe, and Banámichi, and Don Domingo [Durón] also gave me one to his father at Banámichi. After finishing the letters and settling with Don Domingo ($9.25), I went to examine the outskirts of the village. There are ruins of large houses and corrals, on a much larger scale than the ancient ones. They form hollow squares and rectangles; there is red pottery about, and foundations of rubble protrude, similar to those in the other ruins. But the other features are very markedly different. Wherever the others are, [they are] always small patches, but here there are large complexes. Don Domingo assures me besides, that these ruins are positively those of former Spanish settlements, which had to be abandoned less than one hundred years ago! This is interesting as it shows the nature and degree of decay. It is much more rapid here than farther north. The climate is more humid also, and therefore also the mezquite trees which have grown up in the ruins do not, by their size, indicate the same age as they would farther north. It is clear to me that neither the decay, nor the size of trees growing inside of the ruins, is a sufficient indication to determine absolutely the relative age of ruins in different degrees of latitude.

Ruins on the narrow crest, extending west of the ranch of Marco Romo, three miles northeast of Arispe.* These ruins are the most perfect ones which I have seen. The place is now called: "Jitisórichi" but formerly "Tiji-so-richi" and the title to the ranch dates back to the beginning of 1700. This survey was taken on the 1st of March, but I had no other paper and thus put it here. The foundations are of very heavy blocks set on edge, and small mounds commonly indicate the houses, whereas the enclosures are indicated slightly similar to those at Bonorand's, namely: smaller cobble stones. . . . There may have been more houses than those which I measured, but they are so destroyed that only scattered blocks of large and small stones remain. Many of the usual fragments of metates remain, and much broken pottery, but not a single painted piece, nor corrugated.

We left at noon, Don Estanislao Alvarez and I. He led me down into a deep cañada and thence, as the river engulfs itself into rocky cañones, whose base the main road follows, we took a so-called short cut over rugged hills and footpaths, to join the cañón again about ten miles below Bacuachi. The sides of the cañón are precipitous rocks, very picturesque. Wherever there is room, the pitahaya (distinct from the zahuarro) clings to the clefts or crags, very much like the zahuarro itself. The narrow river bottom is sandy, covered with leafing cottonwoods, willows, Botamotes [?], and other trees, and a dense thicket. On the side hills which we traversed before, cedars grew. The landscape along the whole route is exceedingly wild and handsome.

It appears that on the whole route to Ures, nearly, the river flows through a succession of gorges of that kind, with a fertile but narrow bottom. The Sierra Manzanal is to the right of the river. As we approached Chinapa, we sallied from the cañones and entered a broad and fertile cañada, whose abrupt edges are treeless; a few mezquites excepted. Here are the cultivated fields of Chinapa. The place itself, a poor hovel of adobe, rests on the bluff above the river, in a fair exposition but barren, and surrounded by ruined foundations. We stopped at Doña Angelita de Arvisu, whose husband is in jail. The house is mostly in ruins (it was the former monastery); its walls are thick and it still shows in part the construction. Chinapa was formerly a large place, but it has been even completely abandoned at one time, and the Apaches burnt down the houses. The uprising of the Apaches took place in 1830 (?). Previous to that time, they had been living quietly in rancherías among the people. I was soon in conversation with several of the old men, Don Feliz Ruiz and Antonio Morales. They assured me that foundations of ancient villages were abundant along the river, and at a place two miles north of the pueblo, in a very narrow cañón with rocky perpendicular sides, there are paintings in red ochre. They are said to be very rude, and on the hill above them there are traces of a ruin. Metates are abundant, but I am informed that the same kind of rude dish-like metates is found and made today at Arispe! This is important. From here, the distance to Cumpas is fourteen leguas only, and direct, though broken, road.

M A R C H

MARCH 1: Started about 8:30 A.M. We passed down the cañada and followed the river, crossing it almost every hundred yards. The country preserved the same appearance. Farther down we entered a very picturesque cañón, similar to the others, but with higher rocks. Pitahaya clings to the slopes. The general course of the road is more to the west. About 11 A.M., we emerged from these gorges to the distillery of Ignacio [blank], where a round basin is formed. The Sierra de Arispe [Arizpe] is now due south. It is picturesque but almost treeless, though not barren and denuded. At the southern end of this basin is the rancho of Marco Romo, on the site of "Ti-ji-so-richi," and above it, to the west-northwest, is the ruin.* The slope is abrupt, the soil red, and the rocks on the other side of the cañón look like dark red sandstone. Many horrible choyas and some pitahayas cover the ruins. It looks almost as if there had been two or three streets or lines of houses, with a plaza between the third and fourth row. I am still in doubt as to the age of this ruin; still the uniformity in size and shape of the houses, mostly square and without partitions, the situation, etc., show, that it may have been an ancient village. Although most of the sites are plainly discernible, the foundations are not always clear. Still, I found several houses where a singular disposition of the entrance is noted.* Something similar to the entrances on Salt River and Tonto Creek.

In another place there was a shadow of a doorway and a sill 0.70 [meter?] wide. But these signs are still doubtful owing to the distribution of the rubbish. The circular enclosures, two of which I found, are about the size of the bake-ovens of the Pueblos in New Mexico, and consequently suspicious also. The stones composing them are small, like those of the so-called enclosures or corrales mentioned before. It is evident that the pueblo had abundant arable soil in the bottom, and for a lookout and for defense the place is well selected.

From that one we enter the cañada and, having finally rounded the Sierra de Arispe, left it to the left or east. A fertile valley, with leafing

cottonwoods, expands to the south; through it runs the Rio de Bacanuchi which joins the Sonora at Arispe [Arizpe].[51] The town stands
on the right bank of the Rio Sonora, and below the junction of the
rivers. In front of it rises, to the east, the sierra in a series of vertical
terraces of rock, finally crowned by the green, but mostly treeless, slopes
of the higher bold peaks. The tower stands on a low bluff and steep
grade or slope, is regularly laid out, and is a heap of distressing ruins of
once handsome adobe buildings, which are like those of Cholula, often
two stories high, and show a state of considerable former prosperity.
But now it is a terrible sight, almost whole blocks are decaying ruins;
the church, with valuable paintings, is partly rubbish; there is not one
good or good-looking house in the place. It is a sad prospect! All this is
due to the Apache! And a beautiful valley, fertile, with a handsome
climate. In the gardens, enclosed by crumbling adobe walls, stand
orange trees, green and laden with golden fruit, immense platiopuntia
in groves, as large as young apple trees two to three years old, which are
kept for the fruit alone.

I called on Don Leonárdo Gomez, the Prefect, who assured me that
the Apache had left the state, and gave me a letter to the Cura Urias.[52]
I stopped at Señora Mariana de Herrano's, and called on the Cura, who
told me to call again after 5 P.M.

Here, the corn is planted in June and gathered in November; wheat
is sown in January and harvested from June to August. At Bacuachi, two
crops cannot be raised annually, neither at Chinapa. The population
here almost disappears in the day time, reviving at sunset, but its appearance is in accordance with that of the town. It is a dreary sight. At
the Agua Caliente, two-and-a-half miles from Arispe on the Chinapa
road, there is a warm spring, though not hot at all. Chico feels much
better today.

I finally found the Cura after 6 P.M. He promised his assistance. From
the statements of the Padre, it appears that there are ruins all around.
They are scattered on both sides of the river. He also mentioned stone
axes as having been found here or in the vicinity. There is a family
named Elias here, which is said to own several stone implements. On
the whole, the hills along the river are much broken, and do not afford
room for large populations. Their tops are not wide enough. The Cura
is of the opinion that the old pueblos were formerly inhabited by the
Opatas. There is yet, around here, much ignorance about the antiquities, and a great confusion exists as to what is pre-conquistorial and
post-conquistorial.

MARCH 2: Birds singing. It is Sunday, but I have none. At home they have. I am here, in hopes of a fair result, doing my duty as best I can, but always in fear and in doubt. How are they at home? Oh God! I wish I had *done* [finished my work] this day, and could return to Joe! God, help me! I shall never be ungrateful again. I went to Señor Ignacio Elias. He showed me a small axe of greenstone, and a mortar of lava rock with four legs. The axe probably came from Bamori, three miles south of Arispe, on the Sonora River. The mortar was dug up at Arispe, and in digging for house foundations at a small depth.

Although it threatened to rain, I started on foot for the ruins of Ta-ui-chó-pa about noon, and instead of going up the river, struck into the heights. These are cut up into sharp, narrow crests, high and rocky, overgrown with mezquite, choyas, etc.; on the highest points: pitahayas. The valleys between are only gashes, also sandy and rocky and with less thorny vegetation. There is hardly any room for houses on these knife-like ridges, and as far as I could see, to the very mountains, they presented the same appearance. Only towards the river, the crests occasionally fall off in plateaus or aprons, but these again rest mostly on vertical walls, rounded or columnar at the edges, which skirt the river of Bacanuchi, enclosing it in a cajón and leaving only little space beyond the river bed.

For three miles up the Bacanuchi River from Arispe, there is no room for tillage and hardly any opportunity for dwelling, although there would be space on the top of the vertical banks, and they are scarcely higher than 30 meters. On one of the ridges, about one mile west of the river, I found a trace of a small stone house, very conveniently situated for a lookout perhaps. But there were no vestiges of ruins on the other ridges or in the gashes, called valleys, below it. At Ta-ui-chó-pa, the valley opens to the width of nearly a mile and is cultivated, but the widening, consequently the fields, are on the east bank. A few houses are grouped on the west side on the bare and rocky promontories descending abruptly to the river. Above it is a bare but fertile terrace, about 100.0 [meters?] wide; above it, another terrace, scarcely a meter higher, about three hundred meters wide, and still above the latter is the top of the ridge, running about south to north and 25 to 30 meters above the latter. I did not examine the ridge proper. The ruins are scattered over the terraces; they are much disturbed, so much that only a very few foundations could be measured. These show the usual combination of small, almost square houses, and of enclosures, the latter occasionally independent; in some places I could detect them as a kind of addition to the house, or as a continuation of it. I did not notice partitions anywhere.*

The foundations appear in some places to have been double. In such instances, they consist of huge stones filled in with smaller ones. It is significant, however, that there are no metates, nor manos, and no pottery at all. That is: I saw one or two pieces of the latter, reddish. The mounds indicating the houses are exceedingly low, scarcely over 0.06 to 0.10 [meter?] high, and it appears as if the heavy rains had swept out everything that is not absolutely too heavy for anything less than the current of a river or a torrentuous arroyo. This explains perhaps the fact that only the larger stones are left of the foundations, and the interstices between the several stones. I went to one of the houses and found there a very old woman, Josefa Siqueyros, who pretended to be eighty years old. She lent me a stone axe of dark green stone, that has been found in the ruins above. She repeated to me the statement that in the fields "above" an olla had been dug out containing human bones, and it is supposed that they were the bones of a child. Could not find out anything beyond that the olla was: muy colorada [very decorated]. Her grandson, Bernardo, is a captive of the Apache at San Carlos.

I thence returned by the river in the narrow cajón, wading through the river about ten to twelve times. Only about a half-mile north of Arispe it widens, and an arable expanse begins, but beyond, the perpendicular walls of the Sierra de Arispe rise again precipitously. I made a rapid sketch of the stone mortar from Elias, of the stone axe, and I also painted some pottery. This was a Sunday in Arispe. Visited the church, and prayed in it! I need praying very much! Tomorrow I shall paint and do other work, and then leave for Cinoquipe [Sinoquipe] and Banámichi. Chico eats well, but still he suffers from the hava [haba, mange]. Of course, Alvarez did not show himself to cut it. These people are more intent upon drinking and enjoying themselves than upon anything else. Doña Mariana told me today that she also had a mortar (almirez) of lava, which was found somewhere in town. There is every indication that there was an old pueblo here too, and the position is entirely favorable.

MARCH 3: Copied the "almirez" of Doña Mariana. It is of lava. Called on the Cura, but without any effect at all. Painted. Wrote to Joe, enclosing a hundred dollar draft. In the afternoon, I took a walk through the place to the south and to the ridge which rises above the town to the west. There are traces of old buildings and much pottery, but it is evidently of Spanish date. From the top of the ridge, I looked into a chaos of ridges and vales or gashes, the mural fronts of the terraces on which stands the Sierra de Arispe closing the view to the east. The bottom is light green, everything leafing. It appears that the more recent and more populous part of the town is to the south. The old town, which was abandoned very soon after 1836, is where I lodge. Painted all afternoon.

Took leave of the Prefect and of Elias. So far, it is the most unsatisfactory visit which I have made. The people are polite, but, with the exception of the ladies of the house and of Elias, useless for my purpose. Gomez, the Prefect, is a blown-up official. Without official papers I cannot get much support; besides, it looks to me as if the visit of Pinard [Pinart][53] had made the people rather suspicious. My nose and lip trouble me again, effects of a late cold. In the yard of this house, there is an enormous ancient metate, of bluish rock, 0.48 [meter?] long, 0.27 high, 0.27 wide. The [depression] is 0.24 wide and 0.14 deep. There is also a specimen of a flat dish-like metate. Copied both. The latter is of lava, very porous, and now gray with age. The manos are thin, small, and prismatic. Have decided to leave tomorrow at all events. The ladies here are very kind to me, but I must at least go to Cinoquipe, seven leguas from here, and thence to Banámichi. It is better that way than by Chinapa, principally now when the danger from Apache is over.

MARCH 4: It began to rain at 2 A.M. but soon subsided into a drizzle. So I left at 9 A.M. for Sinoquipe. It drizzled, but again turned into a rain which continued, slightly but steadily increasing, the whole day and most of the night, so that I got a fearful drenching. On leaving Arispe I noticed a fan-palm, about 25 feet high, in one of the gardens. Riding down the river I soon was in the cajón again. It is narrow and exceedingly picturesque, the luxuriant young green of the trees of the valley standing in very strong contrast to the dark hill slopes, with green pitahaya and opuntia on them, or perpendicular rocks descending abruptly down to the river bed.

I stopped at a rancho about two leguas from Arispe. It appears that on the heights above the river, and wherever there was any room for them, there are ruins of foundations indicating isolated houses. Thus there are such at Bamori, etc. The pottery is mostly plain red; the people denied having seen any painted or corrugated ware. Stone axes and metates, the latter always broken, were mentioned to me as frequent finds. Lower down, the cañón becomes very grand. Lofty rocks, nearly

1,000 feet high, tower up in vertical crags, grand spires, and pillars. They assume different hues: red, white, yellow, brown, etc. The river, which is rapidly becoming turbid because of the rain, and is also rising a little, runs and winds foaming and rushing in the plain. The latter is covered with soft light green.

At Tetuachi the cañón suddenly opens. The hacienda is handsome, the scenery around is soft, though romantic, and particularly interesting are a group of rocks in the northwest, which [rocks] are as absolutely perpendicular as a wall of masonry. They form an oval mesa with a rounded top. The height of the wall is certainly 300 feet.* They look somewhat like light grey basalt.

Farther down comes the abandoned mill, where Frank Bryan is lonely watchman, and where I met four Americans returning to Tombstone. Farther down still the valley or bottom opens still farther, and the almost completely ruined and abandoned Hacienda del Tren—large buildings of adobe, stands on the right bank of the river.

One mile farther I reached Sinoquipe, a heap of adobe houses on an abrupt bluff on the west side of the river, with a large church partly in ruin. It presents a suspicious appearance. The people appear lazy, dirty, and addicted to drinking. There are at least five or six stores with mezcal. Went to Santos Moreno and there met Colonel Buffum,[54] fearfully tomado [drunk]. It kept on raining. Slept in Colonel Buffum's room, perfectly drenched, and with a leaking roof.

MARCH 5: I was very much annoyed the whole day by the Colonel, who, under pretense of work, did nothing else but to occupy the table, and thus to prevent me from using it myself. Besides, I have a fearful cold. The country is handsome. The mountain scenery around, tempered by the dark green of a scrubby vegetation, is accidented [rugged] and picturesque. In the north, several pillars of rocks arise, one of them imitating perfectly one of the columns of Baalbec,[55] or rather several of them seen in line. To the south-southwest the Picacho de San Benito stands out like a huge lump with a round top and vertical sides. East, the perpendicular crests and peaks of the Minas arise like a contiguous craggy chain. In the south the light green valley of the Sonora River extends below the mill. This mill (San Agustín) is the place where Pechazzari [?] lives, but his behavior upon my presentation to him was very unsatisfactory. Sinoquipe received its communal lands in 1735 by act of Philip V. It is, or was, an Opata village, but today the natives are mixed with the population, they even deny their language, and few of them speak it yet. Still, Buffum assures me that they have preserved much of their aboriginal organization, and that they were in various tribes located in valleys. For instance, the tribe of the Opodepe River [San Miguel drainage] was not friendly to that of the Sonora. One of the old chiefs still lives nine miles north of Sinoquipe, on the latter river. It cleared up gradually, after a most beautiful sunset. My clothes dried only in the afternoon.

MARCH 6: Left at 11 A.M. The river is swollen and the overflow extends across the banks in sheets and some in very shallow streams and channels. The valley is narrow, but fertile, encased in low abrupt bluffs. The green madroño [strawberry tree], very thorny, appears, and the pitahaya is frequent on the heights and slopes, the choya on the tops or mesas. At the rear of the little mesas (narrow ridges frequently) bordering the river, higher and narrow ridges or crests, with similar vegetation rise, with deep gashes between them, to the higher ranges in the distance. In the southwest rises the Sierra de Rayón, in the south the Sierra de Ures. Beautiful birds about, many flocks of ducks in the river, and an occasional grey heron.

At Motepán, I measured along the road, a perfect foundation.* The edges are clearly rounded, the lines are made of heavy stones. Some red pottery is about. I reached Banámichi at 1 P.M., a small pueblo but far different from the others in that it has a number of good, substantial, newly painted houses, and that everything shows signs of more activity and greater neatness. It is located on a bluff on the east side of the river, has its old, large church, partly ruined, and presents on the whole a more wholesome aspect.

From it a scene of exquisite beauty expands. The valley beneath is green with wheatfields, and beyond it, to the southwest and west the Sierra de Opodepe, Sierra de Rayón, Sierra de Ures, form dark green and very accidented curtains. The valley is broad and entirely in [agri]culture.

I stopped at Joaquín Corella's and met Ygnacio Pesqueira. I was turned over to Manuel Romero, who took me home to his simple but pleasant adobe house in the valley. Fig trees, peaches in bloom, pear trees, many vegetables, all green, and luxuriant wheat patches extend all around. It is a very beautiful sight. My host exceedingly kind and officious. He does not have exceedingly great confidence in the mines. His opinion is that the little stone foundations are those of the former houses of the Opatas. At Batonapo, about a mile southeast, he says

there is a fortification of stone about which an Opata tradition exists
to the effect that, previous to the coming of the Spaniards, the tribe of
here and that of the next river east (Oposura!), were at war with each
other, and the people here used to retire thither to defend themselves
from their enemies. He positively asserts that at any distance from the
permanent water courses there are no settlements except a few strag-
gling houses, probably temporary for the hunt only. There is another
extensive ruin at Motepán.

I heard of stone axes, many broken metates, and pottery painted red.
There is no available large timber outside of the highest mountains, but
still the cottonwoods, willows, and even the palo blanco, which covers
so abundantly the hills in places, would yield vigas whereas there is
ample small wood for the other parts of the little roofs. He [Manuel
Romero] is of the opinion that the Seris did not occupy the Cananéa.

MARCH 7: Left on horseback with Romero for the Santa Elena [Helena]
Mines. They are, in a direct line, about one-and-a-half miles from
Banámichi, but the trail and the road both wind around so as to make
it fully three miles of way. The hills are, as usual, steep and covered
with low mezquite. Pitahaya, green madroño, choyas, and palo blanco
in parts. The mine is large and was once very rich in gold and silver.
Today it is—as usual—rich in "large quantities of low grade ore." It is
not working today and has stopped [has not been in operation] since
the fourth of February. The works are extensive and must have been
expensive. There are some tanks of permanent water around, and an
almost permanent arroyo to the south of it. Along the latter there are
traces of foundations, and on some scattered blocks of stones there
are carvings, one of which at least is old and aboriginal. The others are
doubtful. I talked to Mr. Olcott[56] about my money affairs. He did not
say no, but at the same time it is evident that he cannot jump into the
matter.

Upon our return, Romero led me to the volcanic mesa of Batonapo,
a plateau of lava or malpaís proper, very rugged and overgrown with
hateful choyas, palo blanco, madroño, pitahayas, etc., and descending
abruptly to the west into the bottom valley of the river, on the left hand,
there is the narrow valley of Bácachi, on the north, a ciénega with very
dangerous, deep holes of mud. The east of the mesa is not inhabited,
but the west is crossed by very remarkable fortifications, rude, but huge
breastworks of lava rudely piled on top of each other, of great width,
with projections, interior courts, and a central quadrilateral. Houses

are scattered about in irregular squares. There are also houses along the foot, at the ciénega, on the neighboring bluffs, and at a height not a quarter-of-a-mile north of it. I have to examine this very closely yet.

I am also assured of large ruins near Huépaca, and of ollas painted red filled with human bones found there and at Fronteras. The latter are said to be of various sizes, according to as they were adults or of children. At the end of Holy Week, the rehearsal of the dance of Da-ui begins and lasts 15 days. It lasts three days, and is, from the description, a perfect and well-conditioned Indian dance. The men go naked to the waist, and to above the knees, they paint red and white figures. Feet naked. Head of men with a white band and painted, hair long, and costly feathers which they preserve for the occasion. The women with feet naked, a red dress up to half the breast and down to below the knees, probably the left or right breast exposed. Many ribbons adorn the dress. Hair of women long and loose, and a headband too. There are commonly three or four singers with guajes [gourd rattles], but there is no drum.

From what I can gather, it is a dance which contains much of the original. Finally, the perfect caballito with a figure made of the pith of the pitahaya called Moctezuma [Montezuma] at the top of a high pole, which is finally shot down. At the end of the dance, when Moctezuma has been killed, private dances are held in the houses. It is a function which is absolutely public and calls for the many spectators. Many different figures of the dance, and the step, according to the description, is that of the cachinas [kachinas]. Solo dances appear, and the dancers change dress and insignia several times during the feast. The kilts of the men are embroidered. They promised me the words of the dances and song.

In the month of May, they used to hold a great rabbit hunt, the first rabbit was presented to the band. This is now abolished. They had, up to 1857, annual elections of a Governor, of a topile and of a mada, or alguacil. Now the officers are all abolished; still there is, in each municipality, a kind of chief elected during [for] life-time, to whose voice they listen very strictly. The municipalities are absolutely independent. Thus, Pedro Calixto [Calistro] is of Banámichi; Rafael Palominas, of Sinoquipe; Miguel Sinotéz, of Huépaca. Each one has his substitutes. Here, there are two. Besides, there are in case of necessity, councils held in private houses. A council-house is unknown. (The fable of Moctezuma's return is dished up also.) The chief holds all of the titles to the lands and church, etc. At certain intervals, they hold festivals of tis-uin [tiswin, maize beer] in a private house and all the aborigines of the pueblo are forced to concur [participate?]. When the husband or wife dies, the children all inherit; otherwise Spanish and Mexican laws of inheritance.

The Pima still inhabit Onavas, Movas, Rio Chico, San Antonio de la Herta, Soyopa, etc., all south of Oposura and on the west bank of the Rio Yaqui. The Seris occupied the country from Guaymas upwards; they used poisonous arrows. They reached north as far as south of Yuma, touching the Yumas there. The mode of making pottery among the Opata is like that of the Pueblos: in coils, afterwards covered with red ochre and not decorated. They burn it in dung too. Up to 1859, regular caravans of Pueblo Indians from New Mexico visited Sonora annually, about October. Until they reached Magdalena [Sonora], they were under one common head or captain. Then, they separated into three bands to trade. They had zarapes, buffalo hides, etc., and traded them for rebosos, oranges, etc. On the last day of November, the bands met at Hermosillo, and whichever did not come in until the third of December was given up for lost and all the rest left for home. In 1859, owing to an attempt at collection of duties, they never returned since.

MARCH 8: My cold is abominable, and the nose principally is sore. I went with Don Manuel [Romero] to the loma adjoining the pueblo to the south. It is overgrown with choyas and every kind of spine and thorn. The measurements are almost impossible owing to these thickets and also owing to the fact that the hill is covered with large drift and gravel, which makes it difficult to distinguish between the ruins and the gravel and boulder heaps. There is hardly any pottery on the place, but there are a few fragments of old metates and some other stones slightly ground to concavities, which may have been the beginning of new metates. Chips of basalt or lava.

Ruins south of the pueblo of Banámichi.*

There are some flint chips, but they are not very common. The leading feature, however, is a concavity surrounded by heaps of gravels, rocks, and boulders, extending afterwards into a heavy wall, about one [meter?] wide. . . . Width of wall about 0.70 [meter?] to 1.0 [meter?] varying in width. The double walls consist of heavy stones with mud between and small rubble or gravel. Width about 0.50 [meter?].* This is the type of wall in the ruin, except where the walls are single. There are evidently corrales too, with the usual foundations of single rubble.* [There] appears to have been a tank; it is about 0.65 [meter?] deep, and at the bottom grows a willow plant and [there are] traces of moisture. . . .

Everything is terribly overgrown and the measurements very difficult. The general plan of the hill is as follows.* To the northwest of it extends the present town. Last night Don Manuel Romero told me that there are still, in the barrios, some old Indian houses similar to those whose foundations are so frequent. They are thatched with palm leaves, as fan-palms, low and scrubby, exist between here and Cumpas. The manufacture of fan-palm hats is one of the industries of the Opatas at Aconchi. (Opata is evidently a Pima word: O-op-o-tam.)

I called on Don Ramón Durón in the morning. He is a very pleasant old gentleman. In the afternoon, I fixed my groundplan and then painted pottery. No news from the mine until 5 P.M. so far. The Opatas play, one pueblo against the other, several games: The Ua-qui-mari, or runners with two balls [kick-sticks?] of wood (Gomi), a kind of football; the game of "shinny," or Uachícori; the Patol [Patolli], or Quince, with little sticks, four in number, marked respectively, fifteen, ten, six, and four, and with the ring of stones as in New Mexico. The captains of the footraces are called Maynate, one in each pueblo. If such a footrace was to take place, they used to sit in a small, low place all night, smoking long and thick cigars filled with the fungus of the mezquite (called To-ji) which is exceedingly narcotic. They used the flower of it to smoke, and drank tisuin to it. Commonly, Sinoquipe and Banámichi ran against Huépaca and Aconchi, Sinoquipe and Aconchi having the most famous Maynate.

They also had a deer dance called Batespar. One of them wore a deer's head and moved about very lightly. Another one beat, in place of a drum, a Papago basket filled with water, in which they placed a Xicara, mouth downward, and thus the beating, moving the water, produced the sound. [This occurred at the?] eclipse of the moon. They made much noise, beating the war drum, picking metates, etc. Everybody who could walk made some noise, and all pregnant women had to turn around three times. They had a war drum (tambor), small and low, hide on both sides, with one drumstick. Of feathers, the eagle feather (used singly), buzzard (in rows), crow (two only). They scalped, taking the ears along; and danced the scalp dance with the scalp on a pole, and the women began the dance by throwing ashes at the men. The man killer now has a distinctive mark, a red scarf of cotton, and also a badge of buckskin with a little satchel pending from it with tassels and iron-pendants which rattled. The badges they wore when they went to a dance. Their paint was white with red spots except on the knees where there were white stripes. Bows of mulberry wood, arrows of reeds, and of the flower stalks of the yucca. Length of bow: four-and-a-half feet. Points of arrows of the wood of buchuta hardened by fire. No flint points. The arrowheads of iron followed immediately upon those of the buchuta. The latter is very hard and dangerous. (Therefore no arrowheads in the ruins!!)

They used a macana of Palo de fierro, 22 inches long, tied to the wrist by a leather string, 15 inches of it formed a triangular club. Had shields with rawhide covers; the diameter was one foot by 15 inches, convex, painted. A wrist-band of leather on the left wrist. Quivers of fur, for 50 arrows each. Sandals. Hair-tress, tied up behind. Breechclout and huipil. The women, naguas and huipiles, all white. They did not tinge [dye]. Cultivated cotton and wove in estacas [probably a loom fixed in the ground]. Spun with a malacate of wood. Cotton culture abandoned in [within the last] 20 years, owing to the cotton worm. Wrote and mailed letters to Dr. Thomas (with a draft), to Dr. Girard, and to Mr. Parkman. It was midnight when I went to bed.

MARCH 9: Don Manuel's son-in-law, Jesús Romero, came with his whole family to spend the Sunday. I left the house at 9 A.M. for the Cerro de Batonápo, and followed the road, then struck across the fields. There are two foothills on the western slope of the main mesa. These foothills are bare. To the northwest of them is the ciénega with some very deep holes, overgrown with grass, where a woman may yet sink and disappear, as it happened some time ago. The first of these hills I measured in two directions.*

As to habitations, which there are traces thereof, in the shape of a common red pottery (never ornate), metates (even of granite), manos, and many chips of basalt, a very few of red flint. I was unable to discover foundations of any kind. The whole is so strewn over with lava rubble, dykes and ledges protrude so much on the surface, that it is hardly safe to determine what is natural or not. Thus much appears positive that parapets exist, but in regard to houses, if these ever existed, they were few in number and small. The whole looks much more like a place of refuge than like a permanently inhabited fortress. The lomas and mesas around are thickly settled, in proportion, although the groups are small, and it appears as if their population had been pressed from the outside and, instead of fortifying each point, had resorted to the expedient of a central place of refuge for all the surrounding settlements. . . .

I omitted to state that Mr. Olcott, at the mine, showed me a very large stone axe from Ures. It is exceedingly handsome and has the lower end, not with a crease, but with a triangular slit or groove. My upper lip and nose are much inflamed and sore. Called on Pedro Calistro. Drunk.

MARCH 10: Groups of starlings and blackbirds singing. I went to Pedro Calistro, who was drunk again. But he told me to come back tomorrow night, and that they would then tell me all about their traditions. This willingness is rather suspicious on their part and I may get "salted" if I am not careful. The corral or fortification at Bato-napa (boiling or bubbling water) they say was made by *los antiguos* [the ancients]. The name for Opata in their language is *Jay-rana* or *Jayl-dana*, as I understood it. The proper name for Batonapo is Batonapa Vácatz. They promised to get me *Tivinaua* (not *Tivinaui*).

Returned home and finished at last the pottery plate. In the afternoon, I started for the Prensa, or Punta de Agua, in the Cañada de la Cruz. It is about two miles in a straight line from Banámichi, but at least three by the crooked and winding trails, which pass over the broken mesas or ridges of lava and of rubble or drift.* About half way I met a single house which stands on a point. Farther on, I met other groups. They are rather distinct and some of them show double walls, the stones being on an average .027 [meter?] apart, thus giving a total thickness of about 0.40 [meter?]. Pottery is about, plain red, also metates, etc., and an immense number of basalt and lava chips are strewn about. As I neared the ruin and the place where the acequia starts from it, I reached a high mesa rising abruptly above the acequia.* At its northern end it turns a sharp angle, and then descends to a lower mesita, which rests on broken rocks standing abruptly over the beginning of the acequia proper. They form a broken rocky wall, about twenty to thirty [meters?] high. The acequias run at the very foot of the mesa so that there is no space left below. The slope is mostly rocky, or else covered with thick scrubby brush. The mesa itself rises, behind the ruins, to a ridge crowned by lava. The houses are, as on the plan, strung out almost on a line and are the best preserved foundations which I have as yet seen. The stones are all set on edge, sometimes single, and again in double rows, as I marked them, and the buildings, although small, are very regular in shape. . . . Many metates of lava; very flat manos, elliptical and thin; red pottery, some exceedingly thick; little flint. Palo verde, or rather green madroños, are growing inside of the ruins, and to a thickness of 0.20 [meter?] in diameter. It is a handsome group, and I secured every house of it. Returning, I got the *Tivinaua* which is evidently the Yerba de San Pedro,[57] and met Jesús Uchi. He told me that he was properly the real Gobernador, and that Pedro Calistro was a subaltern only; that the Opatas called themselves *Je-ue* and when I spoke of the clan of Alamo he interjected: *Esa es la de este Rio* [They are of this river]. He insisted upon my calling at his house. Spent the evening with Ramón Durón.

MARCH 11: Left early in the morning for Motépan. It was evidently a pueblo, but it is so ruined and destroyed that it is impossible to take any measurements. It may have contained 30 to 50 scattered houses, but only two or three foundations are visible. Few metates are about, and very little pottery. Some basalt chips and little flint. Returned at 1 P.M.

On the brink of the first hill north of the pueblo, after the first crossing of the river, there stands a ruin which I measured, though with doubts!! It turned out, after inquiry, to be a recent house and corral abandoned during the Apache troubles. This, however, is not without importance. It shows the difference between the ancient and the modern ruins. The former, even when made of the same material, are much more obliterated. This is very plainly shown in the case of the walls at Batonapa and here. Both are made of lava, but the former are black, the edges are worn; here the lava is grey, bright, the leucite is very plain in the druses, whereas in the other it is obliterated mostly. I spent the whole afternoon at home painting. The nose is improving under the effects of the *tivinaua*. Have my opinion now of Jesús Pesqueira. He is a fop, a dude, and very ill-bred. This is mostly the case with the Mexican youth.

MARCH 12: My nose decidedly better. This *tivinaua* is a splendid plant. This affirms it is also excellent for hemorrhoids! I painted at pottery all day without much progress; it was difficult work and not very interesting at that, all plain pottery and very much decayed.

At night, by a most beautiful moonlight, I went to Pedro Calistro, who was sober this time. He declared that the old men had all died out, and that he had no ancient traditions. I got, however, the following replies: They call themselves *Joy-ra-uas*. The Pimas they call *Jovas*: the the Apache *Apa-tzi*, whereas those of Arispe call the Apache: *O-Paua*. The Apache are hereditary enemies. The Opatas are divided into two dialects: those of Bacuachi, Arispe, Chinapa, Huépaca, Aconchi, and Babiácora being one; Banámichi, Sinoquipe, Opodepe, Toapa, Cucurpe, Soyapá, Tres Alamos, etc., forming the other. Previous to the [Spanish] Conquest, the pueblos of Banámichi, Huépaca, Aconchi, Sinoquipe formed one, which was at Ba-dé-uachi, near Las Delicias, where the ruins are still visible. After the Conquest, they divided into the four pueblos mentioned. Bá-na-michi (not Banámichi) stood formerly in the river bottom in the fields of Figueroa, but an inundation of the river compelled them to seek the bluff, which was formerly called San Nicolás. Batonapa was a pueblo of Yaquis,[58] and he supposes that the fortifications above were those of these Yaquis. (Cucurpe from "Cucur," dove; Toapa from "Toja.") Sinoquipe from the rock in front of it, on the other side of the river. At the mine, there is another fortified hill.

He showed me the headdress of the *Da-ui* and told me that the women wore the medal of the moon (*metatz*) and the men that of the sun (*ta-ui*). He told me that they formerly had many other dances, but that now they had only the *Da-ui* left. I finally took him aside and told him about the clans. He then affirmed that they had the same organization here, and went on to enumerate them. He counted up: Bear, Tiger, [Jaguar?], Wolf, Coyote, Squirrel, Fox, Skunk, Raccoon (*Batipé*), Eagle, Turkey-buzzard, Lion [Puma], Crow, or Raven. He himself belongs to the Crow. Some of his statements are not clear, however, and he is either not clear himself, or deceiving me. Another clan is the Hare, and still another the Snake. All this is doubtful as yet, and he may have misunderstood me. From his talk, I infer that the Opata live in houses.

MARCH 13: I went to Pedro Calistro but did not find him; his brother was there, and so I copied the Corona [headdress], at least sketched it, and then returned home to finish it. I painted, in fact, the whole day, finishing the Corona, some pottery, etc. Am tired, anxious, and lonely. The people are very kind, but still they are strangers, and the longing for Joe and Papa becomes daily stronger and stronger.

The painted pottery alone is burnt in a cylindrical oven, the common pottery in dung. To tan their buckskins, they shave the hair off with a knife or glass, then rub it with the brains of the animal; afterwards wash it and dry it, even wringing it out. Then they prepare a decoction of plants or barks, and wash it twice, soaking it well. After that process, it is fully tanned. For cowhide they use tallow in place of brains—like the Apache. To make the white or red buckskin yellow, and thus avoid shrinkage in wetting, they pass it twice through the smoke of the olote (Olotl) [corncob]. For tanning they use willow bark, cozahin. (This is probably the Caña agria of New Mexico, as it is used now for ink too.) Their ancient mode of weaving, I am going to see tomorrow. It is still used by the mother of Miguel Valencia. Night quiet and calm; my nose improving very slowly.

MARCH 14: Nose better and had an excellent sleep. Copied the skirt made of reeds, also the reed pole, rattle, and other things. Painted the whole day.

MARCH 15:[59] I went and got shaved early. It was a difficult operation, and somewhat painful. I then met Captain Bell,[60] who gave me letters of introduction to Babiácora and to Oposura. I spent the day with him very agreeably. He presented me to Don Mateo Felix Diaz and to Don Manuel Canillo. The latter told me that the proper name of the Da-ui was: Da-ui-na-ma-ca, that is, "I give thee, because thou givest me," and that it is a dance of the Indians instituted in consequence of their friendly relations with the Spaniards after long and continuous hostilities. He found this in a fragmentary document, signed or written by a certain Zuñiga! The document has disappeared since. The destruction of the archives of Arispe, of Matape, by the revolutionary bands, is certain.

Rain streaks on the Sierra Rayón. The Apache wars commenced in 1834, through the refusal of General Ramón Morales, then Governor of Sonora, to issue rations to the Apache as before.

MARCH 16: In the day it sprinkled occasionally, and I did not therefore go to Huépaca as I intended, but stayed at home painting. It is tedious to be painting at pottery, especially this pottery here, which is very uniform, being simply plain, and at the same time much decayed, thus requiring an infinite number of intricate and very difficult details. I also finished the loom, which was an easy job. Was told tonight that there was, at Babiácora, a Mexican by the name of José Antonio Ruiz, who spoke the Opata language perfectly well, and who could give me much information. I resolved to go to Huépaca tomorrow at all events.

MARCH 17: I started for the Ojo de Agua late. It is a road in the very bottom of the river, first along the lowest terrace and then, about three miles from Banámichi, it descends into the sandy bottom proper, always remaining on the east bank. Here it has a width of two-and-a-half miles. In other words, the foothills recede after leaving Banámichi and touch the river front only at the Ojo de Agua again. It looks very natural, therefore, that the ruins should crowd over the hills near the two places.* At the Ojo de Agua, the few houses stand at the foot of a sloping mesa or ridge about 20 meters high. Its narrow top is flat, overgrown with shrubs, thorny as usual, and with the ruins on the other side. The latter show nothing different from the others, beyond that there are little, low mounds of rubbish. The walls are all double. Pottery the same, metates of granite. Much basalt in chips, but hardly any flint. No trace of circumvallation, etc. I went home soon and caught a slight shower on the road.

MARCH 18: I painted nearly the whole day. In the afternoon, Mr. E. E. Olcott of the Santa Helena Mine came and brought me some drawing paper which I needed very much. Don Rafael Corella told me that the Apache wars commenced in 1831, and in the manner stated before. Painted all night.

MARCH 19: Painted in the forenoon. Left for Las Delicias at noon. The river sinks in the sand here. The west bank is more open, and the mesas are lower. Las Delicias itself stands on the lowest terrace above the river and adjacent to the fertile fields.* It is a genuine hacienda, but not as awfully handsome as told. I at once hunted for Badéuachi, and found that it was a mesa, or rather a series of mesas, with flat tops running parallel with the fields. Of course, it is thickly overgrown with the usual thorny vegetation. Signs of houses are everywhere, but there is nothing measurable forming a large complex. The pottery is as usual. There are many basalt chips, no flint, and very few metates.* It looks as if there had been an entrance like that at the small ruins on Upper Salt River and on Tonto Creek.

In the evening went to see the dance in Joseph Rinaldi's house. Well received and cordially treated. He is the man who, after killing one man at a house in Nevada, killed four men at Globe, Arizona Territory. Met Antonio Marieta, nephew of the celebrated Joaquín.[61] He says that Joaquín died peaceably in Lower California in 1876. There is another ruin close by here at Baynorpa.

MARCH 20: This place here, when well fixed up, is a handsome place. Now it is almost in ruins. Went to hunt for the ruins of Baynorpa. If there was ever any population up there, its vestiges are now almost completely obliterated. Besides, the height is not one contiguous level, but a series of more or less long ridges, affording little room for extended villages. Traces of habitations are faintly visible, and one plain foundation which I measured. Mr. Olcott came to visit the hacienda. Painted groundplans all day. The mail came and no letters. I was very despondent. At night, however, Mr. Olcott sent the boy from the mine with the message, that the money ($97) had arrived. Thank God.

MARCH 21: Left for Banámichi at 9 A.M. and then called on Don Jesús Figueroa. He told me that the Da-ui consisted of three parts. The first is aboriginal and refers to their mode of planting their crops. The other is imported and historical insofar as it commemorates the [Spanish] Conquest, and last is the church dance of the Moros,[62] these being substituted by the Apache. He positively denies that the Opata know anything about Montezuma. The figure placed on top of the pole, and at which they shoot, is Tahuaro, their evil genius. He promised to tell me more about their superstitions, but says that they have lost all their recollections and traditions almost completely. They are modernized.

I then rode out to the mine, and missing the trail, came out on the water pipe between the mine and Banámichi. All of this country is well broken-up, thickly studded with spines, and so rocky that there are no chances for habitations. Kindly received, and Mrs. Olcott and Carlton [son?] started with me to the top of the Santo, a very bold height east of the mine. Its southwestern side is precipitous for about one hundred feet.* It is separated from the mine by a valley, and is about a half-mile distant in a straight line. [Elevation of mine and the nearby valley].

To ascend, we followed a trail southeast then wound up due north to a crest on which there are some rough rounded stone enclosures or foundations, and following that crest nearly due west, struck the only slope on which an ascent is practicable. It is exceedingly steep, rocky, and from the base to the top the height is 200 feet. On this slope, there are five lines of parapets, or rather broken, irregular curves of rocks piled up on the edges of ribs, or ledges cropping out, forming curves around the periphery of the bluff. Behind these there is invariably a space of open ground, like a little platform, whose width is of course variable.*[63] Whether this is natural or artificial I am unable to determine. A strong rude wall then runs up, connecting with a rounded enclosure, of rude rocks, seven [meters?] in diameter, forming the top fortification. Some pottery is strewn about; there is a sign of old metates, but still all the structures look more like enclosures than like houses. The top of the Santo is rocky, but has no signs of human work. A beautiful view extends in every direction.

Mr. Olcott tells me that the hills of the river side are quaternary deposits, but the mountain northeast of Banámichi is a flow of solid lava, whereas the surrounding eminences are deposits of lava detritus. At Téhuachi, there may be primordial deposits. There is obsidian near, in veins. It is a black and opaque. Returned to Delicias at night, and wrote letters to Mr. Parkman, Dr. Thomas, and Lieutenant Scott.

MARCH 22: Mr. McCarran told me of an important ruin near Huachinera. Left Banámichi with J. G. Chism at 9:30 A.M. The abandonment of the old pueblo of Banámichi took place in 1710 or 1715. The old mission mill was founded in 1766.

The mesa is 15 feet above the river, and the river rose seven feet above [at flood level?]. At Aconchi, Doña Guadalupe Durón; at Babiácora, Don Eusebio Santín. I straightened up everything at Banámichi and took leave.

MARCH 23: Wrote to Joe in the forenoon, and painted in the afternoon. I was very sleepy, but at nightfall we were told the blacksmith's shop was on fire. It was soon quenched, however, and we sat still talking in my room, Jim Chism and I, when, about 8 P.M., the fire alarm was raised again. The town had all gone to the wedding of "Nigger Jim" with a Yaqui girl, so that Jim and I were alone in the house. I then thought of the possibility of it being a decoy, to draw us out and rifle the money drawer in the meantime, and therefore stayed at home prepared. There were evidently people about, but nobody came in. The fire broke out a third time, so that Jim and I kept watch until 4 A.M. The roof was pretty well destroyed.

MARCH 24: Stayed at home and painted. Am very tired and need rest. Therefore, I stayed here and shall only leave tomorrow for Aconchi. Jim is as kind as possible for me. So are all the rest, and I am becoming quite attached to the place. As late as one year ago, the Apache killed people around here. Jim was arrested at Banámichi this afternoon, but it seems to be nothing of importance at all. He returned late. "Nigger Jim" had put the plea that he was afraid of violence, and prayed that he be put under bond. Released. Wrote to Dr. Girard; packed up my drawings to send to him by way of Tombstone.

MARCH 25: [Here, Bandelier listed a series of vocabulary items.] These data I got from Pedro Balvestro. He positively denied knowing anything about the gentes, but finally acknowledged that, in former times, there used to exist Indian appellatives like "Coyote," "Venado," "Lobo," etc.

The oldest book of the church (Partida de Bautismo) dates back to 1666 and has a Visita [inspection certificate] of 1697. This is not, however, the first book of San Pedro Aconchi, and of Babiácora. It contains numerous Indian names, as usual, but as Pinard has been here, it is needless for me to bother with them.

I left Las Delicias about 10 A.M. and rode on, crossing the dry bed of the Sonora about the Ojo de Agua. The bottom seems to narrow on the east side, and the Sierra de Aconchi, a very high and rugged, broad ridge, covered with pine timber in its upper tops, approaches from the west. But that bottom is one contiguous strip of fertile soil, all cultivated, and now dark-green, lined with light-green álamos, and the road is one succession of ranchos. The village of Huépaca stands as usual on a high bluff, facing the bottom abruptly to the east. Like the others, dilapidated houses, some painted, others mere mud walls. Below Huépaca, the thorny vegetation becomes lower and more uniform. Aconchi, where I was handsomely received and treated by Don Gavino Durón, stands also on a high bluff; its church is somewhat repaired. The Cura Moctezuma also treated me very well. There are ruins on all the hill tops, of the same kind and pottery as elsewhere, but none measurable.

MARCH 26: In front of Aconchi are the hot springs. There are little ruins, almost obliterated everywhere on the bluffs. Left Aconchi early and reached Babiácora about 1 P.M. The valley narrows, the bluffs on the east crowd the river, and the mountains on the west are very near and bold. Babiácora is like the others with a rickety church. Little pueblos all around, obliterated, unmeasurable. Wrote to Joe, to E. C. Springer, and to Dr. Eggert.

MARCH 27: Left at 9 A.M. with Jesús Villegas, a young and pleasant Yaqui half-breed. Entered the valleys at almost a level, hills and tops covered with brush, mostly mezquite. Arroyos, but no water except one spring and a few holes. Reached the foot of the Sierra de la Palma, and then the ascent began, first through a beautiful cañón, very grand and picturesque. Here oak trees began to prevail. There are almost interminable cuesta—steep, terribly rocky, and very high, lasting for upwards of an hour; tiresome, had to be done all on foot, miserable trail, to the first crest, where an extended view is had over the deep valleys and on the mountains in front of Babiácora and Aconchi. The rock appears to be granitic with dykes of trachyte. Copper stains plentiful. The tops of the Sierra, though steep and rugged, are still covered with oaks, and the slopes carry rich grass. Afterwards down, rugged and bad, trail almost obliterated, to an arroyo with a salt water pool, where an isolated fan palm stands. Thence up another long, horrible slope, to the highest crest. Here a glimpse is had of the Sierra de Oposura. Then at an imperceptible decline, winding along dizzy slopes, the trail almost impassable through land or rock slides, down a great depth, at least 1,500 feet, into an arroyo. Pines and oak constitute a forest all around, but the trail is horrible, running always in the bed of the arroyo. Walked. Towering heights all around, partly wooded.

As we descended very gradually, palm trees appeared, mingled with the oaks, and the pines were left behind. A little water trickled down the arroyo; it is slightly alcaline [sic]. As we proceeded, winding around and between the heights, the trail mostly unfeasible on horseback, the high Sierra gradually went out of sight, and hills lowered, the forest thinned, and the slopes finally grassy and bare. Fan palms occasionally in the bottoms. The Mesa de los Morenos, flat, grassy, and level, was reached after a short but tedious ascent, and in the east, another mountain range arose before us. This we had to cross before reaching Oposura.

I then saw it was impossible to get there tonight, the more so as there are said to be horrible passages ahead. On the mesa I at last put Chico to a lively trot. But it grew dark when we reached the eastern border. A horrible descent, lasting upwards of three-quarters of an hour, over grey trachyte, steep, rugged and slippery, brought us to the grassy bottom of Bacachi. This is a hacienda, now abandoned, since the Apache killed three men there last June (1883). It was dark now, and we concluded to pass the night here, without food nor fire nor water. But Chico had good grass, and so we laid down in an open space. The bottom as well as the surrounding heights bears many fan palms, as high as 25 feet.

MARCH 28: Left before day break and ascended to the barren and grassy pass over the Sierra de Bacachi. Reached the crest at sunrise and had the Sierra Grande in front of us. The descent was similar to that from the

Babiácora Range, but after following an arroyo for an hour or more, we ascended a high trachytic mesa. All around a scene of wild and sublime grandeur, deep clefts, with red and yellow rocks shooting up out of them in vertical pillars and walls. Cactus (pitahaya) growing out of fissures. It was again a horrible descent, then a very rocky arroyo, finally the ascent to another mesa, and after crossing the latter to the northeast for about two miles, landed at the bottom of Oposura, very glad and very well tired out, after our ride of 42 miles, of which at least 20 were walked.

I stopped at the house of Don Manuel Moreno, and soon found Mr. Frank [?], who is exceedingly kind. Oposura (2,000 souls) is on the banks of the Rio Oposura, or the same stream as Cumpas is on. In 1693, that river suddenly dried at Cumpas, and now has remained dry periodically as far as Tepachi, nine leagues south. Twenty-nine leagues (of 5,000 varas each) south of here, it flows into the Yaqui. The Yaqui flows past Huassavas and joins the Yaros or Aros 17 leagues southeast of here. Ruins are everywhere, but especially in the Sierra Madre, where cliffhouses, caves, and other ruins abound, and in the Sierra Huaynopa. But it is still dangerous. On the 31st of January last, the Apache killed two men here, three miles away, and ten or twelve days ago, they stole horses near Babispe.

The statement that the Opatas used wooden points in place of arrowheads is confirmed here, but the Apache used only arrowheads. (Apache War began in 1833.) The more I hear, the more I come to the conclusion that in the Sierra Madre the main ruins exist. There is, furthermore, a very important ruin near the rancho of Moreno, six leagues from here. Called on Dr. Moore, and saw George Woodward.

MARCH 29: I crossed the river and ascended the mesas. On the first tier of hills, I found Spanish remains; on the third tier a few completely destroyed houses in the brush, and on the north end of the mesa a little pueblo with 12 still distinguishable and mostly measurable houses. They are identical with those on the Rio Sonora, but the pottery is mostly in smaller fragments. The latter is red with the streaks of corn-cob (*olote, olotl*) around it on the exterior. Hardly any flint chips accompany the ruins; few broken metates (of lava), manos, no arrowheads, and I found one hatchet-like implement which everybody told me was used for the picking of metates. It is of very hard grey rock, probably quartzite, and has the shape of a flat axe. The edge alone is evidently sharpened.

An arroyo divides the settlement into two groups. The houses are small, very large blocks alone remaining to indicate foundations. [Measurements given here.] Its appearance is about as follows.* The center is occupied by a bush or shrub. I did not notice any of the single-walled enclosures; as on the Sonora, all appeared to be double walls and houses therefore. Returning, I found the vestiges of another group on the south, both groups being separated by an arroyo only.* . . .

I then returned home and met Epitacio Paredes. He had visited Magdalena. He told me that, near Bacanuchi, there are large ruins of groups of small houses, and that the pottery is plain red, brown with stripes of Indian red, and red with black, also white with black, and black with white! He told me of Pinart's thefts at Magdalena, and of a collection of rare archives, hitherto unknown, near Magdalena. He also told me that there had been an Apache War from 1762 to 1774 when the Apache, defeated near El Paso, sued for peace. They were then settled near presidios and churches, and rationed, and kept quiet until 1833 when, the Mexican Government refused to supply them any longer, they went to Arispe to complain. The reply came for them to go to work like the whites. Returning dissatisfied they passed through Bacuachi where the Mexicans went gambling and horse racing with them. The Apache beat the Mexicans and left with the stock they had won, but the Mexicans followed and fired at them, and one Escalante, with a whip, cut out the eye of a chief, *Skilli-cané*, who threatened vengeance. The Apache thereupon began the war, and Escalante was the first man killed. At night, pleasant visit from Epitacio. Captain Kostalitzky[64] promised to attend to my horse. The alfalfa is not good for him.

MARCH 30: I went to Captain Kostalitzky to get some teguas [boots] made by one of his soldiers. Afterwards, to the priest, Don Angel Monje. He promised me [access to] the archives. Then mailed my letters. The postmaster, Don Espiridión Arvisu, told me that at Joriquipa he had found a house still standing. It was of thin plates of stone superposed, the rock cleaving easily in such. The walls were 0.30 [meter?] in thickness. At each corner there was a post of wood with a forked upper end, and in the middle of the wall another such post, but higher, making six posts in all. The doorway was about 0.75 [meter?] wide.* The walls and outer (corner) posts were about 1.50 [meters?] in height; the middle posts, 2.30. This indicates a frame of a pitched roof. It was probably covered with palm leaves. Painted.

In the afternoon, Epitacio called on me. His call was, as usual, useful and profitable. He is the best informed man in Sonora, full of good, solid information. At Ymuriz, there are two ruins. There are important ruins in the Valley of San Lázaro also. There are Apache about. A cow was killed by them yesterday, on the Cumpas Road, four leagues from here. This is positive. The moon is increasing now, and caution is needed. Spent the evening with Kostalitzky. Music in the plaza.

MARCH 31 [Misdated by Bandelier, APRIL 1]:Got shaved, and left for the Volanta. The latter is three miles south of town, on the east bank, at the outlet of a cañada which comes from the east, down a high mesa of volcanic rock, probably rock of lava, since they call it malpaís. It is steep, and has a rim of vertical crags. The valley is very narrow. I crossed the river without difficulty above the Volanta to the west. Opposite, the lomas grow into high sandstone crags, jutting out, the slopes overgrown with dense brush; little mezquite and much thornless shrubbery. Here, the inner seam of my pants (right leg) opened as far down as the knee, and I was in a sorry plight.

I reached the fields of the hacienda of Ramón Aragón. Could not get through, so I followed the thorny fence to its southern end, then turned north along the base of the slope and the western fence, and entered the hacienda again near the house, which was closed. It was thickly surrounded by brush. The boys in the fields fled hurriedly. It was clear that they took me for an Apache. My pants grew worse every minute. I could not do anything at all, and so I went back, after having made about eight miles for nothing. Colonel Torres[65] had arrived, but he was taken hold of by "friends" and beer. I was earnestly warned by Don Gregorio Moreno, as the people are naturally very much intimidated by the terrible raids of the Apache, and suspicious of every stranger who goes out away from the roads. There is positive danger in every way. No wonder the people are afraid! But otherwise they are good and kind, and much more sincere than those of the Sonora River. Epitacio [Paredes] told me that the Tarahumaras of the Chihuahua frontier still use sandals of yucca slats like those found in the caves. Spent the evening with Colonel Torres and W. C. Streeter. The Colonel strongly advises me not to travel in the daytime.

APRIL

APRIL 1 [Misdated by Bandelier, APRIL 2]: Called on the Cura [Monje], who showed me what is left of the archives. It is a poor remnant, going back to 1816 only. At the church there are only some old church authors —Suarez,[66] etc., but the church itself, though badly rifled, still shows some remnants of splendor. It is of adobe, faced with brick and stone, and there are many handsome paintings in it. . . . The Seris use poisoned arrows today.

APRIL 2: At Tonibabi, three leagues east of town, there are hot springs. Epitacio tells me that, opposite Huépaca, there is another fortified hill, a Cerro de Trincheras. He went with me and Julian Moreno to the cemetery, to show me the famous Piedra de Oposura. It is simply alabaster, of which there is a hill nearby. It is white and also veined. Cuts easily with the knife. There are two cemeteries. The old one, on the hill, is now abandoned, as the Apache troubled the people even here. There are ruins on the same hill, but only one foundation remains.*

I concluded to leave today with the mail carrier, who goes on foot. So made my rounds. Mr. France, I could not meet, but the other people all came. Got my pockets full of letters, and the kindest greetings and wishes came along. We left at sunset, and travelled by bright moonlight till nearly midnight when, in an open grassy plot, we camped. It was a delightful camp, warm and quiet. This was in the height of the Sierra de Cumpas. What I could see of the country did not exhibit any difference from the rest, except a scantness of vegetation. No signs of Apache.

APRIL 3: Started before daylight, and had a long but not very difficult ascent through the Sierra de las Bolas, so called from the numberless round blocks of granite, which sometimes even hedge in the trail. If there are Apache about, this part of the road is very dangerous. After having crossed this, traversed a long carrizal, caves ten to fifteen feet high. We are now approaching the Sierra de Granados. Trail rough, but by far not as bad as the trail from Babiácora to Oposura. Beyond the carrizal, we came to the Encino, a rocky hill on whose slope Colonel Torres has been surprised and wounded by the Apache. An occasional view is had towards the Sierra de Joriquipa, and even the mountains on the other side of the Rio Yaqui. The trail grew rougher and rougher, the slopes, while very steep, are covered with grass, and there is little or no pine at all. Vegetation seems to change and to resemble more that of Arizona and of southern New Mexico.

After leaving the main trail at La Palmita, where we met a conducto of at least a hundred pack mules, with Don Francisco Moreno of

Guassavas [present-day Huásabas], we struck a cross-trail towards Granados. The rock became volcanic, and the trail fearful. It equalled, even surpassed, in dizzyness, the trail from Babiácora. Finally, through gorges with vertical rocks, we struck the sandy bed of the arroyo, and followed it almost in a plane, and through a mezquite thicket to Granados, a pueblo of four hundred souls, rather low, and near to the Rio Yaqui on the west bank. A green valley extends like a basin to the north; in it the Church of Huassavas [Huásabas], looms up at the distance of three miles to the north, on the east bank. To the south, the vale narrows. Directly in front rises, on the east, the Sierra de Bacadéuachi [Bacadéhuachi] to a towering height, like the Sierra de Sandía, a fearful step-ladder of red tenacles, mesas, broad columns, mostly precipitous, and only in part covered with vegetation. I should estimate its height above the river to be at least four thousand feet. The trail to Bacadéuachi is plainly visible.

Reception here most charming. Don Fadrique Arviza took me in, but Don Lauriano Durazo and his father, Don Manuel, in fact, all the people of the town, united in giving me a very delightful reception. According to the land titles of Don Manuel Durazo, eight brothers Durazo and one Arviza entered this land in December, 1826, and the whole population descends from these two families. Marriages of first cousins are common, and the "stock" is handsome, well built, and sound. Pleasant and intelligent. They have suffered much from the Indians. The last depredation (horse stealing) was committed by them at Opoto [present-day Oputo] last week only.

In the evening, I met Dr. Holm,[67] a German. He tells me that, in Sinaloa, there is a basin enclosed by perpendicular rocks, in which basin there are at least four to five hundred ancient houses. In the rock, and of very dangerous access, above the houses, are two caves, one of which is full of mummies or skeletons, whose skulls are of enormous size. In the center of the cave is an "altar" around which are their weapons: bows, arrows, stone axes, etc. Don Manuel Durazo told me that, on the site on which the town is located, they dug up many metates, etc., and tresses and braids of human hair. Ruins are everywhere, and the more I hear of them, the more I become convinced that these ruins are the houses on the hill tops and that the dykes built across the arroyos are formed for the purpose of accumulating soil and retaining humidity. If so, it is a very ingenious and creditable process.[68]

APRIL 4: I left with Don Zenón Durazo for the next mesa and the

arroyo at its foot, the same arroyo which we descended yesterday. To the
left of the trail (going up), and above the bed of the arroyo which
hugs the northern steep height, the outlet of the cañada is covered with
sandy but arable soil, mezquite, and with rows of stones of different
sizes, laid on the ground or faintly set into it. They compose lines,
tapering towards the base of the southern hills and diverging towards
the arroyo. (I am interrupted by Don Zenón who tells me that the
Opatas used for their bows and arrows *huasaraco* and *basisicota*. The
latter is striated and thus left like worm-tracks which made the wounds
more dangerous. The arrow points, of buchuta wood, were triangular.*
He thinks that these are pueblos of Opata.) They look about as follows.* There are no regular rectangles, but cross-lines, and there are
two systems, one running alongside of the other, and one serving the
main course of the arroyo, the other a depression to the right of it.
Farther down there is another expanse of such walls of rocks, or lines,
but they are very indistinct.* It shows that the main lines were, rather
than for the purpose of slightly damming the currents descending the
cañada along the arroyo, preventing it from being washed away, pre-
serving the humidity, and maintaining the movable sandy soil. The
necessity of resorting to such measures shows a state of great insecurity!!

The pueblo is small, a wall of stones has encompassed it at one time.
It runs along the eastern brink of the mesa and follows a cut or gash
running into the top. The hill is almost all gravel, thickly overgrown
with thorny shrubs, mezquite, palo de fierro, opo, pitahaya, uña de gato,
choyas, etc. The foundations are very indistinct; they are composed
of huge rocks and they are mostly set on edge. The floor is generally
indicated by a depression. Metates of granite, broken, lie about. No
flint, but some red pottery, resembling that of the Oposura River. The
houses are large, some twice as large as on the Sonora River, so large
even that it suggests the idea that they were not of stone, and not of one
family alone.

Everything is much washed, so that it is difficult to determine
whether the walls are all of stone or not. At all events, they cannot have
been high [judging] from the rubbish left. Mesa of the Pueblo.* [Sketch
and measurements]

They did not seem to be double walls, but the size of the stones com-
pensates for this nearly. At all events, it is clear that the pueblo was a
fortified one. The question now is—did they cultivate only the small
patches in the arroyos, or did they also cultivate the fertile bottom? It
would appear to be the case that they cultivated the latter too. But

then, the query arises, were the people of the bottom the same as those on the hills? It does not look unlikely that the former were later inhabitants, gathered together by the missionaries and settled in the bottoms, but the reverse is also very possible, or they may have been distinct tribes, and not at all contemporaneous. These are important questions to decide. Don Zenón told me that the Opatas evidently inhabited these old pueblos, and he knows at least four of their dances: the *Daui*, the Venado, the *Batupari* (which is *not* the Deer Dance), and the Trenza. The latter is a Spanish name and means a tress or braid. They held up a pole, from whose top hung colored ribbons, and danced around, so as to wind up and unwind the ribbons alternately. (How those people of Banámichi have lied to me!) It is noteworthy that not a bit of pottery is found in the arroyo, and not much of it on the hills. Don Ygnacio Corella of Babispe came in. He says that there are Apaches about Babispe. Gave me a letter to Don Juan J. Samaniego. I shall start for Nacora tomorrow on foot with four men, so as to reach it tomorrow night. Don Fadrique offered to guide me to Huachinera.

On the top of the high, towerlike peak east of us, there is a fortified pueblo, very similar, according to description, to the Santo near Banámichi. The mountains between here and Oposura are waterless and arid, but the Sierra Madre itself is rich in water. From the statements of Don Manuel Durazo it appears that there was no pueblo at Granados, and that the hair tresses may not have been old. Went to the river with Lauriano. It is neither broad nor deep, but very clear and limpid. At night, the Cura of Huassavas came. He is old and crippled, but a very good man. He told me that many ollas have been excavated at the Curacy of Huassavas, containing human bones, which shows that they cremated, like on the Sonora. One of the contained, besides, three flints, two flint arrowheads, and three polished stones.

APRIL 5: Everything arranged for my departure. Father Moreno told me that Huaynopa was properly a mine (Réal) and that another such mine was Huaynopita. It looks as if these places were somewhat fabulous for their riches, especially in regard to the treasures of bullion which are said to have been left there when the Apache destroyed them. It seems that the interior of the Sierra Madre was largely inhabited by Spaniards, also by Opata Indians, in the 17th and 18th centuries, but the Apaches drove them out. Many mines were worked out then.

Met Tio Teodosio. He is over ninety years old, having been a soldier under Hidalgo,[69] and still he came on foot, hale and hearty, from

Buenavista (opposite Guassava) three miles, fording the Yaqui on foot. He confirms the statements about the Opata word for Apache (*Opaua*) and for their expression for themselves, *Joyraua*, but states that the *Hovas* are Tarahumaras[70] and that the Pimas are called *Pi-mas*. He has all his senses yet, but was mortally afraid lest I might shoot him.

Started, at last, about 2 P.M. The ascent was really severe. The grade is not only steep, but continuous almost without rest, for almost one-and-a-half hours. The trail winds around and up slopes, very rocky, often cragged, covered with the usual thorny shrubs and succulent plants. The two picachos in front of Granados loom up as bright red, or rather sienna, Mogotes, capped with slight shrubbery. Beautiful is the view down into the valley, with its fields of green wheat divided by hedges into squares, with the pueblo of Granados. Beyond it rises the sierra which I traversed coming from Oposura, and which, while being a continuation of the Puríca, ought to be called the Sierra de la Madera de Huassavas, looms up in folds and slightly indented ridges. After this ascent, follows a short, rocky level, intervening pillars to the right hiding the view down. Until then, the trail has followed the slope on an average to the south-southeast, now it turns almost due east, into a basin, wide and terribly rocky and craggy, scrubby vegetation fastening itself in the crags and dry arroyos. An amphitheatre of vertical cliffs, culminating in a towering picacho almost due east, surrounds it; the only outlet is due southwest, where a part of the green valley south of Granados remains still visible. The rocks northeast are frightful, and the cliff or picacho presents its umber-colored front facing west, absolutely inaccessible from that direction.*

We descended into the Arroyo de la Tinaja where, in washed out basins by the roadside, we found water. The thirst was intense and the heat also. Clambering over the terrible trail winding up and down the slopes and cutting across the slight curve to the northeast, we finally reached a higher basin at the foot of the picacho. Here the sight of the valley disappears, only the tops of the mountains beyond being visible. A fearful cuesta, rocky and very steep, carries us to the southeast of the picacho, and high above its base of cliffs, though still below its summit. This is the narrow pass crossing the cumbre. Pillars and steeples of red rock loom up from the basin which we have just left, both right and left; before it, is a narrow cañada, somewhat rocky, the trail following the course of a rocky, dry arroyo. Grass grows everywhere almost; oak trees are the principal vegetation, beneath their crowns occasional trunkless fan palms, large yucca, even magueyes. The slopes around are not precipitous, but rocky with grass, the tops show crags. The rocks on the ascent are often grey trachytes, alternating with red and brown lava. The trail winds on an average slight incline to the east and after about one hour, the shaggy crest of the first spur of the Sierra Madre, also called the eastern Sierra de Nacori, appears in the east. At the Palmita, water pools appear in the arroyo; here we rested and ate. It is a dangerous spot. Beyond, the Sierra de Bacadéuachi, or rather Sierra de Teras, appears, running west-northwest to east-southeast. Its tops are covered only with pines, the slopes grassy but mostly treeless.

Night soon closed, beautiful moonlight, but horrible trails, fearful slopes alternately to right and left. I kept on stumbling over the terrible gravel and lava; we finally reached an arroyo with water, and following its course, reached Bacadéuachi after 9 P.M. On this whole transit, the heart of the sierra affords no room for population; there is not enough soil and water. It was a horrible, exhausting task.

APRIL 6: The village of Bacadéuachi, with a ruined Jesuit[71] church, and a splendid, though dilapidated, edifice of brick and adobe, with two high octagonal towers and an elaborate facade, a dome, etc.,* of even modern date, stands on a rocky loma above a little valley, sparsely watered by the waters of a spring (Ojo) that rises one league north-northwest of the pueblo near La Galera.

In that vale are the little fields of the pueblo. The village is very dilapidated, small, and the people good, kind hearted, but dirty and lazy, and also addicted to drunkenness. Their past history is one of terrible woes through the Apache, and the feeling of insecurity owning to the presence of that ferocious enemy is ever prevailing and pervades every soul; almost every action of theirs. The Apache is the subject of every conversation.

With Manuel Galas, the priest, I went to copy their pottery with fictile ornaments. It is plain red. There are many Opatas here. The church books, I am told (could not see them), go back to the 17th century. There was a squabble among the people concerning sweeping of the plaza. Of ruins, I heard a great deal, even of corrugated pottery—painted, but everything is confused as between old and post-Conquistorial ruins.

The valley of Bacadéuachi is, aside from the fertile bottom, very rugged and all covered with thorns and exceedingly rocky, mostly mal-país. It describes a curve, is about two leagues wide, counting in the lower mesas, and opens to the north upon the Yaqui, the Sierra de

Teras facing it in the northeast and fronting the Sierra de Bacadéuachi. In the east lies the Sierra de Nacori proper, not as high as that of Bacadéuachi and correspondingly less rugged. No stream runs through this valley, except what trickles out through the bottom lands of the pueblo from the ojo. On the whole, I was well received at that place; they showed me the interior of the church. It is not as large, in the interior, as that of Oposura and of Arispe, but far better preserved. Some fair paintings and a host of images, some of which are not bad at all, even artistic to a certain extent.

We managed to leave a little before sunset, and crossing the dry and gravelly bottom, ascended the slopes, gravelly flats with shrubs, then rocky, higher, trachytic lomas, to Bamui, where, in a little basin, very much exposed to an eventual Indian attack, we camped for a few hours without fire. We were then seven men, six of them with rifles, one horse, two machos [stallions], and ten burros about. I stuck by my good boy, Pedro Fimbres!

APRIL 7: Got up at 1 A.M. The moon was on the decline. It took nearly two hours to get the animals together, build a little fire, and take something to eat, so that it was nearly 3 A.M. when we started. We wound up the gradual slopes, then went down an interminable descent into an arroyo; this descent was, owing to the usual ruggedness of the trail, exceedingly painful for me, the more so as the moon went down, and it grew correspondingly dark. Finally reached the arroyo, where there was some water and timber, and stumbled through this long and dark bottom, apparently, as far as I could see, encased by high crests with precipitous rents and crests. It began to dawn as we crept up a long and exceedingly steep slope with treacherous, rotten rocks, and as we reached the top, fully three hours after we left Bacadéuachi, the sun had risen. The racket which the boys made while going down into the bottom, through it, and up to the crest, driving the animals who often wandered astray, was deafening with its fine echo. The top or crest is not as craggy as that of the Sierra Bacadéuachi, but in vegetation and type otherwise very much alike. Then we followed an analogous decline, only the downward slope being to the left, and very steep and deep, some gorges being frightful. Soon the sierra east of Nacori loomed up, a shaggy crest with its peak on the south side. Before it, the peaks of the lower sierrita. In the far east, the Huaynopa loomed up as a dark undulated line. In the southeast the Sierra Tyó-pari.

APRIL 7 AND 8: South of Nacori, abandoned pueblos: Mochopa, Cervas. East Satachi, Huaynopa, Huaynopita (on the other side of the Aros River). North, [at] Los Metates, two pueblos. One of them near the crest.

Dykes west of Nacori pueblo.*

On the whole, it looks as if the dykes had been built in order to give the ground an opportunity to consolidate, and the boulders to settle in cuts, forming little flats, from which the remaining rocks could be picked very easily. This is shown by the fact that while there are hardly any rocks on the space dammed up, the level north of it is literally covered with them.

The profile of the mountain is as follows: The sierra east of Nacori is a jagged saw descending to the northwest from the southeast.*

There follows, from southeast to southwest the following profile.*

We took rest at the Saucito, a place very much alike to the Palmita, with water. Nearly due north of it rises the Sierra de los Parapetos, a spur of the Teras, so-called for ancient breastworks on its tops. We then gradually descended down over barren slopes of malpaís. The barren valley of Nacori lay before it. Like that of Bacadéuachi it is a curve, and has a narrow outlet northwest. But the slopes are barren, little shrubbery, much grass in bunches, and stony, though less so than farther west. We descended into a valley with a few álamos and poor fields, then a bleak ridge in the center of the valley, and, on the eastern brink of that valley above the bottom where the fields of the pueblo are situated, stands Nacori. It is a quadrangular fort, the little adobe houses connected with rude stone walls. Two gates offered entrance. An immense plaza forms the interior.* . . . A few corrales are outside of the northwest corner. It was 11 A.M. when I entered. Don Carmen Fimbres received me with the greatest kindness, and I stayed with him.

The hot springs are at the western foot of this hill, between it and the Cerro de las Vellotas, a very high conical hill or mountain, which alone is crowned by stone parapets and fortifications. It is at least six hundred feet higher than this one.

Mesa of the Agua Caliente, Tonibabi, about three miles east of Nacori in the sierrita.* Rock, a yellowish trachytic rock. A few metates and some pottery, red, striated, but otherwise plain. Very little flint. The metates are very large. I copied two stone axes. There was a pueblo on the site of Nacori.

It is a terrible life, the one these poor people are leading today. Harrassed by the Apache constantly, completely abandoned by the Mexican government, they have been unable to raise cattle, scarcely able to raise crops in their scanty, ill-watered lands. The arroyo is not permanent, and even now their crops scarcely amount to anything at all, and they raise cattle, which is, in fact, what the valley is fit for, in constant fear of the Apache. Nowhere have I seen such wild cattle as here, particularly on the slopes. The mere sight of a man stampedes them, and it is a sure sign of the presence of Apache, when the cattle come running in from the slopes.

In February, 1882, the Apache, driving an equipata [pack train], and in hopes of that the people had only simple guns, so that the powders might be wet, attacked the pueblo, but were driven off. On the 17 July 1883, after Crook's raid (!!),[72] they surprised the able-bodied men of the pueblo (there are about thirty of them) outside, interposing themselves between them and the village, but the boys fought them and escaped without loss, except one wounded and one killed. They complain bitterly about the Mexican government. On the 8th, I went with Juan José Coronado to Vayuababi and the Aguas Calientes, in the sierrita. There are ruins, in the shape of groups of few houses everywhere, on the hill tops, on the mesas along the streams or rather arroyos, and most of the latter are dammed up. The whole country is so covered with rocks, that only through damming could the slopes be utilized. Once past the bottom, which is only one-sixth of a mile wide, the country east to the highest tops of the sierra is a thicket of spines.

APRIL 9: I started with Pedro Sonogui, Commission of [commissioned by] Don Jesús Figueroa of Arivechi, but whose address is "Nacori." Twenty-six years ago the Apache captured his brother, José María Figueroa, and now a certain Melchiádes told him that Rafael Anchieta told him [Melchiádes] that the Captain Elias of the Apache was José María Figueroa!! [I am to] tell him that his brother Jesús is the husband of Gertruda Soto, that when the Indians captured him, she had borne the following children: Francisco, Luis, Blas, and Feliz, in chronological order. Tell him that his bride, Antonia Enriquez, is still alive, but twice a widow since, one of her husbands having been killed by the Apache. When they captured him, he was going to Mulatos with a load of mezcal on three mules, together with a certain Bárbaro, who was killed there, and three others.

My teguas had given out, so Pedro, the good boy, put new soles inside. I left at 9 A.M., and visited these different places, which are within one league west of the pueblo.*

Hue-shtyoptz.*

Las Pilas. Here obsidian is found scattered in small fragments.*
Brow of hill, no dykes.

There are also ruins at Bacadéuachi, but I could not measure them.
From the top, we had the same view to the Huaynopa, and I saw
plainly where the Metates [Los Metates, rock formations] are, in the
gap between the last notch of the Sierra Teras and the main body of
that chain (also called Sierra de Bacadéuachi) and northeast of the
Sierra de los Parapetos. Traveling in the daytime I could now see the
wild and rocky gorge of Tereverachi at the foot of the crest, and into
which the long and steep descent is made to the west. There is running
water in it.

Reached Bacadéuachi at 3 P.M. and stopped with Manuel Galas.
They told me that at Ceupa, one league northwest of the pueblo, across
the bottom, on the brink of the steep mesa, is a considerable ruin, and
that ruins are scattered all along on the heights or lomas, however terribly rocky they are. They repeated the statement about the painted
pottery, and that on high points along the Sierra Teras above Ceupa,
there stand ruins of small buildings, one on each peak, like watchtowers.
Day windy but cloudy and therefore not unpleasant, and we made the
trip in less than six hours without any hurry at all. The kindness of
the people is remarkable.

APRIL 10: While at Nacori, I heard of another Reál whose fabulous
riches are extolled—Tayopa, but they do not know where they are.
Here, I was assured that in the Sierra de Opoto there are inhabited
caves!

I went to see the ruins south of the pueblo. The Comatete is about
one mile distant. The lomas are terribly broken, and covered with black
and brown lava, shrouded in a thorny thicket. I measured some ruins on
the Mesita Montosa and on the Mesita de San Marcos. There are more,
but it was not possible to define them. The stones are large and seem
to be simply boulders, picked up and piled together as walls. Probably
with earth. (At Nacori they told me that the ruins at Metates contained
walls and one post. The metates around Nacori are enormous.) The
pottery is common and striated, plain red.

We started at 10 A.M. From the top of the crest I saw, not only the
sierra east of Nacori, but the Huaynopa beyond, and even the Sierra
Ceseri (Cachorrón). My teguas went through in the descent, and I had
a very bad time. Pedro tied them together as best he could, but it hardly

lasted. I got to the pueblo of Granados at 3 p.m. and was very tired. Almost the whole tribe had gone to Huassavas, it being the Jueves Santo [Holy Thursday]. Already in the morning, at Bacadéuachi, they had celebrated it with a very, very, very barbarous music. Dr. Hone (Hohen)[73] called very kindly, and Don Fadrique [Arviza] came as usual, a good, kind, honest man. No news.

APRIL 11: Took leave and went on horseback to Huassavas. The road is, as usual, a trail, and winds around the fields on the mesa. At Guassavas, I stopped at Padre Moreno's, and the fariseós, clowns, attempted, as is their custom, to take Chico [a]way from me. These clowns rule from Friday to the Misa de Gloria, but I escaped.

Nacori is the watershed; most of the waters run north into the Yaqui, but some also run south into the Aros. The Aros springs in the Canton of Guerrero of Chihuahua, [an]other branch at Dolores, the southern branch at Pino Alto and passes through Mulato.

The whole town in fiesta. The fariséos take, beg, or steal every horse they can get, and use it until tomorrow noon, feed it well, but sometimes ruin it too. Had they insisted on taking Chico, I would have certainly fired. It is better this way. At Granados, I copied a stone hammer. Here I meet a host of friends, and they are all as kind as ever. Dr. Hone, Don Polycarpio Moreno, [and] his son. Lauriano Durazo. Had an interesting talk with the Father who told me that in the old church of Bacadéuachi there are two ancient idols of stone, dug out and placed in a niche. One is sitting or rather squatting, and other is standing. They are not very large. Human forms, with very large heads. How sorry I am not to have seen them! We chatted until midnight, and I then still wrote. This sketch of the orography of the western part of the Sierra Madre is by Padre Moreno himself. It is at the same time a keepsake.* [The sketch referred to by Bandelier was very simple and of little present value.]

APRIL 12: Went to High Mass. It was decent and the church crowded. The people here are strictly and sincerely religious!

The Indians formerly lived also upon the following plants: pé-chi-tá for atole, these are the mezquite beans. Matures fully in June; then it is dried. For use, it is boiled, pounded, and then it makes atole. This was laid up for the whole year, although it is very heating food. Pitahaya green, and cooked as cajeta [jelly]. Tuna only as fresh fruit. It lasts from June to November. This is used much at Nacori and Baseraca. The dátil [fan palm fruit] as in New Mexico. Mezcal, the head of the maguey, toasted; they also made tesuin of it. Temaqui, a root like the potato, which is used raw and cooked. Very common in the whole district except in the valley. The gyótes toasted; this is the flower stalk of the maguey and the same thing as the mezcal of the Pima. They do not use only the flower stalk of the maguey, but also that of the Lechuguilla and of the yucca. The vellota, or Cuci, or taller oak, rather its acorn. Chichiquelita boiled with salt and chiltepin, and they call it damoua when they cooked [it] with pinole. Petota, oyvari, chuál, mustard, chinita, vachata, garambuyo, the latter gives two crops annually. Tescaláma, or wild fig tree, very frequent in rocky recesses, growing in rents and clefts. Among medicinal plants, there is the copaquin of which they obtain chinin today.

Near the valley of Bacadéuachi there is a mine of epsom salt, and much fibrous gypsum. The skins of deer they tanned with brains, and now colored red with willow bark. The ollas they did not paint; the red color is natural to the clay; they rubbed it outside with a corncob, and, in order to have the vessel porous whenever it was destined to hold water for drinking, sometimes did not smooth it with stones. In Nacori, the subsoil holds so much water that after having planted one year they have to change or to drain it heavily the next, as it becomes a swamp. This is the case at the Teguito, in the little valley northwest of the pueblo, where the Jesuits had their gardens. At Bacadéuachi, there are commonly seven dry and seven wet years. There was formerly a mill there founded by Father Carranco. In the partidos which are left with his name and signature, the O-pa-uas (Apache) are mentioned as killing the Opatas in the mountains, where the latter mostly lived in huts and caves (adentro de las cuevas, endonde vivian antes de cristianizarar, y les daban Sagrado, porque esteban catequizandoles [inside of the caves in which they lived before being Christianized, and they were given asylum (by the missionaries) because they became converts]).

The Opata dance still the Mariachi, a rather slippery dance, which they dance often at night. It has been prohibited. The singers are seated, and they dance in pairs, embracing each other, and the man often covering himself and the woman with a blanket. The scalp dance they also danced formerly. On King's Day they danced Apache! They formerly had sorcerers, and in the cañada of Vaymodachi these were initiated. They were kept strictly secret and have been abandoned now for eighty years at least.

They were very much afraid of the great meteoric shower of 1832, and of the great aurora of 1859. Baseraca was the first place occupied by the Spaniards. In 1879, church ornaments were stolen from Bacadéuachi by two from Chihuahua, to the amount of two thousand [pesos? dollars?].

Wrote nearly all afternoon at the office of Dr. Howe.[74] The church of Bacadéuachi was begun in 1790, and that of Babispe afterwards, both by the same priest, Father Simó. (Fray Lorenzo Simó from Puebla, Franciscan probably.) He died at Huachinera in misery about 1826. There was an immense convent at Bacadéuachi, and at Guassavas there were at one time nine priests as missionaries.

APRIL 13: Left on foot for the Cara Pintada with Tio Miguel. He was on horseback. We crossed the innumerable ridges to the west-south-west; sharp, rocky crests, with gaps, rents, and arroyos, little valleys between them. In a few of these I noted dykes on the plane, and ruins of a very few houses. The ridges increased in height as we went westward. The Cara Pintada consists of a number of figures cut out about twelve meters above the bottom of a narrow arroyo, at the latter's entrance into the Arroyo de la Culebrilla, through which runs the trail from Granados to Oposura. It is a natural recess of red rock. The figures are evidently ancient and Opata. There was no water, so we had to go about one-and-a-half miles farther southwest through a perfect labyrinth of arroyos, rocky, almost impassable, sharp crests, rocky points and ridges encasing them. We finally dug out some water, went back the same way, and I painted the principal designs.

Afterwards, we described a curve to the west-northwest through a similar broken region, without traces of ruins, and finally turned east-northeast. As we approached the river, at a distance of about four miles from it, traces of ruins appeared, as the one on the other side, in the Cañada de las Tinajitas. The ridges here are so narrow and sharp that there is no room at all for houses, so that the latter are in the valleys. We finally reached Mochubabi, a cañada, about one-fourth, or one-sixth, of a mile in width, at whose eastern extremity stands Huassavas. This is all divided into dykes, though most of them are destroyed or at least deranged. No traces of houses, though I saw some red pottery. Otherwise the dykes are absolutely similar to those in the Arroyo de la Culebrilla.

Cañada de las Tinajitas.* Did not find any pottery here. The stones of the foundations are large and there is no trace of double walls.

Cañada de Mochubabi,* one to one-half leguas west-northwest of Huassavas. To this belong the four plates marked A.B.C.D. The surface of the cañada is much cut up by small arroyos, but in the case of C. it is plainly visible that the arroyo was formed previous to the dykes, as the rows of stones of the latter descend into the gulch itself.

Topographical sketch of the Rio Yaqui and its confluents by R.P.J.P. Moreno of Huassavas, 13 April 1884.*

I inquired of Tio Miguel if the mesas on both sides of the cañada showed traces of houses, etc., and he positively and repeatedly stated that there were none. Reached Huassavas again at 2 P.M. It appears that this morning there had been matachines. Here these are little girls only, and they danced in the church before mass, then accompanied the padre home, and danced at the house. At Babispe they even receive him with matachines. The oldest Libro de Partidas here, dates from 1677, and these are only fragments. Extracts from them: Difuntos de este Pueblo de Opoto desde el año de 1677 [Deaths in this pueblo of Opoto since 1677] (evidently a fragment only). Shows deaths from the Apache in 1684 (fol. 82 flechado por el [shot by arrows] . . . -murió en la guerra flechado) 1688 (fol. 83. Killed los Indios enemigos, 3 young men). In 1692 (Peste de viruelas [small pox] fol. 84) died 64. In 1693 (Peste de sarampion [measles] fol. 85) died 32, the epidemic ceasing in June. In 1695 the enemy killed one (fol. 86). The mines of Nacosari are mentioned as early as 1680 (fol. 81). 1706, the Apache killed two (fol. 93). 1707, mataron los Xanos, en la Sierra [they killed the Janos in the mountains], (fol. 93). 1713 (fol. 96) killed one on the road to Huachinera. No murders are recorded until 1724 (fol. 102) when they killed four on the 21st of March. Thence none to 1737 (fol. 110), one on 12th of February, and on the 28th of March, Don Juan Demaras, Capitán General deste Pueblo . . . fue cojido con traición en un cerco demás de 80 Apache . . . [Don Juan Demaras, Captain-General of this pueblo, was captured by treachery in an ambush by more than eighty Apache]. 3 April 1738 (fol. 112) five, in an ambush of more than 100 Apache. None until after 1743, when the fragment ends. Entierros en Guasabas [Huásabas] de 1766 (fragment) one in October (fol. 162). 1769, two (fol. 164) three Yaquis. 1770, their bodies were found and buried. 1771, eight on the 26 March (fol. 167). 1778 mataron los Apache [the Apache killed] three, among them Thomas, Captain de Opoto (fol. 173). 1780, one (fol. 174). This goes against the statement that the Apache War lasted from 1762 to 1774 only ([Mr.] France).

The worst part of the sierra is the western border of it, from Huachinera to the Rio Aros. General Crook entered west of the Tahuaro, because the latter is terrible, and impassable.

APRIL 14: The customs here are perfectly medieval in some respects. [An]other herb which the Indians used as food: bebeláma.

Huassavas (written Guazaca in the 17th century) 1200 souls, 2000 cattle. Granados, 600 souls, 7000-8000 cattle. Nacori, 300 souls, 500 cattle. Bacadéuachi, 500 souls, 2000 cattle. Huachinera, 290 souls, 2000 cattle. Opoto, 500 souls, 2000 cattle. Baseraca, 1000 souls, 2000 cattle. Babispe, 800 souls, 1500 cattle. San Miguelito, 300 souls, 500 cattle.

20 years ago, there was in Nacori all the cattle, even that of Oposura, 2800 head. The reason why the cattle were all in Nacori is, because the sierra east of it is totally impassable, so that the Apache had to take out the cattle, crossing the promontorio at the Yaqui, and then driving them through the sierra past Nacosari, to the north, and thence towards Fronteras to the Chiricahui Range.

The Indian chief whom Leonárdo Escalante wounded was Tutihe, and he [Tutihe] killed E. and P. Robles between Bacuachi and Arizpe at Mababi. That Tutihe thereafter tried to conquer Sonora, but Colonel Narbona attacked them near Cumpas, defeating them, and Tutihe was killed. Besides Narbona, Don Heraclio Escalante was the most plucky and successful captain. He was killed by the Apache himself. The number of people killed annually in all these pueblos reached 80 to 100 sometimes. All the fertile bottoms of the river were formerly densely wooded; this explains why the Indians formerly did not cultivate them; even when these pueblos were founded, the Indians selected high ground to cultivate corn and did not use the bottoms at all.

Spent a pleasant evening at Don Polycarpio [Moreno] with the Doctor [Hone] and the Padre [Moreno]. Got so sleepy that I could not write. But painted all day. It was very warm during the day, though the night fresh, cool, and quiet. My stomach is out of order.

APRIL 15: Painted in the forenoon; then news came that an escort had arrived from Baseraca to get the Padre, and at once arranged to leave with them tomorrow. Took leave of Dr. Hone. Not well, but took pills. Ba-ca-dé-ua-chi, Carrizo agugueado [water reed]. Guazavas [Huásabas], en donde madura la fruta temprano [where the fruit ripens early]. Babiácora, en medino del agua [surrounded by water]. Wrote and

mailed letters to Joe, to Scott, to Don Joaquín [García Icazbalceta] at
Mexico, and to Jim [Chism] at Las Delicias. News came at nightfall
that Don Fadrique [Arviza] was coming with us tomorrow. Wrote a
long letter to Manuel Moreno.

APRIL 16: Left about 9 A.M., a whole caravan, Padre Monje, Don Fadri-
que, Don Reynaldo Samaniego of Babispe, the "Huero" ["Blondy"],
Don Cesario, Espiridión Lucero, and about eleven more of Huachinera.
We started due north, following the bottom to a crossing of the Yaqui
River, which here is more narrow and deep and rapid than at Granados,
but still has the same beautiful clear water. We then entered the foothills, which here resemble somewhat those on the Rio Grande near El
Paso, though more rounded, and with an equally thorny vegetation.
The yucca is growing taller, showing stems of three to five feet high,
and flowering white. Enormous *Dasylirium*. There appears to be no
room for houses on the hill tops, and there is certainly no cultivable
soil, not even along the river who winds around and around these bluffs;
while on the east bank, the Sierra de Bacadéuachi rises in bleak slopes,
bunches of palisaded rocks, culminating in towering cliffs and mogotes,
whose vertical sides face the river. After crossing the Yaqui three times,
we struck almost directly east into a long winding gap, where the rise-
and-fall is first through an arroyo, very gravelly and with boulders,
finally up a long and steep slope. [Here, Bandelier listed several vocabulary items.]

Ruin above the *Tinaja* at the foot of the *Jarato*.*

The vegetation of these up-slope valleys is similar to that of the
higher valleys in the Sierra de Bacadéuachi, but the arboriferous yucca
prevails in exceedingly tall specimens. The gap is more like the upper
basin of the ascent from Granados to Bacadéuachi; the sierra above it is
fearfully craggy, especially about four miles from the river, the arroyo
runs at the foot of a red cliff of terrible proportions. It is at least 1500
feet above the bottom. We turned north into the Cajón del Alamo, and
oak trees began to appear, then northeast and landed, gradually rising,
into the almost circular elevated basin of the Tinaja, about twenty
miles northeast of Huassavas. This basin, as well as the Alamo, is covered
with excellent grass; some mezquite trees border the arroyo, in which
a tank, tinaja, affords water through digging. To the north are pinnacles, towards which the ground slopes up in broken hills, covered
with grass and tall yucca. Here we stopped to camp. I soon noticed
ruins, but they were few and almost obliterated. Scarcely foundations

remained. A space without grass mostly indicated the houses, together with pottery. Found a foot of a *metate!!* The pottery is red, plain, and striated. There are also signs of dykes. The ground is rocky; still, with the assistance of these dykes a limited amount of soil could be saved. It is a wild, quiet spot, by far the [arche]type of solitude, but at all events dangerous in time of war. Consequently, it has a very bad reputation.

APRIL 17: Left at sunrise. We followed an awful cañón, very deep and picturesque, and finally began to climb the crest of the Jarato. As we rose on the slope, very rocky but with fine grass, the view to the west expanded immensely. The whole mountain range as far as the Sierra de Cumpas rose in long and serrated ridges up from the west. About one-fourth of the distance from the top, the valley of Bacadéuachi opened to the south, the church was plainly visible, and beyond the valley rose the Palmar and clearly to the Sierra of Zahuaripa. When we reached the top of the Jarato the mountains east loomed up, part of the Tahuaro became visible, and behind it the Sierra Huachinera: to the south the Sierra de Nacori and even the tops of the range east of Nacori, which range, it now appears, is properly the eastern rim of the Sierra Madre and belongs therefore to Que-va-hue-ri-chi [Que-hua-ue-ri-chi]. A very strong and cold wind, almost a gale, blew all the time, increasing in violence, but it was a cool bracing air, very vivifying, and totally different from the air below. But not only the air, principally vegetation was different. The crest was a slanting plain, inclining to northeast covered with high grass, and tall oak trees scattered at long intervals. The slopes beyond appeared similar. The soil is very rocky, all brown malpaís or lava. This is the beginning of Huépari. (By the way, the Padrecito had told me that, in the rocks northwest of our camp, there is a deep cavern, containing water.)

We continued our way, horrible trails of lava, grass very high, descending and ascending alternately: the Sierra de Nacosari appeared, very bold and picturesque in the east, also the Sierra de Opoto, and branches of the Sierra de Teras. On the whole, we descended, until finally we reached the Llanos of Huépari. The change in scenery is very remarkable. The rugged cliffs and rocks have completely disappeared; the slopes, though still high, are gradual; the tops of the heights round, even gentle; there are no thorns, no bristles, everything looks bleaker; the air is cool, and almost northern; wintry is the appearance of the landscape.

By Huépari passes an arroyo, very clear and limpid water, but it is not permanent. Splendid oak trees, part of them just budding, line the arroyo. We ascended the steep hill of Bamochi and crossed it. It is over one mile long, and an agglomeration of lava filled with nuggets of black obsidian. There is an enormous quantity of the latter. The hill is the same as the others. From its eastern flank, the Sierra Huachinera is seen in front and at its whole extent. It resembles somewhat the Huachuca only it is longer; the flanks are treeless up to the middle, thence oak, and the crests are covered with tall pines. Behind its southern end rises the Que-va-hue-ri-chi.

General Crook entered the sierra through the Cajón de Bamochi, crossing the crest, and found the Apache on the eastern flank, near the Metates and almost in Que-va-hue-ri-chi. The sierra is not craggy, but the cañones are deep and the slopes steep. From the sierra's southern end, a wall of low parallel ridges communicate to the west with the Tahuaro; they close the valley of Tesorobabi, which runs along the foot of the Huachineras from south to the north. The scenery north is very extended; the mountain ranges are distant; the Teras, high and bleak, rise due north; the Sierra Babispe northeast—it is low. Between Babispe and Huachinera extends a sierrita. All the flanks, slopes, and folds are bare, level, and high, and treeless mesas jut out, grassy and white, from under the tops: they enclose or encase the Rio Yaqui, who sallies from behind the south Huachinera through an impassable cañón. The valley of Tesorobabi is a narrow cañada filled with trees, álamos, oak, much yedra, and cedar, encased by low mesas.

We reached Huachinera at 4 P.M., the trip having been pleasant and profitable. The Cuchilla which ends in the Arroyo of Bamochi is one of the worst passages for the horse that I ever met. It is not the steepness alone, but principally the rock, boulders, and pebbles of lava. The obsidian is exceedingly abundant, although I saw no pebble larger than a walnut. In the valley of Tesorobabi, the heights are all bare, with the exception of a few occasional mezquite bushes, but the grass is abundant and, on the whole, they are not as rough and rocky as those on the Yaqui. The analogy between it and the landscape of New Mexico is remarkable. The same bleakness, the same barren mountain chains in the distance. The Sierra de Teras rises directly north, culminating to a high peak. The Sierra Madre itself is not visible here, as the Sierra Huachinera conceals it. The pueblo proper lies on a precipitous bluff above the milpas [corn fields], and the latter form a semi-circular áncón [recess] with rather precipitous rocks, about 40.0 [meters?] high. The flowers are abundant here at Tesorobabi, and between it and Huachinera, and they show forms very similar to, if not identical with, those of New Mexico. On the road we met ruins, but I did not stop to measure them, as Chico was exceedingly wild and gay. Towards Huachinera, even at Tesorobabi, the rock changes into a reddish sandstone; otherwise all appears grey. Tesorobabi is an abandoned ranch, which Don Fadrique and others are buying for $5500. I have to make here a correction. The high sierra in front, north, is the Sierra Babispe, the Teras lie northwest and are almost hidden by the hills of the Corazón. The low range this side of Babispe is the Sierra de Baserac. Stopped at Don Leonárdo Dávila.

APRIL 18: The kindness of these people is astonishing. In the morning we composed together the statistical report of valuation of the pueblo. It contains the ranchos of San Ygnacio del Nori, of San Antonio de Cobora, 52 dwellings, which they estimated together with the ground at $2000. (The costliest houses at $100.) Rents annually at $300. Products of the milpas, $750 net; of the mezcal distillery at $350; of the cattle increase, $1000. Total annual rents of the population, $2050. Got new teguas.

Started with Espiridión Lucero about 2 P.M. Tahuaro, gavalán [sparrow hawk]. Ta, sun; Metza, moon. Ba, cave. Va, water; de-ua, hondo [deep]. Badéuachi, cañada de la cueva honda. The Tesorobabi River flows through a fertile and narrow bottom, rather a strip of land, well wooded with álamos, etc. The mesas on both sides are mostly bare, though the tops are covered with mezquite. We found ruins opposite Huachinera at Juribán on the lower and on the upper mesa.* They are similar in character to the others, all of stone, scarcely broken, but piled up rocks only with earth. This is the character of all the ruins at Terapa and Horcóncitos; the latter is on the east bank of the arroyo. At H[orcóncitos] the double walls of the houses are plain, in distinction of the single walls of the enclosures. Pottery handsomely painted and often thin, corrugated. Much obsidian and flint. One foot of a metate, also metates without feet, and large broken manos. Espiridión told me that an old woman informed him that the sun and moon were made at Cobora. The people built two fires, and then began to tickle each other. Two were found to be not ticklish, a man and a woman. They threw the man into the fire, and he became the sun; then threw the woman into the other fire, and she became the moon. The sun appeared first, in the west, and thence proceeded east there to begin its course, the moon followed afterwards from the same direction. The same old woman told him also that the dams had been made for represas de agua [water catchment areas] and that the people sowed their crops in them. At home they told me that the corrugated pottery was made [porous] for the purpose of keeping the water cool. They say it is easily achieved. About Nacori, much fine mineral paint.

Hueri-uachi, or Horcóncitos, three miles north of Huachinera, east bank of arroyo.*

Ruins on the mesa Juribán opposite Huachinera, northwest across the river.*

Terapa, red earth, about one-and-one-half mile north of Huachinera.* Terapa is on a high bluff of greyish red sandstone, steep on the south and southwest.

APRIL 19: Upper ruin of Quitamac.*

Ruins on lower plateau below Quitamac on the riverside.* Much grass and some mezquite. Pottery painted, very much like that of Casas Grandes and the Mimbres, exceedingly handsome. Much obsidian and flint.

We left about 8 A.M. on foot, going due east. Traversed the mouth of the Arroyo de la Calera, with steep banks, rocky, and wide, forming a cañada, so that Huachinera is properly bounded by that arroyo on the east and the Rio Tesorobabi in the west. We then traversed an accidented country, thickly overgrown with mezquite and occasional álamos, until we reached the bare hills, which rise to the northwest merging into the Sierra de Baserac. Crossing these we descended into the valley of Cobora, on the banks of the Rio Yaqui. After issuing from the gorge west of the Sierra Quevahuerichi and east of the Sierra Huachinera, the Yaqui turns north sharply right here and forms a really handsome little valley or rather a series of basins, composed of a narrow and very gravelly bottom, overgrown as a rule with álamos and not tillable on account of the masses of drift and boulders. This valley lies on the north and east side and partly on the south and west side of the river.

Cross-section of dykes in arroyo forming the north side of Quitamac.* 1. is Quitamac; 2. and 3., Baguigopa; 4., Batesopa.

Beyond are fierce cañones which lead to Taraisitos [Taraycitos], and thence to the Sierra de las Casas Grandes. The distance is five days journey at most, but it is a terrible trip, and not safe on account of the Indians. Generally speaking, in this valley, the first terrace has very good soil in spots, but even that is divided into round mesas, whose brims are very rocky, and very rocky spaces intervene between. Large mezquite trees grow on the plateaus or terraces.

Los Otates, south side.*

Arroyo de la Calera. Eastern border.*

These dykes are built across the arroyo; on both sides, the slope is steep. The bottom, absolutely untillable, is not over 100.0 [meters?] wide: above it rise platforms, and at Baguigopa, on the north side of the river, the second terrace rises steeply almost in a vertical front.* On the west side of the river, after it has made the bend, lies a fertile plane. Above that plane, the bluff rises steeply and denuded, exposing in the clefts of the arroyos grey breccia. Here there is a cave, walled up, with wooden posts, but evidently modern.*

Quitamac lies on a slope, rather steep, covered with mezquite and backing to the west against a denuded slope. The ruins are on that slope. We forded the river, after I had measured another village low down, which is only a series of mounds encompassing a plaza. It seems to be the rule here in these ancient pueblos. The pottery is everywhere the same, very handsomely painted, and of excellent quality, though rather thin, but rather approximating in quality the pottery of Guadalajara. Much obsidian and some flint.* Metates are scarce, but the manos, all broken, are large, even surprisingly large. The Otates are on the other side of the river, and they lie on a round mesa, very low, and partly covered with high mezquites.

Peñasco ádonde rodéan. [They(?) surround a rocky hill.] Civanorago.* New metate.* Height .29; Depth 0.02 [meter?].

This pueblo or ruin shows the pecularity that it is composed of a series of high, irregular mounds forming a semi-circle, and higher than any other mounds which I have seen in Sonora. Still, the height of these mounds is not altogether artificial, but partly natural. The depression between the mounds indicates the size of the houses, and these were small as usual. Only they appear to have been built closer together for protection! East of the pueblo is a low terrace, grassy and of very fertile soil. In it, although it is almost a perfect level, there are dams, and in connection with the dams, little foundations of very large stones, planted on edge, which appear to have been guard-houses.* Such guard-houses are quite frequent.

We forded the river again, and went to Batesopa. This pueblo was large, the largest I saw in Sonora, but it is so completely ruined that only the very indistinct mounds of earth are left. Large mezquites grow on these mounds. There is much pottery about, some metates, blocks of stone, slightly ground and without feet, although broken; it seems to have been a custom to break the metates. South of the pueblo the ground rises, becomes rocky, though grassy, and here is the basin where they say that the sun was created. It is a round depression, with a rim of stones, now destroyed. The basin itself is covered with burnt fragments of stones, showing that fires were built here. There are guardhouses, or rather enclosures, formed by heavy flags planted on edge, on the same slope.

Espiridión then told me, that in order to create the sun and moon, not only the people of Batesopa, but those of all the surrounding pueblos, including Tamichopa, were summoned together. After the burning of the man and woman; the old people sat together all night in order to invent a name for the sun. At sunrise they had not yet found a name, when a cricket, sitting under a metate, near which an old woman was crouching, began to chirp: Ta-senide, Ta-senide. Thereafter they called the sun "Ta" and they looked for the cricket and placed it in a safe spot, and cared for it until it died of old age. She also told him, that the people of Batesopa entertained constant warfare with those of Casas Grandes, who were Opata also; that they made incursions to Casas Grandes; and those from there crossed the mountains to make war upon Batesopa, frequently.[75]

Finally the people of Casas Grandes became so troublesome, that the pueblos of Batesopa and Baguigopa retired to Terapa. After the incursions from Casas Grandes had ceased, a part of the people returned to their old abodes, and these lived there until the Jesuits came, and gathered them all to Huachinera. He denied all knowledge of the gentes, but spoke a good deal of witchcraft. Stated that all the gentiles feared the coyote, the tecolote [owl], and the lechuza [barn owl]. Says the Opatas came from the north! The Rio Tesorobabi is not permanent, and of no use for irrigating corn, so that the natives were reduced to rain and arroyos for their crops [floodwater farming]. Returned to the pueblo at 4 P.M.

APRIL 20: Went to mass and then to painting. Painted all day. Espiridión brought me a worn-out ancient hammer, and a mortar of stone, low, without feet. At night I wrote to Joe. The Cura told me, and Luis and Manuel Dávila confirmed it, that some of the black designs on the pottery may have been made with feathers. The vessel is heated to red heat, and then the butt of the quill is passed over it, and wherever it touches the heated surface, it leaves a black mark. It is evident that the people who inhabited these old ruins were the Opatas. Even the white-and-black pottery is today made here in Huachinera by an old woman, who also makes pottery in the shape of animals, birds, etc. The white clay is abundant on the trail to Cobora, and, in general, mineral paints seem to exist around here in various places. In the valley, beyond Batesopa, there are wild fig trees, but soon the fierce cañones begin. On the cliffs above these fissures and rents which issue into the Yaqui River, there is a fortification, similar to Batonapa and Tonibabi, otherwise I am told that there are not many ruins in the highest part of the sierra. Baile [dance] at night.

APRIL 21: Made a sketch of the worn out hammer and of the mortar. I am told that at the Tahuaro, eight leagues from here, there is a ruin, well preserved, which contains houses with walls, and the posts still standing, and many metates. Heard the story again that the ruins of Casas Grandes were inhabited by Opata. There may be something to it.

About 9 A.M. Don Romualdo Dávila, Cristóval and Ygnacio Dávila of Baserac came after the Padrecito, and we left together with Trinidad and Jesús Dávila. Chico was wild with joy and fire, and the whole trip was one constant run. We followed the Arroyo of Tesorobabi to the Estancia, a large hacienda; here the valley forms a broad, open cañada, rather bleak; the heights on both sides are low and somewhat rocky, still not as rocky as farther south. There is little vegetation except low cedar, mezquite, and Opuntia arborescens. Everything looks New Mexican. Don Antonio Samaniego was at home.

We then crossed the Yaqui,[76] a broad, swift, and limpid river, which here has emerged from the cañones of the sierrita, and soon after turns north, and we continued our course over hills and through gulches, until we emerged into the valley again which here takes an almost semi-circular form. The village of Baserac lies directly above the river on a steep bluff, not as high as Huachinera. It is larger, and the houses, all of adobe, are low, but all in streets. We stopped at Cristóbal Dávila.

I painted pottery in the afternoon, it being quite warm, and then went to the church, which is of adobe, and evidently the most ancient edifice of that kind I have seen in Sonora as yet. Still, the paint of the vigas, the gilding of the pulpit-box, are intact. There are some old paintings, but none of merit. On the outside, and in the convent, there are still traces of arches recalling the 17th century. Spent a very pleasant evening and prepared for tomorrow's expedition to the Metates, three leagues west of here. The people are exceedingly friendly and kind. There are ruins all around. I tried to get a guide to the Metates, about three leagues west of here, but cannot get one before day after to-morrow.

APRIL 22: Left early with Jesús Dávila, Remigio Andrada, and Trinidad Enriquez, for the Estancia. We took the other road, that is, the western hand, which is much more broken than the one we followed yesterday. Soon came to Los Banquitos, an arroyo winding through a series of basins, which open up and narrow down as the hills on both sides, which are of reddish gray shale and easily crumbling, close down upon them or recede. These hills are barely 15.0 [meters?] high, small; the rock protrudes in ledges and benches, occasional sabinos and a few mezquite grow on them and the tops are grassy. The cañada thus formed is traversed by trincheras at every imaginable angle almost; some are left standing like walls, but in every instance there are heaps of fertile earth left behind them, often sabinos growing out of it, and showing that behind each parapet there was a terreplein, which the wall in front held up. This wall is not vertical, but receding inwards; it is of plates of shale, imbedded in mud and of various heights, but nowhere thicker than 0.50 [meter?].* When the declivity disappears, the wall is a mere foundation, sometimes not even 0.10 [meter?] high. The arroyo has burrowed a bed, sometimes 2.0 [meters?] wide, and 1.50 [meters?] deep, in a winding course; it has divided into branches also, destroying the dykes, and sweeping away the soil behind them, so that they stand out like isolated walls. In several instances they form a triangle, even a rectangle, a perfect garden bed. It shows conclusively that they were formed for the purpose of irrigation and cultivation, perfect garden beds.

Some bits of pottery we found there, but I did not notice any flint or obsidian. The grade is not very steep. But the most remarkable thing is the fact, that sabinos, measuring as much as 0.40 [meter?] in diameter, have grown out of the walls themselves even. (See fol. 73.) *

They are the most interesting part of the dykes that I have seen as yet. There are no houses on the hills adjoining, but nearly every arroyo in the vicinity has its trincheras. We kept on our way south, over hills and through cuts of the bottom, crossed the Yaqui, and got to the Estancia, where I was received by Don Antonio Samaniego in the friendliest manner. He is first cousin to the doctor. After the question of the statistics had been settled, he accompanied me to the Mesa de la Puma, on the south bank of the Yaqui, where there are well preserved foundations left.

In one instance, the terreplein is very plain. It expands behind the wall at least 6.0 [meters?] on a perfect level with the top of the wall. . . . The whole shows that the level of the present arroyo has destroyed the dykes and dams! The name of the place is Arroyo del Suspiro and the Suspiro lies above it, a bare level height, from which both the valley of Baserac and the bottom of the Yaqui are to be seen. . . .

The river bottom here appears to be wider, still there are no traces of cultivation in former times. This is evidently due to the fact that it was wooded. Beyond it, in the east, the slopes of the Sierra de Baseraca are strikingly bare of trees. We crossed the river again to the north, reaching the plateau of Tamichopa. There has evidently been a pueblo here, but there is barely a trace of it left. It stood on a mesa, on the north bank of the Yaqui. On the south side, there are ruins on the top of a little mesa, forming a foothill almost to the high sierra of the Hermanas. On the site of the old pueblo stands the ruins of a rancho. There is some painted pottery about. Don Antonio Samaniego told me that in Taraisitos there are cave-dwellings, and the Casa Blanca, a house, still nearly perfect, built against the walls of a rock. There is also a cave about five leagues from Baserac, east-southeast, with walls in it, and upon the return to the pueblo I was assured that near the Banquitos there are a number of small caves, which have been used as dwellings, and walled up. Called upon Gregorio Enriquez, who was ill, however, and told me that the old Pueblo of Baseraca is on the other side of the river. He confirmed the fact that the people of Batesopa had wars with those of Casas Grandes, and that the latter were Opatas. He is slightly deaf.

Ruins on mesa above Yaqui River, north of the Presa [dam].*

APRIL 23: I started with Alberto Gomez, an Opata, of course, about 8 A.M. on foot. We followed the river for about two miles, hugging it closely, as the bottom is narrow, so much that it completely disappears, and we had to clamber over very rotten and dangerous rocks, on a narrow brim. The river runs through a channel with vertical sides almost; on the east side they are absolutely vertical.*

After crossing this passage we turned southwest and ascended the steep, bare and grassy slopes, very rocky and hard, then descended into the bed of the Arroyo de los Metates, and climbed to the crest of a high cuchillo. This cuchillo is typical from the appearance of the slopes, descending from the mountains to the river. It is high, very narrow, sometimes a perfect blade, and exceedingly rocky and difficult. It rises to the west-southwest so that it forms an uninterrupted steep ascent for two hours at least.

As we approached the Sierra de Teras, oak trees began to appear. The Cerro Boludo, a spur of the Teras, with its bands of vertical crags, remained to the left and the wooded tops of the sierra, resting on fearful crags and walls, ran in immediate proximity in the west and northwest. From the highest step of the almost interminable cuchillo we looked down into a basin, rocky but with trees and grass, out of which a rocky and bare slope rose up.

In this basin, which they call Las Escobas, there are a number of dykes, two of which I measured. There are no houses visible.* The walls of the dykes are of boulders and not bound with earth, they rest on rock, forming natural steps. . . .

Beyond that basin, a rocky slope bars the easy progress. We ascended that slope and descended with great trouble into the deep cañón of the Arroyo de los Metates. The narrow rent is encased by steep slopes, tortuous, on which high grass covers the rocks and boulders strewn over it.. A circle of crags and pillars encloses the narrow valley, the crest of the Sierra de Teras frowns, apparently inaccessible in the west; the vale is in appearance completely shut up. From the heights there descend, steep branches, covered with crags and pillars, and terminating in rocky mesas. The second one of these mesitas, from north to south, is that of the Metates. Its profile from east to west is as follows.*

The surface is reddish sandstone, but although very rocky, it is covered with high grass, and tall oak trees grow sparsely on the western half. The top surface is very narrow; at the eastern extremity of the pueblo it is not even twelve steps wide; at the western end thirty-two on nearly a plane, and eleven on the first declivity towards the south. The ascent from the east is over rocks and boulders to a naked table of rocks, across which rude parapets, of boulders or rather rocks broken evidently with hammers, are laid.* These are mostly only one block high, and they evidently were used by the man lying down behind them. On the northern and southern side low parapets continue. The foundations are plates of rock set on edge, the natural cleavage of the rock, a bluish, hard, and brittle limestone or quartzite, forming plates.*

Very large metates, some with the manos still in them, are about the whole place, showing that it was very hastily and suddenly abandoned, leaving the metates intact. The pottery, which is similar to the other painted pottery, also evinces signs of having been left in a fair state of preservation, though broken by the later crumbling of the walls. The peculiarity of construction of the walls and parapets of this fortified village consists in that the hard rock has all been broken, evidently with stone hammers, into pieces of the size of two to five heads, rough and angular, but still artificially broken.

The majority of walls indicate low parapets or dykes, even lengthwise from east to west, as the longitudinal axis of the mesa is higher than the southern half, forming an evident terreplein . . . the number of habitations is small. . . . The walls are sloping inwards, but show a painstaking work, in fitting the broken fragments, and filling interstices with smaller debris. But it does not, at the same time, show signs of binding material. The wall is perfectly dry in appearance. There is an upright post which they call a picote [picota, pillar], but it was hewn with iron implements, and is therefore of later date altogether.

It was a strong place, accessible only from the west, where the parapets appear to have been strong, and from the east. The arroyo, which here is permanent, runs about 100 yards from the eastern end of the hill. It was hot, and the work, owing to the abominable rocks, very tiresome and difficult. At 3 P.M. we left and took a circuit, following the slope of the sierra closely, curving around by the northwest to the northeast. Towering cliffs, pinnacles, pillars, and columns, often very picturesque and isolated, stare up to the right. The path is difficult clambering over large rocks hidden by high grass, until we reached a perfect plane, lying parallel with and to the north of the bad cuchillo which we followed in the morning, and gradually sloping to the east-southeast. This we followed for about two hours, good level walking, though very high ground above the Arroyo de las Flechas which empties at Baserac. We descended into that arroyo, the painted arrows [pictographs] have been rudely destroyed; they are high up on the south side, on perfectly vertical rocks. Reached the pueblo at nightfall, very tired. On the road, Alberto told me that the caves mentioned by Antonio Samaniego, are but an ancient distillery. He speaks of two caves of sorcerers, one near Joitudachi and the other, west of the river, in the Cerro Boludo, at Chicorchi, and of processions, going from one to the other. Confirms the talk of Espiridión about Casas Grandes, and its people being Opatas.

APRIL 24: Left for Mechapa at 8 A.M. with Alberto. We followed the arroyo for two leagues to the southeast until a deep cañón, very perfect and picturesque, where a gushing brook runs in the shade of high beautiful trees. The spot is most romantic; the crags, painted, tower over steep and green slopes. They are in part, about 1000 to 1500 feet above the arroyo, and there is no space left except for the latter and the distillery where we stopped. At 11 A.M. proceeded to the east following the arroyo up, and then across two high and steep cuestas, rising, about on an aggregate, 1000 feet, down into the bed of the same arroyo again. All around are high steep cones and nests, with craggy tops. It is a bleak and barren landscape; the slopes are rocky but craggy, no possibility of cultivation except through dams in the arroyos.

Joitudachi is the name of the ruin. It is on a rocky crest on the slope, south side and is one house, double.* The walls of that double house are 0.30 and 0.45 [meter?] wide; those on the south side are gone.* On the north side, they are built of thin plates of rock embedded in the earth; the southern cross-walls are of polygonal fragments, artificial. Pottery painted as usual. No obsidian. Below on the north side, about 400 feet, and steep descent, are the usual dykes in the arroyo. Water permanent on the south side of the crest. From it the crest of the Sierra Madre is about 15 miles off to the east. It is well wooded with pines.

Returned at 5 P.M. There are ruins on the mesas right and left of the outlet of the cañón of Mechapa! Called on Gregorio and on Desiderio Enriquez. They confirm absolutely the tradition of Casas Grandes, its being built and inhabited by Opata, its war with Cobora, etc.

Va-serac [Baserac]—where the water comes forth.

Vabispe [Bavispe]—at the headwaters.

Vabiama [Babiama]—bend of the river.

Sinoquipe—snake on top of the mesa.

Chinapa—cotton.

Vacadeuachi [Bacadéhuachi]—water in the cañon of reeds.

Huachinera—temporary cornfield.

Ne-si-pa—I, in the other group.

Guazaca [Huásabas]—where there is early fruit.

Oposura—fierce hearted.

Confirm the statement, that the Opata formerly wore guaraches [huaraches, sandals] of yucca; also the Cahuias [Cahuillas] of California! Say that, three leagues east of here, in the Sierra de Baserac, is a cave-dwelling in which such sandals have been found, also a painted mat of yucca. Baboquivaic and Babocomari are not in Opata; still I believe Espiridión. Last night, Jesús Escalante came, and invited me to his house. He says Juh is not dead, but concealed somewhere, also that there are Apache left in the sierra. But I am worn out and tired. The little star of stone which I painted is from La Calera. Don Antonio Samaniego told me that he exhumed small fetishes of stone at San José, Chihuahua, the hacienda of Don Samaniego.

APRIL 25: Junta Auxiliar [a sub-council] met for statistical reports. The Sierra Madre begins south of the road from Babispe to Janos.* The Sierra de Teras divides into two branches, the one opposite Babispe is the Sierra de la Madera de Babispe; the other, the main branch, rises behind it, in the west. I attended to the meeting of the Junta Auxiliar and fixed up their report as at Huachinera.

Ruins south of the house of Jesús Escalante, at the Galerita, one league south of Babispe. Pottery, etc., identical. Same obsidian and flint, also broken metates. Above river bottom.*

There results from it that the fabrication of serapes is quite an important item at Huachinera and at Baserac. They report a net profit, above cost of wool, of $1000 annually. They also report 107 householders at Baserac; 68 millions of square meters of municipal ground; of which 8 million are cultivated. The two pueblos, Baserac and Huachinera, together with the two ranchos and the Estancia, comprise 195 millions of square meters of ground, of which about 17 million are in culture. I left the good, kind people at Baserac, about 3 P.M. and rode over to the Galerita, two leagues north of the Pueblo of Baserac, where Don Jesús Escalante had his rancho.

Here, I found the ruins above.* They stand on the brink of the mesa above the rich bottom of the river, and it appears that there are others all along the road on the heights. They told me that they had found an arrow sharpener of stone here, and stone axes, but I could not see any of them; they had, as usual, been lost. Spent a very pleasant evening at the rancho. Don Jesús is exceedingly kind and instructive. I heard of many cave dwellings; for instance, at Tasábiri, or Cara Pintada on the river north of Babispe, on the road. It appears that they are quite common, except in the heart of the Sierra Madre, where there are none, and in general, hardly any ruins. Heard it again confirmed that the people of Casas Grandes were Opatas.

APRIL 26: Left for "Vabispe" at 9 A.M. with Angel Escalante. The whole river bottom, from Baserac to Babispe, is one contiguous [i.e., continuous] narrow field, wheat almost predominating. This whole bottom still shows traces of having been covered with wood once, as there is still much of it left. I am positively told that the timber grew all over it formerly, so that the Indians did scarcely cultivate it, not being able to cut off the timber with stone implements. This fact, and the rockiness of the slopes, explains the existence of dams and dykes in the arroyos, forming milpas. These are all along the river as at Baserac and at Huachinera, etc. The country grows more open towards Babispe. In the far north is seen the Sierra de la Cabellera; in the far south the Sierra de Bacadéuachi looms up like a jagged isolated nest. Behind the Sierra de Baserac, the Sierra Madre (Tesahuinori) appears in place; Ochetahueca (*ádonde el viejo está parado* [where the old man rests]) is very bold in the northeast. Babispe stands on the northern apron of a hill, on whose top is the Centinela and the Presidio. The pueblo forms a hollow square enclosing a very large church, yet unfinished which, when completed, will be the finest edifice of that sort in Sonora; a beautiful cupola or dome, and two towers. It is all of brick and arched, and painted inside. Painted all day. Had, as usual, many callers. The view from above Babispe is very fine to the north, and the fertile bottoms expand as the same narrow strip, to beyond San Miguelito, which is one league west or northwest of Babispe. The cúmaro is used, or was, for pinole.

APRIL 27: Distances, from Babispe to Fronteras—30 leagues; from Babispe to Guassavas, 30; from Granados to Oposura, 14; from Oposura to Babiácora, 17 to 18; from Babispe to Janos, 26; from Janos to Casas Grandes, 22 leagues. These are the correct data, as obtained from Don Juan Bustamante, uncle of Reynaldo Samaniego. He is seventy-six years old, and a man of great experience and knowledge. He tells me that the Apache outbreak took place in 1831, that the incident of Tutihe and Leonárdo Escalante is correct, and that the Apache were to blame for the whole affair, as they were lazy, indolent, and always robbing and even murdering on the sly. This is another version of the story.

   I painted all day until night, when I was interrupted by the visit of Ygnacio Dávila, Ynocente Moreno, and soon a host of young fellows gathered in my room. I now recollect many things which I had forgotten to note. So for example: Dr. Moore at Oposura told me that syphilis was rare, that in two years he had treated only three cases; all of a tertiary character. The prevailing sickness here seems to be fever, with chills. There are very few lung diseases, but these, when they come, are fatal. I do not devote any time to ruins right here, for the reason that they do not afford anything new, and the paintings at Tasábiri are, I am told, Apache work! Still, I may yet go out.

   Went to mass this morning; church crowded; and the really beautiful building presented quite an appearance inside. Music as usual, and the singing particularly awful. The wind blew heavy from the south all day. The population is friendly and natural; there is nothing affected at all. Dr. Gottlieb Schramm, (translated into Jesús) of Berlin, but residing at Tucson, whom I had met at Baserac, called again on me. I spent a pleasant half-hour. He cured Padre Moreno of inflammatory rheumatism. I then called on Lorenzo, or Lázaro, Colosio. He is horribly ugly and brutal, but evidently a good Apache fighter. He is, of course, an Opata Indian.

APRIL 28: In the morning I had the visit of Lázaro Colosio. He confirmed the fact that the ruins in the sierra were never large pueblos, only groups of one, two, to a half-a-dozen small houses, also caves. The pottery he identified with that of Huachinera. Of the Apache he thinks that they have mostly retired to the Sierra de Teras. I painted the whole day.

APRIL 29: Wrote and mailed letters to Joe, Lieutenant West, Father Grom, Meysenburg, Mr. Parkman, and Epitacio Paredes. Rumors of Apache about, so that Reynaldo took Chico home tonight. I did some painting also today. Distance from Opoto to Huachinera, 12 leagues, but a horrible road. Today the boys came with the statistics. Baserac, 693 inhabitants; Huachinera, 298. Tomorrow Don Leonárdo will be up at last!

APRIL 30: Don Fadrique came, and Don Leonárdo passed [failed to come?]. Wrote to Elliott, and to Don Joaquín Bonorand, and finally to Epitacio Paredes. Waited and waited, and nobody came. At last Jesús Escalante came, and he insisted upon leaving at once. So we left in the night and, after stumbling over rocks scattered in the river bottom, which we crossed, then following, crossing and recrossing, the bed of the Arroyo de la Cañada which has alternately dry and humid spaces, in the clear moonlight, through much thorny brushes, past cliffs and pillars to the right, we reached the Puerta de la Cañada about two leagues from Babispe, where Don Leonárdo was encamped, with 38 mules, the aparijos [gear] forming almost a line of fortifications. It was an oblong and narrow basin with vertical cliffs in the south and sloping mesas in the north. I have to add here, that according to Lázaro and others, General Crook crossed the road of Babispe to Janos at the

Lagartos which are, in an air line, six leagues east of Babispe. Chiricahui is an Opata word. Chiri, hummingbird; caui, sierra.

MAY

MAY 1: I rose at 2:30 A.M. The little flat in which we rested is skirted by the Arroyo de la Cañada, on the south. At its very edge, the bluffs of grey conglomerate rise perfectly vertical, capped by rounded tops, covered with grass, very rocky, and many arboriferous yucca. On the other side of the little flat, the water of the arroyo forms a series of clear water pools in a thicket of high reeds. Beyond these, rocky lomas and slanting mesas rise in terraces, with little else than grass. Here I found some bits of pottery.

We started at 8:30 A.M. and the whole cortege, consisting of 78 horses, mules, and donkeys, and 24 men; the load consisting of mezcal, panoche, tobacco, pipitoria, etc., began to move. We wound up the course of the arroyo, which is narrow, and covered with thickets of thorny shrubs, while the high and steep slopes, very rocky and covered with grass and arboriferous yucca, close in more and more. We reached the foot of the Cuesta Chica and began to wind upwards. It is not very steep, but undulates up and down, along the slopes, a narrow ribbon which is often a stepladder of rocks, with fearful and dangerous slopes to the right. In all this [area], there is not a sign of ruins, dams, or dykes, and it is easily explained through the fact that there are no small arroyos. The slopes terminate in cuchillos, and the great arroyo carries, in general too much water. The whole slope appears to have been uninhabited.

As we rose, the Sierra de Teras appeared at full length, a formidable mountain chain, terribly steep and dark; the Sierra de Opoto in the distant southwest, and even at intervals the Sierra de Bacadéuachi. At the top of the cuesta, Ochetahueca loomed up in the immediate north, a high imposing ridge or peaked crest,* sharp and long, clad to the base in tall pines. In the south, ramifications of the Sierra Madre, lower and undulating, very dark and pineclad, appear. This must be the Sierra Tesahuinori. We passed through a deep and narrow valley, and then began the ascent of the Cuesta Grande. It is the same undulating band or narrow path, but in the beginning very narrow, and a succession of exceedingly dangerous steps and ledges, where frightful accidents often happen. It is not steep, but very perilous, for the precipices to the right are fearful. At the top is a stonepile, and here I took leave of Sonora, and entered Chihuahua. The wind had begun to blow as we ascended the cuestas; on the top it blew high and cold. A very gradual descent begins to the east, and [we traversed] a high plateau, interspersed with naked, high expanses. The Sierra Madre gradually disappears behind naked grassy slopes in the south; oaks and yuccas drop behind it; and the landscape, completely changed, presents the appearance of a bleak, grassy, cold, table-land. In the far east looms up the Sierra de en el Medio; in the northeast, the Sierra de las Espuelas. The descent is almost imperceptible; the wind blows fiercely and cold from the southwest, and the ground becomes soft, with patches of lava. The hills are all of black and brown lava; so are the mountain spurs coming in from the south. To the north the plain expands, tapering up into the wooded and steep ridges of the Cabellera. No water.

We reached the abandoned rancho of Canetas lying in the plain at the western base of a high spur of lava, about 1 p.m. It was abandoned about 30 years ago, when the Apache burnt it, killing the inmates; then [it was] revivified, and finally abandoned for good. The Arroyo de Canetas flows past. We crossed lava beds again, then a fertile plain in which stand the ruins, about 300 yards from the arroyo (here permanent) north, then rounded a high and rocky hill of black lava, and finally stopped at the Vado [Ford] where the arroyo is a rippling stream with splendid water, skirted with álamos, and a narrow bottom with high grass and reeds or canes. I returned on foot to measure the ruins. They show traces of foundations of lava, but are mostly heaps of gravelly earth, not unlike those on the Gila. Pottery like that of Huachinera, etc. Manos as large as those in the Sierra de Teras; flint, but no obsidian. The mounds seem to indicate larger houses, in fact, a style of architecture similar to that on the Gila!

There are traces of ruins on the other side of the arroyo, on the declivity of the first terrace, and Benigno Reyes told me that to the northwest of the Vado, on the west bank, the lomas above the bottom have ruins also. The arroyo here runs from north to south through a plain; the bottom is widest on the west side. In the east, mesas and hills of lava close the view. On the whole, it is a completely different country, calling forth a distinct architecture. The country has nothing but grass, no other nutritive plants, so that agriculture required greater expansion and progress. But it is evident that the garden plots were contiguous to the houses, and then crowded together also, for purposes of defence.*

MAY 2: We started at 8 A.M., and after traversing about one league of ugly malpaís at the foot of the Lagartos, almost imperceptibly descended into the plain beneath. The Lagartos where General Crook crossed the road to go north, are a slope of lava to the north of the road, and they derive their name from some very homely lizards which still live in rocks on that slope. They are described as large and very repulsive.

General Crook crossed a little east of the ridge or slope. The view to the east is very extensive. In the plain rises the Sierra de en el Medio, to the north of it the Sierra de las Espuelas, and to the north still, the spurs of the Cabellera; they surround a level basin, out of which knolls of lava protrude. The road (for hereafter there are tracks of wagons) is excellent. The plain has no vegetation except grass; Oejvari [?] with its white flowers, appears to be the only nutritive plant. There are some other flowers— Opuntia (Cylindropuntia) occasionally, but no yucca. In the distance appears, behind the Sierra de en el Medio, low ranges; first the Sierra de Janos; then the Escondida; and the Palotada. We hug the barren slopes coming down from the south. They appear to be lava, and there is no vegetation on them except grass. No mountain tops are visible yet in that direction. The Espuelas shift to the north; Ochetahueca disappears; the Cabellera looms up in place of it. We still descend and descend, slowly and almost imperceptibly, past the Peñuelas, rocky palisades facing a hill on the south. Between them, the Lagartos; Don Luis García was attacked and the whole conducto almost destroyed by the Apache about sixteen or eighteen years ago. It is a level, sloping from the south. The Sierra de en el Medio shifted northward, between it and the Espuelas; in the background, the low and barren hills of the Burritos appear, above them towers the Sierra de la Hacha.* Between the Espuelas and the Cabellera in the dim north-northwest appears the Sierra de las Animas. The south continues a series of bald slopes. We reach the Alisos, a dry arroyo coming down from the south, with grassy slopes, some trees, but no water. Here Colonel García fought, 30 April 1882, his clumsy fight with Geronimo.[77] It was an accidental meeting. The Sierra de en el Medio shifts to the northwest, and the Sierra de las Animas appears east of it in the northern background. At the northwestern foot of a high hill, grassy and of lava, on the bank of a series of little springs, always permanent, grassy level, and one single álamo, we halted and went into camp.

These are the Ojitos about three miles east of the Alisos. One-half mile west of the grove in which the pools of water form a string in the grassy plain, rise the ruins on the other side. The highest mounds are not quite two meters high; on the whole, the ruins are more indistinct than those of the Vado, but they present much of the appearance of the mounds around Agua Dulce [present-day Sweetwater], Zacaton, and Florence, in Arizona. Pottery red and plain; no foundations visible; no metates, one or two broken manos, flint, but no obsidian at all. It was well situated, near permanent water, and so disposed, as to permit observations over a vast extent of area. Here the Sierra de en el Medio stands northwest. We passed here a rather pleasant night, as the wind stopped again after nightfall. There are quite heavy snowfalls in winter, and even as late as March and April over this plateau. Before reaching Peñuelas, near the Peñasco, we crossed a few dykes and dams of stones, so that I conclude that there must be vestiges of houses near by. At the Vado and at Ojitos there are no dams and no acequias, but the fields are sloping, and as water falls frequently, they must have rain [moisture] only by means of rain [i.e., dry farming].

MAY 3: Started at 7:45 A.M. Horses and mules went beautifully, Chico always ahead of the big atájo [lead animal]. We slowly descended, always in the same open, grassy plain. The bald slopes in the south sloped down finally, and in the southeast rose the Sierra de San Pedro, with the Aguja, which was the place of refuge and watch tower of Geronimo, protruding boldly. There, between it and the Sierra de Carcai [Carcay], rises the Rio San Pedro. At the foot of the south San Pedro, and in the plain yet, lies the old abandoned ranch of the Casa de Janos. The dangerous journey between Canetas and the Ojitos lay behind us, still this level base of the sierra, an open plain extending to the eastward until the eastern bank of the Rio, has always been much exposed to the incursions of the Apache watching the plains from the tops and cuts.

As we rounded the last spurs of the bald southern slopes, the Sierra del Carcay appeared boldly, extending from southeast to northwest and almost running parallel, at its northern end, with the southern end of the Sierra de San Pedro. It is a long wall, descending abruptly into the plain to the east, and above which rises, to a great height, a craggy peak, shaped like a huge castle.* The Sierra de San Pedro is divided from it by a gap, and this gap is visible where the two chains are seen in front. The plain through which the Rio de San Pedro advances, past the Casa de Janos, is very slightly convex, sloping to the east towards the river. It is about eight miles wide. From the northeast, running north and south, the Sierra de Janos advances into it. At the south it rises to a bleak, ocean-like horizon. Above the latter protrudes the Sierra del Pajarito like a long, shaggy detached ridge or mass. On the east, bleak heights form a little sierrita. At its western foot, almost always dry, runs the riverbed; the spaces, where clear and good water comes to the surface in it, are indicated by isolated álamos. We arrived at the Montón de Alamo, where there is always good clear water in the river bed, at 1:30 P.M. Before sunset went to Janos and stayed there with Don Leonárdo, at the house of Don Pablo Zapata.

MAY 4: I continue from yesterday: Don Benino Reyes told me that in the Espuelas, in the Burritos, the Hacha, he had not met with any signs of ruins. There is little if any water there. All the mountain ranges in the east are low, but the whole country has the appearance of great aridity. Not a tree is visible except the álamos along the river bed. It is terribly desolate. We reached the Agua Fria, about one-and-a-half leagues south-southwest of Janos, crossed the river, and then followed its course down, on the east side there being another bleak plain, partly dotted with mezquites and extending to the mountain ranges beyond, at the foot of which runs another string of álamos, indicating the course of the Rio de Casas Grandes, which is almost permanent. The hills and lomas skirting the Rio San Pedro to the east are called the Lomas de San Pedro, the bald and sterile range, beyond the Rio de Casas Grandes is the Cerro Colorado.* The Rio de San Pedro arises west of the Carcai, and east of the Sierra de San Pedro, and the latter is the same as the Sierra Tesauinna [?] of the people of Baseraca.

Janos lies on the southeastern spur of the Sierra de Janos, above the dry river bed, and a mile from the Monte de Alamos. It is a small place, which only now begins to revive, as since the garrison was removed in 1857, the place was left abandoned to the Apache and the people gradually left. In 1831, Janos had 4950 inhabitants, and in 1857, it was reduced to 500. Now it has about 600. Not a single rancho in its neighborhood is still occupied today.

South of it, in the triangle formed by the two rivers, there is a pass formed by the lomas between them, and beyond that pass lies Corralitos!

The reception at Janos was very kind. I was informed positively that, on the 6th of April last, the Apache had robbed horses and cattle, and killed one horse, in this neighborhood, and had taken refuge in the Sierra del Carcai. Juh is positively not dead. He is the son of Baboso, or rather his grandson, his mother being the well-known Zumba. The Captain Elias is not dead, but neither is he the brother of Figueroa.[78]

There are ruins at Casa de Janos similar to those of Casas Grandes, only smaller; many ruins around Ascención,[79] some along the Rio de San Pedro between here and Casa de Janos, and many along the Rio de Casas Grandes to San Diego. That river flows into the Laguna de Guzmán.

In the morning I started with Don Damasio Rueda to the northeast of Janos, and in the fields at the foot of a volcanic cerro, about two miles from the village, I found the ruin, A.* On the opposite side of the river, southwest about a mile, the ruin B.* The former is only a series of mounds one meter high; the latter a bare flat, in which the foundations have been excavated. The walls were of adobe. Many tepalcates [potsherds] like those of Huachinera, corrugated pieces like those of the Mimbres; manos and metates of lava. The landscape is terribly barren and bleak, not a tree on the heights, and the Sierra de Janos is a succession of steep high hills, rugged from lava and not even with mezquites. The lands are fertile, but there is not a drop of water beyond the purposes of agriculture. The place is a poor one, and has been constantly robbed by Indians, etc.

In the ruins I found obsidian again. I was assured, today, that old documents mention a tribe of Jánotos as living in this vicinity. Of the depredations committed by the Apaches in here, no idea can be given. The road from Janos to Babispe, a distance of 26 leagues, or seventy miles is, for the eight leagues, or twenty-one miles,[80] from the Vado to Ojitos, almost one cemetery. In fact, the dangerous part of the journey lies between Janos and the Cuestas. The great openness of the country, lying as it does, at the very foot of the high mountains in which the Apaches take refuge, and from whose tops and crests they observe and see at immense distances every object in the perfectly treeless plain, makes it very difficult. The intercourse here with them has been very frequent. They often came to Janos peacefully, and the house of Don Pablo has been the roof that sheltered Juh, Nané, and many, many others. In May, 1882, the act of treachery was attempted to exterminate them, while peaceably at Janos. It failed, although there were at least three hundred soldiers and citizens, and only resulted in the death of 16 of them.

They also came frequently to Casas Grandes. It appears they often got drunk, possibly were made drunk on purpose, either to humor them or out of fear or to other purposes. On the whole, the character of the country, once on the top of the Cuesta Grande, which ridge is not far to the southeast of Ochetahueca, is that of a high table-land. It is cold in winter, treeless, exposed to high winds, which in the summer are from the southwest and very hot. The rains also come from that quarter, so that the conditions of the atmosphere are almost reversed from those of the western slope.

In regard to ancient population, the only streams of permanence on the whole route are the Arroyo de Canetas, which comes from the Cabellera in the north, and Ojitos; the Alisos not being permanent. The whole gap therefore was scarcely inhabitable except at those two places. The unsheltered exposure of the houses here, necessitates stronger walls, and more compact building, therefore thicker walls and, here, resort to adobe. Here, the same conditions exist as in southern New Mexico, and adobe being handier than stone, it was consequently adopted. The pottery, etc. is identical. The massacre, or rather the intended massacre, of May, 1882, took place at Casas Grandes, and not at Janos.[81]

I am told that the Laguna de Guzmán is large, surrounded by flats, which in some places are miry, in other places firm. The Laguna de Palomas is surrounded by médanos, and has many fertile springs, but no good lands. The third lagune of this interior basin is the Laguna de Santa Maria. There is a good reason here why the ruins are on the flats and not on the heights. The latter too far from the watercourses, and there are no arroyos to dam up and to cultivate. The slopes are naked, and terribly rocky; all malpaís of the worst kind. But the apparent sterility of the whole region is most striking. Still the bottoms are very fertile. Snow falls in winter.

I am told of many ruins in the interior of the Sierra Madre. Caves of two-story houses, etc. The story that Victorio is of Opata origin is denied here, and he is said to be pure Apache. The people here know nothing of the frogs sculptured out of green stone, said to have been found at Casas Grandes. Neither of metates with feet. This place pertains to the Canton of Galeana; capital is Casas Grandes. It contains only two rivers, the Rio de Casas Grandes and Rio de Galeana, both of which have their source in the Sierra Madre and empty into the lagunes, thus running on an average from southwest to northeast. Had a long talk with Don Luis Perea. He is of the opinion that the existence of Huaynopita is the origin of the tales about Huaynopa and positively declares the latter, as a mine, to be a fable. Don Damasio Rueda brought me a letter to Don Silvestre Quevedo, the Gefe [Jefe] Político [Chief

Officer] of Casas Grandes. Will have to be very careful there, on account of the superstitions of the people about the ruins. Don Leonárdo returned to the camp, while I remained.

MAY 5: Walked over to the camp and then rode back with Don Leonárdo to Janos. We left there at 9 A.M. and had to gallop across the loamy plain dotted with grass and occasional mesquite until 10:30 A.M. to catch up with the train, which had left and gone ahead on the Janos. This plain extends from the Puertecito to Janos in an almost due southernly direction. It forms an oval, and the Rio Casas Grandes leaves it soon, engulfing itself to the southeast between the Capulín and a low range of lava and trap, which forms the eastern border, and the western rim of the Puertecito is formed by a similar range, which forms the eastern border of the Rio San Pedro. The plain gradually rises, and there is not a tree on it, arboriferous yucca forming the highest plant. The mezquite is scarcely three feet high on an average, but that part of it on the ground is strongly limbed, so that it furnishes firewood. The high winds have stunted and obstructed the upward growth of the shrubs, so that the lowest limbs have thickened beyond measure. From the ridge, or saddle, the Sierra Florida [in New Mexico] appeared dimly in the north, and to the south a large and also oval basin expands below, flanked on the east and southeast by the Sierra Escondida, which merged south into the Pass of Chocolate. South-southwest is the Sierra [. . .]; southwest, the Sierra del Cristo. Here, in advance of the latter two, lies Casas Grandes, at the eastern foot of the sierrita, and northwest of it, the Pajarito advances as an abrupt mass into the plain from the west. To the north of it, lower and isolated, very steep mesas, and the Carcai expands at full length along the western horizon. Behind it rose a column of smoke high into the air. The basin is mostly grassy ciénega. The eastern curve of this basin, along an escondida, is formed by the Rio de Casas Grandes, indicated by a string of álamos. Corralitos we reached at 2 A.M. and were hospitably and kindly received by Mr. Adolph Muenzenberger and by his two ladies. Both are from Belleville [Illinois]. Here I heard of the death of Dr. Engelmann![82] Of the Cincinnati riots,[83] etc. The river is dry here, up to a large tank. The hacienda is large, 45 x 40 miles. The formation is lava, and carboniferous. Height above sea level, 4500 feet by aneroid. Much snow falls in winter.

Between here and Casas Grandes, there are at least four ruins. At Santa Maria, thirty-four miles east of here, there are ruins which are identical with that of here and of the Mimbres. Much obsidian. Metate with one foot found here. Obsidian is met with abundance in the hills. The Galeana River drains into the Laguna de Santa Maria. With the exception of the álamos along the river, not a tree is visible; the mountains, the Carcai excepted, are absolutely bare to the very tops. The tillable part of the bottom is not very wide, and extends almost exclusively west of the river. The main part of it is ciénega and lava swellings which occasionally protrude.

MAY 6: Had Chico [shoed?], got my pants to the tailor's, and got shaved. Don Leonárdo left for Casas Grandes early this morning. People here very, very kind. Painted pottery the whole day. Wrote letters at night to Joe (enclosing two drafts of $100 each), to W. W. Griffin[84] (with draft of $60), to Elliott, and to Mr. Parkman. There are ruins at Santa Maria, thirty-five miles east-northeast of here, four villages.

MAY 7: The ruins at Santa Maria are described as fortifications with pottery. Painted all day. Wrote to Mrs. Black, to Ad. Mennet, to Scott, to Jim [Chism?] and to [Mr.] France. A very high wind blew all day and night from the east. The whole southwest side of the Pajarito appears to be on fire tonight which is a sure sign of Apache. At sunset Frank Sheldon, and Don Donaciano Mápula came from Casas Grandes. The fact of the meteorite being [wrapped] in a petate [mat] originally, is confirmed.

MAY 8: The fire seen last night has been made by Joaquín Terrazas.[85] Took leave of Don Leonárdo and finally left at 9 A.M. for Casas Grandes alone. The road keeps on the right side of the dry river until it reaches the Barranco, a little village now broken up and almost abandoned. Here the river runs almost constantly, and the road crosses over to the west side, as the river runs almost due south to north. The spurs of the Escondida hug the river closely on the east side, but the west is a perfectly flat bottom which the road traverses diagonally from northeast to southwest. The river describes a curve and closes in upon the lomas about four miles north of Casas Grandes, so that Corralitos and Casas Grandes form the ends of the basin. A fine and continuous growth of álamos skirts the river on both banks. This plain is very fertile and grassy; the lomas along the foot of the [sierrita?] are covered with a growth of bright green mezquite not over three feet high. In this plain, about half-way between Corralitos and Casas Grandes, groups of mounds stand. Besides the three which I measured, there are at least 14 more.

FIELD-NOTES OF CASAS GRANDES

[Because of the obvious significance of this tremendous site, we have elected to reproduce Bandelier's complex sketches and notes on Casas Grandes in their entirety. Accordingly, the front and back of his pages 86, 87, 88, 89, and 90 are reproduced here.][86]

(PAGE #86, FRONT)

Field-Notes of Casas Grandes

Little pottery in general, but the indented kind handsome.*

The interior of the buildings generally marks a depression or hollow.*

(PAGE #86, BACK)

I continue from yesterday. The mounds are of gravelly earth. They are mostly bare, and thus easily distinguishable from natural swellings. Their tops are commonly crowned by small rocks and stones, accidentally thrown together.

There are many metates, of lava, and all broken. Small manos, and much pottery, painted, and very handsomely and regularly indented and incised. They are the finest pieces of that kind that I have ever seen. I found some more [?] cream colored specimens. The plain, which must be traversed diagonally, is of interminable length. At last the edge of the álamos is reached, and here the river turns almost south-southeast in another curve, the lomas reaching to very near the grove. This curve forms a smaller bottom, which is cultivated, and four miles south of the turning-point stands the little town of Casas Grandes on a bluff, which is a promontory of the lomas. It is a pleasant and rising place of 1600 to 1700 souls. The valley is exceedingly fertile, well tilled, and the river, as far as it is visible to the south, is one continuous line of large álamos. I stopped at José María Mápula and was well received by him as well as by Don Silvestre Quevedo, the Gefe Político. About two miles north of town, on the lomas, stand the ruins of edifices of adobe, which are stated to be a convent! But I doubt it and think that they are older.

(PAGE #87, FRONT)

MAY 9: Excavation a. Wall 1.20 [meters?] thick with the holes for five vigas. Diameter of each viga 0.17 and the distance from viga to viga 0.13. The fifth viga is inserted where a separation or partition-wall was built latterly, as it is shown by the fact that the plastering still remains. Nothing but the round holes remain. No wood.

From *b.* 147 feet north 52 west to rim of arroyo, then 25 feet across, and 202 feet to *h.* which is the corner of the ruins of an enclosure, forming the arm of the southern edifice. This edifice still stands on the loma and above the bottom. The whole loma is studded with the usual low mezquite. The direction of the walls is to west, 12° south. The door *b.* appears to have a stone-lintel, which has now fallen out. Its height is not full, but partly buried.

The rows *B.* and *C.* appear like first stories, lower than the others and perhaps like those of New Mexico.

The mound *A.* is very large, and exceedingly high. It must have been formed by the decay of buildings two and three stories high. There is very little pottery about. Metates are plentiful, and of lava. The plan continues at X: on the other page.

(PAGE #87, BACK)

They are of very regular adobe, but have no windows, and the doors are very small and oval.

I went with Melchior Quevedo, the youngest brother of the Gefe. The ruins stand on the brink of the loma, above the fertile bottom, and about a half-mile south of the town. Their appearance is exceedingly impressive, and the huge mounds show that the edifices were very high. Probably three stories, but not all of the same height. See fol. #88 beginning at the brink (northern) of the arroyo where the distance of 19 feet terminates, running thence northward.

The walls are exactly alike to those of Casa Grande on the Gila, not of adobe, but a kind of marly concrete, mixed with pebbles and small stones. This cajón, as they call it here, is in layers of unequal thickness, and when it crumbles, as on the Gila, in almost cubic blocks. The walls I measured are of various thickness,

(PAGE #88, FRONT)

from 1.20 to 0.40 only. They are covered inside with a thin plaster, which still appears whitish, but in some places shows traces of carbonization by fire. No wood is left, but the holes for the vigas, and the grooves, are still plainly visible. The site for the ruins has been well selected. It commands the view of the whole valley, and at the same time it runs back over the entire lomas and up the mountain slopes south as far as the Paso de Chocolate, in fact, it embraces a wide slope of country.

(PAGE #88, BACK)

The river is not very far, though not very near either. The lomas are covered with gravel and even with rocks, mezquite is of course quite abundant. I measured the whole of the ruins in two times. They are intricate on account of the hills and bluffs that intervene, of debris, making the fragments of walls stand out like pillars. Some of these pillars are still very high. As regards doorways, they are larger, that is, higher than in other ruins, but also very narrow. After measuring the main ruins, I went to the surroundings. There are a number of regular hills west and northwest of the houses which appear to be artificial. A. has been opened and a trench dug almost to its very back. It revealed only drift and gravel, nothing like houses or walls. B. is now level on the top, there is much pottery on it, and about at one-half of its height there is a rim of stones laid artificially, which communicates with the wall or walled-up platform below. This is very evidently artificial, but to what purpose I can't tell as yet. The basin D. is perfectly smooth, and appears to have been moist at one time. It is free of every rock or stone.

(PAGE #89, FRONT)

To give an idea of this mound (B.) only a section can represent it. Low mound, wall. Top with pottery. Rim of stones laid by hand, not very regular, possibly moved.

The groundplan, more in detail, appears as follows: The low mound (a.) formerly extended all around the basin, and formed a corral, which is now almost destroyed, the people having carried off the stones to build with. There is not, therefore, any doubt as to the fact that it was an enclosure. The other mounds of stone, or stone-pile (t.t.t.t.t.) are much smaller, and they are, as excavations have shown, simply stone piles without earth even. The wall (b.) is perfectly alike to the small dykes or dams of Baserac. It inclines inwards, and is well made. Its height is about 0.70. It may be very difficult to get objects here. They are mostly broken. I am again assured that the metates have no feet, and that copper figures (a turtle and fish, for instance) were found in the ruins. The dozen houses, east of the ruins, still partly stand on ruins, and some of them are built on ancient walls. On the whole, the settlement has been very extensive, and has expanded into the river bottom proper. I am told of several acequias which run from the distant mountain sides toward the pueblo, but there is only one of which I can hear very positive information. In regard to other ruins, I only heard that at the hacienda of Reyes, there are large Montezumas. I am also told that there are large ruins in the Escondida east of here. Of caves I hear about two or three days journey west, in the Sierra Madre. The Cuevas, of which I heard at Corralitos, are east-southeast of here. From here, the Paso de Chocolate is plainly visible. It is a perfectly bald, denuded, gap, and surmounted by heights, whence

(PAGE #89, BACK)

I finished my measurements early, and returned, very tired and weary. The conduct of José María Mápula is that of young Mexico. They are impertinent, overbearing, and cross. Wrote some pages. It is time for me to abandon the work, because I am getting weary, and useless. But this valley was admirably [?] for the site of a large pueblo. It is fertile, has wood in proximity, and enough water to irrigate with. The mound (t^1) see fol. 88 p. 2, on close inspection, forms a cross. The sides of the cross are plainly built of stone, like those of the corral or enclosure described on the other side. What may have been the end, purpose, and object of this cross I cannot guess at. It evidently is artificial, and had in its center a stone heap which now is partly excavated, so that it forms a round hole. The whole thing is an enigma to me.

The height of the mounds formed by the arm of the cross does not exceed 0.25, the original height of the central mound, was probably one meter, or a little more.

(PAGE #90, FRONT)

MAY 10: Started at 8 A.M. with Melchior Quevedo, and a certain Dr. Brenan[?] joined us, to my great annoyance. Still, he was, after all, to some profit. I took some sections and details. From all appearances, the houses have been perhaps four stories high. Three stories certainly are visible. The construction is evidently cajón, that is, in so far as it is not adobe. The doorways had lintels, which now have fallen out, decayed, or disappeared, but there are some indications that make me suspect that these lintels may have been stone. Still, Melchior, when I uttered that idea to him, remarked that only wooden lintels were indicated by the grooves left. It is very strange, too, that the buildings show rather large windows! There is, here, an evident progress, or else I have forgotten my past observations. I could not do as much work as I wished on account of the doctor!—but still he was of some use. Upon our return we descended into the bottom where many of the houses are still built on ancient mounds, and even on foundations of old buildings. These foundations are plainly and easily describable, since they are of solid compact cajón, and at least 18 inches wide. Among these houses there runs an elevated ridge, which the doctor showed to me as the ancient acequia! It is evidently a raised stretch, and while it could hardly have been anything else but a ditch, still it appears much more like a chaussée [road] than anything else. I measured it in the bottom and found the following plan. The whole width is 4.30 meters, and I followed it up to the road, and from northwest to southeast for 45 meters. The lines a.b.c.d. are marked by stones, laid in the ground so that the whole divides into these parallel bands, whose cross-section is as follows. But all this does not show a ditch; on the contrary, an artificially elevated surface!!

MAY 10 [Continued]: We then went across the elevated part, back of the bottom. These are the lomas. About a quarter-of-a-mile northwest, in the direction of the pueblo and west or southwest of it, a deep and abrupt arroyo intersects the plateau. On both sides of this arroyo, the ditch, or elevated convex chaussée, appears again. The calcareous concrete, on which the ditch rests, is plainly visible in the cut on both sides. It is also plain that there was no casing of stone to the ditch, only a parallel line of stones laid on the top. The moveable earth is four feet deep, so that the whole structure appears to be four feet deep and ten feet wide.* How the arroyo was crossed is a mystery, unless it was, as the people suppose, by the means of wooden troughs. But this is hardly possible. There would be some trace of it left, and there is absolutely nothing visible. Still, what has been the object of this construction, if it should not be an acequia, I cannot guess. The people all say that it starts from an ojo northwest of town, and about one league off. Thus much of it is evident that it runs straight from the ojo down into the bottom, almost hugging the last houses of the old pueblo, and between it and the river.*

There is said to be a similar acequia on the other side of the river, and there are also ruins there too. Upon our return, we found the remarkable cross-shaped mound. These mounds are yet another enigma to me. They seem to be in part of loose gravel and stones heaped or piled up artificially; then again, they appear to be natural. I returned home

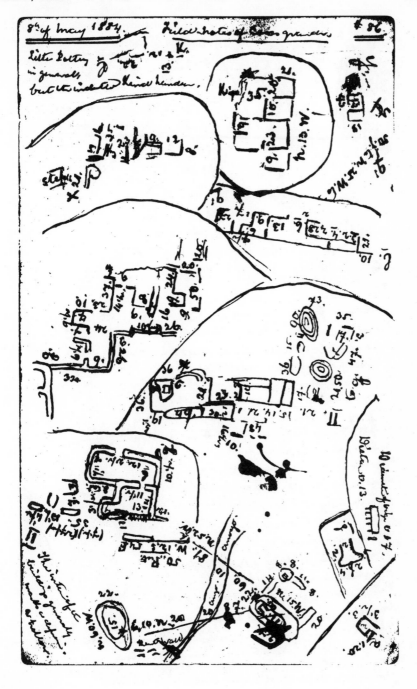

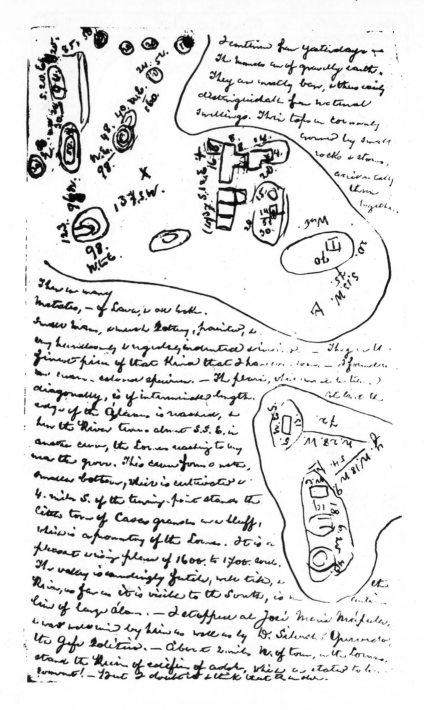

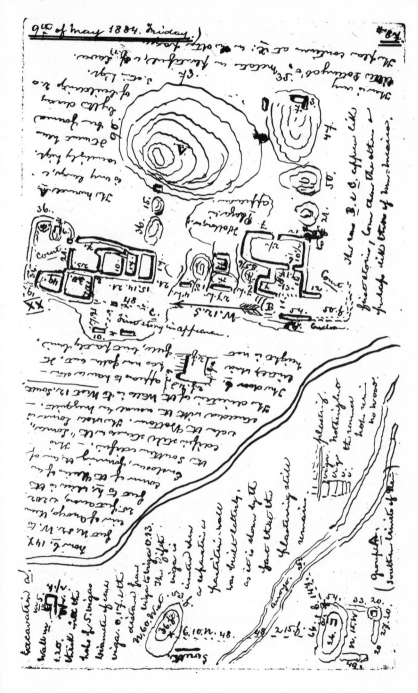

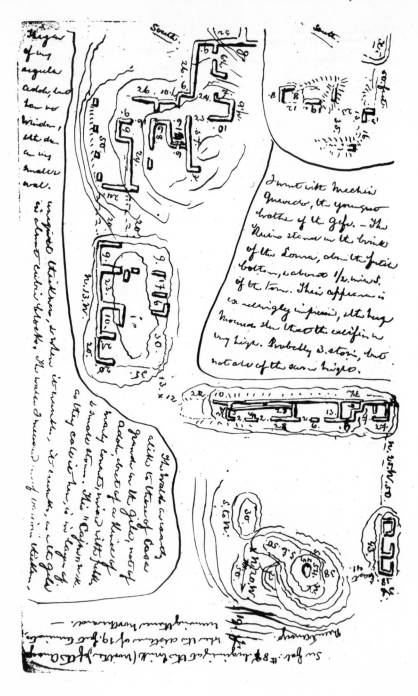

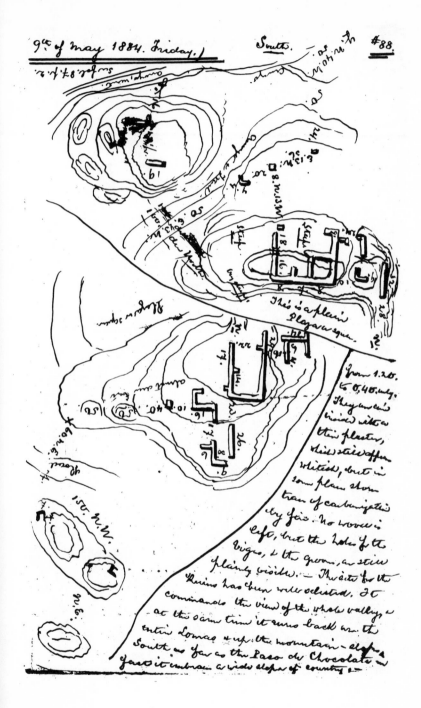

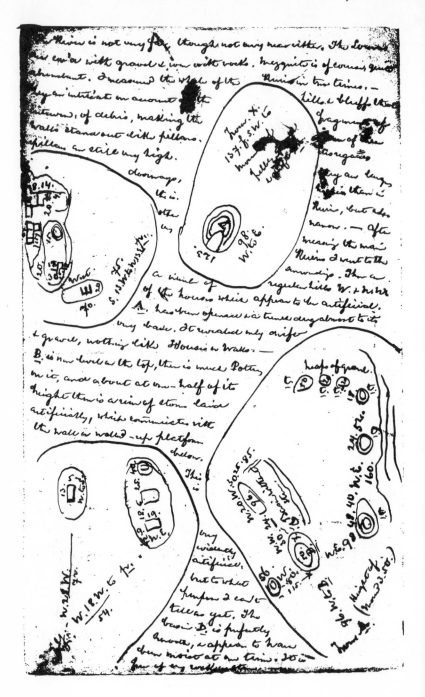

9th of May 1884. Friday.) To give an Idea of # 89.
this mound (B.) as a

I can represent it.   Topwith Pottery.

Low mound. Walls   Rise of Stone laid by hand
not very regular, partly

The groundplan, now in detail, appears as follows: The low mound (a.)
formerly

around the
a "Corral."
almost

people having carried off the stones to build with. There is not,
therefore, any doubt as to the fact that it was a Corral. —
The other Mounds of stone, or stone-piles (c. c. c. c. c.) are much
smaller, & they are, as I said above show, simply stone-piles without
earth even. The wall (b.) is perfectly alike to the small Cliffs or
dams of Bascas. It inclines inwards, as well — . Its height is
about 0.7.0. — It may be
very difficult to get objects
from. — They are mostly broken.
I am again assured that the Metates
have in fact, & that copper-figures (a turtle & fish frints)
were found in the Ruins. — The dozen down, East of the Rivers,
state partly steenks in Ravin, & some of them are built in across
Walls. — On the whole, the settlement has been very extensive, &
has expanded into the River-bottom proper. — I am told of
several Acequias who run fourth distant mountain side
toward the Pueblo, but there is only one of which I can have very
positive information. — In regard to other Ruins, I only
heard that at the Hacienda of Reyes, there is lying
" montezumas ", — I am also told that there is a big this
in the "Escondida ", — East of here — Of "Cavos, I hear about
3. days Journey West, — in the Sierra Madre. The "Cuevos"
of which I heard at Corralites, are E.S.E. of here. — From here
the Cerro de Chocolate, is plainly visible. It is perfectly
denuded of oak, — & surmounted by heights, the

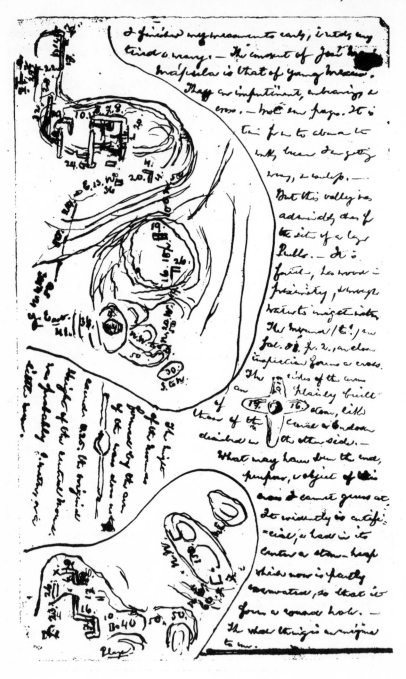

10th of May 1884. Saturday.) Beautiful day, #90
but hot. Windy as
usual, started at 8. a. m. with Melchior Quando, a certain
Dr. Brenn joined us, to my great annoyance. Still, he was,
after all, to some profit. I took some sections and detail.
From all appearance, the houses have been perhaps four stories high.
These stories certainly are visible. — The construction is evidently
"Cajon", it is, in so far, as it is not adobe. — The doorways had
lintels, which now have fallen out, decayed, or disappeared, but
there are some indications that make us suspect that these lintels
may have been stone. Still, Melchior, when I uttered that
idea to him, remarked that only wooden lintels or indicated
the grooves etc. — It is my story too, that the buildings then
rather large indoor! — There is, however, an evident progress, as also
I have forgotten my past observations. — I could not do as
much work as I wished on account of the Doctor! — but still
he was of some use. Upon our return we descended into the
bottom where many of the houses are still built on ancient mounds
or were on foundations of old buildings. These foundations
are plainly or easily distinguished since they are of solid compact
"Cajon", & at least 18 Inches wide. — Among these houses there
was an elevated ridge, which the Doctor shows to me as the
ancient Acequia! — It is evidently a raised street, &
while it could hardly have been anything else but a ditch,
still it appears much more like a "chaussée", than anything
else. — I measured it with the bottom & found the following
plan. The whole width is 4.30 meter, and following it, up to
45.0.

S. E. Road,
N. W. is
45 meter.
lines

The
L. side or marked by stones, laid or bituminous so that
it whole divides into 3 parallel bands, whose cross-section
is as follows. ———— But all this does not the
qualities, with entering an artificially heated surface!!

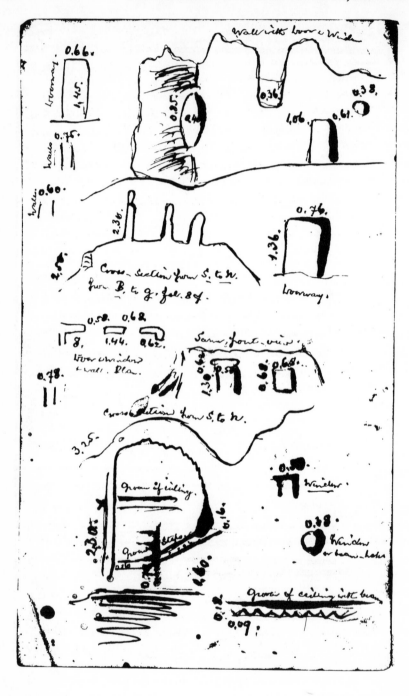

early and then went to painting. Left José María Mápula for good and moved over into the empty house of Don Silvestre Quevedo.

MAY 16: I can easily [make a] resumé [of] the work of the past days [May 11-15]. It consisted exclusively in painting. There are many handsome objects here, principally pottery. Of these, I copied five pieces, three of which are painted, one corrugated, and one plain black. One stone axe, one mortar and pestle, one pestle with the head of a mountain sheep, and many sea shells (snails, univalves). Everything appears to show considerable art. The pottery for example is very beautiful. They talk of copper objects, but I cannot find any trace of them. Thus they mention fish and a turtle of copper, and variously assert that such objects were forwarded to Chihuahua but lately. The same with pottery in the shape of men, women, and animals. I was shown a bird's head, but it is still rather doubtful whether that is really ancient. Turquoises are found abundantly in the ruins after heavy rains; they call them chalchihuites. Of obsidian I have heard only; I have not, as yet, been able to see any, but it is certain that it appears frequently in the volcanic ranges east of here, and I saw a nugget of it, of the size of a large hen's egg, which had been but recently brought in. Of stone axes, I saw one also, though broken, which is exceedingly large. Of course it is of greenish-black trap, diorite, or basalt. Metates are said to be without feet, yet I know positively that some have been found with one foot, and I even heard of some with three feet. Manos are flat, disklike, and not large nor heavy. A picklike implement of trachytic rock, possibly ancient, I found myself in the ruins.* It is rude, but of suspicious origin nevertheless. May have been made latterly.

The people here are excavating constantly, and furthering objects to light. The valley is one of the most fertile, if not the most fertile, I have seen on this trip. It has a beautiful growth of álamos, sufficient for timber of roofing and ceiling, and there is an abundance of water. The people, were they not so abjectly lazy, could easily raise two annual crops. But they are a set of worthless, shiftless, good-for-nothing vagabonds, too lazy to beg, and too silly to steal. Inhabitating, as they do, one of the most favored spots in all northern Mexico, they still have nothing to eat. There is considerable military force here, which of course needs food, but instead of improving the opportunity in order to sell and gain money, they complain of it.

There is much building going on here, though, and the town is rapidly growing. Population about 1,600 souls today.[87] One of the caves, the one nearest to here and situated near the head of the river, has twelve rooms; the other, in the same direction, and about two days journey, has thirty-four rooms.

MAY 17: Painted. In the afternoon, Don Donaciano came. The same evening we took a walk together to the ruins, for the special purpose of investigating the acequia. The latter approaches the ruins almost straight from the northwest, passes two arroyos, and when past the last one before reaching the pueblo ruins, seems to divide into two branches. One of these probably goes around the ruins on the west; the other deflects to the east and passing around the northern end of the ruins enters into the bottom. How the crossing of the arroyos was effected, if not by wooden troughs, I cannot imagine.

The mound which contains the excavation was opened by Nabor Gomez on the strength of a treasure story. He says (but I doubt his statements) that the stones were piled up together with great care, even laid in mud, and that immediately under the top was a bed of ashes. If such were proven, it might explain the purpose of the mounds—cremation of large numbers of bodies. Certain it is that nobody knows exactly what they were for, but the best informed believe that they had something to do with burial rites. No urns with ashes found.

MAY 18: Plenty of visitors. Don Donaciano, Major Valentín Oñate, Don Genovivo Portillo, Capt. Mauro Cándano, Mr. Fahy, and the Gefe Político [Don Silvestre Quevedo]. The Major sent me four fine ollas to copy. Set to work at once and painted the whole day. At night sent a letter to Mr. Muenzenberger. Pleasant walk with Don Donaciano.

MAY 19: Occasional blows with thunder. Called on Capt. Cándano. Painted the greatest portion of the day. At night, call from Mr. Coville and wrote to Mr. Whyte.

MAY 20: For sudden blows and whirls, this a remarkable place. Went to the ruins. I found, beyond the most westerly mound, another building, partly excavated, which is a hollow cuadrilateral [cuadrilátero, quadrilateral], and has been only one story high. Besides, to the southeast of it, there is a huge tank! The analogy between this place and the ruins on the Lower Gila becomes more and more apparent. There is no doubt anymore about it. Whatever differences exist, consist in the effects of local variations. Here, the buildings rest and could rest, on a solid foundation; there was no need for such thick walls, but otherwise the features are nearly identical.

Burial rites may have been different—urn cremation on the Gila, cremation on a large scale here. The metates here are square blocks, well and regularly trimmed; on the Gila they are oblong. The pottery here is much more handsome, but this results from the abundance of fine clay, and the proximity of paints. Found a fragment of indented pottery which is painted. Had a visit from Captain Cándano. The usual walk with Don Donaciano. Three Americans came today, from Eureka.

MAY 21: It is evidently the May wave of cold. It soon cleared fine. Painted pottery all morning, and then went to Don Donaciano, who gave me a letter from Corralitos, which put me in a terrible stew. No letters! What can it mean? Still, there is evidently a misunderstanding somewhere. Mr. Fahy came. Painted the whole afternoon. Much dejected. Mr. Muenzenberger came at last to resolve my doubts. The mail had not arrived yet. Determined to start for the sierra day after tomorrow.

I then went out to the ruins again. There is no doubt but that the cross of mounds is artificial, and made on purpose. I refer to the other side of this sheet for explanation. I went back to the ruins for the purpose of examining the acequia, and while there stumbled on a very large tank, with a broad rim, or border. The tank is 20 meters across, two meters deep, and the rim is on an average twelve meters wide, and about one meter above the surface of the soil. It is of earth, a broad embankment, and there is some stone in it. There is every evidence that it was a tank and for no other purpose.* To the west-northwest of the tank there is another ruin of a one-story building, forming a hollow rectangle, with a distinct court in the middle. This is evidently the last

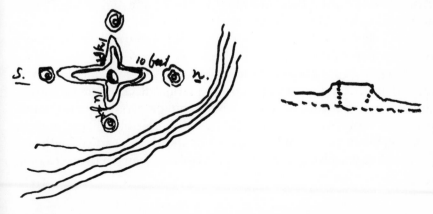

one of that kind (dwellings) in that direction, the most westerly one of the whole pueblo.

See fol. 88 p. 2 and 89 p. 2. This is the cross marked (t^1). Its section from south to north is as follows, and it is similar from east to west. All these little mounds, are merely piles of stones heaped up, and without any sod and earth between them. Attempts at excavations are met with in nearly all of them. I spent the evening partly in Don Silvestre's, partly with Don Damasio Rueda.

MAY 22: I shall begin with the last part of the day, that part spent at the ruins for the second time. I went due west, then turned south, and finally struck the acequia at the crossing of the first arroyo. The dimensions are in feet, English. Direction of acequia here from north 15 west to south 15 east. (The width of the arroyo is at the top; below, it narrows to about 10 feet.)* The acequia here is totally obliterated, but I went due southeast about 950 feet to another arroyo where the same appearance of crossing presents itself, with the difference that it is clearly visible that a casing of unhewn blocks of stone or rocks, lined the side of the acequia to the calcareous concrete forming its base, or, as far as I could see, about four feet deep. This is a front view of the south side of the embankment.* I forgot to state that, here, the filling actually done is about 1.25, while at the upper arroyo, it is fully two meters. [Here, Bandelier recorded several pages of dimensions and azimuths of the acequia and several mounds.]

As it stands, the plan indicates courts, where walls were of concrete also, and extending around the building on the south and southeast. The largest room is on the south wing, but I could not determine as to whether or not it was really one room, or whether the partitions had simply been removed. The corner (north) is a little knoll, showing like a house twenty by twenty and this feature is plainly identical with Casa Grande on the Gila and the ruins at Tempe and on the Verde and Salado. Beyond this large house there is nothing at all, except a low ridge of pebbles west of it. It is very indistinct, and barely visible except to an experienced eye.

Of the acequia, I could not find any trace at all, but Don Donaciano assured me that it does reappear farther south, deflects to the southwest, and finally terminates in an arroyo. One thing is certain: it was carried through the western portion of the pueblo, probably for the purpose of filling the two great tanks or reservoirs, and thence carried southwest for the purpose of irrigating a tract of tillable soil lying in that direction.

The arm, which irrigated the bottom, probably deflected at the second arroyo, so that not the river, but the spring, or ojo, furnished irrigation and, in case of necessity, drinking water. The tanks plainly show, that there was apprehension of danger from enemies, who might cut off the water supply of the acequia as well as impede approach to the river. Besides, the latter here floods part of its bottoms at times. I reach the conclusion almost, that the southern group of the building was only two stories high. The rubbish, however, leaves the point yet undecided. The whole southern front today is at the same height. Arranged with Teodóro Alvarado to go to the mountains. Mr. Coville left for Chihuahua again.

MAY 23: Painted metates. At Nabor Gomez there is a round flat disk of reddish stone, 0.65 x 0.63 and 0.05 thick [meter?]. It was dug up in the ruins, and others of the same kind, often perforated in the middle, are met with. The metate of Gomez is 0.41 x 0.33, and 0.16 high. In the house of Mr. Shaw-Eady,[88] there is another metate 0.47 x 0.38 and 0.26 high. Captain Cándano came and paid me a pleasant visit. I had an offer to go with Captain Ponce and Colonel Terrazas, but could not accept, since they move very rapidly. Got my teguas and shall start for the sierra tomorrow, at least, with Alvarado. Had the pleasure of quite a talk with Don Urbano Zubia. He positively assures me that the aerolite was found in a small house of the ruins and still with the remains of a mat which had been put around it. Of copper utensils or figures he knows nothing, except of a frog (possibly the turtle of others) which, however, is gone long ago. I left Chico with Captain Cándano. Mr. Shaw-Eady left for Galeana tonight, so that I had to say good-bye to him. Beautiful night, warm and pleasant. No letters; still I am not much worried, and I don't know why.

MAY 24: Yesterday, the Gefe Político told me, when I asked him about the disks of stone which Nabor Gomez had shown to me, that the perforated ones had been found in the ruins, inserted in walls, the hole forming a window or loop hole!! He positively said, that he himself had seen them in that condition, in old walls still standing. This statement is very important, and deserves close scrutiny and attention. Don Silvestre is a very reliable man and deserves much faith and credit in what he says.

Two expeditions left for the sierra today. [Colonel] Don Joaquín Terrazas goes in one direction; Captain Ponce in another, to meet at a given point. The day opened beautifully, the mountains are hazy, the air quiet, but promises to become hot. Everything and everybody at Casas Grandes is as quiet and as lazy as ever. Hope to be able to leave today at last. Don Silvestre gave me a clear explanation of the situation of the caves. They are both on side creeks of the Rio de Piedras Verdes: one is on the Arroyo Nombre de Dios; the other is near the river. The junction, near San Diego, of the Rio de Piedras Verdes, with the Rio de Palanganas, forms the Rio de Casas Grandes. There are several villages on this side of the Sierra, which have Opata names: Temósachi, Namiquipa (Nami, inside of; Qui, house).

The day grew very warm, and at last, about 2:30 P.M. Teodoro came, and we left, accompanied by his son-in-law, Severo Parra, Teodoro riding a burro. We followed the west (left) bank of the river. The lomas soon begin to close in upon the bottom, the latter narrowing in proportion. About a league south of the main ruins, there is a small group of others on the loma, afterwards nothing more is visible on that side, except the broad acequia. It is visible for about 300 meters, the river forms nearly an arc to the eastward leaving an ancón to the west. This ancón is bounded by a compact range of gravelly bluffs, traversed by an arroyo coming in from the west.* The arroyo is perfectly dry now, and its level is that of the bottom. The acequia is deeper on the east than on the west side, the respective heights being 1.75 and 1.00 [meters?]. There is no lining to the acequia; it is simply a trough in the loose sandy earth. I learned that, while there is no ruin on the west bank, there is one nearly opposite, on the east side.

We then ascended the course of the river, and the lomas became volcanic and finally to lava! It is a regular malpaís. The Sierra del Ancón looms up boldly in the southwest, and we are approaching it fast. To the northwest, the southerly spur of the Cerro de Montezuma closes in upon the river which now flows almost due southwest and finally due west. In the malpaís, about two-and-one-half leagues from Casas Grandes, there is the ruin on the other side. It is evidently built of the same concrete or large irregular adobes, but there are a great many blocks of lava strewn about, and some lava walls. One hill is peculiar. It is roof-shaped but rounded at the top, and the base is encased by flags set on edge.* Its height is only 1.50 but on the southwest side the declivity down to the arroyo emptying into the river is 3.50 high, and very steep, and it thus increased the height on that side to five meters.* . . . All the mounds are not high. Metates are as usual, and the pottery, though old and dilapidated, still shows the same painting as on the pottery of Casas Grandes. There is very little flint, and no obsidian. Beyond, the malpaís and Cerro de la Boquilla approach the river so as to compress it into a narrow pass. The map gives a better idea of the topography than any description.* This cerro is an almost isolated volcanic rock, somewhat resembling the Cerro San Diego on the Rio Grande near Rincon. It bears no ruins. Through the pass, the Sierra Madre became visible in the west, a dark, solemn mass, somewhat indented, with a solid front extending from south to north along the entire horizon like a black threatening curtain. We crossed the river, then the Rio de Palanganas, and camped in the bottom, in sight of the ruins of San Diego.

MAY 25: The hacienda, from the number of buildings, was quite an important concern. The Apache compelled its abandonment about twenty-five years ago. It is situated in a great plain, which plain extends to the very foot of the sierra, and from the southern end of the Sierra del Ancón to north beyond the Rio Piedras Verdes. The course of both streams, the Palanganas and the Piedras Verdes, is plainly visible, and it is skirted, as usual, by álamos. The Sierra del Ancón approaches close to the Palanganas on the east side. Near the abandoned rancho there is a ruin exactly alike to the other kind of mounds.* Pottery similar also. Metates of lava. The ruin stands on the loma, which here is very low, and also approaches the Palanganas. Thence they follow that river up. [Another] ruin stands right on the river, about one-and-a-half mile to two miles south of [the first]. [A third] ruin is nearby, but about a half-mile from the river, on a commanding point of the loma, and rather high above the plain. [A fourth] is still farther on, on the loma also, and there are said to be other ruins on the same side of the river, also—perhaps, on the other side—to the end of the plain, where there is said to exist a stone wall (trinchera). The grass is all burnt up here to nearly the foot of the high sierra. After the usual useless delays and dallyings, we left the river and began to cross the plain to the westsouthwest towards the Puerto de San Diego. It is a constant steady rise with few undulations, grassy, treeless, and with many antelopes. The antelopes were not very shy, even so little as to come down straight towards us. My companions did some very bad shooting indeed, missing every shot.

As we approached the foot of the mountains, we touched the course of the Arroyo de la Cuerda, along which there are some trees; oaks mostly. Here, at the distance of one legua, about, from the foot of the range, are the dams. They are exactly similar to those in the Arroyo de la Culebrilla near Granados, but more especially they resemble those of Mochubabi. The inclination of the ground, while not perceptible in walking, is still steady and uninterrupted.

On both sides of the arroyo, the plain is traversed by trincheras, which divide it into a number of more or less regular plots or lots. As a general thing, these plots are raised one higher than the other, though but very little only, so that this profile is rather an exaggeration.* As to the width of the whole area covered by these dykes, I could not form any opinion, beyond that it extends on both sides of the arroyo, and is also situated in the groove or cañada formed by the latter.

As we approached the base, the ground grew more and more rocky, or rather, strewn over with lava blocks and pebbles. In that series of cultivated plots (labores, as the people call them here), there are several ruins.* Pottery identical, also metates. The mounds indicate small buildings, of two to four apartments at most: they also indicate walls of earth and little volcanic fragments, exactly similar to those of Casas Grandes. Stone constructions are connected with these mounds; they are sometimes like small enclosures appended to them. In one instance, there is a little square of stones on the upper edge of the mound, over-looking the arroyo, and the enclosures are connected directly with the dykes or dams, so that the mound, on three sides, stands surrounded by the fields. (I noted a second case of this.)

Here we stopped for dinner, and from here we entered the cañón of the Puerto de San Diego. It is a beautiful, narrow, mountain pass, with very gradual ascent. To the right (north), the towering slopes rise very steep, and the crests and tops are pine clad. To the left another ridge, at least 2000 feet high, terminates in vertical crags of columnar rocks, exceedingly picturesque. In the groove and on the very steep slopes, there is an uninterrupted thicket of oak, cedars, pines, some agave of mezcal, some yucca, etc. The path creeps up on the north flank. The rise is about five to six miles long, where the height of the pass is reached, the cañón closing in fully, and only a few small hills, pine clad, on both sides remaining. We then entered a magnificent pine timber, cool, lofty, and majestic, and descended five miles to the west, very gradually, to the Ojito.

MAY 26: Birds singing and the green Guacamayos [macaws] screeching in the tops of the high beautiful pines. We slept in a little arroyo where, from time to time, there are tinajas of permanent water, and sparse tufts of broom grass. It is a beautiful timber, and I at once recognized the prominent features of the country as described by Lieutenant West. We started early, rising to the top of a rocky cordón [ridge], where the high pine timber left us and we had a beautiful view across the whole Sierra Madre to the west. It is all pine clad, the ridges are softly moulded, long, and without peaks or pinnacles at all.

Out of the narrow valleys occasional crags arise. In the far west, there is an apparent break, or pass, and in it looms up the Sierra de Teras very distinctly, and also the top of the Sierra de Baserac, and the northern point of another distant range, which is probably the Sierra de Opoto or Nacosari. In the north the low range beyond which lies the Taraycito [Taraycitos], appears near, and almost in continuation of it follows the Puerto de San Pedro beyond which runs the river of the same name. From a point higher up the crest, the Sierra Quevauerichi is visible in the southwest (here they call it the Sierra de Checui-chupa). The Sierra de las Tapiecitas, which is a southern spur of the Carcay, also looms up in the northeast. The south is closed by pine clad ranges and crests. With the cool, bracing air, the dark blue sky, the brisk northwest wind, and the dark pine clad ridges, still, with only a few turkey buzzards flying above them, the scenery and landscape is invigorating and refreshing.

We descended from the cordón into the bed of the same arroyo of the Ojito, to which arroyo, Teodoro gives the name, "del Portal." This arroyo is very picturesque, beautiful high crags of red and yellow conglomerate, full of caves and recesses, some of whom [which are] deep, but all without walls and buildings. One of them contained a heap of corn cobs. The bottom is narrow, with pines and oaks and brush; in the beginning it is exceedingly rocky, lower down it widens and becomes fertile, grassy and even partly sandy. Fresh bear tracks are visible, and turkeys are cackling in the tree tops. I again admired the clumsiness of my companions at hunting, and their very bad markmanship. Missed every shot.[89] We descended the Arroyo del Portal to where it enters the Arroyo de [los] Pilares, and then followed the latter, which is broad, open, and grassy, to the mouth of the Arroyo de Nombre de Dios. Both arroyos have water even now, in limpid pools, so that the water is certainly permanent in them. The same conglomerate formation forms the banks of the Arroyo de los Pilares, but the bluffs are lower, and less columnar. The soil is exceedingly fertile, though sandy, and very light and moveable. The Arroyo Nombre de Dios, near its mouth, is very much alike.

We went up that arroyo a quarter-of-a-mile, and then I saw, on the left side, a beautiful natural arch, formed out of and in a pillar of red conglomerate. The pillar is about sixty feet high, ten feet thick and perhaps twenty-five feet wide, and the arch, or hole, has a diameter of twelve to fifteen feet, about. Not one hundred meters higher up, on the same side of the arroyo (east), stands the cave in a very much sheltered, even concealed, position, so much so that only by approaching close to the base of the two high pillars in whose further recess it is situated, an uninterested stranger will notice them. The access is from the west, and there is only one trail or path. From any other side it is inaccessible. The walls are of white concrete, and they are plastered inside as usual. Wood is still fairly perfect, and there is no trace of burning. Little pottery, some painted. One metate, barely indented, is lying outside. Everything shows that the caves were evacuated with much care and deliberation, removing everything useful and valuable. From the caves, water, permanent and good, is only about a hundred meters off.

I explored the arroyo for about a mile higher up, where the pillars of reddish conglomerate cease to stand out, and a very hard, greyish rock appears in which there are no more cavities. Beautiful pines grow in the valley, and the grass is high. Turkeys and bear tracks are met with and followed, but without success. No signs of Apache, except old trails, one of which passed here.

[Here, Bandelier recorded detailed measurements of the cave ruins.*]

MAY 27: We left early in the day, at 6 A.M., which is even remarkably early. Instead of taking the arroyo, we rose directly to a cordón, from which we enjoyed the same glorious air and view as yesterday. This cordón led us back exactly to the Ojito, so that we retraced our steps clear back to the foot of the Puerto de San Diego. Here I measured several ruins. . . . We then followed the mountains, crossing the plains to the north-northeast. There are two ruins in this waterless waste, one of which I measured.* They are exactly similar to the others. We crossed the plain until we reached the Rio Piedras Verdes, on whose southwest bank we made our camp. Today I made forty miles on foot, still I could walk clear to Casas Grandes yet. I have now a very good, clear, idea of the Sierra Madre and the interior of it. It is rather a big valley traversed by ridges, and encompassed by elevated crests, or rather chains. On the Sonora side, there are several parallel chains. On the Chihuahua side, south of the Babispe road, there is the Sierra

Carcay followed by the Tapiecitas, and west of it the Sierra de San Pedro, and the Tesahuinori.

MAY 28: Early at sunrise the two fellows went out to hunt and as usual without result. So they finally placed a blast into the river and killed quite a number of fish, some of which were quite large and good to eat. At 9 A.M. I left alone on foot for Casas Grandes. I first measured, on the west bank of the Piedras Verdes, the ruins.* One is very large, though not as large as those at Casas Grandes. Along the front towards the bluff, part of the mound has been washed away and tumbled down, probably by inundations, as the bottom, which is overgrown by trees, is occasionally flooded. Excavations have been made in that embankment, exposing walls of the same kind as usual, and of about 0.40 [meter?] in thickness.

I then followed up the river for about one-and-a-half miles, to beyond the Vado, and in this space measured three ruins, two of which are, however, so small that they appear to have been guard houses only. Farther on, there is a very large ruin of which I am only able to make a sketch. The mounds run from southwest to northeast. This sketch, however, is but an approximation.* I waded the river, which is not very deep, but very clear and limpid. On the other side, the road cuts across to the northeast partly following an arroyo, on whose banks are two much decomposed ruins. The road rises and I thus actually, in this tour, described a complete circle around the Cerro de Montezuma. It is all bleak, waterless, and waste; rocky hills of lava, high and treeless, rise on all sides; and the chain of the Cerro descends very abruptly to the Piedras Verdes River, exceedingly steep. There are not the least signs of ruins visible, neither can any be expected, as there is no arable soil, everything is too rocky, and there is no water at all. After describing almost a perfect circle I got out of the lava hills surrounding the Cerro de Montezuma nearly in front of the great ruin and then crossed the lomas to the pueblo. No letters.

At last I met Don Hilario Maeze. He has in his possession a column of burnt clay, one meter long, and eighteen centimeters in diameter, which was exhumed from the ruins. It is yellowish brown on the outside, and the cut shows a rose-colored clay inside. Object of this column impossible to guess at. Of copper objects, none are authenticated except a rattle and that so-called turtle. But in regard to the aerolite it appears certain that it was found wrapped up in a double mat, of which, however, only the dust, showing the texture, remained. It, of course, crumbled at once. In a ruin north of Casas Grandes a similar vestige of a skirt, made of yucca slats or braids, was found. It was also reduced to dust, plainly showing size and texture of the object, and also crumbled immediately. Moved over to Mr. Shaw-Eady's.

May 29: Very tired and worn out. Day as usual. Could not do much, on account of Laurent, who is drunk, boisterous and bothersome. Painted the plans of the caves. Night beautiful and clear, always cool and nice to sleep. Got letter from Mr. Muenzenberger stating that nothing had come as yet, except the money. Am in a terrible state of anxiety.

May 30: Started for the Cerro de Montezuma early, with Severo Parra. We struck to the southwest across the lomas, and when we reached due west of the ruins and began to rise very gradually on the north side of the arroyo, which arroyo is not permanent, we struck an old trail, of which it is stated that it connects the ruins below with those on the top of the Cerro. It is only visible in parts, and where it is yet on the level loma, marks a broad trail, well trodden out, about a meter wide at most, and it seems as if this trail had been made by picking out the stones and rocks, and piling them up on the side. This gives it the appearance of having been excavated. Here also there are trincheras.* They seem to extend on the north side of the arroyo only, but in the arroyo itself there are two dams which appear to be new. They look as if they had been made only yesterday. Their relative position is as follows:*

Nearby, the road takes the appearance of a cut through a hill, which cut is partly by hand, picking up the stones and piling them on the sides, partly by wear. Nearby also, the arroyo enters the cañón, winding up due west to the lowest part (northern spur) of the crest. It is in fact a high pass. On the right hand (northern) side, are the blocks rudely carved, forming part of a rocky gate or of a promontory, at whose foot the road or trail passes. The figures are rude and clumsy scratchings, one of which evidently intends to represent a shield with feather ornaments.* Finally, in the trail proper, a slab was found which has a carving on it, very much like a horse's hoof and horseshoe.*

It is singular that the trail nowhere shows any artificial filling, only cutting or rather grooving out. This trail widens out to apparently two to three meters, but in fact, it is never wider than one meter, the greater apparent width being due to washing. Its grade varies.* There is, for instance, a cut east of the pass.* In the pass itself the trail hugs the slope, the rocks and stones picked up being on the side of the declivity. Here it has in appearance the width of a carriage road, but this is due to wear and to rains.

The whole plan of the Cerro is about as follows. Roads or trails branch off across it.* The one which we ascended divides at the foot of the rocky hill of the Pueblito and while one of them goes directly up to that ruin, another one crosses over the ridge below, and descends into the bottom of the Piedras Verdes. The Pueblito is a very singular ruin. It stands at the base of the second hump of the chain, north of the top. Crags and pillars skirt it on the west and north, still there are two trails leading up to it through these crags, one from the west, and another from the north. We ascended and descended by the northern one. On the east side is a gradual slope, and this slope is crowned by a handsome wall, faced by larger blocks on both sides, and filled in with stone rubbish. This wall is five feet thick, its height is impossible to determine. A gateway, well-faced on the sides, and two feet wide, enters it from the east; it has a stepping stone across the entrance. The singular feature is the nearly square mound of stone, encircled by a half-moon stone wall outside of the main wall.*

It appears to have been like a lookout or a point of defense, for it has been opened and is absolutely solid. Plates and flags, set on edge are the face of the base; above, it is faced by regularly broken rocks, and inside it is filled with loose gravel, as also the top. A similar structure stands on the brink of the western precipice, overlooking it. There is hardly a continuous wall along the latter. Large and small rocks are piled up, wherever an opportunity is afforded, sometimes semi-circles and circles are formed by them which resemble somewhat the rude Apache structures built out of the ruins at the Carrizo and on top of the mounds there. The principal structure is a large mound, partly excavated, revealing walls 0.55 [meter?] thick, of the usual concrete, and showing, by its height, to have been possibly of two stories.

East adjoining, there is a rectangular depressed court, and narrow rectangular mounds enclosing it, connected with the main structure. The one on the north seems to have been an oblong house, on the south also, on the east a wall of concrete, and the southeast corner is plainly formed by a one-story house containing but one room. Therefore, this part of the ancient settlement is not extensive. But structures and enclosures of stone plates, somewhat irregular and in appearance hastily erected, are scattered north of this complex; they are also built in and on the enclosure mounds of the south, and the northeast of the real Montezuma. The structures at first struck me as possibly Spanish, but upon closer investigation I found that they were aboriginal, but more recent than the solid house of the Montezuma and possibly constructed hastily as a refuge for a small band of fugitives fleeing up here from below. The eastern wall, however, is so well constructed that it naturally seems to belong to the same period as the Montezuma. It is also a very significant feature inasmuch as it shows that they guarded against the east also, indicating that their relations with the Rio Casas Grandes bottom were not exclusively friendly alone. Pottery, metates, etc., as usual. From the Pueblito a well defined trail leads up to the top of the Cerro, rising gradually along the western slope, and in full view of the Palanganas and Piedras Verdes rivers beneath, to the foot of the highest rise, which it finally ascends. The top is occupied exclusively by a round tower, walls of stone plates without binding material, five feet thick, and still eight feet high. There is no entrance nor door to the tower, so that it must have been scaled in order to enter it, and this was probably done by stone steps outside as, where the trail reaches the wall, there is a stone pile outside, as if of some tumbled structure originally built outside against the tower on the north.

On the east side of the wall, inside, there is a niche, and a ruined structure, of stone, walls two to three-and-a-half feet thick, occupies the center. On the southeast there is a semi-circle built against it, inside also, of stone, with thin walls. From the rubbish accumulated around the central structure, I would judge it to have been of concrete above, and probably two stories high at least in part. Not a trace of pottery or any other remains are on the surface, and it appears certain that the place, if ever permanently occupied, was so by a limited number of people. It looks much rather as if it had been a lookout and place of refuge for the people of the Pueblito beneath, with which place there has been a direct communication. Below this tower and at a distance of ten meters from it, and seven feet lower on the north side, there is a lower and rude wall, much ruined, running all around it. It is, now, scarcely over four feet high, and two feet thick, the rocks appear to have been piled up without any earth or mortar between them, and there is no visible entrance. Aside from the path leading up from the north, there is another one—at least it is positively stated—from the south. I confess that I neglected to look for it in time.

The position of the Cerro is a very remarkable one. Isolated, dividing the valley of Casas Grandes on the east, from the valley of San Diego and the Piedras Verdes in the west, it absolutely dominates both, and the whole plain at the foot of the Sierra Madre from its farthest southern termination to the Pajarito. Every flank, fold, pass, and crest of the Sierra Madre on its eastern wall is seen, to the east every plain, valley, and range and pass, from the Boquilla to beyond Corralitos, and in the far north the Sierra de la Hacha [New Mexico] and even the Florida [New Mexico] are dimly visible. The view is immense and the access to the tower, except from north and south, very steep and highly difficult. But neither at the tower, nor at the Pueblito, are there any traces of water! Still, they must have had a water supply somewhere. We returned to Casas Grandes at noon, and in the evening I had a long talk with Don Hilario Maeze. He says that the ruins extend from the headwaters of the Palanganas beyond San Miguel de Babícora all along the streams, and wherever there is permanent water, in the escondida, towards the laguna. Even south of San José there is a Labor de Montezuma [work of Montezuma]. But he also affirms that, while the Sierra Madre is full of ruins which is true to a certain extent only, there are none, south of the Babispe road. I make, after his statements, the following sketch.*

MAY 31: Got a splendid axe of stone to copy. It weighs six pounds. Also saw an immense double metate (cuate). It is squared as usual, has no feet. Height 0.29; at the same place, there is a platter of stone, painted red.* Finally I found some more shells, turquoises, shell beads, and turquoise beads, also a few glass beads, evidently recent, and a regular fetish of green veined stone, representing a bear, and a larger head, representing a similar beast, of the same stone. I am reliably informed that, here as well as at Corralitos, pottery has been found with obscure figures in relief, that there are very large cave dwellings along the Rio Temehuaqui or Piedras Verdes, and that the proper name for the Rio Chuichupa is Rio del Gavilán. From Nombre de Dios, Chuichupa is only about one day's journey, so that, if the Sierra Queuaverichi was traversable, it would be possible to reach Nacori from Casas Grandes in four days, on foot.

JUNE

JUNE 1 AND 2: Mr. [Shaw-] Eady left for El Paso. Laurent drunk all the time. Painted, fixed up all matters, ready to leave. Am tired, weary, and anxious. Here there is trouble with Señor Eady's business. The Dr. [Laurent?] is released and begins to drink again. Captain Cándano and Don Urbano Zubia are the most decent and respectable men here. Took general leave. As to the ruins in the Pajarito, it is yet doubtful if they exist or are aboriginal at all.

JUNE 3: Reached Corralitos at 2 P.M. Got letters from Joe, Mr. Parkman, Greenleaf, Meysenburg, and Elliott. Thank God, Joe is all right; so is Papa. But poor Charles Lambelet![90] What a terrible blow to Bertha. Poor children. Am almost sick. Wrote to Joe and to Mr. Parkman. Home as fast as possible.

JUNE 4: Half sick. Wrote all day. In the afternoon I was slightly better; still lumbago is very painful, and cramps in the lower limbs below the knees. Don Hilario told me that there were very large caves about the Rio Temehuaqui or Piedras Verdes, and spoke of three wooden arches in front of one of them. These arches I very much regret not having seen as, from the description, they may be something like religious symbols. Spent the evening very pleasantly at Charles Beery and John's.

JUNE 5: It soon grew hot and very windy. Wind southwest, raising clouds of dust. Ready for departure tonight. Travel in the daytime is almost impossible on account of heat and dust. On the whole, I am well satisfied with the results of my explorations. But it is decidedly the last trip. These protracted absences from home, the anxious suspense, etc., they are worrying and wearing out far too much, and Charles' terrible death is a warning from God, not to abuse of His leniency and clemency. It is certain that, once at home, other trials will expect me, but He will also grant me the power to go through these.

Examined the map at Mr. Muenzenberger's office. The Janos River flows through a gap in the northern part of the Carcay,* deflecting from a southwesternly course to a northeasternly one. Near the outlet of that gap, on the eastern plain, is the Casa de Janos. The so-called Arroyo Seco issues from the Sierra del Ancón and runs almost north into the Rio de Casas Grandes, and the Cueva, with paintings, is at the head of the Arroyo Seco. It contains no buildings, only paintings, which may be more recent, possibly Apache. Wrote to Reynaldo Samaniego. Left after nightfall.

JUNE 6: Yesterday's entry, "Left after nightfall," was made in sure

anticipation of what did not happen. Chico did not return at nightfall. I hunted for him everywhere, at a distance of nearly one-and-one-
half leagues around, but no trace of him or of any horse of Mr. Muenzenberger's could be met with, so that I was quite exercised over it. This
morning I continued the search diligently and found thereby a little
Montezuma on the other (west) side of the river, about a mile west of
the hacienda, about 0.80 high,* showing it to have been a house of only
one room, possibly a guard house only. As there has been a ruin near
or at Corralitos, that isolated little mound may easily have been erected
only for purposes of watching the fields.

   Malcontent and quite dejected, I went back to the hacienda. Crosbie
had left, forgetting my pottery! The ladies kindly ventured to offer me
to send it by express. This morning at breakfast I met Captain Cándano,
who is going to Ascensión in order to investigate the case of an officer
who has ill-treated a citizen. I was glad to see him again. As to Mr.
Muenzenberger, he is cold and rather uncivil, but I do not mind it, as
the ladies are so much the kinder for all that. Finally, he sent a man to
look after the horses, and at 3 P.M. Chico came at last. At night, two
big bugs [important personages?] arrived, and it required strong re-
minders from the ladies, to have Mr. Muenzenberger introduce me to
them! I left finally at 9:30 P.M., by a very bright moonlight, alone for
Janos.

JUNE 7: It was bitterly cold, particularly in the Puerto, so that I walked
a good part of the way, in order not to freeze. Reached Janos at sunrise, and slept the whole day, as I must confess to my shame. What I
saw of daylight proved, that the weather had been fine.

JUNE 8: Gathered up my pottery and left late with a companion. We
struck east, and after crossing the perfectly level and very fertile bottom
for two leguas about, crossed the Rio de Casas Grandes, which is lined
by the usual álamos, and skirted by high, barren, and volcanic slopes, a
continuation of the Cerro Colorado. Here the road enters between two
of these steep hills of lava, and rejoins the river again beyond that little
pass, in a grassy plain, which is only bounded at the distance east by
the range of the Corral de Piedras, west by the low Sierra de Janos. The
Carcay disappears gradually.

   In the north-northwest looms up the Sierra de la Hacha, and in the
north the Sierra de la Boca Grande, part of which isolated, pointed
group is formed by the Espía. The river, which here is permanent, runs

in the open plain, leaving all heights behind it. The vegetation is grass in high tufts, considerable yucca, and few cacti. In general, cacti are not very common hereabout in Chihuahua, and the *Cylindropuntia*, while blossoming now (pink flowers) are rare. In the sierra I saw a beautiful scarlet *Mamillaria* with double flowers, and some *Plati opuntiae*, also about Casas Grandes, flowering red, and yellowish. I saw no agaves here. Between the Boca Grande and the Corral de Piedras, there is a wide flat gap.

Reached Ascensión at 2 p.m. Stopped at Don Crispín Zapata. Called on the Padre Cabeza de Vaca and on Rafael Anchieta. Ascensión is a new town on a perfect level, founded twelve years ago. Its population is not over nine hundred souls, and its reputation very bad.

There are many mounds here, of the size and disposition of those about Casas Grandes. Found good feed for Chico. Am told that there is one little ruin with a big wall of stones, in the Corral de Piedras, and several in the valleys around it. Large fires in the Sierra de Janos. I wrote to Don Tomás Moreno, and mailed the letter to Don Mariano Samaniego at Janos.

Got a terrible warning tonight! God may help me through this imminent danger.[91] He is indeed infinitely good. Shall stay here and work a few days yet!! The fires on the mountains are very grand tonight.

JUNE 9: Had a very bad night; still it passed without trouble, except a few suspicious signs. Went over to Don Rafael Anchieta. Attempted to paint in the afternoon, but with little success. Slept, and afterwards took a little stroll. It appears that in the ruins about here, the same pieces of pottery, and whole jars at that, are found as at Casas Grandes, the same metates, and I was told of the figure of a bird, which was exhumed. The ruins extend east to within two to three miles of the river banks; they are much decomposed. At night I heard the talk of one of the unfortunate fools who staked everything on the expected treasures of the ruins at Casas Grandes. It was he who, with Nabor Gomez, excavated the mound. He pretends that on the top of that mound there were signs of the ruins of a building, that a metate was found, with an olla nearby, that in the center of the top there was a floor, sunk partly, that there were nine strata of stones and earth, with one of ashes (at the depth of six feet about from the top), that two skeletons, extended full length, were found three feet from the top, etc. Nothing positive can be gathered from this disconnected talk of his. He is a monomaniac and a lunatic.

Night quiet and warm. Those here who know, also affirm that the string of ruins extends along this river clear to the Laguna de Guzmán, and also along the Rio de Galeana clear to the Laguna de Santa María.

JUNE 10: Tonight I intend to leave. Wrote to Fadrique Arviza and L. Dávila, leaving the letters with Don Rafael. Last night, Bastidas told me that in the mound which he excavated, he found bones of deer, and fragments of matting. Left at night with Epifanio Tellez.

We rode over an apparently bleak, grassy country, sprinkles of rain occurring, till 1:30 A.M. and then laid down. So the homeward march began at last! God alone knows what I may expect, but it would be unjust on my part to fear and quake too much. Trust to Him, is the best. It was weary travelling over the moonlit plain, the horses stumbling, rather than walking, their way through them in the night.

JUNE 11: When we awoke, about 4 A.M., it was nearly daylight, and we found ourselves in the midst of a vast plain, not far from the Rio Casas Grandes. That stream is indicated by the usual bunches of álamos along its banks. The plain contains some yucca; the agave seems to have completely disappeared; cacti are scarce. East of the river, and in front of us, the chain of the Corral de Piedras, barren and rugged, appears to sweep around to the Boca Grande in a curve. Southeast towers up the Sierra del Ojo Caliente. (The Ojo is about twenty-five leguas from Janos.) North is the depression of the Boca Grande, and west of it, the Sierra de la Boca Grande, towering up to a low pyramid. Farther west of it, the plain, behind which the Cerros de las Minas Ricas loom up in the distance, stretches across to the powerful group of the Sierra de la Hacha, due northwest. Then follow bleak ridges, behind which the Sierra de las Animas is faintly visible as also the Espuelas and part of the Sierra de en el Medio.

Finally, in the distant southeast the Carcay still appears, partly concealed by the Sierra de Janos and the Cerro Colorado. This is the visible panorama all around, bleak, treeless, hot in the blazing sun. Aside of the river, which becomes again a permanent stream here, there is no water west until the Ojo del Mosco, at the northern foot of the Sierra de la Hacha, north to the Ojo del Carrizalillo, beyond the Boca Grande. We traversed the plain almost due north to the Espía, an isolated volcanic hill, seven leguas south of the Boca, on the western shore of the river. Here the man called Chapman was lately murdered.

The river henceforward runs in a groove with vertical borders, generally about ten to fifteen and twenty feet high, loamy and mouldy, and therefore covered with a luxuriant vegetation of wild grapes, high grass (grama and even wild rye), which extends into the bottom of the river filling up the channel from bank to bank. For over thirty-five miles, and until the river issues from the Boca to turn east to the Laguna de Guzmán, this remarkable feature prevails. The water is only approachable at long intervals, and then through steep trails. For eight to ten miles sometimes, one can ride along the edge of this border peeping down into the water through the high grass and the cottonwood leaves of the trees growing at the very edge and often so inclined (through undermining of the roots) as to meet with the tops across the channel, without being able to allay the thirst of his animal.

It is a peculiar and dangerously tantalizing feature, for the grass is so tall (four to five feet) and rank along the edge as to completely conceal the few trails to the river to anyone not well acquainted with them. We camped at the Espía on the bank of the river, in a shady hollow, until 3 P.M. There was good grass. Then followed the road into the Boca. The pass is not high; it is a series of rocky hills, with mezquite and grama, extending between the sierra and the Corral de Piedras, and the river breaks through it to the east-northeast, sinking permanently at its outlet towards the Laguna de Guzmán. It is wild and dreary, flat in appearance, but very rugged, in fact, no steep inclines, but broken and rocky. Full of vermin in the wet season. Killed a large rattlesnake in the road. We could scarcely get into the river bottom to water the horses; it is full of musquitoes and the water brackish. So we retired to about a mile on the side of a rocky hill, where there was grama.

JUNE 12: Went to the rim early and passed the day in the hollow, by the side of the brackish water, and high tulas [reeds], perfectly concealed, until 1 P.M., when we started. The ruins gradually drop off on the riverside until near the Espía, when they disappear until around the Laguna Guzmán. Here white mounds are visible again. Neither the Boca nor the Sierra de la Boca, nor the Hacha, have any ruins at all. The Sierra de la Boca has no trees, except a few oaks on the tops; its strata dip from north to south or northeast to southwest. The slopes are gentle, and its front, cut from north to south, may be about 15 to 18 miles long. A branch of it, or sierrita, much lower, shoots off to the north, coming around to the east, about 15 miles farther. A short and barely perceptible incline leads to the plateau; another endless plain, waterless, from which Cook's Peak, the Sierra Florida, and the Tres Hermanas appeared almost simultaneously in the north-northeast and northeast. We crossed the waterless sierrita or northern spur of the Boca Grande, and in its northern foothills, in a dreary arroyo, found the rancho of the Cariza-lillo. Not a tree, scarcely a shrub, soil loamy in the narrow bottom, rocky on every little slope. No ruins at all. A dreary desolate spot. Kind reception and good fare. Slept on a counter, at least, much worried by rats, but very kindly treated by John Woods and Mr. Morgan.

JUNE 13: Left across the dreary plain at 5 P.M. going by the trail due northeast. Camped at night, about half-way. Grass poor. No water, of course. Very tired and feeling filthy. Chico rather poor too.

JUNE 14: Reached Deming at 8 A.M. Thank God!! Met Mr. Moorhead at the depot; he advanced me $50. Met Brewer. All railroads terribly washed out.[92] Hardly any trains. Telegraphed home. Wrote to Meysenburg and to Mr. Parkman. Rented a room. Met Lorenzo Carrasco and Mr. J. B. Magruder of the Ivanhoe. Troops out of Fort Bayard, going west, and the Sixth Cavalry coming in from Arizona, are to meet at Lordsburgh [Lordsburg], so Ford of Fort Cummings told me. Met Mr. Carpenter[93] and A. Schutz. Drew $75. also.

JUNE 15: Wires all down east. Western train got in after 9 A.M. Complete disorganization on the Rio Grande. Met Henry Holgate.[94] My room is small, but good, and in my clean clothes I feel like a different man altogether. But until I get news from home I have no relish for any work. May God have protected them! No telegram. Wires all down. Spent evening with Mr. A. Schutz.

JUNE 16: Wires all right again, but no telegram as yet. Painted all day.

JUNE 17: Had an exceedingly bad and despondent time. At nightfall, I suddenly met Dr. and Mrs. Girard. They are on their way east, but stopped on the way, as all travel is completely interrupted. Met Don J. Miguel Vasconcelos of Guatemala. He assured me that the natives of Guatemala still build trincheras today, in the arroyos, and plant trees, etc. on them, thus raising fruit on the soil accumulating behind the wall.

JUNE 18: Painted groundplans. In the afternoon, a fearful sandstorm from the east, caused by thunderclouds moving from northwest to southeast. East of us along the Rio Grande.

JUNE 19: A repetition of yesterday. Dr. Girard still here. All travel is interrupted, and I am out of money.

JUNE 20: Started for Tucson at 7 A.M. Mountains perfectly clear. On the south side of the railroad, the Boca, Sierra de la Hacha, Sierra de las Animas, loom up. Beyond Lordsburgh, Pyramid Range is very clear. Steins Tank (Peloncillo) is very near (north side) in its nakedness. But the most marked sight is the Sierra Chiricahui. It is a formidable chain, and terribly rugged, abrupt ledges, cut up and twisted, pinnacles, crags, and precipices. There is hardly any vegetation at all. Beyond Paso del Dragón, the Sierra Huachuca presented an imposing appearance. Reached Tucson at 5 P.M. Found letters. All good. Thank God.

JUNE 21: Saw Dr. Thomas. Lieutenant Elliott not yet here. Wrote home. Nothing definite about trains. Drew $25 on account salary. Bishop Salpointe lent me: *Crónica Seráfica y Apostólica del Colegio de Propaganda fide de la Santa Cruz de Querétaro en la Nueva España, dedicada al Santísima Patriarca el Señor San Joseph.* [Here, Bandelier noted, in Spanish, extensive data from this source.]

The night was fine, but the incertitude about all trains is very painful. Bishop Salpointe wants to go to Santa Fe too, but we do not know which road to take. Spent the evening very pleasantly at Dr. Thomas'. Night very starry, but exceedingly dark and hot.

JUNE 22: Father Antonio Jouvenceau and I left about 8 A.M. for San Xavier del Bac (Vac, Vat-q'i).[95] We passed the Rio Santa Cruz, an inconsiderable stream, but with permanent water until a mile northwest (about) of Tucson. Beyond it, we went past Silver Lake, a pleasure resort, based upon the fact of a pond (probably a widening of Santa Cruz River) which is deep enough and wide enough for swimming. Reeds encircle it, and tall mezquites and álamos overshadow its banks and the new frame (!) hotel.

We then entered a mezquite brush, assuming in places the proportion of a mezquite forest. It was very hot in it, and exceedingly dusty. Our course was due south. Beyond it, that is where the mezquite became lower, the view extended over the same dreary, whitish plains, enlivened by mezquite alone. There is no perceptible rise nor fall on this whole road. We left the Sierra del Tucson behind us and finally saw the Pico de Baboquivari (about 8000 feet high) very plain and distinct. Reached San Javier [Xavier] after about two hours drive (the distance is nine

miles). It is in a gap between two mountains, or high hills. The western
has exactly the shape of a high pitched roof. At its foot are several
hillocks. All these elevations are malpaís, and the low, scrubby vegetation is that of Tucson, of course.

The church stands on a rise between the two mountelets, and is like
that of Babispe, only it appears smaller, but its interior is still fairly preserved, except the altar, which has almost disappeared, like at Arizpe
and Oposura. Houses of the Papago are scattered about, but it is barely
a village. Father Antonio led us to a little hill, very rocky, west-southwest
about a half-mile from the church. At the foot, but principally on the
slopes, are the graves of the heathen Papagos! They are all recent. The
dead are buried on the ground, as there is no soil to dig into, and a little
chamber of rocks is built around them to an average height of at least
three feet. Then beams, poles, and brush are laid across, and these are
again covered with small and large rocks. Removing the stones, we could
look into one of the chambers. It contained a dismembered skeleton and
rags. Much pottery, broken, baskets, even fragments of quijos [kiho,
carrying basket] are scattered over and among the tombs. It is the custom to deposit all the objects belonging to the deceased, partly in the
tomb, partly on it. If it has been a man, his bow and arrows, macanas,
gun, etc., if a woman, the ollas, quijo, baskets, etc. Father Antonio
opened one of the graves and found in it a well-preserved female corpse,
sitting, with the staff of a quijo in her hand. I measured several, and
found [they were] two and one-quarter steps [in diameter], and one of
them, five steps. This was a group of three.

Father Antonio told me a great deal of the Apache wars, and also
about Pima and Papago customs. They sing to the sick, in order to drive
evil spirits away. In one case of a consumptive, after all other remedies
had failed, they built a hut of bark outside and, although it was very
cold, took him out naked, washed him from head to foot, and then the
twelve men (naked, and painted blue) stroked him one after the other
with the feather of an eagle, each one running off afterwards and blowing away his feather at a distance. This was done in the belief that the
eagle plumes draw out the malady, and in order to prevent its return,
the plume is thrown away at a great distance. At certain times, they
fasten eagle plumes to their houses. They have the war dance and the

scalp dance. No headdresses, the men only wear eagles' feathers on their heads.

JUNE 23: Telegraphed to H. Holgate [Deming] and got bad reply. Painted a piece of pottery, entire, belonging to Bishop Salpointe and from Pueblo Viejo on the Gila [present-day Solomon]. At supper, met Mr. W. S. Ouray [Oury],[96] and arranged with him to go tomorrow to the Estanque Verde. Got information about large ruins in Durango and Xalisco [Jalisco, Mexico].

JUNE 24: Left at 7 A.M. with Mr. Ouray and family. At the Fort [Lowell], met [Lt.] Elliott (the good boy), Mason, and Wheeler. Elliott gave me a letter from dear old Papa, Good news! Thank God! Also one from Lieutenant West.[97] Went out to the Estanque Verde: it is nine miles east-northeast of the Fort, in the Rillito Valley, which, there, is narrower. High álamos line the banks; the bed is dry sand. A thick and rather high mezquite brush covers the first terrace, on the lomas above, on both sides, zahuaro and palo verde appear. On these lomas are some much obliterated pottery, and corrugated, also yellow pieces with red lines. Ruins almost all destroyed, enough left to show that they were small houses. The Estanque, a natural and permanent pond with reeds, is on the north bank and has an abundant supply of water. Mr. Ouray talked very interestingly. He, and also Father Antonio, justify the Arivaypa Massacre. Killed 140 to 180, but only 14 men.[98]

JUNE 25: Walked back to the post. Feet all burnt up. Saw General Forsythe.[99] Drove into town with Elliott, who dined with me. Blow and squall at 5 P.M. Telegram from H. Holgate. Road alright. Thermometer, 113.0.

JUNE 26: Fierce heat, and often sultry. Impossible to do anything, and impossible to sleep also.

JUNE 27: Forced myself to write, but it is nearly impossible. The heat is stifling. Notes on manuscript of Bishop Salpointe:
    Libros de Partidas of San Xaxier. Jesuit Priest, 1720, Reverend Padre Alejandro Rapuani. 21 November 1751, uprising of all the Pima, San Xaxier was abandoned until 1754, the Priest, Francisco Parra, retiring to Tumacacori. He remained Priest until 1760 and was succeeded by

Reverend Miguel Gerstner. In 1761, Reverend Pfefferkorn.[100] 1766, Custodio Ximeño. 1771, the first Franciscan, Fray Ygnacio Zuñiga. The mission appears to have been abandoned between 1810 and 1821. The new church at Tumacacori in 1822. In 1826, the Sobaipuris[101] still existed; they had moved to the San Pedro and finally were so molested by the Apaches that they joined the Pimas. The Pueblo of Santa Ana was previously called Quikiurtajq or Monte Redondo. Fray Francisco Garzés signs Partidas in 1777.

Mails still irregular and sporadic trouble on the A.T.&.S.F. About 11 A.M. it cooled quite perceptibly. I felt better at once. Returned the papers, etc. to the Bishop and suddenly decided upon leaving, as the train was announced regular time at last. Left about 6 P.M., travelling all night.

JUNE 28: Reached Deming at about 2 A.M. and slept in the parlor of the hotel, so full was it. No news from Santa Fe. Telegraphed there, also to the Bishop [Salpointe]. Uncertainty about trains. Met Judge and Mrs. Prince[102] here; also; Conway.[103] Met Fray Pedro Moro.

JUNE 29: Spent nearly the whole day with Mr. Priber of St. Louis and his family. At night, Bishop Salpointe came with Dr. Cochran, and we all started at 9:40 P.M. At Rincon, the overflow became appalling, all the country south of the depot being under water completely. The Jornada is, as usual, dry.

JUNE 30: Reached Albuquerque at 9 A.M. At San Marcial, the waters had greatly subsided, but above it, the expanse of the sheet and the great force of the roaring current were appalling. Transit slow, and had to be effected with a great deal of care and some danger. The lower parts of Socorro are still under water, and above it, between Limitar and Alamillo, is at present the main washout—currents and counter-currents are rushing back and forth, under and around the track. It is exceedingly interesting for the past history of the country, and explains many features connected with the occupation and abandonment of the country. It shows that the Rio Grande bottom, perfectly habitable and safe during long periods of time, may suddenly be swept by a flood obliterating, in many places, human habitation, and burrowing new channels, thus permanently changing the distribution of arable plots and sites for pueblos. Such floods as the one now are not frequent, but they have occurred before, the tendency of the river now being, south of Alamillo, to encroach upon its western bank, whereas north of it, the inverse occurs.

At Albuquerque, I found everybody except Pauline [Borchert?] who is at Jemez. Letter from Joe to Annie [Borchert], all right and all well. Very hot here, and musquitoes bad.

JULY

JULY 1: Terribly hot. Wrote to Joe, to Mr. W. F. White,[104] to Henry Holgate, and a card to Fort Cummings. Called on Candelaria,[105] took dinner at the Jesuits, called on Mrs. Huning, and finally at Annie's. Spent night with Eddy.

JULY 2: Train came in about 11 A.M. As we approached the Alameda, the overflow reappeared and it seems as if the river was turning back into its old channel. At Albuquerque the bridge is gone, and the current also threatened to deflect to the left in which case the new town would have been completely ruined. They saved it, however, by strenuous efforts in constructing a dyke at night, the water rising to within one inch of its top. Since that time it has spread out south of the old town and is coming in to the east gradually. The Alameda is fully under water, and the bottom at Bernalillo is also flooded but the town itself is safe. North of it there are only a few traces of inundation. At San Felipe the water has risen but little, but at Santo Domingo it reaches the foot of the bluff on which the western tiers of houses stand.[106] It looks rather threatening.

At Santa Fe, very kind reception everywhere. Took a room with Jake Gold. Met Father Bourdier; he is at Belen now, whence Father Gromm is at Tierra Amarilla. Pitiful reports come from above. Everything is not permanently under water, but the rivers and arroyos are high and all intercourse is interrupted.

JULY 3: Another hot day. Called as much as I could. Mr. Cole has secured a handsome collection and is actively having [specimens] dug at the Arroyo Hondo, at San Marcos, and in a recently found ruin east of the Arroyo Hondo, called Peña Negra [Peñas Negras]. Also at Fort Marcy. There is some deeply indented and rather regular corrugated pottery, but not painted. Painted pottery, glossy, black-upon-white, no black-upon-red. Innumerable stone axes, and some stone hammers similar to those of the south, that is, with the crease only on three sides, from Peña Negra, fine collection of bone implements from Fort Marcy and San Marcos, fetishes, whistles, pipes, etc. The collection is a very handsome one. He has also a complete hammer of stone with the handle, very fine. Metates are common, but he has some small ones. A vase from Nambé is peculiar; it bears an ornamentation (fictile) clearly from the Spanish period. A corrugated pot similar in shape to the one from the Estanque Verde, a very beautiful bone implement, curved, evidently a badge. Mr. Eldodt told me that he had secured a lot of valuable pottery, etc. from Abiquiu. The inundation would not have affected at all the old pueblos up there. Spent part of the evening at Mr. Meysenburg's.

July 4: Am very unwell. Must have taken cold. Went to S. Ellison's at the archives, and copied documents. The procession was, as usual, music and music, then speeches. Very hot, and I am in a high fever. In the afternoon, I went to Meysenburg, and then up to Reed's for supper. Illness rapidly increasing. Am evidently worked down and now prostration sets in. At the bank today, the draft at last arrived. Last night I had written to Holgate, to Joe, and to Eddy. Am direly sick, and cannot imagine how it came to be so.

Archives of Santa Fe.[107] [Here Bandelier made several pages of notes.]

The procession was as good as no good, and as I felt very badly and in fever, I continued to remain at home as much as possible. Took supper at Reed's and there met J. Pearce.

July 5, 6, 7, 8: Was very ill until Tuesday [the 8th]. Scarcely able to move. Crawled around merely. Got letters from Joe, and finally also the report and letters from Fort Cummings. The old doctor is very kind to me. [I] made as few visits as possible and wrote but very few letters. Copied a few of the bone implements from San Marcos which Cole has in his possession. At headquarters I made arrangements to have the geographical material made use of for a map of Chihuahua and Sonora. Mr. Hartmann[108] is drawing it.

July 9, 10, 11, 12: Felt better gradually. It rained occasionally, which cooled off the air, and made it more pleasant. Juan José [Montoya, of Cochiti Pueblo] came to see me. The poor people [of Cochiti] are in a bad plight, the river is encroaching on the east side, and washing away or cutting up their fields. Below Albuquerque, new breaks have occurred. Mr. Cole showed me a fish hook of chalcedony found at the big ruins of the Arroyo Hondo [L.A. 12].

Got a letter from the A. T. & S. F. R. R.; also one from Henry Holgate. Wrote to Eddy and to Annie. Examined the wool factory matter. At present, nothing can be done, as everything is flat, disorganized, and capital therefore suspicious. Meysenburg is not very hopeful either; he thinks of selling his waterworks.[109] I continued my abstracts at the archives, old Mr. Ellison assisting me with a great deal of kindness. The title of Diego de Vargas' Journal properly is: *El Diario de los Procedimientos del Gobernador y Capitan General del Reyno y Provincias del Nuebo México*. It begins in 1692 and continues at least until 1696.[110] At least thus far I could consult it. [Here Bandelier recorded additional notes.]

I made calls as fast as I could, preparatory to leave at last. Shall I ever return? It is impossible to tell. God alone knows! At all events I believe it will not be very soon, if ever. I leave Santa Fe as quietly as I came into it, four years ago, without noise and fussing at all, no state dinners nor banquets, hardly noticed by the papers. But the military is very kind. General Bradley volunteered a conveyance to Pecos. I had a long talk with Major Tucker,[111] about General Crook, and we agreed upon arranging some pretext for defending his last campaign publicly.[112]

JULY 13: Left at 6:30 A.M. in a buckboard, with young Anastasio Sandoval. At Peñas Negras, seven miles from Santa Fe, stopped and examined the ruin west of the road. It is a small one-house [block, or unit?] pueblo, with walls of adobe and little stone. It appears to have been but one story high. Cole has completely cleaned it out, excavating every room. Found some little pottery. The pueblo is small and could hardly have sheltered more than 100 souls. It stands on the very brow of a rocky hill fronting south and facing in that direction the steep pine clad heights of Peñas Negras, from whose base it is only separated by the periodic Arroyo de Peñas Negras.*

The arroyo empties into the Arroyo Hondo, so that the pueblo really belongs to the drainage system and group of the Arroyo Hondo. About a quarter-of-a-mile beyond, on the east of the Peñas Negras and [east] of the road, at what is called La Cruz del Pértigo there are traces of a ruin also on a knoll by the roadside. We reached Glorieta about 11 A.M., the road thither is destroyed partly by arroyos, but everything is as green and beautiful as it can be. Noticed an occasional small-house, on elevated spots beyond Glorieta.* They are much ruined and hardly any pottery is left on them. Reached Pecos at 12:30 A.M. [sic] and was most cordially and handsomely received by Father Mailluchet and by Mr. Rousse.

Pecos is a lovely spot, and now especially so, since everything is of the most intense green. The crops have been partly flooded, as the Pecos was higher last June than it was ever known to be before. Father Mailluchet's island is cut in twain by the still gushing and foaming current, but the valley is lovely. There are many remains of small houses here, some of which may have been summer houses of the Pecos, but the majority are too far away from the bottom, and are probably older. The bulk of the small ruins, however, is scattered along the foot of the grand, beautiful mesa, in the very high timber skirting its foot. These ruins which I noted already in 1880,[113] are undoubtedly very old,* and prior to the date of the large pueblos.

I am now told and even positively assured, on reliable authority, that there are two old ruins on the top of the mesa above Pecos. One is in the Valles de San Miguel and the other at the Ojo de la Vaca. Both are large-house type. They lie on tributaries of the Arroyo de San Cristóbal and consequently belong to the upper Galisteo group.* From the descriptions, they are large houses, probably of the two and three house variety. But they are described as being much destroyed. At Pecos, on the east side, Father Mailluchet opened a vault, which contained the bodies of a man and child. With the bodies he found a bone needle. On the east side of the Pecos, runs the Rio de la Vaca, east of it the Arroyo del Toro, and the latter joins the former above Fulton, where (at the Gusano) the Rio de la Vaca enters into the Rio Pecos. There are ruins on the Vaca and on the Toro, and on the former there is a fertile ciénega about five miles east of the Pecos Pueblo. This might possibly be the ciénega with the seven pueblos, spoken of in 1598, since there are some faint traces of ruins there. Company pleasant.

JULY 14: 1. Pueblo of Pecos. 2. Town of Pecos. 3. Pueblo de las Ruedas (Kingman). 4. Pueblo del Gusano (Fulton). 5. and 7. Ruins at San Miguel. 6. and 8. Ruins at San Antonio del Pueblo. 9. caves.

These caves are about three miles south-southeast of Pecos; they are described as not large, without partitions, but with traces of whitewashing. In the afternoon, we ascended to the top of the rocky ridge which separates the village on the south from the valley and houses on the north. There I found the observatory, partly natural, partly walled in.

Little is yet visible of it, but below we found arrowheads of red jasper, some obsidian, and pottery. The lookout is a good one, as small pine trees partly hide it, while the watcher has a full view all around. The mountains of Santa Fe (Baldy) are plainly visible and have streaks of snow on them; so has the Juanita. Left Pecos for Kingman at 4 P.M. with Father Mailluchet. We drove up to the ruins and then to the house of Ramón Archuleta. I visited the ruins. Northwest of the middle plaza, about 60 feet, separated by a depression and partly overgrown by trees (sabinos) I found ruins. They are much flattened, and there is one slight rubbish heap about the remnants of foundations.* Otherwise the ruins are the same as 18 months ago, only I found more pottery.

Spent the evening pleasantly, talking. Don Ramón Archuleta came here in 1842, and there were no Indians there any more. They had all left.[114] But the buildings were all intact, although the southern building had been abandoned long previous to the northern square pueblo. The arroyos have changed their course often in late years too. Don Ramón spoke of painted bowls excavated at the ruins, and of a number of small ruins scattered in the timber at the foot of the high mesa.

JULY 15: Handsome. It looks as if the statement of Father Mailluchet, that there would be no rainy season at all, would certainly be fulfilled. The country is beautifully green and very handsome; handsomer than ever. I reached [Las] Vegas at 8 A.M. and drove up to Father Coudert's where the reception was most cordial, but the house being full of priests on account of the commencement exercises of the Jesuit Academy,[115] I went to the Plaza Hotel and took rooms there. Saw Father Defouri,

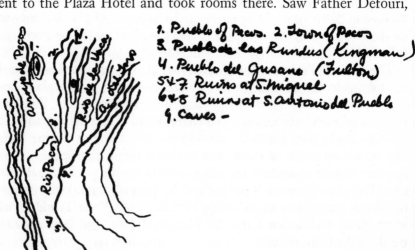

1. Pueblo of Pecos. 2. Town of Pecos.
3. Pueblo de las Rundus (Kingman)
4. Pueblo del Gusano (Fulton)
5 & 7. Ruins at S. Miguel
6 & 8. Ruins at S. Antonio del Pueblo
9. Caves —

Father Fayet,[116] and Father Ribera. The latter had a long confidential conversation whose contents I do not wish to put down here. On the street I met Father Personné and Father Baldassare[117] of Trinidad. Called on Mr. Blanchard.[118] Dr. Cunningham[119] is not here. I left Dr. Eggert's letter at the drug store. At night, wrote to Mr. Parkman and to Elliott. Also to Walter Neil. Was assured today that, a half-mile from Raton, there are traces of ruins, but the same party also assures me that he knows of no other remains of any kind, both in Colfax and Mora counties.

JULY 16: Most of the day was spent at Father Coudert's. He told me that the ciénega where Nazario Gonzales lives, or a place very nearby, is also called Ui-cu. This seems to be an Indian word. Called on Frank Kihlberg.[120] He is alone and always the same. Father Rivera also has not changed, but is sober now [in contrast to yesterday's time of confidences?]. This is my last day in New Mexico, perhaps forever. How many memories, good and bad! May God bring it to a favorable end. At night wrote to Dr. Eggert, for whom I have been unable to do anything at all. Got $30 in money on a draft.

JULY 17: Left Las Vegas at 8 A.M. The mountains soon reappeared, deeply snow-clad. The Sierra de Mora first, then to the north of it, opposite to Springer and due west of it, the Sierra Morena, with the white-clad peak of Taos forming its culminating point. Northeast of the Sierra Morena, and north-northwest of Springer, the Costilla, to which the Culebra is appended to the north, appeared partly snow-clad, and in very good plain view. After crossing the summit of the Ratones and descending, the Huajatoyas plainly and grandly loomed up north, and followed by the Trinchera to the southeast of it.*

The Spanish Peaks (or the Huajatoyas) are the advanced posts of the mountains to the east; they present their enormous masses plainly and seem to rise directly out of the plains east of them. Singular, they show no trace of snow, whereas the Trinchera is still deeply snow-clad.* The Spanish Peaks keep plainly in view afterwards, and the Cuerno Verde also looms up north of them, and between them, the Spanish Peaks, another distant mountain chain apparently running north and south also. The plain between Trinidad and La Junta is remarkably dry; it is the driest part of the whole route. Met B. Ruppe[121] at Trinidad, who went along to Garden City. At Timpas, Pike's Peak also appeared dimly in the far northwest.

July 18: Kansas very beautiful and rich in crops and green. Some improvements and growth are visible. Reached Topeka at 3 P.M. and made arrangements about Chico. Very hot and damp at Topeka. Delivered letter to Mrs. Ruppe from her husband.

July 19: Reached St. Louis at 7 P.M. Was at once bothered by reporters. Called on Pretorius and borrowed $5 from Mr. Thomann.

July 20: Reached home at 9 A.M.[122] Joe well and Papa too. All day quietly at home. Thank God, everything is allright so far. This closes my journey this time;[123] God has protected me wonderfully. He will now guide and protect me at home.

July 21: Spent the day in visiting. I am tired, but very glad and happy. I got a letter from Dr. Girard.

July 22: Letters from Hilder, Dr. Kinner, and Mr. A. Weber. Wrote cards to Ribera, Dr. Eggert, and O. Collet. Letters to George, to A. Weber, and to Mr. Thomann with $5 in it. At the office part of the time. Sent a copy of the *Fifth Annual Report* of the [Archaeological] Institute [of America][124] to Fort Craig to Lieutenant West. At night I went to the priest.

July 23: Sent Mr. Muenzenberger *Tenure of Lands, Social Organization;*[125] also to Donaciano Mápula and Captain Cándano. To all three, I sent the *Fifth Annual Report,* and the *Pecos* report,[126] to Muenzenberger, and to Don Urbáno Zubia. Layne Bernays[127] called. Sent to General Bradley *Pecos* report and *Fifth Annual* of Institute. To Captain Dougherty, *Fifth Annual Report,* also to Pradt [George, of Laguna, N.M.].
I got a telegram from Henry [Kaune] announcing the birth of Lizzie's girl [Alice Amalia Kaune] last night. Wrote at once to Henry and began writing to Pradt. At night, 19 *Cereus* open. F. Meckel[128] and Kersting came to see them and stayed until 10 P.M. Pleasant.

July 24: Was at the office. Wrote letters to Pradt and to Bishop Salpointe and mailed them. I also wrote cards to Sister Euphrasia, to Mrs. Black, to Dr. Thomas, to Jake Gold, to Governor Ritch, and to J. C. Pearce. I mailed *Fifth Annual Report* and *Pecos* to Bishop Salpointe, and *Fifth Annual Report* to Lieutenant Torrance and to Barthelmess.

Got letters from Mr. Parkman and from Henry. Continued in the afternoon. Calls from John Fischer and from Mrs. Balsiger. Wrote to Major Tucker about General Crook's [campaign].

JULY 25: Last night's storm was a very beneficial one. Letter from German consulate which I answered enclosing one of Cushing's [?] Wrote to Mr. Parkman and card to Greenleaf. Mailed to Eldodt report on *Pecos* and *Fifth Annual Report*, also a postal card. In the afternoon was called to Seybt's about coal (Krapp's deed and brick machine). Mali came home from Breese [probably from helping with the new Kaune baby].

JULY 26: Mail train late two hours. Wrote card to Cushing. Spent an hour with Graffenried at L. Appel's.[129] My drawings came from Boston. What a difference with those of this year! Mr. Balsiger dined with us. Painted in the afternoon.

JULY 27: On the whole a very dull day. Got a card from Hartmann, letter from Udo Brachvogel, and one from Peet[130] (of course, a petty, smallish proposition, to exchange old numbers of the *Antiquarian* for new ones. It is ridiculous, simply). In the afternoon went out to the farm and had an exceedingly pleasant time. Saw Cushing's pamphlet on Zuñi fetishes;[131] it is highly valuable. In the morning I painted, copying pottery. There is no doubt but that I have made progress, especially in the treatment of shadows and, therefore, shapes.

JULY 28: One of the convent sisters died today. About 10 A.M. news came that Mathias Kircher had been crushed by a wall of clay falling. He survived until evening and then he died. He was the successor to poor Charles [Lambelet]! Wrote to Udo Brachvogel, to Dr. Kinner, to Hilder, card to Peet! [I also wrote] to Henry Holgate. My saddle, blankets, etc., etc. came. Poor Chico, I will have to sell him at last. Painted a little. Uncle Bernard Suppiger took supper with us. Evening clear but sultry. Papa had, of course, disagreeable business news.

JULY 29: Letters: to Elliott, with my picture, to S. T. Reed,[132] with that of me and my wife. Exceedingly quiet in town all around. Yesterday I got some new paints which are quite hard and useful. Card from Hartmann. Painted and wrote.

July 30: I painted, and I got a letter from Hilder. At nightfall, a visit from Dr. Schloetzer.

July 31: Painted the whole day. Slow work. No letters.

AUGUST

August 1: Got letters this morning from Hartmann, with draft of map. From Pradt, with vocabulary. Valuable additions by him. From West and from Meysenburg. Wrote to E. C. Springer, with old coal mine titles. Saw Seybt! Allright so far.

August 2: Painted and wrote. Complaints of Papa as usual. No letters of any importance.

August 3: In the afternoon went to Graffenried's and to Wachsmuth. Very pleasant.

August 4: Left for St. Louis at 6:45 A.M. I went to George and to Dick Hospes. Very kind reception. Afterwards called on Dr. Alt and on Miss Matilda Meysenburg.[133] Arranged to go out to Mr. Robert Carr's[134] tomorrow. Returned, called on Collet. Evening with Hospes to 12:00 [o'clock]. Streif. Pleasant. George came along.

August 5: Beautiful again. Drove out to Mr. Carr's with Miss Matilda Meysenburg. It is eight miles drive, through Forest Park. Very pleasant. Inside of the timber, low mounds appeared. Reception kind and very agreeable. A handsome farm. Returning, we called on Mrs. Clementine Meysenburg.[135] Met David Ball. Called at the library. Evening pleasantly at George's.

August 6: Returned home. My 44th birthday! Letters from Cushing, etc.

August 7 & 8: Finished to correct the map for Hartmann and mailed it. Left for Breese, Friday at 3:20 P.M. and got there about 6 P.M. Very kind and pleasant reception.

August 9 & 10: Stayed at Breese. Gustav [Bandelier] came Saturday evening. Pleasant all around; only Henry was ill. Got better on Sunday.

AUGUST 11 TO 15: Returned on Monday, in time to be bothered by Papa's usual complaints. Was ill in consequence of it. Bilious, feverish, etc. Papa is ill too. Wrote to Dr. Girard; cards to Greenleaf and to Consul Baum. Got few letters. Painted a good deal. But I was sick and unable to do any writing of consequence.

AUGUST 16: Clear, very hazy, and warm. E. C. Springer came last night, and we had a long and serious talk.[136] He left this morning. At the office the usual discouragement. It becomes very monotonous, but we must stand it. Finished my letter to Hartmann and mailed it. Commenced to write to Dr. Eggert. In the evening Mr. Streif's Ida came.

AUGUST 17: The whole day is very quiet and dull. Card from Hartmann. Spent the day with Streif pleasantly.

AUGUST 18: Clear, and warmer. Papa's birthday today. Across the street, the usual discouragement and dejection prevails. It is almost insufferable. Not the slightest energy or vim, only apathy and cowardice. Wrote to Dr. Eggert and to Henry. Wrote and mailed. Agreed to go to the coal mine this evening and to Belleville in the morning. I went to the mine and found everything in very good condition. But it would be imprudent to sell land now. Reported to Seybt.

AUGUST 19: Clear, but very stifling and sultry. Went to the city and got good news in regard to the coal mine. They are not very splendid, far from it, but still they are good in relation to what I used to hear. $2500 are paid off on the debts, and the notes of $3500 on the Lindell Glass Co. is not lost. The debts now amount to $10,200, and I hope to reduce it to $9000 up to the first of October. Went to Belleville. Very kind reception, especially by Dr. Patrick.[137] His aims are exceedingly sensible and true. But he stays up too long entirely.

AUGUST 20: Unwell. Useless talk and running after absent people. Spent evening pleasantly at Bunsen's.[138]

AUGUST 21: A little less sultry. Had a long talk with G. Hilgard[139] and with Ropeiquet [Ropiquet].[140] Land reported good, and also its future prospects. Took dinner at E; Abend [evening] with Governor Korner [Koerner].[141] Afternoon at Dr. Patrick's. His collection is really handsome, so is also that of Mr. Hilgard. Many flint hoes and shovels.

One fetish! Nearly every implement now used is represented in flint and stone, and well executed.

AUGUST 22: Very sick. Spent the day at East St. Louis. Very unwell. Slept awhile at F. Busson's,[142] but awoke much worse. Saw F. This, but did nothing.

AUGUST 23: Was very sick on Saturday. In bed all day. On Sunday felt better, but bad news has agitated me greatly. Today we at last came to a final resolve, and I am going to try a last resort. God grant a good end may turn up after so many years. Circus today. Papa went with the children. Finished writing to Mr. Hebler.[143] Am down, but much quieter, though weak. Painted and wrote till 10 P.M.

AUGUST 26: Letter from Dr. Eggert. Painted mostly. Mailed letters to Collet and to Padre Ribera; cards to Streiff and to Dr. Eggert.

AUGUST 27: Went to Mr. Rod. Graffenried.[144] He was terribly shocked, but told me not to give up yet. He promises aid. I am somewhat relieved; still it is terrible, terrible. And had I been listened to in time, had I not been constantly hampered and held down in the most cruel manner, this would not have happened.[145] But poor dear Joe! Why must she suffer also!

AUGUST 28: Left for St. Louis. It rained hard. Talked to Hospes. He also says, "Do not give up." Saw Bohn and August Becker. Returned home tired and worn out.

AUGUST 29: Mr. Graffenried came early and gave us 15,000 [Swiss] francs. Good, noble, friend. I wrote to Hospes.

AUGUST 30: Left at 9:35 A.M.[146] Oh, my God, help me. Poor Joe! Was all alone in the car until Indianapolis. Then a few passengers came in. It had rained until to the limits of Indiana and Illinois, that is, to the Wabash River. East of it was all dry and dusty.

AUGUST 31: Crossed the Alleghanies [sic] in clear weather. But how tame the scenery, in comparison with the mountains west. Reached New York at 10:20 P.M., a clear, cool handsome night. Took quarters at the Belvedere.

SEPTEMBER

SEPTEMBER 1: Went to the chemical, and apparently spoiled everything by telling the whole truth. Perhaps not. Called on Richard C., on N. Ponce de León,[147] and on Mr. Ottendorfer, who was very kind. Went to bed at 8 P.M. No word from Professor Ware.[148]

SEPTEMBER 2: Got a definitive negative answer from Mr. Williams, but also a letter to his broker, L. Thomas, #31 Nassau Street, Room 6. They think they can do something. Called on Frank Squier,[149] and he came at 3 P.M. and looked at my pictures. Very favorable opinion. Wrote home and to Hospes. Called on Mr. Christian. Retired at 8 P.M.

SEPTEMBER 3: No reply from Thomas as yet. Called on Garrison[150] of *The Nation*, who was exceedingly kind. Saw Mr. Rittich of the *Staatszeitung* who advises me strongly in favor of the novel.[151] So does Garrison. Returned at 7 P.M. and went to bed at once.

SEPTEMBER 4: Stayed at home until noon, and then I went down town to hear my judgment. But when I was about to start, Valentini[152] came into my room quite unexpectedly. Was very glad to see him. Went to Lieutenant Thomas. No reply as yet. Reported at the bank, and then home. Wrote to Joe, dear, good, poor Joe. Spent evening quietly but agreeably with Valentini.

SEPTEMBER 5: Did not go down town. Called on Mr. Lathrop. Feel miserable and dejected. The constant strain is almost too much for me. Went to bed at 1 P.M., but I could not sleep at all. Afterwards got up, feeling very miserable. At 5 P.M. a dispatch came, that the bonds were sold at 92%, and soon after the statement came also. Thank God. Felt happy, and yet weak. Wrote home and to Hospes. Made a short call at Mr. Lathrop's. Met Mr. [G. H.] Braun.

SEPTEMBER 6: Went to Thomas and the bank, to adjust matters. Called on Mr. Ottendorfer, Frank Squier, and C. B. R[Rittich?]. and C[Christian?]. Kind. Went to bed early, after a pleasant talk with Señor Cusa of Bellinzona.

SEPTEMBER 7: Passed a few quiet hours with Valentini; started for Boston at 4:30 P.M.; and reached there at 10:30 P.M. God, God, help me now!

SEPTEMBER 8: Called at the [Boston] Museum and then, as it was still closed, to Cambridge. Everybody is away. Found Greenleaf at last. Polite, but officially only. Spent a miserable evening again. Wrote home and to Mr. Parkman. Met Mr. Scudder.[153]

SEPTEMBER 9: Went out to the [Peabody] Museum, painting all day (that is until 2 P.M.) at the fine old jar from Cochiti. But the heat and sultriness became too much, and so I rode back to town and to the [Boston] Museum. No letters as yet, from no place whatever. It is distressing in the extreme. Saw my poor Mexican book[154] at last [in press]; the text is fair; but the illustrations are, to say the least, of the most ordinary kind. It is all printed; as to the pictures, I do not know whether they are all done or not.

Retired to my room early, and sat down to write these lines, of sorrow, pain, and disgust. Oh God, my God! Will You never relieve me of a part of my sufferings. And Joe, poor, dear, good Joe! Oh, have mercy upon us at last! Sat up until nearly 10 P.M., writing on my novel.

SEPTEMBER 10: Slept, passably at least. Many musquitoes about, but not very troublesome. Morning too bright only! It announces another frightfully sultry day. Not a breeze is stirring. Found an exceedingly friendly letter of Mr. Parkman to which I replied for tomorrow. I went out to Cambridge and saw the University Press again. Then I copied the jar. At 6 P.M. we had another shower, but the day was terrible. (Thermometer at 98°) Found another card from Mr. Parkman. I hope a little, but that same feeling has deceived me so often, that I cannot trust it at all. God will tell me all tomorrow. Wrote at my novel for a while.

SEPTEMBER 11: I sent a postal card home, and one to Mr. G. H. Braun. Mr. Parkman came, good and kind as ever, and we arranged for me to come out to Jamaica Plain tomorrow. I went to the Museum and got a letter from Joe, dear, good Joe. Thank God for it and for every line in it! Then I went out to Cambridge and painted. Had a talk with Mr. Allen of Johns Hopkins University but tried to reveal nothing. Then I returned to Boston. Returned to my room at 6 P.M. to write. I drew $20 today. Wrote a few lines to Joe. Finally got a painless diarrhea.

SEPTEMBER 12: Diarrhea violent all night. Went to the Museum, took my drawings, and called on Mr. S. P. N. Triscott, #433 Washington Street. Met Mr. Linton and Buehler there. They gave me some advice, but only diffuse. The thing is new to them entirely. Returned home and arranged matters according to sections. I am too weak to go to Cambridge, and therefore prefer to rest previous to leaving for Jamaica Plain. God grant that my drawings may "draw"! Reached Jamaica Plain at 5 P.M. and spent a very pleasant evening.

SEPTEMBER 13: Wrote nearly all day. In the afternoon I drove to Cambridge with Mr. Parkman.

SEPTEMBER 14: I spent the whole day at Mr. Parkman's. We called, after a beautiful walk over and through splendid grounds, on Mr. Lyman,[155] and met there Mr. Lowell. In the afternoon I wrote to Major Tucker and to Lieutenant West. Evening most splendid, though cold, and every appearance of a frost for tomorrow. Finished Chapter II of my novel today. Mr. Parkman admired my drawings very much. He is of opinion that they are very saleable.

SEPTEMBER 15: Got letters from Joe and from Papa this morning. All right, thank God. Then went to Cambridge, mailed my letters, and finally found a fair room at #28 Holyoke Street, Mrs. Cowdin. Met Putnam[156] who is home for a few days. Called on the Misses Riekli at Cambridge.

SEPTEMBER 16: Sunday I had begun to write to Lieutenant Scott. I went to the Boston Museum and had a short talk with Greenleaf. Then to Cambridge, and spent until 3 P.M. at the Peabody painting. Putnam is there, but he is unwell. Finished letter to Scott, wrote to Joe, and to Professor Norton. Poor, dear Joe. Mailed my letters. Began to write my report.

SEPTEMBER 17: Wind somewhat abated. Was struck by a name. (What's in a name?) St. Ermenigilde. Herrmansgilde, the guild of war men! (Order of the Bow, among the early Germans!)[157] Musquitoes very troublesome all night. I went to the University Press and got my Mexican report, then to the library, where Mr. Justin Winsor received me most politely and allowed me to take a book home. I took therefore: *Apostólicos Afanes de la Compañia de Jesús, escritos por un Padre de la misma Sagrada Religion de su Provincia de Mexico*, Barcelona, 1754. The author appears to have been Francisco Xavier Fluvía. Speaks of Indians of the Nayarit. [Here, Bandelier added notes on his reading.]

SEPTEMBER 18: Returned the print of my Mexican report to the University Press; then copied somewhat, and afterwards went to the Peabody Museum. [Additional notes occupied pages 128 through part of 151 (front and back) covering the period September 18 through October 1. These notes were on several volumes from the Peabody Library. Aside from these notes there were only minor references to the painting of specimens and occasional weather reports.]

OCTOBER

OCTOBER 2: Messquitoes bad overnight. Went to the University Press, then to Professor Norton; then to Agassiz,[158] who treated me very badly. Much discouraged and dejected. Still, I trust God will keep me above water. No letters. I remained at Cambridge until the 7 A.M. [train?]; then went to Newport. Much discouraged, dispirited, and disheartened.

OCTOBER 15: Thus far I have not achieved anything. But Dr. Moore[159] and Mr. Garrison have been excellent friends to me. I saw Mr. H. G. Marquand[160] at Newport, Professor A. Marquand[161] at Princeton, and they hold out but little inducement. Still I do not give up all my hopes yet. Wrote home yesterday, after my return from Princeton.

Saturday I wrote a review for The Nation, but it may not be accepted. I was in a very grim mood when I wrote it and therefore very ill disposed. It is exceedingly cold, and there is great political excitement in town. E. E. Olcott of San Elena, Sonora, got married, [at] last in pomp and state. Well, God bless him and may he and his wife never have to go through what Joe and I have had, and still have, to suffer. It is fearful, but God has his reasons for it.

[Bandelier continued here with notes on volumes from the Lenox Library, New York City.][162]

Called on Mr. [Henry] Dronne, when Professor West and Mr. Arnold came. Very pleasant and hopeful interview. They are to call a meeting. Thank God. Wrote home and to Mr. Parkman. A gleam of hope at last. [Presumably, these remarks pertained to possibilities regarding Bandelier's paintings and manuscripts. It is possible, though not probable, that the comments related to potential solutions to the family business problems in Highland.]

NOVEMBER

OCTOBER 16—NOVEMBER 5: I have not been able to keep my journal, owing to dejection, turmoil, business, and everything else. I draw a veil over my stay at New York; it is useless to comment upon it. Times are dark, very dark, and threatening. Still, there are some redeeming features. At the Geographical Society at New York, I found the earliest map which contains any data about New Mexico to be *Ptolomeo, la Geografía* by Messr. Pietro Andrea Mattioló Senese Medico. 1548. (This is the copy partly gone over with ink.) [Other notes followed.]

I returned home [to Highland, Illinois] on the 30th at 7 P.M. and finished my lecture, mailing it to Dr. Moore on the second (Saturday, P.M.). I also wrote to Hospes three times, with note and $55 interest. I wrote to Springer twice, to Bishop Salpointe, to Charley Elliott, to Governor Ritch, to Father Grom, to Father Mailluchet, to Dr. Eggert, to John Pearce, to Dr. Moore, to Greenleaf, to J. H. Gerdes. Mr. De Graffenried lent me $200 for the note of Brewerton; it was a hard job, but thank God, he showed the way to succeed. My drawings I left with National Fire Insurance Company, #60 Wall Street, New York. I also corrected a manuscript for E. A. Allen of Cincinnati, Ohio, and sent it back to him on the 4th, A.M. Wrote to Murray and Andrews and to Henry on the 5th. Election, but the result as yet is uncertain. Weather is ugly. Papa, very ill-humored.

NOVEMBER 6: I wrote to Epitacio Paredes, Magdalena, Sonora; Don Joaquín,[163] Greenleaf, and Cushing. [Grover M.] Cleveland's election [as President of the United States] confirmed. Called at Dr. Knoebel's at night. Address of Rudolph Minor, #298 South Street, New York City, New York. Some excitement in town over election results.

NOVEMBER 7: Johnny Bruckner died at 3 A.M. Letter from G. S. I., from Murray and Andrews, and from Dr. Moore, a receipt. My lecture came too late. Great excitement in town on account of election. J. Bruckner died.

NOVEMBER 8: I went to St. Louis, and I paid off the note of Brewerton. Coal meeting very satisfactory. Henry came to take leave. Good boy; he is exceedingly affectionate. Everything about the mine is promising. J[ohn] B[ruckner] was buried.

NOVEMBER 10: Left at 9:30 A.M.[164] It was sad to leave poor Joe and poor old Papa! But it must be.

NOVEMBER 13: Arrived at New York at 8 P.M. on Tuesday, and Dr. Mohr came to the hotel at once. On Wednesday, I had a busy day. Attended to business down town, got my drawings, and then went to the Lenox Library, where I found my books [Mexican Report] and letter from Greenleaf. Left one copy at the Library; [sent] one to Don Joaquín, one to Governor Ritch, and one to Dr. Eggert. At Lenox and Mr. Dronne's, very satisfactory reports. Spent evening at Dr. Mohr's, #201 Clinton Street, Brooklyn, with Mr. Bill Willis. On Thursday early, Professor Ware called. I left on board the [S. S.] Lessing[165] at 2:30 P.M. We have 24 cabin passengers only, and 100 steerage passengers. Very pleasant. Sea quiet and fresh. Among the passengers there is Mr. Armand Guys, a Frenchman, of Boston. Henry P. Bradley, of Bangor, Maine; and E. McCormick, of Boston.

NOVEMBER 18: Until today noon, we have made 1542 miles in four days and 19 and one-half hours. We ate, this noon, in latitude 47° 56′ and longitude 40° 19′. The sea is beautiful, the ship rolls, but still it is remarkably handsome, and not too cold. All the passengers are slowly recovering from sea sickness; as for me, I was never so well. Passed three steamers. Spent the evening with Dr. Hahn.[166] It grows warmer.

NOVEMBER 19: It had been raining and kept on raining. Motion of ship bad; pitching as well as rolling, very difficult to write. Today 302 miles. Total, 1844 in five days and 19 and one-half hours. The latitude is 49° 20′; the longitude is 30° 1′. Now there is less motion.

NOVEMBER 20: Excellent night, but suffered from asthma. Going more rapidly. At noon, 269 miles. Total 2112 in six days and 19 and one-half hours. Going more at a latitude of 50° 7′ north and longitude of 26° 11′ west. In the afternoon, quieter and handsome, but the gulls have almost completely disappeared, only three to four being visible and following. Spent last evening pleasantly with Dr. Hahn; began telling the tale of the Poor Boy of Pinaua. The doctor spoke enthusiastically of Brazil.

NOVEMBER 21: All the passengers at the lunch table. We sail 14 knots again. At noon 293 miles. Total 2405 in 6 days, 19 and one-half hours. The latitude is 50° 4′ and the longitude is 18° 34′, in seven days and 19 and one-half hours at sea. Last evening at the doctor's, very fine and pleasant. Slept ten hours. Met two ships.

NOVEMBER 22: Sea beautiful. Passed two steamers. Reverend Mr. Schmidt, Rajahmundry, East India. Reverend R. Andersen, #193 Ninth Street, near Third Avenue, Brooklyn, New York. Lecture on the Vedas, by Reverend H. C. Schmidt—a very interesting man. He gave me an East Indian idol and a bracelet. I mailed today four letters; two to Garrison, one to Joe, and one to Mr. Dronne. At noon, latitude 49° 50′, longitude 10° 24′, 315 miles. Total course 2720 miles, eight days and 19 and one-half hours.

NOVEMBER 23: Awoke in sight of Plymouth. The English coast is beautifully green; the sky is clouded but quiet, and the channel beautiful. We crossed the channel and, after 2 P.M., came in sight of Alderney and Jersey [probably Guernsey]. The latter is one hour's sail from France. Behind Jersey, the French coast appeared, low, but crowned by a ceja of rocky hills covered with a brushy vegetation. The harbor of Cherbourg is beautifully and picturesquely fortified, but, with the exception of a few modern forts, they are all rock fortifications that would not stand before a thorough modern fire. There is only one ironclad in the harbor. We landed, in a small tug, at 4:30 P.M. and went to the Hotel de l'Aigh et d'Angleterre. Quaint, but pleasant. There is a beautiful equestrian statue of Napoleon I on the Quai, and there is a bust of Bricqueville almost in front of the hotel. We went to the theater, where they gave the Masque de Fu and Les Mousquetaines au couvent. The theater is most beautiful, and the costumes are correct. The main actress as the Mosquetain was lamentably hoarse. Poor girl, she cried. French officers were very handsome and tastefully dressed.

NOVEMBER 24: Left Cherbourg at 8:30 A.M. Original and picturesque scenery. Quaint Norman houses, large orchards, and small fields. Parcellation carried into extremes. I noticed the peculiar style of houses* with the two gable chimneys, which characterizes our own older style at home. It appears to have been originally Norman. Passed Caen, a city of 45,000 inhabitants, Lisieux, finally Mantes, with its beautiful cathedral. It rained nearly all the time. Reached Paris at 5:20 P.M. Strolled about. Stayed at the Hotel de la Commune. Guys and Henry R. Bradley with me.

NOVEMBER 25: Left Paris at 8:55 A.M. Passed Fountainbleau, San Florentin, Tonnerre, Dijon, Dole, and reached Pontarlier at 7:48 P.M. Deep snow on the pine-clad hills of the Franche Comté. Pontarlier is a quaint and queer looking place. I stopped at the Hotel de Paris where I met a Mr. Ernest Christen of Basle [Basel], and spent evening with him.

NOVEMBER 26: Left Pontarlier at 6:55 A.M. The country until Auvernier, above which place the Lake of Neuchatel bursts into view, is very picturesque, although covered with deep snow. The mountains are higher than I supposed they would look (the Jena); the gorges are picturesque; and the tall pine trees grow on the slopes until to the very bottom of the brook; and the railroad winds itself on dizzy precipices. At Neuchatel everything is covered with snow. Met Dr. Virchau[167] on the train. Reached Berne at 11:20 A.M. and went to Mr. Hebler. Exceedingly kind reception, but when I told the truth, there was little hope. So with Mr. Aebi. Oh, my God!

NOVEMBER 27: With the most discouraging prospects, I went to G. H. and Company [Gruner-Haller and Company] and told everything. No reply, of course. In the afternoon I went with Mr. Hebler to the café, where I met Professor B. Studer,[168] Mr. Moschard, and Mr. Boivin. Then to the Museum of Natural History, where I talked to Professor Studer. In the evening at Alphonse's [probably Bandelier's cousin, Alphonse Bandelier].

NOVEMBER 28: Morning with Berchthold Haller and with Edmond de Fellenburg. How different. Mr. Hebler is very much discouraged. In the afternoon, at 4 P.M., Berchthold Haller called for me, and so we went together across the Tiefenau Bridge to the Enge and back. In the evening, I talked with Mr. Hebler and with Alphonse.

NOVEMBER 29: Very, very despondent. Mr. Hebler regards any salvation utterly impossible. I am getting fairly crazy, and see no hope but in suicide. This is awful. In the afternoon, I went with Berchthold to the historical museum, where we met Edmond. It is very beautiful. Then to Dalp, and to F. Lips, where I left 30 plates for examination. The night was spent with Alphonse. Horrible, horrible.

NOVEMBER 30: Today, will, to some extent, decide. We held the con-

ference at 11:30 A.M., Mr. Hebler, Alphonse, Mr. Mauderli, and Mr.
Burckhardt. The result was not absolutely unfavorable. Still it is difficult, exceedingly difficult. Alphonse is brilliant and beautifully devoted
in every respect. I spent the evening with him and had it very pleasant.
The weather is turning cold.

DECEMBER

DECEMBER 1: Had a good night. Feel better, but still in much doubt.
It is better for me to go to Geneva and await further developments
there. I went to the city library with Berchthold. Pleasant reception.
They have little on America, except the description of Guyana, pub-
lished at Berne in 1670. Afterwards I went to Mr. Lips, who asks 200
francs for each plate. My cold is far better. Spent the evening at the
Café Mutzenberg with Berchthold, Edmond, Dr. Bloas, Professor
Vetter, and Mr. de Rodt. Pleasant. Wrote home.

DECEMBER 2: I went to Alphonse at 10 A.M. He showed me the interior
of the Erlacher-Hof. I then went to Professor Studer, who received me
most charmingly, and with whom I spent a pleasant hour. Afterwards to
F. Lips, leaving all my drawings there, in order to have him make a
selection. [Notes on the Guyana manuscript follow.]
   There is a map, on which is Parime Lacus and at its northwestern
edge name: Manoa o el Dora. It is a pamphlet intending to encourage
emigration to Guyana. I returned home and had another conversation
with Mr. Hebler. Went to the Café d'Jura and met Edmond de Fellenburg. There is a Spanish chargé d'affaires here. A good deal depends
again upon tonight's talk. If unsuccessful—but—I dare hardly think of
it! There is a map of Sanson[169] at the library, dated 1650, which has
Santa Fé, Taos, etc., etc., and a map of 1703, on which there is Casas
Grandes! I shall see more of it tomorrow.

DECEMBER 3: Ugly weather, as usual. Wrote home. Conference with
Hebler, Gruner and Company, and with Alphonse at night. No result.
There is an evident tendency to withdraw on the part of Gruner-Haller
and Company, and Hebler also is weak and shaking. Alphonse alone
stands firm.

DECEMBER 4: The same gloomy and dreary atmosphere. Called on
Gruner-Haller and Company. They were very energetic in appearance

and threatened to compel liquidation. I left for Geneva at noon. Reached Geneva at 4:45 P.M.

DECEMBER 5: Had a long conversation with Moisé. His advice is to go to Berne at once, call on Mr. de Bùren and ask of him a letter of introduction to A. Chenevier[?] and Company here. I stayed at Geneva overnight. Left for Berne late in the afternoon.

DECEMBER 6: I fail to write impressions of today. Mr. de Bùren is a perfect gentleman; the others are cowards and fools. It was a horrible day, but I stood it—thank God! I have at last the cooperation of Mr. de Bùren. He promised it fully.

DECEMBER 7: When the train issued from the tunnel of Chexbres [?], the lake and mountains were magnificent beyond all description. James met me at the depot, and we went home together. I feel somewhat relieved and quieter.

DECEMBER 8: In the meantime I kept on corresponding with Alphonse and with home. At Berne, the horizon cleared up considerably but slowly; they are taking their time of course. In the business, there is nothing new, except that Fritz Ryhiner makes a fool of himself again. I hope to get even with that dirty dog yet. Here, always the same kindness and affection. I made acquaintances, Mr. Limer, Mr. Révillior, Dr. H. Gosse, Professor C. Vogt, and a number of political gentlemen. The museums are very handsome in part, and the Ariana of Mr. Révillior is magnificent. Of course, while it is pleasant here, there is always a pressure within. Absence from home, fear, etc., etc., are unavoidable. Adolphe is here;[170] he is charming beyond all measure.

DECEMBER 26: [Bandelier's next entry after that of December 8]: Letters from home and from Alphonse. Wrote to Alphonse and home also. It [the situation] is again exceedingly dark, and it is hardly possible to write. I am much dejected, thinking of my poor folks at home. The day is cold, and I am unwell. Took magnesia which helped a good deal, but still I am not well. Took a walk in the afternoon and then to the theater, after having seen a Christmas tree at Camps! I went with James and Héléne, Brun [?] and Jeanne, and Adolphe. The play was *Babolin*, fairly rendered. Returned, late as usual.

DECEMBER 27: No letters at all. In the afternoon, Adolphe and I went to visit Mr. Charles Desgranges who showed us his manufactory of pottery. The material is imported from Germany and from the Jura. Part yellow clay, part burnt lime, part sand. Everything by machinery. Night at the city with Adolphe; very nice and pleasant.

DECEMBER 28: In the afternoon, we started on foot for Bossey, James, Adolphe, Mr. Rouge, and Mr. Burdallet. Returned at nightfall, and then went over to Geneva with Adolphe. Nice, but quarrelled with N [?].

DECEMBER 29: Very ill. Bile came up at last. Remained in bed nearly all day. Letters from Alphonse. Fair, though nothing positive yet.

DECEMBER 30: Called on Mr. Desfro, and visited his manufactory for refining gold dust. In the afternoon, Adolphe and I went to Geneva to buy presents. Got 140 francs from Berne. Evening at James's. Am much better. Card from [Lieutenant] Breisacher.

DECEMBER 31: Weather alike [cloudy, chilly, and quiet].

NOTES—PREFACE

1. An unsigned note, "Bandelier Material Enriches School Library," in the *El Palacio* of August-September, 1937, briefly announced the arrival of various items of Bandelieriana, according to the will of Fanny R. Bandelier who died in Nashville in the fall of 1936. The most significant part of the collection was the series of notebooks, extending from 1880 to 1907 and containing his journal pages for those years. (*El Palacio* 1937: 49-50.)

2. These notations on the weather undoubtedly reflected an early interest of Bandelier's. Goad (1938: 78) stated that "Bandelier showed his scientific bent by publishing in the *Bote*, . . . a series of meteorological observations. The last of these articles was published in *Die Union* in January, 1869." The Smithsonian Institution (1874: 92) reported that A. F. Bandelier, Jr., made observations for Highland, Illinois, for the period of 1860-64. An earlier report of the Smithsonian (1864: 65) had listed him as Adolphus F. Bandelier jr., making observations for Highland, Illinois, Madison County, 38' 45" North Latitude, 89' 46" West Longitude, using the barometer, thermometer, and psychrometer. It was noted that it was fairly common for scientists of that period to do this. Dr. George Engelmann reputedly kept meteorological records over a period of 47 years, a longer period, it is believed, than that of any one man in America. (National Academy of Science 1902: 9; also footnote for entry of October 16, 1883.)

NOTES—INTRODUCTION

1. White (1940: I, 2n4) stated that Bandelier once wrote Charles Eliot Norton (December 27, 1889) that von Humboldt was "one of the four men who had wielded the greatest influence upon my inner and outer life, and my scientific career in particular." In this regard it might be pointed out that von Humboldt had travelled in the southwestern United States and, in 1855, had written a report on the geology of Mt. Taylor, the Zuñi area, and the San Francisco Mountains (De Terra 1955: 354). Bandelier must surely have known of this research, and it may well have influenced him in choosing fields of work in later years.

It is interesting to speculate on the identities of the other three men who so greatly influenced Bandelier's life, or career, unnamed insofar as we are aware. Undoubtedly, Lewis H. Morgan would have been one; quite probably, Joaquín García Icazbalceta was another; but the fourth individual would be difficult to select. However, it is quite conceivable that Bandelier would have considered his father as the fourth person. Particularly in the 1870's, as Bandelier was gaining status as an established scholar, he repeatedly mentioned to Morgan that his father had critically read various manuscripts and had discussed and argued points of interpretation (White 1940: I, 87-88). Hobbs (1940b) credited the senior Bandelier with stimulating the spirit of scientific inquiry in his son in childhood. Another possible candidate for the fourth influential person was Frank H. Cushing; there may well have been others who could have been so designated by Bandelier.

2. Aside from major monographs, Bandelier, in the 1870's wrote reviews, comments, and brief notes published primarily in *The Nation*. White (1940: I, 105) compiled a list of nine such items. In the accompanying bibliography of this volume, they may be found under Bandelier's name, designated as follows: 1874-78, 1877b, 1878b, 1878c, 1879b, 1879c, 1879d, 1879e, and 1880b.

3. Anderson, in an article on Santa Fe at the time of Bandelier's first visit, gave a population of 6,635 for the city. A gas system would not be installed until late in 1880;

a water system was still two years away. Railway travel to Santa Fe had only been possible since February 9, 1880, only six months prior to Bandelier's trip (1947: 107-110).

4. The full title of this work was *Histoire de la colonisation et des missions du Sonora, Chihuahua, Nouveau Méxique et Arizona, jusqu'á l'an 1700.* There were 1,400 foolscap pages in French and 400 watercolor drawings, comprising four volumes and an atlas. As noted in our first volume (Lange and Riley 1966: 52n36), the text portion of the manuscript had been the object of a futile search extending over several decades. In June 1964, the missing volume was found in a room of unclassified manuscripts by Alberto Magistri, a worker in the Vatican Library. Magistri had been instructed to keep a watch out for the manuscript by Father Ernest J. Burrus, Institutum Historicum, S. J. (Burrus 1966.) At present, Father Burrus is editing the *Histoire* for publication.

NOTES

1883

1. This Ciénega is in the Abo-Manzano area rather than the Santa Fe area.

2. Bandelier had known Padre Louis Bourdier at Manzano in 1882. (Lange and Riley 1966: 386, 388.) Bandelier met him again at Manzano as he started his travels in 1883. However, in his July 2, 1884, entry, Bandelier wrote, "Met Father Bourdier, he is at Belen now." Salpointe (1898: 282) listed him as one of the priests added by Bishop Lamy to the New Mexico clergy. He was ordained in 1868. (Chávez 1957: 134.)

3. In the first volume (Lange and Riley 1966), this name was spelled as Gromm. Salpointe (1898: 282) listed him as Ignacio Maria Grom who was brought to New Mexico by Bishop Lamy. Chávez (1957: 259) listed him as M. I. Grom, noting that he served at Belen from May 1822 [sic; this would have been at least 1852, and, possibly, later]—April 1884.

4. This was W. Henry Brown, Santa Fe photographer, "west side of the plaza, upstairs," with whom Bandelier had worked almost since his arrival in the Southwest in 1880. Various directories of the time and other references mentioned Brown often alone and again together with G. C. Bennett. (Lange and Riley 1966: 72n57; *Santa Fe Daily New Mexican*, July 12, 1882, p. 4; McKenney 1882-83: 339.)

5. Charles Eliot Norton (1827-1908), scholar and man of letters, was an idealist and reformer by temperament, who exhibited remarkable energy in a wide range of activity. Born in Cambridge, Massachusetts, and graduated from Harvard in 1846, he opened a night school in Cambridge; he was director of a housing experiment in Boston. He worked zealously as an editor for the Union cause and was co-editor of the *North American Review* and one of the founders of *The Nation* (1865). From 1874 to 1898, he lectured on the history of art at Harvard, where he was one of the most popular teachers of the day and an "oracle of the humanities." A friend of many literary greats, including Carlyle, Emerson, Ruskin, Longfellow, and Lowell, he contributed valuable editions of their letters and other biographical material.

Norton also wrote on art and edited collections of poetry, notably the poetry of John Dunne (1895, 1905). Probably his best literary work was his prose translation of the

Divine Comedy (1891-92). (See Encyclopedia Britannica 1967: XVI, 642.) Norton was the founder and first president of the Archaeological Institute of America, in the program of which, he favored classical archaeology over that of the Americas.

6. This individual was erroneously identified in our first volume (Lange and Riley 1966: 387-88) through a misinterpretation of Bandelier's handwriting. His "u" became "ri" with the help of a small speck on the page; this, together, with Bandelier's phonetic use of "ss" rather than "sz," resulted in Kriss rather than Kusz. With the correction made, Charles L. Kusz, Jr., has emerged from a variety of sources as a prominent figure in the Manzano area. Green (1882: 181) noted Kusz as postmaster, the office at Manzano having been established February 28, 1881; also noted was Kusz & Co., Assayers, Surveyors, etc. Kusz was the Commissioner for Valencia County in 1884. For that year, Polk and Danser (1884a: 337) listed Kusz as postmaster and also as a livestock breeder, real estate dealer, and proprietor of the "Gringo and Greaser," a newspaper. Anderson (1907: I, 241-42) added, "The assassination of Charles L. Kusz, Jr., editor of the *Gringo and Greaser* at Manzano, Valencia County, on March 26, 1884, caused high feelings throughout New Mexico. The editor was killed while seated at supper table in his home by two rifle shots fired through a window. He was entertaining Dr. John M. Bradford at dinner, and they were alone. His paper was an authority on mining and ranching in New Mexico and the only paper in the world printed entirely in italics. It is believed that the assassination was due to his fearlessness in discussing public affairs, especially on account of his efforts to expose cattle thieves."

7. This was probably the complicated story of a brother and sister sent out as scouts by the Zuñi (who had newly emerged from the inner earth). The two young people committed incest and then in horror at their deed, mutilated themselves and, with their children, the koyemshi (mudheads), chose to live alone. Eventually, their oldest brother found the two, whereupon the koyemshi took the brother to the gods who instructed him in the correct way to live. By this method the Zuñi learned the correct and moral life.

8. This was probably *Aplopappus sp.* an herb widely used in the Greater Southwest as a topical application for snakebite or taken internally for colds and fever.

9. This town name was derived from sabina, the correct Spanish term for certain species of fragrant juniper. Early colonists applied it to the common scrub cedar, or juniper, covering most of the hills. In time, the word acquired a masculine ending, sabinal. The town is in Socorro County, on the AT & SF RR, 11 miles north of Bernardo, on U.S. highways 60 and 85. It was a post office from 1866 to 1907. (Pearce 1965: 139.)

10. Although Josephine Bandelier is mentioned many times in the journals and is always treated gently, this is practically the only entry in which Bandelier gives any real indication of the relationship between husband and wife. Josephine Huegy Bandelier, the daughter of Moritz, or Maurice, Huegy and Josephine Suppiger Huegy, was born October 11, 1836. (White 1940: I, 64.) She and Adolph were married January 5, 1862, in Highland. There were no children from this marriage. Joe died December 11, 1892, in Lima, Peru.

11. In a letter to Collet (Burrus 1967a: 72), Bandelier spoke of the so-called "médano," or sand drift, being a feature of the pueblos of this area.

12. This mission is now a prominent portion of the Gran Quivira National Monument. Excavation of the associated and underlying pueblo ruins was carried out by the National Park Service in 1965, 1966, and 1967 under the direction of Alden C. Hayes. Pueblo ruins contemporary with the mission were to be left exposed and stabilized to present the visitor with as complete an impression as possible of the historic occupation. In the first volume (Lange and Riley 1966: 385, 435, 459), Gran Quivira and Tabira were equated as synonyms rather than simply cross-referenced. This error should be corrected; as Hayes

has pointed out, Gran Quivira was the Pueblo and/or Mission de los Jumanos while Tabira was Pueblo Blanco (personal communication). See also Burrus 1967a; Kelley 1955; Scholes and Mera 1940.

13. The pre-Spanish Pueblo Indians never used an overall glazed ware. The pottery technically called "glazed ware," or, better, "glaze-paint ware," by archaeologists has a lead preparation applied to the body of the pot, usually in poorly drawn patterns characterized by uneven thickness and margins, runs, and similar "sloppy" qualities. When fired, this gives a partially glazed surface to the pottery. The description here suggests that Bandelier was speaking of such wares, though the reference may possibly have been to one of the Spanish colonial wares, some of which had overall glazed surfaces. It is noteworthy that Bandelier used the term "glossy." He had used the term "glazed" in 1880, but in his 1881 journal he stated that F. W. Putnam objected to this usage in Bandelier's Pecos manuscript. Rejecting the proposed substitution of "varnished," Bandelier had settled on "glossy" as of his 1882 journal entries and continued using the term as of this time.

Writing to W. H. Holmes of the Bureau of American Ethnology in July 1904, Bandelier, then at the American Museum of Natural History, closed his letter with these comments, "By the way, another point that I have insisted upon, and fruitlessly too, a quarter of a century ago is: an analysis of the coarse glaze on Pueblo Pottery from the time of the so-called conquest. Cannot it be done at the capital?" (From Bandelier correspondence in files, Bureau of American Ethnology, Washington.)

14. Dry farming is carried on extensively even today in the Salinas corridor east of the Sandia and Manzano mountain ranges.

15. Father Peter Eguillon was Vicar General at this time. In 1854, Bishop Lamy (not Vicar General Machebeuf as stated in Lange and Riley [1966: 71n55]) had gone to Clermont, France, to recruit priests to assist him. The first to respond was Eguillon, at that time an assistant priest of one of the principal city churches. He was kept for about a year in Santa Fe to teach theology to some seminarians and to prepare them for their ordination. In October 1855, he was sent to Socorro as a parish priest, where he remained until November 4, 1858, when he was appointed parish priest of the Cathedral and Vicar General of the diocese. It was Father Eguillon who brought Reverend J. B. Salpointe to Santa Fe from Clermont, France, in 1859. In 1875, Eguillon gave a brief address in Spanish at the ceremonies which elevated Bishop Lamy to Archbishop. He died in 1892. (Salpointe 1898: 165, 207, Appendix VII.)

16. In other words, the monument was placed there by (or dedicated by) someone whose name did not survive weathering of the stone.

17. "Quarai (Torrance). Tigua Indian, kwa-ri. Site of a Spanish mission 10 miles northwest of Mountainair, founded in 1629 and now in ruins. The remains of the old Church are the most imposing left of the 'Cities that died of Fear.' The stone walls were over 60 feet high and 5 or 6 feet thick, but have crumbled to 20 feet in height. This was a Tiwa pueblo which was abandoned between 1671 and 1680 when the road to Salinas was blocked by Apache Indians. It was created a state monument on February 20, 1935." (Pearce 1965: 127.)

18. Comments, much later, regarding Bandelier's field gear are of interest here. Hodge (1932: 356) noted, "He traveled armed only with a stick a meter long and graduated for measuring ruins, and relied on the meager hospitality of a pitifully unsettled and arid country for the means to keep body and soul together." Lummis, in his remarks at the beginning of The Delight Makers (p. xiv), noted ". . . So we went always by foot; my big camera and glass plates in the knapsack on my back, the heavy tripod under my arm; his aneroid surveying instruments, and satchel of the almost microscopic notes which he kept fully and precisely every night by the camp-fire (even when I had to crouch over

him and the precious paper with my water-proof focusing cloth) somehow bestowed about him. . . . No blankets, overcoats, or other shelter; and the only commissary a few cakes of sweet chocolate, and a small sack of parched popcorn meal. Our 'lodging was the cold ground.' When we could find a cave, a tree, or anything to temper the wind or keep off part of the rain, all right. If not, the Open. . . . He was in no way an athlete— nor even muscular."

19. Rosa de Castilla may be one of the domesticated roses. It is impossible to identify it from Bandelier's statement here.

Manzanilla here is probably *Arctostaphylos sp.* (perhaps *A. pungens* or *A. patula*) an evergreen shrub widely used for various medicinal properties in this area.

20. Here we have a good example of Bandelier's background and familiarity with the German language. In German, the definite article is used with parts of the body, i.e., "the head" instead of "my head."

21. This is one of two ranges in New Mexico bearing this name. (See fn 409.)

22. John Becker became postmaster at Belen, New Mexico, in 1873 (Dike 1958); he was in that same position at the time of Bandelier's visit (Polk and Danser 1884a: 310).

Ellis and Baca (1957: 22) mentioned Becker as a general merchant. Parish (1960: 22-23) noted that "It was the larger general merchant who conducted this intimate trade with the hinterland in a two-way flow of imports and exports with the financing mechanism built in. With some notable exceptions, like John Becker of Belen, and Harry Kelly of Las Vegas, it was the German Jewish merchant who, in competition with his own immigrant people, had risen to a pre-eminent economic position. He was the commercial revolution."

23. Captain George H. Pradt, surveyor, came to New Mexico in 1869 to survey the Navajo Reservation. In Bourke's journal, the name was spelled Pratt. Pradt had served in the 40th Wisconsin Infantry in the Tennessee campaign. In 1872, he was on the staff of the Surveyor-General's Office in Santa Fe. In 1876, he moved to Laguna Pueblo and married a Laguna woman. He served as governor of the Pueblo for a time and later homesteaded to the south. In 1882, Pradt organized a company of Laguna volunteers against raiding Apaches and Navajos. During this period he also conducted surveys for the Surveyor-General and held various county positions. Pradt died in 1927. (McCreight 1927: 208-212; Walter 1927; Bloom 1937: 373.)

24. Rosalie in the 1880-82 journals (Lange and Riley 1966: 343) was identified as a sister of Adolph F. Bandelier. This identification has proved to be incorrect. (See Preface for details relating to this.) Actually, Rosalie, neé Lipps (1835-1924), married Emil Bandelier in 1858 and was the mother of Elizabeth, Gustave, and Emma Bandelier. Widowed in 1873, Rosalie assumed the care of Adolphe E. Bandelier after the death of the Swiss maid, Annali Näfiger (Hobbs 1940a). Rosalie died and was buried in Stillwater, Oklahoma.

25. "Poor Evans" has thus far remained unidentified; over the span of his journals, Bandelier met or otherwise interacted with several individuals by this name. However, the Bandelier Scrapbook contains printed extracts from a letter addressed by Bandelier to S. B. Evans of Ottumwa, Iowa, and dated January 21, 1883. The printed extracts dealt with Abo, Gran Quivira, and the Piros and appeared in the *Saturday Evening Post*, Burlington, Iowa, December 1, 1888. Although there was no mention of writing to Evans in Bandelier's entry of January 21, 1883, it seems possible that this may have been the "poor Evans" from whom Bandelier received a letter on the 18th, at which time he had just completed his trip through the Abo and Gran Quivira area, homeland of the Piro Indians.

26. A remedy for headache and other pain made by boiling herbs (varying in number

and kind from one locality to another) with lime. The mixture is strained, and only the liquid stock is used as medicine.

27. Polk and Danser (1884a: 310) listed Oscar Goebel as operator of a general store in Belen.

28. This was a time of considerable labor unrest in France and Bandelier may possibly be referring to a labor protest against the Chapelier law prohibiting unionization and strikes.

29. It is not exactly clear to what the references of January 21 and 22 pertain. In September 1882, General George Crook, an able and well-respected officer, and a previous commander of American forces in Arizona, was again put in charge of the military forces of the Territory. One of Crook's first actions was to loosen the stringent and bureaucratic regulations that made life so difficult for the reservation Apache. Crook appointed Captain Emmett Crawford as head of the San Carlos Reservation and Lieutenant Charles B. Gatewood, head of the Fort Apache Reservation. The Indians were encouraged to govern themselves and to concentrate on agriculture and stock raising.

It may be that Bandelier's "bad news" had to do with suspicious movements by the non-reservation Chiricahua Apache band of Geronimo.

30. This was Mrs. Lewis Henry Morgan. Lewis H. Morgan, himself, was, as mentioned in our introduction, one of the key persons in the formation of Bandelier's scientific career. White (1957: 259) provided the following brief sketch of Morgan: "Lewis Morgan was born near Aurora, New York, in 1818. He was graduated from Union College in 1840. He went to Rochester, New York, in 1844 where he engaged in the practice of law. Profitable investments enabled him eventually to give up his law practice and to devote himself to ethnology. All his scientific work was done as a private citizen; he never held a position with an institution of higher learning, a museum, or other scientific organization. The two highest honors that American science can bestow were conferred on Morgan: election to the National Academy of Sciences, and the presidency of the American Association for the Advancement of Science. He died at his home in Rochester on December 17, 1881." Elsewhere (p. 257) in this paper, White stated that "In 1871, the Smithsonian Institution published one of the most significant anthropological treatises ever written: *Systems of Consanguinity and Affinity of the Human Family*, by Lewis Henry Morgan. It has been called 'monumental' by A. C. Haddon and A. R. Radcliffe-Brown, and a 'towering monument' by Robert H. Lowie; George P. Murdock has termed it 'perhaps the most original and brilliant single achievement in the history of anthropology.'" (For further data on Morgan, see Stern 1931.)

Bandelier had visited the Morgan home in Rochester from time to time. After Morgan's death in 1881, Bandelier continued to correspond with Mrs. Morgan until the time of her death in 1883. This letter from Belen is contained in the Bandelier-Morgan letters. (White 1940: II.)

31. "QUEMADO (Catron). Span., 'burned.' Ranching and vegetable-producing community on US 60, 81 mi W of Magdalena in north-central part of county. About 1880, Jose Antonio Padilla and his family moved from Belen to a place they called RITO QUEMADO, because both sides of the creek had the sage and rabbitbush burned off by the Indians. He brought sheep and started the stock industry in this part of the state. A few years later the name was shortened to QUEMADO. A second explanation has been that the town is located on an extinct volcanic area and appears to have been scorched. Post office, 1886-. . . ." (Pearce 1965: 128.)

32. According to his 1881 journal, Bandelier met Padre Dr. José Vicente Campos at Cholula, March 8, while on his first Mexican trip. At that time, the Padre made various

church records available to Bandelier and otherwise showed interest in his work. It was Padre Campos who officiated at Bandelier's entry into the Catholic faith, July 31, 1881, with García Icazbalceta serving as his Padrino, or sponsor. (See White and Bernal 1960: 233, 248-249.) In a letter from Cholula, dated March 8, 1881, Bandelier included these remarks, "The priest of the place, Padre Campos, has placed at my disposal the church records, which go back to 1531. He himself, an old man of 75 years, has been priest in the place since 1830, speaks Mexican, and will introduce me to the Indians." (Hammond and Goad 1949: 71.)

33. Don Joaquín García Icazbalceta (1825-94), a famous Mexican historian and writer, who in the mid-nineteeth century became one of Mexico's leading authorities on history, linguistics, bibliography, and geography. García is perhaps best known for his *Colección de documentos para la historia de México*.

García Icazbalceta and Bandelier began corresponding in 1875 but did not meet until March 1881. García's sponsorship of Bandelier in the latter's entry into the Roman Catholic Church gave the two men an additional bond, and they maintained their close friendship for many years—though mostly through correspondence. (See also Riley 1968.)

34. Frank Bigler was a friend of Frank H. Cushing, as well as of Bandelier. This friendship endured after Bandelier abandoned active fieldwork in the Southwest and continued even with Bandelier's widow, his second wife, Fanny, following Bandelier's death in Spain in 1914. At that time, Fanny replied to Bigler, then in Detroit, Michigan, accepting his offer to help disseminate the news of Bandelier's death. Writing from Spain, July 20, 1914, Fanny wrote in great detail regarding Bandelier's final days and asked Bigler, as a true friend of long standing, to let their many friends know. (Bandelier Collection, Library, Museum of New Mexico; Fanny's letter comprised a major part of an article, "Adolph Bandelier's Last Journey," which appeared in *El Palacio*, August, 1949, pp. 241-51.)

35. This was probably Charles L. Bernays. During the 1848 revolution, numerous highly educated people had to flee from Germany, and some located in Highland. Among these were several brothers named Bernays. Two were physicians, and all had received technical education in their native land. About 1854, Charles L. Bernays started to manufacture beer in Highland. The ground floor and cellars of their building were used for the brewery, and the second floor was a residence for the Bernays family. Both Dr. Bernays and C. L. Bernays were among the lecturers in a series of winter lectures which the Library Association sponsored in the reading room of Turner Hall. The Highland Library Association had been founded as early as 1859 and Adolphe E. Bandelier was president. Adolph F. Bandelier, as well as his father, also lectured in this series. (Spencer 1937: 84, 154.)

The two physicians cited in Spencer were identified in Eggen (1933: 36) as Dr. George and Dr. Jacob Bernays. From Hyde (1896: 14), it is known that Charles L. Bernays had moved to St. Louis and become a prominent journalist. In seeking additional information, the editors wrote to Edward L. Bernays, President of the Edward L. Bernays Foundation, who referred them to the book, *Augustus Charles Bernays, A Memoir*, by Thekla Bernays, the latter's sister. This eminent St. Louis surgeon was born in Highland, October 13, 1854, a son of Dr. George and Minna Döring Bernays. A fourth brother, and uncle of Dr. A. C. Bernays, was Bernard Bernays, crippled from childhood, who came with Jacob Bernays and his family to Highland in 1854. He had a great love of art and after fleeing Germany in 1848 had picked up a few Flemish paintings "for a song" in Holland. His Highland walls were covered with art works, and this collection he gave to Dr. A. C. Bernays. When cleaned, it was found that the Flemish paintings were of rare value and were placed in the keeping of the St. Louis Museum of Fine Art. (Bernays 1912: 54-55.)

Prior to 1860, both George and Charles L. Bernays had moved to St. Louis, Dr. George establishing a medical practice and Charles L. Bernays, in conjunction with Henry Börnstein, taking an active part in the newspaper, *Anzeiger des Westens*. (Bernays 1912: 32.) Neither brother lived exclusively in St. Louis. There were periods of residence in Europe; and under Lincoln, Charles L. Bernays had two brief consulships, one in Switzerland and one in Denmark. (Bernays 1912: 57.) At the time of these journals, the two brothers lived in adjoining houses in St. Louis, and both were active in their professions. (Bernays 1912: 103.) Dr. Jacob Bernays had sold his residence and drug store and moved to St. Genevieve, Missouri, in 1865. (Eggen 1933: 36.)

On the basis of this entry it is impossible to establish definitely which member of the Bernays family Bandelier meant here. That it was George, A. C., or Charles L. is supported by the October 19, 1883, entry when he was "in St. Louis" and "went to Bernays." Charles L. Bernays seems most likely as the journal entry of October 9, 1883, summarizing several days' activities, recorded a lecture on September 25 for the Missouri Historical Society in St. Louis; in the Bandelier Scrapbook was found an account in German of this lecture published September 26, 1883, in the *Anzeiger des Westens*, the newspaper of Charles L. Bernays.

36. Washington Matthews, 1843-1905, was born in Ireland and was named Washington as an American appreciation. While still an infant, his mother died and his father brought him to America, settling in Wisconsin. Later they moved to Dubuque, Iowa. After a common school education, he studied medicine with his father, took a course of lectures at the University of Iowa, and received the degree of M.D. in 1864 (LL.D., 1888). Immediately, he volunteered in the U.S. Army and was appointed post surgeon at Fort Union, Montana. His many assignments in the West acquainted him with various tribes of Indians and incited him to investigate their languages and mythology. Few of the old army had more extended opportunities to become acquainted with the Indians, and few knew better how to handle the Indian.

Dr. Matthews was post surgeon at Fort Wingate from 1880 to 1884, and spent as much time as he could spare from his military duties studying the customs, ceremonies, and language of the Indians. He spent the summer of 1884 under the auspices of the Bureau of Ethnology making further studies of the Navajo. Originally his materials were housed in the Department of Anthropology, University of California. The Matthews Collection is now in the Museum of Navajo Ceremonial Art in Santa Fe.

37. This may have been Frank P. Smith of Rochester, New York. The Smithsonian Institution's files contain a letter of October 23, 1882, from Bandelier in which he offered to send a vocabulary of the Cochiti dialect of "Queres" to the linguist, Pilling. He also requested a copy of "the last work of Mr. Morgan's" be sent to "my friend," Frank P. Smith, *Democrat & Chronicle* Office, Rochester, as well as any other publication of the Bureau on archaeology, as Smith "is an ardent & aspiring student, & ought to be 'pushed.'"

38. This letter was published in Burrus (1967a: 70-71). Oscar Wilks A. Collet was born on a farm near Edwardsville, Illinois, August 4, 1821. He attended the Jesuit University in St. Louis and was later associated with numerous historical societies and contributed articles on archaeology, genealogy, and history to their reviews and bulletins. He held various offices in the Missouri Historical Society. He corresponded with such historians as John Gilmary Shea and Francis Parkman. Among the interests was the exact area traversed by La Salle. A by-product of this concern was an inquiry into what the Spanish explorers meant by Quivira, Gran Quivira, and Teguayo. For aid in this research, Collet turned to his friend Bandelier. Collet died in July 1904. (pp. 67-68.)

39. Father Clement(e) Peyron was ordained in 1868. From December 1869 to March 1873, and from February 1874 to January 1875, he was at Cochiti. (Chávez 1957: 134,

261.) He was listed in Salpointe (1898: 283) as one of the priests brought to New Mexico under Lamy. Sadlier (1882: 206) noted Father Peyron at Isleta in 1882.

40. José, or Joseph, Tondre was probably one of "the two boys of Mrs. Tondre at Isleta [who] have learned the language well because they had to speak it with Indian children with whom they were raised, and who did not speak Spanish themselves." (Anderson 1947: 109.) See also fn 468. Dike (1958) listed Joseph Tondre as the first postmaster at Isleta when the post office was established there on September 26, 1882. Baxter (1885: 697) noted "The late Madame Josephine Tondré of Isleta was favored for her wine." The editors would like to correct their erroneous rendering of this family name, Tonche, in the first volume (Lange and Riley 1966: 88).

41. The buildings of Isleta Pueblo are even today dominantly of adobe; however, in recent decades there have been tendencies to use other materials, especially cement blocks made of volcanic tuff, or pumice.

42. The Piro formed one of the more important divisions of Tanoan speakers in the sixteenth and seventeenth centuries. As late as the Benevides period (1621-1630), there were fourteen villages of Piro Indians reported.

The Piros were grouped in two major divisions, one in the area from San Marcial, in the Rio Grande Valley, to about 50 miles south of Albuquerque. The second division, sometimes called Tompiro, was in the Salinas area east of the Rio Grande across the Manzano Mountains. For a concise listing of Piro and Tompiro towns (which included both Abó and Quivira), see Hodge (1910: II, 261-262, 347).

43. Fray Juan José Padilla was a missionary at Laguna for more than twenty years, with short terms of service at Acoma, Zuñi, and San Felipe. Upon his death, he was buried at Isleta, February 5, 1756. At more or less twenty-year periods, the well-preserved body of Padre Padilla was said to rise to the surface of the adobe floor in the old Mission Church at Isleta Pueblo. In time, the legend grew that this was Fray Juan de Padilla who had come with Coronado in 1540 and was later martyred by the Quivira Indians on the Great Plains. The body was brought back to Isleta where, since that time, it had been rising periodically from its grave. The church made at least three exhumations: one in 1819, one in 1895, and one as recently as 1948. From the 1948 account, the coffin was of cottonwood but not a canoe. An account of the 1895 exhumation was found in Spanish in a small tin box within the coffin. Similarly, a letter in English was placed in the tin box in 1948, and a copy made of the earlier Spanish account. For greater detail, see the various papers by Chávez (1947: 251-268; 1952: 386-389; and 1957: 83-84). Defouri (1887: 8-9) referred to Father Juan de Padilla and the "coffin made of a hollow alamo." Bandelier (1890b) published on Fray Juan de Padilla of Coronado's party. In Parsons' study of Isleta (1932: 457), she included a version of the story, "The Priest Who Resurrects," but gave the name of Fray Francisco Lopez.

44. Isleta has been traditionally organized into moieties, with five ceremonial "corn groups" associated with colors and cardinal directions that cross-cut the moieties. Children are assigned alternatively to moieties. The moieties control the two curing societies and also own the kivas. There are no clans but, rather, a bilateral kin system with men owning the houses. (French 1948.)

45. This is a Tiwa pattern of the common Mesoamerican and Southwestern color and cardinal direction association. Even within a given group, different colors and direction relationships might be used for separate ceremonial occasions (Riley 1963a: 54). The most common Isleta usage, however, was north, black; west, blue or yellow; south, red or blue; and east, white. (P. 59; see also fn 156.)

46. The cacique at Isleta, as at other pueblos, functioned primarily as a priest, holding the top position in the religious hierarchy with extensive ceremonial responsibilities.

47. Occasionally, Bandelier explicitly noted the basis of his calculations of heights, distances, or other measurements. While actually not precise, these notations provide some insight on how he worked in the field. (See also fn 170.)

48. For a more detailed account of Isleta funeral practices, see Parsons (1932: 248-250). Some of Bandelier's details varied from those reported by Parsons.

49. Note the similarity between Ya-añe and the Keresan, Chai-añe, medicine man, or doctor.

50. While variations in detail existed from one pueblo to another, there has been a general conformity to the pattern in which the "doctors," or medicine men, control the secular elections. At Cochiti, for example, the cacique and two other head medicine men, those of the Flint, Giant, and Shikame, select the war captains, governors, and fiscales, respectively. No alternates were named, and the people, almost without exception, endorsed the selections.

51. Such heirlooms still persist in the various villages, preserved by families or by society members on behalf of the tribe. Because of the decline in numbers of native artisans, these items are slowly disappearing without proper replacement. (For an example from Cochiti Pueblo, see Lange 1959: 279-281.)

52. Padre Rómulo Ribera was one of the priests added to the New Mexico church by Bishop Lamy. The journal entry of August 27, 1880, is Bandelier's first mention of him. "Saw and conversed with Padre Rómulo Ribera of Peña Blanca. Invitation to stay with him next week." (Lange and Riley 1966: 74.) Actually, Bandelier's Pecos trip and writing took more than a week, and it was not until September 23 that he arrived at Peña Blanca. The next day Padre Ribera took him to Santo Domingo Pueblo to live. This chance contact with Ribera, then, started Bandelier on his ethnographic field work and throughout his journals his visits to and correspondence with Ribera are dutifully recorded. The "bad news" here mentioned is not further elaborated upon. In spite of the frequency of Bandelier's references to him, the reader of the journals forms few impressions of Padre Ribera. The following data concerning him and his family were given in Lange and Riley (1966: 415).

"RIBERA, REVEREND JOSE ROMULO, at Peña Blanca; one of priests added to New Mexico clergy by Lamy. In the 1880's, Don Tomás, his father, together with his mother, kept house for Father Romulo at Peña Blanca. FRANCISCO, JESUS, JOSE LINO, AND URBANO RIBERA, all of El Pueblo, San Miguel County, all related to Father Romulo. José Lino, operated general store and raised livestock; was postmaster; mentioned in 1886, as nominee, on Democratic ticket, for County Commissioner, Third District, San Miguel County. Urbano, blacksmith and wagon maker."

53. Padre John B. Brun was of French ancestry. He was a brother of Mrs. Dumas Provencher and was ordained by Bishop John B. Lamy on August 15, 1868. After serving briefly at Taos and Pecos, he was given charge of the churches and chapels of Cebolleta, Cubero, San Rafael, San Mateo, Laguna, Acoma, and Zuñi. (Jenkins: personal communication.)

54. This distinction between "Old Town" and "New Town" has persisted to the present time. Old Town dates to 1706. The modern section (Pearce 1965: 5) was founded in 1879 by the New Mexico Townsite Co., an auxiliary of the AT & SF RR, which entered the new station on April 22, 1880. For a time the post office was referred to as New Albuquerque, but by July 1, 1882, it had become evident that the newer town would experience the more rapid growth because of the railroad. Accordingly, the post office became Albuquerque. Many early travel accounts noted the rapid expansion between 1880 and 1882.

Polk and Danser (1884a: 297-298) described Albuquerque as having three public schools employing twenty-five teachers and having an average attendance of 800. Catholics had erected a large brick school house which was to be entirely unsectarian [sic] and several private schools and institutions of higher learning. A public library of 1500 volumes, two flouring mills, a soap factory, a foundry and a machine shop, smelting works, wine and vinegar works, a brewery, carriage factory, bottling works, a Mexican filigree jewelry factory, two banks, an opera house capable of seating 500, many handsome and substantial public and private buildings, and the usual number of professional men, special and general stores, blacksmith shops, etc. Two daily newspapers, which also publish a weekly. Lighted by gas and electricity with two lines of street railway, good hotels, etc. Shipments comprised wool, livestock, hides, pelts, gold, copper, and silver, lead, gypsum, sandstone, soap and beer. Population 10,000. Stages semi-monthly to San Pedro and Golden. Telephone, Western Union, Wells Fargo & Co. This, then, was Albuquerque as of the period of these journals. For a contemporary account, see Baxter (1885: 692-697).

55. See fn 121 for 1884.

56. Though families by the name of Candelaria were among the founding settlers of Albuquerque in 1706 (Chávez 1954: 156), precise identification was not found for this entry. Polk and Danser (1884a: 300) listed a José M. Candelaria who was a livestock dealer and owned a general store eight miles north of Albuquerque. From the context of this entry, it would appear that the visit took place nearer to, or in, the city.

57. William M. Borchert and his wife, Annie, were Albuquerque friends, or possibly relatives, of the Bandeliers. Borchert was a partner in the firm of *Scott and Borchert*, furniture dealers, located on Front Street in the new part of Albuquerque in the early 1880's. (*Albuquerque Morning Journal*, September 2, 1882: 4.) Earlier, William Borchert had been the first postmaster of Sabinal, June 12, 1866. (Dike 1958.) In the summer of 1878, prior to Bandelier's initial visit to the Southwest, he wrote to Morgan, sending the letter, dated 19 June 1878, "through Willie Borchert . . ." Morgan and a son of his nephew had visited a few days before that in Bandelier's home in Highland on their way westward. They were in Cañon City, Colorado, June 21, 1878. Bandelier's letter of June 19th included a postscript relaying, through Morgan, "Best love to Willie & the balance." (White 1940: II, 99-100; 1942: 3.)

58. This may have been a misspelling of Saunders. J. T. Saunders was an attorney in Albuquerque. (See fn 176.) In the first volume (Lange and Riley 1966: 317), Bandelier noted that he had "dined with Sanders," June 9, 1882. It could be that Bandelier did not realize his erroneous spelling for the period of his initial contacts with this man.

59. Polk and Danser (1884a: 302) listed Otto Dieckmann as a notary, west of the Plaza in Albuquerque. Twitchell (1917: III, 42-43), in a biography of Otto F. H. Dieckmann, noted that he was born in Germany, May 29, 1847, and that at the age of 16 or 17, he had come to St. Louis and in 1879 to Albuquerque. He was engaged in clerking in a store and was identified with mercantile interests until 1890, when he turned to real estate, and later to fire insurance. He was President of the Southwestern Brewing and Ice Co. He died November 3, 1913.

The "college" Bandelier referred to was the Holy Family College, which was opened in the Jesuit residence in 1873 by Father Donato M. Gasparri. For a short time, Father Gasparri was asked to direct the public school, which he did. In curriculum, there was really very little distinction between the public school and the college. After Las Vegas College was founded by the Jesuits in 1877, there was little interest in the College in Albuquerque; and in 1885, it was given to the Sisters of Charity. (Vollmer 1952: 298-299.)

60. Father Salvador Personé [Personnet], S. J., was stationed in both Las Vegas and Albuquerque in his earlier years; in 1874, he returned to Las Vegas as President of the

Jesuit Academy there. (Defouri 1887: 128.) Polk and Danser (1884a: 306) listed him at the Cathedral San Felipe de Neri in Albuquerque [Old Town]. There he replaced the late Father Gasparri. (*The Daily Optic*, Las Vegas, December 30, 1882.)

61. *Das Ausland* was published in Stuttgart and München, Germany, between 1828 and 1894, volumes I through LXVII appearing in that interval. (See Hodge 1910: 1181.) Hobbs (1942: 113n12) named Friedrich Ratzel, German geographer, anthropogeographer, and writer, as one of the editors of *Das Ausland*, "in which many of Bandelier's works were published." Through the kindness of Dr. Christa Bausch, formerly of the Landesmuseum of Stuttgart, and a visitor on the Anthropology staff at Southern Illinois University, Carbondale, in 1967-68, the editors have obtained xeroxed copies of Bandelier's *Das Ausland* publications for the years of his Southwestern journals, 1880-1892.

62. This was E. J. Post & Co., wholesale and retail hardware, stoves and tinware, guns, pistols, ammunition, wagon timber and paints and oils, in New Albuquerque. (McKenney 1882-83: 330.)

63. Parish (1960: 2) said that Franz [also Frank] Huning was a German Lutheran who arrived in Santa Fe in 1849. In 1857, he established a general merchandise store in Albuquerque [Old Town]. In his study of Jews in the New Mexico economy, Parish commented that Huning "may have been the only non-Jew to have contributed significantly to the early commercial revolution in New Mexico." Baxter (1885: 696) spoke of Mr. Franz Huning as one of the "old residents and a leading merchant and wine-grower." He was also the owner of the Molino [Mill] de Glorieta in Albuquerque [Old Town]. From Germany, he brought with him a German's love of the forest and in 1881 he had set out 1,500 trees. Polk and Danser (1884a: 298, 304) stated he was president, Albuquerque Gas Co.; president, Albuquerque Hotel and Opera House Co.; and general merchant, West Plaza, Old Town. His beautiful Victorian home was referred to as "Huning Castle."

Fierman (1961: 242n28) added the following data: "Francisco Huning no doubt is Franz Huning who was born at Melle, Germany, in 1827, but left Germany during the troubled days of 1848. He went from Hamburg to New Orleans, then to St. Louis, and from there to California in search of gold. In the middle 1850's, Huning moved to Albuquerque and prospered as the proprietor of a general merchandise store and owned the steam-powered Glorietta [sic] Flour Mill."

64. Patol, or patolli, was a gambling game played by the Aztecs of Mexico. It utilized a board and counters with rules of play somewhat like those of parchesi. At Isleta, as elsewhere in the Puebloan area, a simplified form of "board and counter" game was played, the "board" normally being marked out on the ground with small stones. In 1878, Mr. E. B. Tylor had read a paper before the Anthropological Institute on the "Game of Patolli in Ancient Mexico and its probable Asiatic Origin." (Mason 1879: 403.) Bandelier had already noted this game at Cochiti Pueblo in his October 29, 1880, entry. (Lange and Riley 1966: 179, 179n114.)

65. Here, Bandelier was equating, with some justification, these groups at Isleta with what he had become acquainted with in the Rio Grande Keresan Pueblos.

66. Polk and Danser (1884a: 824) listed Dr. R. H. Longwill (allo) of Santa Fe in a roster of New Mexican physicians. The *Santa Fé New Mexican Review*, No. 194, October 6, 1884, showed R. H. Longwill as one of three directors of the First National Bank of Santa Fe. Wharton (1952: 314n4) noted that Dr. R. H. Longwill was a resident of Cimarron, New Mexico, in the 1870's. Anderson (1907: I, 437) stated that Dr. R. H. Longwell (the name appears in both forms, though the Longwill is more common) obtained great notoriety in later life in connection with the assassination of Reverend Talby

at Cimarron. He practiced in several places, but principally in Santa Fe. After an attempted lynching following the Talby murder, Dr. Longwell escaped to Fort Lyon until feelings died down. He originated the first legislation in the Territory regulating the practice of medicine. He was a politician as well as physician; free to express his views, he had numerous enemies. He was a graduate of Jefferson Medical College, but possessed but a limited classical education. At the time of his death in 1895, he was reputed to be the richest physician in New Mexico.

67. S. S. Robinson was listed in Greene (1882: 80) as General Manager of the Mimbres Mining Company of Georgetown. From another journal entry (December 26, 1883), we learn that operations had ceased there about the time of Bandelier's arrival.

68. Julius H. Gerdes was listed by Polk and Danser (1884a: 350) as a merchant in clothing and gentlemen's goods.

69. William G. Ritch was born in New York in 1830. He moved to Michigan in 1855 and later to Wisconsin. He held various public offices and had Civil War service. He was a state senator from Wisconsin and later, a Presidential elector for Grant. He was also a newspaper editor. In 1873, he went to New Mexico for his health and was appointed agent for the Navajos at Fort Defiance in relief of William F. M. Arny. He became Secretary of the Territory in 1873 and served three terms. In 1875, he became acting governor of New Mexico. He was the first president of the new New Mexico Historical Society in 1880 and served as president until 1883. He was also president of the Bureau of Irrigation. He led an active political life and was also a prolific writer. He died in Engle, New Mexico, in 1904. (Lange and Riley 1966: 415.)

70. In various sources, these names are rendered in a variety of ways though there is no doubt that the references are to these men who were wine growers at Belen. Variations include the following: Leyn and Danckyny, Lyns and Dankner, Lyons and Danckenzny. (Ellis and Baca 1957: 23; Polk and Danser 1884a: 310.)

71. This was probably Pottery Mound where a large quantity of glazed wares, Zuñi, Hopi, and Little Colorado pottery in general, appears. (See Hibben 1966: 522-523.)

72. Francis Parkman (1823-93), best known for his multivolume work, France and England in North America, and sometimes called America's greatest historian, was born in Boston and entered Harvard College in 1840, eventually taking a degree in law in 1846. That same year he began a journey across the Great Plains that took him from Independence, Missouri, westward along the Oregon Trail. Pushing on beyond Fort Laramie to the basin of the Medicine Bow River, Parkman lived for a time with the Sioux. He returned to Independence by Bent's Fort and the Santa Fe Trail. These travels were reflected in The Oregon Trail (1849).

Parkman was a very active scholar. Although suffering from partial blindness and recurring head pains, he published in 27 years several volumes of history as well as an autobiographical novel and a book on rose cultivation. Parkman studied the Sioux in order to write about the seventeenth-century Iroquois, thus pioneering in comparative ethnography. He was, also, one of the founders, in 1879, of the Archaeological Institute of America, serving subsequently on its executive committee. (See Encyclopedia Britannica 1967: XVII, 373-374.)

Francis Parkman was an enthusiastic supporter of the work of Bandelier. The two men exchanged letters, and Parkman at least once helped Bandelier with money when the latter was in financial difficulties. In addition, he seems to have been instrumental in arranging publication of Bandelier's The Delight Makers. For relations with Bandelier and for other insights into Parkman's life, see Jacobs (1960).

73. Belief in witches and witchcraft was widespread in Bandelier's time, both among the Indians and the neighboring Spanish-Americans. As education has become more

prevalent, such beliefs have steadily declined. However, a certain amount persists, especially among those of the older generations. It is a difficult topic to study, however; silence on the subject cannot be interpreted as meaning an absence of belief but rather a reluctance to discuss an extremely dangerous subject with strangers.

74. Here, it would appear that Bandelier was simply referring to a masked, or kachina, dance. In a paper on Laguna ceremonialism, Parsons (1920) discussed at some length the various meanings of the term, Chakwena, citing examples not only from Laguna, but from Zuñi and elsewhere. Variations extend from an approximate synonym for shiwanna, or kachina, categorically speaking, to a specific type of kachina, often with direct associations with witches, or witchcraft (pp. 97-99).

75. Frank H. Cushing (1857-1900) went with Major Powell's expedition to New Mexico in 1879, and he lived at Zuñi Pueblo until the spring of 1884. He wrote a number of major publications regarding various aspects of Zuñi culture. Bandelier was not always as complimentary in his views on Cushing, however, as he was here. In 1889, when the Hemenway Southwestern Archaeological Expedition was in financial difficulties (and Bandelier's own future was in jeopardy), Bandelier wrote, "Cushing, it seems is in disgrace. Well—while I am very sorry for it, still it is his own fault. I worked and saved, what he did I do not know." (See McGee et al. [1900].)

76. It is impossible to tell from his entry whether Bandelier was referring to Walter G. Marmon or to Robert G. Marmon, a younger brother of Walter. Walter Gunn Marmon had come to New Mexico in 1868 to survey the Navajo Reservation, and in 1871 he had opened a trading post at the Pueblo of Laguna. From 1871 to 1875 he was a government teacher at the pueblo. In 1875, he returned to trading, and, with his younger brother, Robert G. Marmon, also a resident of Laguna, did extensive surveying of land grants for the Surveyor-General's Office. Both Marmons married Laguna women, and their descendants are still important in the affairs of the pueblo. Both were Laguna governors, Robert in 1880, Walter in 1886. In 1883, Walter secured a patent to a homestead south of Laguna still known as the "Marmon Ranch." He died in November 1899. (Lange and Riley 1966: 331n151.)

77. Cebolleta Mountain was the old Spanish name for Mount Taylor, the highest of the San Mateo Mountains. (Pearce 1965: 105.)

78. The Zuñi believed that originally they came from the fourth level of the earth and were aided in reaching the surface by the Twin War Gods.

79. Canyon de Chelly (Navajo tsegi or canyon) is actually a complex of deep canyons in northeast Arizona of which the two most important are De Chelly and Del Muerto. De Chelly was occupied during much of the Anasazi period and was used, at least seasonally, by the Hopi well into historic times. In the eighteenth century, the canyon complex became a center of Navajo occupation, and it is now for the most part in the Navajo Reservation, with a major section set aside as a national monument.

80. As the corrections in brackets indicate, Bandelier either misunderstood or was misinformed regarding the native name for La Tetilla Peak (7,060'). Earlier, Bandelier had recorded the name as Qqah-sishcotsha (Lange and Riley 1966: 145); in the Final Report (Bandelier 1890-92: II, 80n1), he gave it as "Shkasi-sku-tshu," the pointed height. Goldfrank (1927: 59) rendered it as "Gasickurtc," Nipple Mountain. Here, Bandelier's "Qotit" was a variation of Ko tyīt', the name for Cochiti Pueblo itself.

81. These heaps of stone (sometimes called huacas in Peru) were widely known, both in the Central Andes and in Mesoamerica. They were placed at difficult spots along trails, and adding a stone to the pile gave magical assistance to the traveller.

82. The editors were not aware that in the Register of Persons for the 1880-82 journals

they were combining the careers of two Presbyterian missionary brothers into the one career of Dr. John Menaul. (Lange and Riley 1966: 413.) In doing additional research for the present volume, this note by Bloom was found: "The Rev. John Menaul, M.D., Presbyterian missionary. He had met his future wife while both were on shipboard going to Africa. They had begun their work at Laguna in 1876. John Menaul has been confused with his brother, the Rev. James A. Menaul, who had been sent out in 1870 as a Presbyterian missionary to the Navajos and who, in the 90's, was a synodical missionary to New Mexico." (Wasson 1930: 277n6.)

Wasson (p. 278) noted that John Menaul had a printing office at Laguna, and was engaged in translating American schoolbooks "for the benefit of the heathen." Bloom commented that a bibliography of the issues from this press would be interesting, noting that he himself owned a copy of a Laguna hymnbook from this press, and the Historical Society, another. A reader in the Laguna language was issued in 1882, and it is likely that this was the book to which Bandelier made reference here. It was thought that this press was moved to Albuquerque about 1889 and was used by Dr. Menaul in printing Spanish tracts. Bancroft mentioned La Salona, published at Laguna in 1878. (P. 278n7.)

Gunn (1917: 97-98) said Dr. Menaul was sent to Laguna as a missionary by the Presbyterian board of missions and was also appointed government teacher in 1875, Mr. Marmon having resigned. The printing press at Laguna was devoted principally to missionary work, but Menaul translated and published in the Queres language McGuffey's first reader. In 1884, a bell was placed on the school building by pueblo subscription. Dr. Menaul left Laguna in 1887, loved and respected by many but by no means all.

Undoubtedly Wasson and Gunn were referring to the same Keres reader. With his interest in the Keresan language, Bandelier must have been especially pleased to receive this book.

83. Because of the importance of snakes in Zuñi ceremonial life (they are, among other things, messengers to the gods) the Zuñi are reluctant to kill them.

84. Captain David J. Miller was a translator and chief clerk of the U.S. Surveyor-General's Office, Santa Fe. He exchanged letters with Lewis Henry Morgan concerning fieldwork among the Pueblo Indians. White appraised his field notes (Taos) and an interview with a Pecos Indian (from Jemez) and one from Zia, all of which were in the Morgan Archives, University of Rochester, as "meager and of little value." (1940: II, 216n8.) Miller was active in the New Mexico Historical Society chartered in 1859 but which failed soon after because of the Civil War. He helped organize a second New Mexico Historical Society in 1880, and from 1882 to 1883 served as corresponding secretary. (Lange and Riley 1966: 414.) In the Second Annual Report of the Archaeological Institute of America, p. 13, Miller was listed among the Annual Members as of 1880-1881.

85. In 1856, Bishop Lamy sent his Vicar General, Reverend Joseph Machebeuf, to France to recruit new missionaries. Among the six procured was Joseph M. Coudert, also referred to as José María Coudert, who was ordained on December 12, 1856. In 1859, he was parish priest at Albuquerque. Coudert accompanied Bishop Lamy on an arduous trip from Santa Fe to visit the missionaries in Arizona and to see the principal settlements of that Territory in the fall of 1863. As secretary to Bishop Lamy, he went to Rome with him in 1866. (Salpointe 1898: 208, 223, 240, 257, 282.) Chávez (1957: 259) listed Coudert at Sandia Pueblo in February 1857. In 1880, Bandelier made his acquaintance in Las Vegas, New Mexico, and they visited a number of ruins in the Las Vegas area (Lange and Riley 1966: 342). In 1899, he was pastor at Bernalillo (Salpointe 1898: Appendix VII).

86. Bandelier made the acquaintance of José de Jesús de Armand and his brother, José

María de Armand, in May 1882. (Lange and Riley 1966: 289, 297.) This was a family of part French ancestry that had settled in the Cubero area in the early 1870's. There were various members of the family in the region. A spring called "De Armand" is approximately ten miles northwest of Cubero, and the old De Armand family cemetery is in Cubero. (P. 289n142.)

Polk and Danser (1884a: 314) listed the Alexander De Armand and Sons General Store in Cubero. Dike (1958) listed Alexander De Armond as the first postmaster at Cubero Post Office, Valencia County, established February 24, 1879.

87. In these entries Bandelier is renewing friendships he had made in 1882. In the 1880-82 journals (Lange and Riley 1966: 279n136), the three Bibo brothers, Simon, Nathan, and Solomon, were identified as merchants in the Fort Wingate, Laguna, Cebolleta, and Grants area. In doing subsequent research, the editors used Fierman's "Nathan Bibo's Reminiscences of Early New Mexico" (Fierman 1961, 1962) and fn 469 incorporates added data about Nathan Bibo. The Bibos with their extensive trading in, and knowledge of, western New Mexico and eastern Arizona could give Bandelier invaluable and up-to-date information about the areas he was to visit in 1883-84.

Solomon married an Acoma, Juana Valle (Parish 1960: 150) and was governor of Acoma in 1885 and 1886. Fierman (1961: 234, 234n11, n12) said that Solomon's marriage brought him into controversy with the U.S. Government. Accused of exploiting the Acomas, he was subsequently legally cleared and reappointed governor by the Indian agent, W. C. Williams.

88. Moqatsh, or mokatch (mountain lion), is also the term applied to a kiva firebox at Cochiti Pueblo; Kohaio, or bear, similarly a strong medicine animal, is also used in this way. (Lange 1959: 54.)

89. Yapashi, at present, specifically refers to the Pueblo of the Stone Lions (L. A. 250), being located very near that shrine on the Potrero de las Vacas, within the boundaries of Bandelier National Monument. (See also fn 95.) It should be explained that here and elsewhere in the volume, "L.A." numbers refer to the inventory of archaeological sites in New Mexico kept at the Museum of New Mexico's Research Laboratory, formerly the Laboratory of Anthropology, Santa Fe.

90. Actually, only cornmeal was, and is, sacred; tortillas, in contrast, are traditional and hence proper in ceremonial contexts as present-day packaged or purchased foods are not.

91. Among the Pueblos, men normally were the weavers though women did also occasionally weave (cf. Lange and Riley 1966: 216). The nearby Navajo Indians were also weavers and, though this trait was clearly adopted from Pueblo models, Navajo women did most or all of the weaving. Underhill (1956: 47) has pointed out that following the Pueblo Revolt (1680) and up through the De Vargas reconquest period (1692-1700) there were numbers of marriages of Navajo with Pueblo refugees. She made the intriguing suggestion that skilled Pueblo weavers, unable to teach their trade to sons (who were by custom hunters and raiders) imparted the knowledge to their Navajo wives and daughters.

92. Lizzie, or Elizabeth, was born in Highland, Illinois, the first child of Emil and Rosalie Bandelier. (See Preface and fns 24, 96, and 374.) In the obituary appearing in the Santa Fe New Mexican, July 19, 1954, the birthdate was given as June 23, 1861; this was confirmed in the family bible now in possession of Mrs. R. L. Ormsbee, Santa Fe, Elizabeth's youngest child. However, the First Book of Records of St. John's Church, Breese, Illinois (p. 7), shows the year of birth as 1860 in the entry on Elizabeth's baptism, January 18, 1863, at which time her name was given as Elise Caroline. The obituary erred in stating that Elizabeth was the daughter of Mr. and Mrs. Gustave Ban-

delier and the "niece of Adolf Bandelier." It does seem definite, however, that the terms "niece" and "uncle" were commonly used rather than the technically proper "cousin."

93. These data accurately illustrate the Western Pueblo pattern of kiva association with clan as contrasted with the prevailing Eastern Pueblo pattern of kiva and moiety affiliation. It is interesting to note further that Acoma is the only Keresan Pueblo with the Western kiva pattern of association.

94. See fn 89 for the present meaning of this term. The interpretation recorded by Bandelier has not been verified.

95. This is the only known interpretation of the two figures in the enclosure on the Potrero de las Vacas being *Qohayo* [Ko-hai-o, or bear] and *Shyayaq* [Hunter—animal—mountain lion]. Aside from this instance, they are consistently referred to as the "Stone Lions of Cochiti." In appearance, mutilated and/or weathered as the figures are, they are essentially the same, and there is no valid reason for accepting the data which Bandelier recorded here.

96. This letter probably concerned Elizabeth, or "Lizzie," Bandelier, mentioned in Joe's letter of February 17. Lizzie was to marry Henry Kaune at Highland later that year.

97. This generalization is too gross to have real significance or validity. Innumerable archaeological remains are along the eastern slopes of the Mogollones, or the Mogollon Mountains. Most prominent of these would be the Gila Cliff Dwellings, designated a National Monument in 1907; these are located west of the Continental Divide, however, and this may have been what Bandelier had in mind.

98. This letter is to be found in Burrus (1967a: 71-72).

99. Fort Wingate, McKinley County, New Mexico, is today a mining and ranching community, as well as the site of the fort. It is 12 miles southeast of Gallup and three miles south of Wingate Station. In 1850, the U.S. War Department established a fort at Cebolleta, north of Laguna, naming it for Captain Benjamin Wingate. In 1862, Captain Wingate was killed at the battle of Valverde. In this same year the fort was moved to El Gallo Spring (Ojo del Gallo) three miles south of Grants, where Kit Carson made it his headquarters when he rounded up the Navajos. In 1868, the fort moved again, this time to its present site, which was called the Big Bear Spring (Ojo del Oso). Here there was already a military establishment called Fort Fauntleroy, founded in 1860 by Colonel Thomas T. Fauntleroy and named by him. In 1866, the name was changed to Fort Lyon after Colonel Fauntleroy had resigned his command and joined the Confederacy some years before. In 1868, the two forts were consolidated. Today the Fort Wingate Military Reservation still has storage plants for explosives, but most of the area (64,000 acres) is used for Indian grazing land. Near the highway is a school for Navajos, established after 1925, with dormitories and recreation areas. There has been a post office since 1874. (Pearce 1965: 59.)

100. For the various components of the "Seven Cities of Cibola" and other archaeological sites in the general Zuñi area, the reader is referred to the publications of Spier, "An Outline for a Chronology of Zuñi Ruins," "Notes on Some Little Colorado Ruins," and "Ruins in the White Mountains, Arizona." (1917, 1918, 1919.) The publications afford the best means for identifying Bandelier's sites in terms of more recent surveys and publications.

101. Here, Bandelier appears to have been a bit hasty in his conclusions. Zuñi politics, as is true of other Pueblos as well, exhibit certain democratic qualities. However, factionalism, intrigue, and various devious maneuvers commonly characterize the continual power struggle.

102. Later in life Bandelier spent a number of years in the Peruvian and Bolivian

areas. At this time, however, he had never been to Cuzco nor, as far as is known, to South America.

103. It is difficult to interpret this comment. Zuñi has (had) multiple plazas; in several instances, these are normally indistinguishable (at least to the stranger) from surrounding streets and alleys. The one rather obvious plaza might be the area in front of the campo santo and mission church, but this area could hardly have been described as "small but neat."

104. Houses of seven stories at Zuñi were essentially an illusion. In reality, the houses were (and are) no more than two or three stories in height. However, the fact that they are arranged on a considerable mound, or hill, creates the impression of as many as seven stories when viewed from a distance.

105. The unusually large houses at Zuñi have quite probably been a functional correlate of the ten-foot tall Shalako kachinas dancing indoors as they play prominent roles in the dedication of newly constructed or renovated houses. (See Stevenson 1904; Bunzel 1932; Parsons 1939.)

106. This was true in Bandelier's time and is still true to some degree today. The western Pueblos were never under as firm control of the Spaniards as those of the Rio Grande, and after the Revolt Period, 1680-1692, remained virtually autonomous. This lack of Spanish control plus isolation in the American period have meant for Zuñi and Hopi a much slower pace of acculturation to both Spanish-American and Anglo-American ways.

107. "Principals," or "principales," are the leaders among the various Puebloan and other tribes. The bases for their selection have differed from one tribe to another and also with the passing of time as far as a specific tribe is concerned. Principales normally comprise the tribal council, and they are customarily the older men of the tribe though this latter quality is changing as more tribes are taking advantage of the educational and other experiences, military, etc., which their younger men have acquired.

108. Again, Bandelier was only partially correct. Not knowing the individuals involved (as was undoubtedly also true in large part for Bandelier), it is impossible to know what was happening. One strongly suspects, however, that a number of the old men, if not actually most of them, were also leaders in the theocratic structure of Zuñi. Age merits deference, it is true; but age is often coupled with important leadership status and it is quite impossible to specify which is really dominant. Councils are composed of these oldsters who, over the years, have frequently risen to leadership roles in various society or other contexts.

109. The "Washington party" referred to here was the Stevenson Expedition. In 1879, the Bureau of Ethnology (redesignated in the Sixteenth Annual Report, for 1894-95, as the Bureau of American Ethnology) was established in the Smithsonian Institution. It was decided to send an expedition to the pueblos and ruins of Arizona and New Mexico and to make a detailed study of one existing pueblo. Zuñi Pueblo was selected for the detailed study. James Stevenson (1840-1888), a geologist with the U.S. Geological Survey, was in charge and other members of the expedition were his wife, Matilda Coxe Stevenson, Frank H. Cushing, and J. K. Hillers. Stevenson continued his collecting throughout much of the 1880's. (Anderson 1907: I, 374-375.) For an illustrated catalogue of the collections for 1879 and 1880, see James Stevenson (1883: 307-465). In addition to Zuñi, specimens were collected from Laguna and Acoma, the Rio Grande Pueblos, Canyon de Chelly, and from the Jicarillas. Specimens numbering 3,095 were deposited in the National Museum. This catalogue did not indicate articles specifically taken from the old Zuñi church as Bandelier reported they had been. However, according to Matilda Coxe Stevenson (1904: 16-17), "Two images of saints and portions of the altar of the

old Catholic Church were obtained, the enamel finish on the faces and limbs of the figures showing much artistic skill. The church objects were in the custody of one Mauritio, and in order to determine whether they might be removed a council of religious and civil officers was held. It was finally decided that it would be well to have these objects go with the other Zuñi material to the 'great house' (National Museum) in Washington, where they would be preserved." Extended collections from Acoma and Zuñi were also indicated in the 6th Annual Report, Bureau of Ethnology, (Powell 1888: xxviii-xxix). Those from Zuñi were related primarily to shrines, sacred springs, caves, etc. A series of photographs was noted. The total Stevenson collection for 1884-85 was given as 8,500 specimens from the Southwest which were also deposited in the National Museum. Consult the first volume (Lange and Riley 1966: 89) for Bandelier's meeting with the "Stevenson Party," in 1880. For added material on the Stevensons' work in the Pueblo area, see Lurie's "Women in Early American Anthropology" (pp. 29-81) in Helm (1966).

110. As of this time, Bandelier may or may not have been aware of the inscriptions made by the early Spanish and later explorers and travelers on the rock faces of El Morro. He did not visit the site on this trip. However, as evidenced in his Final Report (II, 328-333) and in his journal entries of October 14-16, 1888, Bandelier did visit El Morro, or Inscription Rock. Aside from his own observations and notations, Bandelier made liberal use in his Final Report of the notes made by General Simpson, who, as a lieutenant, had visited El Morro in 1849 and with R. H. Kern, artist, copied the inscriptions. These notes were published in Simpson's "Journal of a Military Reconnoissance" (1850).

111. To elaborate upon the small, black-and-white sketch made by Bandelier of the mi-le, the reader is referred to colored plates in Stevenson (1904) for a better appreciation of this colorful ceremonial piece. It was pictured alone in plate CI; and in plate XXXV, among others, it was shown in association with various other objects in the layout of a ritual altar.

112. Both the Western Pueblos and those of the Rio Grande Valley identify these six directions for ritual purposes. (See Riley 1963a: 59-60.)

113. This story apparently made an impression upon Bandelier; he told it, himself, subsequently on a number of occasions. (See entries of August 12 and 18, 1883, for example.)

114. The Zuñi "Lake of the Dead" is a rather small body of water a few miles west of the pueblo. When a person dies, he goes to the lake, descends a ladder there, and joins his departed ancestors in villages and circumstances similar to this life on earth. (See Cushing 1896: 409-411.)

115. Interestingly, the Pueblos are monogamous though their deities are polygynous and perhaps reflect a polygynous past for Pueblo Indians. The present-day monogamy is, in fact, very brittle with easy divorce, and it has been described as "brittle monogamy."

116. Although not too much emphasis should be placed on this myth, it is probable that the Navajo and Apache came from the north, breaking off from a Northern Athapascan stock perhaps around, or before, A.D. 1000. These groups, now known collectively as the "Apachean speakers," gradually infiltrated the Southwest. By the time Spaniards began to infiltrate the area, the Navajos at least were growing corn and had adopted other Pueblo Indian traits. (Riley 1954.)

117. These masked impersonations continue as important Zuñi kachinas. They are clowns, yet highly potent and dangerous individuals. Their unusual masks represent neither fish nor pigs, but deformed individuals resulting from an incestuous brother-sister union.

118. Even today the tempo of most dances is faster among the Western Puebloans

than among the Eastern. Items of ceremonial paraphernalia continue to be traded throughout the Pueblo area, though most seem to originate in the western villages as crafts have persisted among those tribes to a considerably higher degree. Throughout recent decades, Zuñi Pueblo has continued to be commonly recognized as the center of the kachina cult, with various traits diffusing both west to the Hopi and east to the Rio Grande villages. Inevitably, there has been a certain amount of reciprocity between these villages.

119. This was probably nothing more than a well-preserved section of the pueblo which in its isolation seemed to Bandelier to be a separate defensive unit.

120. To the best of our knowledge, Frank H. Cushing never left a published corpus of poems. Some idea of his literary style may be gained from articles in the *Century Magazine*, his papers in the Annual Reports of the Bureau of American Ethnology, and his volume of Zuñi Folk Tales. (See bibliography.)

121. A famous story in Norse mythology in which the god Thor visits the evil giant Thrym to recover his magical hammer which had been stolen by the giants.

In the story Thrym demands the beautiful maiden goddess Freya as a price for the hammer. Thor dresses as Freya and pretends to go through with the wedding ceremony. When the love-intoxicated giant places the hammer in Thor's lap, the god uses it to slay the giant and the assembled wedding party.

It is not clear from the journals why Bandelier chose this particular story. Certainly it would be interesting to have had the Zuñi reaction to it.

122. There are indications from archaeological sites in the Southwest that the macaw was known even farther north and east than Zuñi in pre-Spanish times. For a recent summary discussion of macaw and parrot distribution in the aboriginal Southwest, see Hibben (1966: 526-527 et seq.).

123. In puebloan culture, the number four has almost universal ceremonial significance. In many instances, four, itself, is prominent; in others, multiples of four are used. (See Parsons 1939: I, 500-01.)

124. Bandelier's use of the term "gens" was incorrect here. The matrilineal form of sib found at Zuñi (e.g., the Parrot), is properly called a clan, or a matrilineal clan, but not a gens which is patrilineal.

125. It must be remembered that Bandelier was doing an archaeological survey while Cushing was engaged in studying Zuñi ethnology. Bandelier's very involvement with ethnological problems is interesting for it grew out of his firm conviction that data on contemporary peoples could be important or even essential in the interpretation of archaeological data. As we have pointed out elsewhere (Lange and Riley 1966: 67), this is a very "modern" point of view. (See also fn 137.)

126. The use of ground sherds as temper for pottery is well known for Zuñi and other pueblos. It has also been reported for the wares of many prehistoric puebloan peoples.

127. The "planting" of fresh-cut branches, or small trees, of various conifers, or of cottonwood, has been noted widely among the pueblo villages as a part of the ceremonial decorations of plazas or other dance areas. (For examples, see Lange 1959: 329 for Cochiti Pueblo; Parsons 1962: 152, 226, 230, for Isleta Pueblo.)

128. Several times Bandelier has described Pueblo dancers as "naked." This in fact was never the case as his further account demonstrates here. The Pueblo Indian men often dance bare-chested and bare-legged but always wear some sort of loin cloth. Women seem to have danced bare-breasted in early historic times, but in the nineteenth and twentieth centuries the breasts have been generally covered.

129. The young godlike heros of the Quiche Maya, Hunahpú and Xbalanque, destroyed

the evil monster Vucub-Caquix by removing his teeth and putting out his eyes. Cabracan was a son of Vucub-Caquix, also killed by the two youths.

These stories certainly have a generic resemblance to Pueblo myths especially in certain elements (the "twin" motif, for example). The similarities, however, are general and probably point to a common, and ancient, source for these stories. Among the Pueblos, the Twin War Gods are known by variations of such names as Ma'sēwa (Older Brother) and O'yo-yēwa (Younger Brother).

130. Various researchers (Bertha P. Dutton [1963] and J. Charles Kelley [1966], among others) have recently pointed out the generalized Mexican flavor of Southwestern and especially Western Puebloan culture. This is not, however, Mayan and no specific Maya parallels exist despite Bandelier's seeming failure to differentiate between (Central) Mexican and Mayan cultures.

131. This was W. L. Metcalf, one of the Cushing party and an illustrator for Cushing. Bourke referred to Mr. Metcalf as the "young artist whom I met with Cushing and Baxter in the Zuñi country in 1881." Bourke's first meeting with Metcalf was recorded in a May, 1881, entry. In addition, Bourke commented that Metcalf was an artist for *Scribner's* and *Harper's Weekly* who had filled his portfolio with very successful sketches in oil, water, and crayon of the people and places seen on his tour. (Bloom 1936b: 204, 242, 245-46.)

The Baxter referred to above is Sylvester Baxter, whom Bourke said was a correspondent for the *Boston Herald* (p. 242). Baxter was also associated with the Archaeological Institute of America and, later, with the Hemenway Southwestern Archaeological Expedition. For an interesting account of Cushing and a description of Zuñi by Baxter at this time, see Baxter 1882: 72-91. Several of the illustrations he used are signed by W. L. Metcalf.

132. It is difficult, if not impossible, to identify precisely the wares to which Cushing was referring. However, a number of spectacular and well-made wares have been found in the general area of Pinedale, Forestdale, etc., southwest of Zuñi. (See the papers by Colton and others in the Museum of Northern Arizona, Ceramic Series, beginning in 1952.)

133. Bears and lions, as well as eagles, are widely believed by the puebloans and other tribes to possess strong medicine. They are the medicine animals; the medicine men are sometimes referred to as "bears," etc. Paws, claws, talons, feathers, and skins are important parts of the necessary paraphernalia of these native doctors.

134. ". . . dressing stone with stone" refers to the "picking," or sharpening, of the grinding stones, both manos and metates, with hammer stones in order to increase their grinding efficacy. Even today, sounds of this sharpening often precede the preparation of native meal, especially corn, in anticipation of the extensive bread baking prior to various feast days and similar celebrations.

135. Christian Barthelmess, in 1883, was principal musician of the 13th Infantry's regimental band at Fort Wingate. This was his second enlistment in the U.S. Army. Having come in his youth from Bavaria, he enlisted in 1876 as a private and was assigned to the Sixth Cavalry at Fort Apache, Arizona Territory. From the beginning, his life had more direction than that of the average soldier serving on the frontier. He began taking photographs and his musicianship put him into the regimental band. He was discharged on November 14, 1881, at Fort Apache. He re-enlisted the next day (this time in the infantry) and was assigned to Fort Wingate where his contacts with the Navajo and Dr. Washington Matthews added new interests, as he began to make observations on the Navajo. Two of these were published in *Der Westen*, a Chicago German newspaper. He translated one of Dr. Matthews' papers into German for publication, and his knowl-

edge of music enabled him to transcribe a Navajo song for Dr. Matthews. (Frink and Barthelmess 1965.)

136. "Dr. Cushing" was most probably Frank Hamilton Cushing's father, Thomas. Bandelier consistently referred to Frank, of whom he was a great admirer at this point in time, as "Mr." J. W. Powell (1900: 360) noted Thomas as a "practicing physician and a man of learning, who gradually retired from the practice of medicine and devoted himself to the study of philosophy." The father encouraged Frank in his studies but was apparently less enthusiastic about his interest from very early years in archaeology.

In a series of references to the family of Cushing, the precise designation of "Mrs. F. H. Cushing," and later to "Mrs. E. L. Cushing," the wife of Cushing's brother, it would appear that all of these were at Zuñi Pueblo while Bandelier was visiting there. Mrs. Frank H. Cushing was Emily Tennison Magill of Washington, D.C., before her marriage, July 10, 1882. (Who's Who, vol. I, p. 170.)

137. Here again, Bandelier expresses his appreciation of the need and the potential benefits of blending archaeological and ethnological data. Unfortunately, this interest was largely ignored, if not abandoned, until about the time of World War II. It is proper to view his ideas, nonetheless, among the antecedents of Taylor's conjunctive approach (1948: 7 et seq.) and the "new archaeology" of the present time. (See also fn 125.)

138. The Aztec Emperor, Montezuma II, who was killed in 1519, was later made into a supernatural figure and ceremonies connected with him and with Maria, the mistress of Cortez, became widespread in the greater Southwest.

139. Pusha may here be equated with the Cochiti Po'shai-añĩ. At that pueblo, Po'shai-añĩ is remembered as an extinct medicine society—the highest of the three degrees within the Flint Society (Curtis 1926: 87-88). Bandelier was elsewhere told that the name for Montezuma, a relatively modern name, was really "Pu'shaya." In an effort to check these data, Lange's Cochiti informants could only associate "Po'shai-añĩ" with the "Little Horse," or Santiago, of the July 25 celebrations. (Lange 1959: 267-268.)

140. Fray Marcos de Niza was supposed to have visited Zuñi in the year 1539. It is unlikely that he reached this far north (in spite of his claims) but very likely his Negro companion, Estevanico (Estevan or Stephan), did so. There is a story that Estevan was killed outside one of the then Zuñi pueblos and quite possibly an old memory of him lingered into the nineteenth century. Fray Marcos de Niza did visit Zuñi in 1540 as part of the Coronado Expedition but it seems unlikely that he erected a stone pile on Thunder Mountain (or anywhere else in the area). In any event, stone piles throughout this area were constructed by natives in high or dangerous places for supernatural reasons.

Bandelier, here, seems to be recording a mixture of folk memory, latter-day tales, rationalizations, and myths.

141. This was a very interesting and perceptive observation by Bandelier on puebloan social organization. The unique qualities of the individual villages have persisted to the present day, despite such common denominators as the several linguistic groups, affiliated and interrelated secret societies, intermarriages, and other shared features.

142. Stevenson (1904: 116, pl. xxi) provided a colored plate of an indoor shrine for the Elder War God, showing a number of prayersticks. Another plate, black-and-white (pl. xxii), showed an outdoor shrine to the Younger War God on Toyoalana, Thunder Mountain, or Corn Mountain.

143. This taboo on the telling of folktales at times of the year other than winter has persisted to the present day. Would-be violators must weigh the enforcement of the taboo by rattlesnakes.

144. Ceremonial calendar lapses, or losses, are difficult to gather data on. Many cere-monies are not scheduled regularly; as long as a ceremony is remembered, it could poten-tially be staged. The greater the interval, obviously, the greater the chance of innovation, intentional or unintentional. Pride in perpetuating ceremonial traditions serves to deny that ceremonies have actually lapsed, or been lost. However, without periodic perform-ances, these ceremonies cannot help but pass out of general awareness, then particular awareness, and finally complete loss results. Without various written notations by various kinds of people, but rarely natives, such losses are seldom, if ever, realized.

145. For a description of the dress, or manta, of the Malinche at Cochiti, see Lange (1959: 279-281, 302, 327).

146. Such tragic events, though not common, have been sporadically reported. Alfred Herrera, 1963 Governor of Cochiti Pueblo, died of a heart attack suffered during an autumn ceremony in 1963. In earlier days, witchcraft was commonly the explanation; in recent years, this feeling has diminished but not entirely disappeared.

147. As Bandelier's comments, here and elsewhere, suggested, Cushing was deeply in-volved in the Zuñi ceremonial structure. The following excerpts from various sources are of interest on this point:

"In March last [1882] Mr. Frank Cushing visited the Museum with several Zuñi chiefs and Moqui from Zuñi, where Mr. Cushing had lived for some time. The visit was one of great interest. A reception given at the Museum was attended by several hundred persons who were glad to see representatives of the Pueblo tribes and hear Mr. Cushing's remarks about them. By those among us who are especially engaged in ethnographical studies, this visit will be valued from the insight which it gave into the character of these people and from many little things which were learned from them in regard to objects in the Museum; while the impressive religious rite performed by the party on the shore of Deer Island, when Mr. Cushing was formally admitted into one of the higher grades of a religious order, gave, to those who were so fortunate as to witness it, new ideas in relation to Indian character, and impressed upon all the sacrifice which MR. CUSHING was making for ethnological science as well as for the well-being of his Indian friends. It is a satisfaction to know that he has returned to Zuñi accompanied by his devoted wife to share his labors." (Peabody Museum 1887b: 181.)

On August 30, 1882, Cushing took the Zuñi Indians who had accompanied him on the eastern trip to the Seneca Reserve. They returned to Zuñi on September 23rd. (4th A. R., B. [A.] E. 1886: xxxvii.)

During the last six months of 1883 he [Cushing] successfully exerted himself to in-crease his influence among the Zuñi Indians with special reference to securing his complete initiation (begun by the seaside at Boston, in 1882) into their ka-ka or sacred dance organization. (P. xxix.) Early in March (1884) it was expedient to recall Mr. Cushing to Washington. This prevented his initiation into ka-ka. Still by virtue of his membership in the Priesthood of the Bow, he was permitted before leaving to be present at initiation of others. This proved to be of 6 hour duration and he could not get it recorded. (5th A. R., B. [A.] E. 1887: xxv-xxvi.)

148. Albinos at Zuñi Pueblo were mentioned in an article by H. C. Hodge from the New York Sun, no date, in the Bandelier Scrapbook. Albinism has been noted for a num-ber of Southwestern tribes, perhaps most frequently for Jemez Pueblo and the Navajo.

149. Samuel Gorman came to New Mexico in 1852 under the auspices of the Amer-ican Baptist Home Mission Society and was among the first Protestant missionaries to Pueblo Indians. From 1852 to 1859 he lived at Laguna Pueblo, conducting services and maintaining a school. From 1859 to 1862 he was in Santa Fe, returning east with other Union sympathizers in 1862. While at Laguna, Gorman was a frequent and vigorous

spokesman for that tribe against white encroachers and in disputes with other Indian groups. His home became the residence of the Walter K. Marmon family. (Lange and Riley 1966: 332n 152.)

150. This was Charles Franklin, of Arizona. He had once lived with the tribe three years and been formally adopted by the Zuñi. (Bloom 1936b: 120.) He was described by Bourke as "not a man of fine education, but [one who] is unusually clear-headed." The two had an extended conversation about Zuñi clans, or "gentes," or what Franklin called "cliques." (Pp. 192-194.) Part of the information Franklin gave Bourke was the following story. "At the commencement of their new year, some time in December when the days are short, (Winter Solstice?) they put out all fires and sweep the chimneys clean; sweep and clean out all their houses. New fires are kindled from the sacred fire, which is either a fire made and blessed by the caciques or else is one which they preserve, I don't know where. When I was first with them I had been for a long time sick with scarlet fever, and about the time this fire feast came on, I was lying on my bed, alone in the house and feeling chilly, got up and kindled a little flame to warm myself. The smoke, escaping from the chimney, betrayed [me] and aroused the indignation and fears of the caciques who hurried to the house where I was living and found me suffering from a relapse brought on by over-exertion. They cautioned me against my indiscretion and said my sickness was a just punishment for having committed the crime of kindling that fire, that [since] I was now a Zuñi, I must conform to their ways, unless I wished bad luck to pursue me, when I violated them. For (10) ten days, they allowed no fire at all, except in cases of great necessity, such as cooking a small amount of food. No one is allowed to smoke in the streets and nobody eats any meat for the first (4) days. If a man should eat any meat during those four days, he would die." The ten-day period Franklin described was the tesh'kwi, or fast, which precedes the new year; for a detailed account of the events of this period, see Stevenson (1904: 108-128).

151. In each case of a "studied" pueblo, whether by Bandelier or by virtually any of his contemporaries, the approach was at best haphazard. This is regrettable in terms of the potential in the context of the generally unacculturated nature of native life, but it is completely understandable in terms of a general absence of any formal training of those doing the fieldwork.

152. This was a rather enlightened attitude for that period, illustrating a considerable range in degrees of acculturation even in one pueblo. It is also possible that anthropologists have tended to exaggerate retention of the more contrasting, and dramatic, "primitive" views, portraying them as relatively viable long after their virtual extinction.

153. It is noteworthy that Bandelier's reactions to Zuñi Pueblo and to the Zuñi Indians were generally favorable. Whether this was the result of his prior residences at Santo Domingo, Cochiti, Laguna, and Acoma or a difference in the time of their respective visits, late winter or early spring as opposed to late spring and summer, or simply a personality difference, the contrast with the observations of Captain Bourke is striking. Bourke noted, "The smell in Zuni is outrageous. Decayed meat, sheep and goats' pelts, excrement human and animal, unwashed dogs and Indians, fleas, lice and bed-bugs (the houses in Zuni are full of the last), garbage of every kind—it must be regarded as a standing certificate of the salubrity of this climate that a single Zuni is in existence today." (Bloom 1936b: 122.)

154. The "Good Kachina" dancers, comprising a line of identically dressed impersonators, continue to be a favorite among the many masked characterizations at Zuñi.

155. Bandelier's account was ambiguous here; the white masks were worn, but not by women. The wearers were actually male impersonators, as is true of Kachina impersonations categorically.

156. The association of colors with cardinal directions was very strongly developed in the American Southwest and probably represented another example of Mexican-Southwestern contacts. The specific colors given by Bandelier are valid for Zuñi, Hopi, Jemez, and, generally speaking, for the Keresan pueblos. Tanoan-speakers, other than Jemez, had different specific color direction associations as did the Navajo and Apache. (Riley 1963a: 49-50 et seq.)

157. This Zuñi account is quite garbled. (Cf. fn 140.) Cabeza de Vaca was never within hundreds of miles of the Zuñi towns. Possibly, however, there was in Bandelier's time a genuine folk memory of Estevan and of the Coronado Expedition.

Estevan was a Negro slave who helped guide Fray Marcos de Niza from West Mexico to the Southwest in 1539. Fray Marcos never reached Zuñi, but Estevan may have been killed there.

Fray Marcos returned to Mexico and his fanciful accounts of the Pueblo area led to a major expedition commanded by Francisco Vásquez de Coronado, that in the years 1540-42 explored much of the Southwestern area.

Bandelier was later to publish on both Cabeza de Vaca and Fray Marcos. (See Bandelier 1886a; 1886b.)

158. On earlier occasions, here, and in entries yet to come, Bandelier noted disturbed ruins, "pot-hunting" by individuals searching for treasures, curios, building materials, or utilitarian objects such as metates and manos. While in many instances the population was sparse, and travelers few, there were occasional visitors even in the most remote areas. While pot-hunting was often too much of a diversion, many did engage in it from time to time. This is by no means a phenomenon of only recent years.

159. For a relatively complete account of silver work in the Indian Southwest, the reader is referred to Adair's study, The Navajo and Pueblo Silversmiths (1945).

160. A bias from his Pueblo Indian friends, no doubt.

161. See entry of January 28, 1883.

162. This was possibly 2nd Lt. Guy Evans Huse of the 4th Cavalry. He was commissioned June 13, 1879, and was promoted to first lieutenant November 26, 1884. He resigned in 1886 and died in 1893. (Heitman 1903: I, 559.) However, Fort Wingate at this time had eight companies of the 13th Infantry and 9th Cavalry. Bourke (Bloom 1936b: 79) listed a Lieutenant Hughes, but not Huse. Heitman (1903: I, 552) listed a Martin Briggs Hughes, first lieutenant as of May 24, 1873, and captain, as of June 6, 1885. This period of his service was with the 9th Cavalry. It is difficult to decide which was the person Bandelier had mentioned, or that Bourke noted. It would appear that one or the other had misspelled the name.

163. Abies douglassii seldom appears in modern botany. Probably Bandelier meant Douglas fir, presently Pseudotsuga taxifolia Britton.

164. Now usually written Diné, an Athapascan word meaning "people." The Western Apache groups use a similar word with the same meaning, which Bandelier, in his entry of May 24, 1883, rendered as N'de.

165. Dr. Gibson, here, was presumably the same person who drew a sketch of a tipi with a floor plan and signed it "Charles T. Gibson, A. A. Surgeon, U. S. A.," on the back of page 39 of Bandelier's journals. However, a careful examination of Heitman (1903) has failed to reveal any mention of this person, and the editors have no further data on Dr. Gibson.

166. There may be similarities in the house types of these two areas, but there are no demonstrable direct affiliations.

167. D. M. Riordan was sent to Fort Defiance as Indian Agent for the Navajo in 1883

and was appointed postmaster that year. Riordan was at Defiance for only a year, later moving to Flagstaff. (Barnes 1935: 35, 125; Theobald 1961: 99.)

168. Founded on Bonito Creek in 1852 as a control point for the Navajo. (Barnes 1935: 125.)

169. Composite in the sense that many Navajo, even before Bandelier's day, had taken up farming while others herded or hunted. All Navajo spoke, and still speak, a single language in the Apachean or Southern Athapascan group.

170. This is another of the very few instances in which Bandelier included his basis of calculating measurements or distances. In the margin of the journal entry of March 21, accompanying a sketch of ruins, was the following: 270 steps + 807 = 1077 × 0.73½ = 792 [791.595] total length [meters or yards?].

171. Dr. William Eggert was the first homeopathic physician in New Mexico Territory, living in Santa Fe in the 1880's and 1890's, specializing in women's diseases. Born in Germany, Eggert was a graduate in medicine at the New York Homeopathic College. He came to Santa Fe from Indianapolis. Governor Sheldon appointed him to a seven-man territorial medical board; he served as its secretary from its organization in 1882. He aided in writing a new bill on the practice of medicine which passed in 1895. Eggert ranked high in his profession and was a medical writer of national reputation. The December 7 entry, 1882, suggested that Dr. Eggert was assisting Bandelier with German as he wrote, "And then went to see Dr. Eggert . . . , and dragged him over to the room, to read my letters to the *Ausland*." (Lange and Riley 1966: 372.) Bandelier visited Dr. Eggert often and carried on extensive correspondence with him. The July 24, 1883, entry also indicated that Dr. Eggert did some translations for him. (See Anderson 1907: I, 439; Lange and Riley 1966: 409.

Other people also helped Bandelier with his translations; Reverend and Mrs. Meany, Santa Fe, assisted with the translation of *Die Köshare* into *The Delight Makers*. With his *Histoire*, the Golden Jubilee presentation for Pope Leo XIII, Bandelier was aided by Father Augustine Navet. Bandelier, though familiar with several languages, seemed to be really proficient in none. For a discussion of his deficiencies, see White and Bernal 1960 and Lange 1950.

172. This was probably W. W. Griffin of the First National Bank of Santa Fe. (*Santa Fé New Mexican Review*, 1884.) For further data, see fn 84 for 1884.

173. Luther Prentice Bradley reentered service after the Civil War; he served with the 27th Infantry and the 9th Infantry as a lieutenant colonel; he became a colonel with the 3rd Infantry in 1879 and transferred to the 13th Infantry two months later, in June. He retired in 1886. He had held the rank of brigadier general at the end of the Civil War, and in 1867 had been breveted brigadier general for action as Resaca, Georgia, during the war. (Heitman 1903: I, 239.) At Fort Wingate, in the 1880's he was in command of eight companies of the 13th Infantry and the 9th Cavalry.

174. W. S. Woodside was a notary public in Santa Fe. (McKenney 1882-83: 341.)

175. John M. Gunn was first lieutenant under Captain R. G. Marmon, of Troop I (Laguna), 1st Regiment, Cavalry, New Mexico Volunteer Militia. (Official Reports 1884: 114-15.) He was the author of Schat-Chen: History, Traditions, and Naratives [sic] of the Queres Indians of Laguna and Acoma, published in Albuquerque in 1917.

176. This may have been J. T. Saunders, an Albuquerque attorney, with an office in #5, Cromwell Block, according to Polk and Danser (1884a: 306). The October 17, 1882, issue of the *Albuquerque Morning Journal*, announced that "James T. Saunders has severed his connection with the Review. He will probably commence the practice of law either in Albuquerque or in some other point in the territory." (A. J. O. Anderson File.)

177. Father León Mailluchet was from near Porrentruy, Franche-Comte, France. He was a parish priest in the Pecos-Las Vegas area during the 1880's. He lived with his brother and family. (Lange and Riley 1966: 412.)

178. Probably the wife of Matthew McCarty, a settler on disputed Acoma lands. On October 18, 1884, McCarty testified for the San Rafael settlers, stating that he had lived on his ranch for twenty years. A station of the Atlantic and Pacific Railroad some fifteen miles west of Cubero within the limits of Pueblo-claimed land was named for him. Today, this is an Acoma village. (Lange and Riley 1966: 297n 145.)

Pearce (1965: 98) gives this added information. "McCarty's (Valencia). Trading community on Acoma Indian Reservation on US 66, 13 mi SE of Grants. Named for the contractor whose camp was here when AT & SF RR was built through this section. Just above the settlement is a beautiful church recently built by the Indians, which is an exact replica, half size, of the ancient mission church of old Acoma. Its wood carvings are notable works of art. Called Santa Maria de Acoma by some residents. Post office, intermittently, 1887-1911, as both McCarty's and McCarty."

179. James M. Latta was a cattle rancher near Grants in Valencia County. (Polk and Danser 1884a: 320.) In the Santa Fe Daily New Mexican, October 18, 1882, p. 4, Latta was mentioned as being from Albuquerque.

180. Dumas Provencher was a settler of French ancestry, who, with various other members of his family, settled in the Ojo del Gallo, or old Fort Wingate, area about three miles south of Grants after the Navajo campaign of 1862-64. This region, long claimed by Acoma Pueblo, was renamed San Rafael in the early 1870's. Provencher was shot and killed on November 7, 1888, while acting as an election judge at San Rafael. His wife was a sister of Father John B. Brun of San Rafael. (Lange and Riley 1966: 277-278n135.) Polk and Danser (1884a: 320) indicated that there was a firm of Provencher and Brun which operated a sawmill in Grants. In 1882, Provencher was mentioned frequently in the Albuquerque Morning Journal as a prominent lumber dealer. Later, he was a captain (Commanding Officer, Troop K [San Rafael], 1st Regiment, Cavalry, New Mexico Volunteer Militia) under Major George H. Pradt and Lieutenant-Colonel W. G. Marmon in the Apache troubles of the middle 1880's. (Walter 1927: 210, 211, 212; Official Reports 1884: 114-15.) Bandelier had enjoyed the friendship and hospitality of the Provenchers in 1882. (Lange and Riley 1966: 276, 277, 280, 281, 308-309.)

181. In writing of the history of this name, Father Chávez pointed out the name of Chaves (Latin, clavis: plural claves) is the old Spanish and Portuguese word for "Keys." As related by the poet Zapata de Chaves, it was first given to the Ruiz brothers who were knighted for wresting the Portuguese town of Chaves from the Moors in 1160; its coatof-arms of five keys was also bestowed on them. The correct spelling of the name is "Chaves," for it is not a patronym to merit the final "z" like most Spanish names of this ending. But in all Latin America, Portugal, and in some instances in Spain, the "z" ending is used. (Chávez 1954: 23.)

Pearce (1965: 32) gave the the name of this town in Valencia County as Chaves.

182. Dr. Benjamin Morris Thomas (1834-92), trained as a dentist, went to New Mexico for his health and promptly, in 1870, entered the Indian Service (1870, Fort Defiance; 1872, Southern Apaches; 1874-82, Pueblo Indians, Jicarilla Apaches, Southern Utes). McKenney (1882-83: 309) listed Thomas as Pueblo Agent and General Agent for United States Indian Affairs in New Mexico. In his last decade, he was Register of the Land Office (Tucson, A. T.), a dentist in Santa Fe (1886-89), and Territorial Secretary (1889-92). He was known as the "Father of Education" in the Pueblos for his instituting day schools and a boarding and industrial school in Albuquerque, and for sending the first Pueblo Indian pupils to the training school at Carlisle, Pennsylvania. A strong Pres-

byterian, he was an elder of the church in Santa Fe. He died in 1892. Dates vary in the accounts of his life; these data were largely based on notes of A. J. O. Anderson. The 1880-82 journals recorded frequent correspondence between Bandelier and Thomas. In 1880, Bandelier visited twice with Dr. Thomas in Santa Fe, and Dr. Thomas, en route to Zuñi, stopped at Santo Domingo to visit Bandelier. In July 1882, Bandelier obtained the 1880 Census of the Pueblos from Dr. Thomas in Santa Fe (Lange and Riley 1966: 30, 73, 122, 341). Just what "matter" concerning Dr. Thomas was being discussed is not known.

183. This may have referred to the Padre's stand in regard to litigation in the 1880's between the Durán y Chaves heirs and the heirs of Román A. Baca concerning the San Mateo Springs Grant. The original grant had been been made by Governor Mendinueta to Santiago Durán y Chaves on February 5, 1768. Román Baca was a half-brother of Colonel Manuel A. Chaves. Differing accounts have credited each man with the founding of the village of San Mateo. For further details, see Pearce (1965: 147). For the genealogy of this early New Mexico family, consult Chávez (1954: 18-23, 160-164, 324-325). Román Baca became the first postmaster at San Mateo, December 19, 1876. (Dike 1958.)

184. This was James Fornance of Pennsylvania; a West Point graduate, Fornance's career was post-Civil War and primarily with the 13th Infantry which he joined in June 1871. He was promoted to first lieutenant in 1872 and served as regimental adjutant from July 1879 to March 1887. He became a captain in 1889, and he died in 1898 of wounds received at the Battle of San Juan, Santiago, Cuba. (Heitman 1903: I, 429.)

185. One of these, presumably, was used in the book on Barthelmess written by Frink with the aid of Barthelmess' son, Casey. (1965: following p. 56.)

186. Robert Erskine Anderson Crofton, an Irishman; he remained in service after the Civil War. From other units, he became lieutenant colonel in the 13th Infantry in 1879 and colonel in 1886. He retired in 1897 and died in 1898. (Heitmen 1903: I, 339.)

187. Heitman (1903) did not list a Woodbury who could have been this person. Bandelier did not make many errors of such proportions, but this may have been Captain Waterbury, mentioned by Bandelier in his journal of two days later.

188. This was Timothy O. Howe who had been appointed Postmaster General by President Chester A. Arthur in 1881. (World Almanac 1967: 432.) According to the Biographical Congressional Directory, Howe was born in 1816; he died March 25, 1883, at Kenosha, Wisconsin. (1903: 607.)

189. Juan José Montoya was one of Bandelier's best friends and helpers at Cochiti Pueblo, New Mexico, their relationship beginning almost at the outset of Bandelier's first residence there in the autumn of 1880. (See Lange and Riley 1966.) Juan José was born in 1837, was forty-three when he first met Bandelier, and died August 12, 1886.

190. José Hilario Montoya, a good friend of Bandelier's at Cochiti Pueblo. José Hilario was repeatedly put in as governor of the Pueblo and was an acknowledged leader among these people for many years. Father Dumarest (1920: 200n3) noted that "For almost ten years [as of 1905] José Hilario Montoya has held the office of governor. He is a man of rapid and profound thought, incredibly active, and endowed in a high degree with a talent for gentle diplomacy and with unfailing virtue. He has encouraged men to send their children to school and he has always directed the people into lines of progress, retaining the sympathy alike of the Indians and of all Whites who have come into relation with him." Samuel Ellison, first postmaster of Peña Blanca, recommended José Hilario "as the best guide and informant, also as an instructor in their language, which I [Bandelier] might secure." (Lange and Riley 1966: 88.)

191. Don Nicolás Pino was a conspirator, 1846-47, although not involved in the Taos

Revolt. After imprisonment, he took oath of allegiance and remained loyal, joining with Colonel Price in an attack on Taos. He was mentioned as living in Galisteo, 1855, 1857; Nicolás and Miguel (a brother?) fought on the Union side in the Civil War. Pinos were in the Territorial legislature continuously. Nicolás died in 1896, aged 77, a wealthy man; he was buried at Galisteo. Bandelier stayed with Nicolás on a number of occasions when in the Galisteo area (Lange and Riley 1966: 333, 334, 338, 376, 414). Dike (1958) listed Nicolás Pino as the first postmaster of Juana Lopez, Santa Fe County, beginning December 10, 1866.

192. Gregorio was a young married man at Santo Domingo Pueblo who befriended Bandelier in the early days of his residence there. (Lange and Riley 1966: 92-94.)

193. In a review of the first volume of Bandelier journals (Lange and Riley 1966), Father Ernest J. Burrus, S. J., asked, "Is the Brinton of the *Journals* some obscure doctor of Santa Fe (as the Index seems to insinuate) or the renowned Americanist Daniel Garrison Brinton (1837-1899)?" (Burrus 1967b: 121.) Bandelier was equally cryptic here, but no possible alternative has subsequently come to light, and it seems most probable this was indeed Daniel Garrison Brinton.

194. Of these assorted items, the 1882 journals have definitely been preserved, along with other journals of the 1880-1907 period, in the Library, Museum of New Mexico, Santa Fe, where there are also a few original watercolors, photographs, and a miscellany of manuscripts, correspondence, and other materials. These have come from Fanny R. Bandelier, Carl F. Huegy, and others; some may have been included in this shipment noted in the journal entry. Others may have been included in the volumes prepared (essentially scrapbooks) for the Jubilee of Pope Leo XIII in 1888. Still others, primarily a few clippings, may have been incorporated in the Bandelier Scrapbook that Professor Fred Eggan made available to us.

195. Bandelier wrote Mrs. Morgan from Fort Wingate in March 1883, but there seems to have been no journal entry of this fact. "I have increased my collections by 60 colored plates & I cannot any longer accumulate collections. I must paint as much as possible." (White 1940: II, 251.) Conceivably these were the plates referred to here.

196. Eugene Beauharnais Beaumont, of Pennsylvania. He was mustered out of service after the Civil War; reentering service he became a major in the 4th Cavalry in 1879 and a lieutenant colonel in the 3rd Cavalry in 1892. During the Civil War, he had been breveted a lieutenant colonel and had won the Medal of Honor for action at Harpeth River, Tennessee, in 1864. (Heitman 1903: I, 204.)

197. This was William Malcolm Waterbury of New York. After the Civil War, he was mustered out, but reentered service a year later. In 1869, he was assigned to the 13th Infantry as a first lieutenant. He became a captain in 1871. In 1895, he retired with the rank of major. (Heitman 1903: I, 1007.)

198. The use of rabbitskins for blankets was followed by various Southwestern tribes, dating back to pre-puebloan Basketmaker times. The more common form consisted of woven strips of the skins, with fur remaining, rather than pelts pieces together.

199. Bandelier's statement was an oversimplification; literally, it was erroneous. Significant differences, along with similarities, do indeed exist, however, between the Eastern, or Rio Grande, Pueblos and the Western Pueblos.

200. Possibly this account has some validity but the more conventional story was reported later by Bandelier (1890-92: II, 371-372) and told in more detail by Montgomery, Smith, and Brew (1949: 21-22). According to present evidence, Awatovi was sacked by other Hopi villagers (probably late in the year 1700) because of the willingness of Awatovi

Pueblo to accept Spanish priests returning after the Reconquest of New Mexico. (See also fn 456.)

201. This was Mrs. Frank H. Cushing's sister, Miss Margaret W. Magill. She was an artist and, in 1886, was to serve in this capacity on the Hemenway Expedition. (Haury 1945: 6.)

202. This was Professor Eben Norton Horsford (1818-1893), a native of New York, who became well known for his investigations and writings in chemistry. He was nominated by Captain R. A. Wainwright for honorary and corresponding membership in the Historical Society of New Mexico. He was voted into membership in 1860. (Bloom 1943: 281.) Horsford was a life member of the Archaeological Institute according to the Fifth Annual Report of the Institute, p. 10.

203. The reason for Bandelier's back dating of this letter for *Das Ausland* is not clear. It was published in 1884 (*Das Ausland* 1884: 241-243) and titled "Ein Brief über Akoma von Adolf F. Bandelier" and dated May 20 from the the Pueblo of San Estévan of Acoma. Hodge's bibliography (1932: 364) gave an [1883?] date.

204. Ha-ui-cu, or as it is customarily spelled today, Hawikuh, lies west of Zuñi Pueblo, almost at the New Mexico-Arizona line. It was the first Zuñi village to be contacted by the Coronado Expedition. Hodge did some excavations there early in this century, but the major portion of the pueblo remains untouched.

205. If so, this was probably Spanish ware. Prehistoric Pueblo pottery was never wheel (lathe) turned and, even today, Pueblo women utilize the old techniques of shaping pots by hand.

206. Actually, there is no "purple-on-white" pottery in the Southwest. These pieces may have been overfired, with a carmine, or magenta, shade resulting.

207. See entry of April 8, 1883, for further details regarding this person. This was Solomon Barth, forty years of age, St. Johns; in the period 1880-82, he was a member of the Council of the Arizona Territorial Legislature. (Disturnell 1881: 120.) Polk and Danser (1884a: 715) listed him as owner of a general store. A building with Barth Mercantile Co. painted on the outside wall stands today in St. Johns.

208. For a slightly different and more detailed account than Bandelier's, see Fierman 1961: 249n48.

209. Reverend Pedro Badilla, originally from Costa Rica, was sent in 1880 to St. Johns where he built the first church and rectory (Salpointe 1898: 269).

210. This has apparently been a rather common, and certainly understandable, practice. In the excavation of L.A. 70, Bandelier's Pueblo del Encierro, several somewhat large, historic "Spanish" rooms, complete with corner fireplaces and floor-level doorways, were found inserted into the prehistoric Indian rooms of the pueblo. Excavations at L.A. 70 were conducted under direction of Charles H. Lange in the summers of 1964 and 1965, as part of the Cochiti Dam Salvage Archaeological Project of the Museum of New Mexico in collaboration with the National Park Service.

211. José M. Jaramillo, 30 or 31 years old at the time of Bandelier's visit. Jaramillo came to St. Johns from New Mexico between 1873 and 1875. Several members of the Jaramillo family seem to have moved from New Mexico to the St. Johns area in the 1870's. (Census 1880.)

212. A fort first established May 16, 1870, as Camp Ord. The name was later changed to Camp Mogollon, Camp Thomas, Camp Apache, and finally, in 1879, to Fort Apache. The fort was abandoned in 1924 and its buildings turned over to the Bureau of Indian Affairs. (Barnes 1935: 21.)

213. Captain William Edgworth Dougherty, a native of Ireland. After Civil War service, Dougherty was promoted to captain, March 1, 1878, and to major in 1898. Before retirement, he had reached his full colonelcy. Most of his career was spent with the 1st Infantry. (Heitman 1903: I, 380.)

214. This is an example of what W. W. Taylor (1964) has termed "tethered nomadism."

215. Corydon Eliphalet Cooley, a Virginian, was a rancher. He had come to Santa Fe in 1856, at the age of 30 years, and promptly moved on to Colorado for two years, after which he served in the 2nd New Mexico Infantry for another two years, 1861-63. He went to Arizona as a prospector. Cooley was said to have married two Indian girls simultaneously, the daughters of Chief Pedro of the White Mountain Apaches, but one soon died. Nathan Bibo stated that he had been best man at Cooley's wedding but provided no further details. (Fierman 1962: 43n50.) With his wife, Mollie, Cooley established a ranch at the town now known as McNary; about 1875, Cooley relocated, establishing a ranch, sawmill, and trading post at a site which he named "Show Low" after he had won the rights to the area in a card game. In 1881, he served as one of the Apache County supervisors in Arizona; he was 47 when Bandelier met him in 1883. About 1890, he moved back to his earlier location on the Fort Apache Reservation; over the years he had served as a guide and scout for General Crook and other officers. (Thrapp 1964: 79, 79n13; Disturnell 1881: 78; Census 1880.) Fierman (1962: 49) noted that Henry Huning and Coridon E. Cooley were among the first settlers of Showlow. In Polk and Danser (1884a: 603), when Showlow had a population of 50, H. Henning [surely, Henry Huning] was postmaster, and D. E. [surely, C. E.] Cooley was justice of the peace.

216. This is probably Show-Low Ruin described by Haury and Hargrave (1931: 9). The ruin was later called the "Huning Ruin" after Mr. Henry Huning on whose ranch it was situated. Though Bandelier met Huning (April 18, 1883) he made no further identification. (See also Bandelier 1890-92: II, 392-393.)

217. Bandelier was quite right here. Weathering is not a reliable guide to the age of pottery.

218. Instead of societies, as among the Puebloan tribes, the Apache had individual shamans, or curers.

219. Possibly James Buell, a New Yorker by birth, listed in the Arizona 1880 Census as being from Pima County (no city of residence given).

220. The fact that such hunts were at least occasionally of considerable proportions and economic importance is demonstrated by White's account of an Acoma hunt for antelope on the San Agustín Plains. In 1887, the Acoma sent out a party of 74 hunters, 4 cooks, and 8 herders (for burros to bring back the meat); they killed 744 antelope, dressed the animals, and dried the meat, the whole affair taking about two weeks. (White 1943: 335-337.)

221. Fierman (1962: 49) noted that Henry Huning of Las Lunas and Coriden E. Cooley were among the first settlers of Show Low. Polk and Danser (1884a: 603) gave the population of Show Low as 50, and listed H. Henning [certainly Henry Huning] as postmaster, owner of a general store, contractor and stock raiser. Listed with him was D. E. [certainly C. E.] Cooley, justice of the peace. (Se fn 215 for Cooley.) Fierman (1961: 242) also mentioned the flour mill of L. H. Huning of Los Lunas. Whether this was Henry Huning is not clear.

222. There are several men of this name listed in the 1880 census: E. M. Clark, born in New York, and living in Tucson; George Clark from Yavapai County; Henry L. Clark of Phoenix; and Joseph L. Clark of Pinal County, originally from England.

223. This was probably the Alligator Juniper (*Juniperus pachyphloea* Torr.), so called because of its distinctive, checkered bark. It is typically a taller tree with a larger trunk diameter than the more widespread Oneseed Juniper (*Juniperus monosperma* [Engel.] Sarg.). The two species are found in the Upper Sonoran zone (3,500-7,000 feet), but the Alligator Juniper is also in the Transition zone (4,500-8,400 feet). (Preston 1940: 80-81, 86-87.)

224. See fn 81.

225. Given in Polk and Danser (1884a: 593, 709) as Henry E. Lacy, postmaster and owner of a general store and post trader at Fort Apache.

226. This may have been Dr. G. T. Henderson, a physician located in 1881 in Tombstone, according to Disturnell (1881: 229).

227. Captain Henry M. Kendall of the Sixth Cavalry. (Heitman 1903: I, 591.)

228. Downey (1943: 278) described briefly an incident in which "Sergeant Will C. Barnes of the Signal Corps [rode] out of the fort [Apache], climbed the mesa surrounded by hostiles and semaphored the news of Carr's approach. A sortie cleared the way for the oncoming column and rescued the brave sergeant who was awarded a well-deserved Medal of Honor." Will Croft Barnes survived the Apache wars, and has won a permanent place in Arizona history with his volumes, "Apaches and Longhorns" (1941) and "Arizona Place Names" (1935: 2nd Edition, 1960). Whether or not this was the same person Bandelier mentioned as Mr. Barnes later in the day's entry is problematical. It is probable that the two, "Sergeant" and "Mr.," referred to the same individual.

229. These were quite probably Pinedale, or Forestdale, polychromes; these are, indeed, very striking wares.

230. This was another instance of disturbed ruins as noted previously in n158.

231. "Mr." Barnes, here, was probably Sergeant Barnes (fn 228) although Bandelier appears to have been rather precise in his use of military ranks. It may be, however, that the precision was maintained regarding commissioned officers but not non-commissioned officers.

232. This was a common nineteenth century stereotype of the Apache. In fairness to Bandelier it should be pointed out that he was riding into hostile Apache country at considerable personal risk and could hardly be blamed for his jaundiced view of the Apache.

233. Casa Grande in the Gila Valley and Los Muertos in the Salt Valley are major sites of the Hohokam Classic period (ca. A.D. 1200-1400). Representing, apparently, a fusion of Hohokam and an Anasazi group called "Salado," these sites are characterized by high rectangular structures of adobe, the one at Casa Grande being four stories high. Associated are walled compounds, inhumation burial (contrasting with the typical Hohokam cremation), and a distinctive black, red, and white polychrome pottery.

Both Casa Grande and Los Muertos seem to have been deserted by the time the Spaniards arrived in Arizona.

234. Presumably the wife of Captain William Edgworth Dougherty. (See fn 213.)

235. Wife of Second Lieutenant Charles B. Gatewood of the Sixth Cavalry. Lieutenant Gatewood was the officer who, in 1886, persuaded Geronimo to surrender. Lieutenant Gatewood was never given proper credit for this feat and eventually retired on half pay, having lost an arm in an army post fire and explosion in Wyoming. (Davis 1929: 235 et seq.)

236. For discussions of the effect of Apache raids in Mexico for loot and slaves, see Lister and Lister (1966: 162-170).

237. The implications of this remark are unclear; the informant may have believed

that the Apache fled the ruins within the historic period to escape from outside authority. If true this would be another example of a lack of historical sense common to many primitive people. The statement would represent a blend of rather recent history with a period several centuries back. At present there is no evidence that Athabaskan speakers ever inhabited pueblos.

238. This appears to have been the well-known, pitch-covered, basket water bottle of the Apaches.

239. Geronimo was a Chiricahua Apache medicineman, probably born in the mid-1830's in the Upper Gila River area. In 1876, when an attempt was made to remove the Chiricahua to San Carlos, Geronimo fled to Mexico with a band of followers. He later was persuaded to return to San Carlos but fled again in 1884 and remained hostile until persuaded by General Crook to surrender in 1886.

Geronimo and his warriors were deported to Florida and, later, were finally settled in Oklahoma. Geronimo died in 1909. (Hodge 1907: I, 491; see also Davis 1929.)

As is evident from the journal entries, here and on following pages, reports of Bandelier's capture and death at the hands of the Apaches caused considerable alarm. The account by Barnes (1914: 5-6), while very graphic, contains several errors, such as placing the event in June of 1880, weeks before Bandelier's first entry into the Southwest, not to mention the Apache country of Southern Arizona—an event that came considerably later. Barnes also placed Bandelier's family in Rockford, Illinois, rather than Highland.

240. In the Bandelier Scrapbook, there is a brief note, in French, from a Swiss newspaper (no date), telling of the sorrow of Bandelier's family upon hearing of his death and their relief on receiving his telegram of April 28, 1883. Bandelier's letter of reassurance to Mrs. Morgan dated April 28 from Fort Apache was preserved in the Bandelier-Morgan letters. (White 1940: II.) Bandelier's letter, dated April 29, 1883, to García Icazbalceta (Mexico) read as follows (White and Bernal 1960: 271; our translation): "Fort Apache, Arizona, U.S.A. My very dear friend: A few words to refute a notice (an obituary) that has appeared. It has been published that the Apaches killed me in Chihuahua. This is so far from being true that I am not only living among them but am happy and enjoying myself. I shall be in this territory until next month. The terrain lends itself rather poorly to travel and I have to go slowly even if the weather continues good and the people continue to help me. I do hope to continue on although with difficulty."

241. The letter to Cholula, presumably, went to Padre Campos (see fn 32). On several occasions, Bandelier wrote to García Icazbalceta and Padre Campos at the same time. (See entries of January 27 and November 3, 1883, in addition to this entry.)

242. In the Weekly Telephone, June 18, 1884, there is mention of Mr. Emil Preetorius who was connected with the Westliche Post of St. Louis. Kargau (n.d.: 643) stated that the Westliche Post was established in 1857. In 1864, it was purchased by Arthur Olhausen, Dr. Emil Preetorius, and Theodore Plate. This partnership was dissolved in 1880, and Dr. Emil Preetorius and Carl Schurz became the owners. The Westliche Post Association was then organized with Preetorius as President. Dr. Preetorius, Chief Editor, had occupied the editorial chair since 1864.

Hyde (1896: 14) in an article on Newspapers and Newspaper People of Three Decades makes the following statements about Preetorius in his discussion of German newspapers in St. Louis and specifically the Westliche Post in this reference. "It was during the war that the good Dr. Emil Preetorius was evolved, and with him came that lottery ticket of journalism, Mr. Joseph Pulitzer, followed in the spring of 1867, by the distinguished general, senator, cabinet officer, orator, publicist, and 'mugwump,' Carl Schurz. Schurz occasionally wrote political articles for the Post, and they were always brilliant; but the public regarded him as a figurehead editorially. In truth the daily commentaries on events and men were seen to be chiefly by Preetorius, who enjoyed the reputation of being that kind of editor whose judicious work was and is generally found among the sweepings, or in the waste basket." Dr. Emil Preetorius was acting president of the Missouri Historical Society from 1890 to 1893.

Hodge (1932: 364) cited a "Letter dated Fort Apache, Arizona, 29 April, 1883, addressed 'Lieber Herr Pretorius' in which various pueblos and pueblo remains are mentioned." *Westliche Post*, St. Louis [1883]. This is the "long letter . . . on the Apache troubles." (Bandelier Scrapbook.)

243. Sanchez was a leading chief of the White Mountain Apache and one generally friendly to American settlers. He was not involved in the killing of Captain Hentig (fn 246) and others in 1881 nor of Agent John L. Colvig of San Carlos the following year by White Mountain dissidents. (Davis 1929: 10; Thrapp 1967: 254.)

244. John Baptist Salpointe was born in St. Maurice de Poinsat, Puy-de-Dôme, France, February 21 or 22, 1825. He attended seminary in Clermont-Ferrand, and was ordained a Roman Catholic priest in 1851, teaching at the Clermont-Ferrand Seminary from 1855 until 1859. Father Salpointe came to the United States as a missionary in the Diocese of Santa Fe in the latter year and was appointed Vicar General in 1860. Salpointe was consecrated Titular Bishop of Doryla and Vicar Apostolic of Arizona in 1869, where he vigorously opposed the government practice of placing Roman Catholic Indians under Protestant missionaries. Father Salpointe was named Titular Archbishop of Anazarbus and Coadjutor of Santa Fe, 1884-1894, and Archbishop of Santa Fe, 1885, and Titular Archbishop of Constantia (Tomi), 1894. Salpointe died in Tucson, Arizona, July 15, 1898. (Who Was Who 1963: 461.)

245. Bandelier's calculation of 10,670' for Mount Graham differed from that he made two days later (10,600'). More recent maps are not too helpful—World Book (1959: facing 406) gave Mt. Graham at 10,720' while a Rand McNally Atlas (1962: 80) gave the height as 10,713'. In Bandelier's *Final Report* (1890-92: II, 406n1), the height was given as 10,516'.

246. Capt. Edmund C. Hentig, of the 6th Cavalry, who was killed by the Apaches near Cibicu on Aug. 30, 1881. (Thrapp 1967: 221-224; Heitman 1903: 1, 524.)

247. Camp Goodwin was established in 1864 on or near the Gila River above the junction with the San Carlos River. The camp was vacated in 1871 because of its unhealthy site. (Barnes 1935: 182.)

248. Lieutenant Britton Davis of the Third Cavalry. According to Thrapp (1967: 260) Davis, assigned to San Carlos in 1883, was "fresh out of West Point." Actually, he was in the class of 1881 and had come to Arizona in the summer of 1882. Even so, the information on Apache social organization he gave to Bandelier should, perhaps, be taken with some reservation. See also Davis (1929) for his own account of the middle 1880's.

249. Casa Grande, first described by the Kino party, November 1694, is perhaps the most famous ruin in southern Arizona. The most impressive part of the ruin is a four-storied adobe structure; the first floor (possibly originally a platform) was deliberately filled in. This great structure, due to both exterior and interior plastering, has remained more or less intact. Surrounding this, probably ceremonial, compound is a vast series of mounds covering many acres but largely unexcavated. Although the main compound belongs to the Classic Period of Hohokam, there was earlier occupation as well.

Casa Grande was found deserted by the Kino party but there well may have been some proto-historic Pima (the modern descendants of the Hohokam) settlement of the site. Since 1918, Casa Grande has been a National Monument, but earlier had received some protective attention by state and federal agencies.

250. Camp Thomas was established in 1876 on the south bank of the Gila River,

some six to eight miles above old Camp Goodwin, but, in 1878, it was shifted upstream because of its unhealthy location. The name was officially changed to Fort Thomas in February 1883. The military establishment was abandoned in 1890. (Barnes 1935: 442.)

251. Originally Pueblo Viejo, present-day Solomon was earlier known as Solomonville, named after Isador E. Solomon. The community had first been settled by fifteen Mexicans who named the place for the nearby ruins. In 1876, Solomon bought out the first American settler and located there to convert mesquite to charcoal for use in smelting copper at the Clifton mines. A post office was established in 1878 with Solomon as postmaster. William Kirkland carried the mail there on horseback, and it was he who named the place Solomonville.

252. Possibly Rueben Wood, one-time trader at San Carlos. (Thrapp 1967: 254.)

253. Colonel A. W. Evans, a famous Indian fighter. (Men of colonel or general ranks can be found in a number of histories of the time, especially in Thrapp, Bourke, Cruse, etc.)

254. Lieutenant John M. Porter of the Third Cavalry. (Heitman 1903: I, 800.)

255. Isador E. Solomon went from Las Cruces, New Mexico, to work for relatives who had started copper mining in Arizona. He was later sent to locate mesquite to make coke for the smelting operation. He found it at Pueblo Viejo on the Gila River; in time, the community became known as Solomonville and, still later, as Solomon. Solomon was prominent in politics in the 1880's. In 1881 Isador Solomon was treasurer of newly founded Graham County and a brother, Adolph Solomon, was a supervisor of the same county. In that same period Nathan Solomon, also a relative, owned the livery stable in Solomonville. (Census 1880; Disturnell 1881: 169-170; Parish 1960: 148; Reeve 1952: 251n134.)

256. Originally established in 1859 as Fort Breckenridge, apparently at the junction of San Pedro River and Arivaipa Creek. It was abandoned in 1861 but reestablished as Fort Stanford in 1862. The post was renamed Fort Grant in 1866 and was transferred, in 1872, to a point some 25 miles north of Willcox. (Barnes 1935: 125.)

257. Dr. S. D. Pangburn, a physician at San Carlos from 1880 to 1890. (Quebbeman 1966: 362.)

258. Sam T. Gilson, an Indian Agency employee, who established a well and stage station between Globe and San Carlos. The well, built with Indian labor, was later assigned to the San Carlos Agency and Gilson's homestead is now a stockyard and loading station for San Carlos Reservation cattle. (Barnes 1960: 103.)

259. T. C. Stallo, a mining superintendent in the Globe area, and, in 1881, Public Administrator of Gila County. Stallo listed his occupation as "doctor" in the 1880 census and was commonly referred to as Dr. Stallo. He is not known to have practiced medicine. (Quebbeman 1966: 372; Disturnell 1881: 172.)

260. Probably William Harris Cook who began a medical practice at Globe in 1882. (Quebbeman 1966: 335.)

261. See fn 288 for another, and more detailed, description of this form of axe.

262. This seems to be a reference to the Woolsey "Bloody Tanks" massacre, which spot is normally located at the head of Bloody Tanks Wash just west (not east as Bandelier says) of Globe. However, Mr. Bert M. Fireman, Curator of the Arizona Collection, Arizona State University Library, has cogent reasons to believe that the real Bloody Tanks massacre took place on Fish Creek a considerable distance down the Salt River from the Globe area. Bandelier's number of Apache killed is far too high.

The other references are to the early Spanish conquest period. In 1519, Cortez, perhaps at the instigation of his Tlascalan allies, slaughtered large numbers of the inhabitants of Cholula near present-day Puebla, in central Mexico. In 1532, Pizarro massacred the Inca forces of Atahuallpa at Cajamarca in northern Peru. The situation at Cholula is somewhat obscure, but Pizarro's act was wantonly criminal though Bandelier was apparently unaware of this. (See, for example, Bandelier 1882: 6.)

263. A J. H. Eaton was listed by Polk and Danser (1884a: 594) as the owner of a saw mill at Globe. The name also appeared in the Eaton and Bailey General Store and the Eaton and Young Livery of Globe.

264. Presumably the wife of Major Caleb H. Carlton of the Third Cavalry. (Heitman 1903: I, 282.)

265. Perhaps Charles T. Connell, once chief of scouts and later with the Immigration Service. In later years, Connell wrote articles on frontier life. (Thrapp 1967: 254fn.)

266. This was quite possibly the present-day so-called Devil Dance, the name given by Whites to a series of masked dances aimed at producing health or other blessings on such occasions as a girl's puberty rites.

267. The Yuman Indians can be more properly described as riverine peoples. Their languages are part of the Yuman stock which has no known relationship with Chinese.

268. Of the firm of Hitchcock and Company; one of the two druggists in Globe in 1881. (Disturnell 1881: 140.)

269. Both of these tribes used masks in their dancing impersonations of various deities; while there may be occasional similarities, the development at Zuñi was far richer and much more varied.

270. Wheatfields was named during one of the King S. Woolsey expeditions of 1864. In that year Woolsey led a party of 93 men against the Apache. In the region of the Salt River drainage, north and west of what later was to be the city of Globe, Arizona, the party found and harvested considerable amounts of Indian wheat.

In Bandelier's day, a post office named Stanton (but often called Wheatfields) had been established in the area some 18 miles northwest of Globe. In 1876 Mack Morris established the Richmond Silver mine in this vicinity and treated the silver ore at a mill in Stanton, or Wheatfields. This mine was exhausted by 1882, and, as Bandelier pointed out, the mill was no longer in operation by 1883.

After failure of the Mack Morris mining operation, the various ranches and farms in the area were purchased by the Inspiration Consolidated Copper Company. Stanton no longer exists today. It is not to be confused with the ghost town, Stanton, in Yavapai County, Arizona. (Russell 1908: 50n; Thrapp 1964: 84n; Barnes 1935: 480-81.)

271. This would seem to be the half-blood Indian scout, Archie McIntosh, mentioned by Thrapp (1967: 95 et seq.) and by a number of other historians of the period. He is probably also the A. McIntosh listed in the 1880 census as living in the upper Salt River area.

272. See fn 164.

273. Perhaps Charles A. Fisk of the Globe area.(Census 1880.)

274. The identity of this extensive site has not been established. For a discussion of the archaeological remains in this area, see Haury's monograph on the excavation of Los Muertos and neighboring ruins (1945).

275. Possibly remains of ball courts (Schroeder 1949) or, perhaps as a better possibility, of dance platforms. For a discussion of the possible confusion of ball courts and dance platforms in the Hohokam area, see Ferdon (1967).

276. A few copper bells appear in excavations of Hohokam sites, especially in the Sacaton Phase of the Sedentary Period.

277. Bandelier's description of the bell does suggest Hohokam, although Hohokam bells were cast, using the lost-wax method. Possibly, the hammering was secondary.

278. Camp Reno was an outpost of Fort McDowell from 1866 to 1868. At the time of Bandelier's visit, there was a post office there named Reno. (Barnes 1935: 360.)

279. One of the Prather family who earlier had settled the Reno area; possibly Isaac R. Prather who was postmaster at Reno in 1880. (Theobald 1961: 123.)

280. A military post on the west bank of the Verde River, some seven miles above the junction with the Salt River. The fort was established in 1865 and abandoned in 1890. (Barnes 1935: 258.)

281. Lieutenant George Lawson Scott, of the Sixth Cavalry. (Heitman 1903: I, 868.)

282. George Wilcox, probably a relative of N. Wilcox, postmaster at McDowell. (Disturnell 1881: 145.)

283. The Maricopa speak a Yuman language of the Hokan Stock; the Pima, a Piman (or Piman-Tepehuan) language of the Uto-Aztecan family of languages.

284. This mill belonged to Charles Trumbull Hayden (1825-1900), an early settler in Arizona, pioneer judge, and merchant, who built the first gristmill in the Salt River Valley. His son, Carl Trumbull Hayden, was U.S. Senator from 1927 until he retired in 1968. The Senator was born in Tempe in October 1877 and would have been five years old when Bandelier visited the area. (Peplow 1958: 81; Who's Who 1967: 980.)

285. Alex F. McDonald was appointed President of the Mormon communities in the Mesa area (the Maricopa Stake) in 1880. This appointment was confirmed in December 1882 by Apostles Erastus Snow and Moses Thatcher who set up a permanent religious organization in the area. At the same time, H. C. Rogers and C. J. Robson were appointed assistants to McDonald; E. Pomeroy was made Bishop of Mesa; Thomas E. Jones, Bishop of Jonesville; and David Le Barren, President Elder at Tempe. (History 1884: 283, 299-300.)

286. Sandals of hide, or of maguey fibers, worn by the Aztecs.

287. Polk and Danser (1884a: 717) listed a J. M. Murphy as owner of a general store in Tempe.

288. This was the three-quarter grooved axe, the prevalent type throughout Hohokam times in the Gila and Salt river areas.

289. This was probably Pueblo Grande, which has been largely destroyed in the expansion of Phoenix.

290. Presumably F. Gallardo, a saloon and restaurant owner of Tempe. (Disturnell 1881: 171.)

291. Russell (1908: 256) mentioned a cache found in the hills south of Casa Grande, in a former sacred place of the Pima. Among the objects he reported was a "bird carved from stone." According to Russell, both the eagle and hawk were supposed by the Pima Indians to cause disease, and eagle-down and hawk feathers were used in curing. That the hawk had strong mana-like powers was indicated by the fact that a person touching a hawk became supernaturally dangerous and had to go into four days of seclusion. (P. 263.)

292. Sweetwater, or Agua Dulce, was at one time a stage station on the Gila River about ten miles west of Sacaton. Sweetwater was never a post office. It was located near the historic Pima town of Tusonimon, visited by Kino in 1697. (Barnes 1935: 433, 461.)

293. Casa Blanca is another of the large complexes of Hohokam ruins scattered up and down the Gila Valley. It is in an advanced condition of collapse.

294. J. D. Rittenhouse owned a general merchandise store at Sweetwater. (Disturnell 1881: 170.) He was also an Indian agent at Sacaton. (Polk and Danser 1884a: 602.)

295. Russell (1908: 183) reported that women were secluded for four days during the menstrual period. During that period ". . . they lived in the bushes near the village, making little shelters to shade them from the sun and occupying their time in making baskets. They lived on pinole which was brought each morning and left at a short distance from their camp. Sometimes there were several together. They always bathed in the river before returning to their homes."

296. The *kiaha* was a carrying basket equipped with a light wooden framework, the whole attached to the woman's head by a tump line, with the basket riding on her shoulders. (Russell 1908: 140-41.)

297. Here we have another example of Bandelier's willingness to repeat stereotypes about American Indians. Among the Pima, men cleared the fields, planted, and irrigated the crops, while women harvested and did housework. (Russell 1908: 89.)

298. At the time Russell studied the Pima (1901-1902), weaving had been largely abandoned, and this may also have been true in Bandelier's day. Weaving and the cultivation of cotton, however, were reported from the earliest European contact period and presumably were aboriginal. (Russell 1908: 148-51.)

299. This Agency, originally called the Pima and Maricopa Indian Reservation, was established by Act of Congress, February 28, 1859.

300. Records scattered through the *History of Arizona Territory*, including a biographical sketch, and reports to the Commissioner of Indian Affairs in the 1880's identify this man as Reverend Charles H. Cook, a member of the Presbyterian Mission located on the Pima Reservation. Originally a member of the Methodist Episcopal Church, he came to Sacaton, Arizona, to missionize the Pima and Maricopa Indians. In 1881 he joined the Presbyterian Church and was placed in charge of the mission at Sacaton. We were unable to find his death date though he seems to have died or left the area before Russell's time, that is 1901-1902.

301. Scepola may be either Earth Doctor or Elder Brother, both culture heroes of the Pima. (Russell 1908: 206 *et seq.*) Bandelier's statement concerning the origin of the word "Tucson" may be correct. It would be either Pima *sluyk-son* "dark spring" or Papago *chuk-shon*, the name for Sentinel Mountain which has a dark zone at the base. (Barnes 1935: 455; Barnes 1960: 284-285.) The name Arizona may be derived from the Papago *ali-shonak* "place of the spring" (Barnes 1960: xv), though there are alternative derivations; Nahuatl *arizuma* "silver bearing," or even Spanish *arida zona* "arid area." (Barnes 1935: 26.)

302. Thomas E. Ellis, a physician at the Pima Agency in 1883-84. (Quebbeman 1966: 340.)

303. The significance of the "north" remains obscure, unless at one time, there were two communities, one on the Southern Pacific railroad and the other either north or south of it, perhaps the latter is the more likely. (The possibility of this referring to a person seems less probable.) Willcox, founded in 1880, was probably named for General Orlando B. Willcox, Commander of the Department of Arizona from 1878 to 1882. (Thrapp 1964: photo portrait, facing p. 49.)

304. This was probably John Walker, born in Nauvoo, Illinois, in 1840, who settled among the Pima and, in 1865-66, served in the Arizona Volunteers, commanding Pima Indian troops. Walker, at one time, was a probate judge of Pinal County. (Thrapp 1967: 33-36.)

305. Actually, it would be better to describe the Pima-Papago as rancheria peoples rather than puebloan in type. Although they shared intensive agriculture with the Pueblo Indians, the Piman groups lived (and live) in scattered homesteads, rather than in the compact and substantial towns of the Pueblo tribes.

306. Father Kino (Bolton 1948: I, 172) mentioned a large irrigation system in use in the Casa Grande area at the time of his 1697 visit. Though the point has been in some dispute, it is likely that there has been continuous large-scale irrigation in the Gila and Salt river areas since Hohokam times.

307. Pima women abstained from salt following the birth of a child until the child's umbilicus had healed. (Russell 1908: 185.)

308. Even in Russell's time, the clan structure of the Pima was in a state of decay. It was, moreover, patrilineal. (Russell 1908: 197.) Descriptions of Pima clans are reminiscent of those of the Southern Tepehuan and Tepecano, southernmost of the Piman-speaking groups. A more detailed description of these latter is now in press, cf. Carroll L. Riley, The Southern Tepehuan and Tepecano (Handbook of Middle American Indians, Vol. 8, University of Texas Press, in press.)

309. According to Russell (1908: 256), "Those who have power over the crops, the weather, and the wars are called Makai, Magicians. Only one or two women were ever admitted to this order among the Pima. There were usually about five Makai in each village."

The organization of Makai and other Pima shamans was considerably less complex than that of ceremonial groups at Zuñi and resemblances between the Makai and Koko were at best superficial.

310. This situation was also reported by Russell (1908: 195-196).

311. The Hohokam inhabited the valleys of the Salt and Gila rivers, and were the builders of such centers as Casa Grande, Casa Blanca, Pueblo Grande, Los Muertos, and many others, as well as of elaborate canal systems. On present evidence, it would seem that the Pima Indians are Hohokam descendants—the prehistoric Hohokam gradually being transformed into historic Pima as contacted by Kino and others around A.D. 1700.

312. Russell made no mention of Apache-Pima trade. Goodwin (1942: 87-88) also denied that such trade existed. It seems probable, however, that at least occasional trade contacts were established after Americans had occupied and pacified southern Arizona.

313. This is probably true (see Goodwin 1942: 471 et seq.). It should be pointed out, however, that in the nineteenth century the word "Tonto" was applied very indiscriminately to practically all Indians living between the White Mountains of Arizona and the Colorado River. Probably Bandelier, here, is thinking of the Tonto bands of Western Apache, but his informant, Judge Walker, may not have made the same distinction.

314. In January 1864, a party of Americans and Maricopa Indians under the command of Indian fighter King Woolsey fought an engagement at the "Bloody Tanks," probably in Fish Creek Canyon (see fn 262). A band of Apaches was lured into the American camp by the offer of pinole and were then slaughtered. Some nineteen Apaches and one American (Cyrus Lennan) were killed.

This incident has often been confused with another in which Woolsey actually gave the Indians pinole mixed with strychnine. It is not entirely clear to which event Bandelier had reference here; from the context, the Bloody Tanks fight seems more likely. (Thrapp 1967: 27, 29-32; Lockwood 1938: 148-149; Russell 1908: 50-51.)

315. Not having the earlier journals at hand, as these had been left in, or sent back to, Highland, Illinois, it would be interesting to know what additional "running records"

Bandelier kept with him in the field. It may, of course, have been a case of keen memory. No mention has been found of any effort on Bandelier's part to keep such an auxiliary account.

316. Antonio Jouvenceau was one of the early priests at Tucson. He and five other missionary priests were brought to Arizona by Bishop Salpointe in 1869 from Clermont in France. Antonio Jouvenceau was sent to Tucson where Father Francis X. Jouvenceau was parish priest. Fr. F. X. Jouvenceau also came from Clermont (in 1859), but it is not clear if the two men were related. (Salpointe 1898: 211, 222-23, 260-61.)

317. Fort Lowell was established at Tucson in 1864 after that town was abandoned by the Confederate forces. The fort was reestablished in 1866 and, in March of 1873, was moved some eight miles east of Tucson to a point between Rillito Creek and Pantano Wash. At present, some ruins of the old fort are part of the Tucson Memorial Park. One of these presently houses the Fort Lowell Museum. Other portions, privately owned, such as the Sutler Store, lie outside the Park. For additional information, see Old Fort Lowell (Hughston 1911).

318. Presumably one of the Sisters of St. Joseph who staffed St. Mary's Hospital at Tucson.

319. Captain Joseph Basil Girard was born in France and entered the service from Michigan. In 1867, he became assistant surgeon, U.S. Army. He was promoted to major, surgeon, in 1888; lieutenant colonel, deputy surgeon general, in 1901; and assistant surgeon general in 1902. (Heitman 1903: I, 459.) At this time of Bandelier's travels in southern Arizona, Girard was post surgeon at Fort Lowell.

320. This was Joe's brother, Edward B. Huegy. In the first volume (Lange and Riley 1966: 235), Bandelier noted that "Edward came home [to Highland] from Chicago tonight [December 23, 1880]." The next day, he wrote, "Had Eddy again in the morning. Always the same." It is interesting that in this entry, two-and-a-half years later, Bandelier also commented, "Always the same." In the Eggen history of Highland (1933: 88), Ed. B. Huegy was listed in the directory as "book binder, and dealer in picture frames, cords, tassels, etc." The precise date of Edward's move from Highland to Albuquerque remains unknown, but it was probably in the early 1880's. (See footnote for entry of July 20, 1884.) The Morning Journal, Albuquerque, of August 22, 1884, noted that "yesterday was the thirty-sixth birthday of E. Huegy," making him eight years junior to Bandelier.

321. Bandelier arrived during Santa Fe's "Tertio Millenial" Celebration. The day preceding Bandelier's arrival, Frank Cushing had directed "an ambuscade and sham fight by the Zuñi Indians, with an exhibition of their peculiar rites and ceremonies." (Ellis 1958: 129.) (See also fn 126 for 1884 and for further details of this celebration consult Ellis [1958].) White (1940: II, 252n2) stated that "This celebration, which Bandelier later called 'the spurious Tertio millenial jubilee,' was held in 1883 in the belief that Santa Fe had been founded in 1550. The Gilded Man, pp. 285-286." Loomis (1966:44) stated that the United States Court House building in Santa Fe was the center of this "Tertio Millenial." The building had been only partially finished, and the grounds were badly neglected; however, citizens led by L. Bradford Prince and Arthur Boyle prepared the area for the celebration which included Indian ceremonials, chicken pulls, and horse, mule, and burro races.

322. Clara Mary Huning was the daughter of Franz Huning. (See fn 63.) She married H. B. Fergusson, Territorial Delegate to Congress, 1877-1899, and Representative for the State of New Mexico, 1912-1915. (Fierman 1961: 242n28.)

323. Lionel Sheldon was a lawyer and politician, a Civil War Brigadier-General (Union), and a congressman from New Mexico (1868, 1870, 1872). He was instrumental

in securing the nomination for President Garfield (1880), whom he knew, and was appointed Wallace's successor as Governor of New Mexico, 1881-1885. He was a strong and vigorous executive and sponsored or approved important educational, mining and railroad, as well as court procedure, legislation. His term saw some stormy legislative sessions when Las Vegas and Albuquerque delegates attempted to strip Santa Fe of its pride as the capital city. Sheldon favored Santa Fe. In 1884, he called out the national guard to aid in putting down the Apache outbreak of that year under Geronimo. (Twitchell 1912: 490-491n401, 491n404.)

324. In a letter to Mrs. Lewis Henry Morgan, dated July 18, 1883, Bandelier complained about the inequality of interest and expenditures of the Archaeological Institute of America, supporting his view with the following figures: In 1882, the Institute received donations of $5,620 for classical research and $200 for American research. In the same year, the Institute spent $10,266.64 in Greece as compared with $2,456.90 in America. (White 1940: II, 253.)

Earlier, in the same letter (p. 252), Bandelier wrote that "Thus I succeeded in meeting Cushing & his folks again [at the Tertio Milennial Celebration in Santa Fe]. He is well, somewhat exercised over the Logan affair, but otherwise pleased and hopeful . . ." White (p. 252n3) noted, regarding "the Logan affair," that "General John A. Logan and some of his associates tried to dispossess the Zuñi Indians of some of their land, land which contained a precious spring. Cushing endeavored to thwart Logan's plans. Logan attacked Cushing in a published letter with great bitterness, vehemence, and with little regard for accuracy. Although 'somewhat exercised' over the affair, Cushing did not deign to reply to the scurrilous attacks of Logan. See Wm. E. Curtis, *Children of the Sun* (Chicago, 1883), pp. 43-59."

In this same letter of July 18 to Mrs. Morgan, Bandelier provided his summary of "the main, and also undoubted, results of my New Mexican work so far." (P. 253.) Bandelier listed nine points, which were, as follows (pp. 253-254): 1. The boundaries of the area covered with vestiges of sedentary habitations, from lat. 39° to 33°, north. 2. The fact that these remains continue further south, in a chain almost unbroken, as far as Central America. 3. The distribution of the communal house type, reaching as far west in Arizona as long. 111° W., & as far southwest as lat. 33° N., but not going beyond it, whereas in New Mexico it covers the whole area. 4. The existence of the small house type, alongside of the former, and in greater numbers, over the whole territory. 5. The gradual transformation of the small house into a detached house village type, connected by courtyards so as to form a defensive complex, in western and southern Arizona. 6. The appearance, there, of a many-storied house of concrete, & of much smaller size than the Pueblo dwelling, & of different construction, also of artificial mounds supporting buildings. 7. The fact that the so-called cliff houses are not the work of a particular tribe or group of tribes, but are the result of a state of war, over the entire area, wherever the opportunities for the erection of such structures were favorable. 8. A change in mode of life, therefore, to such an extent only, as was demanded by the changes in climate and natural resources. 9. A change in artifacts which, while indicating some progress to the southward, is still only in keeping with the topographical, physical, and climatological variations, or, in other words, with the transformations in the country produced by changes in latitude and altitude.

Continuing his "report" to Mrs. Morgan, Bandelier added the following paragraphs (pp. 254-255):

Without alluding to other details I shall state that the past of these countries, as far as I am able to judge of it, indicates, during the period preceding the 16th century, a state of alternate peace and war, few migrations on a large scale, if any, but rather local shifting only. A moderate population of sedentary Indians claiming tribal ranges, over which they moved their villages, changing their sites at long intervals. These tribes appear to have attained their status of culture in the north, but to have modified it in the south, whereas it is not unlikely that their contact with other, roaming groups has raised some of the latter above the state of savagery. The disappearance of these sedentary Indians took place, in the southern two-thirds of Arizona & over four-fifths of New Mexico, before the arrival of the Spaniards, & it was due to intertribal warfare, "kilkenny cat-fights" between neighbors, to the occasional raids of savages, and to the calamities usual [sic] attending a state of protracted insecurity. Natural catastrophes only appear as local causes, & not as general convulsions.

The remnants of this sedentary population are found today, in the so-called "Pueblo Indians" of New Mexico and Arizona, and among the Pimas and Pápagos of southern Arizona. It is not impossible that the Yumas and Mojaves may also prove to have belonged to them formerly. The Pueblo Indians still possess a degree of culture at least equal, if not decidedly superior, to that which must be ascribed to the builders of the now ruined edifices; the others have receded, previous to the advent of the Spaniards, into a condition similar to that of the Iroquois and of the corn-raising tribes of the Mississippi valley.

There is no doubt but that, at various dates and for various of the causes above stated, remnants of sedentary tribes drifted gradually southward into Mexico. In general, there appears to have been a tendency, on the part of the aborigines, to gradually press south and east rather than north or west. Their history outlines itself dimly as one of slow growth, and of hardly less rapid decay, terminating with a fall and obliteration or displacement. It is evident that this is the work of very long periods of time and that, consequently, while a limited number only of the ruins have co-existed at any time, the existence of sedentary man in these countries goes back to considerable antiquity.

These, my dear Mrs. Morgan, I regard as the results, up to date, of my work. It points to the south as a field for future indispensable action, and I hope to go back there next October to continue my labors with all necessary prudence & caution. I am grateful to God for his protection, for the protection he has given to my family, & for the sympathy he has preserved for me among the kind and good people of the land.

325. Timothy Gruaz purchased the print shop of *Der Highland Bote* in April 1863. He was reported to have been one of the signers of the antiemancipation petition and was much more radical in his opposition to the Civil War than was Voegele from whom he purchased the paper. He tried to be fair in the newspaper but there was continued division about the war in Highland and ultimately a second paper, *Die Union*, was started to give more support to the North. He was elected to the board of trustees of the village of Highland in April 1875, and proposed several ordinances in a special election. In 1877 he was engaged in the insurance business with his stepson, George Ruegger. In 1884 he is listed as being in real estate and in April of that year was also elected city attorney. Earlier journal entries (Lange and Riley 1966) reveal Gruaz as one of the colleagues with whom Bandelier enjoyed discussing politics, books, and such matters. Here, however, relations between Bandelier and Gruaz seem less congenial.

It might be well here to comment on the Highland newspaper situation in general. Since our first volume was published, we have acquired additional information on the history of Highland newspapers. The data cited from Goad (Lange and Riley 1966: 10n3) were essentially correct, but it should be noted that the original name of *Der Highland Bote* was *Der Erzaehler*, which was first published on March 26, 1859, when the country was aroused over the Lincoln-Douglas debates. Publishers were Rudolph Stadtman and John Karlen, who sold out after a month, leaving Stadtman the sole owner. In May, he changed the name to *Der Highland Bote*, which was unenthusiastic about Lincoln's election. Accordingly, a second German newspaper, *Die Union*, was begun October 24,

1863, to espouse the Northern cause, supported by many in the community. Feelings between the two papers were bitter. Both changed owners and editors several times. B. E. Hoffmann and Maurice Huegy were the last owners of *Der Highland Bote*, having bought it in June 1868. They published it for about a year; Hoffmann was elected to county office, moved to Edwardsville, and discontinued the paper. (Spencer 1937: 105, 219, 223.)

Russ Hoffmann, present publisher of the *Highland News Leader* (and no relative of B. E.), informed us (June, 1968) that *The Weekly Telephone*, inaccurately designated in the first volume as *The Highland Weekly Telephone*, was not the first English-language newspaper there. Subsequent research in Spencer (p. 220) revealed this to have been the *Highland Herald*, begun by several businessmen, with Wm. H. Toy as editor, with the first issue appearing April 13, 1881. It changed owners a number of times; the last, Charles Boeschenstein, in 1883, moved to Edwardsville, combining *The Herald* with the *Edwardsville Intelligencer* which he had just purchased. This latter newspaper is still published in Edwardsville, and its files were examined in the course of research for this and subsequent volumes.

Because the people had acquired a liking for an English newspaper through the *Herald*, J. S. Hoerner, editor of the German newspaper, *Die Union*, began printing *The Weekly Telephone* from the same office. This was published for a span of only two or three years. (Goad cited Vol. III, no. 16, June 9, 1885; however we could find no more than one volume: Volume II, nos. 1-52, February 26, 1884-February 18, 1885.)

Until 1892, *Die Union*, continuing in German, was the only newspaper in town; this date coincided with the final date of the Bandelier journals with which the editors are concerned.

Prior to World War II, the volumes of *Die Union* were given to the University of Illinois, Urbana; from there, they were moved to various libraries until, at last report, they are in the Midwest Regional Library, Chicago.

The *Highland Leader*, now the *Highland News Leader*, has been published since 1900, and all files are at the *News Leader* office in Highland. Another English newspaper, *The Highland Journal*, was published from 1895 until 1961. All of these volumes are on microfilm in the Louis Latzer Memorial Public Library, Highland.

326. The journals reveal that Bandelier corresponded frequently with Dr. Gustav Brühl (in the first volume, the umlaut was omitted) and occasionally visited him in Cincinnati. Dr. Brühl, a physician, was born in Prussia in 1826 and educated in Germany. In 1848, he came to St. Mary's Hospital in Cincinnati. In 1869-71, he was editor of *Das Deutsche Pionier* (Cincinnati: 1862-1884). A writer of prose and poetry, Brühl was also interested in the archaeology of the United States, Mexico, Central America, and South America. He died in 1903. (Lange and Riley 1966: 408.)

327. Dr. Ernst P. Raab was a physician in Highland. (Polk and Danser 1884b: 1003.)

328. E. L. Cushing was the brother of Frank Hamilton Cushing (Bloom 1936b: 113); it seems probable that the E. L. Cushings were at Zuñi at the time of Bandelier's visit with the F. H. Cushings, beginning February 21, 1883.

329. Mr. E. M. West was a member of the banking firm, West and Prickett (Edward West and William R. Prickett) in Edwardsville, Illinois. (Polk and Danser 1884b: 871.)

330. The Honorable William P. Bradshaw was a member of the legal firm, Metcalf and Bradshaw of Edwardsville, Illinois. (Polk and Danser 1884b: 870.) The *Weekly Telephone* of Highland of March 26, 1884, speaks of him as a possible candidate for lieutenant governor at the Republican State Convention. He went with Constable Todd and A. F. Bandelier to Edwardsville at the time of the failure of the F. Ryhiner and Co. bank in 1885.

331. Prior to his interests in the Helvetia Milk Condensing Co. of Highland, George

Roth had been in the hardware and implement business. A successful and influential business man with a wide acquaintance, he was at one time the largest stockholder of the milk company in 1893. For a brief time in 1881 he had owned the *Highland Herald*, the first English-language newspaper, in partnership with Louis E. Kinne. (Spencer 1937: 199-200.) However, this was a short-lived venture of two months; two years later, the *Highland Herald* was purchased and incorporated into *The Intelligencer* (at Edwardsville) when Charles Boeschenstein became owner of both papers. (P. 220.)

332. Andrew W. Metcalf was a partner in the legal firm of Metcalf and Bradshaw in Edwardsville, Illinois. One can only guess that Gruaz as a real estate agent and Bandelier representing the F. C. Ryhiner & Co. bank were ironing out some legal problem concerning the property which had originally been the Highland Foundry (1870) built with money borrowed from the bank and to which the original owners, A. T. Vallotton and F. A. Lelauren, gave a mortgage on the lot, building, and equipment. It was not a successful venture and in March 1874 Lelauren sold his interest to Vallotton, who in turn a month later, also gave up and let the bank have the property to satisfy the mortgage (Spencer 1937: 170-171). Undoubtedly, A. F. Bandelier had been involved in the initial transaction as this occurred before he left the business to pursue his scholarly interests. One senses his annoyance in the journals at still finding himself involved in business matters whenever he was in Highland.

333. B. E. Hoffmann was a teacher in the Highland public schools in 1865. In that year he was appointed clerk of the village. From 1866 to 1869 he was postmaster. In 1868, he was appointed village assessor, and, in partnership with Maurice Huegy, bought the German newspaper, *Der Highland Bote*. They conducted the newspaper until 1869 when Mr. Hoffmann was elected county clerk on the Republican ticket and moved to Edwardsville. He discontinued the paper and took the material with him. (Spencer 1937: 130, 215-216, 219, 226.)

334. In 1863, Seybt had been elected president of a society to found a newspaper espousing the cause of the North in the Civil War. The new paper was named *Die Union* and Seybt was the first editor, a position from which he resigned after eight months. In the fall of 1869, he was an unsuccessful candidate for sheriff of Madison County. He was one of many Highland citizens instrumental in bringing a railroad to Highland, and for many years he looked after Highland's interests in the railroad. He also had interests in the Henry Hermann & Co. Flour Mill. In 1884, *The Weekly Telephone* spoke of Seybt as a real estate agent.

Bandelier had an interest with Seybt in the "Confidence Coal Mining Co." and the "Highland Mechanical Works." (Goad 1939: 55.)

That the coal mine ownership continued to plague Bandelier is evident from this and subsequent entries in his 1883 journals. (See his entry of August 14, 1883.)

335. Because of the shortage of funds (AIA 1883: 21), the Archaeological Institute of America was unable to complete publication of Bandelier's Mexican studies, much to Bandelier's disappointment. The publication (Bandelier 1884a) did appear, however, the following year. (See 154 for 1884.)

336. Bohn's precise identity remains obscure. He appears to have been a St. Louis business man, perhaps a banker or realtor. In the 1881 journals, the entry of January 24, while Bandelier was in Boston, stated that Bandelier "wrote to Bohn about the house, having also received a letter from him today." Later, February 19, in St. Louis, Bandelier noted, "Failed to meet Mr. Leder, but took leave of Bohn." Bandelier left St. Louis the next day for his several months of research in Mexico.

337. Richard Hospes entered the employ of the German Savings Institution of St. Louis (organized 1853) as a mere youth and was promoted steadily. In 1864, he was

appointed cashier and had managed the Institution ever since. (Kargau n.d.: 165.) Bandelier wrote Hospes and consulted with him on business matters in St. Louis, but one feels there was a friendship between the two beyond their business affairs.

338. This was Edward H. Greenleaf, Secretary of the Executive Committee of the Archaeological Institute of America, 1880-81, when Bandelier began his work for the Institute. Greenleaf served until the spring of 1884, at which time he was succeeded by Arthur L. Frothingham, Jr., of Baltimore. Upon leaving the Executive Committee, Greenleaf became Secretary of the Boston Society of the AIA, 1884-85. (Archaeological Institute of America, Second, Fifth, and Sixth Annual Reports.)

339. A. T. Vallotton was one of the original owners of the Highland Foundry built in 1870. Many buildings built in Highland had metal sills in the doorway which bore the imprint "Highland Foundry." (Spencer 1937: 170-71.) See also fn 332.

340. J. Brunnschweiler and F. A. Gleyre formed a partnership, the F. A. Gleyre and Co., otherwise known as the Highland Mechanical Works in 1874. The property had first been the Highland Foundry (see fn 332), and it, too, had financial backing from the bank. Work was mostly confined to farm machinery and equipment, but the business was not successful. It had almost been discontinued when the building burned in 1882. Title reverted to the bank and was sold along with some other assets at a public sale in 1886 after the bank had failed. (Spencer 1937: 171-172.) It is evident from the text of the journals that some sort of settlement was desired in 1883.

341. Spencer (1937) wrote of two men by the name of Blattner, both of whom were important in the history of Highland. One was J. N. Blattner who in the summer of 1840 built what was known as the "knob-house" which upon its completion was occupied by Dr. F. Ryhiner who moved his family at this time from St. Louis to Highland. This was probably the same John Blattner (p. 88) who was said to have built the Methodist Church in 1849, first making the brick himself. The other was John R. Blattner who arrived from Switzerland in Highland either in 1848 or 1849. He erected a building hoping to produce silk and fitted the building with this purpose in mind. He planted young mulberry trees and hatched silkworm larvae in large numbers only to find that he did not have sufficient mulberry leaves to feed them. He then remodeled his building into a hotel which was called the New Switzerland House, and it was a famous landmark for many years. In 1849, on August 16, President Zachary Taylor appointed J. R. Blattner postmaster, a position which he held for seven years. In 1853, he was instrumental in setting up a shooting range. From Spencer's account, it is impossible to tell which John Blattner was defeated by Jacob Eggen in the election of the first president of the newly incorporated village in 1865 (p. 129). John R. Blattner was also mentioned as buying up the old Market House in 1879 which had become a blight and razing it and cleaning up the street where it had stood (p. 137). John Blattner did the drain work on the new hospital addition in 1890 (p. 183). Spencer did not indicate any relationship between the two men and Bandelier's reference does nothing to clarify the identification. Polk and Danser (1884b: 1002) listed simply John Blattner, real estate.

342. Dr. John B. Knoebel practiced medicine in Highland and the vicinity for a long time. In 1885 he was chosen as the first president of the Board of Trustees of the Helvetia Milk Condensing Co. He resigned from this position at the end of the first year. (Spencer 1937: 199.)

343. This is F. C. Ryhiner, Jr., born in Highland in 1846. He died in the state of Washington in 1899. He was the son of Mrs. Josephine Suppiger Ryhiner and Dr. Frederick C. Ryhiner. A close friend since boyhood, Bandelier refers to him in his journals as "Fritz." Spencer (1937: 192) says he was a bachelor and had few family ties to hold him to Highland. A sister, Mrs. Louisa Thedinga, lived in Dubuque, Iowa.

344. "Mali" (or "Maly" as in Lange and Riley 1966) was Josephine Huegy Bandelier's sister, Amalia Huegy. On several occasions during the years 1880-1882, Bandelier noted sending insect specimens to Maly; her precise identity remained obscure, however, and in our first volume appeared in the index simply as Maly despite a group photograph of Joe, her sister Amalia, Adolphe E. and Adolph F. Bandelier. In the spring of 1967, Amalia and Maly were identified as the same individual through the courtesy of Amalia's grandnephew, Professor Harvey Huegy, Visiting Professor of Marketing at Southern Illinois University, Carbondale. Amalia was born August 5, 1850, the daughter of Moritz Huegy and sister of Maurice and Josephine. She never married and died October 24, 1910.

345. This letter, written on August 6, 1883, from Highland, gives added insights into Bandelier's family relations (White and Bernal 1960: 272 [our translation]):

As it has been nine months since I had news from Mexico, I am going to make a new effort so that [the reply will reach me] before I leave for southern Arizona. [From there] I shall go, if God wills, to Sonora and Chihuahua. I have written you three times this year, once from Manzano, or from Belén, in the Rio Grande, again from Fort Wright [actually from Wingate] and finally from Fort Apache. In my journey, I have had luck, a great deal of luck. Travelling alone and by horse, I have covered 1847 English miles and have traversed successfully the middle of New Mexico and the lands of Arizona. I stayed for six weeks among the Apache, who could not have treated me better. The notice of my death could have been fatal to my wife; therefore, I left my horse in Tucson and returned. Once here, I was able to assure myself that all went well, and relations [with my wife] follow their normal course, being an intimate and perfect union. I have not forgotten the obligations I must fulfill to you and the Church.

Now, my dear friend, please have the goodness to send me some lines that will tell me how you are, and that will show me if I still keep a corner of your memory. My best wishes for your family.

346. Polk and Danser (1884b: 1003) listed Dr. Hans Mohr as a Highland physician.

347. John Balsiger had accompanied Adolphe E. Bandelier to Brazil after they had fled for their lives from Switzerland. (Hobbs 1940: 122-123.) Hobbs reports that Balsiger always had Saturday dinner in the home of the elder Bandelier (p. 123).

Balsiger along with A. E. Bandelier, Jacob Eggen, and others founded the Highland Agricultural Society in January of 1869. (Spencer 1937: 229.) His wife, Julia, was born December 10, 1826, and was the eldest daughter of Reverend Francis Vulliet, pastor of the French Church for a period of years. The Balsigers had four sons and four daughters. Mrs. Balsiger died March 7, 1884. (Weekly Telephone 1884: March 12.)

348. Joseph Speckart was a prominent business man in 1865 at the time Highland was incorporated as a village and was elected a trustee from the first ward. He operated a butcher shop and is mentioned as operating a tannery with Henry Zweck. He subscribed to a fund to bring a railroad to Highland and his name is identified with every move for the good of the town. In 1878 he served on the building committee for the hospital. (Spencer 1937: 129, 140, 175, 179.)

348a. This was Mrs. George Hoffmann of St. Louis, a cousin of Josephine Huegy Bandelier. Hobbs (1942a) stated, "Mrs. George Hoffmann and Mrs. August (Emily) Becker were cousins of Josephine Huegy Bandelier on her mother's side; Hubert was George's son, who came to Santa Fe for his health (after 1882) and died in Denver of tuberculosis. Cilla H. (Sept. 13, 1883), George's wife." [See entry this date this volume.] In the journals, Bandelier referred to her either as Cilla or Celia.

It is curious that in the published article in El Palacio, in which many other data from this interview were utilized, Hobbs (1942b: 112n5) identified George Hoffmann, rather than Cilla Hoffmann, as the cousin of Joe.

349. This referred to Part I of his "Report on Investigations in New Mexico during the years 1883-84," which was published as an appendix, along with Part II, to the Fifth Annual Report of the Archaeological Institute of America. See also fn 124 for 1884.

350. See fn 35.

351. J. Wildi, a member of the general merchandising firm of Ammann and Wildi, was the son-in-law of John Spindler, an early Highland settler. In 1883, he became a partner in the Highland Embroidery Works. The wool factory about which Wildi was approaching Bandelier was to become the Helvetia Milk Company in 1885. In time this became one of Highland's most important industries. Wildi sold his interests in the Embroidery Works when he became interested in the milk company. He was the youngest member of the board of directors and served as secretary-treasurer for a number of years. Due to differences, he founded another milk company and built another plant in Ohio in 1907, retaining more than one-third of the Helvetia stock. He died in Highland in 1910. In the early 1900's he had erected a residence on the site of the former Blattner's New Switzerland House. Remodeled and with an addition, this building is known today as the John Wildi Masonic Temple. (Spencer 1937: 55, 200, 201, 206, 207, 211, 218.)

352. Plans for a wool factory were started in 1843 by N. Smiley. He interested others in this enterprise and in 1845 erected a building and equipped it to manufacture a rough sort of woolen cloth from raw wool, much of which had to be shipped in. Smiley had invested heavily and was forced to mortgage the factory and was unable to make it pay. It passed through a succession of owners but none of them was able to pay off the mortgage. In 1874, all attempts at running a wool factory ceased, and the F. C. Ryhiner & Co. bank took over the building and machinery and the plant lay idle. (Spencer 1937: 71-72, 197.) Apparently Mr. Wildi and Bandelier did not reach an agreement before Bandelier left for New Mexico on October 15th. In the 1883-84 journals, there are entries which continue to refer to the wool factory.

353. The precise identity of this person has not been established. (See fn 35.)

354. "Uncle Kinne," referred to here, was Charles Kinne (original form of the name was Kuenne), the father of Louis E. Kinne, identified by Hobbs (1940a) as a cousin of Josephine Huegy Bandelier.

Charles Kinne first emigrated from Saxony, Germany, to Louisville, Kentucky. Because of his dislike for slavery, he moved in March, 1840, to Highland. He was a saddler and harness maker and, like Bandelier's father, contributed much to the early growth of Highland. He was postmaster during the Civil War, having been commissioned by Lincoln in 1861. In 1869, he was elected president of the board of trustees of the village of Highland. (Spencer 1937: 42, 158, 225, 232.)

355. Louise Vulliet was the daughter of Rev. Francis Vulliet, who arrived from St. Louis on the same stage that brought A. E. Bandelier to Highland. From 1851 to 1874 he was the minister of the French Church. His son, Louis F. Vulliet, succeeded him as pastor and early in his pastorate the church revised its constitution and identified itself with the Congregational Church. He served as pastor until his death in 1883. Since the Bandeliers also came from what was called French Switzerland undoubtedly the ties between the two families were close. Fn 347 has already cited Julia as another Vulliet daughter. (Spencer 1937: 101.)

356. A Mrs. John Widmer, who lived one mile east of Highland, died April 22, 1884. (Weekly Telephone 1884.) Hobbs (1940a) identified Widmer as the hired man, seemingly on the farm of Adolphe E. Bandelier. He was born in Switzerland and came to Highland independently of the Bandeliers. Later, Widmer returned to Switzerland where he died. Descendants of this family operate the Widmer Florist Shop in Highland today.

357. Reverend G. R. Wallace was Assistant Pastor of the Congregational Church of Highland from 1883 to 1886. (Spencer 1937: 103.)

358. Reverend William Fiegenbaum was the pastor of the German Methodist Church in Highland, having been pastor since 1848. Spencer says he was very active and resourceful and that Highland became the center of Methodism in that part of the country. During the cholera epidemic of 1849, Reverend Fiegenbaum and others were kept from traveling their rounds for fear they would spread the disease. Reverend Fiegenbaum devoted himself to the care of those suffering from cholera in Highland. (Spencer 1937: 88-89.)

359. This was Reverend Louis F. Vulliet. See fn 355.

360. These names appear in the journals from time to time. Charles was Charles H. Lambelet, the person whom Bandelier took to St. Louis for eye surgery as noted in the September 6, 1883, entry. Charles was listed as an employee of the Highland Tile Works (Weekly Telephone, April 16, 1884). See fn 90 for 1884 for the circumstances of his death. Bertha was a sister of Bandelier's wife, Josephine Huegy Bandelier, and wife of Charles Lambelet. (Weekly Telephone, April 20, 1884.) There were three Lambelet children: Fanny, Edmund, and Oscar. Rosalie was the widow of Emil Bandelier (See Preface and fns 24, 92, and 374.)

361. The deaths that occurred were due to an argument regarding a land-grant claim at Estancia Springs, New Mexico. Actually, Whitney was not mortally wounded. Killed at Estancia Springs on August 17, 1883, were Manuel B. Otero and Alexander Fernandez, a brother-in-law of James G. Whitney. Both Otero and Whitney were prominent men. For details, consult Otero (1939: II, 99-108) and the Santa Fé New Mexican Review, August 18 and August 20, 1883. These sources, however, were not in complete agreement in regard to various details.

362. Alban Jasper Conant, artist and author, was born in Chelsea, Vermont, in 1821. He was curator of the University of Missouri for eight years. He was commissioned chairman under the United States land grant. He founded the school of mines and metallurgy and was supervisor for three years. In 1880 he was appointed Délégué Correspondent, Institutional Ethnographique, Paris. He painted portraits of Lincoln, Sherman, Anderson at Sumter, many judges of the Court of Appeals and of the Supreme Court of the United States and cabinet secretaries, four portraits of Henry Ward Beecher, Dr. James McCosh, Bishop H. C. Potter, Burial of De Soto, etc. He wrote The Archaeology of the Missouri Valley (published in many European translations), Footprints of Vanished Races in the Mississippi Valley, My Acquaintance with Lincoln, etc. He died February 3, 1915. (Who Was Who n.d.: 248.)

363. This was the first wife of B. A. Suppiger (See fn 365), née Miss Mariette Wickenhauser whom he married December 9, 1848. They had two children, a daughter, Cecile, and a son, John Xavier, who died in infancy. Bandelier's exact relationship to her is not known to the present writers.

364. Robert Suppiger, maternal cousin of Josephine H. Bandelier (Hobbs 1942: 112n6), was a dealer in Providence and in anthracite coal and wood in nearby Trenton, Illinois (Eggen 1933: 88). He also had an interest in the David Suppiger & Co. Highland Mills (Polk and Danser 1884b: 1004). The Weekly Telephone, though making no mention of the suicide, noted October 22, 1884, that Bernard Suppiger had purchased the late Robert Suppiger's share in the flour mill.

364a. George Hoffmann's wife Cilla, or Celia, was related to Josephine Huegy Bandelier. (See also fn 348a.) George Hoffmann's profession in St. Louis has not been determined, nor has it been possible thus far to learn whether he was related to the Highland and Edwardsville Hoffmann family. Besides maintaining frequent social exchanges, Bandelier frequently consulted George about family and business matters, as the journal entries repeatedly indicate. George was often at the railroad station in St. Louis to welcome Bandelier home or to bid him farewell. A further indication of their mutual esteem is evidenced by the fact that the Hoffmann son, Hubert, because of poor health, accompanied the Bandeliers to New Mexico in 1885.

365. Mr. B. A. Suppiger was born July 13, 1823, at Sursee, canton St. Gallen, Switzerland. On May 10, 1833, he came with his parents, three brothers and eight sisters to the virgin district on which in later years the town of Highland was platted out. At the time of his death in 1910 he was the last one of these pioneer settlers. He was a blacksmith by profession. See fn 363 regarding his first marriage. After being a widower for several years he married Mrs. Anna Catherine Menz (née Kamm), January 1, 1887. (Obituary, Madison County, Illinois.)

366. Hilder appears to have been an official of, or at least active in, the Missouri Historical Society. He introduced Bandelier at his lecture for this Society on September 25, 1883 (Anzeiger des Westens, September 26, 1883). In 1884, Colonel H. H. Hilder of St. Louis was elected a corresponding member of the Anthropological Society of Washington (Anthropological Society of Washington 1885: 51). Presumably, this was the same person.

367. This is the first known journal entry which referred to the German version of the novel, Die Köshare. In January 1890, the Belletristisches Journal, New York, purchased Die Köshare, and the novel was run serially from January 1 to May 14, 1890. The English translation, The Delight Makers, was not completed until January 17, 1889; its publication came some time after that.

368. This was Henry Spencer Kaune of Breese, Illinois, who was a partner in Kaune Brothers (William G., Henry S. and Charles A.) Roller Process Flour Mill at Breese. As these journals show, Henry was married September 13, 1883, to Lizzie, Bandelier's cousin, who since her father's death had made her home with the Bandeliers in Highland. (See fn 92.) From various sources (Casey et al. 1956: 27-28; Twitchell 1917: IV, 64-65; the Kaune family bible in possession of Henry's daughter, Mrs. R. L. Ormsbee, Santa Fe; and Henry S. Kaune's obituary, Santa Fe New Mexican, July 5, 1933), the following data have been compiled. Henry was the son of Charles H. and Ernestina Weidner Kaune, born in Jamestown, Illinois, January 8, year uncertain. The family bible and obituary state that Henry died at the age of 78, making his birth year 1855; however, both sources specifically state that he was born in 1857. Twitchell gave the birth year as 1855; Casey et al. gave the age at death as 72, making the birth year 1861. The editors have, as yet, been unable to determine the correct year. In any event, Henry moved to Santa Fe in 1887 for his health, and he was joined there shortly afterward by his wife and children.

369. Mr. Wilborn is spoken of in a Weekly Telephone of 1884 as having two daughters, Mrs. M. Huegy [probably Mrs. Maurice Huegy] and Mrs. A. Beck. [Alexander Beck was an early assessor of Highland. (Spencer 1937: 226).]

370. Dr. Adolf Alt was a physician who was born in Mannheim, Germany, in 1851. He received his M.D. from the University of Heidelberg in 1875 and came to St. Louis in 1880. He became Professor of Opthamology, Medical Department, St. Louis University. (Leonard 1906: 21.) Dr. Adolph [Adolf] Alt belonged to the St. Louis Society of the Archaeological Institute of America. He was listed as an annual member. (AIA 1909: 80.)

371. August J. Pagan was a distiller of apple, peach, and grape brandies, wine grower and manufacturer of cider and cider vinegar. (Polk and Danser 1884b: 1003.) He was also president of the Helvetia Shooting Club in 1884. (Weekly Telephone 1884.)

372. This was Professor Adolf Bastian, prominent German ethnologist (1826-1905). With Berlin as his base, he traveled widely. He became Curator of Ethnography in 1868,

and in 1869 he founded the Königliches Museum für Völkerkunde. Lowie (1937), in his *History of Ethnological Theory*, devoted Chapter IV (pp. 30-38) to a discussion of Bastian's work. White (1940: II, 106n3) stated that Bastian became Director of the Berlin Museum für Völkerkunde in 1886.

373. The *Weekly Telephone* of 1884 reported Ida Becker's marriage to Rudolf Streiff on March 27, 1884.

374. This was Gustav, or Gustave Adolph, Bandelier, son of Emil and Rosalie Bandelier; Gustave was born in Breese, Illinois, July 7, 1865, and baptised October 22, 1865, with Adolph and Josephine Bandelier serving as sponsors. (See also fns 24 and 92.) Emil was Bandelier's cousin, who had lived in nearby Breese, Illinois, where he died August 10, 1873. In several references to Gustave, or Gus, in the journals, relations between him and Bandelier seemed somewhat less than cordial. In the winter and spring of 1882, for example, the entries suggested considerable friction. January 6: "Had a fuss with Gus at dinner, the boy is getting decidedly rude, coarse and sulky, and I told him plainly that he either had to reform or to go." March 3: "At night, fuss with Gustave. The boy left—I am glad of it. He is and will remain nothing else but a nuisance." Goad (1939: 15n6) reported that Gustave had three sons: George Emil, living in Fort Worth, Texas; Edward Louis, living in Stillwater, Oklahoma; and Eugene Alphonse, of Gallup, New Mexico. In August, 1969, we had the pleasure of a personal interview with George, at that time a resident of several decades in Stillwater. We learned that Gustave had married Lillie Wilhelmina Klein, of St. Louis, in 1895. Gustave died August 15, 1934, and was buried in Stillwater. Since Goad's study, not only George had moved, but Edward had moved to Midwest City, Oklahoma, and Eugene, to Phoenix, Arizona; all three sons were living as of the summer of 1969. From George's remarks, it became quite clear that, again, the complaining journal entries had recorded Bandelier's immediate reactions to specific situations, in this case to a teen-ager's behavior. In reality, the relationship between Bandelier and Gustave was much more one of mutual respect and genuine affection.

374a. Emily (Mrs. August) Becker was a cousin of Josephine Huegy Bandelier on her mother's side (Hobbs 1942a). The Beckers made their home in St. Louis.

374b. Mrs. Hesse (Elizabeth Donne) was a sister of Mrs. William G. Kaune (Sarah A. Donne), whose husband was a brother of Henry S. Kaune. (See fn 368.) Elizabeth and Sarah were daughters of Robert and Gertrude Donne, Breese, Illinois, pioneers. (Breese Centennial 1956: 27.)

375. Dr. Hugo Kinner was born in Woerlitz, Germany, in 1840. He attended several German universities and graduated from Berlin. Kinner was commissioned by his family to settle certain family affairs in America where the family had been represented since early days in Virginia. In 1864, he settled in St. Louis and began to practice medicine. For his own enlightenment and observation, he traveled widely among the tribes of American Indians. Kinner was a member of the American Anthropological Association and of the Archaeological Institute of America. (Leonard 1906: 329-330.)

376. R. von Pfleger was a seventh-grade teacher in the public schools of Highland. (*Weekly Telephone* 1884: 3 June.) The June 25, 1884, issue of the *Weekly Telephone* announced that he would open a writing school on July 7, 1884, for four weeks "$1.00 tuition in advance."

377. Polk and Danser (1884b: 1187) under Millersburgh says, "See Baden Baden." "Baden Baden. Sometimes called Millersburgh, is located in the southwestern part of Bond county, 12 miles from Greenville, the seat of justice and the location of the nearest bank, and 4 miles from Pochahontas, its shipping point. Population, 275. C. H. Williams, postmaster." (P. 183.)

378. Peter Steiff was listed as owner of a flour mill in Baden Baden, sometimes called

Millersburgh [Millersburg], population in 1884, 275. (Polk and Danser 1884b: 183, 1187.) Although Bandelier's spellings were not always accurate, the editors feel that this name was Streiff. The son has not been identified.

379. Andrew J. Henry was given as a county judge of Greenville, Illinois, in Polk and Danser (1884b: 978).

380. A Joseph Miller was listed as a tinsmith in Caseyville (11 miles north of Belleville) in Polk and Danser (1884b: 310-311).

381. An account, in German, of this lecture was found in the Bandelier Scrapbook. It had been published in the *Anzeiger des Westens*, a St. Louis newspaper, on September 26, 1883. The article was entitled, "Die indianischen Ruinen des Westens."

382. Bandelier did not note completing this correspondence but in 1885 *Das Ausland* (pp. 974-975) published "Ein Brief von Adolf F. Bandelier über seine Reisen im südwestlichen Nordamerika," which was dated October 12, 1883, from Highland. In it, Bandelier condensed his travels from November 6, 1882, to June 26, 1883, and noted that he had traveled 1847 miles "by horse and by foot."

383. Bandelier often mentioned Graffenried and Wachsmuth together; one gains the impression that they were possibly neighbors of the Bandeliers, on farms outside of Highland. In the December 22, 1880, entry (Lange and Riley 1966: 235), Bandelier commented, "In the afternoon went to the farm. Graffenried and Wachsmuth are still lazy, almost depressed, and always glad to go to bed." Rudolph von Graffenried was apparently of some financial means and was said to be of a titled Swiss family (Hobbs 1942a).

384. In the first volume of the journals (Lange and Riley 1966: 236), Bandelier mentioned going "out in the afternoon to see J. Scheule," while he was at home in Highland in December of 1880. This is probably the same person.

385. This was Dr. George J. Engelmann of St. Louis. From time to time, Bandelier collected and sent plant specimens to Engelmann and corresponded frequently with him. Born in Frankfurt-am-Main, Germany, February 2, 1809, Engelmann received his M.D. from the University of Wurzburg in 1831. He came to the United States in 1832. He returned to Germany in 1840 and married Dorothea Horstmann. He brought his bride to St. Louis. Their only child, George, also became a physician. The father has become perhaps better known as a botanist than physician. However, his work in botany was sandwiched into a demanding medical practice. The frequency with which "Engelm." follows the genus and species names in plant listings attests to his prodigious work in botany. He was also a pioneer meteorologist and is said to have recorded observations for a longer continuous period of time than anyone else of his era. He was an organizer of the St. Louis Academy of Science and one of the founders of the National Academy of Science. He was the first curator of the herbarium of the St. Louis Botanical Gardens. His works were assembled in the "Botanical Works of the late George Engelmann Collected for Henry Shaw, 1887." He died in St. Louis, February 4, 1884. (National Academy of Science 1902: IV, 3-21; Who Was Who 1963: 171.)

386. Brigadier General Ranald S. Mackenzie of the Fourth Cavalry was Commander of the District of New Mexico at this time. He retired in March, 1884. (Thrapp 1967: 274; Heitman 1903: I, 672.) He appears to have been well regarded; of interest is an editorial, January 17, 1883, which appeared in the *Santa Fe Daily New Mexican* (p. 2):

"Make the Indians go to the free schools after we have them established. Our venerable Uncle Sammy should stick a pin here. [Secretary of the Interior] Teller's proposition to disarm the wild Indians ain't so bad, but if he had gone a step farther and proposed to arm them with the spelling book and appoint such men as Ronald [sic] Mackenzie and "Red" Forsythe [probably George A. "Sandy" Forsyth; see fn 440] as the schoolmasters, the whole of the ground would have been covered. We recommend the secretary to publish an addendum to his report, and to incorporate this idea."

387. This was probably Charles L. Bernays. (See fn 35.)

388. This can only be Mrs. F. C. Ryhiner as her son was a bachelor. Dr. Ryhiner had died in 1879. Whether or not Mrs. Ryhiner was making her home in St. Louis is not known. Her obituary appeared in the *Weekly Telephone* of February 4, 1885. She had died on January 31, 1885, and was survived by a daughter, Mrs. Louisa M. Thedinga of Dubuque, Iowa, and a son, F. C. Ryhiner, Jr., of Highland, and by three brothers: Bernard, Anton, and David Suppiger, also of Highland.

389. Maurice Frederick Hendrick De Haas (1832-95) an American marine painter. De Haas was born in Rotterdam, Netherlands, and settled in New York City in 1858. He became a member of the National Academy in 1867. De Haas's best known painting is *Farragut Passing the Forts at New Orleans*.

390. This was E. G. Savage, manager of the Raton Coal and Coking Company. (McKenney 1882-83: 334.)

391. Thomas Cruse, Sixth Cavalry, later a brigadier general and author of *Apache Days and After*. (Heitman 1903: I, 342; see also Cruse 1941.)

392. Charles Pinckney Elliott, of South Carolina. A graduate of West Point, he became a second lieutenant in the Thirteenth Infantry, June 13, 1882; the following year, June 7, he transferred to the Fourth Cavalry. In 1888, he became a first lieutenant and retired in 1898 as a captain. (Heitman 1903: I, 401.)

393. See fn 476.

394. Jake Gold was a dealer in curios; his store was on the northwest corner of San Francisco Street and Burro Alley. His store was the first of its kind in Santa Fe. Almost from the time of his first arrival in Santa Fe, Bandelier visited Gold's store, finding his collections of manuscripts and ethnological and archaeological specimens of real use. (McKenney 1882-83: 399.)

395. Mr. Robert B. Willison, of Santa Fe, was a civil and mining engineer who also dealt in real estate. (Polk and Danser 1884a: 354.)

Bandelier (1890-92: II, 121) wrote "A gentleman whose long experience in New Mexico and intimate acquaintance with its topography gives great weight to his opinions, Mr. R. B. Willison, C. E., of Santa Fé, . . ."

Later, in the same volume (279n1), Bandelier referred to "my friend, Mr. R. B. Willison of Santa Fé."

396. McKenney (1882-83: 339) listed M. A. Gold as a saloonkeeper; this was probably Aaron Gold. His relationship to Jake Gold is not clear. Dike (1958) listed Aaron Gold as the first postmaster at Peñasco, Taos County, beginning September 10, 1874.

397. This was probably Samuel T. Reed who was listed in Polk and Danser (1884a: 353) as being in the real estate and mining business, with an office over the First National Bank of Santa Fe. McKenney (1882-83: 340) noted Reed as president of the Santa Fe Bonanza Mining and Tunnel Company.

398. John Baptist Lamy was born in Lempdes, France, October 11, 1814. He attended the Seminary of Montferrand, France, and was ordained a priest in the Roman Catholic Church, 1838. Lamy came to America in 1839 as a missionary, first in Wooster and Danville, Ohio, and later in Covington, Kentucky. He was named Vicar Apostolic of New Mexico, and Bishop of Agathon in 1850, becoming Bishop of Santa Fe in 1853, and Archbishop from 1875 to 1885. This Santa Fe Diocese included New Mexico, Arizona, parts of Colorado, Utah, Nevada, and was expanded to take in the whole of Colorado in

1860. Bishop Lamy induced the Sisters of Loretto to found a settlement in Santa Fe in 1852, the Christian Brothers in 1867 and, with their help, actively promoted the building of schools and churches. Lamy died on February 13, 1888, and was buried in Santa Fe. The famous novel by Willa Cather, *Death Comes for the Archbishop* (1927), was based on Lamy's life. (Who Was Who 1963: 301.)

399. Other than a reference to "Father Farini in Santa Fe" in an October 10, 1884, issue of the *Santa Fé New Mexican Review*, no further clue to this person's identity has been found.

400. Captain Fletcher A. Blake was prominent in the 1880's in the general area of Las Vegas. He had been active in White Oaks, Lincoln County, where gold had been discovered in 1879. He became the first postmaster of Vera Cruz, Lincoln County, July 5, 1881 (the office was discontinued June 25, 1883). In 1882, he was associated with the Las Vegas Coal and Coke Company. In 1884, Blake was listed as a cattle raiser at Las Vegas. The same year, Polk and Danser (1884a: 362, 365) listed Blake as editor and proprietor of the *Daily Sun*, on the plaza in Las Vegas. In 1897, he was the operator of a health resort at Beulah, near Las Vegas. (Dike 1958; Lange and Riley 1966: 408; Polk and Danser 1884a: 327.)

401. Mariano S. Otero, Bernalillo, New Mexico, was one of the group that formed a committee with Nathan Bibo in the period, 1873-78, to aid the sheriff in the capture of a gang which was terrorizing the area. (Fierman 1962: 57.)

402. The Pereas were locally prominent in the flour mill, general merchandising, and the post office of Bernalillo. (Polk and Danser 1884a: 310.) Haines (1891: 384) commented that the mercantile house of the Perea Bros. in Bernalillo transacted the largest business in that part of the country. Twitchell (1925: 401n, 474) said that Don Pedro Perea (Facing p. 398) was a councilman from Bernalillo, as well as being president of First National Bank in Santa Fe and delegate in Congress from New Mexico.

403. This name was given in the first volume as Father D. Parisis (Lange and Riley 1966: index.) The initial "D." is in error. Defouri (1887: 54) said Father Stephen Parisis was pastor of Bernalillo. Chávez (1957) stated that Parisis was ordained February 2, 1869; he was one of the priests brought to New Mexico by Bishop Lamy. (Salpointe 1898: 283.)

404. See fn 109.

405. This remark stemmed from the fact that the presence of kachinas, or masked dancers, at Isleta was the result of the immigration to Isleta of the "Laguna Colony," who brought their masks with them, having been driven from Laguna by the progressive element there. The point was a fine example of the attitude that secrecy among the Puebloans was not directed at non-Puebloans, Anglos, for example, but to non-believers whether these were white, Negro, Indian, or other.

406. Isleta (and Isleta del Sur), in fact, represent the remnant of the Southern Tiwas. These people may, at one time, have had as many as twenty villages in the central Rio Grande area. The Tiwa, however, took the brunt of Coronado's invasion of 1540-1542 and, because of their central and vulnerable position, declined sharply in the first century of Spanish rule. During the Pueblo Revolt of 1680, Isleta, by then the paramount village of the Southern Tiwa, remained loyal to the Spaniards. During the confused years that led to the Reconquest of 1692, a number of the Isletans were moved south to El Paso and settled in a new village called Isleta del Sur. From the eighteenth century on, only one main pueblo remained in the Isleta area, though with surrounding rancherías.

407. According to Haines (1891: 383), Felipe Chaves was born in Pedillos, Bernalillo County, November 16, 1835. He received a common school education in Mexico; he

married Josie Chavez, 1856, and they had three children. In 1886, Chaves moved to Valencia County. At one time he was the largest sheep owner in the Territory, but during the Civil War he lost the entire number. He later restocked his ranch, and by 1881 he had sold his sheep interests.

408. JORNADA DEL MUERTO (Socorro, Sierra, Doña Ana). Span., "journey of death." This celebrated topographic feature lay on the caravan routes from Chihuahua to Santa Fe and was chosen for travel because it shortened the route by at least a day. It was a waterless stretch of nearly 90 mi from Rincon to San Marcial between San Andres Mts. on E and Fray Cristobal Range on W. In addition, many miles were sandy, and sometimes the Indians made their attacks from hiding places in the mountains or arroyos. Oñate in 1598 named one of the arroyos *Los Muertos*, "The Dead," and the phrase *jornada del muerto* in Spanish is "journey of the dead man." However, since hundreds perished in this crossing, women and children as well as men, "journey of death" seems a much more fitting translation. (Pearce 1965: 77.)

409. Bandelier (1892: II, 355n1), in writing of the San Mateo Range said, "There are two mountain ranges in New Mexico which bear this name. The one to which I refer here lies west of Fort Craig and San Marcial, and appears like a continuation of the Magdalena Mountains; its altitude is given as 10,209 feet." It was to these mountains in Socorro County that Bandelier referred in this entry. The second range are the San Mateo Mountains in Valencia County, also called the Sierra de San Mateo. Mount Taylor (old Spanish name, Cebolleta Mountain) is the highest of the San Mateo Mountains. (Pearce 1965: 105, 147.)

410. Bandelier probably had reference to the Robledo country here. Pedro Robledo, a native of Toledo, was the first person in the Oñate colony to die in New Mexico. It is thought that Robledo, a settlement on the west branch of the Rio Grande near Doña Ana commemorated the place where he was buried. A nearby promontory may also have commemorated him. A second explanation for the name given this area was that it honored Doña Ana Robledo, the legendary (perhaps mythical) seventeenth-century lady for whom Doña Ana Settlement seemingly was named. (Pearce 1965: 137.) Christiansen (1964) referred also to the death of Pedro Robledo and said that his name remained on Oñate's campsite for 300 years and was then forgotten, being retained only on the nearby mountain. He noted that the site at Robledo was a favorite one during the eighteenth century on the long and arduous route from Santa Fe to Chihuahua. The Spanish talked of building a presidio there as it commanded a critical river ford but nothing was ever built until the Americans built Fort Selden there. Pearce (1965) did not mention Fort Selden in connection with Robledo. He noted the Spanish campground a short distance south of Robledo (p. 137).

411. Major Eugene Van Patten, of the 1st Regiment, Cavalry, New Mexico Volunteer Militia. (Official Reports 1884: 114-15.)

412. Pedro Pedregón, Captain. Commanding Officer, Troop A (Las Cruces), 1st Regiment, Cavalry, New Mexico Volunteer Militia. (Official Reports 1884: 114-15.)

413. The Manso lived originally in the area of Las Cruces and El Paso in the lower Middle Rio Grande Valley. Their linguistic affiliation remains uncertain, but in historic times they showed considerable cultural similarities to the Piro and the Tiwa. (Lange and Riley 1966: 364n161; Hodge 1907: I, 801-802.)

414. A large group of Taracahitian speaking peoples who, today and throughout historic times, have occupied the mountainous areas of central Chihuahua. For a recent study of the Tarahumar see Pennington 1963.

415. Reverend Peter Lassaigne was among the clergy brought to New Mexico by Bishop Lamy. In 1864 Lassaigne and Reverend Peter Bernal volunteered to go to Tucson,

as the Jesuit Fathers had been recalled. They could not get any farther than Las Cruces, as no one would risk guiding them because of fear of the Apaches. The two fathers returned to Santa Fe. However, in 1869, Lassaigne, with permission of the ecclesiastical authority, did join the clergy in Arizona. When Tularosa was made the center of a parish in 1870, Lassaigne became its pastor. (Salpointe 1898: 241, 261, 262, 282.) As this entry indicates, Lassaigne had returned to Las Cruces sometime in the interim. Polk and Danser (1884a: 324) also listed him at Las Cruces.

416. Quitman was 80 miles below El Paso on the Rio Grande. Fort Quitman had been reoccupied after the Civil War but it had been abandoned in 1877. (Crimmins 1935: 141n27.)

417. In view of the widespread incorporation of Montezuma into Southwestern myths, this alleged lack of knowledge is dubious. Probably Bandelier's informants were simply reluctant to discuss the matter with him, a stranger.

418. This was Christopher J. Hildreth, listed by Polk and Danser (1884a: 326) as the editor and proprietor of the *Rio Grande Republican*, a weekly paper at Las Cruces devoted to the interests of Mesilla Valley. The paper was founded in 1881, and after a few years Hildreth was followed by several successors. (Anderson 1907: I, 476; Greene 1882: 50.)

419. Alberto, or Albert, J. Fountain was a prominent figure in New Mexico military, political, and professional life according to Twitchell (1912: II, 494-95, 495-96n409). Colonel Fountain, a lawyer, was in command of the 1st Regiment, Cavalry, territorial militia troops, called out by Governor Sheldon in 1884. Fountain also rendered service to local peace officers in ridding the ranges of Grant, Sierra, and Socorro counties of cattle thieves. An interesting episode of this type was contained in the Official Reports (1884). In 1896, he and his nine-year-old son, Henry, were mysteriously ambushed; the bodies were never found. The criminals were never identified despite strong suspicions of individuals involved in the range wars and power struggles of the area at that time. (See Jenkinson and Kernberger 1967: 131, 145-151.)

420. Defouri (1887: 21) mentioned Reverend Ramón Ortiz, "for forty years parish priest of El Paso."

421. A large unit-type pueblo of several hundred rooms and many kivas in Chaco Canyon, New Mexico; it is one of the principal attractions of this much-visited national monument.

422. In primitive groups, generally, there is a very close relationship between the practice of medicine and both religious and political organization. Medicine men are closely involved with religion and are usually political leaders as well.

423. Bernardo de Miera y Pacheco, a soldier-cartographer and religious image maker, who was a member of the Vélez de Escalante Expedition to Utah in 1776. Adams and Chávez (1956: 13n1, 16n13) referred to him as Captain Miera. He was for some years a citizen of Santa Fe (pp. 268-269).

424. This was William Dessauer, proprietor of a general merchandise store in Las Cruces, New Mexico. (Polk and Danser 1884a: 324.) Dessauer also served as quartermaster of the 1st Regiment, Cavalry, New Mexico Volunteer Militia in 1883-84. (Official Reports 1884: 114-115.)

425. In the Southwest, the owl was, and is, widely considered an evil omen, connected with black magic and witchcraft.

426. This is not really conclusive. There may well have been large numbers of sites of former human occupation that would have been missed by the (presumably) untrained observer, Nicomedes.

427. Actually, it would have been more normal to have the governor, rather than the cacique, act as host to any outside visitor.

428. This was almost certainly Charles Blanchard of Las Vegas who traveled in the southern portion of New Mexico and adjacent Texas in his business as a general merchandiser. On March 12, 1880, Blanchard became president and treasurer of the Las Vegas and St. Louis Mining and Smelting Company. Among the incorporators was Charles Longuemare, metallurgist and superintendent. (Callon 1962: 113.) (See also fns 472 for 1883 and 118 for 1884.)

429. This account of the Queres occupation of Gran Quivira would have appeared little more than hearsay until rather recent archaeological findings. National Park Service excavations of the pueblo at Gran Quivira National Monument under the direction of Alden C. Hayes have revealed such features as a flat stone slab in the rim of the kiva firepits, consistently placed in the right-hand portion as one faces the firepit, deflector, and ventilator complex. This unique trait has also been found in salvage archaeological excavations in the new Cochiti Dam area. While present elsewhere, as at Pindi Pueblo, and in the Chama Valley, such shared features would seem to lend credence to some degree, at least, of common background for Gran Quivira and the Keresan tribes.

430. This was probably prompted by Bandelier's claim of adoption by the Cochiti, with esoteric knowledge to support the claim, and/or Nicomedes' stated belief in a traditional prophecy which seemingly led to his confusing Bandelier with an Indian from the North. (See entry of November 10, 1883.) The editors remain somewhat doubtful of Bandelier's claim of adoption by the Cochiti. No mention of any even slightly related activity has been found in the journals, either in anticipation or in retrospect, of what could only have been a really great event in his life. Of course, another great event in Bandelier's life, his conversion to Catholicism in Mexico in 1881, was also very scantily recorded in the journals.

431. This was Mr. O. W. Meysenburg of St. Louis and Santa Fe. (See fns 109, 133, 134, and 135 for 1884.)

432. It is quite likely that this was Joseph P. Whyte, president of the Jos. P. Whyte Real Estate Co. of St. Louis (Kargau n.d.: 147).

433. Except that Polk and Danser (1884a: 324) listed him as a physician at Las Cruces, nothing more has been found about him.

434. Juh, a Chiricahua war chief and companion of Geronimo. Juh refused to surrender to Crook in May, 1883, but died or was killed a short time later near Casas Grandes, Chihuahua. (Davis 1929: 6 et seq.)

435. Nana, a war chief of the Warm Springs Apache group and contemporary of Victorio. Nana was with Geronimo in Chihuahua in 1883 and surrendered to Crook's forces. (Davis 1929: 6 et seq.)

436. Victorio was a warrior and chief of the Warm Springs and Chiricahua Apache. From the early 1870's until his death in Chihuahua in 1880, Victorio kept the Southwestern border area in turmoil. After his death, Nana inherited the remnants of Victorio's band and continued raiding. He was finally captured by Crook in 1883 and died in Oklahoma. (Lockwood 1938: 324; Davis 1929: 13 et seq.)

437. This may have been William H. H. Llewellyn, listed in the 1882 Annual Report of the Commissioner of Indian Affairs, p. 369, as the farmer-in-charge, October 1, 1881, at South Fork, Lincoln County, where he dealt with both Mescalero and Jicarilla Apaches. (Official Reports 1884: 369.)

438. In 1847, shortly after the Americans took over control of New Mexico, a few Taos Indians and Mexicans from the Taos vicinity attacked and killed the newly appointed

governor, Charles Bent. The rebels began a march on Santa Fe but were quickly scattered by American military forces. (Spicer 1962: 170.)

439. Ruins of Fort Selden are fifteen miles north of Las Cruces on the east bank of the Rio Grande. Garrisons were there from 1865 until April 1879. The fort was named for Henry R. Seldon, 1st New Mexico Infantry, and one-time captain of the 5th U.S. Infantry. (Pearce 1965: 58-59.) (See also entry of November 2, 1883, and the first footnote for that entry.)

440. Lieutenant Colonel George Alexander Forsyth, a well-known Indian fighter. He had been brevetted brigadier general during the Civil War; he was again so recognized for his action in defending Beecher Island during the long, bloody engagement there against Roman Nose and the Cheyennes in 1868. He was also variously known as "Red" and "Sandy." In the 1882 campaign, with the 4th Cavalry, pursuing Loco and his Chiricahuas into Mexico, Forsyth was severely criticized for lack of vigorous action, allowing the Apaches to escape into the rugged Sierra Madre. (Downey 1943: 279 et seq.; Thrapp 1967: 223n25, 235 et seq.)

441. This was D. S. Stanley, brevet major general, who was the commanding officer, United States Army, District of New Mexico, Headquarters at Santa Fe. At the same time, this man held the rank of colonel and was in command of the 22nd Infantry Regiment which was based in Santa Fe. (Santa Fe Daily New Mexican, Jan. 18, 1883, p. 3.)

442. P. F. Herlow was the proprietor of Herlow's Hotel, located on San Francisco Street; a livery stable was in conjunction with it. (McKenney 1882-83: 340; Polk and Danser 1884a: 352; Santa Fé New Mexican Review, 1884.)

443. This was probably Gerard D. Koch, described by Hobbs (1942b: 114n14) as a lumber and hardware dealer in Santa Fe and a personal friend of Bandelier. Earlier, Koch was listed as a partner in Eldodt & Koch, Dealers in all kinds of Merchandise, Dry Goods, Groceries, &c., San Juan, New Mexico, and Abiquiu, New Mexico (Huggins 1876).

444. Robert G. Marmon, younger brother of Walter G. Marmon (see fn 76), was listed by Polk and Danser (1884a: 323) as postmaster; Dike (1958) listed him as the first when the post office was established at Laguna, January 24, 1879. Robert was the first white man to hold the office of governor in any Keresan pueblo, serving in this capacity in 1880. Born in Ohio, in 1872, he came to Santa Fe as a U.S. Government civil engineer. In 1875, he moved to Laguna and did engineering, general merchandizing, and stock raising. He married a Laguna woman. He spent ten years in the New Mexico militia, serving as captain of a Laguna cavalry troop during the Apache wars. He worked for better education at both Laguna and Acoma; in 1884, he headed the first delegation of sixty Indians taken to Carlisle, Pennsylvania, for education. (Anderson 1907: I, 371.)

445. Salpointe (1898: 275) provided the following on this retreat. "After his resignation, July, 1885, the Most Rev. J. B. Lamy retired to a small country place he had purchased in 1853 in the vicinity of the Tesuque River. This place, which the Prelate designated by the name 'Villa Pintoresca,' was commonly called 'El Cajoncito de Tuseque [sic].' [Soon after purchasing this plot] . . . the Archbishop had a modest house and a small chapel built on it, and when he felt the weight of years added to that of the administration of his vast diocese, it was there that he was wont to go at times, for some days of rest. He could not expect to have visitors in a place so remote; still, when any strangers happened to make their way to the solitary picturesque spot, he always cheerfully entertained them in the best possible manner."

446. In 1882, Bandelier had met Samuel Eldodt briefly on two occasions. (Lange and Riley 1966: 272, 372.) Samuel Eldodt had come to the United States and Santa Fe in 1868, at the age of 18, from Westphalia, Germany. Two brothers, Mark and Nathan,

merchants, had come to the United States in 1851 and to Santa Fe in 1862. Samuel became a partner in their firm in 1882. He became treasurer of the Territory of New Mexico, 1894-98; delegate to the Constitutional Convention, 1910; mercantile business in Chamita, as late as 1911. (Lange and Riley 1966: 409-410.) In Polk and Danser (1884a: 705) he was listed as owner of a general store in Abiquiu.

Bourke (Bloom 1936b: 258), while at San Juan Pueblo, wrote ". . . Mr. Samuel Eldodt, the store-keeper, who has been with these Indians for more than 13 years, knows their habits well and something of their language. As a certificate of his general intelligence, I will merely say that he speaks fluently English, French, Spanish and German." Bandelier must have welcomed this opportunity to visit San Juan.

447. Lange and Riley (1966: 408-409) presented the following data on Amado Chavez: "Chávez, Don Amado. Born Santa Fe, 1851; ancestry extended to 1692, to General Chávez, with De Vargas. Educated at St. Michael's in Santa Fe, and at business college in Washington, D.C., Georgetown University, and National University Law School, diploma in 1876. Employed by Interior Department, Washington, D.C. Returned to New Mexico, 1882; attorney-at-law, sheep raiser. Elected House of Representatives, Territorial Assembly Speaker, 1884; Superintendent of Public Instruction, 1892; established education in New Mexico on firm basis; second appointment, 1904-05. New Mexico-Texas boundary litigation, 1912. Married Kate N. Foster, née Nichols, 1892; three children." See Chávez (1954: 19) for importance of this family in New Mexico history. Amado Chávez, according to Fierman (1961: 241), was the son of Colonel Manuel A. Chávez, claimed by some as the founder of San Mateo. See fn 183, noting the alternate spelling, i.e., Chaves.

448. "Pueblo," here, was simply the Spanish for village; San Mateo was not an Indian pueblo.

449. This was Alexander Douglas, named postmaster at Joseph, Rio Arriba County, when the post office there was established September 30, 1884. Formerly (February 3, 1852), it had been called Abiquiu, and on December 2, 1884, the name reverted to Abiquiu. (Dike 1958.)

Polk and Danser (1884a: 295) gave Douglas as postmaster of Abiquiu, population 300, County seat of Rio Arriba County and noted he operated a general store there with Samuel Eldodt.

Frank Bond, whose brother George Bond worked for Eldodt at Chamita, or San Juan, had this to say about Mr. Douglas, "Mr. Alex Douglas was a well educated, polished Scotch gentleman, very exact in his dress and carriage, extremely particular in everything he did. He spoke the Spanish language perfectly; in fact he used to say he dreamed in Spanish. He ran a little store at Abiquiu in company with Mr. Eldodt." In 1883, George and Frank Bond bought out Scott and Whitehead at Española. (Bond 1940: 340-341.)

An advertisement on Huggins' map (1876) showed Alexander Douglas as Business Manager at Abiquiu of the firm Eldodt & Koch, Dealers in all Kinds of Merchandise, Dry Goods, Groceries &c., San Juan, New Mexico, and Abiquiu, New Mexico. This advertisement noted he could "furnish all kinds of forage, Miners' and Emigrants' supplies en route to the San Juan country."

450. This was the site of the Tewa village of Okeh (probably to be identified with the Yuqueyunque of Coronado) where Juan de Oñate, in the winter of 1598, established the first capital of New Mexico, on the west bank of the Rio Grande. This settlement, its mission church, and a little later the town named San Gabriel, met with failure. The Indians of Okeh moved to the east side of the Rio Grande where their village became known as San Juan. In 1601, most of the Spanish settlers at San Gabriel deserted, many

returning to Chihuahua. In the next decade, however, a number of colonists returned and, in 1610, the capital was moved to the site of present-day Santa Fe. (Spicer 1962: 156-157.)

451. Father Camilo Seux was one of the priests added to the Santa Fe Diocese by Archbishop Lamy.

Bandelier, in his *Final Report* (1890-92: I, 220n1), in discussing missionary work among the Pueblos, wrote,

"Witness the great difficulties which my esteemed friend, Rev. Father Camille [Camilo] Seux, priest of San Juan, has lately experienced from the Indians of that village, when, in compliance with the territorial laws, he caused the cemetery to be removed outside the village. It nearly cost his life."

Elsewhere, in the same volume (p. 268n1), in a statement comparing various pueblos, Bandelier added these comments about Father Seux:

"Thus, for instance, the churches at San Felipe, Cochiti, and Acoma are comparatively in good repair. At San Juan, all the work done was performed by the priest, Rev. Father Seux, at his own expense, and almost against the will of the Indians, who while they would not allow any outsider to touch the edifice, still refused to make even the most indispensable repairs."

452. This may have referred to the ruin "on a little eminence, near to the old highway to the north, . . . all that remains of the Garita, the only Spanish fortification, save one, in all our wide continental domain. Against its western wall the revolutionists of 1837 were shot when their short-lived success had vanished in defeat." (Prince 1912: 16.)

453. Far more research is needed in the documentation of evidence of such puebloan migrations for the historic period and in archaeological investigations for the prehistoric period. Already known, but often in only minimal detail, are the moves of the Tewa to Hano, in the Hopi country; of the Laguna Colony, to Isleta; of the Isletans and Piros, earlier, to Isleta del Sur; of the settlement at Tortugas, near Las Cruces; of the Hopi migration to Santo Domingo; the people of San Marcos to Santo Domingo and other Rio Grande villages; of the Pecos survivors to Jemez; and of smaller groups, such as the several families from San Ildefonso to Cochiti. As for the Quivira's associations, "los Queres del Sur," with Keresans or Piros, more investigations are urgently needed. (See fn 429.)

454. Defouri (1887: 20) mentioned Father Francolon as follows: "Father J. B. Francolon, lately parish priest of *Santa Cruz de la Cañada*, has yet in his possession a circular letter from one of the Superiors of the Franciscans to his brethren to gather up all the statistics, all the facts worth knowing, and forward them yearly to the mother house at Mexico."

455. The statement that the Nambé governor was a Navajo is not so important as a startling bit of information in the sense of being unprecedented. Rather, it is important for an on-the-spot clue, which, in combination with similar data, provides valuable insights as to practices otherwise unknown or unsuspected in terms of frequency of incidence. Such instances demonstrate one of the principal values of these journals.

456. The widespread Pueblo Revolt (with Apache help) took place in 1680 and forced Governor Antonio de Otermín to evacuate New Mexico and retire to El Paso. Several attempts were made to return, but all failed until, in 1692, Diego de Vargas Zapata y Luján led an expedition back to New Mexico. After several years of intermittent fighting, de Vargas pacified the Rio Grande area, but firm control was never reestablished in Zuñi and Hopi country. (See also fn 200.)

457. Bandelier here was apparently correcting an entry made in his March 31, 1882, journal where he stated that two men by the name of Abreu and one by the name of

Alarid were killed at Agua Fria. (Lange and Riley 1966: 246.) The "engagement of 1837" spoken of here was also referred to as the Rebellion of 1837 at Santa Cruz (pp. 407, 414). Chávez' account (1954: 120) added that Don Santiago Abreu was captured near Los Cerrillos by the Chimayo insurgents and cruelly put to death at Santo Domingo Pueblo.

458. This term, "cajón—work," may well have referred to what are now called "puddled" adobe walls in which the courses were built up in poured blocks, or units, rather than by pre-cast bricks. Descriptions and diagrams of such walls, shown with matching convexities of the tops and concavities of the bottoms for added strength, were presented by Stubbs and Stallings in their report of excavations at Pindi Pueblo (1953: 24-31).

459. This was John C. Pearce, listed by McKenney (1882-83: 340) as a metallurgist and assayer in Santa Fe. Dike (1958) listed John C. Pearce as the first postmaster at Cribbensville, Rio Arriba County, when the post office was established there October 17, 1884.

460. Captain Louis Felsenthal came to New Mexico in 1855. He joined the Historical Society in 1859, donating some Spanish arms to the society. The society suspended its activities during the Civil War. After serving in the Civil War, Felsenthal returned to Santa Fe and helped in the reorganization of the New Mexico Historical Society about 1880. He was appointed Adjutant General for New Mexico by Governor Sheldon, December 31, 1881. As evidenced in the 1880-82 journals, Bandelier consulted Captain Felsenthal frequently. (See Lange and Riley 1966: 410.) As this journal entry indicates, Bandelier continued to contact him when in Santa Fe.

461. For a detailed history of the stormy and bitter struggle between the Franciscan missionaries and the civil authorities in New Mexico in the seventeenth century, see Scholes (1937, 1942). Scholes, however, mentioned only one letter, dated September 29, 1643, from Salas at Cuarac (1937: 185).

462. This was one of the very rare instances in which Bandelier referred to his wife with her full name; habitually, it was Joe.

463. Samuel Ellison was territorial librarian of New Mexico from 1881 until his death in 1889 and consequently Bandelier's contacts with him were frequent. Prior to coming to New Mexico in 1848, having been born in Kentucky in 1817, he served in the Texas army, 1837-40, as deputy sheriff in San Antonio, 1840-42, and in the U.S. Army, 1846-49. Before becoming territorial librarian under Governor Wallace, he had served under several other governors as interpreter and secretary. He was also active in the New Mexico Historical Society (Espinosa 1938: 1-13). Dike (1958) listed him as the first postmaster at Peña Blanca, March 14, 1867.

464. In this entry, Bandelier was combining comments on the Quivira of the Great Plains with other notes on Gran Quivira, the pueblo and mission church east of the Manzano Mountains. Undoubtedly distinct in his mind, the comments so close together here should not mislead the reader. (See fn 12.)

465. This was Rev. James H. Defouri of the Church of our Lady of Guadalupe in Santa Fe. (Polk and Danser 1884a: 350.) Salpointe (1898: 282) listed him as one of the priests brought under Lamy. Lange and Riley (1966: 409) gave added biographical information. Defouri, born in La Palud, France, 1830; ordained in 1854; came to the U.S. in 1856, various missions among Plains tribes; Kansas, in 1862; Bishop Miege's Vicar-General, 1875-80; private secretary to Archbishop Lamy; rebuilt Guadalupe Church and built the parish house. Wrote several historical items: *Mes de María; Historical Sketch of the Catholic Church in New Mexico; History of the Apparition of the Holy Mother of Guadalupe; Historia de los Mormones.* Moved to Las Vegas where he died. Defouri's *Historical Sketch of the Catholic Church in New Mexico* published in 1887,

is of particular interest as a fairly accurate reflection of what the Catholic Church knew of its history and records as of the period corresponding to Bandelier's Southwestern years. Archbishop Lamy had charged Defouri with this work as the result of a request in 1884 from the *Congregation de Propaganda Fide* in Rome. (Defouri 1887: 159.)

466. When the AT & SF RR was extended into Santa Fe (1880), the junction of the main line and spur into Santa Fe was named Lamy, honoring Archbishop John B. Lamy. On September 29, 1857, he had taken the area referred to as the Lamy Grant, a tract of irregular shape, in trust for the Roman Catholic Church. (Pearce 1965: 84.) Twitchell (1925: 362) noted that when Bishop Lamy brought back the Sisters of Loretto in 1852, they had stopped at the "bishop's ranch" near the present railroad station of Lamy. This is not to be confused with the property known today as the Bishop's Lodge, in Tesuque Canyon, north of Santa Fe, which Archbishop Lamy used as a place for rest and seclusion.

467. In his entry of April 2, 1882 (Lange and Riley 1966: 247), Bandelier noted that Wallace was "now called" Armville. Apparently that name did not last; Pearce (1965: 177) failed even to mention it among the several designations of this community, including Thornton and Domingo. Polk and Danser (1884a: 370) noted Wallace as an important mining town, population of 1,000; deposits of gold, silver, copper, fire and potter's clay, and coal were in the vicinity. Wallace was at the end of a railroad division (AT & SF) southwest of Santa Fe. Some importance was still retained in the early 1900's, the town serving as a railroad connection with Santo Domingo Pueblo and especially with the Cochiti mining district. (Anderson 1907: II, 890.) Greene (1882: 28) listed it as having a weekly paper, the *Watchman*. Pearce (p. 177) stated it had a post office from 1882 to 1887.

468. This may have been the other one of "the two boys of Mrs. Tondre at Isleta [who] have learned the language well because they had to speak it with Indian children with whom they were raised, and who did not speak Spanish themselves." (Anderson 1947: 109.) See also fn 40.

469. Nathan Bibo, one of several brothers who were merchants in New Mexico (see fn 87), had come to Santa Fe in 1867, being met at the stage by Simon, another brother and early settler of western New Mexico, and Willie Spiegelberg, an old school friend from Germany. Immediately, Nathan was employed by Spiegelberg Bros., a wholesale dry goods company in Santa Fe. In 1868, he was employed by the firm of Zeckendorf in Old Albuquerque. When, in 1869, Spiegelberg was appointed Post Trader of the "new" Fort Wingate (see fn 99), Nathan Bibo was selected to manage the store. In 1871, Nathan became post trader at Camp Apache [Arizona] and bought the store. By letter and with maps, he persuaded Quartermaster General Meiggs in Washington that it would be more economical to supply Camp Apache from New Mexico and Missouri routes than from California. His recollections of getting supplies to Camp Apache are an exciting account of this period of territorial history. Later the same year, he sold out at Camp Apache and decided to settle in the Rio Grande, locating at Bernalillo in 1872. There he built a store and home on land purchased from the Honorable Francisco Perea, adjoining Perea's vineyard. Bibo also planted a vineyard and transplanted a number of trees from an old orchard. Both vineyard and orchard flourished and his home received many important personages of the day. He also built the government station, as well as the stable room for the mail contractor and owner of the stage line. In 1884, he established a business in San Francisco, but retained his interests in Bernalillo. In San Francisco, he married Flora Abrams and had a daughter and a son. His business there was wiped out by the fire following the 1906 earthquake. His marriage did not last, and he returned to New Mexico. Later he became a protagonist for the Indians. (Fierman 1961, 1962.)

A brother, Joseph, was apparently a partner in the Bernalillo store, as Polk and Danser (1884a: 310) cited Joseph and Nathan Bibo, General Stores, Bernalillo.

470. Except that Salpointe (1898: 283) listed J. G. Splinters as one of the priests added under Lamy, no further data have been found.

471. This was the person erroneously identified in the first volume (Lange and Riley 1966: 322) as Adolph Mermet. In the earlier editing, Bandelier's handwriting made the "rm" indistinguishable from "nn." Otero (1939: II, 3) noted Adolph Mennet among a group of responsible Las Vegas citizens who formed a vigilante group in 1881-82. No further information has been found, other than the fact that Mennet was one of several to whom Bandelier addressed brief notes on New Year's Eve, 1883.

472. This would appear to have been Charles Longuemare, listed by Polk and Danser (1884a: 364) as the editor and publisher of The Bullion. Ritch (1885: 216) referred to him as Professor Charles Longuemare, Commissioner of Socorro County. Official Reports (1884: 116-67) listed Charles Longuemare as Chaplain of the 1st Regiment, Infantry, of the New Mexico Volunteer Militia. (See also fn 428 for his business affiliation in 1880 with Charles Blanchard.)

473. Here Bandelier is obviously interested in describing the Rio Grande Valley and not the river which, of course, actually flows south and east.

474. William L. Rynerson had resigned his commission as colonel of the 1st Regiment, Infantry, New Mexico Volunteer Militia, sometime prior to the printing of the 1884 Official Reports (p. 125).

As a citizen of New Mexico, he was highly esteemed. Born February 22, 1828, in Kentucky, he entered Franklin College in Indiana, but, before graduating, left for gold in California. In 1861, he enlisted under General Carleton and proceeded to New Mexico. He was discharged in 1866, breveted major and lieutenant colonel for meritorious services. He engaged in mining in New Mexico. In 1871, he married Mrs. John Lemon. He was appointed Adjutant-General under Governor Pile. He was a delegate to the Republican Convention that nominated Garfield. In 1870, he had been admitted to the bar and since then had practiced his profession. (Haines 1891: 326, 329-330.) Greene (1882: 50) listed W. L. Rynerson as attorney and J. H. Rynerson as blacksmith at Las Cruces. Col. W. L. Rynerson and J. H. Rynerson owned the Modoc and the southern extension of the same lode, called the Lebanon. They also owned the north extension, Nestor Armijo sharing in the latter partnership. (Greene 1882: 51.)

475. Fort Craig saw the rise and fall of the Confederacy in New Mexico. Located on the west side of the Rio Grande, 35 miles south of Socorro, it was built in 1853 to protect the Lower Rio Grande Valley and to repel the Indian raids along the Jornada del Muerto. An earlier fort, Fort Conrad, had been built in 1851 at a different location; in 1854, the troops moved south to Fort Craig. (Pearce 1965: 58.) The historic marker at the entrance to Fort Craig says it was abandoned in 1885 and notes that it was the home base of the famous poet-scout, Capt. Jack Crawford. Sufficient ruined walls are still standing to indicate the original extent of this Fort.

476. Fort Cummings is near the entrance of Cooke's Canyon at Cooke's Spring, 6 miles NW of Florida. It was designed by Gen. George B. McClellan with a high wall of adobe entirely enclosing the barracks and headquarters. Built in 1863 near a stagecoach station of the Butterfield Overland Mail to protect mail carriers, emigrant trains, and freighters from the bands of Apaches. It was named for Maj. Joseph Cummings. The fort was permanently abandoned in 1891. (Pearce 1965: 58.)

477. Pearce pointed out that both the town of Cooke's and Cooke's Mountain, or Peak, were named for Capt. Philip St. George Cooke, in charge of the Mormon Batallion

[sic] when the first wagon train of the expedition passed that way in November, 1846. As Bandelier did in this entry, Pearce noted that most maps omit the final "e." Cooke's Peak was also known as Signal Peak because it was used in Indian days as a signal hill by Cooke. He also established a second signal station at Soldier's Farewell Hill. (Pearce 1965: 39, 156, 158.)

478. A number of Masons, lieutenants as of this time, were listed by Heitman (1903: I, 695); however, it seems most likely that this was Stanton Augustus Mason, second lieutenant in the Fourth Cavalry.

479. This was George Russell Cecil, a Virginian and West Point graduate. He became second lieutenant, 13th Infantry, June 17, 1874; he was promoted to first lieutenant, July 24, 1883, also with the 13th Infantry. (Heitman 1903: I, 291.)

480. This was probably Fred Wheeler, from Wisconsin, a West Point graduate, who became a second lieutenant with the 4th Cavalry in 1878. He was promoted Nov. 1, 1881, to first lieutenant. He retired as a major in 1901. (Heitman 1903: I, 1023.)

481. John Henry Hobart Peshine had served as a midshipman in the U.S. Navy and, later, in the infantry during the Civil War. Honorably discharged in 1865, he reentered the service in 1873 as a second lieutenant. He became a first lieutenant in May 1882; ultimately, he became a major, prior to his retirement in 1902. (Heitman 1903: I, 786.)

482. This comment was not too significant as of Bandelier's time, being essentially an impressionistic observation on his part. However, it is now possible, often, to determine sources of obsidian by spectrographic analysis, by neutron activation, or other techniques.

483. This was probably Richard Hudson, listed by Dike (1958) as the first postmaster of Mimbres Hot Springs Post Office, Grant County, established June 24, 1878. On January 28, 1879, the name was changed to Hudson Hot Springs, and Richard Hudson continued as postmaster. Pearce (1965: 56) added, "Faywood Hot Springs (Grant). 22 mi NW of Deming. Originally named HUDSON HOT SPRINGS for the owner, Col. Richard Hudson, who came to NM with the California column in 1862, later settling in Grant County. The springs were once famed for their curative qualities." Hudson was promoted from lieutenant colonel to colonel May 25, 1882, and succeeded Wm. L. Rynerson as commanding officer, 1st Regiment, Infantry, New Mexico Volunteer Militia. (Official Reports 1884: 125.)

484. This was Second Lieutenant George Washington Smith of the Ninth Cavalry; along with several others, Lieutenant Smith died in action against the Apaches near the McEwer's Ranch, August 19, 1881. Lieutenant Smith was a Virginian who entered the service from Kansas, and in the course of the Civil War had risen to the rank of brevet lieutenant colonel. He reentered the service as a second lieutenant with the 9th Cavalry, August 6, 1873. (Heitman 1903: I, 898; II, 37.)

485. This was probably Benno Rosenfeld, listed by Dike (1958) as the first postmaster of Georgetown Post Office, Grant County, established May 21, 1875. Rosenfeld was also listed as first postmaster of the Santa Rita Post Office, Grant County, established December 8, 1881. The two communities were about five miles apart.

486. This may well have been J. B. Risque, secretary and manager of the Albuquerque Foundry and Machine Company (Polk and Danser 1884a: 301). His relationship to the John P. Risque of Silver City (See fn 103 for 1884.) is unknown to the editors.

487. This was probably the same person listed by Polk and Danser (1884a: 319) as S. S. Brennan, operator of a saw mill at Georgetown. In the entry for January 2, 1884, Bandelier visited the S. S. Brannan ranch, traveling through "lofty timber" to reach his destination.

488. As indicated in his Final Report (Bandelier 1892: I, 11) and in his report to the

Archaeological Institute of America on his New Mexico work in 1883-84 (Bandelier 1884b: 98), Bandelier had been asked to investigate aboriginal mining, which explains his frequent reference to mines in the journals.

Much later, July 15, 1904, Bandelier (then at the American Museum of Natural History) wrote to W. H. Holmes, of the Bureau of American Ethnology, that "I have never published anything on copper or bronze for the simple reason that I never could get anybody to analyze them. I have suggested it repeatedly and already twenty years ago, but no attention was ever paid to my entreaties (for I actually begged). With our friend [Professor H. O.] Bumpus, it may be that I will succeed, and then render account of the composition of our bronze and copper instruments." (From Bandelier correspondence in Bureau of American Ethnology files, Washington, D. C.)

The prospecting and mining boom that was taking place in the Southwest at the time of Bandelier's investigations must have greatly facilitated his research. Not only were miners familiar with the location of mines, but many could tell him of the location of ruins as well.

Pearce (1965: 149) said that Santa Rita was settled in 1803 by Francisco Elguea, a Chihuahua businessman, and that originally it was named Santa Rita del Cobre. Sp., "copper." The mine was known in early Spanish times, and continued digging has made it one of the greatest open-pit excavations in the world. The post office was established in 1881, soon after the construction of the AT & SF RR in this area.

Lister and Lister (1966: 106) referred to a Spaniard, Francisco Pablo de Lagera (a variation of the name cited by Pearce above?) as having worked these mines. He was expelled following Mexican independence. Brief mention was also made of Robert McKnight of Missouri as one of the mine operators in the early nineteenth century. He, too, was forced to leave because of repeated Apache raids, one night losing eighty pack mules.

The editors visited these impressive mines, now operated by the Kennecott Copper Corporation, in the summer of 1968. In addition to the open pit mines at Santa Rita, there is a reduction plant at Hurley. Their brochure contained the following information concerning the history of the mine.

Actual history of the mine began about 1800 when Spanish soldiers from Mexico discovered native copper on the surface. Some of the earliest products went into Mexico by mule train for Spanish coins.

Much later there were periods of underground mining which depended on rich ore for success. Steam shovel operations began September 23, 1910. In the early years of open pit mining the copper grade ran about 2%. It has now declined to about 1% and only large scale production makes the operation profitable. It is the fourth largest open-pit copper mine in the country. Every working day about 90,000 tons of material are blasted out and removed from the mine, three-fourths of which is waste. About 22,500 tons of ore are hauled to Hurley, from which about 300 tons of refined copper are recovered. (Kennecott Copper Corporation n.d.)

489. This may have been Dr. Granville N. Wood, who had an office in Silver City for twenty years or more. A native of Massachusetts, and a graduate of Northwestern University in 1878, Wood lived in California, Iowa, and Kansas and served briefly in the Medical Department of the Indian Service in the Indian Territory before going to Silver City. (Anderson 1907: I, 441.)

490. This was probably Mrs. J. C. Winter, whose husband operated a general store at Georgetown. (See entry of January 1, 1884.)

491. Fort Bayard, Grant County, 10 miles east of Silver City began when a troop of cavalry, operating in southern New Mexico, camped at a spring among the foothills in this area in 1863. A regular garrison did not arrive until August 1866, and later that year

the post was established. It was named for Gen. G. D. Bayard, who first watched the process of digestion through a window in the stomach of an injured patient. It was active as a post until 1899. Since then it has been an Army hospital for tuberculars; later its facilities were used by the U.S. Public Health Service and the Veterans' Administration. Presently the New Mexico Department of Public Welfare cares for chronic-disease patients there. (Pearce 1965: 58.) In 1884, Fort Bayard had a population of 400, mostly soldiers. (Polk and Danser 1884a: 318.)

NOTES

1884

1. Polk and Danser (1884a: 319) listed J. C. Winter as the proprietor of a general store at Georgetown, New Mexico. Ritch (1882: 67) listed J. C. Winter as a notary public at Fort Bayard, his term expiring September 2, 1882.

2. Polk and Danser (1884a: 319) listed an Edward Moulton, Lumber, of Georgetown.

3. Mangas Coloradas, or Red Sleeves, a leader of the Mimbreño Apache of southern New Mexico. Originally friendly to the Americans, Mangas Coloradas and his people suffered attacks by miners and settlers in southwestern New Mexico. Eventually he joined Cochise in attempting to block the California volunteers who had reoccupied Arizona and parts of New Mexico after these areas had been abandoned early in the Civil War. Mangas Coloradas was taken prisoner by the California troops late in 1862 or early in 1863. He was killed by the soldiers under rather suspicious circumstances while "trying to escape." (Hodge 1907: 799, 863.)

4. Bandelier did not elaborate upon this fountain pen; its brand remains unknown. It is interesting to note, however, a World Book (1959: 6173) comment that Lewis Edson Waterman produced the first practical one in 1884, though attempts to design one had been made as early as the 1600's. Early in the 1881 journals, there are a number of entries of general relevance here. January 17, while Bandelier was in the Boston area, he noted his kind reception by Professor Ware (fn 148) who was "willing to give me any instruction I may desire as far as architectural & topographic drawings are concerned." January 18, "Prof. Ware gave me very fine directions for architectural drawings & paintings, showed me the use of India ink, & will make me out a list of practical, not compendious instruments, colors, etc., also with explanations." At home in Highland, Bandelier received word on February 4th that "the pen" had been sent by mail, and two days later, "Pen rec'd from Cambridge." In his entry of April 8, 1881, after some weeks in Mexico, Bandelier noted, "I can hardly write anymore with the stylographic pen, it is too capricious. Have bought a regular pen, slightly cheaper than at home."

In the November, 1914, issue of El Palacio, comments by A. D. F. Hamlin (1914:6), School of Architecture, Columbia University, were included as part of other tributes to Bandelier. A few excerpts follow: " . . . I would like . . . to say a word about the late Dr. [sic] Bandelier. I never saw him more than two or three times but he made a great impression upon me then. This was in the early days of the School of Architecture at Columbia University during his explorations and investigations in the Southwest, when he came to New York with his reports on his earlier investigations and sought the advice and counsel of Professor Ware with regard to the matter of drawings. I believe Dr. Bandelier had had no instruction whatever in draughtsmanship and felt greatly the need for some instruction in this line. Professor Ware in two or three interviews or lessons gave him suggestions and counsel which Dr. Bandelier was so quick and eager in adopting that, as Professor Ware put it, he learned more about drawing in two or three interviews than many students do in the three years of study. The meeting of those two keen intellects was a delight to witness and I, who was then on the threshold of my career as a teacher, was greatly impressed and delighted by this experience. . . ."

5. H. B. Ailman was listed as treasurer of Grant County, 1881-82, in the New Mexico Blue Book for 1882. (Ritch 1882: 66.) Meredith and Ailman were in the general mercantile and banking business in Silver City. (Notes made from display case of old photographs with identification in Silver City Historical Society Museum, summer, 1968.)

6. Pearce gave the date of gold discovery at Pinos Altos as 1860. The settlement was originally called Birchville for a Mr. Birch, one of three men who made the discovery. It was later changed to Pino Alto and, then, Pinos Altos. It is in Grant County 7 miles NE of Silver City on NM 25 in the Black Range. It has had a post office since 1867. (Pearce 1965: 122.)

There was a legend of an earlier Mexican settlement called Pinos Altos, from which gold was sent to Chihuahua in 1837, according to records in Mexico. That camp disappeared. In 1866 the name was changed from Birchville to the original Pinos Altos. (Watson 1968: 1.)

7. This is generally a valid statement, but Bandelier's inference of an evolutionary explanation is incorrect. The use of sandal or moccasin is based more on a cultural preference than any developmental aspect.

8. Colonel José Carrasco learned of these rich mines from an Apache Indian he had helped. Realizing the richness of his discovery, Colonel Carrasco with the aid of friends and influence got a part of the Santa Rita del Cobre grant from the Mexican government. (Woods 1968: 1.)

Bandelier (1890-92: II, 363n4) made these observations: "The elevation of Santa Rita copper mines is 6,161 feet. The discovery of this important copper deposit is due to the Mexican Lieutenant-Colonel Manuel Carrasco. About the date of discovery I am not certain; I heard it variously stated as 1801 and 1810. See Garcia-Conde, *Ensayo estadistico sobre el Estado de Chihuahua*, fol. 62."

9. Bandelier did not elaborate on his findings. One version of the Adams' Diggings story has been given by Jenkinson and Kernberger (1967: 36); in this account of the "Lost Adams Diggings," in the Apache country west of Socorro, New Mexico, there was supposed to have been some $60,000.00 in gold buried beneath a burned cabin. Pearce (1965:2) located Adams Diggings in Catron County, 15 miles northeast of Quemado; Adams and several others were reported to have discovered a fabulous gold mine in the malpais west of Grants. All were killed by Apaches except Adams, Davidson who was away from camp with Adams when the Apaches attacked, and a man named Brewer who was said to have escaped.

With his interest in primitive mining, Bandelier undoubtedly was alert to such tales. Efforts to identify Adams' Diggings continued to interest him, as was evidenced by a newspaper clipping from a *Santa Fe New Mexican*, probably of 1890 (Scrapbook, Library, Museum of New Mexico). "If reports are true, the famous 'John Adams diggings' have been discovered in the Navajo Reservation. According to other interpretations of the (still very problematic) story, the 'diggings' should be either in the Arizonian Sierra Blanca, or near the headwaters of the San Francisco river. Under the assumption that they have been found at last, the question arises: What next? Will it be the 'Cerro del Oro' somewhere in central Texas, or perhaps the 'Cerro del Almagre' in northeastern Arizona? The latter might prove the most profitable find of the two, since it is described as a mountain of cinnabar. Quicksilver is more valuable now, in the long run, than either silver or gold."

10. Greene (1882: 80) listed J. D. Waters as bookkeeper of the Mimbres Mining Company of Georgetown, N.M. Presumably, this was the person to whom Bandelier had reference here. However, a J. L. T. Waters was listed in Polk and Danser (1884a: 354) as the hotel proprietor at Santa Rita, N.M. On February 15, Bandelier wrote letters to Rosenfeld (of the Georgetown-Santa Rita area) and to "S. D. Waters." The editors feel that this was the same Mr. Waters as on this page entry and that the initial "S" was an error. Bandelier was in the habit of writing back to his former hosts after reaching his destination.

11. Bandelier had corresponded with a Frank Robinson in March 1882. (Lange and Riley 1966: 245.) Greene (1882: 80) identified him as the first assistant to the general manager of the Mimbres Mining Company of Georgetown, N.M., S. S. Robinson.

12. Corner fireplaces have commonly been attributed to Spanish influence; however, there have been sporadic occurrences of these features in definitely prehistoric sites in a number of Southwestern localities and cultural time periods.

13. This was possibly Elon G. Smith, the first postmaster when the Fort Seldon Post Office, Doña Ana County, was reestablished May 16, 1881. The spelling for the first post office, established November 9, 1886, was Fort Selden. (Dike 1958.) This latter form seems to have been the more commonly accepted.

14. Silver City, originally "San Vicente de la Ciénaga," when founded about 1870. A post office has been in continuous operation since 1871, the name soon changed by Anglos to Silver City because of the mine boom. In 1874, it became the seat of Grant County, and in 1876 the settlement was incorporated. Before the AT & SF RR was built in 1881, twelve- and fourteen-horse teams hauled ore and bullion into the city, and bricks of gold and silver were stacked on sidewalks outside shipping offices. (Pearce 1965: 156.)

15. Steins Pass near the New Mexico-Arizona border was one of three mountain gaps utilized by the old Butterfield Overland Mail route and early emigrant trails to southern California. Named for Captain Steins who lost his life defending Doubtful Canyon. (Pearce 1965: 160.) Numerous sources were also found using the form Stein's Pass.

16. Here Bandelier was actually well west of the Continental Divide. His "Divide" apparently referred to the watershed between the San Pedro and Santa Cruz drainages.

17. A mine near Tucson that was in operation at least by 1774. In 1879 and again in 1883 important copper deposits were discovered at the site. (Barnes 1960: 276.)

18. See fn 316 for 1883.

19. General Bonifacio Topete, in Bandelier's day commander of the Mexican forces in Sonora.

20. Report upon United States Geographical Surveys west of the one hundredth meridian, in charge of 1st Lieut. George M. Wheeler. Published under authority of . . . the Secretary of War in accordance with Acts of Congress of June 23, 1874, and February 15, 1875. In seven volumes and one supplement . . . Washington, Government Printing Office, 1875-1889.

The special report discussed by Bandelier was Volume IV (1878: 404 pp.) and is titled: Botany. Reports upon the botanical collections made in portions of Nevada, Utah, California, Colorado, New Mexico, and Arizona during the years 1871, 1872, 1873, 1874, and 1875. By J. T. Rothrock, surgeon and botanist to the expeditions of 1873, 1874, and 1875, and the following scientists: Sereno Watson, George Engelmann, Thos. C. Porter,

M. S. Bebb, William Boott, George Vasey, D. C. Eaton, Thomas P. James, and Edward Tuckerman.

21. Lieutenant Henry P. Kingsbury of the Sixth Cavalry. (Heitman 1903: I, 601.)

22. In discussion of ethnobotanical specimens collected in the Cochiti area, Lange (1959: 150-151) included *Rumex* spp. Dock; *canaigre*. Leaves of this plant are used as table greens when the plant is young; young stems are eaten as rhubarb; roots are used in tanning. As in this entry, Bandelier consistently referred to this plant as "caña agria." For reference to this plant for use as pottery paint at Cochiti, its distribution, and for tanning, see Lange and Riley (1966: 247, 253, and 271).

23. This was Lieutenant H. T. Reed, United States Army, who found the Dakota Calendar. See fn 28 for additional details.

24. See fn 96.

25. Fort Huachuca was first occupied in 1877 with a post office (called Camp Huachuca) founded in 1879. (Barnes 1935: 214.)

25a. This was Eugene Asa Carr, native of New York and graduate of West Point in 1846. During the Civil War, Carr rose to the rank of brigadier general (March 7, 1862). Mustered out of service, January 15, 1866, Carr returned to service as a lt. col. in the 4th Cavalry Regiment, January 7, 1873; he transferred to the 5th Cavalry, April 10, 1873. He became a colonel, commanding the 6th Cavalry, as of April 29, 1879. Carr again became a brigadier general, July 22, 1892, and retired February 15, 1893. On January 16, 1894, he was awarded the Medal of Honor for his actions at Pea Ridge, Arkansas, March 7, 1862. (Heitman 1903: I, 285.)

Thus, while Carr had held, and would again hold, the rank of brigadier general, he was a colonel at the time Bandelier visited Fort Lowell in 1884.

26. This was published as Part II of the Appendix to the Fifth Annual Report of the Archaeological Institute of America. See also fn 124.

27. This could possibly have been John Fisher. Goad (1939: 16n9) wrote that the back of the Bandelier country home was given over to servants' quarters. John Fisher, an old retainer of the Bandelier family, was left stranded when the family moved away and did odd jobs about Highland. Later he returned to Switzerland where he died.

28. In the Bandelier Scrapbook, in an unsigned article that appeared in *The Nation*, August 23, 1877, there is a review of "A Calendar of the Dakota Nation. By Bvt. Lieut.-Col. Garrick Mallery, U.S.A." Bulletin of the U.S. Geological and Geographical Survey, Washington. The fact that Lieutenant Reed had found the "Calendar" and shown it to Colonel Mallery is substantiated in this review. The reviewer pointed out that this was not a "national calendar but really dealt with events specially affecting that part of the Dakota nation located about Fort Sully and northward." The reviewer took issue with some of Mallery's interpretations, though he credited him with "notes that show considerable research and much acuteness." White (1940: II, 190n2) gave the following biographical sketch of Mallery, which explains why Mallery was consulted: "Garrick Mallery (1831-1894), American Army officer, ethnologist; graduated from Yale in 1850, admitted to the bar 1853, practiced law until he joined the Northern army in the Civil War. He made a study of the Dakota Indians; joined the staff of the BAE in 1879 (the year it was founded); was founder and President of the Anthropological Society and of the Cosmos Club of Washington, D.C.; was chairman of Anthropological Section, AAAS, in 1881; wrote 'Picture Writing of the American Indians,' 10th A.R. B.A.E., Washington, 1894."

Bandelier cited Lt. Col. G. Mallery as a "distinguished friend" in his Pecos Report.

29. See fn 335 for 1883.

30. If not the first and only instance since Bandelier began his Southwestern field-work in 1880, this is certainly one of the very few occasions when various circumstances combined to overwhelm him to the point that he briefly contemplated the possibility of quitting, if not completely, at least his affiliation with the Institute.

31. Fort Yuma (originally called Camp Calhoun) was established by the United States First Dragoons in 1849 at the site of Father Garcés' Purisima Concepción Mission near the juncture of the Colorado and Gila Rivers. The fort served as way station for settlers moving over the southern route to California. In post-Civil War times, the fort declined in importance, and was relinquished by the Army in 1885. (Brandes 1960: 81-86.)

32. Thomas Dunbar, originally from Maine, a rancher in the Tucson area. (Census 1880.)

33. This is a rather mysterious person, a Dr. G. King who lived in seclusion at Hot Springs, near Willcox, until his murder in 1884. (Quebbeman 1966: 352.)

34. The pages for this date's entry were missing when the present editors began their work. However, a typescript of the entry was fortunately available.

35. A famous Chiricahua chief, born in the mid-1820's, who kept Arizona in turmoil in the 1860's and early 1870's. In 1872, Cochise made a treaty with General Oliver O. Howard and remained peaceful for the remainder of his life. He died in 1874. (Thrapp 1967: 145-146, 169 et seq.)

36. Captain William N. Tisdall of the First Infantry. (Heitman 1903: I, 963.)

37. Adna Romanza Chaffee of the Sixth Cavalry. At this time Chaffee was a brevet major with the field rank of captain. (Heitman 1903: I, 292.)

38. Bandelier's impression was overly optimistic. The Indians were more aware of the ephemeral nature of the stream than he supposed and they did not see fit to establish permanent villages there. In fact, Bandelier seemed to have visited Huachuca during a fairly wet period. A serious water shortage hampered operations at the fort in later years.

39. Lieutenant Frank West of the 6th Cavalry. (Heitman 1903: I, 1020.) A New Yorker, and West Point graduate, West's service began in 1872; he became a first lieutenant in 1876; a captain in 1887, all with the 6th Cavalry. He won the Medal of Honor in 1892 for his action, ten years earlier, against the Apaches at Big Dry Wash, Arizona. At that time, he was first lieutenant, commanding Troop I, 6th Cavalry, and a detachment of Indian scouts.

40. Lieutenant William Woods Forsyth, of the 6th Cavalry, who was with Crook on the 1883 campaign into Mexico. (Thrapp 1967:301 et seq.)

41. Lieutenant John M. Stotsenburg of the Sixth Cavalry. Stotsenburg was a second lieutenant at the time Bandelier knew him. He remained in the army, and during the Spanish American war reached the rank of colonel. Stotsenburg was killed in action in the Philippines in 1899. (Heitman 1903: I, 930.)

42. Turquoise mosaic was a typical decorative practice in the Hohokam Culture of southern Arizona.

43. This report was published in Aztlan: The History, Resources and Attractions of New Mexico (Ritch 1885) under the title, "Ancient Pueblos in and about Santa Fe" (pp. 199-202).

44. A post established in 1866 on Babocomari Creek some ten to fifteen miles west of Tombstone. Units of the First Cavalry and the detachments of several infantry regiments were stationed there. The camp was given up in 1869. (Brandes 1960: 73-75.)

45. Captain Gilbert E. Overton of the Sixth Cavalry. (Heitman 1903: I, 763.)

46. Originally established as Camp Lincoln, in 1864, about a mile north of the junction

of the Verde River and Beaver Creek. In 1868 the post was renamed Camp Verde and, in 1871, was moved a short distance to a more healthy location. It was given up by the Army in 1890. (Brandes 1960: 70-73.)

47. General Ignacio Pesqueira (1820-1880), Governor of Sonora in the 1870's and an important figure in the Arizpe area for many years. (Villa 1948: 137-147.)

48. A series of related people of northern and eastern Sonora, speaking diverse dialects of Opatan, one of the Uto-Aztecan languages. The southern Opata, those of the Mocte-zuma and Middle Yaqui rivers formed a separate linguistic unit called Eudeve. The Opata proper lived on the Upper and Middle Sonora River, and Middle Bavispe River and the Upper Moctezuma River, while the more isolated and linguistically aberrant Jova were located on the Upper Bavispe River (Spicer 1962: 90-92). Spicer (pp. 91-97) considered the Opata a ranchería people and estimated their population (including the Eudeve) to have been about 15,000 at the completion of the Jesuit missionization (ca. 1680). On the other hand, Johnson (1950: 7), following Sauer (1935: 29), gave the aboriginal Opata population as 60,000 and considered that they lived in large towns (1950: 10).

49. The Seris were and are a hunting-gathering group living along the Central Sonoran coast between the Concepción and Matape rivers, especially in the area around Tiburón Island. The Seri, speaking languages of the Hokan Stock, related to Yuman, lived in small, scattered bands. There were never more than a few thousand Seri but, because of their isolated position and great maneuverability, the Seri were able to resist most Spaniard and Mexican efforts to missionize them. Today, the some two-hundred surviving Seri are slowly being brought into the mainstream of Mexican life.

Bandelier never visited Seri country. As far as is known, there was never a Seri occupation of the Cananéa area. (Spicer 1962: 105-117.)

50. For response to this letter, see entry for June 24, 1884, and first footnote for that entry (fn 97).

51. Bandelier seemed curiously unimpressed with Arizpe in spite of its long and interesting history. The site, known from Coronado's time, was originally an Opata town and was missionized by the Spaniards in 1648. For a time Arizpe was capital of Sonora, but removal of the capital to Ures in 1832 and subsequent decades of Apache raids had caused serious decline by the time of Bandelier's visit. Arizpe, today, is making a slow recovery, but is off the main commercial routes of modern Sonora.

Of interest in the historical context is an article, "Anza's Bones in Arizpe," in which Carranco (1969: 416-28) provided a brief description of Arizpe and summary of Spanish colonization efforts in the area, as well as on the Pacific Coast, including San Francisco, and also in New Mexico. He placed considerable emphasis on the activities of Juan Bautista de Anza, Governor of New Mexico from 1777 to 1787, who was buried in the cathedral of Nuestra Señora de Asuncíon, Arizpe. Identification of the specific coffin and the remains was made in 1963 by Professors Heizer, McCown, and Howell of the University of California, Berkeley (p. 417).

52. Father Juan Urías, who was still Cura at Arizpe in 1886. (Villa 1948: 146.)

53. In his *Final Report* (1890-92: I, 76), Bandelier mentioned Mr. Alphonse Pinart, "distinguished traveller"; from the comment in his entry of March 25, 1884, it would appear that Pinart was also interested in archival data and in a sense was a rather unwelcomed rival of Bandelier in his search for similar material.

54. In 1881 there was a mining superintendent at Tombstone named M. P. Buffum, and another superintendent, a W. M. Buffum, at Prescott. Conceivably, Bandelier's "Colonel" might have been M. P. Buffum since there were Americans from Tombstone involved in mining activities in the Arispe—Sinoquipe area. Heitman (1903: I, 260)

listed only one person of that name, a Colonel Martin P. Buffum who resigned his commission February 22, 1877, and who died April 20, 1884. Of course, the title might have been derived from territorial or state militia service, an honorary title , or conceivably from service in the Confederate Army, in which case Heitman would not have listed him.

55. An important Greco-Roman site located in present-day Lebanon.

56. This was E. E. Olcutt, associated with the Santa Helena Mines.

57. This could be either *Tecoma sp.* or *Solanum verbascifolium*, both herbs being widely used for medicinal purposes in the southwestern United States and in northern Mexico.

58. A group of Taracahitan speakers who lived on the lower Yaqui River in Sonora. The Yaqui and closely related Mayo of the Mayo River to the south were contacted quite early in the history of Spanish conquest; the Yaqui, in fact, fought a battle with Diego de Guzmán in 1533. For the next two centuries, the Mayo entered into and even sought friendly relations with Spanish missionaries while the Yaquis throughout their history resisted intrusion by first the Spaniard, then the Mexican. At present, most of the 10,000 Yaquis live on tribal lands on the northside of the Yaqui River though the Yaqui are slowly (and rather unwillingly) being assimilated into Mexican national life. (Spicer 1962: 46-85.)

Bandelier never visited Yaqui territory in his travels throughout the Greater Southwest.

59. While far off and in the field, Bandelier, on this date, was elected a corresponding member of the Anthropological Society of Washington (1885: 50-51). Among the twenty-one elected with Bandelier were the following: Mr. H. H. Bancroft, Mr. A. J. Conant, Dr. George J. Engelmann, Col. H. H. Hilder, and Prof. F. W. Putnam. Active members included: Mr. Frank H. Cushing, Col. Garrick Mallery, Prof. Otis T. Mason, Mr. W. J. McGee, Maj. J. W. Powell, and Mr. James Stevenson; corresponding members included: Dr. Daniel G. Brinton and Mr. Alphonse Pinart; honorary members included: Prof. Adolf Bastian, Sr. Joaquín García Icazbalceta, and Dr. Washington Matthews.

60. This person may have been Benjamin F. Bell of New York and Illinois. Bell was an enlisted man in the Seventeenth Illinois Cavalry in the latter part of the Civil War but was commissioned and made a brevet captain in the closing months of the war. He left military service in 1869. (Heitman 1903: I, 207.)

61. Joaquín Murrieta (1829?-1853), the celebrated California bandit. Murrieta was born in Mexico but moved to California where he worked in the gold fields from 1849-1851. After his family was brutalized by American miners, Murrieta became the leader of a robber band and terrorized the state for two years. In 1853, Murrieta and most of his followers were killed by an American sheriff's posse near Tulare Lake, California. (Columbia Encyclopedia 1963: 1441.)

62. This "church dance of the *Moros*" may have been a form of the Matachina ceremonies, widespread among Spanish and Indian communities of the Southwest as well as elsewhere in the Spanish-speaking world (e.g. Philippines). It is a religious dance in which Spanish and Moors engage in mock battle. Substitution of the Apache for the more ancient enemies, the Moors, is an interesting example of adaptation and "updating" of a religious ceremony. (Parsons 1939; and others.)

63. Here and elsewhere Bandelier discussed terraced hillsides, some of which may have belonged to the Trincheras Culture. Trincheras sites (dry masonry walls, forming, perhaps defensive, terraces along the sides of hills) are most common in north-central Sonora and are associated with Trincheras purple-on-red pottery. Some "Trincheras" described by Bandelier, however, are probably regular agricultural terraces, especially in northeastern Sonora, and do not belong to the Trincheras Culture. (Johnson 1966: 32-33; Sauer and Brand 1931: 68-69 et seq.)

64. This was Emilio Kosterlitzky, later a colonel in the Rurales; with his battalion, he waged a relentless war against the Apaches in his portion of northern Mexico. He was something of a mysterious and colorful figure: born in Moscow in 1853, son of a Russian father and German mother; in 1872, deserted a Russian warship in Venezuela; came eventually to the United States; allegedly served in the 8th Cavalry attaining the rank of sergeant; deserted again, fleeing to Mexico where he quickly became an officer in the Rurales. Kosterlitzky exploited the freedom allowed in the Rurales, clothing himself and his men in distinctive uniforms. He was a harsh disciplinarian, but succeeded in forming the "finest body of mounted men in Mexico." Under President Diaz, he ruled virtually singlehandedly; when Diaz was overthrown, Kosterlitzky fled to the United States as a refugee. Ultimately, he performed "invaluable service," from 1917 to 1926, for the Department of Justice. He died in Los Angeles in 1928. (Thrapp 1964: 348-49; portrait photograph facing p. 80.)

65. Perhaps a relative of General Luis E. Torres, governor of Sonora at this time.

66. Presumably the eighteenth-century Mexican historian, Juan Suárez de Peralta.

67. We have not been successful in finding data on this individual. Bandelier was not at all informative in his journal entries, and further complicated the situation, we strongly suspect, by noting this individual's name in several forms. It is quite probable that Dr. Holm, here, was the same person that Bandelier noted as "Dr. Hone (Hohen)," a week later, and as "Dr. Howe," two days after that, and three days later as Dr. Hone again. (See entries of April 10, 12, and 15, 1884.)

68. This would seem to have been a type of trinchera, or dispersion dikes, for flood-water farming.

69. The great Mexican revolutionary leader, Father Miguel Hidalgo y Costilla, who was executed by the Spanish authorities in Chihuahua on July 30, 1811.

70. Actually, the Hovas are not Tarahumaras, but an Opata sub-group.

71. The Jesuits had been, by the late decades of the sixteenth century, awarded considerable sections of northwestern New Spain for their mission activities. In the seventeenth century, they gradually pushed the line of missions up the west coast and highlands of Mexico, effectively missionizing the Lower Pima and Opata by about 1680. In the following years, Kino and his fellow priests contacted the Upper Pima and laid the foundation for Jesuit missions in present-day Arizona.

The entire missionizing program in northwest Mexico, as elsewhere in the New World, was wrecked when the Spanish Crown suddenly expelled Jesuits from Spain and all her colonies in 1767. The Sonoran and Arizona missions were taken over by Franciscans a short time later, and, under the leadership of men like Father Francisco Garcés, a viable mission program was maintained in the area, and, in fact, extended westward to California. (Spicer 1962: 22, 86-104, 132, 195, et seq.)

72. In the spring of 1883, General Crook, after discussing the matter with Mexican officials in Sonora and Chihuahua, led a small force of 193 Apache scouts and one company of the Sixth Cavalry into the Sierra Madre. Their target was a group of Chiricahua Apache who with elements of other bands had fled from the San Carlos Agency under Geronimo, Nané, Juh (Ju), and others. On May 5, 1883, Crook's forces reached Bavispe and Bacerac and, on May 6, Huachinera. The group then swung eastward in the direction of Cumbre and, finally, in the period May 18-29 persuaded Geronimo, Nané, Chihuahua, and others to surrender. By May 29, only Juh and his band were missing (see fn 434 for 1883), and Crook's men escorted a total of 374 men, women, and children back to Arizona. (See map, pages 474-75.)

73. See fn 67.

74. See fn 67.

75. This is of course a possibility. If the ideas of Johnson (1950) concerning the essential urbanism of the Opata are correct it might suggest a tie with the prehistoric urban culture of Casas Grandes. For recent comment see Di Peso (1966: 23-24).

76. This part of the Yaqui River is today normally known as the Bavispe.

77. Colonel Lorenzo García, of the Sixth Mexican Infantry. Thrapp (1964: 238-242) termed him "one of the most famous and successful of Mexican army Indian fighters." Popular on both sides of the border, he kept the hostile Indians confined in the mountains, taking aggressive action only when the Indians entered the lowlands. He attacked the Apaches who were retreating before Forsyth's column in the spring of 1882. While a number of the leaders escaped, considerable damage was inflicted. García protested Forsyth's entry into Mexican territory. On November 9, 1882, the North American residents of Hermosillo, Mexico, presented García with a handsome sword in commemoration and appreciation; he, however, passed it on to his battalion.

78. See beginning of entry for April 9, 1884.

79. There are several versions of this name. Present-day maps, such as those of the U.S. Coast and Geodetic Survey and the National Geographic Society, show it as La Ascención. More commonly in the literature, however (Bandelier 1890-92; Lister and Lister 1966; and others), the form Ascensión appears, with or without the article, La. In his journals, Bandelier used both Ascención and Ascensión, but apparently favored the latter.

80. This is one of the few entries in which Bandelier made any attempt to correlate distances. Even here, the ratio varies betwen one to 2.5 and 2.7.

81. This refers to the attack made by Colonel Joaquín Terrazas y Quezada on a group of Apache led by Juh. The Apaches were attempting a peaceful settlement with the Mexicans and were unarmed. A number of Indians were killed on the spot (at their camp on the Rio Casas Grandes), but Juh, with the main body, escaped. (Lister and Lister 1966: 165-166.)

82. For data on Dr. Engelmann, see footnote for entry of October 16, 1883. Engelmann's death had actually occurred February 4, 1884, in St. Louis; the lapse in time, until May 5, 1884, when Bandelier first learned of this, illustrates his prolonged travels in remote areas.

83. These riots broke out on March 28, 1884, following the refusal of a jury to bring in a murder conviction against one William Berner who had killed his employer with a hammer. The trouble started with a mass meeting to demand better juries and an end to political corruption. A lynch mob was quickly formed and, finding that Berner had been spirited out of Cincinnati, the mob began to raid pawnshops and hardware stores for firearms. Late in the evening, the group attacked and partly burned the courthouse, and it was midnight before the situation was brought under control by militia. In the fighting at least 56 people were killed and some three hundred injured. (Harlow 1950: 272-274.)

84. This was Colonel William W. Griffin of the First National Bank of Santa Fe; Griffin was also active in other phases of Santa Fe life, serving as vice-president of the Santa Fe Academy, and being otherwise mentioned in the newspapers of that time. (Santa Fe Daily New Mexican, files, 1883-84.)

85. Colonel Joaquín Terrazas was a military commander and cousin of Governor Luis Terrazas. (Lister and Lister 1966: 161-63.)

86. Serious excavation at Casas Grandes did not begin until 1957-58 when Dr. Charles C. Di Peso of the Amerind Foundation, Dragoon, Arizona, began extensive

work at this site. For a summary of the recent work at Casas Grandes, see Di Peso 1966: 3-25.

87. A Franciscan mission was established in the Casas Grandes area about 1665. A village gradually grew up along the Casas Grandes River developing by the nineteenth century into the town of Casas Grandes and Nuevo Casas Grandes, the latter a railhead. An influx of Mormons into the Rio Casas Grandes Valley in the late nineteenth century considerably changed the ethnic make up of the area and, today, Casas Grandes is partly Mormon. (Lister and Lister 1966:48 et seq.)

88. This was Sydney Shaw-Eady of Sydney Shaw-Eady & Co., surveyors and civil engineers of Casas Grandes, Chihuahua, Mexico. Their agents in El Paso were Crawford & Co. Identification was on the basis of a letter from Thomas F. Wilson to "Friend Adolph" dated June 16, 1884, on the letterhead of the Sydney Shaw-Eady & Co. The spelling was Cases Grandes on this form. Wilson was expressing sympathy on the "accident in your family." This probably referred to the death of Charles Lambelet. (See June 3, 1884, entry.) He also conveyed the greetings of Don Silvestre Quevedo (see May 4, 1884, entry), Capt. Cándano (see May 18, 1884, entry), and Mr. Julia. (Also referred to as Mr. Zulia in the same letter, this was probably Don Urbano Zubia. See May 23, 1884, entry.) The original letter was found folded and inserted at the back of the original Bandelier 1884 journals. We have been unable to find any specific reference to the receipt of this letter by Bandelier. Mr. Shaw-Eady, as well as the other men mentioned here, had all assisted Bandelier during his stay in Casas Grandes.

89. The second comment of this nature within the period of two days reveals Bandelier's mingled amusement and disgust regarding his companions' poor marksmanship. We recall the involvement of Bandelier and his father with the local and national competitions of the various Schützenvereins while living in Highland in the 1860's and 1870's. He was acquainted with recognized marksmen; his own skill, however, was apparently less than outstanding. His talent seemingly lay in the management and arrangement of these contests, not in the actual competition. Goad (1938: 78; 1939: 19-20) noted that in a national Schützenfest held in Highland, June 3, 1865, Bandelier won the 123rd prize, a wooden saw buck.

90. The Weekly Telephone, April 20, 1884, reported that Charles H. Lambelet died last Saturday at the age of 39 years, 7 mos, and 18 days from injuries in a shredder. He was born September 18, 1844, and was survived by a wife and three children. The Weekly Telephone, April 30, 1884, reported that Mr. and Mrs. H. S. Kaune of Breese were in Highland attending the Lambelet funeral. (See also fn 360 for 1883.)

91. The precise nature of the threat remains obscure. It may have been a personal threat in the "bad" Ascensión community; it may have been real or imagined illness. The opening statement of the following day's entry is not particularly enlightening but suggests the latter.

92. For greater detail regarding this flood, see Ellis and Baca (1957: 22-24); there the notes of Father J. B. Ralliere of Tomé are given in translation.

93. Listed in Polk and Danser (1884a: 709) as S. P. Carpenter, owner of a general store at Fort Cummings.

94. Henry Holgate was listed in McKenney (1882-83: 941) as in Holgate & Raithel, a meat market. Polk and Danser (1884a: 315) listed Holgate as active in livestock at Deming.

95. The foundations for San Xavier del Bac were laid by Father Kino in the year 1700, and it became one of the Jesuit missions in the Upper Pima country. After the

expulsion of the Jesuits in 1767, the mission was taken over by Franciscan Father Francisco Garcés in 1768. San Xavier, today, is a flourishing Franciscan center.

96. William Sanders Oury, a well-known Tucson attorney and one of the early settlers of Tucson. Oury was leader of the infamous Camp Grant massacre of 1870 in which a group of Americans, Mexicans, and Papago Indians slaughtered some one hundred Apache women and eight men, and kidnapped 25 to 30 children. The Apache had been gathered at Camp Grant as part of the U.S. Army pacification program. Attempts to punish the perpetrators of this action came to nothing in spite of pressures from President Grant himself because a local (Tucson) jury refused to convict members of the party (Paré 1965: 121-123). See also Smith (1967: 186-203, especially, p. 198) who points out that the numbers of slain Apache have never been properly determined though the round figure of 100 probably is not far from the truth. According to Smith, 27 children were captured and sold into slavery in Mexico. Only a handful were ever recovered.

97. This letter, dated March 12, 1884, and written from Fort Huachuca, Arizona, was found at the back of the 1884 journals:

Dear Professor:—

I received yours of the 19th ult. [Bandelier actually wrote to West on February 29th; February 18th, he had dined at West's and on the 19th he left Fort Huachuca for Sonora] from Bacuachi yesterday, and was very glad to hear from you. I will answer your letter though I don't think you will ever get this.

The news is that Geronimo and Chatto are all in, the former came in with 150 head of beef cattle which he offered to sell at 5 dollars a head—

I do not think there is an Apache left in Mexico (alive). So that you have nothing more to fear from that score—

I saw some very interesting pictures of ruins recently in the daily Grapphic [?], made by Stevens in the San Francisco Mountains. They are underground, and the entrance had a circular wall or breastwork around it about 2 feet high—

Breastwork around entrance

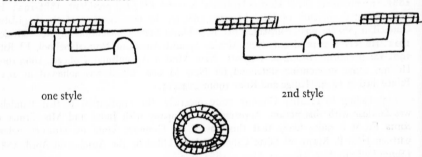

one style   2nd style

Groundplan of wall
around entrance

Everything is quiet in the U.S.—

No news of any great importance. I hope you will come back this way from Janos instead of going to Fort Cummings.

Mrs. West and everyone sends best regards to you. Nothing has been heard from Illinois so your people must be all right.

Yours sincerely,
F. West

98. See fn 96.

99. It seems most probable that this was the same person, George Alexander Forsyth, whom Bandelier mentioned meeting at Rincon, New Mexico, in 1883. Forsyth, or Forsythe, had a brevet rank of brigadier general. (See also fn 440 for 1883.)

100. Father Ignaz Pfefferkorn, S. J., was sent to the New World in 1755-56. He was assigned the Papago mission of Atí in the Altar region, arriving at the station late in the year 1756. Pfefferkorn remained there for seven years, then shifted to the mission of Cucurpe to the east, between Altar and Arizpe where he stayed till the expulsion of the Jesuits in 1767. (Treutlein 1949: 1-20.)

Pfefferkorn seems, also, to have spent a time in a third mission that is nowhere specifically indentified in his own writings. Treutlein (p. 20 fn.) suggested that this mission was San Ignacio, but perhaps it was, indeed, San Xavier.

101. One of the groups of northern Piman-speaking peoples of the seventeenth and eighteenth centuries—others include the "Pima Proper," the Soba, and the Papago. The Sobaipuri lived along the San Pedro River and the middle courses of the Santa Cruz and Gila rivers. They are now essentially extinct as a tribal group but live on as one of the ancestral elements in modern Pima and Papago Indians. (Castetter and Bell 1942: 4-11.)

102. L(ebaron). Bradford Prince was born in Flushing, Long Island, New York, 1840, the same year Bandelier was born. Prince founded the Flushing Literary Society in 1858; he was a member of the Queens County Commission, 1861; he received his B.A. from Columbia University in 1866. He was a delegate to state conventions, 1866-78; delegate to national convention nominating U. S. Grant for President, 1868. He was active in New York state politics, a member of the legislature in 1870, 1871, 1873-75; state senator, 1876-77; delegate to national convention nominating Rutherford B. Hayes. Prince refused appointment as governor of Idaho Territory, 1878; he was appointed chief justice of New Mexico, 1879, and resigned in 1882. Prince married Mary Katherine Beardsley in 1881. He was president, University of New Mexico, Santa Fe, 1881; vice-president, New Mexico Historical Society, 1882-83; president, 1883-1923. He was appointed governor of New Mexico, 1889-93; he was member of the Legislative Council, 1909; he was chairman, First Republican State Convention in New Mexico, 1911. He served as president, New Mexico Spanish-American Normal School, El Rito, 1902-12; president, Board of Regents, New Mexico Agricultural College, 1899-1904. He was active in securing statehood for New Mexico, which was achieved in 1912. Prince died in 1923. (Lange and Riley 1966: 414-415.)

103. Failing to identify Conway more precisely, the implication is that Bandelier was familiar with this person. Apparently in company with Judge and Mrs. Prince of Santa Fe, it is quite likely that this was T. F. Conway, Santa Fe attorney, whose partner, John P. Risque of Silver City, had been killed by the Apaches in April, 1882. (Santa Fe Daily New Mexican, May 2, 1882, p. 3.)

104. W. F. White was general passenger and ticket agent for the AT & SF Railroad at Topeka, Kansas. (McKenney 1882-83: xii.)

105. See fn 56 for 1883.

106. White (1935: 20-21) quoted Bourke, as of 1881, and Poore, as of 1890, citing periodic flooding of the western, lower, portion of Santo Domingo Pueblo. Kubler (1940: 107-108), citing Bandelier, noted several serious floods of this pueblo which forced moving the village. An especially destructive inundation in 1886 destroyed the church on the western periphery; the present structure, on the eastern periphery, was built sometime before 1890 by Father Noel Dumarest.

107. For Ellison's own account of the Santa Fe Archives, see Espinosa (1938: 1-13). This was a manuscript entitled "History of New Mexico by Samuel Ellison, Santa Fe, 1884." The original manuscript is in the Bancroft Library, Berkeley, California.

108. This was probably the map Bandelier used in his *Final Report*. In the Preface to Part I, he wrote, "Map of Sonora and Chihuahua is due to Mr. H. Hartmann, C. E. of Santa Fe." This map showed Crook's Trail of 1883 and Bandelier's route. According to the Sixth Annual Report of the Archaeological Institute of America, 1884-85, p. 40n1, "A map of N. E. Sonora and N. W. Chihuahua has been published by the U.S. War Department, compiled from information derived from these last explorations of

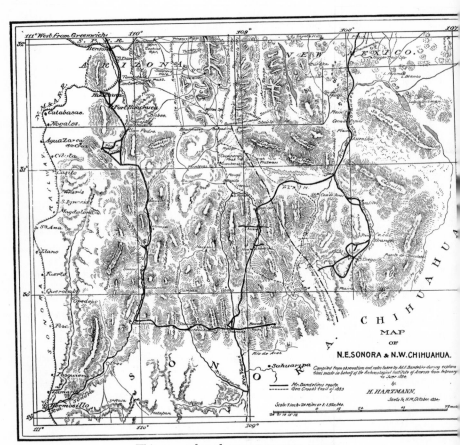

This map, enlarged, appears on pages 474-75.

Mr. Bandelier." Burrus (1967a: 83, 83n86), however, commented that "Bandelier seems to have had little interest and competence in historical cartography." In his review of the first volume (Lange and Riley 1966), Burrus (1967b: 121) made a similar observation, "Although Bandelier frequently mentions in his journals the compilation of maps, and also entered abundant data on printed or hectographed maps, he seems to have neglected historical cartography, which could have helped him solve many a problem. This is one of the most evident weaknesses in his many-faceted and broad scholarship."

109. The *Santa Fe Daily New Mexican* of March 7, 1883, listed the following as directors of the new Santa Fe Water and Improvement Company: Messrs. Robert E. Carr and O. W. Meysenburg of St. Louis, T. B. Catron, W. W. Griffin, and H. L. Warren. "The organization was formed for the purpose of storing water in the mountains and for selling and distributing the same in this county for irrigation, manufacturing, and mining purposes." Polk and Danser (1884a: 354) gave Robert E. Carr as president and O. W. Meysenberg [sic] as secretary and manager of the Water and Improvement Co. Mr. Meysenburg was a son-in-law of Robert E. Carr. (See fn 431 for 1883.)

110. Espinosa (1937: 13), quoting Ellison in his account of Ellison's life in New Mexico, especially as Territorial Librarian, noted a manuscript which may well have been this one: "There is an incomplete journal of Diego de Vargas, gov. & capt. gen. from 1692 to 1697. (He was superceded by Rodriguez & returned to Santa Fé in 1703 as Marques de la Nava de Brasinas.)"

111. Major William Francis Tucker was paymaster at Fort Marcy in Santa Fe in 1884. Heitman (1903: I, 973) noted that Tucker, a native of Massachusetts, entered the service from Illinois; he was promoted to major, February 27, 1882, and made paymaster. He was promoted to lieutenant colonel and made deputy paymaster general, February 19, 1903.

112. These comments apparently had reference to General Crook's pursuit of the Apaches into Mexico in the spring of 1883. (See entry and footnote for April 7 and 8, 1884.) International agreements prevented free pursuit of the Apaches across the boundary between the United States and Mexico, and the Apaches cleverly exploited this fact. However, there were agreements which permitted specific pursuits subsequent to particular damages to life or property. Thrapp (1964: 268-69) explained the U.S. Army's frustrations until a raid by Chato in the vicinity of Tombstone, March 21, 1883, provided Crook with his incident. Crook made a hurried trip to Mexico for advance clearance and returned to begin his pursuit. Seemingly, the incident, technically proper, was not unanimously approved or endorsed by the public and certain government officials.

113. See Lange and Riley (1966: 74-83). Aside from Bandelier's own research (1881b), serious work at Pecos did not begin until A. V. Kidder did his intensive excavations there in the 1920's and 1930's. For major publications resulting from the work of this expedition, see the following sources: Kidder 1924; 1931-36; and 1958; also, Hooton 1930 and Parsons 1925.

114. Bandelier recorded the migration of the surviving Pecos to Jemez in 1840. (See Lange and Riley 1966: 77, 78, 84.) Parsons (1925: 4-5) commented on Bandelier's data.

115. Las Vegas College had been founded by the Jesuits in 1877. (Vollmer 1952: 299.) For a more detailed account, see Callon (1962: 78-88).

116. Juan Bautisto Fayet was the first pastor of the Anton Chico parish of Santa Fe. He was appointed by Lamy to this parish in 1857. He was at San Miguel parish in 1889. (Chávez 1957: 124, 153.) Bandelier had made his acquaintance there in 1882. (Lange and Riley 1966: 351.)

117. A decade earlier, in August, 1874, the Very Reverend Father Baldassare, S. J., replaced Father Personnet as Superior at Albuquerque. In later life, Father Baldassare was stricken with paralysis and returned to Italy to recover his health. (Defouri 1887: 127-28.)

118. Charles Blanchard, familiarly known as Carlos, came to Las Vegas in 1864 from his home in St. Mark, Quebec, Canada. He was 22 years old at the time and

shortly thereafter tried business in Lincoln County. He returned to Las Vegas in 1868 and became a wagon master between Fort Union, New Mexico, and Fort Harker, Kansas. Polk and Danser (1884a: 326) listed him as owner of a general store in Las Vegas.

On one of his many trips to St. Louis, being a devout Catholic and a church trustee, he arranged for the purchase of an organ from George Kilgen, organ manufacturer of St. Louis. On October 22, 1885, there was advertised "The largest and most Powerful Organ west of St. Louis. Buy a ticket to the Concert and encourage Music and Education." (Callon 1962: 34, 48.) (See also fn 428 for 1883.)

119. McKenney (1882-83: 318) listed Dr. J. M. Cunningham as a Las Vegas physician. Callon (1962) mentioned Dr. Cunningham as an early resident of Las Vegas, prior to the arrival of the railroad in 1879 (p. 26) and subsequently cited various Republican party activities of Dr. Cunningham in the early 1900's (p. 217, passim).

120. Parish (1960: 12) referred to Kihlberg as "a much traveled German Jew." Elsewhere (p. 138), Parish stated that "The beautifying of the Old Town Plaza of Las Vegas came as a result of the driving force of Frank Kihlberg, with the strong support of the almost solid square of Jewish merchants facing the oval." McKenney (1882-83: 319) listed Frank O. Kihlberg as a real estate agent in Las Vegas.

121. Captain B. Ruppe went to Albuquerque in 1879 and worked as a clerk in F. H. Kent's drug store in Old Albuquerque. Ruppe embarked on his own in 1883 and moved to New Albuquerque in 1892. Later, he served as a member of the State Board of Pharmacy, under Governors Thornton and Otero; in 1899, he became president of that board. In the early 1900's, he and others were successful in establishing a School of Pharmacy at the University of New Mexico. (Anderson 1907: I, 465.) The connection, if any, between this man and Carlos Ruppe in Albuquerque (entry of February 1, 1883) remains obscure.

122. Bandelier's arrival was announced in the following Wednesday's newspaper July 23, 1884—Weekly Telephone: "We are happy to chronicle the safe arrival at home of our renowned townsman, Prof. Adolph Bandelier, last Sunday morning, after an absence of about ten months. He was expected home some time ago, but in the first place was delayed by floods in the regions he explored, and then upon his return to Santa Fe and other places his many friends would not let him pass without having retained and feted him for at least a week. The Professor looks very healthy and appears in decidedly good spirits, despite the many hardships and perils he experienced on this last research, which from all we can learn is considered by him a very successful one. We are confident that if there are any secrets about the ancient history of the Indians that can be disclosed, he will do the job, since everybody here knows that whenever he undertook to do anything, he always did it thoroughly, and this work being the object and pride of his life, he certainly will go on with all necessary endurance, perseverance and courage, and not rest until he has reached his mark. We do not know anything about Mr. B's future intentions in regard to his work, but feels [sic] safe in saying upon our responsibility that if in his opinion there are any more results to unearth, he will surely leave us again after some time."

In the Weekly Telephone of July 9, 1884, there had appeared this notice: "Adolph Bandelier is expected home this week. His many friends will be glad to see him again after an absence of nearly ten months." In the same issue of this local Highland paper was a story from the Morning Journal, Albuquerque, New Mexico, July 1, 1884: "A. F. Bandelier, who knows more about the Indian and his ways than any other man in America, called at The Journal office in company with his brother-in-law, E. B. Huegy, last evening. The readers of The Journal will remember how many times the report came last year that Mr. Bandelier had been murdered by the Apaches, but these stories seem to have but little effect on that gentleman, who still persists in continuing his studies, under all sorts of difficulties. He has but just returned from a four months trip among the Sierra Madre mountains and, if he would, could give us a whole column of interesting matter. Mr. Bandelier goes north to Santa Fe to-morrow."

123. While one may realize, in retrospect, the full implication of this and other remarks by Bandelier in his journal entries, these comments rather consistently and completely disguise the fact that Bandelier, at this time, was technically concluding the field research that he was committed to do for the Archaeological Institute of America.

In his *Final Report*, Bandelier (1890-92: I, 3-4) observed that, "Since the year 1884, when explorations were discontinued, I have, as often as it was feasible, made short tours of investigation into regions hitherto unknown to me. Although such excursions were wholly independent of my connection with the Institute, that connection terminating officially in January, 1885, I shall include here also whatever observations I may have been able to secure. . . . I have given to the Institute an account of all my trips, with the exception of the last one, which occupied the period from November, 1883, to July, 1884."

124. This report was on the annual meeting of the Institute held in Boston, May 17, 1884. Over half (pp. 32-52) of the Executive Committee's report was devoted to the activities of Bandelier from November 1882 up to March 9, 1884, closing with a note that Bandelier's report of his tour in Mexico, in 1881, "is now nearly ready for publication." (P. 52.) In addition, an appendix presented two reports by Bandelier. The first (pp. 55-87) was written to President Norton from Highland, Illinois, and dated August 11, 1883; the second (pp. 88-98), was written to President Norton from Fort Lowell, Arizona, and dated February 2, 1884. They were titled, "Reports by A. F. Bandelier on his Investigations in New Mexico during the Years 1883-84." (See pages 472-73, a reproduction of Bandelier's map.)

125. These reports were: "On the Distribution and Tenure of Lands, and the Customs with Respect to Inheritance, among the Ancient Mexicans," and "On the Social Organization and Mode of Government of the Ancient Mexicans," which appeared in the Eleventh and Twelfth Reports of Peabody Museum, respectively.

126. The complete citation is: Bandelier, Adolph F., A Visit to the Aboriginal Ruins in the Valley of the Rio Pecos. Papers of the Archaeological Institute of America, American Series, Vol. I, No. 2, 1881, Boston, pp. 34-133. In 1883, a second edition of this report was published in response to a demand from Santa Fe for the celebration that summer of the supposed 333rd anniversary of the city's founding. For the many strangers expected, it was regarded as the best possible guide for studying the history and understanding the character of the most noted ruins in the vicinity. (AIA 1885: 34-35.) For an account of this celebration, see Ellis (1958). His lead sentence was, "The greatest show ever staged in New Mexico ran for six weeks in Santa Fe, in 1883." This celebration, running from July 2 through August 15, was only briefly mentioned by Bandelier since he was in Santa Fe only from July 6 to 10, en route from Arizona and southern New Mexico to Highland, Illinois. (See fn 321 for 1883.)

127. This individual's exact identity has not been ascertained. (See fn 35 for 1883.)

128. F. was here, apparently, an abbreviation for Father. Eggen (1933: 44) wrote of him as "Rev. Joseph Meckel." He was a Catholic priest in Highland and made many improvements inside and outside the church, as well as founding and building the original St. Joseph's Hospital. After a successful pastorate at Highland, he was sent in 1896 to St. Mary's at Alton, Illinois, where he died.

129. Louis Appel ran a saloon in Highland (Polk and Danser 1884b: 1002).

130. The Reverend Stephen Denison Peet (born 1830), of Unionville, Ohio, established the *American Antiquarian*, "the first attempt to publish a periodical purely in the interest of American Archaeology and Ethnology." (Mason 1879: 383.) White (1940: II, 128n1) noted Peet as a Congregational clergyman and antiquarian. Peet was Secretary of the American Anthropological Association, 1879; editor of *American Antiquarian* and *Oriental Journal* from 1879 to 1888. He published on ancient architecture, picture writing, and on effigy mounds in Wisconsin. Bandelier, December 2, 1879, spoke of Peet as an "anti-ethnologist." There was "great danger of his [Peet's] remaining, as long as he lives, nothing else than an archaeological showman, exhibiting his labelled specimens to the admiring gaze of a very unethnological audience." (P. 139.)

131. Cushing's paper on "Zuñi Fetiches" appeared in the Second Annual Report of the Bureau of [American] Ethnology, 1883, pp. 3-45. Bandelier probably saw a published "separate," his term "pamphlet" hardly applicable to the entire volume of 477 pages. It has recently been republished as a separate by Bahti (1966).

132. See fn 397 for 1883.

133. Bandelier was probably bringing greetings from Mr. O. W. Meysenburg, whom he had seen in July in Santa Fe. See combined entries for July 9-12.

134. The March 6, 1883, *Santa Fe Daily New Mexican* reported that "General Robert Carr, the owner of Santa Fe's water works, who has been so-journing among us for several days, leaves for his home in St. Louis today accompanied by his son-in-law, Mr. Meysenburg. . . . General Carr is president of the St. Louis Mercantile Library Association. Mr. Meysenburg returns to Santa Fe in one month when the water works will be generally overhauled." (See also fn 109.) Whether Bandelier's call was social or related to business was not disclosed.

135. The relationships between Miss Matilda Meysenburg, Mrs. Clementine Meysenburg, and Mr. O. W. Meysenburg were not clarified in the journals. Bandelier had recently seen Mr. Meysenburg in Santa Fe and was probably conveying personal greetings in these calls. It is possible that this family was related to G. and Emil A. Meysenburg of the German-American Bank of St. Louis (Kargau n.d.: 163) and that Bandelier had known Mr. Meysenburg prior to their Santa Fe meeting.

136. Cumulatively, the entries for the period beginning August 11, 1884, and continuing through the remainder of the month while Bandelier was in Highland reveal the growing awareness of the family and others that the condition of the F. Ryhiner & Co. bank was rapidly deteriorating. Bandelier avoided explicit notations in his journals, but his commentaries and notations of people with whom he consulted in this period make it very clear that he was now stepping in to try to help save the business of his father and the other partners, F. C. Ryhiner, Jr., and Maurice Huegy, both his longtime friends.

137. John J. Patrick was a dentist in Belleville, Illinois (Polk and Danser 1884b: 212).

138. George C. Bunsen was a justice and insurance agent in Belleville, Illinois (Polk and Danser 1884b: 206).

139. It seems quite likely that this man was of the same family as Henry Villard. Henry Villard was born Ferdinand Heinrich Gustav Hilgard in Bavaria, April 10, 1835. After a series of political disagreements with his father, an influential and conservative jurist, young Hilgard came to the United States in 1853 and settled for a time with relatives in Belleville, Illinois. Villard eventually became a newspaper man, and at the outbreak of the Civil War, a correspondent with the Union Army. After the war, Villard turned to finance and became a leading railroad promoter. In 1881, he obtained control of the *New York Evening Post* but continued mainly as a railroad

financier. He died November 12, 1900. Goad (1939: 38n10) added that Villard was also president of the Edison General Electric Company. He backed the collecting expedition to Peru from 1892 to late 1893 or 1894, when the American Museum of Natural History took over sponsorship of Bandelier's work in Peru.

140. Frederick Ropiquet was a sheriff and collector in Belleville, Illinois (Polk and Danser 1884b: 212).

141. Gustave Philip Koerner (1809-1896). A political figure and writer in nineteenth-century Illinois. Born Philipp Gustave Körner in Frankfurt-am-Main, Koerner became involved as a young man in the revolutionary movements in Germany. Forced to flee because of his revolutionary ideas, Koerner arrived in St. Louis in 1833. Finding Missouri a slave state, he moved to St. Clair County, Illinois, where he practiced law and became involved in Democratic Party politics. From 1852 to 1856, Koerner served as lieutenant governor of Illinois, but in 1856, because of strong personal antislavery feelings, he switched to the Republican Party. In 1862, President Lincoln appointed Koerner minister to Spain. In later years, Koerner withdrew from politics and devoted his time to writing. In 1880, his well-known historical study, Das Deutsche Element in den Vereinigten Staaten von Nordamerika, appeared. Other writings included Aus Spanien (1867) and an autobiography that was completed shortly before his death. (Dictionary of American Biography 1961a: 496-97.)

142. Ferdinand P. Busson was a grocer in East St. Louis, Illinois (Polk and Danser 1884b: 861).

143. Mr. Hebler was in Bern, Switzerland; he was apparently a trusted friend to whom Bandelier was turning as he approached the conferences and negotiations with the officials of Gruner-Haller and Company of Bern. (See entries beginning with that of November 26, 1884, when Bandelier arrived in Bern, and on through December 3 of that year.) Whether Hebler was involved personally, in addition to his acquaintance with Bandelier, is not clear.

144. Rudolph Graffenried was probably the individual noted in fn 383 for 1883, along with Wachsmuth. Both names appeared sporadically in the journal entries; they seem to have been very good friends.

145. Bandelier was here referring to problems of the F. Ryhiner & Co. bank founded by his father, F. C. Ryhiner, and Moritz Huegy, Bandelier's father-in-law. See Spencer (1937: 190-91) for biographical sketches of these three partners. The name of the firm has been given in various forms in different sources; Burrus (1967a: 72) reproduced the letter of August 26, 1884, to Collet from Bandelier, with a letterhead "F. Ryhiner & Co., Bankers, Highland, Ills."

146. Bandelier's departure from Highland was not announced in the paper for more than a week (September 10, 1884—Weekly Telephone): "Mr. A. F. Bandelier has gone east for a stay of several weeks, on matters connected with his archaeological research."

147. Steck (1943: 83) included an item, Datus geográficos y estadicos del estado Chihuahua, 1907, by J. M. Ponce de León. Wagner (1937, 1967: 339) included Dr. Nicolás León, citing his Boletín I, Instituto Bibliográfico Mexicano. Whether Bandelier called on one of these men, or upon an entirely different person in New York, is difficult to determine.

148. This was William Robert Ware (1832-1915), professor of architecture, Massachusetts Institute of Technology, and a member of the executive committee of the Archaeological Institute of America. (White 1940: II, 224, 224n1.) The Sixth Annual Report of the Institute, for 1884-85, listed William R. Ware as an annual member and secretary of the New York Society of the Institute. (See also fn 4.)

149. This was the brother of Ephriam George Squier, well known among early archaeologists interested in the New World. Frank was apparently a dealer in rare books and manuscripts. White (1940: I, 258) noted that Bandelier had purchased the "Monograph of Authors on Central-American Languages" from Frank Squier.

150. This was Wendell Phillips Garrison (1840-1907), literary editor of *The Nation* (1865-1906). He was the third son of William Lloyd Garrison, editor of the *Liberator*. White (1940: I, 62n18) commented that "*The Nation* was a friend and champion of Bandelier for many years. . . . [in an account of his fieldwork in New Mexico, 1880,] Bandelier is called 'one of the most accomplished and sanest of American archaeologists.' [The Archaeological Institute of America] 'was fortunate in obtaining the services of a scholar so well versed in American antiquities, in the story of the Spanish conquest of Mexico, and in the whole body of early literature respecting the Indians and their relations to their conquerors, that he is not liable, like so many of the investigators of American antiquities, to fall into error through ignorance of what is already known. More than this, Mr. Bandelier, although an enthusiast, is a man of science, and understands the difference between a theory and a fact.' "

151. "The novel" was *Die Köshare*. (See fn 367 for 1883.)

152. Dr. Phillip Johann Joseph Valentini was born in Berlin, Prussia, in 1825, of Italian parents. He died in New York in 1899. His studies of the documentary history of the pre-Columbian cultures of Middle America and Mexico brought him into an acquaintance with Bandelier in the late 1870's. (White 1940: II, 103n15.) Otis T. Mason (1879: 384), in his discussion of anthropology in 1878, included these remarks, "On Mexican archaeology, the pamphlet of Professor Valentini, entitled 'Vortrag über den Mexikanischen Calendarstein,' translated by Mr. Stephen Salisbury, in the *Proceedings* of the American Antiquarian Society, No. 71, is a work of rare merit, and may be reckoned among the permanent productions of the year."

Several years earlier, Valentini (1882: 73-74) included the following remarks concerning the work of Bandelier in a lengthy footnote (p. 73n1). The comments merit inclusion here: "This conception of ancient Mexican society will not astonish those who read Mr. Ad. F. Bandelier's recent publications on the subject, and take care to examine the premises by which this gentleman was brought to so surprising a conclusion. He has expounded his theory in three successive articles, which were published . . . [see Bandelier 1877a; 1878a; 1879a]. The author comes to the acceptable results that Ancient Mexico was neither an Empire, nor a feudal Monarchy, nor ruled by a despotical power. . . . These are some of the main results aimed at by Mr. Bandelier in the research he made on ancient Mexican Society. It will readily be noticed that they stand in direct opposition to all which his predecessors had been teaching on the subject. We congratulate him sincerely upon his bold achievement. Not so much, however, because we think to have found in Mr. Bandelier a welcome confederate in our warfare against the extraordinary theories indulged in by the late Brasseur de Bourbourg, to whom he is an equal in enthusiasm, in vast reading and in constructive power, but because he has known how to master his emotional and intellectual agencies, and, in battling the most complex and contradictory historical material, has succeeded in arranging it in an array of lucid premises, which of themselves lead to a series of common-sense conclusions. The foot-notes he has given are indeed of an extension which appears uncommon. They occupy a space five times larger than the text. Yet as their contents are not reasonings, but abstracts taken from the ancient Spanish authors, whose works are not at every student's disposal, and as the author wishes to settle, once and forever, a point important in Mexican history, we think this copiousness of quotations is not only excusable but necessary. It shows the author's circumspection, and the honest interest he has to make his reader judge for himself, the particular reasons why he should be induced to abandon a long-cherished doctrine and adopt the new one, which the author recommends. It will be impossible for this writer to agree with Mr. Bandelier upon each and every point. But this does not hinder him from endorsing the healthful tendency that pervades the whole work, nor from admiring the author's industry and steadfast earnestness displayed in so laborious a research."

153. This may have been Dr. Samuel H. Scudder who was entomologist, custodian, Boston Society of Natural History, 1864-70; assistant librarian, Harvard, 1879-82; palaeontologist for the United States Geological Survey, 1886-92; and editor of *Science*, 1883-85. (American Men of Science 1906: 284.) Dr. Scudder was listed among the life members of the Archaeological Institute of America in the Fifth Annual Report of the Institute, p. 11. It is also possible, however, that this was Horace E. Scudder (1838-1902) who later became editor of the *Atlantic Monthly*, serving from 1890 to 1898. At this time, Scudder was doing editorial work with Henry O. Houghton at the Riverside Press in Cambridge. (Jacobs 1960: II, 241.) It is difficult to favor one possibility over the other.

154. This was Bandelier's "Report of an Archaeological Tour into Mexico in the Year 1881," Papers of the Archaeological Institute of America, American Series, Vol. II, Boston. The reader is reminded of Bandelier's frustrations over the delays in publishing this report; see entries for August 3, 1883, and February 7, 1884.

155. Theodore Lyman was a member of the Board of Trustees of the Peabody Museum of American Archaeology and Ethnology. In 1881 he was elected treasurer of the Board. (Peabody Museum 1887a: 4, 6.) Born in Massachusetts, he was educated at Harvard, studying under Louis Agassiz. He became a zoologist and, in 1884, was president of the American Fish Cultural Association. He was a member of the House of Representatives from Massachusetts, 48th Congress, 1883-1885. He died in 1897. (Who Was Who 1963: 519.)

156. Frederic Ward Putnam was born in Salem, Massachusetts, April 16, 1839. From earlier interests in ornithology and ichthyology in his studies at Harvard, Putnam changed to archaeology, becoming curator of the Peabody Museum of Archaeology in 1875. In 1886, Putnam was given the Peabody Professorship and then became chief of the department of ethnology, World Columbian Exposition, 1891-1894. Afterwards, he was curator of anthropology at the American Museum of Natural History, 1894-1903; finally, he became the University of California's first professor of anthropology and director of the Anthropological Museum.

Putnam achieved prominence and recognition in a variety of scientific organizations including the American Anthropological Association and the American Association for the Advancement of Science; he served the latter, not only as president, but also as permanent secretary for twenty-five years.

Putnam died at Cambridge, Massachusetts, on August 14, 1915. (Kroeber 1915: 712-18.)

157. For data regarding the Zuñian Order of the Bow, see fn 147 for 1883.

158. This was Alexander Agassiz (1835-1910), who came to the United States from Switzerland in 1849. He studied at Harvard under his father (Jean) Louis Agassiz (1807-73), becoming an authority on fishes. His greatest work was in mining, especially the Calumet and Hecla mines in Michigan. Alexander gave a million dollars to Harvard to continue work in zoology which his father had begun. He was listed as a life member of the Archaeological Institute of America. (AIA 1909: 24.)

159. This was George H. Moore (1823-1892), librarian, historian, bibliographer; in 1879, he became librarian of the Lenox Library, New York City. (Jacobs 1960: I, 121.) In the Bandelier Scrapbook, there is a letter from *The Nation*, November 20, 1879, written by Bandelier, dated November 6, 1879, and addressed to Mr. George H. Moore, Superintendent of the Lenox Library.

160. Henry G. Marquand, philanthropist, father of Princeton archaeologist, Allan Marquand. (Dictionary of American Biography 1961b: 292-93.)

161. Professor Allan Marquand (1853-1924), archaeologist and art historian at Princeton. (Dictionary of American Biography 1961b: 291-92.)

162. The Lenox Library was based on the collections of James Lenox (1800-80); this became a part of the New York Public Library. (Jacobs 1960: I, 119.) On February 14, 1878, Bandelier wrote Morgan that "Perhaps the richest Library in the U.S. is that of Mr. John Lennox [sic] of New York." (White 1940: II, 92.) White added (p. 92n2), "James Lenox (1800-1880), American collector and philanthropist. He specialized in collecting bibles; it was he who brought the first Gutenberg bible to the United States. He founded the Lenox Library in N.Y., which was incorporated in 1870. It was eventually opened to the public." In the Bandelier Scrapbook, there was a clipping, seemingly from the year 1877, of a letter signed "A. D." and addressed to the editor of *The Nation*. It said that Lenox had purchased and still owned "that invaluable lot of Americana which formed the stock of the late Mr. Ternaux-Compan's collection."

163. [Our translation]

Highland, Illinois
November 6, 1884

My Dear Sir and Friend:

Before leaving for Europe where I hope to stay for two or three months, I would like to excuse the silence I have maintained. The last letter I sent you was dispatched from Huasavas on the Rio Yaqui, Sonora. I succeeded in crossing not only the Sierra Madre but also part of the Sierra de Yeras, mountains more rugged and impressive than the main cordillera. Traveling to Chihuahua, I had to rest at Casas Grandes whose ruins I studied for a month. From Casas Grandes I penetrated for the third time the Sierra Madre, going on foot to the heart of these solitary places. Putting my life in danger, I left Mexican territory and, detained at the railroad junction by flooding of the waters of the Rio Grande, I did not arrive home till the 23rd of July, very tired but happy to see my wife again after an absence of nine months.

The results of the last voyage are the most important that I have yet made, and at the same time they conclude my fieldwork. Scarcely had I returned home when I saw an obligation to leave for Boston; now I must cross the ocean to finish, in Spain and Rome, my studies on the Spanish possessions in North America. Consequently, allow me to send you the following address:

Mr. A. F. B. aux soins de [in care of] Mr. le Cmdt, C. Haller.

Berne, Suisse.

I hope to be returning here before the first of February from New York. I shall be able to send you a copy of the book that I wrote on Mexico (Cholula, Mitla, etc. etc.) and that the Institute finally published. In it there is included a facsimile of Rojas' map as well as some photographs and a multitude of sketches.

The time I lost in Boston is to blame for my not having written before. I had to write up the last work that will come out on New Mexico, Arizona, Sonora, and Chihuahua. Because of its extraordinary length, its publication will necessarily be delayed. An atlas of 300 pages of illustrations will accompany the three volumes of text. The cost of reproduction in several colors is more than 25 thousand pesos and is one of the reasons that I go to Europe where this work is done better and more cheaply. I won't fail to write you from there. On the 13th I embark on a course for Cherbourg.

As the hours that remain here are few, I hope that you will pardon my brevity. Many regards to all your family and to friends in Mexico, and for you all the love of your affectionate friend and servant.

Ad. F. Bandelier

164. Bandelier's departure was a news item in the *Weekly Telephone* of November 12, 1884: "After a short stay of only about one week Prof. Bandelier has again left us. He had been absent about two months in the East, attending to the publication of his new book on Mexico, and lecturing at Boston, New York, and other eastern cities. Since the illustrations for his grand work cannot be furnithed [furnished] as desired in this country, he now leaves for Europe to make arrangements there with the most prominent artists, the text of his books, however, will be printed in America. He will be about seven or eight weeks, and after his return here will resume the writing of his book, which will require several years." (See entry of December 1, 1884.) Dissatisfaction with American prices and quality of work had been expressed by Bandelier in his letter of November 6, 1884, to García Icazbalceta.

165. At the back of the original 1884 journals, a handbill of the Steamship "Lessing" was found. It contained a cabin passenger list (twenty-four in all, including two children and a servant) for the November 13, 1884, sailing from New York to Hamburg via Plymouth and Cherbourg. B. Voss was the ship's commander.

166. Dr. R. T. Hahn was the physician aboard the S. S. Lessing.

167. This may well have been Professor Rudolf Ludwig Karl Virchow (1821-1902), German scientist, teacher, and political leader, contributor to archaeology and anthropology but even more importantly to the study of diseases. He is considered by many to have been the father of modern pathology, advancing the theory of cellular pathology, establishing that every cell originates from a previously existing cell and that in pathological, as well as in normal, physiological circumstances, the results come from the interaction of originally normal cells with their circumstances. Virchow brought this approach to bear on ideas advanced by Darwin; he believed Neanderthal Man was a pathological case. (See Penniman 1952: 109-111.)

168. Several entries in the journals for the period from November 26, 1884, to January 27, 1885, when he was in Bern, make it clear that Adolph F. Bandelier met and talked with Professor Studer. During that interval, Bandelier mentioned being with Alphonse [the cousin] and also with Adolphe [perhaps another, younger, cousin; possibly a brother or a son of Alphonse]. Hobbs (1942; 118n25) stated that Alphonse had visited in Highland once when Elizabeth B. Kaune (Lizzie) was a child.

169. For an evaluation of this map, see Bloom (1936a: 210). Bloom's concluding remarks were, "The locating of tribal names and place-names in New Mexico is pretty badly mixed up. It is significant of the lack of correct information in Paris in 1657 about this part of the world."

170. For possible identification of Adolphe, see fn 168.

GLOSSARY

acequia—irrigation canal
adobe—sun-dried brick for house, wall, or other construction
afanes—workers
agua dulce—literally, sweet water
aguardiente—a distilled beverage, perhaps mezcal or sotol
agua sedativa—a herbal headache medicine, varying in composition
aguja—needle or spine
alameda—public walk (also a grove of poplar trees)
álamo—poplar tree, cottonwood tree
alguacil—constable (see also topil)
almagre—ochre
almirez—mortar
amarillo—yellow
ancón—in Bandelier, a recess or canyon in a hill
angostura—narrow pass
apachita (apacheta)—ceremonial stone heap made by travelers
aparijo—travel gear
arroyo—stream bed with deep cut sides, common in semi-desert and desert countries
atajo—short cut; in Bandelier, lead animal of a pack train. This is possibly a misspelling of hatajo (herd or group of animals).
atole (atolle)—corn mush
azul—blue
babosa—silly or dirty; at one point, Bandelier seems to have meant an Indian group
baile—dance
barrial—muddy place
barro—mud; in Bandelier, also a place name
bellotas (vellotas)—acorns, or juniper berries

blanco—white

bolas—balls; in Bandelier also large boulders

bordo—bank (of a stream)

"*buena gente*"—literally, "good people"; in Bandelier, "friends," a form of greeting

caballito—a native dance

cabra—goat

cacica—cacique's wife or female assistant

cactli—sandals (from Nahuatl)

caja—literally, box; in Bandelier, drum

cajeta—jelly or a container of jelly

cajón—a large box or in America a narrow (box) canyon. Bandelier used the term in the latter sense and also for large boxlike chunks of adobe used in house construction

calle—street

canoa—canoe or boat

cañada—canyon or glen

cañón—canyon

cañutilla—wreath made of rushes

capellán—chaplain

capitán de la guerra—war captain

carretero—wagon road

carrizal—land filled with reed-grass

caxete (cajete)—bowl

cedro—cedar

ceja—ridge or summit

cerro—hill or highland

ciénaga—a marshland or swamp

ciénega—alternative spelling of *ciénaga*; Bandelier preferred the form *ciénega*

cofradía—association of persons, especially confraternity, brotherhood, or sisterhood

colorado—red or colored

compañero—companion

conducto—normally, channel through which business is conducted; Bandelier used the word to mean a pack train

coralillo—normally, coral snake; Bandelier, however, used the term to mean some sort of tree or bush

corcho—corkwood

cordón—ridge

corona—crown; Bandelier also used this word to mean ceremonial head-
    dress in native dances
corral—corral or yard
cosa acabada—something old
cuate—double or twin
cuerno—horn
cuesta—ridge
cúmaro—perhaps a variant of comino (cumin)
cumbre—summit or top
cura—priest
chamizo—literally, burned wood; in Bandelier, one of the various shrubs
    of the eastern New Mexico area
chaparro—scrub oak or scrub vegetation
chiquito—small or tiny as a small child
choyo—cholla cactus
chungo—bun hair style, worn, among Southwestern Indians, by both
    men and women
datil—date; fruit of the date palm or fan palm
desagüe—drainage ditch
enagua (see also nagua)—petticoat; originally a piece of cloth wrapped
    around a woman's waist and legs and worn under the huipil; usually
    plural, i.e., enaguas, "petticoats"
encino—oak
encino colorado—red oak
equipota—pack train
estaca—stake; in Bandelier, probably a loom fixed in the ground
estancia—a farm or cattle ranch, also a hill or room
estanque—reservoir
estufa—stove, also used to refer to the underground ceremonial rooms
    or kivas of the Pueblo Indians
fariseo—literally, pharisee; clown in a Spanish-Indian ceremony
fiesta—a celebration often on a saint's day or other religious holiday
flecha (baile de la)—arrow dance
gavilán—sparrow hawk
genízaro—mixed blood
gente—people; in Bandelier, occasionally "clan"
governador—governor
grama—couch grass
guacamayo—macaw
guaje—gourd rattle

guaraches (huaraches)—sandals
guerra—war
hacienda—large ranch
hava (haba)—mange
higuera—fig tree
hondo—deep
horcón—forked branch, also roof, or roof support
huero—blonde person
huipil—a sleeveless blouse worn by Mesoamerican women
Indios bárbaros—unacculturated Indians
jacal—adobe house or hut, brush and pole structure
jarra—jar or pitcher
jefe político—chief officer
jícara (sometimes xícara)—basket or container, cup
kiho—a Piman word for a special kind of carrying basket
labores—works; in Bandelier, cultivated fields
lagarto—lizard
lagune (laguna)—lake or marsh
lechuza—barn owl
legua—league; this is of varying lengths, a common one being some 3
    miles; Bandelier seems to have used a 5-mile league
libella—dragon fly
loma—hill
los antiguos—the ancient ones
llano—a plain or flat basin
macana—war club
macho—stallion
madroño—strawberry tree (madrone, *Arbutus unedo*)
maíz—corn
malacate—in America a spindle or spindle-whorl
malpaís—bad lands, usually lava extrusions
mano—hand stone for grinding corn
manta—a blanket or overgarment
manzanilla—camomile, one of several plants of the aster family, the
    dried leaves sometimes used medicinally
máquina—literally engine; sawmill
matalote—saddle horse, often meaning an old or worn-out animal
médano(s)—dune(s)
médico—medical doctor
medio—half or middle; in Bandelier a small coin

melote(s)—literally molasses or honey; men's hair style
merced—land grant
mesita—small mesa
metate—grinding stone for making maize meal
mezcal—mescal agave, or an alcoholic drink distilled from this plant
mezcla—lime mortar
milpa—corn field
mimbral—osier, willow or willow grove
mogote—flat-topped cliff or hill
mole—chocolate-based sauce
mula—a she-mule; Bandelier also uses the term to mean macaw
muy colorado—very decorated
mygah—gila monster
nagua—see *enagua*
negro—black
Nuestra Señora—The Virgin
ocoteas (ocotillo)—coachwhip plant
ojo—spring
ojos colorados—"Red Eyes"; Indian ceremonial group at Isleta Pueblo
ojos negros—"Black Eyes"; Indian ceremonial group at Isleta Pueblo
olla—pottery vessel used to carry or store water
olote—corncob
padre—Catholic priest
palo blanco—hackberry tree; probably *Celtis sp.*
palo de fierro—tesota tree; *Olneya sp.*
palo verdo—paloverde tree; *Cercidium sp.*
panoche (panocha)—unrefined sugar
paraje—place, or residence
peñascosa—rocky
petate—woven sleeping mat
picacho(s)—sharp-pointed hill(s)
picota—in Bandelier, post or pillar
pinabete—spruce tree
pinito (baile del)—Little Pine Dance
pinole—a drink made of parched corn and water
piñón—piñón tree
pita—agave fiber
plaza—open area in town center
portal—porch or entryway
potrero—pasture-land; in New Mexico, a tongue of high ground

pregonero—town crier

presa—dam

presidio—fort or army post

pueblito—small village or town

pueblo—village, also a group of village Indians in the Southwest

puertecita—small gate

¿quien sabe?—who knows?

quince—15; also another name for the gambling game, patol, or patolli

ramos (baile de los)—Bough Dance, possibly Evergreen Dance

ranchería—hamlet

rancho—ranch or ranchhouse

real—Spanish colonial coin of varying values and sizes, a common variety containing one ounce of silver

rebosa—shawl or stole

rechizero—medicine man

represas de agua—water catchment areas; Bandelier uses the phrase to mean agricultural terraces which retain ground water

rillito—small stream; in Bandelier the name of such a stream in the Tucson area

rio—river

rito—rite or ceremony

rosa de castilla—Spanish Rose; in Bandelier an unidentified rose

sabino—juniper

sahuaro—saguaro cactus

sangrantado—in Bandelier, some kind of wood

sepultura—grave

serape—sarape, a narrow blanket worn by men over the shoulders

sierra—mountain range

sopa—soup

sotol—the sotol cactus or a drink distilled from it

tablas—headboards used in ceremonial dances among Southwestern pueblos

tambor—drum; in Bandelier also, war drum

tapesto—(perhaps tapesco) a kind of roof or shelter supported by poles

tasajo—jerked beef; in Bandelier seems to be used for some sort of plant

tecolote—owl; from Nahuatl tecolotl

teguas—boots

tepalcate—potsherd

tequío—in Mexican usage, a tax

tienda—store or tent

tilma—cloak

tinaja—an earthenware jar; also a natural basin

tío—uncle

ti-suin (or tiswin)—maize beer

tomado—drunk

tombé—drum

topil—sometimes used interchangeably with *alguacil*; a low-grade political office, the kind normally held by young men in Spanish-Indian communities

tortilla—flat corn or wheat cake

tortuga (baile de la)—Turtle Dance

tulas—reeds

túndita—in Bandelier, a tower-like rock

tusa—prairie dog

uño de gato—cat's claw plant

vadito—ford of a small stream

vellotas—see *bellotas*, acorns or juniper berries

venado (baile de)—Deer Dance

verde—green

viga—rafter

visita—inspection by civil or church government official

xícara (jícara)—basket or container, cup

zacate—grass or hay

zahuarro—saguaro cactus

BIBLIOGRAPHY

Adair, John
    1945. The Navajo and Pueblo Silversmiths. (University of Oklahoma Press, Norman, 220 pp.)

Adams, Eleanor B., and Fray Angélico Chávez
    1956. The Missions of New Mexico, 1776: A Description by Fray Francisco Atanasio Domínguez, with other Contemporary Documents. (University of New Mexico Press, Albuquerque, 387 pp.)

American Men of Science
    1906. A Biographical Directory. (The Science Press, New York, J. M. Cattell, ed., 364 pp.)

Anderson, Arthur J. O.
    1947. Santa Fe on Bandelier's First Visit. (El Palacio, Vol. 54, no. 5, pp. 107-10.)

Anderson, George B.
    1907. History of New Mexico, Its Resources and People. Two volumes. (Pacific States Publishing Company, Los Angeles, pp. i-xxvii, 1-522, and pp. 523-1047.)

Anthropological Society of Washington
    1885. Officers and Council of the Anthropological Society of Washington and the Transactions of the Anthropological Society. (202 pp.)

Archaeological Institute of America
    1880. First Annual Report of the Executive Committee, 1879-80. (Archaeological Institute of America, Cambridge, pp. 1-26.)
    1881. Second Annual Report of the Executive Committee, 1880-81. (Archaeological Institute of America, Cambridge, pp. 5-25.)
    1883. Fourth Annual Report of the Executive Committee, 1882-83. (Archaeological Institute of America, Cambridge, pp. 19-22.)
    1884. Fifth Annual Report of the Executive Committee, 1883-85. (Archaeological Institute of America, Cambridge, pp. 5-98.)
    1885. Sixth Annual Report of the Executive Committee, 1884-85. (Archaeological Institute of America, Cambridge, pp. 27-40.)

1888. Eighth Annual Report, 1886-87. (Archaeological Institute of America, Cambridge, pp. 1-48.)

1909. Membership of the Institute. (Bulletin of the Archaeological Institute of America, Vol. I, No. 1, The Norwood Press, New York, pp. 5-123.)

Bahti, Tom
    See Frank Hamilton Cushing, 1883.

Bandelier, Adolph F.

1874-78. Highland, Illinois, Article in Johnson's New Universal Cyclopedia.

1877a. On the Art and Mode of Warfare of the Ancient Mexicans. (Tenth Annual Report, Peabody Museum of American Archaeology and Ethnology, Cambridge, pp. 95-161.)

1877b. Review (unsigned) of E. G. Squier's Peru: Incidents of Travel and Exploration in the Land of the Incas, in The Nation, vol. 25, June 21, pp. 367-69, and June 28, pp. 383-84.

1878a. On the Distribution and Tenure of Lands, and the Customs with Respect to Inheritance, among the Ancient Mexicans. (Eleventh Annual Report, Peabody Museum of American Archaeology and Ethnology, Cambridge, pp. 385-448.)

1878b. Comment on Ph. Valentini and his The Mexican Calendar Stone, in The Nation, Vol. 27, p. 84.

1878c. Same, The Nation, Vol. 27, pp. 176-77.

1878d. Comment on Dr. Gustav Brühl: Die Culturvölkes Alt-Amerikas in the Cincinnati Volksfreund, Feb. 11, 1878.

1879a. On the Sources of Aboriginal History of Spanish America. (Proceedings, American Association for the Advancement of Science. St. Louis Meeting, 1878, Salem, Massachusetts, pp. 315-37.)

1879b. Review (unsigned) of E. B. Tylor's Researches into the Early History of Mankind (1878 edition), The Nation, Vol. 28, p. 170.

1879c. Sources of Spanish American History, signed "A. D.," in The Nation, Vol 28, p. 265.

1879d. Review (unsigned) of Ad. Bastian's Die Culturländer des Alten Amerika, The Nation, Vol. 28, pp. 357-58.

1879e. The National Museum of Mexico and the Sacrificial Stone, in the American Antiquarian and Oriental Journal, Vol. II, No. 1, pp. 15-29.

1880a. On the Social Organization and Mode of Government of the Ancient Mexicans. (Twelfth Annual Report, Peabody Museum of American Archaeology and Ethnology [1879], Cambridge, pp. 557-699.)

1880b. Review (unsigned) of Charles Rau's The Palenque Tablet in the U.S. National Museum, etc., The Nation, Vol. 30, pp. 423-25.

1880-92. Original Bandelier Journals. (Library, Museum of New Mexico, Santa Fe, New Mexico.)

1881a. Historical Introduction to Studies among the Sedentary Indians of New Mexico. (Papers of the Archaeological Institute of America, American Series, Vol. I, No. 1, Boston, pp. 1-33.)

1881b. A Visit to the Aboriginal Ruins in the Valley of the Rio Pecos. (Papers of the Archaeological Institute of America, American Series, Vol. I, No. 2, Boston, pp. 34-133.) A second "edition" of the entire volume, items 1881a and 1881b, was issued. (Boston: published by Cupples, Upham, & Co., London: N. Trübner and Co. 1883.)

1882. Notes on the Bibliography of Yucatan and Central America. (Proceedings of the American Antiquarian Society, New Series, Vol. I., 1880-81, Worcester, pp. 82-118.)

1883. Report by A. F. Bandelier on His Investigations in New Mexico in the Spring and Summer of 1882. (Bulletin of the Archaeological Institute of America, I, Boston, pp. 13-33.)

1884a. Report of an Archaeological Tour in Mexico, in 1881. (Papers of the Archaeological Institute of America, American Series II, University Press, Boston, 326 pp.)

1884b. Reports by A. F. Bandelier on his Investigations in New Mexico during the Years 1883-1884. (Fifth Annual Report of the Executive Committee, Archaeological Institute of America, Cambridge, pp. 55-98.)

1884c. Ein Brief über Akoma von Adolf F. Bandelier, May 20, [1882], Pueblo of San Estévan of Acoma. (Das Ausland, Band LVIII: 241-43.)

1885. Ein Brief von Adolf F. Bandelier über seine Reise im südwestlichen Nordamerika, Highland, Oct. 12, 1883. (Das Ausland, Band LVIII: 974-75.)

1886a. Alvar Nunez Cabeza de Vaca, the First Overland Traveler of European Descent, and His Journey from Florida to the Pacific Coast—1528-1536. (Magazine of Western History, Vol. V., July, Cleveland, pp. 327-36.)

1886b. The Discovery of New Mexico by Fray Marcos de Nizza. (Magazine of Western History, Vol. V. Sept., Cleveland, pp. 659-70.) (Reprinted in New Mexico Historical Review, Vol. IV, No. 1, Santa Fe, Jan. 1929, pp. 28-44.)

1887-88. Histoire de la Colonisation et des Missions de Sonora, Chihuahua, Noveau Méxique et Arizona, jusqu'á l'an 1700. (Manuscript, 1,400 foolscap pages, 400 watercolor drawings by the author, in four volumes, with an atlas.)

1890a. The Delight Makers. (Dodd, Mead & Co., New York, 490 pp., 1946 edition.)

1890b. Fray Juan de Padilla, the First Catholic Missionary Martyr in Eastern Kansas. 1542. (American Catholic Quarterly Review, Vol. XV, No. 59, Philadelphia, pp. 551-65.)

1890c. The Historical Archives of the Hemenway Southwestern Archaeological Expedition. (Congrès International des Américanistes, Septième Session, 1888, Berlin, pp. 450-59.)

1890-92. Final Report of Investigations among the Indians of the Southwestern United States, Carried on mainly in the years from 1880 to 1885, Parts I and II. (Papers of the Archaeological Institute of America, American Series, III and IV, Cambridge, pp. 1-319 and pp. 1-591.)

1892. An Outline of the Documentary History of the Zuñi Tribe. (Journal of American Ethnology and Archaeology, Vol. III, No. iv, Cambridge, 115 pp.)

1893. The Gilded Man (El Dorado) and Other Pictures of the Spanish Occupancy of America. (D. Appleton and Company, New York, 302 pp.) Reprinted by The Rio Grande Press, Chicago, Ill., 1962.

1904a. On the Relative Antiquity of Ancient Peruvian Burials. (Bulletin XX, American Museum of Natural History, New York, pp. 217-26.)

1904b. The Cross of Carabuco in Bolivia. (American Anthropologist, VI, pp. 599-628.)

1910. The Islands of Titicaca and Koati. (The Hispanic Society of America, New York, xviii, 358 pp.)

Bandelier, Fanny Ritter

n.d. Recollections regarding the early years of Adolph F. Bandelier. (Files, Museum of New Mexico, Santa Fe.)

Bandelier Scrapbook.

n.d. Sent to the authors by Dr. Fred Eggan, University of Chicago. Clipped to first page: "A Book of Newspaper Clippings Prepared for Adolf Bandelier."

Barnes, Will C.

1914. Adolph F. A. Bandelier, Tribute and Reminiscence. El Palacio, Vol. II, No. 2, November, pp. 5-6.

1935. Arizona Place Names. (University of Arizona Bulletin, Vol. 6, No. 1, General Bulletin, No. 2, 503 pp.)

1941. Apaches and Longhorns: Reminiscences. (Edited and with an Introduction by Frank C. Lockwood; with a Decoration by Cas Duchow, 210 pp.)

1960. Arizona Place Names. (Revised and enlarged by Byrd H. Granger, University of Arizona Press, Tucson, 519 pp.)

Bartholdi, Albert, ed.

1932. Bandelier, in Prominent Americans of Swiss Origin. (James T. White and Co., New York, pp. 193-97.)

Baxter, Sylvester

1882. The Father of the Pueblos. (Harper's New Monthly Magazine, Vol. 65, Harper & Brothers, Publishers, New York, pp. 72-91.)

1885. Along the Rio Grande. (Harper's New Monthly Magazine, Vol. 70, Harper & Brothers, Publishers, New York, pp. 687-700.)

Bernays, Thekla

1912. Augustus Charles Bernays, A Memoir. (C. V. Mosby Company, St. Louis, 309 pp.)

Bingham, Hiram

1914. Bandelier. (The Nation, Vol. 98, March 26, pp. 328-29.)

Biographical Congressional Directory, A

1903. A Biographical Congressional Directory, 1774-1903. (Government Printing Office, Washington, 900 pp.)

Bloom, Lansing B.

1936a. The Sanson Map. (New Mexico Historical Review, Vol. XI, Notes and Reviews, Santa Fe, p. 210.)

1936b. Bourke on the Southwest. (New Mexico Historical Review, Vol. XI, Santa Fe, pp. 77-122, 188-207 ,217-82.)

1937. Bourke on the Southwest. (New Mexico Historical Review, Vol. XII, Santa Fe, pp. 337-79.)

1938. Bourke on the Southwest. (New Mexico Historical Review, Vol. XIII, Santa Fe, pp. 192-238.)

1943. Historical Society Minutes, 1859-1863. (New Mexico Historical Review, Vol. XVIII, Santa Fe, pp. 247-311.)

Bolton, Herbert E., translator and editor

1948. Kino's Historical Memoir of Pimeria Alta. Two Volumes in One. (University of California Press, Berkeley and Los Angeles, pp. 1-379, pp. 1-296; Index, pp. 299-329.)

Bond, Frank

1946. Memoirs of Forty Years in New Mexico. (New Mexico Historical Review, Vol. XXI, pp. 340-49.)

Bourke, John G.

1958. An Apache Campaign in the Sierra Madre: An Account of the

Expedition in Pursuit of the Hostile Chiricahua Apaches in the Spring of 1883. Introduction by J. Frank Dobie. (Charles Scribner's Sons, New York, 128 pp.) 1958 reprint of the 1886 edition.

Brandes, Ray

    1960. Frontier Military Posts of Arizona. (Dale Stuart King, publisher, Globe, Arizona, 94 pp.)

Bunzel, Ruth L.

    1932. Zuñi Katcinas. (47th Annual Report, Bureau of American Ethnology, 1929-30, Washington, pp. 837-1086.)

Bureau of [American] Ethnology

    1886. Report of the Director. (4th Annual Report, Bureau of Ethnology, Washington, pp. xxv-lxiii.)

    1887. Report of the Director. (5th Annual Report of the Bureau of Ethnology, Washington, pp. xv-liii.)

Burrus, Ernest J., S. J.

    1966. The Bandelier Collection in the Vatican Library. (Manuscripta, Vol. X, No. 2, July, published by St. Louis University Library, Lowrie J. Daly, S. J., ed., pp. 67-84.)

    1967a. Quivira and Taguayo in the Correspondence of Bandelier and Shea with Collet (1882-1889). (Manuscripta, Vol. XI, published by St. Louis University Library, Lowrie J. Daly, S. J., ed., pp. 67-83.)

    1967b. Review of The Southwestern Journals of Adolph F. Bandelier, 1880-1882, edited and annotated by Charles H. Lange and Carroll L. Riley. (Manuscripta, Vol. XI, No. 2, published by St. Louis University, Lowrie J. Daly, S. J., ed., pp. 120-21.)

Callon, Milton W.

    1962. Las Vegas, New Mexico: The Town That Wouldn't Gamble. (Las Vegas Publishing Co., Las Vegas, New Mexico, 352 pp.)

Carranco, Lynwood

    1969. Anza's Bones in Arizpe. (Journal of the West, Vol. VIII, No. 3, pp. 416-28.)

Casey, Mrs. Charles T., et al.

    1956. Breese Centennial Celebration: Souvenir Program and History of Breese. (Breese Journal, Breese, Ill., 82 pp.)

Castetter, Edward F., and Willis H. Bell

    1942. Pima and Papago Indian Agriculture. (Inter-Americana Studies I. University of New Mexico, Albuquerque, 245 pp.)

Census of Arizona Territory

    1880. (Microfilm, Arizona State University Library, Tempe.)

Charnay, D.

    1887. The Ancient Cities of the New World, being Travels and Explorations in Mexico and Central America from 1857-1882. (London, 546 pp.)

Chávez, Fray Angélico, O. F. M.

1947. The Mystery of Father Padilla. (El Palacio, Vol. 54, No. 11, pp. 251-68.)

1952. A Sequel to "The Mystery of Father Padilla." (El Palacio, Vol. 59, No. 12, pp. 386-89.)

1954. Origins of New Mexico Families in the Spanish Colonial Period. (Historical Society of New Mexico, Santa Fe, 339 pp.)

1957. Archives of the Archdiocese of Santa Fe. (Academy of American Franciscan History, Bibliographic Series, Vol. III, 283 pp.)

Christiansen, Paige W.

1964. The Myth of Robledo. (El Palacio, Vol. 71, No. 3, pp. 30-34.)

Colton, Harold S.

1952. Museum of Northern Arizona, Ceramic Series, No. 1—, Flagstaff, Ariz.

Columbia Encyclopedia, The

1963. The Columbia Encyclopedia, 3rd Edition. 1 volume. (William Bridgewater and Seymour Kurtz, eds., Columbia University Press, New York and London, 2, 388 pp.)

Crimmins, Colonel Martin L.

1935. Colonel Buell's Expedition into Mexico in 1880. (New Mexico Historical Review, Vol. X. pp. 133-42.)

Cruse, Thomas

1941. Apache Days and After. (The Caxton Press, Caldwell, Idaho, 328 pp.)

Curtis, Edward S., ed.

1926. The North American Indian. Volume XVI. (Plimpton Press, Norwood, Mass., 322 pp.)

Cushing, Frank Hamilton

1883. Zuñi Fetiches. (2nd Annual Report of the Bureau of Ethnology, Washington, pp. 3-45.) Reprinted by K C Publications, Flagstaff, Ariz., with Introduction by Tom Bahti, 1966.

1890. Preliminary Notes on the Origin, Working Hypothesis and Primary Researches of the Hemenway Southwestern Archaeological Expedition. (Congrès International des Américanistes, Septième Session, 1888, Berlin, pp. 151-94.)

1896. Outlines of Zuñi Creation Myths. (13th Annual Report, Bureau of American Ethnology, 1891-1892, Washington, pp. 321-447.)

Das Ausland (See Newspapers.)

Das Deutsche Pionier

1869-71. Das Deutsche Pionier: Eine Monatsschrift für Erinnerungen aus dem Deutschen Pionier-Leben in der Vereinigten Staaten, Gustave Brühl, ed. (Cincinnati, 1872-84.)

Davis, Britton

1929. The Truth about Geronimo. (Yale University Press, New Haven, 253 pp.)

Defouri, Very Rev. James H.

1887. Historical Sketch of the Catholic Church in New Mexico. (McCormick Bros., Printers, 410 Sansome Street, San Francisco, Calif., 164 pp.)

De Terra, Helmut

1955. The Life and Times of Alexander von Humboldt, 1796-1859. (Alfred A. Knopf, New York, 378 pp.)

Dictionary of American Biography

1961a. Dictionary of American Biography, Dumas Malone, ed. (Vol. 5, Pt. 2, Charles Scribner's Sons, New York, 617 pp.)

1961b. Dictionary of American Biography, Dumas Malone, ed. (Vol. 6, Pt. 2, Charles Scribner's Sons, New York, 647 pp.)

Dike, Sheldon H.

1958. The Territorial Post Offices of New Mexico. (Published by Dr. S. H. Dike, 1611 Bayita Lane, NW, Albuquerque, N.M., 56 pp.)

Di Peso, Charles C.

1966. Archaeology and Ethnohistory of the Northern Sierra. (in Handbook of Middle American Indians, Robert Wauchope, gen. ed., Vol. IV, Gordon F. Ekholm and Gordon R. Willey, eds., University of Texas Press, Austin, pp. 3-25.)

Disturnell, W. C.

1881. Arizona Business Directory and Gazeteer. (San Francisco, Bacon and Co., 327 pp.)

Downey, Fairfax

1943. Indian-Fighting Army. (Charles Scribner's Sons, New York, 328 pp.)

Dumarest, Father Noël

1920. Notes on Cochiti, New Mexico. (Memoirs of the American Anthropological Association, Vol. VI, No. 3, pp. 137-236.)

Dutton, Bertha P.

1963. Sun Father's Way: The Kiva Murals of Kuaua. (University of New Mexico Press, Albuquerque, 237 pp.)

Eggen, Jacob

1933. History of Highland (originally written in German in 1887). Trans., Rev. C. E. Miche; ed., A. P. Spencer. Two scrapbooks. (Louis Latzer Memorial Public Library, Highland, Ill., pp. 1-44 and pp. 45-105.)

Ellis, Bruce T.
 1958. Santa Fe's Tertio-Millenial, 1883. (El Palacio, Vol. 65, No. 4, pp. 121-35.)

Ellis, Florence Hawley, and Edwin Baca
 1957. The *Apuntes* of Father J. B. Ralliere. (New Mexico Historical Review, Vol. XXXII, pp. 10-35.)

El Palacio (Anonymous)
 1937. Bandelier Material Enriches School Library. (El Palacio, Vol. XLIII, Nos. 7-8-9, Aug. 18, 25, Sept. 1, Santa Fe, pp. 49-50.)

Emmett, Chris
 1965. Fort Union and the Winning of the Southwest. (University of Oklahoma Press, Norman, 436 pp.)

Encyclopaedia Britannica
 1967. Encyclopaedia Britannica, Volumes 16 and 17. (Encyclopaedia Britannica, Inc., William Benton, Publisher, 1199 pp., 1223 pp.)

Espinosa, Manuel J.
 1938. Memoir of a Kentuckian in New Mexico, 1848-1884. (New Mexico Historical Review, Vol. XIII, No. 1, pp. 1-13.)

Ferdon, Edwin N., Jr.
 1967. The Hohokam "Ball Court," An Alternate View of Its Function. (The Kiva, Vol. 33, No. 1, pp. 1-14.)

Fierman, Floyd S.
 1961. Nathan Bibo's Reminiscences of Early New Mexico. (El Palacio, Vol. 68, No. 4, pp. 231-57.)
 1962. Nathan Bibo's Reminiscences of Early New Mexico (continued). (El Palacio, Vol. 69, No. 1, pp. 40-60.)

Fletcher, Alice C.
 1900. See W. J. McGee, et al.

French, David
 1948. Factionalism in Isleta Pueblo. (American Ethnological Society Monographs, No. 19, New York, 48 pp.)

Frink, Maurice, with Casey E. Barthelmess
 1965. Photographer on an Army Mule. (University of Oklahoma Press, Norman, 151 pp.)

Goad, Edgar F.
 1938. Bandelier's Early Life. (The Historian, pp. 75-82.)
 1939. A Study of the Life of Adolph Francis Alphonse Bandelier, with an Appraisal of His Contributions to American Anthropology and Related Sciences. (Unpublished Ph.D. Dissertation, University of Southern California, Los Angeles, 229 pp.)

Goldfrank, Esther S.

1927. The Social and Ceremonial Organization of Cochiti. (Memoirs of the American Anthropological Association 33, 129 pp.)

1967. The Artist of "Isleta Paintings" in Pueblo Society. (Smithsonian Contributions to Anthropology, Vol. 5, Washington, 227 pp.)

Goodwin, Grenville

1942. The Social Organization of the Western Apache. (Chicago University Publications in Anthropology, Ethnological Series, University of Chicago Press, 701 pp.)

Greene, Chas. W.

1882. A Complete Business Directory of New Mexico and Gazeteer of the Territory for 1882. (New Mexico Publishing and Printing Company, 256 pp.)

Gunn, John M.

1917. Schat-Chen, History, Traditions and Naratives [sic] of the Queres Indians of Laguna and Acoma. (Copyrighted 1916 by John M. Gunn, Albright & Anderson, Albuquerque, 222 pp.)

Hackett, Charles W., ed.

1923-26-37. Historical Documents Relating to New Mexico, Nueva Vizcaya, and Approaches Thereto, to 1773, Collected by Adolph F. A. Bandelier and Fanny R. Bandelier. (Carnegie Institution of Washington, Publication 330: I, II, III. 502 pp., 497 pp., 532 pp.)

Haines, Helen

1891. History of New Mexico. (New Mexico Historical Publishing Co., New York, 631 pp.)

Hamlin, A. D. F.

1914. Letter to Editor, El Palacio, in appreciation of Bandelier. (El Palacio, Vol. II, No. 2, November, p. 6.)

Hammond, George P., and Edgar F. Goad

1949. A Scientist on the Trail: Travel Letters of A. F. Bandelier, 1880-1881. (The Quivira Society, Vol. X, Los Angeles, 142 pp.) Reprinted by Arno Press, New York, 1967.

Harlow, Alvin F.

1950. The Serene Cincinnatians. (E. P. Dutton and Co., Inc., New York, 442 pp.)

Haury, Emil W.

1945. The Excavation of Los Muertos and Neighboring Ruins in the Salt River Valley, Southern Arizona. (Papers of the Peabody Museum of American Archaeology and Ethnology, Harvard University, Vol. XXIV, No. 1, Cambridge, Mass., 223 pp. and 90 plates.)

Haury, Emil W., and Lyndon L. Hargrave

1931. Recently Dated Pueblo Ruins in Arizona. (Smithsonian Miscellaneous Collections, Vol. 82, No. 11, Publication No. 3069, Washington, 120 pp.)

Heitman, Francis B.
1903. Historical Register and Dictionary of the United States Army from its Organization, September 29, 1789, to March 2, 1903. Two volumes. (Washington, D.C., pp. 1-1069 and pp. 1-626.)

Helm, June, ed.
1966. Pioneers of American Anthropology: The Uses of Biography. (The American Ethnological Society, Monograph 43, University of Washington Press, Seattle, London, 247 pp.)

Hendron, J. W.
1946. Frijoles: A Hidden Valley in the New World. (Edited by Dorothy Thomas, Rydal Press, Inc., Santa Fe, 89 pp.)

Hibben, Frank C.
1966. A Possible Pyramidal Structure and other Mexican Influences at Pottery Mound, New Mexico. (American Antiquity, Vol. 31, No. 4, pp. 522-29.)

History of Arizona Territory
1884. History of Arizona Territory. (Wallace W. Elliot and Co., Publishers.) Reprinted by the Northland Press, Flagstaff, Ariz., with Introduction by Douglas D. Martin, 1964, 322 pp.

Hobbs, Hulda R.
1940a. Notes on interview with Mrs. Elizabeth Bandelier Kaune, Santa Fe, New Mexico. Files, Library, Museum of New Mexico, Santa Fe.
1940b. Bandelier in the Southwest. (El Palacio, Vol. 47, No. 6, pp. 121-36.)
1942a. Notes on interview with Mrs. Elizabeth Bandelier Kaune, Santa Fe, New Mexico. Files, Library, Museum of New Mexico, Santa Fe.
1942b. The Story of the Delight Makers from Bandelier's Own Journals. (El Palacio, Vol. 49, No. 6, pp. 109-24.)

Hodge, Frederick W., ed.
1907-10. Handbook of American Indians North of Mexico, Parts I and II. (Bureau of American Ethnology, Bulletin 30, pp. 1-972 and pp. 1-1,221.)

Hodge, Frederick W.
1914. Bandelier Obituary. (American Anthropologist, Vol. 16, No. 2, pp. 349-58.)
1932. Biographical Sketch and Bibliography of Adolphe Francis Alphonse Bandelier. (New Mexico Historical Review, Vol. VII, No. 4, pp. 353-70.)

1940. Unpublished manuscript of paper presented at a Memorial Conference, August 6-8, 1940, in Santa Fe, as a part of centennial celebration of Bandelier's birth. (Library, Museum of New Mexico.)

Holmes, William H.

1900. See W. J. McGee, et al.

Hooton, Earnest A.

1930. The Indians of Pecos. (Yale University Press, New Haven, 391 pp.)

Horgan, Paul

1956. The Centuries of Santa Fe. (E. P. Dutton & Company, Inc., New York, 363 pp.)

Howlett, Rev. W. J.

1908. Life of the Right Reverend Joseph P. Machebeuf, D. D. (The Franklin Press Company, Pueblo, Colo., 419 pp.)

Huggins

1876. Huggins' Map of New Mexico. (Compiled from Official Records, in Surveyor General's Office; published by New Mexico Stock & Agricultural Association, Chicago, Ill.)

Hughston, Caroline Mary

1911. Old Fort Lowell. (Arizona Silhouettes, Tucson, 20 pp.) Reprinted 1964.

Hyde, William

1896. Newspapers and Newspaper People of Three Decades. (Missouri Historical Society, Vol. 1, No. 12, St. Louis, pp. 5-24.)

Jackson, A. H.

1884. Report to Commissioner of Indian Affairs, 1883. (House Ex. Doc. 1, Pt. 5, 1st Session, 48th Congress in 4 volumes, Vol. 2, pp. 63-65.)

Jacobs, Wilbur R.

1960. Letters of Francis Parkman: edited and with an introduction by Wilbur R. Jacobs. Two volumes. (University of Oklahoma Press, Norman, pp. 1-204 and pp. 1-286.)

Jenkinson, Michael, with Karl Kernberger

1967. Ghost Towns of New Mexico: Playthings of the Wind. (University of New Mexico Press, Albuquerque, 156 pp.)

Johnson, Alfred E.

1966. Archaeology of Sonora Mexico. (In Handbook of Middle American Indians, Robert Wauchope, gen. ed., Vol. IV, Gordon F. Ekholm and Gordon R. Willey, eds., University of Texas Press, Austin, pp. 26-37.)

Johnson, Jean B.

1950. The Opata: An Inland Tribe of Sonora. (University of New Mexico Publications in Anthropology, No. 6, 50 pp.)

Kargau, E. D.
n.d. Mercantile, Industrial, and Professional St. Louis (674 pp.)

Kelley, J. Charles
1955. Juan Sabeata and Diffusion in Aboriginal Texas. (American Anthropologist, Vol. 57, pp. 981-95.)
1966. Mesoamerica and the Southwestern United States. (In Handbook of Middle American Indians, Robert Wauchope, gen. ed., Volume IV, Gordon F. Ekholm and Gordon R. Willey, eds., University of Texas Press, Austin, pp. 95-110.)

Kennecott Copper Corporation
n.d. Visitor's Guide to the Open Pit Mine at Santa Rita and the Reduction Plant at Hurley. (Chino Mines Division, General Office: Hurley, N.M.)

Kidder, Alfred V.
1924. An Introduction to Southwestern Archaeology. (Yale University Press, New Haven, 151 pp.)
1928. Adolph F. A. Bandelier. (In the Dictionary of American Biography, Vol. I, Charles Scribner's Sons, New York, pp. 571-72.)
1931-36. The Pottery of Pecos, Part I and Part II. (Yale University Press, New Haven, pp. 1-166 and pp. 1-636.)
1932. The Artifacts of Pecos. (Yale University Press, New Haven, 314 pp.)
1958. Pecos, New Mexico: Archaeological Notes. (Phillips Academy, Papers of the Robert S. Peabody Foundation for Archaeology, Vol. 5, Andover, Mass. xx, 360 pp.)

Köpfli, Kaspar
1833. Die Licht- & Schattenseite von New-Switzerland in Nordamerika. (Sursee, 61 pp.)

Köpfli, Salomon
1842. Neu Schweizerland in den Jahren 1831 und 1841. (Verlag von Xaver Meyer, Luzern, 82 pp.)

Kroeber, A. L.
1915. Frederic Ward Putnam. (American Anthropologist, n.s., Vol. 17, No. 4, pp. 712-18.)

Kubler, George
1940. The Religious Architecture of New Mexico in the Colonial Period and Since the American Occupation. (Contributions of the Taylor Museum, Colorado Springs, Colo., 232 pp.)

Lange, Charles H.

1950. Notes on the Use of Turkeys by Pueblo Indians. (El Palacio, Vol. 57, No. 7, pp. 204-09.)

1959. Cochiti: A New Mexico Pueblo, Past and Present. (University of Texas Press, Austin, 618 pp.) Reprinted by Arcturus Books, Southern Illinois University Press, 1968.

Lange, Charles H., and Carroll L. Riley, eds.

1966. The Southwestern Journals of Adolph F. Bandelier, 1880-1882. (University of New Mexico Press, Albuquerque, 462 pp.)

Leonard, John W., ed.

1906. The Book of St. Louisans, A Biographical Dictionary of Leading Living Men of the City of St. Louis. (The St. Louis Republic, St. Louis, 630 pp.)

Lister, Florence C., and Robert H. Lister

1966. Chihuahua: Storehouse of Storms. (University of New Mexico Press, Albuquerque, 360 pp.)

Lockwood, Frank C.

1938. The Apache Indians. (The Macmillan Company, New York, 348 pp.)

Loomis, Sylvia Glidden, ed.

1966. Old Santa Fe Today. (Prepared by The Historic Santa Fe Foundation; published by The School of American Research, Santa Fe, 48 pp.)

Lowie, Robert H.

1937. The History of Ethnological Theory. (Farrar & Rinehart, Inc., New York, 296 pp.)

Lurie, Nancy Oestreich

1966. Women in Early American Anthropology. (In Pioneers of American Anthropology: The Uses of Biography. June Helm, ed.) (The American Ethnological Society, Monograph 43, University of Washington Press, Seattle, London, pp. 29-81.)

Mallery, Garrick

1877. A Calendar of the Dakota Nation. (In United States Geological and Geographical Survey of the Territories, Bulletin, Washington, Vol. III, No. 1, pp. 3-25.)

Martin, Douglas D.

See History of Arizona Territory.

Mason, Otis T.

1879. Anthropology. (Annual Record of Science and Industry, 1878, Harper & Brothers, New York, pp. 379-408.)

Matthews, Washington

1900. See W. J. McGee, et al.

McCreight, W. T.

1927. George H. Pradt. (New Mexico Historical Review, Vol. II, pp. 208-12.)

McGee, W. J., et al.

1900. Remarks on Frank Hamilton Cushing, pp. 354-56; by William H. Holmes, pp. 356-60; by J. W. Powell, pp. 360-67; by Alice C. Fletcher, pp. 367-70; by Washington Matthews, pp. 370-77; letter on, by Joseph D. McGuire, pp. 377-79. (American Anthropologist, Vol. 2, No. 2.)

McGuire, Joseph D.

1900. See W. J. McGee, et al.

McKenney, L. M., and Co.

1882-83. McKenney's Business Directory of the Principal Towns of Central and Southern California, Arizona, New Mexico, Southern Colorado, and Kansas, 1882-1883. (Pacific Press Publishers, San Francisco, 941 pp.)

Missouri Historical Society

1897. List of Members and Contributors. (Vol. 1, No. 13, St. Louis, pp. 32-42.)

Montgomery, Ross G., Watson Smith, and John O. Brew

1949. Franciscan Awatovi: The Excavation and Conjectural Reconstruction of a 17th Century Spanish Mission Establishment at a Hopi Indian Town in Northeastern Arizona. (Reports of the Awatovi Expedition, Peabody Museum, Harvard University Report No. 3, Papers of the Peabody Museum of American Archaeology and Ethnology, Harvard University, Vol. XXXVI, Cambridge, 361 pp.)

Morgan, Lewis Henry

1871. Systems of Consanguinity and Affinity of the Human Family. (Contributions to Knowledge, Smithsonian Institution, 17, Washington, 602 pp.)

1877. Ancient Society, or Researches in the Lines of Human Progress from Savagery Through Barbarism to Civilization. (The World Publishing Company, New York; later published by Charles H. Kerr, Chicago, 1910; published again by Meridian Books, the World Publishing Company, Cleveland and New York, Eleanor B. Leacock, ed., 1963, 569 pp.)

1880. A Study of the Houses of the American Aborigines: with Suggestions for the Exploration of the Ruins in New Mexico, Arizona, the Valley of the San Juan, and in Yucatan and Central Mexico, under the Auspices of the Archaeological Institute. (First Annual Report of the Executive Committee, Archaeological Institute of America, 1879-80, Cambridge, pp. 29-80.)

1881. Houses and House-Life of the American Aborigines. (Contributions to North American Ethnology, Vol. IV, U.S. Geographical and Geological Survey of the Rocky Mountain Region, Department of the Interior, J. W. Powell, in charge, Government Printing Office, Washington, 281 pp.)

National Academy of Science

1902. Biographical Memoir of George Engelmann. (Biographical Memoirs of the National Academy of Science, Vol. IV, Washington, D.C., pp. 3-21.)

New Mexican Printing and Publishing Company

1882. A Complete Business Directory of New Mexico and Gazeteer of the Territory for 1882, Anonymous. (New Mexico Printing and Publishing Company, Santa Fe, 266 pp.)

Newspapers

Albuquerque Morning Journal: 1882, 1884
Anzeiger des Westens (St. Louis): 1883
Daily Optic, The (Las Vegas, N. M.): 1882
Das Ausland (Stuttgart and München, Germany): 1882-86
Der Highland Bote: 1866
Intelligencer, The (Edwardsville, Ill.): 1885
New Mexican, The (Santa Fe, N.M.): 1968
Santa Fe Daily New Mexican: 1882-83
Santa Fé New Mexican Review: 1883-84
Saturday Evening Post (Burlington, Ia.): 1888
Weekly Telephone, The (Highland, Ill.): 1884-85
Westliche Post (St. Louis): 1883

Official Reports

1884. Official Reports of the Territory of New Mexico for the Years 1882 and 1883. (Published by authority. New Mexican Review Company, Santa Fe, 140 pp.)

Otero, Miguel Antonio

1939. My Life on the Frontier, 1882-1897, Two volumes. (University of New Mexico Press, Albuquerque, Vol. II, 306 pp.)

Paré, Madeline F., with the collaboration of Bert M. Fireman

1965. Arizona Pageant. (Arizona Historical Foundation, Phoenix, 336 pp.)

Parish, William J.

1960. The German Jew and the Commercial Revolution in Territorial New Mexico, 1850-1900. (New Mexico Historical Review, Vol. XXXV, Nos. 1 and 2, Parts I and II, pp. 1-23 and pp. 129-50.)

Parsons, Elsie Clews

1920. Notes on Ceremonialism at Laguna. (Anthropological Papers of the American Museum of Natural History, Vol. XIX, Part IV, New York, pp. 85-131.)

1925. The Pueblo of Jemez. (Published for the Department of Archaeology, Phillips Academy, Andover, Mass., by Yale University Press, 144 pp.)

1932. Isleta, New Mexico. (47th Annual Report of the Bureau of American Ethnology, 1929-30, Smithsonian Institution, Washington, pp. 193-463.)

1939. Pueblo Indian Religion. Two volumes. (University of Chicago Press, Chicago, pp. 1-549 and pp. 551-1275.)

1962. Isleta Paintings. Ed. Esther S. Goldfrank. (Smithsonian Institution, Washington, ix-xvi, 299 pp.)

Peabody Museum of American Archaeology and Ethnology

1887a. Report of the Curator. (Peabody Museum of American Archaeology and Ethnology, 14th Annual Report, Vol. III, No. 1, Cambridge, pp. 1-41.)

1887b. Report of the Curator. (Peabody Museum of American Archaeology and Ethnology, 16th and 17th Annual Reports, Vol. III, Nos. 3 and 4, 1884, Cambridge, pp. 159-92.)

Pearce, T. M.

1965. New Mexico Place Names, A Geographical Dictionary. (University of New Mexico Press, 187 pp.)

Penniman, T. K.

1952. A Hundred Years of Anthropology. (Gerald Duckworth & Co., Ltd., London, revised edition, 512 pp.)

Pennington, Campbell W.

1963. The Tarahumar of Mexico. (University of Utah Press, Salt Lake City, 267 pp.)

Peplow, Edward H., Jr.

1958. History of Arizona. Volume II. (Lewis Historical Publishing Co., Inc., New York, 621 pp.)

Polk, R. L., & Co., and A. C. Danser

1884a. Colorado, New Mexico, Utah, Nevada, Wyoming, and Arizona Gazeteer and Business Directory, 1884-1885. (891 pp.)

1884b. Illinois State Gazeteer and Business Directory, 1884. (2323 pp.)

Powell, J(ohn) W(esley)

1888. Explorations in the Southwest. (6th Annual Report, Bureau of American Ethnology, 1884-85, Washington, pp. xxviii-xxx.)

1900. See W. J. McGee, et al.

Preston, Richard J.

1940. Rocky Mountain Trees. (Iowa State College Press, Ames, Iowa, 285 pp.)

Prince, L. Bradford
   1912. Old Fort Marcy, Santa Fe, New Mexico. (Santa Fe, 16 pp.)
Quebbeman, Frances E.
   1966. Medicine in Territorial Arizona (Arizona Historical Foundation,
      commissioned by the Arizona Medical Association, Phoenix, 424
      pp.)
Radin, Paul
   1942. The Unpublished Letters of Adolphe F. Bandelier concerning
      the writing and publication of The Delight Makers. (Southwestern
      Archeologica, Charles P. Everitt, New York, 33 pp.)
Rand McNally
   1962. New Cosmopolitan World Atlas. (Rand McNally & Company,
      New York, 248 and 128 pp.)
Rau, C. C.
   1879. The Palenque Tablet. (Contributions to Knowledge, Smithson-
      ian Institution, 22, No. 331, Washington, 81 pp.)
Reeve, Frank D.
   1952. Albert Franklin Banta: Arizona Pioneer. (New Mexico Historical
      Review, Vol. XXVII, pp. 200-55.)
Riley, Carroll L.
   1954. A Survey of Navajo Archaeology. (University of Colorado
      Studies, Series in Anthropology, No. 4, pp. 45-60.)
   1963a. Color-Direction Symbolism. An Example of Mexican-South-
      western Contacts. (América Indígena, Vol. 23, No. 1, pp. 49-60.)
   1963b. Adolph F. Bandelier as Archaeologist. (The Kiva, Vol. 29, No.
      1, pp. 23-34.)
   1968. Adolph Bandelier—The Mexican Years. (América Indígena, Vol.
      28, No. 2, pp. 425-36.)
   In press. The Southern Tepehuan and Tepecano. (In Handbook of
      Middle American Indians, Robert Wauchope, gen. ed., Vol. 8,
      Evon Z. Vogt, ed., University of Texas Press, Austin.)
Riley, Carroll L., and Charles H. Lange
   1961. Review of Correspondencia de Adolfo F. Bandelier by Leslie A.
      White and Ignacio Bernal. (El Palacio, Vol. 68, No. 4, pp. 258-61.)
Ritch, W. G.
   1882. The New Mexico Blue Book 1882: The Legislative Blue Book of
      the Territory of New Mexico. (Charles W. Greene, Public Printer,
      Santa Fe, New Mexico, 154 pp.)
   1885. Aztlan: The History, Resources and Attractions of New Mexico.
      (D. Lothrop & Co., Boston, 253 pp.)
Rothrock, J. T.
   See George M. Wheeler.

Russell, Frank
    1908. The Pima Indians. (26th Annual Report, Bureau of American
        Ethnology, 1904-05, Washington, 389 pp.)
Sadlier, D. and J., & Co.
    1882. Sadlier's Catholic Directory, Almanac and Ordo for the Year of
        Our Lord 1882. (D. and J. Sadlier & Co., 31 Barclay Street, New
        York, 570 pp.)
Salpointe, Most Rev. J. B., D. D.
    1898. Soldiers of the Cross. Notes on the Ecclesiastical History of
        New Mexico, Arizona, and Colorado. (St. Boniface's Industrial
        School, Banning, California, 229 pp.) Reprinted by Calvin Horn,
        Publisher, Inc., Albuquerque, N.M., 1967.
Sauer, Carl O.
    1935. Aboriginal Populations of Northwestern Mexico. (Ibero-Ameri-
        cana, No. 19, 33 pp.)
Sauer, Carl, and Donald Brand
    1931. Prehistoric Settlements of Sonora with Special Reference to
        Cerros de Trincheras. (University of California Publications in
        Geography, Vol. 5, No. 3, pp. 67-148.)
Scholes, France V.
    1937. Church and State in New Mexico, 1610-1650. (Historical Society
        of New Mexico, Publications in History, VII, 206 pp.)
    1942. Troublous Times in New Mexico, 1659-1670. (Historical Society
        of New Mexico, Publications in History, XI, 276 pp.)
Scholes, France V., and H. P. Mera
    1940. Some Aspects of the Jumana Problem. (Contributions to Amer-
        ican Anthropology and History 34, Carnegie Institution of Wash-
        ington, Publication No. 523, Washington, D. C., pp. 267-99.)
Schroeder, Albert H.
    1949. Cultural Implications of the Ball Courts in Arizona. (South-
        western Journal of Anthropology, Vol. 5, No. 1, pp. 28-36.)
Simpson, James H.
    1850. Journal of a Military Reconnaissance from Santa Fe, New Mex-
        ico, to the Navajo Country. (Reports of the Secretary of War,
        Senate Executive Document 64, 31st Congress, 1st Session, Wash-
        ington, D.C., pp. 56-168.)
Smith, Cornelius C., Jr.
    1967. William Sanders Oury. (University of Arizona Press, Tucson, 298
        pp.)
Smithsonian Institution.
    1857. Annual Report of the Board of Regents up to January, 1857. (A.
        O. P. Nicholson, Printer, Washington, 467 pp.)

1864. List of Meteorological Stations and Observations of the Smithsonian Institution for the Year 1863. (Annual Report of the Board of Regents of the Smithsonian Institution for the Year 1863, Government Printing Office, Washington, 419 pp.)

1874. Annual Report of the Board of Regents for the Year 1873. (Government Printing Office, Washington, 452 pp.)

Spencer, A. P., ed.

1937. Centennial History of Highland, Illinois, 1837-1937. (Centennial Commission, Highland, 273 pp.)

Spicer, Edward H.

1962. Cycles of Conquest. (University of Arizona Press, Tucson, 609 pp.)

Spier, Leslie

1917. An Outline for A Chronology of Zuñi Ruins. (Anthropological Papers of the American Museum of Natural History, Vol. XVIII, Part III, New York, pp. 207-331.)

1918. Notes on Some Little Colorado Ruins. (Anthropological Papers of the American Museum of Natural History, Vol. XVIII, Part IV, New York, pp. 333-62.)

1919. Ruins in the White Mountains, Arizona. (Anthropological Papers of the American Museum of Natural History, Vol. XVIII, Part V, New York, pp. 363-87.)

Steck, Francis Borgia, O. F. M., Ph.D.

1943. A Tentative Guide to Historical Materials on the Spanish Borderlands. (The Catholic Historical Society of Philadelphia, Philadelphia, Pa., 106 pp.)

Stern, Bernhard J.

1931. Lewis Henry Morgan: Social Evolutionist. (University of Chicago Press, Chicago, 221 pp.)

Stevenson, Matilda Coxe

1904. The Zuñi Indians: Their Mythology, Esoteric Societies, and Ceremonies. (23rd Annual Report, Bureau of American Ethnology, 1901-02, Washington, pp. 1-608.)

Stubbs, Stanley A., and W. S. Stallings, Jr.

1953. The Excavation of Pindi Pueblo, New Mexico. (Monographs of the School of American Research and the Laboratory of Anthropology, No. 18, Santa Fe, 165 pp.)

Taylor, Walter W.

1964. Tethered Nomadism and Water Territoriality: an Hypothesis. (Actas y Memorias, XXXV Congreso Internacional de Americanistas, Mexico City, 1962, pp. 197-203.)

Theobald, John, and Lillian Theobald

1961. Arizona Territory: Post Offices and Postmasters. (Arizona Historical Foundation, Phoenix, 178 pp.)

Thrapp, Dan L.

1964. Al Sieber, Chief of Scouts. (University of Oklahoma Press, Norman, 432 pp.)

1967. The Conquest of Apacheria. (University of Oklahoma Press, Norman, 405 pp.)

Treutlein, Theodore E., trans. and annotator

1949. Sonora: A Description of the Province by Ignaz Pfefferkorn. (Coronado Cuarto Centennial Publications, 1540-1940, Vol. XII, University of New Mexico Press, Albuquerque, 329 pp.)

Twitchell, Ralph Emerson

1911-17. The Leading Facts of New Mexican History. Five volumes. (Cedar Rapids, Torch Press.)

1925. Old Santa Fe: The Story of New Mexico's Ancient Capital. (Santa Fe New Mexican Publishing Company, 488 pp.) Reproduction of 1925 edition by Rio Grande Press, Chicago, 1963.

Underhill, Ruth M.

1956. The Navajos. (University of Oklahoma Press, Norman, 299 pp.) Revised by the University of Oklahoma Press, Norman, 1967, 292 pp.

Valentini, Philipp J. J.

1882. Mexican Paper. (Proceedings of the American Antiquarian Society, New Series, Vol. I, 1880-81, Worcester, published by the Society, pp. 58-81.)

Villa, Eduardo W.

1948. Galeria de Sonorenses Ilustres. (Impulsora de Artes Graficas, Hermosillo, Sonora, 221 pp.)

Vollmer, E. R., S. J.

1952. First Jesuit School in New Mexico. (New Mexico Historical Review, Vol. XXVII, pp. 296-99.)

Wagner, Henry

1937. The Spanish Southwest, 1542-1794. (The Quivira Society, Vol. VII, Parts I and II, Los Angeles, pp. 13-274 and pp. 275-552.) Reprinted by Arno Press, New York, 1967.

Walter, Paul A. F.

1927. Major George H. Pradt. (New Mexico Historical Review, Vol. II, No. 2, pp. 208-14.)

Wasson, Jos.

1930. The Southwest in 1880. (New Mexico Historical Review, Vol. V, pp. 263-87.)

Watson, Dorothy

1968. Pinos Altos. (Chamber of Commerce History, #37, Silver City, Grant County, N.M., 3 pp.)

Wharton, Clarence

1952. Spruce McCoy Baird. (New Mexico Historical Review, Vol. XXVII, pp. 300-14.)

Wheeler, George M.

1875-89. United States Geographical Surveys West of the One Hundredth Meridian. Seven Volumes and One Supplement. (Government Printing Office, Washington, Volume IV, Botany, by J. T. Rothrock, 1878, 404 pp.)

White, Leslie A., ed.

1942. Lewis H. Morgan's Journal of a Trip to Southwestern Colorado and New Mexico, June 21 to August 7, 1878. (American Antiquity, Vol. VIII, No. 1, pp. 1-26.)

White, Leslie A.

1935. The Pueblo of Santo Domingo, New Mexico. (Memoirs of the American Anthropological Association 43, 210 pp.)

1940. Pioneers in American Anthropology: The Bandelier-Morgan Letters, 1873-1883. Two volumes. (University of New Mexico Press, Albuquerque, pp. xv + 272, and viii + 266.)

1943. New Material from Acoma. (Bureau of American Ethnology, Bulletin 136, Anthropological Papers 32, Washington, pp. 301-59.)

1957. How Morgan came to Write *Systems of Consanguinity and Affinity*. (Papers of the Michigan Academy of Science, Arts and Letters, Vol. 42, pp. 257-68.)

White, Leslie A., and Ignacio Bernal

1960. Correspondencia de Adolfo F. Bandelier. (Instituto Nacional de Antropología e Historia, Seria Historia, VI, México, 322 pp.)

Who's Who in America with World Notables, 1968-69

1969. Who's Who in America with World Notables, 1968-69. (Jackson Martindell, Publisher, A. N. Marquis Co., Chicago, 2563 pp.)

Who Was Who in America

1963. Historical Volume, 1607-1896, A Component Volume of Who's Who in American History. (A. N. Marquis Co., Chicago, 670 pp.)

Who Was Who in America

n.d. Who Was Who in America, 1897-1942, Volume I. (A. N. Marquis Co., Chicago, 1396 pp.)

Winship, George P.

1896. The Coronado Expedition, 1540-1542. (14th Annual Report, Bureau of American Ethnology, Washington, pp. 329-613.)

Wissler, Clark

1914. Bandelier Obituary. (El Palacio, Vol. 1, Nos. 6 and 7, p. 8.)

Woods, Betty
    1968. The Mimbres. (Chamber of Commerce History, #41, Silver
        City, Grant County, N.M., 2 pp.)
World Almanac
    1967. The World Almanac and Book of Facts. (The New York World-
        Telegram, New York.)
World Book Encyclopedia
    1959. World Book Encyclopedia. (Field Enterprises Educational Cor-
        poration, Chicago, Eighteen volumes, J. Morris Jones, ed.)

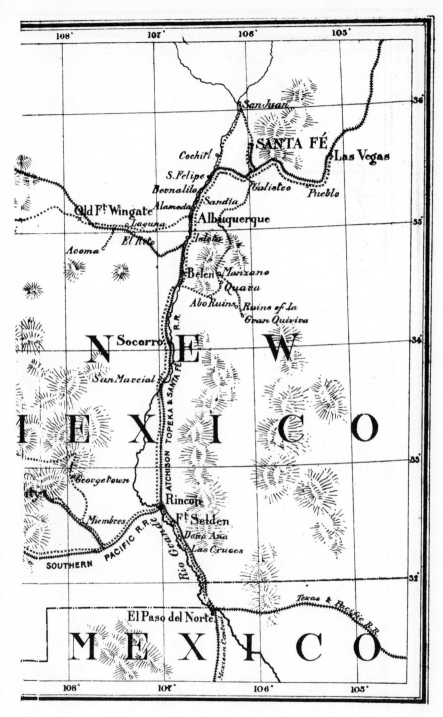

Bandelier's Routes, 1883

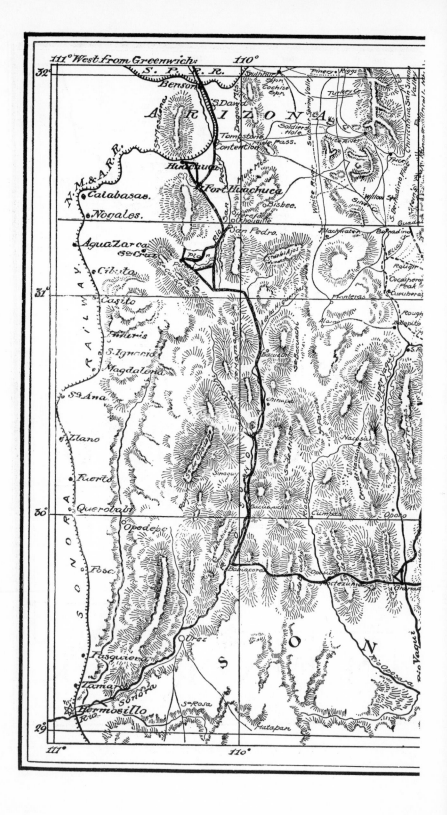

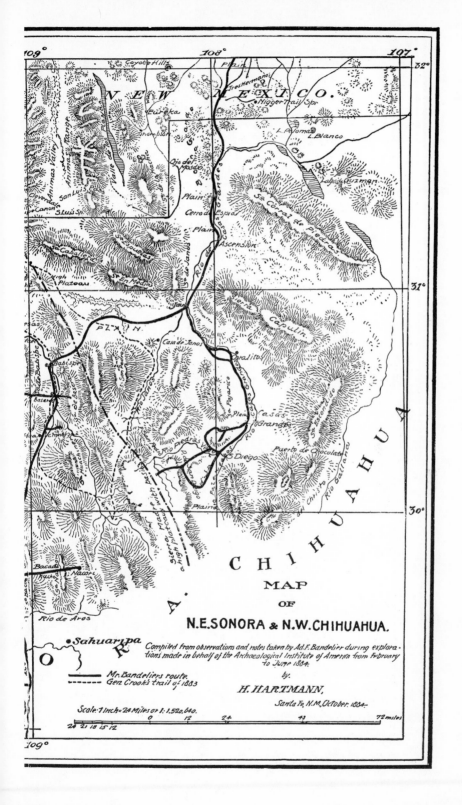

MAP
OF
N.E. SONORA & N.W. CHIHUAHUA.

Compiled from observations and notes taken by Ad. F. Bandelier during explorations made in behalf of the Archaeological Institute of America from February to June 1884.

by.

H. HARTMANN,

Santa Fe, N.M. October. 1884.

———— Mr. Bandelier's route.
- - - - - Gen. Crook's trail of 1883

Scale: 1 Inch = 24 Miles or 1: 1,520,640.

INDEX

(B. designates Adolph F. Bandelier)

Wingate): 46, 60-61, 140, 338; accompanied B. up Thunder Mt., 48, 50; photograph of La Cebolla ruin, 62; B. arranged for him to take his plates, 67, 382n195; influenced by Matthews, 374-375n135; published on Navajo, 374-375-n135

—Mountain Sheep Dance (Zuñi): photographed, 52, 53, 377n152; splendid negatives of, 66, 381n185

Baserac(a), Son.: 281, 287, 294; first place occupied by Spanish, 264; statistical data, 266, 280, 282; oldest Sonoran church seen to date by B., 274; church arches noted, 274; convent, 274; old pueblo, 276, 280; meaning of name, 279; serapes in economy, 280

Basket remains: San José de las Tusas area, 78; Fort Apache area cave, 89, 90, 91, 386n238; Salt River cave, 112

Baskets. See Apache, Pima

Bastian, Dr. Adolf (Berlin, Germany): 148, 150, 402-403n372; honorary member, Anthropological Society of Washington, 424n59

Bastidas (Ascención): excavated Casas Grandes mound with Gomez, 324, 325

Batesopa, Son.: largest Sonoran pueblo seen to date by B., 272; sun and moon creation myth, 270-271, 273; warfare with Casas Grandes, 273, 276, 426n75; fortification in cliffs, 274

Batonapo (Bato-napa), Son.: proper name, Batonapo Vácatz, 240

—fortifications: lava, with Opata tradition, 234-235, 235-236, 240, 274; B. told fort and pueblo were Yaqui, 242, 424n58

Baum, Consul, 341

Bausch, Dr. Christa, 365n61

Bavispe (Babispe), Son.: 168, 214, 215, 249, 255, 269, 270, 280, 281, 282, 321; matachines, 265; population and heads of cattle, 17th century, 266; meaning of name, 279; centinela, presidio, 281; unfinished church admired by B., 281, 281-282; league distances given to Huásabas, Janos, 281

Bavispe River, Son., 426n76

Baxter, Sylvester, 374n131

Baynorpa (near Las Delicias), 244, 245

Beans (spp.?): Salt River, 115; Tonto Creek, 117; Casa Grande, 136

Beaumont, Col. Eugene B. (Fort Wingate), 67, 382n196

Beck, Mrs. A. (Highland), 402n369

Becker, August (St. Louis), 342

Becker, Emily (Mrs. August) (St. Louis), 399n348a, 403n374a

Becker, Ida (Highland), 148, 403n373. See also Streiff, Mrs. Rudolf

Becker, John (Belen), 19, 20, 24, 25, 31, 34, 358n22

Beery, Charles (Corralitos), 322

Belen, N.M.: 19, 24, 155, 176, 332, 355n2, 358n22, 359n27, 359n30; oldest book (1793) of parish, noted, 20

Bell, Capt. (Banámiche), 243, 424n60

Bell, C. G. (Georgetown): sandals excavated from Gila cliffhouses, 199, 200

Belletristisches Journal (N.Y.C.): purchased B.'s novel, Die Köshare, 402n367

Belleville, Ill., 290, 341

Benecke, Mr. (Belen), 24

Benevides period, 362n42

Bennett, G. C. (Santa Fe): photographer, associated with W. Henry Brown, 355-n4

Bennett's. See Houck, Ariz.

Benson, Ariz., 205, 211, 212

Bent, Charles, 167, 409-410n438

Bern (Berne), Switzerland: 1, 2, 19; B. at, 350-352; 1703 map with Casas Grandes in library, 351

Bernalillo, N.M.: 332; Father Coudert, priest at, 368n85

Bernays. For data concerning this family, see 360-361n35, 400n350

Bernays, Charles L. (St. Louis), 20, 150, 360-361n35, 405n387

Bernays, Dr. Joe (Highland), 145, 400n-353

Bernays, Layne (Highland), 338

Bibo, Joseph (Bernalillo), 414-415n469

Bibo, Nathan (Bernalillo), 176, 369n87, 384n215, 406n401, 414-415n469

Bibo, Simon (Acoma area), 369n87, 414-415n469

Bibo, Solomon (Acoma), 33, 369n87

Bigler, Frank: 20, 24, 25, 27, 28, 63, 64, 148, 360n34; friend of Cushing and B., 360n34; friend of Fanny Ritter Bandelier, 360n34

Bishop's Lodge (Santa Fe), 169, 410n445, 414n466

studies by Matthews for, 361n36; name changed from Bureau of Ethnology to, 371-372n109; Stevenson Expedition to Zuñi, 371-372n109

Bùren, Mr. de (Bern, Switzerland), 352

Burial. See Funeral and burial practices

Burnside, John (Carlyle), 180

Burritos Mountains, Chih., 285, 287

Burro Mountains, N.M., 188

Burrus, Father Ernest J., S. J. (Institutum Historicum): editing B.'s Histoire for publication, 355Intr.n4; criticized B.'s work in historical cartography, 430-431-n108

Busson, Ferdinand P. (East St. Louis), 342, 435n142

Bustamente, Don Juan (Bavispe), 281

Butschofsky (Butjofsky), Dr. George (Las Cruces), 166, 409n433

Butterfield Overland Mail, 420n15

Cabellera. See Sierra de la Cabellera

Cabeza de Vaca, Padre (Ascención), 324

Cabeza de Vaca, Alvar Nuñez, 54, 378n157

Cache system: Apache, 91; Gatton's, 188, 189, 191, 192, 202; Silver City area, 192; Casa Grande area, 390n291

Cachorrón. See Sierra Ceseri

Cacique: Isleta, 21, 362n46; Taos, 31; Piros, 158, 159; Keres, 160; Zuñi, 160; Mansos, 160, 164; Senecú, 163, 164; Santa Clara, 172; Cochiti, 363n50

Cahuias. See Cahuillas

Cahuillas (Cahuias) (Calif.), 279

Cajamarca (Caxamarca), Peru: 104; Pizarro's massacre at, 388-389n262

Cajón, cajones: Casa Grande, 85; Pueblo Viejo, 103; Tonto Creek, 103; Casa Blanca, 132-133; Florence area, 140; Tesuque area, 174; Casas Grandes, 293, 295, 296, 310; Casas Grandes area, 312; Arroyo de la Cuerda, 314; Pueblito (Chih.), 319; term defined, 413n458

Cajón de Bamochi: Crook's route through, 269

Cajón del Alamo, Son., 267

Calistro (Calixto), Pedro (Banámiche), 236, 240, 241, 242

Calixto. See Calistro

Calpan (Cholula area): axes from, 108

Cambridge, Mass., 344, 345, 346

Camitria (ruin near San Juan Pueblo), 172

Camp Apache, Ariz.: ruins of Zuñi origin, 69; history of, 383n212; mentioned, 414-415n469. See also Fort Apache

Camp (Fort) Goodwin, Ariz., 97, 100, 207, 387n247, 387-388n250

Camp Grant, Ariz.: 207; massacre, 428n96. See also Fort Grant

Camp Huachuca, Ariz., 421n25. See also Fort Huachuca

Campos, Padre Dr. José Vicente (Cholula), 4, 20, 159, 359-360n32, 386n241

Camp Reno, Ariz., 390n278. See also Fort Reno

Camp Thomas, Ariz., 383n212, 387-388-n250. See also Fort Thomas

Camp Verde, Ariz., 422-423n46

Caña agria, 208, 243, 421n22

Cañada Alamosa, N.M., 31, 36

Cañada Ancha, Son., 221

Cañada Bonita (Venado area), N.M., 72, 73, 74

Cañada de Juan Luján, N.M., 16, 18

Cañada de Mochubabi, Son., 265

Cañada de la Cruz, N.M., 24, 25

Cañada de la Cruz, Son.: 223, 224, 240; El Pueblito ruin at, 226; Punta de Agua in, 240-241

Cañada de la Torneada, N.M., 16

Cañada de las Tinajas (Las Cruces): rock paintings, 157

Cañada de las Tinajitas, Son., 264

Cañada del Agua Escondida, N.M., 31

Cañada del Aguaje, N.M., 11, 16

Cañada del Carrizo, Ariz., 86

Cañada del Leon, N.M., 11

Cañada del Pueblo (San Marcos area), 152-153; second ruin distinct from, 174

Cañada del Puerto Largo, N.M., 17

Cañada del Venado, N.M., 73

Cañada Pintada, N.M., 18

Cananéa, Son., 220, 221, 222, 235

Cananéa River, Son., 218, 219

Cándano, Capt. Mauro (Casas Grandes), 308, 309, 311, 322, 323, 338, 427n88

Candelaria's (Albuquerque), 23, 332, 364-n56, 429n105

Canetas, Chih.: 286; rancho burned by Apaches, 284

Canillo, Don Manuel (Banámiche), 243

Cañón de Juan Tafoya, N.M., 27

Cañón del Gavilán: Apaches fought in, 186, 416n484